THE ORIGINS OF SCIENTIFIC SOCIOLOGY

THE ORIGINS OF

JOHN MADGE

SCIENTIFIC SOCIOLOGY

THE FREE PRESS, *New York*

TO JANET

ACKNOWLEDGMENT

This book is based on a course of lectures that I gave four years ago, as a visitor from England, to a class of graduate students at Brooklyn College. The idea of giving a Methods course in terms of the historical development of empirical sociology was suggested to me by Professor George Simpson. I am deeply grateful both to him and to the able group of students on whom I imposed the rather concentrated lectures that this treatment demanded.

Since the original presentation, the material has been much changed and extended. In the course of this process I have received invaluable help and guidance from sociological friends and colleagues on both sides of the Atlantic and of the English Channel. I will not thank them individually by name, but it is clear that without their support the book would never have been completed.

JOHN MADGE

CONTENTS

THE THEME

The theme of this book is a simple one. It is that the discipline of sociology is at last growing up and is within reach of attaining the status of a science.

A mature science possesses refined and systematic methods of data collection, suitable analytical tools, and an appropriate conceptual equipment. In some measure, all these instruments are now available. Looming beyond them is the systematic theory that is needed to guide understanding and action. The full delineation of that theory still eludes us, but it is certainly true today that the conceptual equipment brought to bear on each fresh problem is increasingly regulated by what has gone before.

Like other young sciences, sociology has devoted and continues to devote much of its energy to descriptive study. Some of the material thus collected possesses immediate administrative utility, and almost all of it helps us toward a better understanding of social life in its complex ramifications. This is the "natural history" function of sociology; apart from its intrinsic value it represents a necessary stage not only in building a language but also in providing the opportunities needed to develop sophisticated techniques of investigation. But, however concrete and accurate the data collected may be, their value is fragmentary until they can be unified with other descriptive findings. This is not merely a matter of gathering comparable information about findings; what is needed at all levels of generality is the formulation and testing of significant hypotheses. Ultimately, the power of sociology rests in its accumulation of provable and applicable ideas, not merely of facts.

The positivist ambition of Auguste Comte was to construct a science of society that would rival in its rigor the established sciences. Comte died over a century ago, and the structure is still incomplete. There are various explanations for this slow growth. Men were reluctant to recognize that every science possesses an individuality determined by the nature of its field, so that some time has been wasted in vain attempts to create a sociology in the image of another science. The established disciplines resisted for generations the establishment of a challenging newcomer, which declared—often crudely —that there were unexplored aspects of social life and neglected methods of exploring them. The unfamiliar and inelegant formulations enjoyed by sociologists won few friends among the humanists. Men of action could see no usefulness in the preoccupations of the infant science. Attention to its teachings, such as they were, promised no financial returns.

One does not customarily speak of a "German physics" or an "Italian astronomy." There are naturally differences in the focus of interest in the various scientific centers of the world, but the natural and biological sciences have developed generally accepted methods of testing the assertions of other scientists, whatever their country of origin. It is not yet the same in the case of sociology. It is true that some cross-fertilization has taken place. As we shall be reminded, Émile Durkheim visited Germany in search of the masters, and more recently there has been a continuous flow of scholars from all continents toward the United States.

In spite of these unifying tendencies there are distinctive features in each national brand of sociology—the ethnological concern of the French, the broad comparative sweep of the German folk science, the administrative empiricism of the English. If one thinks in terms of empirically based studies, the center of gravity today is undeniably in the United States, and the products of American sociology are unmistakable. Although this is not necessarily admitted by all Europeans, the American sociology of the last two or three decades is also the most productive not only of techniques but also of empirically tested ideas.

It is for this reason that all except the first of the following chapters, which are designed to illuminate some of the landmarks of the past half-century, are based on work originating in the United

States, even though several of the leading figures, including Znani-ecki, Myrdal, Adorno, and Festinger, stem from the Old World.

Various criteria were applied in selecting the works to be included. The underlying principle was the belief that science is concerned not merely to formulate knowledge but also to do something with it. Furthermore, consummate techniques are barren without fertilization by realistic and significant ideas. These words are carefully chosen. According to some, all facts are potentially of equal worth, and their value lies in the accuracy of their truth rather than in their applicability to the problems of the world. This is a philosophy of empty plenty to which many will find it impossible to subscribe. It is a fact that the paths to truth are often devious, and that some of the most striking discoveries are arrived at surreptitiously. But it is also a fact that mean and subservient minds can be detected by their concern with the innocuous and the trivial. Almost consistently, the researches to be described were undertaken under the stimulus of major current social problems. In the following chapters we shall meet suicide, social disorganization, Babbitry, race hatred, productivity, totalitarianism, leadership, the uncertainties of sexual behavior. These are not arid abstractions but the very stuff of community existence.

One may therefore summarize by indicating that the selected works must make significant contributions in three areas—in the area of investigational technique, in the area of ideas, and in the provision of understanding and control of social problems.

None of these areas can properly be separated from the other two. It is remarkable how consistently the same train of events occurs. A particular problem impresses itself on an investigator; as he explores its dimensions he also makes himself aware of possible sources of relevant empirical information and begins to devise original methods of collecting and extracting this information; he finds it necessary to conceptualize the problem in a novel way; as likely as not he will develop fresh techniques of analysis. The common strain running through this process is one of innovation. It is a striking feature of the examples given how few of the investigators were able or willing to depend on the procedures evolved by their predecessors.

We now come to the question of how the specific selection of cases was made. It would of course be impossible to satisfy every reader by any selection, but some of the omissions may be felt to be so striking as to require comment. It may appear natural to exclude from the list such early masters as Spencer, Sumner, Simmel, and Tönnies on the grounds that, although they espoused science, their systematic empirical work represented a negligible part of their literary output, but the position of Max Weber is somewhat different and a special apologia is perhaps required.

Max Weber, whose reputation and influence have never been higher than today, was both more sophisticated and more experienced in the empirical testing of ideas than the sociologists previously mentioned. It seems possible that if he had been spared to complete his life's work, he would have undertaken a systematic analysis of the evidence for the brilliant insights contained in *The Protestant Ethic*. As it is, his contribution can be regarded as a fertile source of guidelines but not as suitable for inclusion in this book as a work of scientific sociology.

For all this, Weber's approach to the elements of social structure is still entirely modern. One can only add that his ideas, and indeed those of the other early sociologists, can be seen very near to the surface of the thinking of the contemporary sociologists with whom the following chapters are concerned. The persistence of these ideas illustrates once again the extent to which a science needs not only procedural skills but also a distinctive view of the world.

In recent decades, with the phenomenal growth of interest in and support for sociology, there has been a corresponding increase in the output of sociological research. Research has been institutionalized, and most major universities and other institutions have permanent research centers. The Bureau of Applied Social Research of Columbia University has an international reputation and a very considerable research output. Its activities come under the watchful eyes of Merton and of Lazarsfeld, and theoretical and methodological sophistication are thereby ensured. Across the American continent, the University of California at Berkeley now provides various institutionalized opportunities for sociological research, particularly in the fields of politics and industrial relations; many of the leading figures at Berkeley are products of Columbia University, but the California school possesses a distinctive character. A third great center in the United States, the University of Chicago, continues with an active program, and all over the world sociological research centers are emerging. It is to be regretted that there is no space in the present book to incorporate work from these and other important sources.

This book is an essay in contemporary history, and most of the characters in it are still alive. Others, like Znaniecki, Stouffer, and Kinsey, died in the past few years. Wherever possible, the story of the works described has been brought up to date, but it is perhaps inevitable that such a work can never entirely capture the spirit of the moment.

Having recorded these reservations, we may now return to the contents of the book. Durkheim's *Suicide*, the first work discussed, satisfies all the criteria laid down. It concerns a social problem that was being much ventilated at the time; the author picked up a well-established statistical tradition and put administrative records to novel uses; he devised new analytical instruments, such as his *coefficient of preservation;* above all he evolved an important new sociological concept, *anomie*, which has been the starting point for much subsequent speculation and investigation. In retrospect it appears that Durkheim even erred by being too sociological. Apart from a few rather naïve psychological assertions, he was determined to concentrate on social facts to the exclusion of individual motivations.

The next chapter, devoted to *The Polish Peasant*, by Thomas and Znaniecki, discusses another social problem, the disorganization that Polish families underwent as a result of the massive migrations from Europe to America. Here the emphasis was entirely different. Both the empirical sources, which were largely personal documents, and the conceptual treatment, including the celebrated *four wishes*, were initially concerned with the behavior and attitudes of individuals, and the social facts were seen as projections of these individual responses.

The Polish Peasant helped to establish an empirical tradition in the School of Sociology at the University of Chicago, but the full flowering of this tradition owes much to Robert Ezra Park, who came on the scene while the work was in progress. Park's enthusiasm built up a distinctive school of empirical sociology, which is described in Chapter 4. Every method of data collection then known was made use of—official records, documents of various kinds, informal interviews, life histories, and participant observation. The Chicago sociologists were emphatically interested in the real world of the city, which Park described as "the natural habitat of civilized man."[1] The whole spectrum of social types is surveyed in *The Gold Coast and the Slum,* the book chosen to be the main example of the work of the Chicago school. Their theoretical contribution was less important. Some of the ecological ideas of Burgess and McKenzie were more firmly established by the new data, and the theories of Thomas were again applied, but there was no striking development of theory.

The American twenties were a bleak period for sociological theory, and when Robert and Helen Lynd settled on "Middletown" as the location for a civic survey, they started work in a condition of almost complete theoretical naïveté. What they set out to do was to collect the facts, and under the influence of Wissler they decided to adopt one of the prevailing anthropological frameworks into which to fit their facts. Through an inherently businesslike approach they achieved in their data collection a rigor not previously attained, and through native perceptiveness they grew to recognize the necessity for theory. A natural social purpose informed their work; this became more explicit with the passage of time, and, interestingly enough, development led them toward action theories based on the immanence of power rather than toward perspectival theories.

Chapter 6 is devoted to the social problem of productivity. The celebrated Hawthorne experiment described in *Management and the Worker* by Roethlisberger and Dickson was part of an action program aimed concurrently at improving industrial morale and at boosting output. This study was in many ways more sophisticated than any previously described, not only in its techniques—both the nondirective interviewing and the observational studies were highly developed for their period—but also in its maturing theories of small-group interaction and of the chasm between formal and informal organization. For various reasons this Harvard work has been subjected to much criticism, principally because the idea of "social skills" has been found to connote sinister forms of manipulation. But the ideas as well as the methods evolved in the Hawthorne experiments have so deeply penetrated into industrial thinking that it is difficult now to realize how original they once were. This program was noteworthy because it was expensively sponsored by a large industrial corporation. Presumably it was the most costly sociological study up to that date.

In contrast, Chapter 7 describes an honest and intimate study undertaken by one junior fellow at Harvard. Whyte's *Street Corner Society* could perhaps be described as containing more perceptive insights than the author knew how to handle, and it is remarkable how many theorists have made use of his material for purposes of illustration. Like the original Lynd, the early Whyte strikes the reader as a gifted amateur, but one feels that he was more receptive to ideas as such than Lynd. He found it rather fascinating to contrast the solidary street-corner society with the more ambitious and grasping organization of the local college boys, and he regarded the local racketeers as objects of interest rather than, as some of the Chicago school would have seen them, as a blight to be eradicated. He was mildly sympathetic to all social systems, and reserved his disdain for the do-gooders of the settlement house who were earnestly trying to convert the "roughnecks" into decent imitation bourgeoisie.

At this point we move into the big money. Chapter 8 relates the story of the already distinguished young Swedish social economist Gunnar Myrdal's being brought to the United States by the Carnegie Corporation to undertake a "neutral" study of the Negro problem; of his enlisting the help of an impressive band of social scientists; of the outbreak of World War II, which both interrupted his work and also transformed the bargaining position of the Negro; and of his massive report, sagely named *An American Dilemma* so as to place the problem squarely on the shoulders of all Americans. This chapter shows that Myrdal's masterly and conscientious work broke little fresh ground, except perhaps in his theory of method, but because of its provenance and timing it was to have a profound influence on American attitudes toward race relations.

With the United States precipitated into World War II the full range of talents was inevitably mobilized. The United States Army was extremely fortunate in securing the scientific services of many fine social scientists in a Research Branch under the highly professional leadership of Samuel A. Stouffer. Their achievements offer an excellent example of the manner in which secondary use can be made of material collected for administrative purposes. It is evident that the questionnaire surveys conducted during the war were of immediate value to the Army authorities who were faced with many urgent and challenging problems. It is known that the points demobilization system adopted by the authorities at the end of the war was originally suggested by the Research Branch, but these contributions would have had only local and administrative importance had it not been for the initiative of Stouffer and his colleagues and the enlightened sponsorship of the Carnegie Corporation and other bodies. Their assistance made it possible to collate and analyze the mass of survey material that had accumulated and to record a full description of the highly sophisticated techniques that had been developed, including scalogram analysis and latent structure analysis. This material was published in four massive volumes with the generic title *The American Soldier*. Even this did not exhaust its exploitation. A concurrent *Continuities* volume provided several scholars with opportunities for afterthoughts; in particular, Merton and Kitt picked up the numerous half-formulated statements on relative deprivation and built them into the first full-scale presentation of the reference group concept.

The next chapter sees the incursion into sociology of a team of zoologists. Alfred C. Kinsey, of Indiana University, passed straight from an investigation of 150,000 gall wasps to the far more laborious study of the sexual behavior of certain human males and females. According to Kinsey, he was motivated to undertake this task because he found the literature so unhelpful on the problems put to him as an informal counselor by his students. Kinsey was not only the master mind but also the most assiduous worker. By 1948, when *Sexual Behavior in the Human Male* was published, his interviews totaled over 7,000 out of the 12,000 then completed, the residue being shared among five other persons. His interviewing methods were reminiscent more of the prosecuting lawyer than of the psychiatrist. His statistics derived from astronomy rather than from the social sciences. His theory of sexuality was entirely zoological and so completely without moral judgment that it was widely interpreted as encouraging every form of sexual deviation. In spite of throwing him open to criticism on these and other counts, Kinsey's work survives because of its undeniable greatness and integrity. He was also lucky in that his work coincided with a moment in American history when sexual mores were up for reexamination, and in that he was able to satisfy the questioning public that they were indeed normal, thereby relieving untold anxieties. Wars are a forcing time for morals, but Kinsey's work had started in the thirties. In a much more direct way the inquiries that led to *The Authoritarian Personality* were a product of the times. When Hitler seized power, world Jewish opinion was shocked at the number of ordinary Germans who fell in with the anti-Semitism of the Nazi regime. As the tide flowed toward the United States it was felt that some means should be found of identifying potential anti-Semites in the American population. Various inquiries were therefore sponsored, and of these the best known and the most profound was that entrusted to a mixed team of German social scientists and American psychologists jointly led by Adorno and Sanford. The union of German theory and American empiricism proved highly productive. The idea of authoritarianism, long since formulated in Frankfurt, was built into a highly developed test procedure which in its later forms progressively eliminated direct references to overt forms of racial prejudice or authoritarian attitudes. Use was also made of open-ended projective questions and of the Thematic Apperception Test. Selected individuals whose test scores were either exceptionally high or exceptionally low were subjected to clinical interviewing, and their protocols were then correlated with their test scores. This and subsequent work along similar lines at Vassar and Berkeley strongly support the belief that there is an authoritarian-personality syndrome, perhaps transmitted by parents in infancy. This is one case in which the theoretical approach is more convincing and consistent than the empirical studies, which are vulnerable to criticism, and though the approach is also weak in sociological perspectives, on balance the achievement is impressive.

The next chapter reports on a very different type of investigation. For many years Bales at the Harvard Laboratory of Social Relations had been perfecting an instrument for observing the interactions of small problem-solving groups. This involved the use of an observation room and various special recording and analytical procedures. The technique was designed to analyze the manner of interaction during the process of problem solving rather than the subject matter discussed. When *Interaction Process Analysis* was published in 1950 the results obtained were still fairly elementary, but since then the use of the technique has spread all over the world and has led to many insights. Outstanding among these is the identification of at least two types of leadership: the instrumental leader is the chief producer of ideas, while the expressive leader maintains the cohesion of the group. Although the approach is abstract, many concrete applications have already suggested themselves, for example in relation to committee work, in relation to family roles, and in relation to purposive groups, such as bomber crews.

Another important immigrant to the United States was Kurt Lewin. Under his initiative the idea of *group dynamics* has established itself. Lewin was a believer in the necessity of experimentation, and the method of action research is part of this approach. Among Lewin's most distinguished colleagues was Leon Festinger, who with H. H. Kelley is the author of *Changing Attitudes through Social Contact*. In worldly terms this is a small study that concerns itself with the problem of the 100 families who made up the total population of a government housing project in Baytown. These project families were reluctant to make contact with the town as a whole or even with one another because they believed themselves and their neighbors to be of low status and therefore liable to be rebuffed if they made advances to other supposedly higher-status people. The investigators decided to launch an activity program to increase contacts, but, rejecting the straightforward method of sponsoring joint project-town activities, they attempted to proceed by the more theoretically challenging method of raising the self-evaluation of the project people by stimulating greater contacts on the project itself. It was hoped that this would lead in turn to greater contacts between project and town. As a practical experiment this had very limited success, but the relative failure stimulated some intense theoretical speculation. It became clear that the activities arranged by the community workers did not possess by any means a universal appeal. Those who were overpersuaded to join in the activities might end up more dissatisfied and with lower self-evaluation than ever. Those who were unapproachable by the community workers remained unaffected by the vicissitudes of the activity program. Some very general propositions result from this study.

Finally, an attempt is made to draw together the threads which run through the preceding chapters. These are of three kinds. There are first the social problems which stimulated the research. Some of these, such as the problem of assimilating immigrants and of reconciling groups of different national origins, have been more in evidence in the United States than in most other countries. Others are more or less universal in industrial societies: suicide, delinquency, and other symptoms of social disorganization; social and political intolerance; morale, productivity, and social engineering; moral change; the role of social agencies; problems of leadership and group integration.

The next section concerns the techniques and methodology of social investigation and analysis. This includes consideration of the problem of reconciling individual and group dimensions; of the merits and weaknesses of documentary sources, objective and participant observation, the great range of interviewing techniques; of the possibilities of experiment. It takes in the phasing of investigation from first explorations to the limits of proof. It considers the variety of indices and scales that have been constructed and the manner in which statistical treatment has grown up to meet the need to process new forms of data.

Lastly, there is the question of the increasing coherence of empirical sociological theory. It will be shown that, sometimes using different nomenclatures, many scholars have been concerning themselves with very similar sets of ideas. What once seemed to be a limitless network of ideas that were expanded to accommodate any fresh empirical finding is now developing perceptible regularities. Typical examples are the contrasting of *Gemeinschaft* with *Gesellschaft*, the delineation of social reality, clearer understanding of how the individual moves in relation to groups, a more adequate model of how the group functions as a system.

Behind all these procedural and intellectual issues is the question of the aim and the commitment of the sociologist himself. Science is characterized by action rather than by contemplation, and because the human and social consequences of sociological action are so immediate and profound, it is imperative that society and the sociologist be linked by bonds of common moral purpose.

2

SUICIDE AND ANOMIE

Durkheim's *Suicide*[1] is a practically inevitable choice for inclusion in this volume. It was not the first empirically based study that Durkheim undertook, and there is not general agreement that it is his best empirical study, but it is the appropriate one in this context as being the work in which he pioneered the application of statistical methods to a sociological issue.

Émile Durkheim[2] was born on April 15, 1858, in the small town of Épinal in the province of Lorraine on the edge of France, the child of a scholarly rabbinical family. He had a fairly normal career for a bright boy. He distinguished himself at the local college of Épinal. While still young he decided not to train for the rabbinate but to become a teacher, and so at the age of eighteen or nineteen he moved to Paris to the *Lycée Louis-le-Grand*, which was a necessary steppingstone for admission to the *École Normale Supérieure* in Paris, which was at that time a top choice for French academic students. He did the necessary preparatory work, though the requisite cramming disgusted him, and he passed into the *École Normale Supérieure* in 1879, when he was twenty-one years old.

The École was a tremendously exciting center of learning at that time. It had as students and on the faculty people who subsequently made their mark in a variety of fields. Sociology was relatively weak there because it was a new and immature discipline, but Lévy-Bruhl had graduated just before Durkheim was admitted. Philosophy was flourishing, and Durkheim's contemporaries as students included Bergson, Jean Jaurès, and Blondel. In psychology Pierre Janet, since

12

popularized by Elton Mayo and one of the important psychologists at the turn of the century, was in the same year as Durkheim. The intellectual climate was thus highly stimulating, but although Durkheim was exposed to what to us seem to be a group of giants, he did not get on particularly well with them. In fact he found the atmosphere uncongenial. He felt that his fellow students were rather immature dilettantes philosophizing about nothing very much, and this feeling of being out of sympathy with them must have strengthened his resolve to deal with the real world in as realistic a manner as he could achieve.

The two people for whom he did develop great admiration were members of the faculty. One was Fustel de Coulanges, the historian, and the other was the philosopher Boutroux. But one cannot claim that he derived much direct benefit from the École, except that he gained a very good grounding in the possibilities of a logical approach to problems. It was when he began reading for himself that he found his masters in people whom he did not meet in person but only through their writings: men like Renouvier, the advocate of a literally moral philosophy, and later Auguste Comte. These men seem to have had the greatest influence on him.

It was an exciting epoch in another way. The year 1879, when he was admitted, was just eight years after the creation of the Third Republic in a France which had been defeated by Germany. There was at that time among intellectuals a widespread feeling that the old institutions must be replaced because the country had been ossifying. Therefore, although Durkheim was born the son of a rabbi and was very much influenced in childhood by a Catholic instructress, he was himself an atheist and an anticlerical, an attitude which was normal among his generation of intellectuals in France.

In this setting Durkheim developed a threefold objective. First, he felt that he should denounce the dilettantism around him and become a specialist in the type of social investigation that would apply the objective methods of science to human affairs. Second, he felt that he must re-examine the current philosophy, particularly the philosophy of science, and he was not afraid to take that in his stride. Third, he regarded sociology not as an abstract and remote subject but as one which could be applied to social problems and as a corrective to the undesirable and outdated practices still prevalent in France at that period.

Thus we can visualize Durkheim as a man who had had probably the best and most rigorous training that France could offer at the time—which was extremely good—and one who had earned a reputation as a brilliant though rather difficult and humorless person. He did not rank high upon graduation, being one from the last of his class, but even then he could not be ignored. His contemporaries felt that he had not thus far realized his potentialities, but they were impressed with the clear aim which he had set himself, and to which he more or less adhered during his fifty-nine years, of developing a sociology that would make a contribution not only to social understanding but also to the administration of his country.

Like most of his fellow students, on graduating he took various teaching jobs in *lycées* in different cities, and these helped him develop his administrative and other skills. But he planned to become not an administrator but a scholar, and during his five years of teaching he took one year off, half of which he spent in Germany to explore the land of Kant and Hegel. He lingered in Leipzig, where he was enormously impressed by Wundt as a scientific philosopher and by his psychophysical laboratory, and this influence lasted all Durkheim's life.

In 1887 Durkheim began to gain wider recognition, and he was invited to become an instructor in a newly instituted course of social science at Bordeaux. This was a very important move because there were few such openings at that time. He became a professor at Bordeaux in 1896, at the age of thirty-eight, which confirms that his career was developing at a satisfactory pace.

During those years he was not only instructing. He completed his thesis, called later, in book form, *De la division du travail social* (*Division of Labor*). The subject of the thesis fitted in well with his basic theme. The subtitle of the first edition of the book issued reads *Étude sur l'organisation des sociétés supérieures*,[3] and reflects Durkheim's conclusion that specialization is a necessary condition of higher civilization. The corollary of this conclusion served to reinforce and justify his attack on the dilettantism and amateurism that surrounded him at the École. *Division of Labor*, a creative and thoughtful work, contains in partly developed form many of the ideas and hypotheses, including those relating to the causes of suicide, on which he was to work throughout much of his career.

Durkheim defended his thesis with some difficulty in 1893. He had many antagonists on his jury. It was a serious matter defending theses in those days, as it still is in some European countries, but Durkheim was undaunted and won. The book came out the same year, 1893. In 1895 he published the essays known as *The Rules of Sociological Method*,[4] which pronounced his method as *Division of Labor* had pronounced his philosophy. In 1897 came *Suicide*, which is the main topic of this chapter.

Even during this period Durkheim's literary output was not sufficient to keep him occupied. He was also busy preparing for the publication of *L'Année Sociologique*, which first appeared in 1898 and was a tremendously valuable professional journal for early sociologists and social philosophers. The *American Journal of Sociology*, founded in 1896, had preceded *L'Année Sociologique* by about two years, but the two periodicals together signalized an important step forward. They constituted the first proof that one could use the word "sociology" without apology, and that sociology was a sufficiently meaningful word to support even an academic journal.

Durkheim's life in the 1890's was the fullest and richest period of his career. After 1900 he settled down into more of a routine. He spent another ten years as professor at Bordeaux. In 1906 he moved to Paris to fill the chair as Professor of the Science of Education at the Sorbonne. This subject was not exactly in line with his interests, but while he lectured on the history of pedagogy he also gave courses in ethics, religion, marriage and the family—which gave scope to his sociology. Seven years later, in 1913, the University recognized this formally by giving him the composite title Professor of the Science of Education and Sociology. This was the first important chair in France that included the word "sociology."

Durkheim's interest in the function of religion had grown with the years, and in 1912 he published his last major work, *Les formes élémentaires de la vie religieuse* (*Elementary Forms of the Religious Life*),[5] based on a study of primitive Australian society.

During World War I he became not exactly a politician but rather a professional patriot and was absorbed in ephemeral activities. Heartbroken at the death from wounds of his son André, he died in 1917. Certain ambitious works which he had mapped out were left unwritten. In contrast to the glorious decade in which he produced the *Division of Labor*, the *Rules of Sociological Method*, and *Suicide*, his last twenty years seem to have been dissipated in an eminent scholar's round of engagements.

DURKHEIM ON SUICIDE

We now turn to *Suicide*, the book to which this chapter is devoted. Durkheim was quite clear as to his task, which was to demonstrate that the social sciences can examine an important social issue, on which other people have philosophized for a long time, and can show by the systematic presentation of existing facts that it is possible to arrive at useful conclusions which will help with practical proposals for future action. He chose the topic suicide for three reasons. The first reason was that the word "suicide" can easily be defined, even though he shows later that this is not strictly true. His second reason was that there were many statistics available on the subject. Third, suicide was an issue of considerable and growing importance. Suicide had increased three- or fourfold during the nineteenth century and was likely to become a major problem. Thus he could show that his task was not a minor academic exercise but a public issue on which guidance was urgently needed.

There was also the point—although Durkheim did not think this so useful—that a number of people had already done scientific or near-scientific work on suicide. In several countries the local suicide statistics had been examined, and certain conclusions had been derived from them. For example, Ogle in England had examined the demographic material of the British General Register Office, and in 1886 had published a paper in the *Journal of the Royal Statistical Society* called "Suicides in England and Wales in Relation to Age, Sex, Season and Occupation." This paper provided an early hint that there might be certain correlations between suicide rates and other recorded information. The positivist school of criminology in Italy, founded by Lombroso and his associates, had already paid attention to the problem of suicide. The most important pronouncement of this school was probably Morselli's *Il Suicidio*, published in Milan in 1879, but by that date Ferri had already written monographs on the subject. Furthermore, many European countries (including Austria, Belgium, Italy, France, Bavaria, Prussia, Württemburg, and other German states) and the United States had started keeping regular official publications giving not only the number of suicides but also various related statistics that Durkheim could use for his purposes. He did, in fact, base almost all his analysis on material that had already been published. As we shall see, there was only one point at which he found the published material to be insufficient, and in this case he was able to gain the full co-operation of the French Ministry of Justice, which gave him access to unpublished raw material. Apart from that, practically all the material he used had already been published and was available.

As has been mentioned, Durkheim started by asserting that defining "suicide" was a fairly easy matter, but almost at once he encountered difficulties. Many definitions may be called into question by citing marginal cases. For example, if a man is so unhappy that he refuses to eat and wastes away, is that suicide or is it an illness of some kind? When soldiers march into battle in circumstances such that they are certain to be killed, is that suicide or is it something else? In formulating a definition it is not always possible to be certain whether or not to include particular instances. Durkheim, after many years' examination of these different considerations,[6] started with a preliminary definition, and when he found that it was not sufficient he added to it.

His first definition was: "The term *suicide* is applied to any death which is the direct or indirect result of a positive or negative act accomplished by the victim himself." It is clear why "direct or indirect" is needed and also "positive or negative." If a man refuses to eat, in Durkheim's definition, this is suicide just as much as if he eats something poisonous. If a man commits an act that he knows will be punishable by death, this can be as suicidal as if he kills himself with a dagger. But then Durkheim points out that this is still incomplete because it neglects one important feature, namely, that suicide should be an intended act. It is clear that the element of volition should be made explicit. He therefore arrives at the definition: "Suicide is applied to all cases of death resulting directly or indirectly by a positive or negative act of the victim himself which he knows will produce this result."

Durkheim also finds it necessary specifically to exclude animals. Probably today we would not concern ourselves much about this, but at that time there were credible stories of animals that deliberately sought death when something had happened to their masters.

It has been authenticated that some animals pine to death if something happens to their master, but that is different from suicidal intent. Durkheim appends an extraordinary story reported by Aristotle of a horse which had intercourse with its own mother by mistake and was so shocked by this action that it threw itself over a cliff in shame. This does not seem a credible story. Animals, as we know, do not worry whether or not they are closely related to their mates.

We now have a definition of suicide that is recognizable and plausible and that fits in fairly closely with the system by which official suicide statistics have been kept. The last point is important, for it was of no value for Durkheim to evolve a perfect definition that ruled out the use of existing statistics. In most of his definition all that he is doing is producing a somewhat more rigorous version of the ordinary administrative way of defining suicide. It is only fair to add, however, that some categories included as suicide by Durkheim would not be recorded among any normal administrative enumeration of suicides, and their inclusion in the definition has been widely criticized. Durkheim himself apparently changed his mind on this point. In *Division of Labor* he specifically excludes acts of sacrifice and abnegation as found in primitive societies, and by implication he excludes the altruistic suicides of soldier or doctor.

If the widow of the Indian did not survive her husband, nor the Gaul the chief of his clan, if the Buddhist has himself torn on the wheels of the carriage carrying his idol, it is because moral or religious prescriptions demand it. . . . These voluntary deaths are therefore no more suicides, in the common sense of the word, than the death of a soldier or a doctor exposing himself knowingly because of duty.[7]

Later he includes altruistic suicide (unlike Halbwachs and his other followers). While this does not seem to be an issue of major practical importance, as statistics of altruistic suicides are not collected, it is of theoretical importance as related to Durkheim's thesis, which will be discussed later, that suicide can result from either too little or too much (if altruistic suicide is to be discouraged) integration of the individual in his society. Durkheim was right, I think, in classifying the act of sacrifice as a form of suicide.

A second step that Durkheim takes before proceeding—and this is essential to his whole argument—is to demonstrate that suicide is not an arbitrary patternless act committed by a number of individuals, but that the total incidence of suicides for a country permits us to calculate a suicide rate, which is then an example of what he calls a "social fact," that is a function of the society in question. The general concept of the "social fact" is one of the central themes in all Durkheim's writing and thinking, and we shall be returning later in this chapter to what he means and to the difficulties attached to the concept. But he demonstrates in this specific context that, however much we may worry philosophically that by treating suicide as a social fact we may be reifying what is merely a random collection of activities, this worry is not empirically justified. For Durkheim can demonstrate that the suicide rate stays at a remarkably constant level from year to year and that this constancy cannot easily be reconciled with psychological as opposed to sociological explanations. One has to admit that the suicide rate is a function of a particular area at a particular time, and there is considerable stability in this suicide rate—indeed there may even be more stability in suicide than there is in general mortality. Durkheim compares the three sets of figures between 1841 and 1860 and shows that the total mortality rate varies more for those years than the mortality by suicide.[8]

It follows that this particular voluntary act must have some inherent stability which holds the suicide rate steady. Furthermore, as well as being stable in one particular set of circumstances or in one particular country, it also varies very distinctly from one place to another. This is an additional reason for supposing suicide to be a social fact that is independent of the individual decisions of the people who commit suicide. As Durkheim puts it, "Each society is predisposed to contribute a definite quota of voluntary deaths."[9] There is an influence that makes it, in some sense, inevitable that a given society in any particular year will produce a predictable number of deaths.

It is on these grounds that Durkheim considers a study of suicide as properly a field for sociology. Whereas other people have attempted to explain suicides in terms of the motivations of individuals, he rejects this explanation—most people think that he rejects it too much—and although he works through possible explanations in terms of the characteristics of individuals, this is little more than a necessary step before coming to the main point that concerns him, namely, to account for suicide and for variations in suicide rates in terms of differences in the social characteristics of each community compared.

The first part of *Suicide*, in which Durkheim disposes of the broad extrasocial causes, such as psychological states and what he calls "cosmic factors," despite its analytical importance, is quite short. Durkheim then concentrates on examining the nature of social causes, discussing how they produce their effects and how each corresponds to a characteristic social setting. This is the central and most important part of the book in which he develops his celebrated theories. The volume concludes with a relatively short discussion devoted to a precise examination of what the social element of suicide is and what means can be used to counteract suicide. Characteristically, he ends with the practical question: "What steps can we take to reduce this social problem?" Although this is not the most cogent or lasting part of his treatment of the question of suicide, it is for Durkheim an essential and inescapable part of his task. Some years before, in the preface to the first edition of *Division of Labor* he wrote:

Although we set out primarily to study reality, it does not follow that we do not wish to improve it; we should judge our researches to have no worth at all if they were to have only a speculative interest. If we separate carefully the theoretical from the practical problems, it is not to the neglect of the latter; but, on the contrary, to be in a better position to solve them.[10]

SUICIDE AND MENTAL ILLNESS

We now turn to the first analysis, which concerns the extrasocial factors, that is, the factors directly relating to the actual individuals who choose to be suicides. It will be remembered that Durkheim's purpose was to diminish the importance of these factors, which he felt had been previously overstressed, and it is instructive to see how he set about this task. First, there was the very old belief that suicide is directly connected with insanity. The French in particular tended to hold this view. Several authors in the early nineteenth century had examined this point and had concluded that suicide is a kind of illness. One exponent of this view was Dr. Bourdin, author of the monograph *Du suicide considéré comme maladie* (*Suicide Regarded as an Illness*), published in 1845. Durkheim points out that, if suicide is an illness, it could be either a special form of insanity which manifests itself only in this particular way or a consequence of one or more other forms of insanity which are already known. He disposes very quickly of the belief that suicide could be a special form of insanity. He reminds the reader that alienists used to postulate a category of mental illness called "monomania" whose victims showed symptoms in only certain particular ways, one of which might be a suicidal tendency; but he adds that, at the time he is writing, the theory of monomania has been rather discredited because the only proof of its existence is tautological, and there is thus no need to go further into such an explanation.

That leaves the possibility that suicide is a consequence of one or more forms of mental illness. The manner in which Durkheim elaborates his examination of this possibility is characteristic of the way in which he sets about his work. As soon as possible he quits philosophizing and seeks detailed facts which might enable him to accept or eliminate this particular hypothesis.

He points out that there are four types of mental illness which might lead to suicide. He labels these as follows:

1. Maniacal suicide: the type of suicide that someone might commit as a result of hallucinations.

2. Melancholy suicide: the act of a person who wastes away, who cannot concern himself with anything and drifts out of this life.

3. Obsessive suicide: the suicide of a man who had an obsession of some sort which would compel him to take his life.

4. Impulsive or automatic suicide: for example, someone walking beside a precipice has an irresistible impulse to throw himself over.

It is characteristic of all the above types of suicide either that they are motiveless or that the forces leading to the act of suicide are purely imaginary. In Durkheim's contention, it is clear that many recorded cases of suicide have no history of any other concomitant acts or states of mind, as would be necessary to explain the suicide in these terms. In his view, the vast majority of cases of suicide do not have this particular feature, so that anybody who tries to account for all suicides in terms of individual mental illness is being selective in his choice of material.

Durkheim goes on to apply such statistics as he can find that relate insanity and suicide. In certain respects this connection does seem to be supported. For example, both suicide and insanity are commoner in the city than in the country. They tend to rise and fall together year by year; if insanity is on the increase, suicide may well be increasing too. But there are certain other facts which Durkheim thinks will outweigh those two and that make it much less likely that there is any widespread connection between insanity and suicide. For example, the number of women in mental institutions is slightly higher than the number of men in mental institutions, that is, about 55 women to 45 men, but women in the population as a whole constitute only about 20 per cent of the suicides. Durkheim was constantly alert to the possibility that his conclusions might be due to false statistical inferences, and so he examines the consequences of the fact that, the mortality of insane men being higher than that of insane women, there would be fewer insane men than women in mental hospitals left to commit suicide. But this is only in the ratio of 55 men dying in mental hospitals to every 45 women, not nearly enough to account for the great discrepancy in suicide rates, and his conclusion remains that the greater propensity of men to commit suicide is independent of the psychopathic factors.

Second, Durkheim cites the fact that among Jews the insanity rate is above average but their suicide rate is much lower than average. Catholics are a little less often insane than the average but very much less often commit suicide. This also tends to disprove the direct connection between the two.

The third consideration is that there is a marked discrepancy between the ages at which insanity and suicidal tendencies show themselves. It is a common fact that the suicide rate increases with increasing age; that is, the longer people live the more likely they are to commit suicide. On the other hand, insanity is at its highest in the years of maturity, between thirty and forty-five. So this again somewhat discredits the connection between suicides and insanity.

The fourth objection is that, though high insanity rates and high suicide rates are often found together, some countries with low suicide rates have a high proportion of insane people. When he examined the available statistics country by country, he found that these two sets of data do not correlate. As a matter of fact Morselli drew somewhat different conclusions from the same data; Durkheim includes a table based on Morselli's data which shows a fairly steady direct relationship between insanity and suicide, but he distrusts Morselli's figures because he infers that Morselli's "alienated" include imbeciles (mentally handicapped) who of all groups have the least tendency to suicide. One might expect that this would have strengthened the argument in favor of a connection between insanity proper and suicide, even if appropriate statistics were not then available, but Durkheim rather confuses the issue by including a table based on the data of Koch, whose statistics Durkheim describes as "much more complete and apparently more careful"[11] which show a fairly steady inverse relationship between the suicide rate and the combined rate of insanity and imbecility.

Durkheim's fifth reason for doubting a correlation between suicide and mental illness is that, though at the time both insanity and suicide had indeed been increasing for a century, these increases had not been consistent in any one place. This he lightly brushes over and does not examine in detail. On the assumption that the change is related to the increasing level of civilization, Durkheim forestalls any such argument by reference to the compatibility in lower societies of a high suicide rate and a low insanity rate. This argument is weak, based, as it is, on the incomplete diagnosis of mental illness in primitive societies and on Durkheim's definition of suicide, which includes altruistic deaths.

It should perhaps be mentioned that since Durkheim's time evidence has accumulated that senile and functional psychoses play an important part in precipitating many suicides. See, for example, the report by Sainsbury.[12] Authorities today, without disputing Durkheim's main conclusions, will not be happy about his total rejection of any regular connection between suicide and insanity.

One special clinical condition that Durkheim regards as a mental defect is that of alcoholism. The problem of alcoholism has always been a matter of some concern in France, and he is able to produce some quite interesting data on the subject. He includes some ecological material in the form of four maps showing facts relative to alcoholism and suicide. By means of these maps he is able to demonstrate that areas which have a high suicide rate do not correspond with the areas which have a high number of prosecutions for alco-

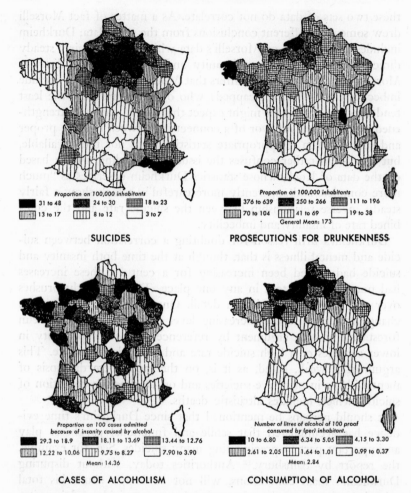

Suicides and alcoholism. (Adapted from Émile Durkheim, *Suicide,*
translated by John A. Spaulding and George Simpson and edited by
George Simpson. New York: The Free Press of Glencoe, 1951, p. 393.)

holism, a high rate of alcoholic disease, or a high rate of alcoholic
consumption. He examines these maps in some detail. One map
shows, for example, that suicides are concentrated either around
Paris or in Normandy or on the Riviera. A second map shows that
prosecutions for alcoholism are concentrated in the tip of Britanny,
in Normandy, to some extent in the Paris region, and also in the

Bourgogne area, where wine is cheap. The third map indicates the incidence of alcoholic diseases at that time, and shows that they were very widely distributed around France, whereas, according to the fourth map, the consumption of alcohol was very much concentrated in Normandy and in the Paris region. There is thus little evidence of any systematic connection between these sets of facts.

In some foreign countries, for example Denmark, a high rate of alcoholism is occasionally associated with a high rate of suicide. But Durkheim describes this as accidental; he does not believe that there is any direct causal connection, although at a later stage in his analysis there are indications why Denmark, as a Protestant nation, is likely to have a high suicide rate. Durkheim attributes the high rate of alcoholism to the fact that because they do not have wine in Scandinavia the peoples drink hard liquor. This conclusion is still encountered. In Germany the districts with the highest consumption of alcohol are also those with the highest suicide rates, and this again seems to have some connection with the division of the country into Catholic and Protestant areas. Durkheim concludes that the evidence does not really support a connection of any importance between alcoholism and suicide.

The next question is whether the suicide rate is perhaps the result of genetic factors. Are certain races intrinsically more prone to suicide than other races? This question brought Durkheim face to face with an issue which is very familiar today but was then somewhat novel. This is the problem of what is meant by "race." Durkheim shows the concept of race to be rather meaningless, and very difficult to pin down in terms of the genetically intermixed countries of Europe with which he is mainly concerned. As occasionally happens, Durkheim's attention to this point seems to be connected with his feeling that he must correct Morselli. Morselli is regularly cast in the role of chief antagonist, perhaps because Morselli's book is a work of substance. In this case Morselli claimed to have demonstrated a significant difference in suicide rates between the four main racial groups found in Europe, namely, the Germanic (German, Scandinavian, Anglo-Saxon, and Flemish), Celto-Roman (Belgian, French, Italian, Spanish), Slav, and Ural-Altaic (small groups very rare in Europe, found in Finland and Hungary and in some Russian provinces).

Durkheim argues that classification into races and racial comparisons of suicide rates based on it are not valid because, when one breaks these so-called racial groups down further, one finds there is even more variation in the suicide rates within each racial group than there is between the supposed racial groups. In the case of the Slav group, for example, the annual suicide rate per million inhabitants ranged from 158 in Bohemia to 14 in Dalmatia. The Celto-Roman group's suicide rates correspondingly varied from 160 in France to 30 in Italy, and even fewer in Spain, for which he does not give a precise figure. In the case of the Germanic group, Denmark had the very high rate of 268, Germany (these figures were before unification) had about 200, whereas there were 84 in Sweden, 70 in England, and 50 in Flanders.

Thus, according to Durkheim, this clearly disposes of the argument that suicide rates can be compared in terms of these racial entities. But he pursues Morselli into his assertion, which appears hard to dispute, that in a country like Austria, which had part German and part Slavonic areas, there seemed to be a connection between race and suicide rate, the predominantly Slavonic parts of the country showing a much higher rate than the predominantly German parts. Durkheim does not agree with this, and he recalculates the figures to exclude Vienna (which even at that date was an important part of Austria) on the grounds that "Vienna, like all capitals, has an enormous annual number of suicides," and by excluding Vienna he shows that there is really not much difference between the German and Slav races when they live in the same social environment. "Accordingly," he states, "the difference observed between them under other circumstances is not one of race."[13]

He undertakes a similar treatment for German and Latin races in Switzerland. When these countries are corrected for religion there seems to be no great racial difference. Durkheim concludes that "Germans commit suicide more than other peoples not because of their blood but because of the civilization in which they are reared."[14] He also very rapidly disposes of another of Morselli's pet theories that tall people are more prone to suicide than short people and that therefore tall races have a higher suicide rate than short races.

Next he considers whether it could be the hereditary factor of filiation—the actual handing-down within families of some genetic propensity—by which suicide is passed on. If not congenital, could a tendency to suicide be transmitted to babies at an early age? On the analogy of tuberculosis, this hypothesis of filiation has a certain appeal to him, but he advances two substantial objections to it. One is that it does not explain the lower suicide rates in women, who are equally exposed to the hereditary factor as men. The second, which is a more cogent argument, is that it does not explain the delay in the incidence of suicide. If a child has caught tuberculosis from his mother, this will show itself at a rather early age, whereas the suicide incidence, as has been mentioned, tends to increase with age, the highest rates being among old people. Thus Durkheim rejected this theory after a quite cursory examination. Perhaps he felt that it was not a threatening type of theory and therefore could be dealt with in a summary fashion.

SUICIDE AND COSMIC FACTORS

The next group of theories examined by Durkheim are concerned with what are described in the English translation as "cosmic factors." This means, for example, the relation between climate and suicide rate. His analysis is based on certain known facts. There are, for example, more suicides in summer. This is a firm trend which occurs in many countries. There are only one or two exceptions, and it is typical of Durkheim's carefulness that he goes into these quite thoroughly. In the Grand Duchy of Baden, in one particular year the suicide rate was highest in the autumn. Durkheim took great pains to show that this did not actually disturb the broad picture of the suicide rate's being at its highest in the summer. Now the obvious hypothesis based on the above facts would be that suicide is due to temperature, a hypothesis accepted by Morselli. Durkheim actively disputes this argument. He admits, for example, that while French soldiers were fighting in Egypt their suicide rate rose sharply. He admits, too, that soldiers and others who go to a tropical country "throw themselves abruptly into the ocean under the direct rays of the sun. . . . The *sirocco*, likewise, which produces a stifling heat, has been observed to have a similar effect on suicide."[15] But, he says, it is also true that during the retreat from Moscow in 1812 the French troops in the intense cold were committing suicide in large numbers. So it cannot be directly the heat which induces people to kill themselves. Secondly, suicides are not necessarily more

common in warmer periods; they are commoner in the spring than
in the fall, which is somewhat warmer, and if one compares the rate
in spring with the rate during a period in the fall which has the
same mean temperature as the spring, the suicide rate in spring is
still higher.

So it seems to Durkheim that the facts cannot be explained in terms
of temperature alone. There is a further argument: the suicide rate
is not higher in southern European countries than in northern European countries. With these considerations in mind, the positivists
Lombroso and Ferri slightly modified their theory and claimed that
it was not the absolute temperature at any time which disposed people to commit suicide but the rise in temperature, such as occurs
in spring. But Durkheim refers the reader to a table which gives the
monthly average temperatures and the monthly suicide rates and
shows that there is no empirical basis for the idea that the change
in temperature corresponds with a change in suicide rate. There is
no conspicuous rise in the suicide rate with the approach of warm
weather.

Durkheim produces another fact which does correlate closely with
suicide and that is the length of the day. It is possible that what is
really responsible for the increase in the suicide rate in the spring is
not the temperature but the longer periods of daylight. As usual,
Durkheim attempts to account for this connection by bringing in
further empirical data. He examines certain statistics which give
the hours at which suicides take place, and shows that there seem
to be two peak times for suicide during the day. One is in the morning between 6 and 11 A.M., and the other is in the afternoon between
noon and 4 P.M. Between these peaks there is a little dip during the
lunch hour (11 A.M. to noon).

Durkheim does not suggest that daylight is the direct cause of
suicide, but he proceeds (by a process that Lazarsfeld has called
elaboration[16]) to suggest that suicide is a function of social activity,
and that the more daytime there is in which to be socially active
(this was before the use of electric light) the more exposure there
is to the likelihood of committing suicide. The lunch-hour calm
(more protracted in the provinces than in Paris) causes a sag in the
suicide rate. He reinforces this by an argument based on the fact
that suicides seem to be more numerous on Mondays, Tuesdays, and
Thursdays than on any other day of the week because these are the

days of greatest economic and social activity. One more cogent point is that the suicide rate is higher in cities than in the country, and this is consistent with the idea that suicide is related to the amount of social activity. The whole argument does, however, remain highly speculative.

IMITATION

The next main theory examined by Durkheim is based on the idea of imitation. Tarde, a contemporary and fellow countryman of Durkheim, had asserted that all forms of behavior, including forms of antisocial behavior such as crime, are essentially a result of imitation. Durkheim treats this assertion in a very characteristic way. First he asks what is meant by "imitation." He arrives at three quite different meanings. One form of imitation is related to what he elsewhere calls "collective representations," that is, the leveling in the consciousness of individuals in society which leads people to think or feel in unison in response to the guidance of their culture. In this sense imitation is a function of assimilation to the group.

A second form of imitation is to follow the manners and customs of a society which lead its members to do what is expected of them, to do the prescribed thing in a given set of circumstances, since conformity possesses social authority. And the third form of imitation occurs when we copy some things just for the sake of copying them, as we might pick up a bad habit from someone else. Durkheim's point here is that the first two are not accurately describable as imitation in a mechanistic sense, but that they involve a certain social element of belonging and subscribing to social pressures. The first type is a constructive act of following through and promoting the common aims and beliefs of the group, and the second reflects a personal desire to conform with the common will. Thus the third meaning is the only one, in Durkheim's definition, that should be admitted as imitation.

How far can this motiveless copying be shown to be a cause of suicide? Durkheim gives some striking cases in which outbreaks of imitative suicide have taken place. There was, for example, the famous example of a sentry box in a Boulogne army camp which was the scene of several suicides in quick succession. There seemed to be no particular reason why they should have occurred, but suicide became a kind of fashion. He cites several other examples of this apparently senseless imitation. He might perhaps have found a place for these transient fashions among the forms of mental disturbance which led to what he called "impulsive suicide"—a type of irrational behavior that does not relate to any objective reality.

Durkheim also looks at imitation from the ecological viewpoint. He states, for example, that the chances of imitation are greater in an urban area, and that the higher urban suicide rate bears out the imitation hypothesis. But this argument fails under detailed analysis. It applies quite well to the *départements* around Paris but not at all to the smaller districts. Durkheim does not labor very long over this point, but he draws the one very interesting conclusion that, since imitation is not a highly probable cause of suicide, reports of suicides in newspapers have little influence. If this conclusion is valid, it would be relevant to current topical questions, such as whether crime is aggravated by certain television programs. The belief that crime programs promote crime is based partly on the theory that people commit crime through imitating other crimes, real or fictional. Certainly it is possible to learn techniques in this way, but that is a different matter.

After his examination of imitation Durkheim is satisfied that he has in general successfully disposed of the nonsocial causes, and thereafter he is directly concerned with social causes and with the social situations in which these causes operate.

We shall turn later to an appreciation of his struggle to achieve a sociology purged of consideration of individual personalities and motivations. At this point we shall merely interpose that this attempt to proceed by successive elimination is methodologically a slippery procedure because not even Durkheim could think of all possible nonsocial causes; he discusses only those that have come to his mind. It is not logically sound to state that there cannot be nonsocial causes because you happen not to have thought of them. Furthermore, although he has in most instances successfully demonstrated that the nonsocial factors which he has considered are not the major causes of suicide, he has nevertheless had to accept many of these factors as subsidiary and partial causes. Nevertheless, he has obviously depreciated the apparent importance of possible explanations, and if he can advance a good positive hypothesis for a social cause, most people would accept his argument that explanations based solely on nonsocial causes are inadequate.

If the suicidal impulse originated in the individual, it is evident that knowledge of the psychological condition of the suicide would be paramount. Apart from theoretical objections to this approach, however, Durkheim also puts forward a practical objection, namely, that although in many countries the officials are required to establish the presumptive motives of suicides, these statistics are of little value.

Unfortunately, official establishments of fact are known to be often defective even when applied to obvious material facts comprehensible to any conscientious observer and leaving no room for evaluation. How suspect must they be considered when applied not simply to recording an accomplished fact but to its interpretation and explanation! To determine the cause of a phenomenon is always a difficult problem. The scholar requires all sorts of observations and experiments to solve even one question. Now, human volition is the most complex of all phenomena. The value of improvised judgments, attempting to assign a definite origin for each special case from a few hastily collected bits of information is, therefore, obviously slight.[17]

If the origin of the suicidal act is to be traced to the social situation, it is necessary to consider not the motivations of the individual but only the background to the act. It would be desirable to proceed by classifying the external causes of a series of suicides, but Durkheim is prevented from taking this first step because no adequate classification of the external causes of suicide has been formulated. So, in his opinion, the right procedure is first to set up a broad classification of social causes of suicide, which can be done on the basis of existing information, and then to take a series of suicides and try to fit each into one or another category of social cause. He describes this solution to a very familiar research problem as an etiological classification rather than as a morphological one—etiology relates to causes and morphology relates to types—but even this basis of classification confronts him with the familiar dilemma of having to devise a classificatory system in advance of systematic data analysis.

In any case, Durkheim feels that it is better to start with an examination of the underlying causes without wasting time on the distant repercussions of these causes on the consciousness of individuals. This is the core of his whole argument. In practice his procedure is to group suicides into three broad etiological types. The first type he calls *egoistic suicides*, the second type *altruistic suicides*, and the third type *anomic suicides*.

EGOISTIC SUICIDE

Durkheim's treatment of egoistic suicide starts not with a theoretical discussion but with an empirical analysis of the relation between religion and suicide. He presents a table which shows a striking difference in the suicide rate between those of different religious persuasions. Protestant states in Europe have a suicide rate three times as high as Catholic states. This table he actually borrows from Morselli. He proceeds to ask whether this could be due to the cultural differences between predominantly Catholic countries and predominantly Protestant countries, and he examines this question by comparing some provinces within the state of Bavaria. Broadly speaking, there was at that time a fairly close similarity of culture in all the provinces of Bavaria, but there were more Catholic families in some of the provinces than in others. Durkheim's analysis shows that even within the same general cultural background the suicide rate will be lower where there are more Catholics. He finds very striking differences. For example, in the nine years 1867–75 the provinces with a Catholic minority of less than 50 per cent had an average suicide rate of 192 per million inhabitants, whereas the provinces which were more than 90 per cent Catholic had an average rate of only 75, that is, only two-fifths as many. This analysis is replicated for the state of Prussia, and although the general level of suicide rates was higher because Prussia had a larger proportion of Protestants, the variation in provincial suicide rates varied in a similar fashion with the proportions of Protestants and Catholics.

Jews, on the whole, seemed to have a suicide rate even slightly lower than Catholics. This leads Durkheim to speculate first whether this is perhaps due to the fact that in many places both Jews and Catholics were minorities within a predominantly Protestant society. Had the need for social cohesion perhaps been the reason for their lower suicide rate? Durkheim gives grounds for supposing that, though this might be true in some cases, it is not the main reason. Protestant minorities, for example, do not show a lower suicide rate.

Durkheim suggests that the real difference between Protestants and Catholics is that the Protestant has the opportunity, and is encouraged, to exercise much greater freedom of inquiry than the Catholic. Whereas the Catholic obeys the rules prescribed for him, the Protestant is free, at least to some extent, to question rules and to think things out for himself. Durkheim says, in fact, that the loss of certainty involved in having to think things out for himself undermines the determination of the Protestant not to kill himself. Because there is less uniformity as to goal, less integration, the individual is less ruled by conscience, less dominated by the group morality, and is therefore more able to take his individual decision about ending his life if circumstances appear to warrant it. Durkheim suggests that this fact is somewhat confirmed by the situation in England, a Protestant country, in which the suicide rate is relatively low because the Established Church exerts more pressure on society than do churches in other Protestant countries.

He connects this emphasis on free inquiry and lack of certainly with the quest for knowledge; this argument was undoubtedly corroborated at that time by the education statistics, which showed that the Protestant countries had a much higher level of education than the Catholic countries. This distinction was found to be true even when Catholic and Protestant provinces were located in the same state, as in Prussia. England was also shown to fit into this pattern because its educational level at that time was relatively low. In that respect England ranked closer to Catholic than to Protestant countries.

Another result which helps to confirm this point is that the best-educated groups in society, namely, those in the liberal professions, are in all countries most prone to commit suicide. Durkheim also suggests that the lower educational level of women would help to explain their lower proneness to suicide. This argument is even supported by an opposite result derived from the United States. Negro women in America were at that time better educated than their Negro men compatriots, and their propensity to suicide was well above average, at times even surpassing that of white women.

This conclusion left unexplained the fact that Jews, with a high level of education, had relatively low suicide rates. Durkheim suggests that this might be explained by the fact that their education was not in the same way the result of a lack of certainty, and that the characteristic Jewish thirst for knowledge was much more instrumental, in that the Jew desired knowledge "not in order to replace his collective prejudices by reflective thought, but merely to be better armed for the struggle. For him it is a means of offsetting the unfavorable position imposed on him by opinion and sometimes by law. And since knowledge by itself has no influence upon a tradition in full vigor, he superimposes this intellectual life upon his habitual routine with no effect of the former upon the latter."[18] And so on. However true this description may be, it is a monumental and classic example of *ex post facto* argument.

The general conclusion, leaving out the special case of the Jews, is that desire for knowledge and the tendency toward suicide both stem from the lack of cohesion in the society, and that it is the lack of cohesion which is the original cause of both these effects. Hence one cannot blame knowledge as such for suicide, for knowledge is an intervening variable. One cannot say that more knowledge causes more suicides, but rather that a tendency to suicide is one of the prices that have to be paid for being in the liberal professions.

After the discussion of religion and education Durkheim turns to the family and its influence on the suicide rate, and this is the context—the only occasion in *Suicide*—in which he constructs his own statistics. There is a common belief, supported by the crude demographic data, that more married men and women commit suicide than unmarried people. These unstandardized statistics are misleading because the unmarried category includes the young up to the age of sixteen and suicide is very rare among children. Furthermore, as has been mentioned, the suicide rate increases steadily with age, and as unmarried persons are younger on average than married persons, there is a constant tendency to exaggerate the suicide rate of married persons. With a full age correction Durkheim estimates that the ratio would be 160 unmarried suicides to every 100 married suicides for a standardized population.

In his detailed analysis Durkheim first concerns himself with the question of the widowed. Do the widowed conform more in their suicide rates to the married or to the unmarried? Is it true, as has been suggested, that widowhood is the most unlucky of all states from the point of view of suicide? He found it very difficult to trace any published statistics to help him answer these questions, and this inadequacy encouraged him, with the assistance of Marcel Mauss, his son-in-law, to make a fresh analysis of suicide rates for the three years 1889–91 in France, making use of unpublished documents in the possession of the French Ministry of Justice. For this purpose 25,000 suicides were classified. Durkheim was able to judge from the similarity of the results relating to these three years that he need not analyze any further data.

His main presentation of this material is in terms of an index, a tool of analysis, which he calls the *coefficient of preservation;* this is the ratio between suicide rates for different categories of people. Thus the coefficient of preservation between married and unmarried would be the ratio of suicide rates for the two (that is, 1.6 in favor of the married). Incidentally, he slightly confuses this treatment in the middle of his presentation when he stops using the coefficient of preservation and substitutes the *coefficient of aggravation,* which is nothing but the inverse of the coefficient of preservation.

Examination of his summary tables suggests to him the following generalizations:

1. Marriages that take place too early tend to provoke suicide, especially for men. Men who marry very young are extremely likely to commit suicide, the coefficient of preservation being about 0.2. (He warns us that this result is based on a very small number of cases.)

2. From the age of about twenty the married of both sexes are less suicidal than the unmarried.

3. The coefficient of preservation varies with the sexes. In some countries, like France, it is men who are favored by marriage, and their married/unmarried coefficient of preservation is higher than for women, but in other states, such as Oldenburg, marriage apparently favors women more than men, and then the married/unmarried coefficient of preservation is higher for women than for men.

4. The state of widowhood (that is, the loss of a spouse by death) reduces the coefficient of preservation but does not bring it below unity. A widower, as compared with someone who has never been married, may have a coefficient of preservation as high as 1.6—there is some residual benefit from the married state, you might say, which makes it slightly less likely that a man once married will commit suicide.

This could be attributed, as Durkheim points out, either to the marital environment or to marital selection. Experience of marriage may permanently diminish suicidal tendencies, or perhaps potential suicides are less likely to marry in the first place. The second possibility was favored by some of Durkheim's predecessors, such as Bertillon and Letourneau, but Durkheim believes that it is confuted by the facts he has collected. His explanation is that, contrary to the general opinion, the state of marriage in fact benefits men more than women. Therefore, as men derive more benefit from marriage, they are more, as he says, protected by marriage than women are, and this is reflected in their favorable coefficient of preservation as compared with that of women.

Durkheim next examines the question whether this preservation is a function of the conjugal group (having a husband or a wife) or a function of the family group (having children). He is able to show that having children very steeply decreases the likelihood of suicide. Indeed, the coefficient of preservation between childless married men and unmarried men was only 1.5, whereas the coefficient of preservation between married men with children and unmarried men was 2.9. According to his calculations, as soon as a man has a child he almost halves his chances of suicide. This effect is so striking that widowers with children are better off than married men without children; if a man's wife dies, leaving him with children, he is still less likely to commit suicide than if his wife is alive but he has no children. The aggravating effect of childless marriages appears with special clarity in the case of women. In Durkheim's figures for France, childless married women were found to commit suicide half again as often as unmarried women.

Taking the analysis one stage further, Durkheim finds that the coefficient of preservation increases with the size of the family, so that each additional child living in the household decreases the chances of suicide.

The results of this analysis thus run counter to another widely held theory about suicide, namely that it is caused by life's burdens and that to support a wife and family is an unbearable load from which people escape by committing suicide. This popular theory is discredited by Durkheim, and he is led to question Malthus' thesis that it is so unpleasant for parents to raise a large family that they should be protected from this eventuality. Durkheim points out that restricting the size of the family in fact has a reverse effect, according to his analysis, in that it diminishes the human desire to live. But he does not seem to consider the alternative hypothesis that family men refrain from suicide through a sense of obligation to their wives and children whom it is their duty to support.

Just as the stability and solidarity of a family are favored by size, so also a strongly constituted political society might be expected to restrict suicide. This theory is tested by Durkheim, who examines the suicide statistics in periods of great political upheaval. Certain kinds of political upheaval, again contrary to common opinion, reduce the suicide rate. This had been shown by Morselli, and Durkheim accepts Morselli's conclusion. It is found, for example, that a state of war or a real crisis that binds a society together will be reflected in a reduction in the suicide rate, which may stay below average for several subsequent years. This can be shown occasionally even in such a mild event as an election crisis; in particular a fairly important local issue has an effect on the suicide rate. One possible explanation of this is that at such a time record keeping is less accurate, but Durkheim does not think this a likely explanation because the result is found so universally and also because of the continuation of the lowered rate for a year or two after the crisis.

Once he has presented his empirical results, Durkheim sets up three propositions: (1) Suicide varies inversely with the degree of integration of religious society, (2) suicide varies inversely with the degree of integration of domestic society, and (3) suicide varies inversely with the degree of integration of political society. This formulation makes it clear why he chose the title *egoistic* for the first type of suicide. As Durkheim sees it, suicide of this type is a consequence of social disintegration.

But society cannot disintegrate without the individual simultaneously detaching himself from social life, without his own goals becoming preponderant over those of the community. . . . If we agree to call this state egoism, in which the individual ego asserts itself to excess in the face of the social ego and at its expense, we may call egoistic the special type of suicide springing from excessive individualism.[19]

Durkheim proceeds in several pages of extremely interesting and highly speculative argument that explain why in his view excessive individualism not only responds to suicidal influences but is itself a cause of suicide. There is a striking parallel here between

Durkheim and the early Freud in their attribution of the death wish to the state of egoism.

ALTRUISTIC SUICIDE

The second group of suicides consists of what Durkheim calls *altruistic suicides*. The justification for including these in the definition of suicides has already been discussed. He reminds us that this type of suicide has been frequently recorded among what he calls "lower societies," and he dredges from the classics and from the early ethnological studies examples of practices that illustrate the self-inflicted deaths required by ritual or social duty. There are certain situations, for instance, in which elderly people are obliged to kill themselves or be killed by their children, quite common situations in which the widows of important personages are included in the funeral pyre, and some others where the close retinues of chiefs are killed or kill themselves when the chief dies. These are what Durkheim calls *obligatory altruistic suicide*, but there are other forms of altruistic suicide, namely, *optional altruistic suicide*, that is, suicides which are respected but not required,* and *acute altruistic suicide*, such as the self-destruction of religious mystics.

The central feature of these altruistic suicides is that, unlike the egoistic suicides, they are impelled by group solidarity. The egoistic suicides are individuals who think that it is for them to decide what to do, because they have no roots in society, whereas the altruistic suicides are those who give themselves up to the will of their particular society and do whatever the rule tells them to do.

As statistics for primitive peoples tend to be deficient, Durkheim concentrates in his empirical analysis on soldiers. He starts with the general fact that the suicide rate of soldiers is much higher than that of the civilian population of the same age, and he sets out to discover the reason for this surprising fact. Soldiers are healthy, the flower of their countries, they have a high *esprit de corps* and live communally, so one would expect on those grounds that their solidarity would hold them together. Is it because they are unmarried? No, because unmarried civilians have a coefficient of

---

* "The readiness of the Japanese to disembowel themselves for the slightest reason is well known."[20]

preservation of 1.6 in comparison with unmarried soldiers. The suicide rates, furthermore, of noncommissioned officers are higher than those of ordinary other ranks, and the rates for officers, many of whom were married, are higher still. So it seems that the military status of the individual is somehow related to his tendency to suicide.

The second possibility is that the high suicide rate is due to alcoholism. Durkheim rejects this on the grounds that everywhere the effect of alcohol on suicide rate is meager, and a marginal cause could not account for the high suicide rate among soldiers even though they might drink rather heavily.

Is it that soldiers become so disgusted with the hardships of army life that they feel the desire to kill themselves? This does not explain it, for various reasons. First, because one would expect soldiers to become accustomed to army life. The fact that they endure it for a time would make them more willing to survive its rigors, whereas according to the data suicides of soldiers increase with length of service and, as with civilians, increase with increasing age. Second, this explanation is not borne out by the fact that, although officers and noncommissioned officers have better lives than ordinary soldiers, they are also more prone to suicide. A third objection is that men who have volunteered to stay in the army longer than they are required to stay or have re-enlisted are more suicidal than the average.

Durkheim's residual hypothesis is that the suicide rate of soldiers is high because soldiers are altruistic, because they are trained to devalue their selves and their own wishes, to immolate their own interests in the interests of the group; consequently, because life itself is made less important, suicide does not mean so much to them. This hypothesis is consistent with the facts already given and is also supported by some other evidence. It is established, for example, that the soldiers' rate is much the same in all countries, considerably more so than civilian rates. There thus seem to be some features in the soldier's life which lead to a constant rate in different countries. Finally, elite troops, who have learned best to discount life and independence, are also the most susceptible to suicide.

We may thus contrast two extremes. At one end is a traditional-type country with a traditional attitude toward the army and also a traditional army ethos. Such a country will have a high altruistic suicide rate but, conversely, is likely to have a lower egoistic rate because there is a well-knit society. At the other extreme, Durkheim finds that political liberalization is leading toward civilian-type armies, so that military suicide rates of the altruistic type are declining, whereas civilian suicide rates of the egoistic type are increasing. Obviously this tendency has progressed greatly since Durkheim was writing.

This, then, is an outline of how Durkheim treats altruistic suicide. He then turns to the third group, which he calls *anomic suicide*.

ANOMIC SUICIDE

It can be shown that suicide rates increase at times of economic crisis; for example, bankruptcies correlate with suicides. The suicides are not necessarily attributable to actual financial difficulties; occasionally, for example, a dramatic political change has led to an economic advance, which may also raise the suicide rate. Durkheim cites the case of Italy, where there was a phenomenal increase in economic activity after the conquest of Rome by Victor Emmanuel in 1870. And yet in the following seven years the suicide rate increased by 36 per cent. This increased tendency to suicide seemed to follow directly from the disturbance of the old social and political order, even though the upheavals had favorable economic consequences.

This apparent anomaly is explained by Durkheim's thesis that an increase in suicides follows any disturbance of what he calls the *collective order*. This leads directly into the core of his argument and into his concept of *anomie*. He shows that in a fixed society people have limited aspirations and know how much they can expect to achieve. In a society in upheaval people no longer have to limit their aspirations. But there is a limit, and when they discover an unbridgeable gap between their aspirations and their achievements they suffer the shock that tends to lead them to anomic suicide.

Durkheim is obliged to account for the fact that certain political crises, like war situations, reduce suicide rates, whereas other political crises, like those that have just been discussed, increase suicide rates. He explains this apparent contradiction by the assertion that certain sorts of political crisis unite a society against an external danger, and that when society is unified in this way, as often occurs during wartime, suicide rates will go down because internal cohesion is increased. On the other hand, there are certain types of political or economic crisis which throw the whole basis of social cohesion open to reconsideration, and in these circumstances anomic suicide will increase.

Durkheim's argument that there is a direct connection between the disturbance of social norms and a high suicide rate is an extremely important contribution to the development of sociological theory. It relates to an embryonic form of the reference-group theory, suggesting that individuals commit suicide not because, for example, they are poor but rather because their living standards are lower than they think is appropriate. In a crisis the reference point becomes indeterminate. The level of aspiration is unlimited, so that people develop an unrealistic view of their potentialities, and when this view fails, they are liable to commit suicide.

If people are really poor, Durkheim argues, "poverty protects against suicide because it is a restraint in itself. . . . So the less one has the less he is tempted to extend the range of his needs indefinitely."[21] People know what they have and what they can hope to have. If they can scrape through, it is enough. Earlier, in *Division of Labor,* Durkheim had pointed out how mistaken outside observers may be in their assessment of the misery of others:

It is true that observers have sometimes painted the life of lower societies in quite different colors. But that is because they have taken their own impressions for those of the natives. But an existence which appears intolerable to us can be quite satisfying for men of a different physical and moral constitution. . . . To pity the lot of primitive peoples, it is not enough to establish that hygiene is badly observed there, that police protection is wanting. The individual alone is competent to appreciate his happiness. He is happy if he feels happy.[22]

This restraint is comparable with the traditional restraints of religion and, as Max Weber later pointed out, is an important point of departure of the Protestant ethic from the Catholic viewpoint. According to the Protestant ethic, the individual is expected to aspire, and it is this accent on individual achievement which, according to Durkheim, helps to account for the high suicide rates in a Protestant country and even more so in a society in which religion has lost much of its influence. The limit is reached in the expanding economy of an open society.

There, the state of crisis and anomie is constant and, so to speak, normal. From top to bottom of the ladder, greed is aroused without knowing where to find ultimate foothold. . . . A thirst arises for novelties, unfamiliar pleasures, nameless sensations, all of which lose their savor once known. Henceforth one has no strength to endure the least reverse. . . . We may even wonder if this moral state is not principally what makes economic catastrophes of our day so fertile in suicides.[23]

This vivid description of anomie was one of Riesman's starting points. To him, suicide was a natural conclusion for the inner-directed man if he should be overwhelmed by guilt at his own inadequacies. "Durkheim was right to see comparatively high suicide rates in the advanced industrial countries as symptoms of a psychological malaise uncontrolled by any cultural tradition";[24] but we could add that Durkheim's image of the fickle, pleasure-seeking society contains more than a foretaste of other-direction.

Durkheim examines his empirical material for tests of his theory of anomie. He points out that just as suicide rates are high in the liberal professions so they are highest among those social groups connected with trade and industry because here are occupations in which the potential rewards are greatest.

He then passes to an examination of the relation between divorce and suicide, and shows that the divorce rate is very closely connected with the suicide rate and that the consequences of divorce are thus quite distinct from those of widowhood. This question had been studied by Bertillon in a detailed analysis of the different Swiss cantons, some Catholic and some Protestant, and also in a study of French *départements*. Durkheim accepts Bertillon's analysis but rejects his interpretation. Bertillon had postulated that different areas contained a different proportion of families suffering from what he called "unstable equilibrium"—people of irregular lives, with poor character and intelligence. Durkheim discounts the idea that some districts have more than their fair share of genetically psychopathic personalities, but suggests that the coincidence of high divorce and high suicide rates stems from a single social fact, namely, that a state of anomie is in operation.

Mention has already been made of Durkheim's rather surprising conclusion that, if a low suicide rate can be treated as an index, marriage favors the husband more than the wife. This conclusion is extended if consideration of divorce is introduced. The facts reveal that in societies in which divorce is permitted marriage reduces a woman's likelihood of committing suicide, whereas in societies in which divorce is not permitted marriage increases the likelihood of her committing suicide; when a woman is unable to escape from the marriage state her status is correspondingly depressed, and this is reflected in the manner indicated. This argument has to be closely reasoned, and Durkheim (or his translator) appears to have slipped into the erroneous statement that "only husbands contribute to the rise in the suicide rate observable in societies where divorces are frequent, wives on the contrary committing suicide more rarely than elsewhere."[25] The latter assertion is in contradiction to the suicide rates indicated in his Table XXVIII; it is only the married/unmarried coefficient of preservation for wives which is relatively high in societies where divorces are frequent.

Finally, Durkheim brings up other data in confirmation of his theory which aims to account for the parallelism between divorces and suicides. First, since matrimonial instability is more complete with divorce than with mere separation, this fits in with the fact that the suicide rate for divorced persons is much higher than that for separated persons. Second, support is given by the fact that the male unmarried suicide rate grows steepest at the age of maximum sexual feelings for men, between twenty and forty-five, and this reflects the sexual anomie from which young men suffer if they have no institutionalized sexual life. This effect is not seen in the case of females, which "is just what we should expect if, as we have granted, woman is not very sensitive to this form of anomie."[26] Lastly, Durkheim harks back to some points made in an earlier chapter relating to the comparative advantage that men gain from marriage in France and certain other countries. I have not seen any later examination of these data, but it is a point which could well have been studied in a wider context, particularly in the United States, where women are believed to have a very privileged position both inside and outside marriage. In the United States too the divorce rate is exceptionally high, a fact which at least bears out Durkheim's theory even if it does not clarify it.

Durkheim devotes one more chapter to a summary of his typology. While suicide is always the act of a man who for some reason prefers death to life, it must be made abundantly clear that there is not one form but various forms of suicide. Given his etiological classification of the three forms of suicide—egoistic, altruistic, and anomic—Durkheim claims that suicides can then be examined in their morphological aspects, and study can be made of what features are present in the actual states of mind or other distinctive properties of the individual suicides. He summarizes the individual states of mind as follows. The egoistic suicide is in a state of resignation; he is opting out of a society which, he feels, has no further hold on him or on his right to take his own life. The altruistic suicide has what Durkheim calls inner conviction; he knows that he is doing what is prescribed by his value system. And it is because he is so closely bound up in the mores of his society that he will kill himself without hesitation. The anomic suicide is a person whose passions are out of control. The fact that the external restraints and moral values around him are in confusion will mean that his passions will determine his actions in this case.

While Durkheim suggests this contrast between the despondent egoist and the overexcited anomic, it seems that the distinction between egoistic and anomic suicide, at least in terms of personality, is not completely clear. In terms of culture the difference is more discernible. At the one end there is the stable society containing a minority of deviant egoists some of whom end in suicide; at the other end there is a measure of social disorganization in which individual anomie is a recognizable norm. These are perhaps sufficiently different to be subdivided, possibly not sufficiently different to be considered extremes, as Durkheim attempts to use them.

However, though Durkheim's classification remains imperfect, his distinction between personal motivations and cultural pressures has proved enormously stimulating to sociological theory. In particular it is in the foundation of Merton's classic paper "Social Structure and Anomie," in which he sets out "to discover how some social structures exert a definite pressure upon certain persons in the society to engage in non-conforming rather than conforming conduct"[27] and in which he sets forth a logically powerful typology of modes of individual adaptation. Five modes are distinguished: conformity to the prevailing goals and means; innovation, the acceptance of goals and the rejection of means; ritualism, retention of means and their elevation as goals; retreatism, rejection of both goals and means; rebellion, the attempt to institutionalize substituted goals and means. Of these, it is clear that innovation bears a relation to Durkheim's anomie and that retreatism bears a relation to his egoism.

Durkheim has retained one last empirical surprise. He is able to show by the use of data from France, Prussia, England, and Italy that, contrary to expectations, there is no obvious relation between the etiology of the suicide and the method of suicide chosen. It seems, rather, that social factors determine the choice of means and are stable in a given society for quite long periods. Even seasonal or other cosmic factors do not seem appreciably to affect the choice. Suicide by drowning, for example, is as frequent in winter as in summer. But opportunities vary and are reflected in modes: firearms must be available before they can be used; jumping from high buildings is commoner in cities because the buildings are higher; the development of railways led to a crop of suicides on the tracks. Perhaps the most influential factor was the dignity attached to different types of death. Some are considered noble, some degrading; but the honorable choice—decapitation, poison, hanging—varies with the society.

SOCIAL THEORY

This concludes Durkheim's main empirical findings. But it does not conclude his book, for he returns to a reconsideration of the underlying causes of suicide. Here he is concerned, not with the data, but with their essence and with the conceptual guidelines that inform all his thinking—the *social fact, social normality*, and *collective representations*.

Belief in the existence of *social facts* is a fundamental feature of Durkheim's methodology, and his *Rules of Sociological Method* is predominantly concerned with the recognition of social facts. These concepts of Durkheim's have been ascribed a certain mystical quality by some of his critics, but this was not justified by what Durkheim himself wrote, at least in the 1890's. For him a *fact* in the social category is one whose incidence and regularities are conditioned by the social context and vary with the social context. This does not lead to universality. "A thought which we find in every individual consciousness, a movement repeated by all individuals, is not thereby a social fact."[28] On the contrary, social facts are products of their environments. "Currents of opinion, with an intensity varying according to the time and place, impel certain groups either to more marriages, for example, or to more suicides, or to a higher or lower birth rate, etc."[29] Hence, "the relations of suicide to certain states of social environment are as direct and constant as its relations to facts of a biological and physical character were seen to be uncertain and ambiguous. Here at last we are face to face with real laws, allowing us to attempt a methodical classification of types of suicide."[30] Today, when social causation (or functional interdependence) is taken for granted, this claim seems commonplace, but at the end of the nineteenth century it was still very necessary to assert that at least some regularities derived from social rather than individual influences.

Another concept used by Durkheim and often misunderstood is that of *social normality*. As a scientist he is determined not to be misled into the sterile belief that good and evil are irrelevant for science. For him science is senseless if it does not offer assistance in the selection of ends and in the choice between alternative means to these ends. At the same time he recognizes that it is necessary to have some criteria by which normality may be judged and which are arrived at independently of immediate moral judgments. To him, the fault of the morally committed lies not so much in the determination to distinguish the normal from the morbid but in the fact that normative judgments are interposed too soon.

The common flaw in these definitions is their premature attempt to grasp the essence of phenomena. They presuppose propositions which, true or not, can be proved only at a more advanced stage of science. . . . Instead of aspiring to determine at the outset the relations of the normal and the morbid to vital forces, let us simply seek some external and perceptible characteristic which will enable us merely to distinguish these two orders of facts.[31]

The simplest answer is that what is most commonly found is the normal, and this statistical definition has a great attraction for him. "We shall call ‘normal’ those social conditions that are the most generally distributed, and the others 'morbid' or 'pathological.' "[32] But this definition, which may be the only viable definition in physiology in which normal functioning has a more or less constant and recognizable sense, is undermined in social phenomena by the constant processes of social change. Here an emergent feature still statistically unimportant may yet be a normal response to changed conditions and should sometimes be recognized as the norm even before it is numerically predominant. Conversely, "a phenomenon can persist throughout the entire range of a species although no longer adapted to the requirements of the situation,"[33] and this should become the "pathological" form as soon as its usefulness is seen to be ended.

In *The Rules of Sociological Method* Durkheim embraces the identity of average with normal,[34] but in *Suicide* he categorically rejects Quételet's theory of the average type, at least in relation to suicidal tendencies, principally for the very reason that it makes no allowance for social change or for the *collective representations* peculiar to a given social environment which lead to a suicide rate which is at once remarkably constant and almost negligibly small in its incidence. If the French rate of 150 suicides per million citizens per annum is expressed as an average intensity of the suicidal inclination, it would have to be described as 0.00015, which is unimpressively weak. Therefore, although it may be stated that some occurrence of suicides is normal, just as some incidence of crime is normal, the incidence of suicide cannot be traced back to a latent tendency which is evenly but miscroscopically to be found in every individual.

It is thus that Durkheim hovers on the brink of describing machinery by which the social facts of a given environment operate to influence the actions and attitudes of the individual in that society. Perpetuation of suicide rates, or of any other social fact, is not mediated by interpersonal transactions. Transcending the personal transmission is the irresistible pressure of collective representations. "Collective tendencies have an existence of their own; they are forces as real as cosmic forces, though of another sort; they, likewise, affect the individual from without, though through other channels."[35] Just as mortality rates depend on the climate or the nature of the soil, so also moral acts, such as suicide, are reproduced with even greater uniformity because they also depend on forces external to individuals. But at this point Durkheim holds back. Just as in an earlier generation Florence Nightingale had refused to believe in the existence of germs which could so plausibly account for the cross infection of overcrowded hospital patients, so here Durkheim fails to seize the mystery of the unconscious.

Today it is generally recognized that psychical life, far from being directly cognizable, has on the contrary profound depths inaccessible to ordinary perception, to which we attain only gradually by devious and complicated paths like those employed by the sciences of the external world. The nature of consciousness is therefore far from lacking in mystery for the future.[36]

Durkheim's antagonism to individual psychology was partly aimed polemically at Tarde, his distinguished contemporary, and the immaturity of the introspective philosophizing which constituted much of the psychology of their time made his position tenable. Even when he claimed that social facts should be explained in terms of other social facts and not in terms of individual facts, he found it necessary, as Alpert has pointed out,[37] to postulate an abstracted kind of individual, considered as he would be were he to live in complete isolation. In other contexts Durkheim speaks of the individual "as he really is," and here he is a recognizable individual motivated by both society and self. Durkheim's stress on man as a social animal was an essential element in his campaign to supplant the individualistic theories that had prevailed in the nineteenth century, and it is primarily as a polemic device that it must be judged. It was left to his pupil Maurice Halbwachs[38] to state the more balanced relationship between social and individual determinants of suicide.

It has also been mentioned that Durkheim went into the question of suicide, as into the other social questions he studied, with the intention of changing society and eliminating social evils. He therefore quite naturally devotes the end of his book to what he calls "practical consequences." In view of his studiously objective view of normality he has first to consider whether suicide should be regarded as normal or abnormal. He concludes that the presence of a modicum of all three of his etiological types of suicide—egoistic, altruistic, and anomic—is to be regarded as normal. But he tempers this conclusion by the suggestion that the enormous increase in the number of voluntary deaths, many of them traceable to anomie, is "a pathological phenomenon becoming daily a greater menace."[39]

By what means are we to overcome this menace? Would an increase in legal penalties reduce suicide? Durkheim believes that public opinion would not support harsher penal action, though moral penalties—refusal of a regular burial, deprivation of certain civic, political, or family rights—might be acceptable. But it might easily not be an effective deterrent.

Durkheim rejects education because education is too much in the image of society, and if society produces suicides, education cannot be expected to counter suicide.

This leaves the possibility of strengthening the social institutions which will increase social control of the egoistic individual and will moderate the influence of anomie. But political control is too far removed from the individual, and religious control is too much merely a symbolic idealism. This leaves the family, but the modern family has lost its entity as a collective being. Families become smaller; individuals live alone in pursuit of their careers.

Durkheim then turns to the possible power of the work group institutionalized into some kind of corporation made up "of all workers of the same sort, in association, all who co-operate in the same function."[40] This idea of the corporation, which will act as an intermediary third force between a bureaucratic central government and the individual, has been found attractive by generations of social theorists. The form, though not the substance, of the corporation was taken over by Mussolini's Italian fascist dictatorship as an instrument of central control, and this misuse has done to the idea a disservice which will take a lot of living down.

Durkheim proposes the corporation as an antidote to egoistic suicide, but it is interesting that at this point of his exposition he states that anomic suicide is closely related to egoistic suicide and could be combated by the same means.[41]

Finally, among his practical measures, Durkheim turns to the question of combating the suicides resulting from conjugal anomie. Here he reaches the apparently logical conclusion that as there is a correlation between divorce and suicide, "the only way to reduce the number of suicides due to conjugal anomie is to make marriage more indissoluble."[42] He advocates this even though he recognizes that in society as then constituted the protection of marriage against divorce would favor the man and might actually increase the number of female suicides. In the long run this would be modified by forging a society in which man and woman have become "creatures of the same nature," so that "man and woman are equally protected by the same institution." But all this cannot be achieved without profound changes in social structure, and in Durkheim's view it presupposes what is nothing less than a total reversal of the trend of social development, away from the supposed economic benefits of large-scale organization and toward what he calls *occupational decentralization* by which, without prejudice to the division of labor, each individual would have a local center to which he could owe his social allegiance without losing his larger patriotism. This idea, like that of the corporation, is an attempt to come to terms with an industrial civilization which has found many latter-day supporters.[43]

We are here concerned more with Durkheim's concepts and methods than with his substantive findings. But these findings were of considerable importance and have been mainly refined rather than materially challenged by subsequent work. In 1933 Dublin and Bunzel listed the prevailing factors accepted at that date. These have been summarized by Alpert[44] as follows:

1. The rates of suicide are higher in the summer than in the winter.

2. They are higher among people suffering from mental diseases than among the mentally normal population.

3. Men have a higher suicide rate than women.

4. In the United States the suicide rate for whites is higher than that for Negroes but lower than the rate for Chinese and Japanese.

5. Older people have a higher suicide rate than younger people.

6. The suicide rate is higher in urban than in rural areas.

7. Soldiers have a higher rate of suicide than the civilian population.

8. Protestants have a higher suicide rate than Catholics.

9. The suicide rate is higher among single, widowed, and divorced persons than among the married.

10. Among the latter it is higher for those who have no children than for those who are parents as well as spouses.

Of these ten statements all except No. 2 and No. 4 are found in Durkheim's volume. Number 4, which is partially treated in

Suicide, is a purely local application of a more general affect, and No. 2 is one on which Durkheim did comment but on which the psychiatric evidence has since been enormously improved. But far more important than these isolated assertions is the conceptual frame welded by Durkheim to hold them in position, and much of the fresh evidence collected during the twentieth century has gone to enlarge the applicability of his sociological concept of anomie, pre-eminently by the ecological studies of Cavan, Schmid, and others, and of his psychological concept of egoism, which in one form shades off into the entirely morbid and withdrawn individualism of the psychotically depressed.[45]

In the development of method his use of statistical correlations, though perhaps naïve by present-day standards, was strikingly advanced and rigorous for his day. Even more important, Durkheim was the early master of the indirect clue, or what has later become known as the *intervening variable.*[46] For example, he came to believe that the explanation of an important class of suicides lay in the absence of social cohesion. But social cohesion as such was not recorded in any census or official report and had thus to be approached by examination of such facts as were available—divorce rates or economic and political crises. This use of the indirect clue is common enough in all sciences—compare the use of the spectrum for qualitative analysis in chemistry—but in sociology it is indispensable. And it is because he was able to show the fruitfulness of an analysis of the indirect clue that his *Suicide* will stand as a monument to Durkheim, the first great empirical sociologist.

3

PEASANTS AND WORKERS It is sometimes implied that the importance of a book can be gauged by the number of copies sold. This is certainly not true of *The Polish Peasant in Europe and America* by William I. Thomas and Florian Znaniecki. The first edition of 1,500 copies was issued in five volumes[1] by the Gorham Press in Boston between 1918 and 1920. A second slightly rearranged edition was published by Knopf in 1927 and also had a printing of 1,500 copies. The situation has now been changed, forty years after the first edition, by the publication of a paper-back version, but in all these intervening years a total printing of 3,000 copies of this immensely influential work has had to serve the whole world.

In the preceding chapter it was stated that Durkheim chose the subject of suicide for his study because suicide was developing into an important social problem, with suicide rates increasing and no very good explanation of why they were increasing. In the same way the subject chosen by the authors of *The Polish Peasant* reflected a somewhat pressing social problem of their time. In the early twentieth century Polish emigration was extensive. In 1913 there were 130,000 Polish immigrants into the United States; another 800,000 Poles, while still nominally domiciled in Poland, were each year moving seasonally into Germany in search of work. This was therefore a massive movement, and it was associated with very rapid social and economic changes of all kinds in Poland itself. It was therefore not difficult for the authors to select this as a problem worth examining.

W. I. Thomas had become interested in the subject of migration many years earlier. After some years as a student and teacher of philology, he became a graduate student of the University of Chicago in 1894 in order to study sociology in Professor Albion Small's newly founded department. His interest in sociology appears to have been aroused during a visit to Europe when he was much influenced, like Durkheim before him, by Wundt's *Völker-psychologie*, but he also seems to have derived more from his reading of Herbert Spencer, George H. Mead, and Charles H. Cooley than from the formal courses provided at the University of Chicago. Thomas was an independent thinker able to draw inspiration from many sources.

On receiving his doctorate in 1896 Thomas returned to Europe, and as he traveled he became fascinated by the cultural differences between the countries that he visited and by the ways in which new forces were stirring in the traditional life of the peasant societies. So when later he joined the faculty of Chicago his interest was centered on the subject of immigration from Europe, on the transformation of peasant society and of peasant social attitudes, and these were the fields in which he was giving courses of instruction some time before he began to make empirical contributions to our knowledge of them. Now that the study of attitudes is taken for granted as a proper activity for sociologists, it is difficult to imagine how novel it must have appeared at the beginning of the century.

It will be remembered that all Durkheim's analysis was based on objective official records of one kind or another, and that his ambition for scientific sociology lay in making what use he could of the objective recorded facts available to him. In this respect *The Polish Peasant* is at the opposite extreme. Where Durkheim exploited objective data, Thomas and Znaniecki sought to bring into their net all the subjective information that they could accumulate. To them this was essentially a problem about people, and they were determined to approach the people themselves and to derive what knowledge they could from them. So in complete contrast to Durkheim and his official records, they were concerned wholly with documents of various kinds, all of which were either contributed directly by people or contributed very directly about people, as with case histories.

It is easy to understand how Thomas set out on this great enterprise. Quite early, probably when he was preparing this course, Thomas realized that not nearly enough was known about the problems of immigration. It is a fairly familiar experience to offer a course on a certain subject and then discover that rather little is known about that subject. Thomas was determined to overcome this ignorance. Fortunately in 1908 he found a sponsor in Miss Helen Culver, heiress of the founder of Hull House in Chicago, with which Jane Addams was associated. Miss Culver offered him $50,000 to conduct a study of the problem of immigration. At that stage he was still undecided which stream of immigration he would study, but as the Polish immigration was numerically very important at that time, Thomas decided to concentrate his attention on the Polish population—the Polish peasants in Poland, the forms of social disorganization and reorganization they were experiencing in Poland, and correspondingly the Polish immigrants as they arrived in the United States, with their progress and difficulties in assimilating into American culture.

His collaborator, Florian Znaniecki, was associated with this inquiry only after the main lines had been established. Znaniecki was a brilliant young man, a professor of philosophy in Poland, whose field of interest was similar to that of Thomas. He was much concerned with forms of social organization and disorganization, and although Barnes[2] refers to his participation as "mainly in the rôle of a translator,"[3] this description may well be an understatement of his practical and theoretical contribution. Znaniecki came to the United States at the beginning of World War I, and from then on he and Thomas, who seem to have acted as very good foils for each other, worked up and worked over the material they had gathered.

The volumes that they ultimately presented are very ambitious. The material itself is fairly extensive, and it is interesting to examine the sources they raided and the use to which they put their material. But this is only part of the value of their report. In their Introduction the authors contribute a long and very illuminating description of Polish life as it was and as it was changing at that time. They also explain their methodology and express a number of important general theories regarding the focus of sociological research.

The wide scope of *The Polish Peasant* is reflected in the fact that those who have tried to introduce and discuss the volumes have found it rather difficult to decide where to start, where to stop, and on what features to concentrate. In the present book the methods and the immediate empirical concepts are the principal concern, and so I propose to lean heavily on the empirical material, to discuss the various ways in which the material was used, and to look at the methodological problems that the authors encountered—and these last are extremely important. A brief look at the substantive findings and at the authors' theoretical positions will also be necessary, to make sense of the rest, but this will be curtailed as much as possible.

SOURCES OF DATA

First, the material. The authors were able to tap a wide variety of sources. The largest single source was a collection of letters comprising fifty separate sets and all together 754 letters, and occupying 800 printed pages. These letters were mainly to or from immigrants to America. Thomas acquired them through an advertisement in *Dziennik Zwiazkowy*, the American Polish *émigré* journal, in November, 1914, apparently by offering 10 to 20 cents for any letter received from Poland by an immigrant to the United States. It must be reported in passing that Thomas and Znaniecki were not explicit as to how they obtained their material. There is in *The Polish Peasant* no statement on the sources of these letters or of the other materials that they used. The fact that there was an advertisement in the Polish *émigré* journal was only made known in 1938, more than twenty years later, at an important conference held to discuss *The Polish Peasant*. It was also by chance revealed in the letters themselves by the inclusion of a letter written by a peasant who by November, 1914, had come to America. In his letter addressed to Thomas he asked whether it was true that Thomas was offering 10–20 cents for each letter and that these letters would be returned. "I beg you to send me a guaranty, for should I lose these letters, I should prefer not to have the reward at 20 cents each."[4]

The rather arbitrary and unsystematic inclusion of this letter is the only clue in the book as to how the letters were obtained. Nor is it stated anywhere how many letters were received. It is possible that the authors obtained a great many more letters than they used.

The technical points of handling the material did not seem to concern the authors very much. They wanted to get on with the job and to suggest ways in which their material could be organized and illuminated, and they were not too much concerned with whether the letters were in any way representative. At this remove, all that can be said is that the letters used were collected in the manner indicated. They are probably genuine; the Polish immigrants probably had neither the wit nor the desire to forge them at 20 cents a letter. Naturally the originals were in Polish, and Znaniecki translated them into English. We can also probably discount the possibility that they might have been written with a view to publication; some date back to 1905, whereas they were not collected until 1914.*

One interesting feature of these sets of letters is that they come from a wide range of social class levels. The whole book is called *The Polish Peasant*, but this description extends from the nobility—not quite the aristocracy, but landed farming families—at one end to the manor peasants, who were only slightly higher than serfs, at the other. The collection also included examples from the peasant proletariat, who were wage earners, people who moved round to do seasonal work on farms, and there were even a number of letters to and from peasants who had moved to the towns. During this period, at the beginning of the twentieth century, some industrialization was occurring in Poland and the characteristic shift to the towns was taking place. As we shall see, migration to the towns was often a first step toward emigration to America.

It is perhaps surprising how many of the letters come from middle-class sources. However, at that time many immigrants to America—even from middle-class families—were extremely poor. The money inducement would presumably weigh more with the poorer lower classes, but this would possibly be balanced by the greater literacy of the less poor immigrants. By definition, almost all of them were probably more mobile than the Polish peasantry as a whole. In any case, these are mere speculations, and it is obvious that the letters cannot be regarded as revealing the statistically

---

* While this defect does not apply in the present case, it is liable to diminish the research value of letters. Fairly adequate safeguards have, however, been devised. In my *The Tools of Social Science* there is a detailed description of the different ways in which documents can be validated, together with various examples of the opportunities for falsification of documentary material.

typical experiences and attitudes of Polish immigrants as a whole.

The authors say that they have arranged these series of letters as far as possible with reference to the presentation of two questions: the dominant situation in which the group or its member finds itself and the progressive disintegration of the family group.[5] Probably by the "dominant situation" they mean mainly the social class, and by the "disintegration of the family group" they are concerned with the disorganization and reorganization which relate to the process of emigrating and assimilating to the American way of life.

This very large batch of material is presented in fifty sets, each set referring to one family. At the beginning of each set of letters there is an introduction, sometimes of several pages, explaining the background of the family and accompanied by some theoretical points to explain their situation. In addition there are copious footnotes throughout the text to explain the meaning or the significance of particular passages.

The second set of materials comes from the archives of a Polish newspaper, *Gazeta Zwiazkowy*. These were bought by Thomas on a visit to Poland probably in 1909 or 1910. Here again there is no mention in the book of the origin of this material, and although quotations are given their proper references, the source of the material was again first revealed at the 1938 conference. Thomas rather casually mentioned on that occasion that he had come across a man who had run a weekly journal in Poland, and that he had been able to search the journal's files covering a period of twenty years.[6] Again we do not know how many original documents there were, but Thomas mentioned that all together these and certain other documents he had brought back totaled 8,000. Certainly nothing like that number are used in the book. Most of the other material was from published sources, such as copies of newspapers. There was a mimeographed German publication called *Umschau in Polenlager*, which tried to collect from Polish periodicals all current material bearing on the Polish national movement for use by German editors and politicians. The authors make much sporadic use of quotations from this journal for the years 1908, 1909, and 1913. This suggests perhaps that there was not a complete set but that while Thomas was in Poland he bought this publication for a few weeks and used it when appropriate. It must therefore be regarded as being primarily illustrative material which may or may not be representative of the whole contents of the journal.

Rather unfortunately, a batch of documents comprising about one third of all the Polish material was lost. The loss of these papers was also described at the 1938 conference.[7] Thomas had somewhat strained relations with some of the Polish politicians, but he finally persuaded them to agree to hand over a mass of documents if he went to Poland to collect them. Thomas did not have time to go himself, so he sent one of his assistants, Mr. Kulikowski. Unluckily, Kulikowski's visit coincided with the beginning of World War I. He had collected a large pile of material and had also made copies of many other documents, but he had to leave everything behind when he rushed out of Poland. Thomas says, "I have speculated on how much difference in our final results this loss meant," and he added, "I do not think it was very much."

The next batch of material concerned people who wished to emigrate from Poland. This had been collected personally by Znaniecki, and resulted from the period (1911–14) while he was director of a body in Warsaw called the "Emigrants Protective Society," which had been set up to carry out various functions connected with emigration, including the securing of employment for would-be emigrants, the making of arrangements for their emigration, and apparently also the deterring of some people from leaving Poland if the society thought they would be particularly valuable citizens to retain in Poland. Znaniecki used some of the letters written to this society to illustrate the preoccupations, hopes, and fears of Poles who wished to emigrate to America.

The next three groups of material relate to Poles who had already arrived in America. First there was a set of documents in the nature of histories of particular parishes.

An interesting development in the same line is the so-called "album" of the parish, a commemorative publication which in older parishes is issued on important anniversaries by the parish committee presided over by the priest and contains an illustrated history of the parish up to date, with brief records of all the institutions included within its limits, collective photographs of all the associations, portraits and short biographies of the most prominent members and families, etc.—in short, a perfectly standardized synopsis of everything which social opinion considers worth knowing and remembering about the community.[8]

The *Memorial Album of the Golden Jubilee of the Parish of Stanislas Kostka* in Chicago, which was apparently the largest and most conservative Polish parish in America, came out in 1907.

Next in the list of sources is a description of a number of Polish bodies which the authors term "superterritorial organizations," meaning that they were not linked to particular parish groups in Chicago.

Various categories of Polish *émigrés* had banded together for different purposes, and the histories of the societies thus formed were supplied on request by the secretaries. The records are therefore rather uneven in quality. The best-documented material relates to the Polish National Alliance, which seems to have been an important society. Characteristically the Polish National Alliance at first intended to include parishes, but since no parish joined it, the Alliance developed exclusively as a system of associations. The authors were concerned with these superterritorial organizations not so much for their ostensible purposes as for their function in the system of immigrant social institutions, and they were interested to find that such organizations had little direct influence on the character of the local associations of which they were constituted. They found that almost any association could bodily transfer from one superterritorial institution to another merely by adjusting its political slogans and also possibly by adding to the range of its activities but without having to modify its social organization. As time went on, the main character of these associations converged into the same general form.

The next set of papers consists of extracts from various bodies located in Chicago which were concerned in one way or another with Poles suffering from the effects of social disorganization, or what they label collectively as "demoralization."[9] The first of such bodies was the United Charities, which had amassed much material on the economic dependency of adult Poles. Certain cases from these records are quoted and discussed. Further material comes from the archives of the Legal Aid Society, which are taken to illustrate the breaking-up of conjugal relations by Polish immigrants and its connection with the escape from traditional Polish morality. There are also some case histories of murders committed by Poles drawn from records of the Cook County Criminal Court and the Chicago coroner's office. Finally in the Juvenile Court of Cook County there is material on the demoralization of children, on the vagabondage and delinquency of boys, and on the sexual immorality of girls.

Last and most famous of all is the long, racy, and very well written life history of a young Pole, Wladek Wisznienski. Wladek had lived in Poland until shortly before the end of his story, which is essentially about his experiences in Poland. He was induced to write this story by Thomas' offer of payment. He became so enthusiastic when he began to write that he set about his task very rapidly, and about three months later he delivered an immensely long but well-constructed story of his life. The authors themselves admit that they could use only half of what Wladek had written, and as the printed version is 300 pages long, it was quite a novel. Here again there are considerable difficulties about the truthfulness of what Wladek writes, so his story has to be considered at a variety of levels. The first question is, Was he sincere? On this count he does not appear to hold anything back. He makes himself out to be at times a somewhat doubtful character. The number of girls he claims to have seduced and deserted is impressive rather than honorable. At the same time most of the events he describes are presented as ending in his favor, though in practice it is clear that economically and socially he is actually drifting down. He starts as a baker's apprentice, yet he does not persevere to become a master baker and indeed holds no job very long. Yet he succeeds in showing himself in a good light.

The only direct validation offered, which Thomas and Znaniecki probably take too seriously, is that Wladek produced some letters supposedly sent to him by his family and in the authors' opinion the facts in the story are corroborated by the letters. But again it is not made clear how many letters there were. Only a few are published at the end of the life history, and these are certainly not enough to validate the whole story. So we must reserve judgment on validation.

How much it matters whether Wladek's story is true or not is another question. You might say that at one level the important point is that he should reveal how he thinks he ought to have behaved as a young man in Poland, and that this is a faithful reflection of his own idealized version of himself. In that case, the difficulty is to discern whether his idealized image is of himself as a Pole or of his own and Thomas' image of him as an immigrant to the United

States. In all, it is rather tantalizing not to know how much of this is embroidery for the drama and how much is the truth.

R. E. Park reviewed *The Polish Peasant* when it appeared, and he suggested that there had been a number of life histories and that only this one was published. The source of Park's statement is not known, but as head of the Chicago school and as a close friend of W. I. Thomas, Park was probably informed. Furthermore, the authors themselves state that this is a typical life history, and they give several reasons for believing so. But there is no proof, and we are left with the authors' celebrated challenge:

We are safe in saying that personal life-records, as complete as possible, constitute the *perfect* type of sociological material, and that if social science has to use other materials at all it is only because of the practical difficulty of obtaining at the moment a sufficient number of such records to cover the totality of sociological problems, and of the enormous amount of work demanded for an adequate analysis of all the personal materials necessary to characterize the life of a social group. If we are forced to use mass-phenomena as material, or any kind of happenings taken without regard to the life-histories of the individuals who participate in them, it is a defect, not an advantage, of our present sociological method.[10]

As we shall see, the life history is much used by the authors for the purpose of illustrating their sociopsychological theories, and pre-eminently Thomas' theory of the four wishes, but it is sill probably safe to conclude that Wladek's story reveals more about the personality of the writer than about the general background and typical behavior in the Poland from which he came. It is perhaps indicative of some uncertainty on the part of the authors that Wladek's life history was placed in the middle volume of the first edition of *The Polish Peasant*, whereas in the second edition it was placed at the end. It is no detraction from the vividness and attractiveness of the narrative to state that it is somewhat difficult to tame and difficult to place.

One general feature of all the sources that have been described must be pointed out. The various documents presented are not employed as a collection of sources to be used throughout the five volumes. In fact the authors use their materials successively in the different sections of their analysis. First, they present a part which is primarily concerned with the traditional way of life in Poland and with the stirrings of social change, and for this purpose they make use of the fifty sets of letters. Second, they examine the forces making for disorganization and for reorganization in Poland, and for this purpose they use the archives, newspapers, and the other Polish materials described. Third, they look at the process of reorganization and disorganization in America, and for this purpose they use the parish albums, the data from the extraterritorial groups in Chicago, and the records from the law courts, coroner's office, Legal Aid Society, and so on. Finally (taking the order of the second edition) they use Wladek's life history, not so much to illuminate all the preceding sections as to examine other aspects of their theoretical premises, and for this purpose they again write quite a long, fresh introduction which presents some of the best-known of the theories first formulated in this book.

It will thus be seen that this monumental work, first published at intervals during three years, is like a succession of almost independent studies strung together on the logic of the order in which the analysis is presented. There is an inevitability in the idea of the breakdown of traditions in Poland, in spite of certain forces which favor reorganization in Poland, of demoralization of the immigrant peasant in America, and then of the attempt to re-create a workable set of Polish groups in the new country. Apart from this logical sequence, any one part of this book is fairly complete in itself, so much so that certain formulations are widely scattered and even the theory of the *four wishes* is stated, slightly differently, in two places. Given this succession of themes, it is obviously appropriate that the materials with which the themes are illustrated should also be used successively.

METHODOLOGY

The authors' contribution to sociological methodology is perhaps the most famous and most controversial part of the whole study. It consists of a long presentation of between eighty and ninety pages, and is thoroughly and profoundly worked out. It is an impressive piece of work, but even on casual reading it seems to bear rather little relation to the actual empirical research that the authors were reporting in *The Polish Peasant*. In fact, when taxed with this criticism twenty years later at the 1938 conference, Thomas admitted that it was quite true. He—and toward the end both he and Znaniecki—had been working on their methodology for some time independently of their empirical research, and although many of the ideas were obviously affecting their research methods, the formulation of their methodology was complete only after they had finished the research work reported in the book.[11]

The starting point of their thinking is that the study of social reality involves a concentration on social change. They assert from the start that any conceptual scheme that is concerned only with the static condition of society at a given time will be of little value. The need for conscious social control is itself largely a product of the current speed of social evolution, so that any approach that neglects the dynamic of social change is radically incomplete.

The next point made by the authors is that it is disheartening to observe how society normally controls social change, to see how ineffective the familiar social controls are, being centered on the crude technique of what they call "ordering-and-forbidding," which is no more and no less effective than the magical techniques formerly used in the attempt to control nature, and takes no account of any theoretical understanding of human or social motivation. Thus ordinary legislation is essentially an act of will, an exercise of power to enforce the disappearance of the undesirable or the appearance of the desirable. The results will sometimes be as intended, but they may be accompanied by great and often unnecessary tensions. Furthermore, if conditions change or become less stable, the legislation previously effective may fail for reasons not accounted for in the magical formula.

The substitute for this, which is normally tried when neither litigation nor recourse to the powers of the state are involved, is what the authors describe by the rather pejorative name of "practical" sociology, as exemplified in business, philanthropy, diplomacy, and in personal relations generally. This "common-sense," or "practical," sociology is based on certain assumptions as to how society operates and, with somewhat inadequate conceptual apparatus, attempts to understand social phenomena in terms of causes and to control the phenomena by manipulating the causes. As the authors point out, this attempt springs from the widespread fallacy that because we live in society we must therefore automatically understand it. In truth, the individual's practical understanding is obviously limited, first, by the exterior limitation that every individual's experience can constitute only a small part of the whole complexity of social facts, and, second, by the even more effective limitation that prevents the individual from seeing things that he is not inclined to see.

If, in spite of this low level of understanding, we succeed to some extent in controlling social processes, we tend to be overimpressed by our control and to neglect the enormous proportion of failures. This may well mean that we have adopted an exceedingly low standard of success for social control rather than that we have achieved any very impressive capacity for control. Furthermore, little of such practical wisdom as some individuals do achieve can be communicated to others because the conceptual apparatus is inadequate.

The second fault of practical sociology is one to which the authors attach much importance. This is the fact that the investigations instigated in the name of practical sociology are designed with too immediate a reference to practical aims. It is in no way implied that the scientist should neglect problems of actual practical importance. The sociologist may study crime or war as the chemist studies dyestuffs. But too close an identification with social reform means that the investigator has prejudiced his norms, has already decided what the proper standards should be. He first sets up an arbitrary norm and then, either explicitly or implicitly, compares what he actually finds with this norm, which may be either intrinsic (whatever is, is right) or extrinsic (based on certain moral, religious, or aesthetic standards).

The fact that the authors emphasize that one should start by building a theoretical framework does not mean that they want to choose a field of operation which has no social significance. "Sooner or later," they assert, "science must pay her debts." They are very anxious to focus their investigations on urgent social problems, and they are quite prepared to take the current concept of normality as their starting point, but they believe that the only way to study social problems is to have no previous normative commitment. This is particularly important in the case of an issue exhibiting signs of social change. Unlike Durkheim, who, as we have seen, ran into difficulties by attempting to isolate one unique norm in respect of any issue, Thomas and Znaniecki recognize explicitly that, at least in the short run, conflicting social norms can coexist, and that social change consists essentially of supplanting the old dominant social norm or system of norms by a fresh system.

The third fallacy that the authors expose is the widespread assumption that any group of social facts can be isolated, theoretically or practically, from the rest of the life of the given society. In practice it may be inevitable that administration be compartmented, but it is absurd to conclude from this that one can study a factory or an army or prostitution or education or any other social institution as a thing in itself rather than by looking at it as a subsystem of the whole social system.

They also mention two further fallacies that, they claim, are outmoded, but that persist to this day. The first of these fallacies is the belief that different individuals react identically to identical influences. Courts still try to infer people's reasons for acting in certain ways in the belief that one can interpret behavior in terms of motives. Psychological science has equipped itself better in the last forty years to probe into individual motivations and consequences, but it is still incontestably an inexact branch of science.*
The second surviving fallacy is that people develop spontaneously a capacity to profit from improvements in material conditions. Thus, certain housing reformers can be heard to claim that it requires only the provision of decent houses to make everyone happy, healthy, and well adjusted, while some temperance advocates claim that abolishing saloons will solve the problem of alcoholism. Assertions of this kind can be contradicted by the most elementary empirical tests.

Here the authors begin to work into their central thesis, which is that both *tendencies* (social attitudes) and *conditions* (social environment) must be changed if social control is to be efficient. They make the interesting point that when it is not possible to bring about a simultaneous modification of conditions and tendencies it is better to concentrate on adjusting tendencies, because a change in social attitudes will lead to modifications in environment, whereas the

* This may be compared with Durkheim's discussion of the morphology and the etiology of suicide. See p. 31.

consequences of a change in environment are not predictable. They illustrate this by instancing the respectable poverty of the peasant in Poland under conditions which would lead to crime and pauperism in the United States, by the decay of family life in the favorably placed Polish aristocratic circles, and by other apparent paradoxes.

In every problem examined one can find the two factors, namely, the dependence of the individual on social organization and culture and the dependence of social organization and culture on the individual. So it is necessary in their formulation to study simultaneously two aspects, which they call *social values* and *attitudes*. Both terms are carefully defined in the Methodological Note. Briefly, a *social value* is any object which has a meaning to a member of a social group so that it may become an object of activity to that member. Thus a foodstuff, an instrument, a coin, a piece of poetry, a university, a myth, a scientific theory is a social value.[12] Each can take on a meaning in connection with human actions—food because it is to be eaten, an instrument because it is to be used, and so on. Conversely, an object which has no meaning for human activity is "valueless." Meanwhile, "by attitude we understand a process of individual consciousness which determines real or possible activity of the individual in the social world. Thus, hunger that compels the consumption of the foodstuff; the workman's decision to use the tool. . . ."[13]

It will be noted that these definitions are not only action-oriented but are also both positivistic and behavioristic, in that inferences as to social values and attitudes are made to await empirical verification by what would normally be observable acts.

It is very tempting at this point to go into the whole question of how the authors use the concepts of social value and attitude. This question has been thoroughly explored, and somewhat whittled away in the exploration. In brief, one is forced to conclude that, while their explicit recognition of the need to explore what might today be called culture and personality marks an important advance on Durkheim's stubborn exclusion of the role of the individual, their attempt to separate social values and attitudes is not successful as an empirical device. Blumer, in his analysis which preceded the 1938 conference, is extremely hard on their attempt, and at the conference itself Thomas substantially shifted his position. He then admitted that, though this conceptual separation was a useful device to force them to think the question through, there was no known empirical method of separating social values from attitudes for purposes of examination. In view of Thomas' own abandonment of these concepts in their original application it would clearly be incorrect to pursue the matter further.

As Blumer points out, however, the exploration of the value-attitude system can proceed at different levels. The establishment of the need for a simultaneous formulation of social processes in terms of the individual and of the social group is an important contribution, one that everybody will not accept. It is in no way diminished by the fact that the authors' specific formulation of the relationship between social values and attitudes breaks down on close examination. It was this introduction of the attitude into their conceptual scheme that led R. E. Park to label Thomas and Znaniecki social psychologists, in spite of their own feeling that social psychology could exactly subsume attitudes but was not large enough to take in the integration of social values and attitudes at which they aimed.[14]

What derives from this simultaneous approach at the less empirical level is a definition of causality that is in direct conflict with Durkheim's definition. Durkheim stated: "The determining cause of a social fact should be sought among the social facts preceding it and not among the states of the individual consciousness."[15] Thomas and Znaniecki state that the cause of a social or individual phenomenon is never another social or individual phenomenon alone but always a combination of a social and an individual phenomenon. In terms of their value and attitude concepts this can be put very concisely; the cause of a value or of an attitude is never an attitude or value alone but always a combination of a value and an attitude.

This is made clear by a number of examples taken from the succeeding volumes of *The Polish Peasant*. The first is of two brothers who have a tyrannical father. One son shows submission, becomes a "good" son; the other son responds by secret revolt and resentment. The response of each son is here an amalgam of two different components of the situation. The tyranny of the father is a factor precipitating some responses, but the attitude of submission in the one son is caused by the tyranny of the father combined with the sense of family solidarity of the son, while the attitude of revolt of the other son is caused by the tyranny of the father combined with a tendency to self-assertion in the son. All these tendencies are recognized as possible in Durkheim's *Suicide*, but his formula is less able to accommodate one altruistic and one egoistic son in the same household.

This seems very elementary, and in considering specific examples it is difficult to imagine that individual differences of this kind might not be universally taken for granted. Theirs is the prototype of a typical contemporary formulation. For example, in a certain delinquency area some children become delinquent and some do not. To account for the response differences one must take into the picture the character of the individual personality as well as the social background.

Another interesting practical example is given in *The Polish Peasant*. The authors found that the Poles who went each year in very large numbers to Germany as seasonal laborers to help with the harvesting were willing to work very hard and to be paid on a piecework basis, so that they earned good money, whereas the Poles who remained in Poland were unwilling to accept piecework, which they refused under the most ridiculous pretexts, and also did not work very hard. In terms of the social situation, it may be said that the Poles were responding to the tradition of hard work which prevailed in Germany. But there is also a difference in the motivations of the two groups; the Poles who went to Germany were self-selected and had a direct motive, as they went there with the specific purpose of making money; as they were working in novel conditions, they were temporarily released from the traditional Polish attitude that work is a necessary evil.

Another example relates to the difficulty that the American social workers at that time were experiencing when they tried to buttress the marriage—group organization among the Polish immigrants. Social workers were baffled by finding that the more they interfered by trying to bring about reconciliation between the Polish couples, the more in practice they succeeded in undermining family solidarity. The fact was that they were underrating the survival among the Polish immigrants of their traditional social coherence; the intervention of the social workers was introducing a strong external force the main effect of which was to dissolve the only feature that was holding the family together, namely, the principle of family solidarity.

At this point the authors become a little ambitious. They say that if the above methodological rules are applied in making a simultaneous study of social values and of attitudes, they will lead in a completely different direction from the one traditionally followed. The final result would be not a system of definitions, as in law and political science, or any other form of philosophical or sociological systematization (here they insert an oblique thrust at Spencer and other system builders), but rather *a system of laws of social becoming* in which the definitions and other conceptual schemes are means rather than ends; "that is, . . . either instruments helping to analyze reality and to find laws, or conclusions helping to understand the general scientific meaning and the connection of laws."[16] The authors elaborate on what they mean by "the laws of social becoming" at great length in this chapter. But unfortunately, although they claim that the formulation of laws of social becoming is what they are working toward, the examples of the laws cited are entirely hypothetical and incomplete. In spite of the valuable clearance work the authors have done in this book they fail to formulate laws of social becoming or even to indicate clearly how a single law can simultaneously introduce both attitudes and values.

In his critique Blumer stresses the point that Thomas and Znaniecki give no description of how an attitude influences a value or of how a value influences an attitude. At certain points in their argument the words appear to be interchangeable. Furthermore, there is a specific statement that values may influence attitudes in a variety of ways. As soon as you admit the possibility of different consequences to a given action you are renouncing the use of the causal relationship as a predictive instrument. To be scientifically applicable and usable a generalization must effectively limit the list of possible outcomes of a given cause. If this condition is not met, or is not likely to be met in the foreseeable future, the laws of social becoming will have a restricted value.

Some other points discussed in the Methodological Note, though perhaps not so central to the total argument, are nevertheless important. The first of these points concerns laboratory experimentation. It is an incontrovertible logical assertion that without experimentation results can never be fully verified. This methodological issue and its implications for the social sciences were much discussed by J. S. Mill and other nineteenth-century pioneers, and the question is carefully re-examined here by the authors of *The Polish Peasant*. They begin by pointing out the extent to which natural scientists rely on laboratory experimentation. This normally differs from practical application in two main respects. First, the ordinary laboratory experiment is much simplified in various ways; the experimenter eliminates all variables that do not immediately concern him in order not to disturb the directness of the experiment. Second, in the laboratory the effects of failure, in terms of cost or pain, can be minimized, or may in any case be well within the price worth paying for new knowledge, whereas the cost of a practical full-scale failure might be prohibitive.

In the authors' view the smallest social experiment, even on a laboratory scale, should not be allowed merely for the sake of knowledge if there are possible harmful effects on the participants.

Now in all so-called social experiments, on however small a scale, the question of practical value is involved, because the objects of these experiments are men; the social scientist cannot exclude the question of the bearing of his "experiments" on the future of those who are affected by them. He is therefore seldom or never justified in risking a failure for the sake of testing his theory.[17]

On the other hand, it is obvious that no social change can occur without innovation, and a social scientist is as justified as any other practical man in taking risks once he is convinced that the chances of benefit are greater than the chances of harm for those with whom he experiments. He should therefore perfect his theories and generalizations before applying them or handing them over to the social practitioner. His theories can be tested prior to experimentation only if he seeks out "new experiences" and applies to them systematic forms of observation. He is particularly required to seek out new experiences that might contradict his previous observations.

While it is only natural that a scientist in order to form a hypothesis and to give it some amount of probability has to search first of all for such experiences as may corroborate it, his hypothesis cannot be considered fully tested until he has made subsequently a systematic search for such experiences as may contradict it, and proved those contradictions to be only seeming, explicable by the interference of definite factors.[18]

Beyond the small-scale social experimentation the authors definitely envisage an increasing impact of the social sciences on social practice, so as to eliminate the present strange situation by which "persons of merely good will are permitted to try out on society indefinitely and irresponsibly their vague and perhaps sentimental ideas."[19] Instead of this they foresee a type of theoretically backed *social technology* which will apply to practical situations the knowledge accumulated by the social scientists, just as other branches of science have their practical technologies.

This notion of the need to explore, gradually converging onto the experimental and social-action phases, has been elaborated in *The Tools of Social Science*.

The authors give some details of how they think a social technologist would set about controlling a social situation. This would entail the possession of three kinds of data: (1) the objective conditions under which the individual or society has to act (i.e., social values), (2) the pre-existing attitudes that will frame his behavior (i.e., attitudes), (3) the *definition of the situation*,

that is, the more or less clear conception of the conditions and consciousness of the attitudes. And the definition of the situation is a necessary preliminary to any act of the will, for in given conditions and with a given set of attitudes an infinite plurality of actions is possible, and one definite action can appear only if these conditions are selected, interpreted and combined in a determined way and if a certain systematization of these attitudes is reached, so that one of them becomes predominant and subordinates the others.[20]

This is the first, almost casual, introduction by the authors of their celebrated concept of the definition of the situation. While it gives greater theoretical precision to the somewhat loose reference to *meanings* in their first formulation of social values and attitudes, it still fails to meet the main practical objection to this part of their theory, which is that it in no way helps the investigator (or social technologist) to determine in advance which of the available plurality of possible actions the subject will actually take.

The authors then make the interesting suggestion that we may be somewhat misguided in trying to apply a form of social control in which individuals are no more than passive objects of our experimentation. It may be that the intervention will do no good, or may even do harm, simply through faulty technique—because we are treating subjects like objects. They suggest that it might be more correct to regard the subject as an active participant in an experiment, to bring him along with it, and to take advantage of the fact that he is a reflective human being.

And, indeed, from both the moral and the hedonistic standpoints, and also from the standpoint of the level of efficiency of the individual and of the group, it is desirable to develop in the individuals the ability to control spontaneously their own activities by conscious reflection.[21]

This implies that, while the testing of rats in mazes may be a justifiable activity for learning about animal psychology, for testing people in real-life situations it is possible both to learn more and also to behave in a morally much more correct way toward your subjects if you take them into your confidence and if you take advantage of the fact that they can think constructively and by doing so can help you, as you can help them, toward a correct definition of the situation. Their suggestion is quite casually introduced and is not pursued at this point but it may be regarded as an early and vivid statement of a point of view which is of first importance in the social sciences, and one which raises a genuine methodological point of difference among social scientists. When you are investigating human beings your subjects will to a greater or less extent be aware of what you are doing. Either you cheat them in one way or another —for example by telling them that you are investigating something quite other than what you are investigating—or you take them into your confidence. By taking subjects into your confidence, Thomas and Znaniecki rightly claim not only that you are acting correctly toward them in that you are respecting their human dignity but also that the resulting investigations will be more realistic and fruitful.

It does not follow from this that subjects should be bored with elaborate details they do not need, any more than a child should be bored with overelaborated explanations. Examples will be given in later chapters of investigators who learned by practical experience how to enlist support without overdoing the explanations. In these contexts the importance of the role of the opinion leader will become clear.

As they near the end of their Methodological Note, the authors make their first formulation of the celebrated typology of the *four wishes*. Here the wishes are enumerated as (1) the desire for *new experience*, for fresh stimulations; (2) the desire for *recognition*, for sexual response and social appreciation; (3) the desire for *mastery*, whether domestic tyranny or political despotism; and (4) the desire for *security*, based on the instinct of fear. This is a typology that has been used in a great variety of contexts, and, as has been stated, occurs twice, somewhat modified, in *The Polish Peasant*. Thomas elaborated his idea of the four wishes in *The Unadjusted Girl*,[22] in which the desire for mastery has disappeared and the desire for response (sexual companionship) has been separated from the desire for recognition (status, fame). According to Barnes,[23] Thomas was both surprised and somewhat shocked at the popularity of his classification of unconscious motivation. Four years later, at a symposium published as *The Unconscious*,[24] the wishes had become "fields" or "classes" of values, but finally Thomas abandoned his attempt at a satisfactory typology. What he did retain was the principle that humans are endowed with strong subjective urges that are canalized, repressed, or blocked by social pressures. At this level his pursuit of the four wishes represents an important contribution to the clarification of the relationship between personal aims and social needs.

TECHNIQUES OF INVESTIGATION

Nowhere in these volumes is there what would today be regarded as an adequate detailed description of the methods used. There are, however, in the Methodological Note two pages[25] that give a possibly not altogether trustworthy answer to some of the questions raised elsewhere in this chapter.

The best way to do justice to the authors' intentions on method is to quote from their description.

We use in this work the inductive method in a form which gives the least possible place for any arbitrary statements. The basis of the work is concrete materials, and only in the selection of these materials some necessary discrimination has been used. But even here we have tried to proceed in the most cautious way possible. The private letters constituting the first two volumes have needed relatively little selection, particularly as they are arranged in family series. Our task has been limited to the exclusion of such letters from among the whole collection as contained nothing but a repetition of situations and attitudes more completely represented in the materials which we publish here. In later volumes the selection can be more severe, as far as the conclusions of the preceding volumes can be used for guidance.[26]

This paragraph indicates that the material is being used for qualitative and not for quantitative analysis. It follows inevitably from the method by which the letters were collected that there is no basis of representativeness, so that there are no means of determining the frequency with which given situations and attitudes repeat themselves in the relationships between Polish immigrants and their peasant families still in Poland. The actual and legitimate use of such material is to illustrate the fact that certain situations and attitudes may be found.

The authors continue:

The analysis of the attitudes and characters given in notes to particular letters and in introductions to particular series contains nothing not essentially contained in the materials themselves; its task is only to isolate single attitudes, to show their analogies and dependences, and to interpret them in relation to the social background upon which they appear. Our acquaintance with the Polish society simply helps us in noting data and relations which would perhaps not be noticed so easily by one not immediately acquainted with the life of the group.[27]

These points are clear. There is no need to minimize the intimate knowledge of the Polish peasant which was brought into the collaboration by Znaniecki, or the profound thinking about the dynamics of social change in peasant societies which was contributed by the interaction of both authors. But in their formulation the authors perhaps exaggerate the inevitability of their own conceptualization, as though the model which they "notice" has an independent reality over and beyond its functional utility in aiding the processes of scientific generalization and prediction.

I should repeat their final plea in this section. They regard *The Polish Peasant* as a monograph, and they do not wish to overstate their conclusions or present them as a substantive set of results, either theoretical or practical. They claim rather that this is a type of approach using methods which they would like to see applied to similar problems of social becoming, whether in Russia, France, Germany, or America, or to Jew, Oriental, or Negro. All studies, whether of migrants or of societies undergoing internal changes, would add to the knowledge of social reality, and the authors would like to see a great number of such studies made so that results could be compared and findings confirmed or confuted.

At the time *The Polish Peasant* was in preparation the orthodox procedure in sociology was still the *comparative method*, by which the social institutions or social problems as they existed in different, often simpler, societies were compared one with another. Although the authors handled the comparative method gently, it is clear that they were striving to find a method that would give a more integrated picture of the total life of the group.

In selecting the monographic method for the present work and in urging the desirability of the further preparation of large bodies of materials representing the total life of different social groups, we do not ignore the other method of approaching a scientific social theory and practice— the study of special problems, of isolated aspects of social life. And we are not obliged even to wait until all the societies have been studied monographically, in their whole concrete reality, before beginning the comparative study of particular problems. Indeed, the study of a single society, as we have undertaken it here, is often enough to show what rôle is played by a particular class of phenomena in the total life of a group and to give us in this way sufficient indications for the isolation of this class from its social context without omitting any important interaction that may exist between phenomena of this class and others, and we can then use these indications in taking the corresponding kinds of phenomena in other societies as objects of comparative research.[28]

SOCIAL THEORY

Let us take a brief look at the authors' statement on social theory, even though this is not our chief concern. Their social theories are mostly concentrated in the introduction to Wladek's life history.

One subject of interest is their theory of personality. Here, as always, they are concerned with the idea of personal development, of change—the dynamic side of personality. They treat this by postulating that the individual is born possessing a fundamental original group of attitudes which they call the *temperamental attitudes*. Later on, these temperamental attitudes are worked upon by external social influences and become what they call *character at-*

titudes; these are the set of organized and fixed groups of attitudes with which the individual faces the world. The process by which the temperamental attitudes change to the character attitudes is what they call the *life organization* of the individual.

Of particular interest about their exposition, although the point is not discussed elsewhere, is the fact that it seems to have a close affinity to the psychoanalytic formulation. Where Thomas and Znaniecki postulated the development of the *temperament* into the *character,* Freud postulated the idea of the *id* developing into the *ego.* As I understand it, one important feature of the ego, and of the superego as well, is the adjustment of the original innate impulses to the needs and bounds of external reality—first of physical reality, as with the ego, and then with social reality, as with the superego. It is interesting that this apparently independent thesis fits so closely with psychoanalytic thought. Even Dollard, with his psychoanalytic interests, does not call attention to the parallel in his discussion of Wladek's life history, though he does point out that, in contrast with Freud's "Little Hans" case history, Thomas and Znaniecki are very weak in explaining the kind of mechanism by which temperament turns into character.[29] They give the mode of transformation a name when they call it "life organization," but they do not explain what forces are working on the individual temperament to turn it into character. And in this respect Dollard's criticism is irrefutable.

The concept *definition of the situation* is reintroduced at this point to describe how the character attitude derives from a particular social value; indeed, a key difference between character and temperament is that temperamental attitudes are not capable of defining the situation but merely generate an instinctual response to a situation. It follows that a capacity in the individual to define the situation presupposes the previous development of his character attitude. Here again we are reminded of Freud's reality principle, but in the Thomas and Znaniecki formulation the definition of the situation is what determines reality. As Thomas stated at the 1938 conference, "if men define situations as real, they are real in their consequences."[30]

The manner by which the individual's impulses are brought into line with social values is here again discussed in terms of the *four wishes.* In this context, however, there is an interesting distinction between the wishes. The desire for *new experience* is the only wish that involves a break from custom, a departure of the individual from the social prescriptions, whereas the other three wishes (the desire for *security*, *response*, and *recognition*) all imply the acceptance of social or parental norms in the desire of a reward from one or more other members of the group. But even the four-wishes typology is not very helpful, for the number of possible modes of conduct that would in some way reconcile these four wishes is extremely large, and reference to the four wishes does not in any way predetermine the actual response, whether conformist or deviant, that will occur in a given social situation.

One example used elsewhere in *The Polish Peasant* is the report, which recurs from time to time in history, that unmarried mothers are glorified for bearing children. One such report must have been in the news at the time Thomas and Znaniecki were writing, during World War I, when propaganda was being used against the Germans on the grounds that Germany was "officially impregnating its unmarried women and girls and even married women whose husbands are at the front."[31] A similar report was used as propaganda against the Nazis during World War II, and in 1956 in Hungary exactly the same story was being used by opponents of the regime. This took the form of a widely disseminated story that the Hungarian Communist regime put up posters in a hospital which proclaimed: "To have children is a duty for mothers but it is a glory for unmarried girls." Whether these stories are true or false, they unquestionably have a strong impact on those who hear them and are believed. Under stable conditions, at least within the Judaeo-Christian tradition, the official defloration of unmarried girls is unthinkable, but under certain conditions of war or revolution it is at least credible to people that the social values may be so transformed that the importance of childbearing may entirely overshadow the traditional importance of chastity, so that a radical change in behavior can be accommodated by a society without violating the character attitudes of its members.

At a more descriptive level the authors throw out a typology that is of considerable interest. This is their division of the population into what they call the *Philistine*, the *Bohemian*, and the *creative individual*. The *Philistine* is the person with such a rigid set of beliefs and values that he is unable to strike new attitudes, so that he relies on a few narrow rules of behavior and conduct with which to steer himself throughout life. He is not a questioning person, and he is rigid in his thinking, but he knows how to adapt to any situation that he can recognize. The *Bohemian*, on the other hand, is a person whose character has never completely formed, so that his character attitudes have never been worked into a coherent system. His life organization is therefore built up of a number of inconsistent chapters with no clear line of development linking them together. The *creative individual* is the one for whom we reserve our praise; he has within himself the possibility of systematic enlargement and exploits this possibility in pursuit of some definite aims. The constancy of his purposes enables him to accumulate experiences, and his adjustment to his situation helps him to develop throughout his life.

Blumer refers to all these theories, commenting that they are provocative, suitable for the study of change, empirically and logically plausible, and that they give evidence of profound and experienced knowledge of the world. Furthermore, he believes that they have had a great influence on the subsequent development of sociology and social psychology. On the other hand, he feels that these, like almost all the theoretical and methodological points presented in *The Polish Peasant*, are not in any direct sense derived from the material cited.[32]

Another of the authors' highly stimulating theoretical models is concerned with the processes of social disorganization and reorganization. They give a fairly simple half-operational definition of *social disorganization*, which they describe as "the decrease of the influence of existing social rules of behavior upon individual members of the group." And if one could describe the existing social rules in an equally simple form, one could apply their definition to obtain a measure of the degree of social disorganization. They do derive from this the hypothesis—and it is nothing more—that social disorganization occurs in a country because new attitudes arise, either by importation or by internal changes in the economic and social structure, and when the new attitudes are applied to the old rules (rules in this sense being a manifestation of social values) the rules themselves are undermined. When this occurs the situation will not be restabilized until new attitudes have generated new social values more in keeping with the new economic and social realities.

In the case of Poland, Thomas and Znaniecki discerned four new attitudes that were in process of undermining the traditional rules of Polish peasant society. The first of these attitude changes was the growth of *individualism*—the break-away from the family system which had persisted in the Polish countryside to a system in which each individual looks after his personal interests, having a career, being paid for what he does. The second attitude change was the growth of *hedonism*—the introduction of the idea that it is proper to do things for pleasure and to use money to gain hedonistic ends. The third tendency was an increase in *success seeking;* you might say that the Puritan ethic was prevailing. The fourth was the *transformation of all values* from what the authors call "qualitative" values to what they call "quantitative" values; with this attitude change, people cease to consider whether a thing is beautifully made and begin to think instead whether it will sell well in the market.

In the case of the peasants remaining in Poland, the authors attribute these attitude changes to the increased industrialization of the whole economy, to the fact that the villages are no longer isolated but are visited by the merchants and peddlers who bring the urban values with them, and to the improvements in communications which result in people's visiting the towns. And this introduction of the new Puritan ethic, in their opinion, is breaking down the old familial system in the Polish villages, so that the old primary group ties, in spite of the response and the recognition they offered, are not enough to restrain the formation of these new attitudes. As far as the people who emigrated are concerned, the reasons for the change are much clearer. Here the immigrants are bringing their old values, or slightly modified old values, with them and are attempting to apply them in the midst of a set of new rules, the rules of the host American society. Here again the conflict and lack of correspondence between the attitudes and the values leads to social disorganization. Only the development of an institutionalized expression for the fresh attitudes will make it possible to enter into the phase of social reorganization.

As Blumer points out, this theory is much larger than can be supported by the material adduced. At least it can be said that the material published in the book is not in conflict with the theory, but it cannot be properly claimed that the theory of social disorganization and reorganization is derived from the material produced by the authors. On the other hand, the theory is a very plausible one. It fits in with much of other thinking on the subject. Though there had not been much previous empirical work on the subject, the theory is consistent with earlier historical analysis. And its presentation in an abstract form, which can be applied to a variety of circumstances, is very suitable for a theory in this context.

Before leaving the topic of social disorganization we should examine its relationship with Durkheim's concept of *anomie* and his quasi-independent concept of *egoism*. As has been shown, the distinction between anomie and egoism was not made clear by Durkheim because he was reluctant to probe into personality differences. This self-imposed restriction was not operative in the case of Thomas and Znaniecki, who therefore seem to come closer to the truth. In discussing demoralization they state:

We have seen that individual demoralization is not in any regular and unmistakable way connected with social disorganization, i.e., with the decay of existing social rules of behavior and institutions. Its existence in a social group certainly does indicate that the rules and institutions prevailing in this group at a given moment are in some respects inadequate, do not correspond to the real attitudes of the members and cannot furnish the latter with a life-organization adapted to their individual temperaments and at the same time capable of regulating their behavior in accordance with the demands of social life in the given conditions. And there is no doubt either that prevalent social disorganization, in those periods when the old system which controlled more or less adequately the behavior of the group members is decaying so rapidly that the development of a new social system cannot keep pace with this process of decadence, is particularly favorable for the growth of individual demoralization, whereas the prevalence of social reconstruction—a new system taking the place of the old even before the latter has completely decayed—is a factor of moral progress. But differences between individuals account for the fact that, even in the face of a rapid disorganization, many members of the group are still able to preserve an old or create a new life-organization of their own, and even in the midst of intense reconstruction many members are yet unable to adapt their life-organization to the new social demands and remain or become demoralized.[33]

DESCRIPTIVE MATERIAL

The discursive description of the breakdown of the Polish peasant economy and its re-creation in the new terms is absolutely brilliant, a tour de force. We are not here concerned directly with substantive results, but for an understanding of how a peasant economy operates and how under current conditions it is liable to be undermined from outside, Thomas and Znaniecki offered one of the first and probably still one of the best and most detailed, formative, and comprehensive explanations.

This exposition is published as the Introduction to the letters in Volume I and occupies over two hundred pages. The structuring of the treatment itself is of interest, particularly in relation to another attempt at total description of a community, namely *Middletown*, by R. S. and H. M. Lynd, discussed in Chapter 5. Thomas and Znaniecki have seven sections: The Peasant Family, Marriage, The Class System in Polish Society, Social Environment, Economic Life, Religious and Magical Attitudes, Theoretic and Aesthetic Interest. The Lynds have six sections: Getting a Living, Making a Home, Training the Young, Using Leisure, Engaging in Religious Practices, Engaging in Community Activities.

Comparison of these two sets of headings alone reveals the difficulty of making a balanced cross-cultural study. In Middletown, "it became more and more apparent that the money medium of exchange and the cluster of activities associated with its acquisition drastically condition the other activities of the people."[34] Among traditional Polish peasants the dominant institution was the family, and most other functions of life revolved not merely around the individual-in-his-family but around the family itself. Marriage was a familial duty designed to strengthen and perpetuate the family solidarity and had nothing to do with romantic love; social class was ascribed by family membership and was not achieved by personal attainments; education was a function of the family rather than of the community; economic life was familial, based on a network of obligations to labor and rights to support. Much of the analysis in *The Polish Peasant* is designed to show how this traditional pattern was being obscured by the individualistic infections of an acquisitive society. With the disintegration of the familial life there was developing a certain liberation from the claims of the family in matters of marriage. The young man beginning the process of emancipation, living away from home, might neglect to consult his family, but he would still judge his future bride according to his family's normal criteria; more individualized, he would consult his personal needs in selecting his partner; finally comes the romantic love-marriage of the adaptive socially mobile society.

Similarly, social mobility was becoming possible, using the universal levers of "instruction, economic development—rather as an increase of income than as an acquisition of property—wit, tact, a certain refinement of manners, and, in general, qualities which assure, not the influence upon a given social environment, but the adaptation to a new social environment, including marriage above one's own class and breaking of familial solidarity."[35]

Finally, economic attitudes were similarly responding to the development of capitalism. The old ideas of co-operative family effort and economic security within the family were being replaced by individualization, secured by the acquisition of new general and technical skills, and capitalization, the acquisition of personal property. Economic well-being was measured decreasingly in terms of the good life in the family and increasingly in terms of possession of the means to buy goods and services.

This is only one aspect of Thomas and Znaniecki's presentation, which throughout is clearly written and neatly worked out. It is a beautifully formulated piece of work, the basis of which is decidedly more solid than the empirical material alone would allow. The description derives from profound and long-standing knowledge of the Polish peasantry. Obviously Znaniecki must have immersed himself in the history and antecedents of the rural areas of his mother country. One can imagine Znaniecki and Thomas sitting together, Thomas asking questions and Znaniecki elaborating this and that, then perhaps consulting his sources for additional details, with the result that they built up a very clear and beautifully articulated description of the peasant way of life in Poland.

EVALUATION

The general evaluation of *The Polish Peasant* as a contribution to social science was well summarized by Blumer in the paper he prepared for the 1938 conference.[36] Blumer begins by setting up the aims of the authors as he sees them. The first aim was to devise a conceptual scheme that fits the circumstances of complex and changing societies. The authors were not content to confine themselves to the study of primitive societies, and they were not satisfied with an analysis which took a static view of any society. They wanted the changes in social organization to be the central point in their analysis.

According to Blumer, the authors' second aim was to have the analysis take into account the fact and the consequences of human interaction. Here again the stress is on the dynamic aspects of the situation. Their third aim was to "catch" the subjective factor; this is reflected throughout in their selection of material. The fourth aim was to set up an adequate theoretical framework.

As has been stressed, the authors explicitly stated that they were interested in an approach and in a method. They pleaded that a similar approach be adopted for studies of other societies, and it was always part of their purpose to interest other scholars enough to ensure replication of their studies. But their hopes have not materialized.

As a total evaluation of the work Blumer reaches four conclusions. The first conclusion is that the particular materials used are not a decisive test of the theoretical interpretations. This is abundantly clear. From the letters and the other documents alone one could not derive the theoretical and descriptive conclusions presented in the book. Nor can the materials be organized to prove or to confute the theoretical interpretations. But, confronted with the theory unaccompanied by these materials, one would be justified in replying that theirs is a highly speculative and dogmatic theory; the fact that the description is presented in conjunction with the theory gives greater confidence in the theory and greater insight into its meanings. In this way, as Blumer points out, Thomas and Znaniecki undoubtedly provide more than a selective illustration of points in the theory.[37]

Blumer's second conclusion, in the light of *The Polish Peasant*, is the rather gloomy generalization that human documents are probably not adaptable to the validation of theories of any kind. In this conclusion he is explicitly criticizing the authors' choice of human documents as source material for the validation of theories, which he believes to be an unsuitable choice that could not have been rectified simply by putting the material to other uses in the analysis.[38]

Blumer's third conclusion is that human documents, although not useful for validations, are invaluable sources of hunches, insights, questions suitable for reflection, new perspectives, and new understandings.[39] Thus they are pre-eminently material for exploration, for the formulation but not for the testing of hypotheses. One difficulty with this kind of material is that its complexity requires a subtle interpretation rather than a rigorous analysis. Blumer states as his fourth conclusion that valid interpretation depends on the "experience, intelligence, skill and fruitful questions"[40] of the investigator. As these factors vary, so will the interpretation.

Perhaps, only the judgments of those who are similar or superior in competence and familiarity to the investigator are significant in the critical evaluation of a report. Other readers would have to temper their own judgments by some acceptance, *on authority*, [my italics] of the analysis which the investigator makes of human documents.[41]

This means that ultimately belief in the truth of the investigator's results depends on one's faith in his knowledge, integrity, and perspicacity. For this reason alone the comparable studies that the authors called for could never have been replicative in the formal scientific sense. One can only say that these authors have penetrated very deeply into the material, and that their results look so decidedly plausible that there is no reason to suppose that they are untrue.

It is perhaps characteristic of Blumer that he is rather pessimistic as a methodologist. He is reluctant to accept any proof except proof by experiment. This is logically correct, but his objection to the methodology of *The Polish Peasant* is an objection that applies in equal measure to almost all investigation so far conducted in the social sciences. The debate was by no means silenced by his conclusion. In the 1938 conference several of those present objected that it is unrealistic to stipulate this degree of validation. Blumer had stated that the scientific procedures in *The Polish Peasant* did not "work." The use of the word "work" was criticized by Max Lerner, who countered:

Can you define the word "work" to mean anything more than the shedding of illumination upon a new situation? When you say can it be applied successfully to a new situation, which I gather to mean a new set of data, again we may ask what you mean by "successfully" and what you mean by whether a thing "works." You have not only the quantitative question of how much illumination it sheds but also the subjective question of whether it sheds illumination for Mr. X and not for Mr. Y.[42]

The gist of this argument, as I understand it, is that proof is not the only desirable end. In a situation requiring action the best available advice is what is needed. If a report conveys to the reader confidence in the truth of its results, and if it throws new light on the question, it is serving an invaluable function as an exploration, even if proof is still unattainable.

The 1938 conference appears to have been a successful and stimulating occasion. The Committee on Appraisal of Research of the Social Science Research Council, which had sponsored Blumer's original critique and the subsequent conference, decided to initiate another series of examinations on the specific question of the suitability and use of personal-document material in social science. Four authorities were commissioned to describe the use of personal documents in their own disciplines. In 1942 Allport contributed a two-hundred-page monograph on the use of personal documents in psychology. This monograph is full of interest, both as a description of the many ways in which and purposes for which personal documents were at that date being used by psychologists, and as a conscientious mustering of the arguments for and against the use of personal documents. It is soon clear that Allport's criteria of science are less exclusive than Blumer's.

What does science aim to do? The answer, as we piece it together from the writings of many authorities, seems to be that *science aims to give man an understanding, a power of prediction, and a power of control, beyond that which he can achieve through his own unaided common sense.* If we abolish preconceptions as to what the scientific method *must* be, and fix firmly in mind this threefold *goal* of science, we conclude that the study of personal documents unquestionably has its place in science.[43]

In 1945 the Social Science Research Council published a volume of monographs from three additional authorities. Gottschalk wrote "The Historian and the Historical Document" and showed how well rooted the personal document is in historiography. Kluckhohn wrote "The Personal Document in Anthropological Science" and demonstrated the well-tried methods of the anthropological field investigator, many of which entail the recording of personal-history material. Angell contributed "A Critical Review of the Development of the Personal Document Method in Sociology 1920–1940," the core of which is a description of the major sociological works in those two decades that had made use of personal-document material.[44]

Perhaps because of the fact that of these three only sociology traditionally pretends to the status of an analytic science, Angell's paper is the one that devotes most attention to the scientific function of personal documents. Angell lists various points in the scientific process at which personal documents may be useful: the securing of conceptual "hunches"; the formulation of new hypotheses, either rigorous or common-sense; the verification of hypotheses and the corresponding validation of the conceptual schemes in terms of which they are formulated. Personal documents can also supply the facts on which administrative decisions ultimately depend, and finally they can be used illustratively to facilitate the communication of scientific abstractions.

Angell appears to have a less harsh view than Blumer on the possibility of using personal documents for testing hypotheses; he is inclined to criticize Thomas and Znaniecki not so much for their choice of personal documents as a source of information as for their misuse of the material—the failure to randomize in their selection of material, the failure to state their hypotheses with operational precision, the failure to present all the evidence on which they based their conclusions. Angell concludes:

There is probably no such thing as a decisive test of the usefulness of a concept. Only the accumulation of research results over long periods can indicate whether certain "slants," or approaches to reality are productive of significant theory. Human documents will certainly play their part in this gradual accumulation of scientific experience, but no one study or group of studies can be expected to be conclusive.[45]

No two works of stature could be more different than Thomas and Znaniecki's *The Polish Peasant in Europe and America* and Durkheim's *Le Suicide*. *The Polish Peasant* derives its conceptual momentum from the overwhelming richness of its material: *Suicide* proceeds to its destination by the relentless precision of its analytic apparatus. *Suicide* is based on administrative records, *The Polish Peasant* on personal revelations. *Suicide* reaches a conclusion which, with successive enrichment, has survived mainly intact for sixty years: *The Polish Peasant* presents us with a treasury of ideas. These were two great pioneering works that set the pace for the subsequent development of sociological research.

To this day there is the same need for proofs and the same need for explorations. Each work represented an important break from academic social philosophizing; each sought answers to pressing social problems; each made important, and in no way opposing, contributions to sociological theory; each was firmly based on the belief that truth has to be sieved painstakingly from empirical material.

4

THE CHICAGO SCHOOL AROUND 1930

For this chapter the subject matter is the entire output of the Chicago school during its early blossoming toward the end of the 1920's and the beginning of the 1930's. The fame of the Chicago school of that period rests not on one book or on one author or even on one particular topic. Rather it lies in a highly characteristic approach and a highly developed interest in the real world. So although *The Gold Coast and the Slum* is used as the main illustration of the Chicago approach, it should not be inferred that this book is markedly superior to a number of other books in the series to which less detailed reference will be made.

The Department of Sociology at the University of Chicago was founded in 1892 and was thus the earliest school of sociology in the United States. The first head of the department was Albion Woodbury Small, one of the key figures in the foundation of American sociology, the first editor of the *American Journal of Sociology*, and one of the founders of the American Sociological Society. A year later Small was joined by W. I. Thomas, coauthor of *The Polish Peasant*. The Chicago Department of Sociology had been an important place for some time before the phase with which this chapter is concerned.

It was in 1914 or 1915 that Robert Ezra Park left his newspaper job to join the department. He was the force behind the tremendous surge of fieldwork for which the Chicago school became celebrated at that time. He was perhaps the first major figure in sociology whose interest was primarily in human beings and their normal social behavior rather than in their historical development or in their social problems. He wrote much later:

I expect that I have actually covered more ground, tramping about in cities in different parts of the world, than any other living man. Out of all this I gained, among other things, a conception of the city, the community, and the region, not as geographical phenomenon merely, but as a kind of social organism.[1]

He gives us this picture of himself and of his passionate curiosity, his love of people, just walking about and watching the crowds, standing for a moment to listen to what they are saying, and then passing on. All his life he was a journalist in the highest sense of the word, a man who was always ready to see something of human interest in the ordinary behavior and ordinary events of the street and the meeting place.

Very soon after Park went to Chicago he began to formulate the idea of a massive research program centered in the normal features of the city of Chicago. In the March, 1916, issue of the *American Journal of Sociology* he contributed an article called "The City: Suggestions for the Investigation of Human Behavior in the Urban Environment." This famous article has since been published many times. First Park and Burgess used it in their *Introduction to the Science of Sociology*, next it was reproduced in *The City;* and recently it was reprinted in *Human Communities*, one of the three retrospective volumes devoted to Park's writings.[2] It is included in the volume of readings by Hatt and Reiss, and extracts are found in various other places.

In this article Park outlines the program which later for many years constituted the major research activity of the Chicago school. Park calls for the application to urban life and culture of the same patient methods of observation that anthropologists like Franz Boas and R. H. Lowie had expended on the life and manners of the North American Indian. So far, he states, this field had been left to writers of fiction, such as Émile Zola. In elaborating this theme he describes in detail the specific directions in which he feels that research should be undertaken.

He not only lists the established sources of data, such as demographic data on the growth of the cities, sex ratios, age structures, but he also outlines some of the ecological problems which had at that date been inadequately examined. He advises that study be focused on the neighborhood, to ascertain what constitutes the floating population, in terms of race and social class; to discover how many people live in hotels, apartments, tenements, how many own their homes, and what proportion of the population consists of nomads, hoboes, or gypsies. Though he loved humanity, his curiosity was disciplined by a sense of reform, and he asks how an isolated neighborhood can be reconstructed to bring it into touch with the larger interests of the community. He sees this question as related, on the one hand, to the great improvements in communication and transportation and, on the other, to the apparent isolation of the immigrant waves and racial minorities into ghettos and areas of population segregation. From this he concludes that more should be known about the segregated areas of the city that are peopled with racial minorities.

At that date many of his questions were still unanswerable. For instance, of what elements were these isolated neighborhoods composed? To what extent were they the product of a selective process? How did people join and leave the groups so formed? What were the relative permanence and stability of their populations?

He also calls for an examination of questions of industrial organization and of what he describes as "the moral order." Under this heading he includes the consequences of the division of labor and the divergences of values and attitudes between those of different occupations. He therefore suggests a series of studies of vocational types, such as the shopgirl, the policeman, the peddler, the cabman, the night watchman, the vaudeville performer. Furthermore, perhaps reflecting the then ongoing work of Thomas and Znaniecki, he suggests a study of social control and social disorganization as seen in the home, in the police court, in the street, and in city life generally.

This ambitious program was formulated in 1916, and by 1925, when the article was next published in full,[3] it was possible to add a chapter by Ernest W. Burgess describing the work that had already been done. In this chapter Burgess looks back at the comparative statistics already collected, as in Adna Weber's book on the growth of cities and Bucher's work, and notes the general urban trends that these books reveal, contained in such facts as that there are in cities more than the normal proportion of women, fewer old people, more immigrants, and a greater division of labor. Burgess points out, however, that the authorities cited deal with aggregation and not with the expansion of the cities, and it is in this paper, some years before the fresh empirical data were available, that he introduces the famous concentric-ring diagram of Chicago—the business area in the center, the slum area (called the *zone in transition*) around the central area, the zone of workingmen's homes farther out, the residential area beyond this zone, and then the bungalow section and the commuter's zone on the periphery.

This formulation by Burgess constitutes the primary ecological idea on which the Chicago studies of Park's era were based. Burgess here also puts down some of the other ideas which were followed up in the later studies. One is the concept of *succession*, used to describe the fact that these concentric rings, built up one after another historically as a city grows, are also invaded successively from the inside. The succession hypothesis suggests, for example, that when an area which has been occupied by wealthy families begins to run down the homes are taken over as rooming houses, while the wealthy former residents move to a more suburban locality.

Burgess also puts forward here his other rather clumsily titled theory of *centralized decentralization*, which postulates the development, as the city grows, of new nuclei which on a smaller scale reproduce the characteristics of the central core of the city. He also takes over and reintroduces the idea of organization and disorganization, as expounded by Thomas and Znaniecki in *The Polish Peasant*.

Finally he repeats the practical suggestion that there should be studies of "hobohemia," of the slums, of the rooming-house districts, the racial ghettos, the black belt. But by this date the explorations originally suggested by Park were well under way. In fact, Nels Anderson's *The Hobo*[4] had been published two years earlier, in 1923. Many of the other most important studies had already been started. For example, Thrasher began working on *The Gang*[5] about 1920, and his report was published in 1927, so that work was well advanced by 1925. Another study in progress was Louis Wirth's *The Ghetto*.[6]

One other point from Burgess' paper should be mentioned. It is here that he suggests ways in which facts collected for normal administrative purposes are adaptable for use in this quite different ecological context. A simple example is the growth of communication indicated by the fact that streetcar rides in Chicago had increased from 164 per person per year in 1890 to double that number in 1921. Another indication of the same tendency was the fact that the number of letters and telephones had doubled in the ten years between 1912 and 1922. He also shows that his hypothesis of *centralized decentralization* may be confirmed by reference to land values. He remarks that in his experience the changes in land values in different parts of the city provide the best index of the way in which the city re-forms itself, to the extent that the emergence of a new center can be recognized first by increase in land values in that area.

This ecological work has its limitations, but it also has very definite uses; it has perhaps become somewhat isolated in the last twenty years. Although there are modern exponents,* and many valuable demographic ecological analyses have been undertaken, after the mid-thirties the idea of pursuing ecological studies in conjunction with detailed field inquiries seems somehow to have lost favor. Possibly Chicago had been slightly overstudied, but perhaps what is needed is a steady review of a city's ecological changes based on field studies as well as administrative records and using some of the routines which were worked out in Chicago. If this were carried out as a matter of course in a city, it might be very useful to those who need to discern subtle changes in the pattern.

Conversely, it will become apparent in later chapters how completely the ecological approach is missing in some area studies. Possibly in the Chicago series there is too much emphasis on the influence of geography, but that is no reason for omitting geography altogether, as some researchers have done. They identify a class of person as, for example, a suburbanite or exurbanite and proceed to discuss members of this class without attempting to pin down in any systematic way their relations with their workplace, or the fact that a district has a history and a life span that can be both more complex and more interesting than the history and life span of an individual.

* Notably Professor Schmid of the University of Washington.[7]

There seems to have been more consciousness of ecology in English field studies than in American. But the emphasis recently in that respect in Britain has been laid more on family studies in the neighborhood and on general studies of the interaction network rather than on people and social groups as they relate to the physical structure of the city.[8]

The third paper of note in *The City* is by Professor Roderick McKenzie, who was stimulated by Park to use the ecological analogy in human affairs. And it was McKenzie who did most to think of these problems specifically in terms of human ecology. He wrote some time later a book called *The Metropolitan Community*.[9] But he died early in the mid-thirties, and his death may explain the failure of this line of approach to make as great an impact as might have been expected.

THE GOLD COAST AND THE SLUM

We now turn to a more detailed discussion of the work inspired by Park and regulated and organized by Burgess. At least twelve such studies were published in the twenties and early thirties. The first and fullest attention will be paid to *The Gold Coast and the Slum*, by Harvey Warren Zorbaugh, first published in 1929 and frequently reprinted since that date.[10] *The Gold Coast and the Slum* deals with the district of central Chicago known as the "Near North Side." This area lies immediately north of the Loop, the central business area, across the Chicago River; it comprises an area one and a half miles from north to south and one mile from west to east, where it is bounded by Lake Michigan. This area had seen the growth of Chicago but had not by the 1920's yet been submerged in the busy commerce of the Loop. At that time it had a population of 90,000 people, "a population representing all the types and contrasts that lend to the great city its glamour and romance."[11]

The point of particular interest to Zorbaugh was that in that very small area there was an exceptionally steep gradient of social and living conditions, of wealth and poverty. Furthermore, it "is not only an area of contrasts; it is an area of extremes"[12] in which the heights of wealth and fashion and the depths of poverty and slum living were equally represented.

The Near North Side has the highest residential land values in the city, and among the lowest; it has more professional men, more politicians, more suicides, more persons in *Who's Who*, than any other "community" in Chicago.[13]

A map of the Near North Side makes the ecological pattern clear. The main north-south street is Clark Street; two blocks east of that is State Street, which divides the district in two. To the east of State Street is a much-favored section; Lake Shore Drive and the beautiful apartment buildings and private residences overlooking the lake make this one of the most desirable living areas

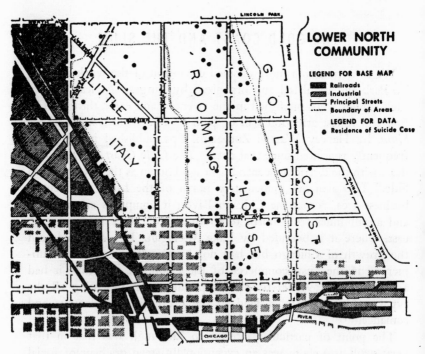

Map of the Near North Side, Chicago, showing the principal areas described. This map was first used to show the incidence of suicides, and it will be seen that many of them are clustered along Clark Street.

in Chicago. This is the district known as "the Gold Coast." Between Lake Shore Drive and State Street lies another area of residences, definitely upper-class, the nearer Lake Shore Drive the more favored and fashionable. But the landward part of this area had already declined entirely into an area of rooming houses. Behind that again was the area of bright lights on each side of Clark Street, aimed at a lower-class clientele. Apart from Clark Street itself, this was the area of what Nels Anderson had called "hobohemia," the last resort of the criminal and the defeated. In the middle of this slum, but not of it, was one small district called "Towertown" or "the Village," at that time the main artists' colony in Chicago. The river itself was edged by industry, so that it offered no beauty and no space for recreation, and was in fact the most depressed part of the whole area.

Further inland again was a rather interesting zone which had been the first home of successive waves of immigrants. This had had an Irish period and a Swedish period, and when Zorbaugh was making his study it was known as "Little Sicily," being inhabited mainly by Sicilian immigrants, who were trying quite successfully to follow their traditional Sicilian way of life. But even during Zorbaugh's study a Negro wave was moving in and the Sicilians were tending to move out.

Thus in a very small area it was possible to study a microcosm of the whole city, with the added advantage that "all the phenomena characteristic of the city are clearly segregated and appear in exaggerated form."[14]

The greater part of Zorbaugh's book is devoted to a detailed examination of each area in the Near North Side. First was the area of the Gold Coast, where many of the four hundred really upper-class families of Chicago lived. One of the best addresses in Chicago was, and still is, Lake Shore Drive, and on this street itself or on one or two streets just behind it lived two thousand of the six thousand families who were listed in the *Chicago Social Register* at that time. These families were highly conscious of their neighborhood and of their role in society. They were very careful not to allow outsiders to break into their circle.

Some of Zorbaugh's informants described the old days when gracious ladies gave balls which were attended by families from all the important houses, but these informants added that this was no longer happening. The old caste system of an upper-class society seems to have been replaced even then by what some informants called the "social game." This referred to the fact that certain people had quite deliberate techniques for breaking into the *Social Register*. What you had to do was in some way to win a dinner invitation to the home of one of the really established families. Once you had done that, you would be included on other people's invitation lists and thus become eligible for membership in certain exclusive clubs. At the end of the road was the vista of the *Social Register*, which would set the seal of approval upon the social aspirant.

The crucial beginning was the first invitation, and quite cynically ambitious people developed ways of obtaining invitations. The use of children was quite common. The climber would set her children to play with the children of an established family living in the same hotel or apartment building, or her children would meet other suitable children at their schools. And through the children of these well-established upper-class families they would win invitations for themselves. Another method was to discover the pet charity of an upper-class lady and then yourself develop a great interest in this charity; you would attend an open meeting of the charity that the lady was moderating or addressing, and after the meeting you could approach her, express interest in the wonderful work of her charity, and offer a small donation. Apparently she then felt more or less obliged to ask you to tea. If you played your cards right, in the end you would receive a dinner invitation.

By such stratagems the inviolability of the old upper caste had already been destroyed by 1930, and this class has probably dwindled even more since then. At that date there were obviously certain people in society who selected the names for the *Social Register*, but nobody seems to have known who they were or upon what basis they operated. "Society" simply accepted its rulings without question. If people were in the *Social Register*, it was proper to invite them to your home. In the same way the names of eligible young bachelors were added to the list of "five hundred dancing men." If they were on that list, they could have as many dances as they might wish.

This is the idle and spectacular side of life on the Gold Coast. On the other hand, as Zorbaugh points out, although there is much stupidity in the way of life of the upper four hundred, there is also a genuinely serious side. Not all charities are "pet" charities. There was a concentration of civic leadership on the Gold Coast. The society was almost the only group in Chicago at that time that supported cultural and musical activities. They were the people with sufficient leisure and wealth to be able to devote some of their time to charity and the arts, to philanthropic and un-remunerative activities generally. They were led to this at least partly by a sense of obligation that people of culture, wealth, and leisure owed to "the less fortunate."

Zorbaugh makes it plain that the families of the Gold Coast did not often act as a group, at most forming cliques of ten or twelve families. Although conscious of their common tradition and bound together by class solidarity, they were less neighborly and com-munity-conscious than at first appeared. The families prided them-selves (as perhaps upper-class people always do) on not knowing their neighbors, and this happened to be in keeping with the anonymity of a big city, the social barrenness of hotel life, the effect of transience created by the fact that they were always traveling between home and pleasure resorts in different parts of the country and abroad. They also had their "summer places." It was right to be in your own home for only four months of the year. All this suggests that though the Gold Coast families retained a vestige of social leadership, this was a fairly faint echo of the social leadership which survived in the countryside and which had been at one time much more significant even in the city.

It may be remarked in passing that the connection between hotel life and anonymity was also examined in a small study, about twelve pages long, by Norman S. Hayner under the title "Hotel Life and Personality."[15] This is not specifically about Chicago but is based on material from a large number of places, and constitutes a neat com-mentary on the breakup of family and social ties that is a con-sequence of living in hotels, whatever the social class.

The next chapter is focused on the world of furnished rooms located in the area back of the ostentatious apartments, hotels, and houses of the Lake Shore Drive. The buildings here appeared to be highly respectable but extremely shabby and run-down. They were, in fact, the former residences of the upper classes that had been deserted. House after house carried the card "Rooms to Rent." But there is a corollary to this odor of gentility, for the people living in the furnished rooms were on the whole strangely unconventional because they had few roots in the society. At the time of Zorbaugh's survey a rather high proportion of those living in this rooming-house district were unmarried. He found that 52 per cent were single men, 10 per cent single women, while the remaining 38 per cent were married "with or without benefit of clergy." The implication is that there were a great many fairly temporary liaisons. The abnormality in population structure was also signalized by the remarkably small number of children in the area. There was a correspondingly modest demand on school places, which was in particularly marked contrast to the teeming child population in the adjacent slum areas. Some measure of the prevailing transience is given by the fact that the whole population on average turned over every four months. Even the keepers of the rooming houses were transient; one half of them at the date of Zorbaugh's survey had been there only six months. Facts such as these reveal the fantastically high rate of turnover of the whole population.

The rooming house was radically different from the boardinghouse. The boardinghouse had something of the character of a home away from home. Boarders ate together, played games together, and the landlady "took something of a personal interest, even if remote, in her boarders." A boardinghouse could place a newcomer in a definable social situation, but as early as 1930 it had passed out of existence in the American city mainly because of the increasing commercialization and depersonalization of social relationships. The rooming house was the modern substitute; in this the dining room, the parlor, and every other common meeting place was eliminated, thus inhibiting all social relationships between fellow roomers or between roomers and the rooming-house keeper. The keeper's only concern with what goes on in his house was that the roomers were not disturbed. "A woman who was asked by one of the census workers how many married couples there were in her house said, 'I don't know—I don't ask—I want to rent my rooms.' "[16]

What lay behind this sort of life was well brought out in a long personal document, the life story of a "charity girl," which described her arrival in Chicago from the small city where she was born, and how her initial excitement gave way to almost intolerable loneliness. During her first year in Chicago she was keyed up by her ambition to be a concert pianist, but after a year or two she was shocked when told by her music teacher that she would never be an artiste. All she had lived for was destroyed. Her mother was dead, her father had disowned her, she was rejected as a musician. And so she drifted into the life of a kept woman, a pitiable victim of social disorganization. It is a vivid and rather touching story which gives the whole flavor of this area—a hiding place for people who are desperately lonely, unsettled, rootless, anonymous.

In this atmosphere "there can be no community tradition or common definition of situations, no public opinion, no informal social control."[17] Political agents had long since found that it was useless to try to persuade people to vote, or indeed to show any interest in politics. All man's normal wishes as defined by W. I. Thomas were thwarted. "He finds in the rooming house neither security, response, nor recognition."[18] There was a high rate of suicide, as could be expected; the *anomie* that Durkheim saw in times of national disorganization was concentrated and endemic in an area such as this. Ruth Shonle Cavan's study of suicide in this Chicago area[19] had been published in 1928, and Zorbaugh publishes a map of the area prepared by Earle and Cavan showing the extent to which suicide was concentrated in this rooming-house area (see p. 94).

If the inhabitants avoided suicide, they sometimes apparently resorted to the weaving of a fantasy life in which they lived out an imaginary and more satisfying existence. There is a story of two shopgirls who lived in an entirely fictitious world writing to Doris Blake to ask what a young girl should do if a man she liked but didn't love tried to kiss her. Of course this had never happened to them.

For those who avoided suicide and were not satisfied with pure fantasy there was another type of substitution; this was the solution of those who bought a parrot or some other pet and devoted all their love to it as the rock upon which they tried to build their life. In Merton's typology this is the *retreatist* mode of individual adaptation.[20] Finally, and most frequently, there were those who reached some kind of accommodation with the rooming-house life, who lowered their sights, cut off their old associations and ties, and settled down to a narrow, loveless but bearable existence.

Not far from the rooming-house section was the area known as "Towertown." It had acquired this name because after the Great Fire in 1871 almost the only building that remained in the district was a masonry water tower that stood high above the area. Tower-town was the artists' quarter. By the date of Zorbaugh's survey it seems to have become a second-rate Bohemia. Zorbaugh was obviously not impressed by what he saw there, and he labeled the population as "egocentric poseurs, neurotics, rebels against the conventions of Main Street or the gossip of the foreign community, seekers of atmosphere, dabblers in the occult, dilettantes in the arts, or parties to drab lapses from a moral code which the city has not yet destroyed."[21] Symptomatic of this, of course, would be the free love, the unconventional types of sex relationship that were much paraded to sustain Towertown's reputation for promiscuity. One informant told of mailboxes with two names—John Jones; Mary Smith—indicating a man and a woman living together unmarried. Homosexuality was said to be fairly widespread. There was, however, an impression that the unconventionality with regard to sex as to other matters, a by-product of the artistic temperament, had attracted to the district many individuals that were not genuine artists but were seeking an escape from the repressive conventions of the larger community.

The next area was what Zorbaugh colorfully described as the "Rialto of the half-world," which is marked on the map as North Clark Street. This offered cheap stores by day, bright lights by night. It constituted the business quarter for the really disorganized families, for the hoboes, the radicals, the squawkers, the stick-up men, panhandlers, prostitutes, dopeys, jazz hounds, gold diggers, and charity girls—all the residue of the city could be found using that area as their Main Street. It provided vast numbers of lunchrooms, probably because such people had no cooking facilities where they lived and depended on places where they could buy cheap meals. There were seventy-six lunchrooms and restaurants in a short stretch of North Clark Street. Other stores dealt in the various needs of the homeless man—secondhand-clothes places, resale shops, clothing exchanges. Barber shops and missions served as gossip centers. Bookstores offered stalls of free reading for the browser.

Zorbaugh's book has something to say about the characters here and about the extremes of personal and social disorganization that they reflect. There was the "squawker" standing on every corner and peddling his useless wares—shoestrings, safety pins, pencils, postal cards. Most of the squawkers were able-bodied, but the physically handicapped would exploit their disabilities. The elite of the profession were those who could simulate paralysis or epilepsy. There were the "street fakirs," the men who would show you the sun through a long telescope for ten cents, or the ones who would sell you your horoscope for half a dollar. Finally there were the "wobblies," the reds and agitators from all over America, fervently reading newspapers or crowding round soapbox orators.

By night this area had a reputation for vice throughout the city. Before prostitution was suppressed, it had been a red-light district, and it was still a good place for people to come for illicit love because they could take advantage of the anonymity that it offered. In 1930 there were still seven cabarets that gave opportunities for not very carefully hidden prostitution.

There is a good description of the area by a pawnbroker who conveys well the flavor of economic destitution. His customers were actually living from hand to mouth, but at the same time they wanted to have a good time and were willing to pawn everything they had to get it. This pawnbroker's description is reminiscent of those of the English journalist Mayhew, whose well-known reports in *London Labour and the London Poor* in the 1870's are equally vivid. Mayhew's stories were elicited from London's underworld and constitute the first elaborate nondirective interviewing tried anywhere.[22]

Behind the bright lights of North Clark Street were the slums— the streets in which these destitute people lived. No new residences would be built there; any fresh building would be for stores or one or two offices, and the general air was one of dereliction. Within the slum there were two distinct parts. One, the tenement area, was the world of foreign tongues and foreign cultures. The other, the area of cheap lodging houses, was a jungle of human wreckage; here were economic failures, broken families, no families at all. They were all derelict, for this was the lowest point to which they could drift. They all had the touch of economic misfortune or failure; physical inadequacy, dope, and gambling were almost universal features of their stories—a loss of grip and hope and a resulting sense of defeat, a set of attitudes that meant the acceptance of the slum, and a final isolation from the world. There are many vivid descriptions of what life of that kind meant, and in most of them it seems that alcohol and drug addiction played an important part in the story.

Although there was relative isolation of the outcaste, the slum also housed a variety of racial minorities. The immigrant to a big city customarily arrives without financial means, and it is in the slum that he finds not only a place to live that he can afford but also a social world whose traits, being transplanted from his own corner of the Old World, are familiar and comprehensible.

In the colony he meets with sympathy, understanding and encouragement. There he finds his fellow-countrymen who understand his habits and standards and share his life-experience and viewpoint. In the colony he has a status, plays a rôle in a group. In the life of the colony's streets and cafés, in its church and benevolent societies, he finds response and security. In the colony he finds that he can live, be somebody, satisfy his wishes—all of which is impossible in the strange world outside.[23]

There were, for example, in that area between three thousand and six thousand Persians, mostly young single men who had come from the vineyards and orchards of Persia to seek their fortune. They seem to have worked mostly in hotels or as janitors, since they had no particular industrial skills. But they were relatively well off because, unlike the Italians, they did not send their money to the home country. There was a small Greek colony of the same sort, but, although its members were people of low status, they avoided destitution by availing themselves of the ethnic solidarity which led Greek restaurant owners to give them work.

The survey also showed traces of earlier racial invasions from Sweden, Germany, and other European countries. Most of these immigrants had long since become established citizens and had moved out into more favored districts, and those still found there with their shops and clubs were little more than remnants of waves that had come and passed on.

In the late 1920's the colonists of this district were predominantly from Sicily, and they were studied in detail, but Zorbaugh also called attention to yet another invasion that was then starting—the arrival of poor Negroes from the cotton fields of Georgia, Mississippi, and Arkansas. By the time of Zorbaugh's survey they were moving into dwellings that even the Sicilians had abandoned, meeting the high rents by overcrowding and slowly but steadily driving the Sicilians northward into the former German slum. These waves of immigration and displacement observed by Zorbaugh will be seen to fit well into Burgess' concept of *succession*, already discussed.

The point that Zorbaugh wished to bring out was that the slum has a sociological reality as well as an economic reality. It starts by being an economic haven for the destitute, but comes to exhibit certain characteristic social patterns which distinguish it from adjoining areas. The attitudes and behavior problems of slum dwellers are typical and are peculiar to themselves.

The first feature of the slum is its cosmopolitanism. The Near North Side slum contained twenty-eight distinct nationalities. But there is a further effect of racial segregation, which is that families of very different social status are drawn together if they share color or culture. No other area of the city possesses such a wide social spectrum.

The consequence is more than merely a polyglot culture. Those who live in the slum seem to become genuinely tolerant of others. Social distance is reduced to a minimum, and there appears to be very little racial feeling. It is as though these slum dwellers felt that they were all in the same boat, segregated from the conventional world, and that they were not going to struggle with one another. Nor would they cultivate a conventional sense of responsibility. Practically their only external contacts with society were through the social agencies and through the law, and neither of these was particularly respected. They thought that the social agencies were bodies to be exploited. One notable slum character, "Honest to God Sam," boasted that he was being simultaneously helped by fourteen charity organizations and that in the main he had succeeded in keeping each agency unaware of what the others were doing. If the slum inhabitants despised the agencies, they hated the law, which they regarded as a natural enemy and a source of constant interference and oppression.

It would not be correct to label all these slum dwellers as defeated people. A certain proportion of them are always moving out and up. But the individuals and families that characterize the slums are defeated people, men and women who have no energy, no drive, no ambition, no spirit left in them. They are the people who have been trodden on by the rest of society, and they are going to stay at the bottom. It must be understood that the problems of the slums and the problems of, for example, delinquency do not necessarily co-incide. Delinquent peer groups in their teens are seeking adventure wherever it may be found—in the junk yards, on the railroad tracks, and everywhere else—and for reasons that are incompletely under-stood they sometimes engage in wanton violence and senseless de-struction. But despite this they are potential pioneer material and represent a quite different stratum from the hoboes.

What seems to characterize the hoboes is that they are unwilling to commit themselves to anything or to anybody; they are not prepared to settle down to having family relationships, work rela-tionships, or social relationships with others. A pioneer or a member of a delinquent gang cannot be anxious to withdraw; he must have the urge to be a member of a social group, to feel some dependence on his society.

Zorbaugh establishes empirically that there are three classes lo-cated in the slum—hobohemia, recent immigrant families, and boys' gangs. His explanation of the boys' gang is that it is a second-generation effect.

The immigrant generation, feeling little other pressure than the necessity of learning the minimum of the English language required to get along economically, shuts itself off in a Little Sicily or a ghetto and lives to itself. The American-born generation, however, is not able to live to itself. The law requires it to attend American schools; and in many other ways it is precipitated into American cultural life. It finds itself living in two social worlds, social worlds which define the same situation in very different ways. At once cultural conflicts arise; perhaps merely vague bewilderment and unrest, but often definite problems of personal be-havior. In the normal native community the family and the community meet these problems for the child. But the foreign family and com-munity are not able to do this completely or successfully. Their attempts as likely as not but serve to make the child as a delinquent in the eyes of the *American law*.[24] *

* This passage may be compared with Louis Wirth's generalizations derived from his study of the ghetto: "On the one hand there is the strange and fascinating world of man; on the other, the restricted sectarianism of the little group into which he happened to be born, of neither of which he is fully a member. He oscillates between the two until a decisive incident either throws him headlong into the activities of the outer world, where he forgets his personality and metamorphoses into a new being, or else a rebuff sends

This quotation recognizes the importance of the deviant subculture. But the last two sentences in particular are obscure. Neither here nor elsewhere does Zorbaugh fully trace the development of the deviant boys' gang or show that there is anything but an economic connection between the coexistence in slums of voluntary isolates, such as hoboes, and unassimilated immigrant newcomers. The inadequacies of his formulation are emphasized by his detailed description of Little Sicily, or "Little Hell," to which he next turns.

This is the tenement area, which constitutes the westerly half of the Near North Side. On the maps, confusingly, it is marked as Little Italy, although elsewhere in the Chicago Series[26] it is marked as Little Sicily. The district appears to be a natural reception area for fresh immigrant waves. In two generations it had been dominated first by the Irish, next jointly by Irish and Swedish, and then by the "dark people," that is, the Sicilians. Zorbaugh made a study of six blocks in the heart of the district and found five-sixths of the population to be Sicilian.

It seems that these Sicilian families did not behave in the manner attributed to slum dwellers. For example, they were not noticeably tolerant of other racial groups, and their arrival led to considerable tensions, in children's playgrounds and elsewhere, between the Sicilians and the Swedish families that they were displacing. They also showed little signs of developing the polyglot culture that Zorbaugh has previously described. In fact, these Sicilians, who came mostly from around Palermo, seemed to have continued in almost every respect the mores of the village areas from which they had migrated. For example, they maintained very strict sexual morals. Normally the girls were betrothed by their parents at about

---

him bounding into his old familiar primary group, where life, though puny in scale, is rich and deep and warm.

"This same problem is not only encountered by the individuals in their own lifetimes, but is the problem of succeeding generations in any immigrant group. This accounts for the fact that the immigrant himself scarcely ever is fully assimilated into the new group of his own lifetime, and at the same time is seldom a criminal, but that his children do become assimilated and are at the same time giving rise to problems of disorganization and crime. The ghetto shows that what matters most in social life is not so much the 'hard' facts of material existence and external forms as the subtle sentiments, the dreams and the ideals of a people."[25]

the age of twelve, and after that they were not allowed to go out without the permission of their fiancé. Engaged couples would meet only in the presence of their parents or, suitably chaperoned, at family ceremonies. All the traditional rules of this kind were enforced by the parents, who were determined to maintain their traditional Sicilian code.

Also maintained was another traditional aspect of Sicilian life, namely, the incredibly fierce and persistent feuding between different villages or different families. These customs were imported and reproduced in Little Sicily. Furthermore, the enforcement of the laws against such feuding was even more difficult in America than in Sicily because the methods available to the authorities were inadequate. For example, in Sicily any informer can remain anonymous; if he knows that someone has committed a crime, he may inform the police. But under American law he must appear in court. This constantly caused people to refuse to testify as witnesses, and on several occasions led to Sicilians' being killed for having given information. There was little respect for American law among the Sicilian immigrants.

Little Sicily contained a desperately poor population. It had at that time the highest proportion of families on relief in the whole of Chicago. But this economic destitution led to very few signs of social disorganization. There was little divorce, little desertion, and family solidarity was highly developed at every level. It was quite common for several families from one village to emigrate together, and each village group maintained a lodge in Little Sicily. The Church does not seem to have played a strong role in their lives. Sicilian peasants, even at home, do not entirely accept church leadership, and in Chicago, where most of the priests were northern Italians, the hold was even less effective. Again, the immigrants did not understand local politics. They knew that there were certain bosses who told them how to vote and rewarded them if they did what they were told. This was all they expected to have to do with politics.

This sketch completes the description of the groups that had made the Near North Side their home. As has been said, the contrasts within the area were tremendous. And yet there seems to have been a common strain, in the very great difficulty found in all groups in maintaining or reconstructing any sense of community. The rich socialites on the Gold Coast had no sense of community as such, apart from sharing a good address; the rooming-house people were transients completely detached from society; the hoboes, by definition, were isolates and wanderers. The only place where there was any rootedness was in Little Sicily, and here again there was the feeling of impermanence, of constantly being displaced by a new wave of immigration. And even in Little Sicily the American-born generation did not know whether to look back to the mores of the Sicilian social organization or to look forward to the local confused American way of life.

A chapter is devoted to an examination of the reasons for such glaring inadequacies in the local community institutions. This is on what are now familiar lines of nostalgia for village life.

In the village community the church, the school, and the "town meeting" or political organization exist as community institutions and function under community sanctions. But on the Near North Side the church has ceased to bear any vital relationship to local life; the school, while still in the "community," is part of a great system of schools, centrally directed, and little interested in local problems; and the "town meeting" has become a ward club, where "the boys" and political jobholders gather to take orders from the ward boss, and perhaps to "sit in" on a few hands of poker.[27]

Furthermore, the family, as we have seen, was virtually nonexistent in the rooming-house area and in hobohemia, and was tending to disintegrate in Little Sicily. Thus, only the Gold Coast families were functioning effectively as agencies of social control.

Economically neither the family, nor indeed the Near North Side itself, operated as a functioning unit; individuals would leave their homes and even the district on their daily journey to work. The newspaper, a traditional mode of social control in the small town, was here syndicated and displayed no interest in local issues or local opinion. It might take notice of the Near North Side only when there was a lurid crime or a suicide to report. Such clubs as existed would cater for some cult or some segment of the population rather than concern themselves with larger community issues. Politics fell a prey to grafters who could offer immediate benefits to interested groups—a means of "uplift" to the Gold Coast, a means of protection to Clark Street, a source of bribes for the immigrant. In the absence of a common culture genuine political action had become impossible, so that the greater part of the area did not govern itself but was governed by the police and the social agency.

Thus the law was perceived by most of the population as an instrument of repression which tried to press the Near North Side into the mold of values set up by the city as a whole. The task of the police was, at best, to enforce compliance with the negative values, the prohibitions, of the law.

Where the law did not tread, the social agencies stepped in. There were more than fifty such agencies "endeavoring to set standards of private life and public conduct; to persuade, cajole or force the population of the district to conform to the values and mores of the larger society—values and mores derived from generations of village life, and often unadapted to the life of the city."[28] The practical work of the agencies was focused on physical reclamation —scrubbed floors and washed windows—on approved methods of child raising, on the care of the maimed or sick. Other agencies engaged in the endless and apparently ineffective task of spiritual reclamation.

All these efforts, whether disciplinary or hortative, appear to have met an equivocal response from the population. Those scenting profit give a nominal or calculating co-operation. Others are indifferent, suspicious, resentful, or in open opposition. When social life has disintegrated beyond a certain point, each individual comes to rely upon himself and wishes for neither help, guidance, nor interference from others.

There follows a detailed case history of the Lower North Community Council, which at that date was the latest of a series of essays in community organization, following the nineteenth-century attempts to set up "settlements," which seem to have achieved little lasting effect.

Earnest middle-class people, with the best of motives, came to live in the settlements, among those whom they longed to help. Zorbaugh suggests that their weakness lay in the fact that their goal was understanding rather than uplift, and that this sentimental interest in persons rather than programs was unable to adjust itself to the Sicilian deluge. Later, in 1910, there had been an ambitious attempt to set up a community center. Much money was subscribed in the Gold Coast for this purpose, but nothing came of it. All the activities failed within a year for lack of response from the community.

Then came World War I, which did somehow band people

together in a new way. In 1919 there was a fresh wave of enthusiasm which led to the setting-up of the Lower North Community Council. It looked for a time as though something would come of it. Every attempt was made to ensure that the council was both communal and democratic. A network of committees was created, and on these "every language, race and color, every shade of religious and political belief, every degree of economic and social position was to be represented."[29] The aims were strikingly practical—improvements in sanitary conditions, the elimination of rats, ball games for the kids, campaigns for a cleaner and more sightly community. The emphasis was on neighborliness and fellow feeling through the medium of community singing and community hikes. But gradually the professional men whose drive had set these activities going lost interest and dropped out. After two years there was no denying that the hoped-for community response had failed to materialize. The Community Council passed through a prolonged crisis. Finally those who remained loyal to the idea began to take a realistic rather than an idealistic attitude toward community life in a large city. They became reconciled to the fact that

in the city black and white, rich and poor, Protestant and Catholic, cannot be gotten to rub elbows and be neighbors as people do in small towns. The city just isn't like that. In the city people get together in groups on the basis of their differences, and these groups won't mingle. But if they are taken as they are, they can be manipulated.[30]

Laying aside their ideals of universal brotherhood, the surviving idealists resolved to analyze the forces at work in the community, the crosscurrents of influence, the nuclei of action, in order better to manipulate them.

It is interesting to note how closely this program is paralleled by the concept of *social skill* adumbrated by Professor Elton Mayo and in the Hawthorne experiment, as described in Chapter 6 of this book.

SOCIAL THEORY

The last two chapters of *The Gold Coast and the Slum* are devoted to an attempt to place the findings of the study in a more universal and more theoretical context. In what is perhaps a slightly labored fashion Zorbaugh takes some of the ideas which his studies have thrown up, and tries to build them into a conceptual whole. It is apparent, however, that Park and the Chicago school were interested primarily in people and in living institutions, secondarily in the resolution of social problems, and that to many of the Chicago sociologists social abstractions were little better than an inescapable chore. There were, of course, exceptions, outstanding among whom was W. I. Thomas, who was manifestly the most fertile of the Chicago theoreticians. Some of his ideas presented in *The Polish Peasant* recur time and time again in the Chicago volumes as they apply to different facets of the Chicago situation.

The one important additional ingredient was the concept of ecology and the practice of relating community structure to geographical and spatial realities. As has been shown, this was the contribution of E. W. Burgess. Otherwise the theoretical advances were disappointingly slight. It might, in fact, be said that the Chicago investigators provided the material but that the theoretical organization of the material was left for succeeding generations of sociologists. For example, the ideas in F. M. Thrasher's *The Gang* were put forward with great sincerity but without theoretical sophistication or detachment. Thrasher was committed to a certain point of view in relation to gangs, which he found morally odious and difficult to view objectively. But the material he was able to collect and the way in which he presented it have been very useful in the development of thinking about delinquency. Some of the most advanced theorizing on this subject, as in Cohen's *Delinquent Boys*, borrows raw material from Thrasher's work of twenty years earlier as much as from any other source.

It must therefore be admitted that the set of ideas which Zorbaugh brings together here in presenting his theoretical conclusion does not constitute a very impressive list. It is true that it is directed to community workers rather than to academic sociologists, and it may well have been deliberately pitched at the level that he judged to be most effective in improving their understanding.

The starting point is his earlier conclusion that it is not sufficient to think in terms of an idealized community, but that one must accept human nature, the cultural tradition of the area, and the fixed physical configuration of the "community." Before improving society one must understand it, so the first task is to inquire into the nature of the community, to discover how it acts, how it sets up standards, how it defines its aims and ends, how it gets things done. One must also analyze what has been the effect of the growth of the city upon the life of local areas and how industrialization affects community life.

In this context the community is thought of as a group with shared experiences and a common definition of the situation. Zorbaugh quotes Thomas as offering the best analysis of the community and its control, showing how under ideal conditions the *folkways* become equivalent in force to the instincts and even displace them. He makes the point that absolute unanimity of opinion, which is the essential of community action, may be found in villages but can never properly occur in a city, where, quite apart from the unsettling effects of mobility and external change, the development of sectional interests makes any version of folk solidarity quite unthinkable. It is for this reason that, whereas in the village the basis of political decision is consensus, the political method of the city is democracy based on majority opinion as determined by the counting of votes.

Zorbaugh next turns to the growth of the city, which he describes in the terms already propounded by Burgess. He repeats the three concepts set up by Burgess—expansion, succession, and "centralized decentralization"—and he repeats Burgess' claim that these are displayed, at least in modified form, in the growth of every city. These concepts, and their limitations, were discussed at the beginning of this chapter, but Zorbaugh makes an extension of the ecological theory in introducing the concept of *natural areas*. This is perhaps a slightly pretentious way of describing the fact that a combination of terrain (hills, rivers, and coastline) and of man-made features (railroad tracks, canals, industrial areas) tend to divide a city into relatively isolated zones. For instance, in Chicago the Loop cut off from its hinterland would appear a very distinctive natural area. But the very example of the Near North Side shows that a natural area does not necessarily constitute a single community. Its definition is geographical or economic and not cultural. And this is a point that some planners have neglected. Planners have been known to divide their cities into *natural areas* or *neighborhood units* that were separated from one another by railroads or canals, green wedges, or other barriers. And they are sometimes rather surprised when these artificially isolated zones do not automatically turn themselves into communities.

The case of the Near North Side is more telling as an illustration of the way in which natural change in the city, and the appetite for expansion shown by business and industry, act to create the slum. The idea of the transitional zone is also attributable to Burgess, but Zorbaugh can point to the example of this area in which disorganization occurs because the old function of the buildings has ceased and the new function has not quite arrived. Landlords hope that if they hold on a while, their lots will increase in value. Meanwhile they are content that the old buildings on the lots are used inefficiently, for purposes other than those for which they were designed. On this account the slum is constantly eating into adjacent areas, dragging its surroundings down, converting apartments into tenements and rooming houses, while the single-family houses beyond are being converted into apartments. These changes can take place incredibly fast, particularly in the United States. In Chicago, it is reported, "a generation is as long a period as any area has been able to maintain itself as a fashionable residence area."[31] At this rate of change the fact of succession is unmistakable.

Zorbaugh points out the way in which, in the interests of tidy planning, urban renewal tears down the old landmarks—churches and memorials—which, as physical symbols of local communities, held the city together. Another change that undermines the local community is the increasing separation of functions. Even by 1930 only a minority still worked in the district in which they lived. An accountant, for example, would go to the business center for his office, and might even go elsewhere to meet other accountants with whom to share his professional social life. Recreation is commercialized and increasingly concentrated in a few "bright-light" areas.

A local consequence of the division of labor is an exaggeration of social distance in the residential locality. In the village, which the Chicago school are constantly idealizing, practically everybody has some economic and cultural relationship with everybody else. In the city such relationships no longer occur in the local community, and social distance consequently increases.

The increase of individuation of behavior is another point picked up from Thomas and related to the Chicago scene. In their description of the breakdown of the old Polish peasant, it will be remembered, Thomas and Znaniecki stressed the extent to which the old qualitative relations were giving way to quantitative relationships. The "job well done" was being supplanted by "the right price for the job"; the idea of family solidarity was declining in the face of individual competition. This is an undoubted characteristic of cities everywhere, and this too had been noted by Burgess.

Burgess describes individuation in terms of what he calls *mobility*, under which he includes both the individual's physical movements about the city and also the number of contacts and stimulations which he experiences. On these counts, as has already been mentioned, statistics disclosed an extremely rapid increase in mobility. It is pointed out that the experiences of second-generation immigrants when they go outside their own colonies to work or to attend school expose them to contradictory definitions of the situation and open the way to a dissolution of public opinion and a decay of social solidarity. Using a quotation from *The Polish Peasant*, Zorbaugh calls attention to the similarity between the disorganizing effect on second-generation immigrants of their daily commuting from the colony to other parts of Chicago and the disorganizing effect on Polish peasants of taking seasonal jobs in German cities. In each case the result is seen as the replacement of face-to-face and intimate relationships by casual, transitory, disinterested contacts.

There is within [the city] no common body of experience and tradition, no unanimity of interest, sentiment, and attitude which can serve as a basis of collective action. Local groups do not act. They cannot act. Local life breaks down.[32]

This quotation epitomizes the highly dramatized nostalgia for village life which recurs in the work of the Chicago school. This nostalgia does not stem from Robert E. Park, who perhaps was not at all sentimental, except as a great journalist can afford to be sentimental. He was prepared to enjoy and to accept anything that was human because it offered one more of the incredibly varied manifestations of social life.

Even though Zorbaugh was less sentimental than some of his colleagues, notably than Thrasher, his conclusions were too one-sided to be quite realistic. What he fails to take into account is the extent to which individuation is a general cultural tendency in industrial societies and the extent to which people positively choose city life for what it can offer, quite apart from possible, if uncertain, economic benefits. It is interesting to note that a new generation of sociologists is bringing forward similar arguments in favor of city life as the city succumbs to the largely economic charms of suburbia. Disintegration appears to be the fate of all twentieth-century Western communities as physical continuity is progressively improved, division of labor is perfected, mobility and individuation increase. While it is true that, under the influence of technological change, the physical character of the city is being transformed into vast suburbias, the attracting power of urban life is in no way diminished. It appears that there are some features of metropolitan life which, far from destroying the means of social life, offer this fulfillment to an increasing portion of the population.

TECHNIQUES OF INVESTIGATION

So much for the substantive material and its conceptual organization. We shall now take a look at Zorbaugh's techniques of data collection. It must be admitted that a careful reader of any of the early Chicago authors who pays attention to their scientific method will find that they are all remarkably casual in describing the sources of their facts. Standards have advanced so rapidly in this respect that by modern standards their procedures fall somewhat short of being scholarly or scientific. This is not to say that the intention to be systematic is lacking. For example, in *The Gold Coast and the Slum* documents are assigned numbers between 1 and 73. Each quotation in the book is referred to a particular document number, so that the reader can grasp the continuity in what individuals have said. This is a very helpful scheme, impeccable in principle, but in practice there are various anomalies, such as two documents numbered 14 and several documents lacking numbers. In certain places in the book Zorbaugh is careful to describe his documents. In the chapter on the Gold Coast, for example, he says in a footnote, "The documents in this chapter were contributed by residents of the Gold Coast who wish to remain anonymous," and this comment accounted for fourteen essays.

In two places in the book use is made of large groups of school essays, each group consisting of several hundred essays. On balance it appears that there are two separate groups, and they have two document numbers, but this is not quite clear from the evidence. In certain other places it seems very likely that documents to which Zorbaugh gives different numbers are in fact the same document being quoted twice.

There is also one house-to-house survey that was the source of Zorbaugh's information on the ages, racial origins, and other facts about the rooming-house population. No details are given of what this rooming census comprised, but the schedules are said to be filed at the University of Chicago. It is strange that not more was made of this source of information, as a house-to-house survey of rooming-house families would be extremely difficult to conduct efficiently. An area like that, with its cult of anonymity, its lack of respect for the law and for social agencies, would have been an exceptionally difficult sample to crack open. In the absence of details of how it was done one must have some reservations about the facts presented.

Certain existing records are mentioned as having been used. The *Illinois Lodging House Register* sounds like a semiofficial register and correspondingly reliable. A school census sounds as though it had been conducted on behalf of the board of education. Reference is also made to the records of the Juvenile Protective Association, a voluntary association, and to the case histories of the United Charities. These sound systematic and professionally conducted. Then there are various life histories, such as that of the charity girl and that of the pawnbroker, which have already been noted in this chapter. These individuals have clearly been approached and invited to contribute life histories, but no particulars are given of the techniques used. Perhaps some were interviewed intensively and gave their answers verbally; perhaps others wrote their stories. But this is mere speculation. There is equally little explanation of the source of the many reports by social workers and others who had some expert knowledge of the area.

Many of the documents are merely given a number without a description of source, and it is therefore not possible to know how much credence to give to their contents. One does not want to be too pedantic about this aspect of the study, but on the occasions when Zorbaugh wishes to draw what is essentially a statistical conclusion about an issue, as opposed to an illustration, it is not satisfactory and may not be really necessary to be as inexact as he was about sources. Presumably Zorbaugh had knowledge of all his sources but did not think it worth while to state them. Such casualness is a reminder of the date at which the work was conducted, but it is a fact that this aspect of the research technique showed little, if any, advance since *The Polish Peasant*.

The license to generalize must be paid for by precision as to sources. In other contexts, when the purpose is to illustrate by presenting some case material, free use of a well-expressed phrase or of a striking occurrence is justified. For that purpose it need not be systematic material. But Zorbaugh asks us to accept his evidence as derived more systematically than merely drawn from a ragbag of cases, and the authority of his work suffers because we have to take his sources so much on trust.

It is understandable that the various Chicago authors differ considerably in their attention to this component of scientific procedure.

Thrasher, for example, was considerably more conscientious in this respect in his presentation of *The Gang*. Thrasher, who spent seven years collecting and preparing his data and located 1,313 gangs in Chicago, made use of about 270 sources, numbered consecutively, and it is possible in his book to ascertain their origins. He had, it is clear, done careful work interviewing boys who were members of gangs, and 61 gang boys are separately identified. He does not use this material in a statistical way, but brings it in to provide examples from which he can draw certain conclusions, in a manner that is generally acceptable. The second largest group of informants were social workers, who in most cases prepared or made available written reports. Thrasher probably asked them to write their views on some particular topic, but in a few cases reference is made to interviews. Also interviewed were 12 policemen, 6 politicians, and 16 other people who were identified in one way or another, such as attorney or club director. In all there seem to have been about 130 interviews. Furthermore, he persuaded 21 of the gang boys to write their early life histories. Some of these are rich sources of information. Thrasher drew 37 relevant clippings from newspapers and 44 unpublished reports from various sources. He records 10 of his own observations. Thus, he offers a very clear picture of how he obtained his material and gives a good impression by internal evidence of the quality and reliability of the material. And yet, although his procedure is much superior to that of Zorbaugh, it falls short of what would be expected today. If the Chicago researchers had taken this side of their work just a little more seriously and been a little more painstaking in their final revision of the text, they could each have come up with a noticeably tidier and better-authenticated report.

It is clear, however, that a concern with method was left very much to the initiative of each investigator. Another contributor to the Chicago series was Paul G. Cressey. While special investigator for the Juvenile Protective Association he was requested during the summer of 1925 to report on the new and questionable phenomenon which later came to be known as the "taxi-dance hall." When Cressey started work he found that this type of establishment, at which girls could be hired as dancing partners for "ten cents a dance," was an institution with which even social workers were not familiar. Published material was found to be scanty and of little value. Many relevant data were secured from the case records of social agencies, notably his own organization, the Juvenile Protective Association of Chicago.

These sources were, however, found to need supplementation, and Cressey's first endeavor was to gain further information by formal interviews. He soon abandoned this method; for he found that as soon as a proprietor of a taxi-dance hall or any of his associates was approached and told of the interests of the interrogation he fought shy of co-operation.

It was therefore decided to try another method.

Observers were sent into the taxi-dance halls. They were instructed to mingle with the others and to become as much a part of this social world as ethically possible. They were asked to observe and to keep as accurate a record as possible of the behavior and conversations of those met in the establishments. Each observer was selected because of his past experience, his training and his special abilities. These investigators made it possible to gather significant case material from a much more varied group of patrons and taxi-dancers than could have been secured through any one person. The investigators functioned as anonymous strangers and casual acquaintances. They were thus able to obtain this material without encountering the inhibitions and resistance usually met in formal interviews. Further, the independent reports from different observers upon their contacts with the same individual made possible a check upon the consistency of the documents obtained. Moreover, this information concerning patrons and taxi-dancers made it feasible to secure much ancillary social data from the records of social agencies.[33]

One interesting feature of this use of observation techniques is that it was nearly contemporaneous with a very powerful, and ultimately influential, book by Eduard C. Lindeman called *Social Discovery*, which was published in 1924. Cressey's field studies of the taxi-dance hall began in 1925.

Lindeman was severely critical of the then current methods of social investigation. His objections to these methods are familiar today, but although they are now more widely held, there is still a great deal of social scientific work which chooses to reject or ignore the difficulties inherent in the simpler survey methods. He wrote:

Investigators conducting social surveys must be naïve indeed if they assume that their observations do not change situations. That they do possess a naïveté of this sort is evident from the refinements of their technique which all tend to eliminate the personal factor, to make the observers increasingly impartial, neutral. . . . This is particularly true of studies based upon schedules of questions for which the investigator finds answers by making enquiries of persons. Analysis of such schedules reveals that the questions all contain premises which imply simple conclusions.[34]

He goes on to quote Bowley's "absurd" advice that bias can be avoided by posing questions in simple "yes" or "no" form, and points out that the real difference in feasibility is between the sorts of issue in which the investigator already knows the form of answer —"how many farms of a particular size there are in a given area, how many people live in a single city block, et cetera"[35]—and those that entail not only the "what" of life but also the "why" and the "how."

In Lindeman's view the conclusion to be drawn from this is that more emphasis should be given to observation as a method of social investigation. Up to a point he agrees with the behaviorists, who for slightly different reasons reject the objective accuracy of answers to questions. Lindeman paraphrases it thus:

If, say the behaviorists, you wish to know what a person is doing, by all means refrain from asking *him*. His answer is sure to be wrong not merely because he does not know what he is doing but precisely because he is answering a question and he will make the reply in terms of you and not in terms of the objective thing he really is doing. . . . Thus, . . . if you wish to know what a person is *really* doing, watch him (don't ask him).[36]

To Lindeman, as to the behaviorists who classified talking as "verbal behavior," observation was a form of asking questions. He even claimed that "the method of objective observation in relation to all phenomena connected with behavior which are subject to measurement is superior to any other conceivable method of interpreting these phenomena."[37] This was the task of the *objective observer*, "from the outside." In Lindeman's scheme this is complementary to, and equally important as, the task of the observer "from the inside," or *participant observer*, and since, obviously, no single investigator would be capable of simultaneous observations from the outside and from the inside, a joint investigation is imperative.

It happens that Lindeman's name is associated with his more novel proposal for participant observation and not with the need for objective observation, but the investigators sent by Cressey into the taxi-dance halls, checking the consistency of one another's observations and of the documents obtained, were undoubtedly in Lindeman's category of objective observers. Even earlier, Nels Anderson, who later produced a text in collaboration with Eduard Lindeman,[38] had been living the life of a hobo to be what was perhaps the first deliberate participant observer.[39]

The wide range of approaches adopted by the Chicago school is by no means exhausted by the examples given thus far. As we have seen, some personal documents were used by Zorbaugh and by Thrasher, but in one instance a report is substantially a carefully prepared life history. This is Clifford R. Shaw's presentation of *The Jack-Roller*.[40] A "jack-roller" is a criminal who robs drunken men, with or without violence. Shaw's book is the carefully annotated story of one young criminal psychopath and the description of his crimes and of his experiences in detention home, reformatory, and house of correction. William Healy, a pioneer in criminology in the United States, had based his book *The Individual Delinquent* on an analysis of the case histories of several hundred young Chicago delinquents, and it was left to Shaw to develop the technique longitudinally by eliciting the boy's own story.

The life-record itself is the delinquent's own account of his experiences written as an autobiography, as a diary, or presented in the course of a series of interviews. The unique feature of such documents is that they are recorded in the first person, in the boy's own words, and not translated into the language of the person investigating the case.[41]

Shaw recognizes that there are distinct possibilities of falsification by the boy, and he takes exemplary measures to minimize this possibility. He had known the boy for six years, from the age of sixteen until the age of twenty-two, when he produced his final manuscript. Shaw was counseling him throughout this period, except while he was in the Chicago House of Correction, and had clearly got to know him very well. Shaw had evidently helped the boy organize his material, and the final version was only gradually arrived at. The first stage had been to secure a list of the boy's behavior difficulties, delinquencies, and commitments. These were put in chronological order and returned to the boy to provide a framework for his "own story." His first document was a brief account, and

we pointed out to him that his first story was an excellent summary of his life, but lacked detailed descriptive material. In response to our suggestion that he write a more detailed story, the original document was increased to its present length. All of the suggestions and illustrations used to indicate the sort of material desired were drawn from his own experiences.[42]

Both long and short versions are published in the book.

Furthermore, Shaw had checked and built up the story from outside sources of data whenever this was possible.

As a safeguard against erroneous interpretations of such material, it is extremely desirable to develop the "own story" as an integral part of the total case history. Thus each case study should include, along with the life-history document, the usual family history, the medical, psychiatric, and psychological findings, the official record of arrest, offenses, and commitments, the description of the play-group relationships, and any other verifiable material which may throw light upon the personality and actual experiences of the delinquent in question. In the light of such supplementary material, it is possible to evaluate and interpret more accurately the personal document. It is probable that in the absence of such additional case material any interpretation of the life-history is somewhat questionable.[43]

Precautions such as Shaw describes may be regarded as safe-guarding the authenticity of his life-history material. There remain, however, two questions that require satisfaction before the utility of such material can be established.

The first is how far the narrative is objectively told and interpreted by the informant. Shaw has a direct answer to this question. Both he and Burgess, who contributes the theoretical analysis of the life record, make a clear distinction between the delinquent boy's defini-tion of the situation and that of society at large. They were there-fore not surprised to find a disparity between the "objective facts" and the boy's interpretation of them.

The boy's "own story" is of primary importance for ascertaining the personal attitudes, feelings, and interests of the child; in other words, it shows how he conceives his role in relation to other persons and the interpretations which he makes of the situations in which he lives. It is in the personal document that the child reveals his feelings of inferiority and superiority, his fears and worries, his ideals and philosophy of life, his antagonisms and mental conflicts, his prejudices and rationalizations.[44]

If it is asked what is the utility of knowing such intimate details of an individual's mental processes, the answer may be that such knowledge has two major uses. The material provides a clue to the appropriate methods of treatment of the individual case, and equally it provides insights into the nature of the deviant subculture to which the boy belonged.

The other main question is the generality of a life record such as The Jack-Roller. The answer to this is a little more difficult. The case for generality may be claimed to rest on the convergence of various studies. Shaw himself collected other life histories, including The Natural History of a Delinquent Career and Brothers in Crime.[45] Many case histories have also been constructed from the contributions of various lay and professional expert informants and from available records. An early instance was Walter C. Reckless' Six Boys in Trouble.[46] But the life history can also be justified as the embodiment in an actual case of the theories of attitude and be-havior information built up in a less localized context. Burgess com-ments on The Jack-Roller:

To many readers the chief value of this document will not consist in its contribution to an understanding of the personality of Stanley and other delinquents or of the methods of treatment of similar cases. To them its far-reaching significance will inhere in the illumination it throws on the causation, under conditions of modern city life, of criminal careers and upon the social psychology of the new type of criminal youth.[47]

It is also of interest that Clifford Shaw himself regarded the detailed study of an individual as only one approach to the study of delinquency. Concurrently with his collection of life histories he was working with Henry D. McKay on the analysis of delinquency areas. "Delinquency areas" constituted a special variety of the "natural areas," which have already been mentioned as one of the most celebrated products of the early Chicago School of Sociology.[48]

The method used was to plot court cases of delinquency on a map of Chicago, marking the place of residence of the delinquent, or in some cases the location of the offense. The scatter map was subsequently corrected for density of population, so that the incidence of delinquents in each area of the city could be stated as a proportion of all youths of the age in question, say, ten to sixteen years.

It was confirmed by this method that certain areas had a consistently higher incidence of delinquency, and these areas were given the name *delinquency areas*. Furthermore, this method of quantification made it possible to show that delinquency rates vary inversely with the distance from the center of the city, and that areas of high delinquency are likely to display other symptoms of disorganization, such as dependency, transience, or suicide. These results stand even if the concentric rings around the center are not so perfect in other cities as they appear to have been in Chicago, and even if modern post-Sutherland criminologists are more sophisticated about the correlation of social class and antisocial activity than the Chicago pioneers of ecological analysis.

One prerequisite of the detailed comparative study of the different areas of the city is that there be an adequate breakdown of population data. The Chicago sociologists were able to take advantage of the fact that the Bureau of the Census in many districts makes a secondary analysis of the decennial census by small city areas, or *census tracts*. In the case of the city of Chicago there were seventy such census tracts in the 1920 census and seventy-five such census tracts in the 1930 census, and these were used for a number of the Chicago sociological studies.[49]

A good example of the usefulness of the census-tract data is given by Reckless,[50] who was concerned with the incidence of prostitution in Chicago. Reckless began in 1922 on one of the earliest Chicago studies and submitted his first report for the University of Chicago as a doctor's dissertation in 1925. Up to that date the data in the possession of certain of the social-welfare agencies interested in organized vice had not been released for his use, and he had had to lean heavily on official statistics. Later, in *Vice in Chicago*, he used more case material that had been made available to him, and the fresh data were well knit together with the official statistics.

As was customary in the Chicago ecological studies, the basic seventy-five census tracts which together cover the city were somewhat coalesced, in this case into seventy statistical communities, so that 1920 and 1930 census material could be compared. From the census data the actual population of these statistical communities could be derived. Concurrently the records of the Committee of Fifteen, whose full-time job it was to investigate and suppress vice resorts[51] were analyzed for the years 1910–29, and note was made of every place at which investigators in any given year found evidence of commercialized prostitution. In all, during these years there had been 5,895 such places. It was shown by this procedure that the vice resorts were very unevenly distributed and were, in fact, to be found in only 38 of the 70 statistical communities; in any one year vice resorts were to be found only in a maximum of 24 such communities. Furthermore, many instances were isolated, and only 16 tracts were classified as vice-infested on the grounds that they had an average of at least one resort per year. Narrowing the distribution still further, Reckless found that the 12 most infested tracts, containing 30 per cent of the city's 1920 population, harbored 96.3 per cent of the total number of places of commercialized vice from 1910 to 1929.

Rapid population changes were taking place in Chicago, and a comparison of the data around the time of the 1920 census and around the time of the 1930 census showed that there had been spectacular changes in the apparent distribution. One tract, Grand Boulevard, a few blocks south of the Loop, rose from seventh place in 1920 (18.67 vice resorts per 100,000 population) to top position in 1930 (100.33 vice resorts per 100,000 population).

The next step was to determine whether there was any regular correlation between the incidence of vice resorts and any other demographic features revealed by the census data. There had, for example, been a hypothesis that vice resorts were likely to be found in areas where men greatly outnumber women. It was found that, whereas in 1920 a strong preponderance of men or of women in the local population was associated with a high vice rate, this was no longer the case in 1930. A suggested explanation was that this change was associated with the dispersal of vice resorts away from the near-central regions of the city. Accordingly, it was suggested[52] that the correlation of high vice rate with unbalanced sex ratio was spurious, with the demographic characteristics of the near-central area as the intervening variable.

It was shown that tract vice rates were strongly positively correlated with high proportions of adults and low proportions of children in the population. This was correlated with the low incidence of children in the socially disorganized rooming-house areas, as described by Zorbaugh, as the analysis also showed that tract vice rates correlated negatively with home ownership. "They indicate areas of non-family or loosely knit family life—areas in which commercialized vice can thrive."[53] On the other hand, contrary to the ethnocentric stereotype, it became clear that there was no association between a high incidence of foreign-born whites and a high vice rate. In fact, vice was concentrated in the tracts with the lowest percentages of immigrants.

Reckless goes on to compare the tract vice rates with other symptoms of social disorganization—liquor-law offenses, venereal-disease cases, adult-male crime, juvenile delinquency, poverty, and divorce. Statistics on all these points related to the locality of the offense or the domicile of the offender were derived from various sources: Federal records for liquor offenses; a sample of clinics for the incidence of venereal diseases; home addresses of male county-jail inmates (collected by Shaw) for adult-male offenders; juvenile-court cases (male and female) for juvenile delinquency; United Charity cases for poverty; court records for divorce.

It appeared that there was a concentration of many of these in the vice areas of the city, but that this concentration was by no means as total as in the case of vice resorts. "In other words, almost two-thirds of the chief social problems of Chicago fell outside the important vice areas of the city."[54] In some instances, notably in the case of male juvenile delinquency, the correlation with vice rate was very slight.

This study illustrates a very different type of inquiry from Shaw's *The Jack-Roller* or even from Thrasher's *The Gang*. But it was equally characteristic of the Chicago Sociological series, as is shown by two other celebrated books—Cavan's study of the ecological distribution of suicide[55] and the later study of the distribution of mental disorder by Faris and Dunham.[56]

These few examples illustrate the wide range of research techniques pioneered and developed—the use of personal documents, the development of participant observation, fresh forms of ecological analysis. For the first time a start was made in the more or less systematic study of deviant groups with mildly antisocial features, such as the hoboes and the taxi-dance hostesses. Perhaps the abiding fact about the Chicago series is that it is unified by its field of interest rather than by its methods. Probably more than with any other school of sociology, there is a distinctive quality in Park's creation in Chicago, with its determined concern with locality, its faith in human betterment, and an intrinsically American hatred of deviation and radicalism which cohabits strangely with the school's grasp of the wonderful richness and variety of human institutions. In later chapters of this book the fruits of the Chicago heritage will be regularly in evidence.

LIFE IN A SMALL TOWN

Even to a sociologist one of the interesting and important objects of study is to see the development of thought of an individual. The primary subject of this chapter is the preparation of two extremely influential books, but there is an important secondary theme, which is the story of Professor Robert Lynd, of the man who walked in to the first study of Middletown and who, after a great extension of knowledge and experience, which he gained at Columbia University and elsewhere, went back to Middletown to produce his second report, *Middletown in Transition*.[1]

Robert S. Lynd was born in Indiana in 1892 and moved at the age of eighteen to Louisville, Kentucky, where his father was to be a bank employee. He received his bachelor of arts degree from Princeton University and then, intending to become a Presbyterian minister, went on to the Theological Seminary and received a bachelor of divinity degree. Soon thereafter the United States entered World War I, and Lynd joined the United States Army.

After the war, in the early 1920's, Robert Lynd and Helen, his wife and collaborator, worked at the Institute of Social and Religious Research. The research program of the institute was to include a survey of religious provision and practice in a typical small American city. By various criteria that will be described later the town selected for the survey was Muncie, Indiana.

When consideration was being given to the question of what facts were relevant to the study of religion in America, the study came under the influence of Professor Clark Wissler, of the American

126

Museum of Natural History. Wissler, an anthropologist, in his studies of North American Indians had paid considerable attention to religious observances and practices. While Lynd was pondering the problem of a suitable frame of reference Wissler was on the point of bringing out his *Man and Culture*,[2] in which he presented a ninefold classification under which the activities of any culture could be described. Almost concurrently W. H. R. Rivers, in his *Social Organization*,[3] had presented a sixfold classification, which was the one Lynd decided to adopt. But it was to Wissler that Lynd owed his realization that, just as the study of primitive religion requires an understanding of a primitive society in all its aspects, so also the method and approach of social anthropology could legitimately be applied to the study of American religion in its total setting.

Years later, when *Middletown* was due to be published, Clark Wissler was invited to contribute a foreword. He wrote:

So this volume needs no defense; it is put forth for what it is, a pioneer attempt to deal with a sample American community after the manner of social anthropology. To most people, anthropology is a mass of curious information about savages, and this is so far true, in that most of its observations are on the less civilized. What is not realized is that anthropology deals with the communities of mankind, takes the community, or tribe, as the biological and social unit, and in its studies seeks to arrive at a perspective of society by comparing and contrasting these communities; and whatever may be the deficiencies of anthropology, it achieves a large measure of objectivity, because anthropologists are by the nature of the case "outsiders." To study ourselves as through the eye of an outsider is the basic difficulty in social science, and may be insurmountable, but the authors of this volume have made a serious attempt, by approaching an American community as an anthropologist does a primitive tribe. It is in this that the contribution lies, an experiment not only in method, but in a new field, the social anthropology of contemporary life.[4]

In spite of the bold form of his claim, one can perhaps detect in the above quotation Wissler's feeling that *Middletown* might be received by its readers with something less than enthusiasm. It seems that the Lynds and their associates, whose original object of studying local religious practices had so greatly expanded, found it an extremely difficult task to encompass in one report the manifold institutions and activities of a modern community, and that even three years after the completion of the fieldwork they were not entirely satisfied with their handiwork.

In a preface to *Middletown* the Lynds write:

No one can be more aware than the writers of the shortcomings of the report—the lack of adequate data at certain points and frequent unevenness of method. Furthermore, the field work was completed in 1925; the point of view of the investigators has developed during the subsequent years, and the treatment would be at many points more adequate were the investigation to be undertaken now.[5]

Later, in his preface to *Middletown in Transition*, Lynd wrote:

In the case of *Middletown* it was three years and a half—in a mood alternating between enthusiasm and weary disgust as the job worms its exhausting course through rough draft, revision, checking and cross-checking, and compression for publication.[6]

But if the authors had sometimes despaired, there was no justification for their lack of confidence, for the book was an instantaneous success. In 1929 alone there were six printings. *Middletown* had succeeded in its attempt to set down "the facts" about a small American city. Nearly ten years earlier, in *Main Street* and *Babbitt*, Sinclair Lewis had described in devastating parody the deplorable deficiencies of the American small-town businessman's life and ethos. Veblen's astringent analysis had had a quarter-century to undermine the entrenched beliefs of the American people. Although the country was still prosperous, the great depression was in the offing. And then *Middletown* appeared, the first scientific and ostensibly uncritical, objective description of small-town life. Here for the first time, without reformist overtones and without dramatization, was a mirror held up to the ordinary American.

Furthermore, this work, unlike many another popular success, was equally acclaimed by the Lynds' learned peers. The success of *Middletown* created an imperative demand for more social surveys. In 1930 W. F. Ogburn, president of the American Sociological Society, devoted his presidential address to the subject. On all sides there was a call for more facts about American society, even though there was perhaps a certain tardiness at explaining what the value of facts as such might be.

Lynd himself became executive secretary of the Social Science Research Council. This body had been organized in 1923, and was formally incorporated in 1924 to link the activities of anthropologists, economists, historians, political scientists, psychologists, sociologists, and statisticians. The declared purpose of the Council was, and is, to plan, foster, promote, and develop research in the social field. When Lynd became executive secretary in 1930 there was not the present range of foundations prepared to sponsor research, and the Social Science Research Council was used by the Rockefeller Foundation as the agency for distributing research funds earmarked for the social sciences. Partly for this reason Lynd's position in the Council could have been one of considerable power and responsibility had he not soon thereafter chosen to move into the center of the academic circle.

At the same time, as has been made clear, Lynd was a self-taught man as far as the social sciences were concerned. It therefore reflects great credit both on him as an individual and on Columbia University as an academic institution that, when in 1931 Columbia was looking for a professor of sociology, the university was able to overlook Robert Lynd's formal shortcomings for a post of such seniority and bring him into this important faculty.

The chair of sociology at Columbia University had been created in 1894 and had been filled from that time until 1931 by Franklin H. Giddings. At his death Giddings was over seventy-five years old, and though in his earlier years he had been a distinguished scholar and an inspirer of scientific method, his contribution, it seems clear, had deteriorated during his last ten to twenty years. Furthermore, he seems, according to Harry Elmer Barnes,[7] to have been a casual teacher and a difficult personality, so that he was unable to build up a team as impressive as that which Small and, later, Park had created at Chicago. Finally, although he had encouraged the application of scientific method to sociology, Giddings himself, it seems, did not engage in empirical work. And although R. M. MacIver's arrival had strengthened the school, there was still nobody with actual experience of field research.

Sociology at that time came within the faculty of political science, and the appointment committee consisted of representatives of the graduate departments—history, economics, government, and public law as well as sociology. The rumor at the time was that the sociologists wanted a leading theoretician but were outvoted by the other schools, who felt that the need was for a research man. Even when this point was conceded, it was still found difficult to agree on a suitable person. Although *Middletown* had made him a sociological celebrity, Lynd had not advanced to doctor of philosophy. Sensibly the faculty overcame its scruples and granted him a doctorate on the basis of parts of *Middletown* which were indisputably entirely his own work, and in the fall of 1931 Lynd was installed at Columbia University as professor of sociology. Another advance for empirical sociology had been signalized.

Lynd's immediate contribution to Columbia was a renewed emphasis on the contemporary scene—on the consumer in modern American society and on the modern family. He must also have stimulated the young graduates—Lundberg, Komarovsky, and McInerny were just setting out on their study of leisure in Westchester County. But the stimulation was undoubtedly in both directions. For the first time Lynd was exposed to rigorous theoretical thinking and disputation. Znaniecki was in the United States for two years as a visiting professor at Columbia. Lynd could respect Znaniecki as a field researcher as well as for his mastery of theory, and through him Lynd began to realize the impracticability of recognizing two breeds of social scientist—field investigators who go out and get the facts and theoreticians who fit the facts into their theories. Only then did Lynd emerge from his position of raw empiricism and realize that he must conduct his field investigation from an informed theoretical position.

Meanwhile the great depression was leaving its mark on Western thought. As we shall see, Lynd had almost instinctively divided his Middletown families into two groups, which he calls "working class" and "business class." It seems that the Lynds had had no help from Karl Marx in deciding on this two-way classification,* but later, in the climate of the thirties, they did read deeply in the writings of Marx and Engels, and partly from this source they began to revise their thinking about the American community in terms of its class structure and the operations of its pressure groups.

---

* "However, there is no reference to Marx in *Middletown*, and from the best of authorities we know that the authors had not read anything by Marx when this book was written."[8]

Lynd's opportunity to apply his new theoretical equipment occurred in 1935, when he was persuaded to return to Middletown to ascertain how well the city had surmounted the depression years and how much the community had changed. He arrived in Muncie in June, 1935, with five assistants. On this occasion his wife did not participate directly in the study, although she was coauthor of the subsequent report. This investigation and the reporting were much less prolonged than in the first survey—fieldwork in 1935 involved less than a tenth of the man-days of research time spent in Middletown on the 1924–25 study, and the report was published two years after work commenced (as compared with five years for the first study).

Into this report, *Middletown in Transition*, Lynd packed all his militant and evangelical feeling about the shortcomings in American society. While he retained something of the structure of the earlier Middletown, this time he substituted for his dead-pan "getting at the facts" a hard-hitting exposure of the sources of power in what he still regarded as a typical American city.

When his second volume was completed, in the spring of 1938, Professor Lynd was invited by Princeton University to deliver the four Stafford Little Lectures. This series, which provided the substance of his book *Knowledge for What?*,[9] was his opportunity to demonstrate how far he had traveled since he first came to Muncie in January, 1924.

He proclaims in his opening chapter:

Contemporary social science contains within itself two types of orientation that divide it into two blocs of workers: the scholars and the technicians. Both work within the protective tradition of free intellectual inquiry: and both assume continuity and relevance between their respective realms in the common task of exploring the unknown. Actually they tend to pull apart, the scholar becoming remote from and even disregarding immediate relevancies, and the technician too often accepting the definition of his problems too narrowly in terms of the emphases of the institutional environment of the moment.[10]

He proceeds to show that it is possible for the social scientist to avoid both pitfalls; he is able to concern himself with immediate practical problems while raising them to a higher order of abstraction so that they fall into place in a less transient conceptual setting.

But at Princeton, and in his subsequent book, Lynd has a double task. He is speaking to an audience that is largely skeptical of the capacity of the social sciences to contribute either to science or to practical affairs. At the same time he is speaking to a smaller circle of specialists who are so absorbed in their narrow specialisms— history, political science, economics, sociology, anthropology, psychology—that they do not notice the dynamics and the contradictions of contemporary American culture.

Lynd devotes the last chapter of *Knowledge for What?* to the presentation of what he describes as "some outrageous hypotheses." One feels here that he is determined to demonstrate to his readers that he personally has emerged from the age of innocence and naïve empiricism into an age of maturity, in which he can face and formulate at a high level of abstraction the basic dilemma of modern society. His ideas constitute a highly stimulating challenge to the assumptions of modern American society—the need for more social planning and control to facilitate the human ends of living, the need to extend the reality of democracy in government, the need to explore alternatives to private capitalism, the need to analyze closely the substance of class conflict, the need to replace the myth of individual equality by the achievement of equality of opportunity, the need to recognize and make allowance for the creative, spontaneous irrationality in the human make-up, the need to re-examine the basis of popular education, the need to discover a modern substitute for the dying reality of traditional religion, the need to build a culture that rejects the inevitability of war, the need to solve the problems of urban living, the need to develop a congruent hospitality to change, the need to remove the obstacles to the application by social scientists of the foregoing measures.

This list is perhaps slightly dated in its emphases, but it does comprise the sort of political program that many European and American liberals would have been prepared to support in the late 1930's. As such it has few surprises, but what does seem less justifiable is the form in which it is presented. Each of the above twelve points is first introduced as a problem, and when this problem has been discussed for a few sentences, it is restated in a form which thinly disguises it as a hypothesis. For example: "*The hypothesis:* it is possible to build a culture that in all its institutions will play down the need for and the possibility of war."[11]

The fact that everyone but a lunatic wishes to outlaw war means that Lynd would find no sane critic of his aspirations. But sympathy with his aims should make one no more receptive to the idea that these constitute a hypothesis. One can only ask by what practical method, short of conquering the world for a benevolent dictatorship, could any social scientist hope either to confirm or to nullify this suggested hypothesis in the form in which it is stated. Clearly this series does not constitute a set of testable hypotheses. Nor does it noticeably interlock or suggest a structured theory. Unlike the bricks of theory—anomie, disorganization-reorganization, the four wishes—Lynd's set are in fact not abstractions at all but rather generalized political aims.

Lynd's 1938 Stafford Little Lectures at Princeton University and his subsequent published version were immensely influential. They undoubtedly helped put the social sciences on the midcentury map, even though Professor Lynd did not at that time find the synthesis which would combine the contribution of the man of scholarship and the man of action.

METHODS OF INVESTIGATION

We shall now return to a more detailed examination of these books. The fieldwork for *Middletown* took about eighteen months, and was completed in June, 1925. There was then a long period of gestation; the foreword was not written until June, 1928, and the book came out in 1929. Thus all together it took approximately five years from the beginning of the fieldwork to the publication of the book.

This is the first instance in the present series in which the authors give a full and conscientious description of the materials they have used and the methods they have employed in collecting them. In *The Polish Peasant* and in the works of the Chicago school it is possible to pull these facts out from footnotes and other inferential sources, but the work is done for the reader in *Middletown*, which includes a concise five-page appendix describing the methods used. Here it is told how, early in 1924, a small office was set up unobtrusively in Middletown by a group of people who had come, they said, to "study the growth of the city." When they started work—Mr. and Mrs. Lynd and two assistants—they had no fixed schedule other than the decision to collect material in terms of the six main life activities proposed, as we have noted, by W. H. R. Rivers. Thus the work was organized from the beginning in terms of these six activities: Getting a Living, Making a Home, Training the Young, Using Leisure, Engaging in Religious Practices, Engaging in Community Activities. It is important to remember that this is essentially an anthropological frame of reference.

The next decision was the selection of the community for their survey. Why did they choose to go to this small city of thirty-odd thousand inhabitants in the state of Indiana? The Lynds claim that no ulterior motives guided their choice, that Muncie was not consulted in advance, and that no organization or person in the city contributed to the cost of the survey. It appears that they listed the characteristics a city should possess as representative of contemporary American life, namely, a temperate climate, a sufficiently rapid expansion rate to feel the growing pains that accompany contemporary social change, an industrial culture with a moderate amount of modern high-speed machine production, no single plant dominating the city's industry (that is, not a one-industry town),* a substantial and largely self-contained local artistic life, no outstanding peculiarities or problems, a location in the Middle West as the common denominator of the United States. It was also necessary that it be compact and homogeneous enough to be manageable for purposes of study. This they interpreted to mean that it should have a population between 25,000 and 50,000; that it should be reasonably self-contained, that is, not a satellite of a larger city; and that it should have a relatively small Negro and foreign-born population.

One is inclined to be a little suspicious of the apparently complete rationality of the selection procedure. It is true that, as has been mentioned, Lynd came from Indiana and that Muncie is the sort of place he would have known about—not too big, not exceptional or outstanding in any way. When this kind of mediocrity is

---

* The Lynds were not strictly correct in equating a single-plant town with a single-industry town. In the case of *Muncie*, as will be shown, the industrial, and indeed the total, life of the city was dominated by the enterprises of one family, but in terms of occupational opportunities this imbalance was not significant.

formalized, the set of criteria listed above might emerge. But experience suggests that the course of scientific investigation is generally erratic and that it is a common pretense afterward for the scientist to claim that he proceeded in a direct route from beginning to end.[12]

In this instance, however, such a judgment may be unduly harsh. There is the curious fact that when Katz and Lazarsfeld were selecting, by an extremely rigorous procedure, a city suitable for their *Personal Influence* investigation, Muncie was on the short list, ranking very close to the average. It was rejected on the grounds that it would not be wise to select Middletown for a second study and also, strangely enough, because it was a one-industry town.[13] Thus thirty years later Middletown was violating one of Lynd's own selection criteria.

The basic method used at the start of the study was to explore in as detached a manner as possible the activities of the people of Middletown. The investigators therefore set about getting to know people, avoiding any premature attempt to set up definite schedules or questionnaires, concentrating first on getting the feel of the city while gradually working into a more systematic observation of the modes of behavior to be seen there.

In this respect the Lynds were adopting the procedures of R. E. Park and his colleagues in the Chicago school. For although one may be critical of the rather casual use of documents by some of the Chicago scholars, they were, of course, still following the precepts of Park. Like him, most of them were essentially observers who would have spent much of their time tramping about the streets, getting themselves into close contact with the people with whom they were concerned. There had been this receptive, informal observation in Chicago, and it was a feature here also in Middletown. The Lynds and their helpers were entrenching themselves by going around, attending meetings of different kinds, watching behavior, and talking to anybody they could find who might be able to give them information.

From the outset they intended to view the city in its true perspective. Originally they were going to cover the whole period from the eighties or nineties right through to the date of the survey. Later on, in order to simplify their task, they decided to take two key dates, 1890 and 1924, and much of the book is organized about the differences that had taken place in the three and a half decades between those dates.

Another initial decision that had to be made concerned the social classification they would use. The work was to be organized from the beginning in terms of social classes, but here, as has been mentioned, it was decided to have only two classes. The grounds for this decision were local and empirical; the Lynds concluded that there was no significant upper class, and so in fact it was legitimate to divide people into the working classes and the business classes. To anticipate their results at this point, their Middletown studies showed that the working classes represented 71 per cent of the population and the remaining 29 per cent belonged to the business classes. In *Middletown in Transition* the authors correct these figures on the grounds that they had calculated their percentages by counting the number of employed people. As there were more employed people in the working-class families than in the middle-class ones, because the families were larger, this exaggerated the number of working-class families. They later corrected their estimate to 60 per cent working-class families and 40 per cent business-class families. They based their classification on occupation, distinguishing the people who deal with things (the working class) from those who deal with people (the business class). This scheme is marvelously simple, but it does not overcome certain familiar difficulties, such as where one should place the dentist, who is obviously a professional man although he deals with things, that is, teeth, or the sculptor or musician, who equally deals with things. Sensibly they decided not to be too pedantic about such cases but put them in with the business classes.

Their specific field methods are described under five headings. The first is called "Participation in the Local Life." The Lynds and their colleagues either lived in apartments or lodged in private houses with the deliberate intention of living normal Middletown lives, thus achieving spontaneity and reducing what they called the "bug on a pin" aspect. They did not want to appear as a breed of elevated beings who were able to look down, observe, and analyze from a position of superiority; they wanted to be on a level with the people whom they were observing. They made a point of accepting all invitations, so that they dined with a great variety of citizens, attended meetings of a great variety of organizations. Week in, week out, they attended churches, school assemblies and classes, court sessions, political rallies, labor meetings, civic-club luncheons, missionary meetings, lectures, annual dinners, card parties, etc. At these meetings, wherever possible, inconspicuously they took notes of what was going on and then immediately afterward wrote up an account according to a standardized form. When it was impossible to take notes at the time, the record was made immediately afterward from memory.

This is an interesting point. In England, Sidney and Beatrice Webb, who had already completed their most monumental studies, on trade unions and local government, had exactly the same problem and met it in much the same way. Incidentally, the Webbs' book, *Methods of Social Study*, was published in 1932. That was not long after the Lynds were operating in Middletown, and in its detailed advice on points such as note-taking it was, with the possible exception of Lundberg's *Social Research*,[14] the most practical manual on how to conduct fieldwork that had been published up to that date.

The second method used by the Lynds was the examination of documentary material. Here they took all available records relating to Middletown, including census data, city and county records, court files, school records, state biennial reports and yearbooks. The two leading daily newspapers were read in detail for 1890 and 1891 and were supplemented by readings from a Democratic daily and a labor paper which flourished for a time. The two current Republican dailies and the Democratic weekly were read and clipped in corresponding detail during the year and a half of the study. The thirty-five intervening years were covered by sampling.

The minutes of various organizations were read, in each case for 1890–91 and 1924–25 and in some cases for the intervening years as well. This analysis covered the board of education, the missionary societies of two leading churches, the ministerial association, the Federated Club of Clubs, the woman's club, the library board, the Humane Society and many other groups. They also came into possession of two unusually detailed diaries, one the diary of a leading merchant who was also a prominent Protestant churchman and the other that of a young Catholic baker, and these they read through for the years 1886–1900. In addition they obtained parts of other diaries and scrapbooks of clippings, programs, letters, and other similar items which helped to build up a picture of 1890 for comparison with the person-to-person contacts and folk talk of the survey period. Also available were public histories of the state, the county, the city, and city directories, maps, "boom books," Chamber of Commerce publications, high-school annuals, health and other surveys of the city. Thus they acquired quite a full background by reading published material.

Third in the list of methods was the compilation of statistics. Today the word "statistics" commonly connotes some rather sophisticated manipulation and analysis of data, and it is a timely reminder to meet the word in this more traditional context. Official and other sources yielded information on "wages, steadiness of employment, industrial accidents, nearness of residence to plant, promotion, club membership, church membership, contributions and attendance, library and periodical circulation, attendance at motion picture theaters, ownership and use of automobiles, etc."[15] Logically the source of most of this information could probably be given an alternative classification as "documentary records," but this is a correction of little importance.

The fourth method was the interview, of which four main variants are described. One type consisted of what they called "casual conversations"—with streetcar conductors, janitors, barbers, or chance associates at luncheons or club meetings. All such conversations were conscientiously recorded at the earliest opportunity. The second category consisted of carefully planned interviews with individuals who were especially qualified to give information; for example, they interviewed the six leading Protestant ministers and the secretaries of the Y.M.C.A. and the Y.W.C.A. Each of such interviews took about four hours, and was conducted only after the investigators had got to know these people through close contacts over many months. It is claimed that the interviewers thus elicited almost complete frankness of response.

As the study progressed the investigators began to feel the need to test in individual families certain hypotheses that had suggested themselves, and the last two sets of interviews were designed for this purpose, one to question working-class wives and the other to talk things over with some wives of businessmen.

They selected, somewhat casually, a sample of the wives of workers (native-born white Americans) in the three main plants in the city. This sample was to some extent stratified to cover people living in different parts of the city, and families lacking children of school age or lacking either parent were excluded. The design was thus to select ideal rather than statistically representative families, and although the sampling frame was limited to workers in the three plants, the sample was taken as typical of all workers in the city. Another flaw in the sampling method was that almost all interviews took place during the day, thus excluding the wives who went out to work. All together there were 182 of these interviews, and certain simple facts, such as the occupation and duration of employment of the husband, were obtained from that number; while for the main schedule of questions there were 124 completed interviews. Of the 124, one hundred also gave facts relating to their family budgets. So there are full records for 100 and a diminishing amount of information relating to various numbers of informants up to 182. These were fairly tough interviews, certainly for that time; they lasted from two to three hours and were all conducted by three staff members. The success rate was only 80 per cent, which we would today regard as low, but considering the time and the topics, such as income distribution, a 20 per cent refusal rate is not surprising.

The interviews with the wives of businessmen in the city were not designed as a representative sample of all levels in the business class. The investigators deliberately excluded the four richest families, and they picked what they called "just good substantial folks." In this case they wrote a letter asking for an appointment and called only on receipt of a favorable reply. The interview took longer, probably developing into a social occasion with the discussion ranging over a variety of topics, but the interviewers found it very difficult to get the facts from these informants on intimate personal details, such as religious beliefs or incomes. This reluctance to disclose personal data is familiar to all interviewers of middle-class informants.

It must be stated that the authors treat the survey material with complete fairness throughout their book. Whenever they quote figures they are scrupulous to provide the derivation, even when the style of the sentence is rather spoiled by an insertion indicating the sample. There are very few places where they fail to describe their sources. In this respect they show an important advance beyond the authors previously discussed, many of whom were quite casual about describing how they obtained their facts. The Lynds in this book are also very careful never to make it appear that the facts they present are more important or more representative than they actually are. They very seldom quote percentages of answers, but present their results in numbers, for example, "in the case of twelve of the thirty-eight friends of this business group."[16] This is a much safer way, much less open to misunderstanding, even though the results may occasionally appear less spectacular.

Their fifth method, after interviews, was the use of questionnaires. Some of the questionnaires were submitted to certain local experts; for example, a questionnaire on club membership and activities was sent to the four hundred societies and clubs the Lynds were able to locate in the city during the spring of 1924. There is no indication of how many replies were received, but there is a hint that the response rate may have been rather low. They also administered questionnaires to two samples of high-school boys and girls. One was to 700–800 boys and girls attending all sophomore, junior, and senior English classes. In this questionnaire the Lynds were concerned with the life of the high-school population. They also administered a true-false test to all junior and senior social-science boys and girls (about 550) in which they concentrated on points of view relating to certain public questions. It is an interesting fact that no answers from Negroes were included in the tabulations. Other children were roughly classified by their fathers' occupations and religions and political affiliations. In the latter test the procedure was to give the social-science students a series of statements which they were asked to check as true, false, or uncertain. A typical statement was "The white race is the best race on earth," and they report that 66 per cent of the boys and 75 per cent of the girls checked this as true. Another statement was "A citizen of the United States should be allowed to say anything he pleases even if he advocates violent revolution if he does no violent act himself." It is reported that 70 per cent of the boys and 75 per cent of the girls checked this as false. The questions appear to be so remote from the life and experience of the average high-school student that, while there seems to be considerable regularity in the answers, it is very hard to attach meaning to the results. It rather looks as though the Lynds may have felt that way, for they comment:

Since these questionnaires were not used to measure any general "attitudes," scores for the questionnaires as a whole were not compiled, nor were they tested for reliability or validity. The answers to individual questions, representing as they do verbalizations, are, like the interviews, used not as proof but as suggestion of tendencies.[17]

In practice they merely report some of these results, with the claim that "further insight into the stamp of the group with which Middletown children complete their social studies courses is gained through the following summary of answers. . . ."[18] It probably does not help very much to include these results, but it is possible that the Lynds felt they had gathered some statistics and might as well make use of them. In the chapter on *The Authoritarian Personality* we shall see how similar questions were used to test a very definite psychological hypothesis (Chapter 11).

DESCRIPTIVE MATERIAL

One constant feature of the Lynds' work is the straightforward and honest manner in which the material was put down. In spite of his lack of formal research training, Lynd did discover in himself a flair both for fact-finding and for organizing his facts. The result is an orderly description, whatever the subject under discussion. In each chapter the sections lead into one another nicely, and the whole effect is very smooth, maintaining the reader's interest and exhibiting a development of the theme. There are very few points at which the reader feels that the subject matter does not belong where it has been placed. This is particularly noteworthy because the six major headings are in fact not very well suited to a sociological delineation of what goes on in a Midwestern city. In a sense the Lynds' achievement was thus more of a feat than if they had thought out clearly in advance the headings under which to organize the material. What is demonstrated is a great capacity for fitting the material into a conceptual structure that was laid down perhaps somewhat prematurely.

At the present time it is not easy to appreciate the novelty of the picture then presented. Inevitably it has now lost its impact for us in many places. Even in 1929 the authors had to contend with the acid fiction of Sinclair Lewis and other small-town critics, and it seems indisputable that they were well aware of this vein of thought when they were deciding which facts to bring forward. But in *Middletown* the facts are organized in a way that would not be used for a novel.

Of the details themselves it is difficult now to realize that any of them were strikingly fresh to the readers of *Middletown*, but this is probably a measure of the extent to which at that time the public image of such towns remained distorted by a nostalgic belief in the survival of the pioneering spirit. Particularly to someone who had always lived in New York and had had little contact with a small city it could be slightly shattering to be confronted with the narrow frame within which life in a city like Middletown was conducted. This is the case even though the authors' description does not deeply question the particular activities and values to which Middletown subscribed. The Lynds of the 1920's, with metropolitan sophistication, descended on a small Midwestern town and gave us the facts about what they saw. Systematic description and not external judgment was the objective of *Middletown*, and this, as we shall see, constitutes the great difference between the first volume and the more purposeful and political *Middletown in Transition*. The method of *Middletown* is to muster facts in order to convey impressions. This is best illustrated by an examination of a typical chapter, and for this purpose a description will follow of Chapter IX, "The Houses in Which Middletown Lives," which opens the section on "Making a Home."

The Lynds' first step is to give the dimensions of the topic. The previous section had concentrated on the 43 in each hundred who earned Middletown's living, and even these earners divided their time between workplace and home. These were the group least dedicated to home life. The remaining population (23 per cent homemakers, 4 per cent very old or feeble, 11 per cent very young, 19 per cent at school) focused their lives primarily on the home. Middletown's 38,000 people were living in 9,200 homes, of which 86 per cent were in one-family houses and another 10 per cent were in two-family houses. Only 1 per cent of the homes in Middletown at that date were in apartment buildings, and 3 per cent were in apartments over stores, the latter being chiefly in the downtown section. By these statistics the reader begins to get the feeling of the type of small town delineated, with its spread-out single-family houses.

The useful life of a house in Middletown was estimated as being between thirty and fifty years. The oldest houses, built in the 1880's, had occupied rather large lots for their date, usually 62 feet 6 inches wide and 125 feet deep. Later it became common to increase the density of development by dividing off the back of each of these old lots, giving frontage onto the side street—a form of development that can be observed throughout the United States. Concurrently new building lots were shrinking in size; whereas the city blocks in the 1890's usually contained eight lots, by the 1920's the same-sized blocks contained ten, twelve, or fourteen, with obvious implications for children's play, family leisure, and family privacy.

Back yards are ceasing to be ample affairs with grass and fruit trees and grape arbors where the housewife sits and peels potatoes for supper . . . and the family spends Sunday afternoons around the barrel-stave hammock. In many working class families smaller yards and closer neighbors have reduced the back yard to an overflow storage place in this day of no attics, store rooms or barns.[19]

This was indeed a criticism of Middletown; but it reflected, one feels, the nostalgia of well-established citizens rather than an external analysis.

Without comment on its theoretical implications, the authors recorded the fact of ecological succession, ". . . in each new generation the less well-to-do tend to inherit the aging homes of the group slightly 'better off' in the preceding generation."[20] One of the few hypotheses in the chapter is in the realm of aesthetic theory, being an acute speculation—reminiscent of Veblen but not derived from him—on the trend toward aesthetic simplicity.

The disappearance of the ornate houses of the seventies and eighties, decked out in elaborate scrolls and "gingerbread" work, in favor of the plainer homes of today in which the emphasis is upon all manner of new interior devices in bathroom and elsewhere, probably reflects, among other things, a tendency commonly observable in human culture: in periods when improvements in effectiveness in the utility of a tool are at a standstill, human ingenuity tends to spend itself in decorating the tool, but in periods of evolution in the effectiveness of the major use, ornamentation tends to assume a place of secondary importance. The Middletown house of the eighties was still simply a box divided into rooms, with relatively few changes in process in its adaptation as a place in which to live comfortably. The coming of bathrooms, a wide range of electrical equipment, central heating, and other inventions, is today focusing attention upon a wide variety of changes in the interior livableness, with corresponding decline in exterior ornamentation.[21]

The authors go on to describe the changes in house design that had been taking place in the wake of these technical developments. Clearly they regard the main influence to have been the widespread adoption of these various conveniences that had previously been used only by a few of the very wealthy. But they do also give examples of the relation between changes in house design and changes in the pattern of living.

The disappearance of the spare bedroom in these days of high building costs is probably not unrelated to the diminishing tendency . . . for aging parents to come home to live with their children. Likewise, the tendency to throw the former parlor and sitting room together as one large exposed living room, doing away with the privacy that the daughter of the house and her caller used to find in the earlier parlor, may be related to the fact that many a daughter is leaving home with her "date" to "get away from the family" and find privacy in the anonymity and darkness of the movies or automobile. This is in turn reflected in the prominence of the number of evenings children are away from home during the week as a source of disagreement between children and their parents.[22]

There follow a series of descriptions—"composite pictures based upon detailed accounts of the homes visited by staff interviewers"[23] —in which typical homes were delineated. Interestingly, at this point of the report the twofold classification into working and business classes was abandoned in favor of a fivefold classification.

The first type of home was that of the poorer working man and presented an utterly depressing picture.

The poorer working man, coming home after his nine and a half hours on the job, walks up the frequently unpaved street, turns in at a bare yard littered with . . . worn-out automobile tires, opens a sagging door and enters . . . his home . . . the kitchen . . . swarming with flies . . . strewn with bread crusts, orange skins, torn papers, and lumps of coal and wood; the bedrooms with soiled, heavy quilts . . . worn green shades . . . at a tipsy angle. . . . The whole interior is musty with stale odors. . . . A baby in wet, dirty clothes crawls about the bare floor among the odd pieces of furniture.[24]

The other extreme was represented by the "fine old places," the ancestral homes of a group of wealthy families living in the "East End" of town.

Whether the father of one of these families comes home from office or bank to the large parlors and library of the older type of house or to the ample long living room of the new, he is greeted by an atmosphere of quiet and space. The wide rooms, soft hangings, old mahogany, one-toned rugs or deep-colored Orientals, grand piano, fireplaces, cut flowers, open book-shelves . . ., the walls hung with prints . . . may be combined with certain individual touches, a piece of tapestry on the wall, a picture not seen elsewhere, a blue Chinese bowl.[25]

In between these extremes were the equally characteristic and equally depressing respectable homes of three intermediate social strata: the homes of the skilled workingman, with their embroidered pillows and colored religious mottoes; the barer homes of head bookkeepers and schoolteachers who endured present sacrifices for the sake of their children's education; the homes of the business group, with self-conscious period design and imported furnishings.

This systematic characterization, composed of acute observations in the different homes of Middletown, constituted a valuable and original contribution to the sociology of family life. Comparable descriptions would be found in novels, but it is clear that the Lynds were earnestly attempting a full and careful description of life in the different strata. If they were taking sides in their comparison of the classes, they concealed the fact very well. Furthermore, their evidence was not only authentic but also uncommon. Even today evidence on how houses are furnished and lived in is ragged indeed. Chapin, for example, made an elaborate study of social status dependent on the objects to be found in different houses. This is a highly technical piece of work and highly organized statistically by Guttman, but it is vulnerable methodologically.[26]

By chance there is an oblique commentary on the Chapin scale in these very descriptions. It may be remembered how the presence or absence of a sewing machine changed its meaning between the original Chapin scale and the later Guttman version. It happens that the Lynds, in all innocence, inserted into their picture of the better-off workingman's home the sentence "The sewing machine stands in the living room or dining room." Needless to say, there is no mention of sewing machines in the inventories for the three levels of the business group that the book described.

The chapter concludes with an examination of the pressures which were acting to encourage home ownership—"the deep-rooted sentiment . . . that home ownership is a mark of independence, of respectability, of belonging."[27] There was the arrival of the automobile, which made a suburban home compatible with an urban job, the unprofitability of building for rent, the growth of credit facilities for financing home buying. Some forces were also operating as deterrents to home ownership—rival calls on the pocket, for the purchase of a new automobile or the education of children. The authors also appear to be blaming the machinery for house purchase —they make criticisms of both the institutional hurdles and the single-unit handicraft system of production. On balance, they note a slow but definite trend toward home ownership, and they speculate as to whether the extension of home ownership to the working class would counteract their accelerating mobility.

This is one of the nearly thirty chapters in *Middletown*, and it would be quite fair to describe it as typical. Like the other chapters, it is vivid, fresh, trustworthy, informative, thoughtful. Its analysis appears like a distillation of the considered opinions of a highly intelligent group of Middletowners. It is almost entirely without challenge, except indirectly in the sense that bare facts, holding a mirror up to men, constitute a challenge. That such facts were found cumulatively horrific to metropolitan America—Mencken described it as a study of *Moronia*—was due to the cultural lag of Middletown and to the obliteration of the idealized small-town image.

At this point in Lynd's career the record speaks for itself. With his theological background he was a self-taught social scientist. As a fieldworker and as an empirical analyst he had had to feel his own way. In that respect he was no worse off than most of the pioneers discussed in this book. The institutionalization of social research is a late development, and even today some of the most creative researches are born outside the bureaus. We are, it appears, confronted with a classical dilemma. No one should tolerate shoddy material, shoddy methods, woolly thinking, but it must be admitted that there can be something rather stultifying in concentrating on methods of investigation, so that there is almost a negative correlation between the rigor of methods and the importance of results. It is significant that Lynd was meticulous in his presentation; the source of each statement is carefully noted. But his statistical treatment is elementary, and it is rare today to find an author bold enough to come forward with a descriptive portrait of a city without at least a garnishing of statistical tables.

A recent book, *Small Town in Mass Society*,[28] springs to mind in this context. The authors, Vidich and Bensman, are deliberately and most engagingly underselling their product, which is deceptively simple in its presentation. The book contains no tables, but some quite elaborate fact-finding gleams through the chinks. It also is hung on a well-absorbed theoretical structure, and in this respect a comparison with *Middletown* shows the theoretical innocence of the Lynds' first volume.

MIDDLETOWN IN TRANSITION

As has already been stated, a theoretical orientation was much more evident in the second volume, *Middletown in Transition*, which first appeared in 1937.

It is an unfortunate fact that authors who try to repeat an earlier success often succeed only in producing a second volume which is much more elaborate and much duller than the first, or else they may manifestly run out of ideas. Perhaps the most striking fact about *Middletown in Transition* is that it transgresses this rule, in that, although the material is much more flimsy in the second book, what it has to offer is of considerably more lasting interest than in the case of its predecessor. Simplicity rather than elaboration was the aim; the number of man-days of research in the second study was only one-tenth as great as for the original *Middletown*. Some of this disparity can be explained by the fact that the investigators were able to go straight to work with an existing network of contacts. But the saving in time was due basically to the fact that they streamlined all their procedures and eliminated all luxuries and exploratory devices. Instead they went directly into a newspaper-clipping routine, into an analysis of the records that had accumulated since they had left and they straightway undertook "scores of interviews both formal and informal." Thus, with obviously much reduced effort they brought together the material for the second book.

The purpose of the return visit was to ascertain the extent of the changes that had taken place in Middletown since 1925, and the Lynds were prepared for two alternative eventualities. One was that Middletown would be much changed as a result of the great depression of the early 1930's, and that these changes would be reflected in the habits and attitudes of the people. The other possibility was that Middletown would be basically unchanged—that the inertia in the social structure would have been so great that the fresh experiences of poverty and unemployment would not have basically affected the way of life or the values and attitudes of the people. It seems clear that Lynd returned to Middletown expecting some radical changes, or enough change to make a fresh study worth the trouble.

Here is an American city which had been the subject of eighteen months of close study in 1924–25. During the following decade the conditions of its existence had been unexpectedly altered in a way which affected every aspect of its life. Its growing population had been tossed from prosperity beyond any experienced prior to 1925 to an equally unprecedented depression. The opportunity thus presented to analyze its life under the stress of specific interrupting stimuli, whose course can be traced, offered something analogous to an experimental situation.[29]

A number of more precise questions were posed. Had the basic texture of Middletown culture been tough enough to remain intact? Had the deep trust in self-help and belief in the future been maintained? Had the old faiths survived, and were the young embracing them? Had the sense of community developed further, or were latent cleavages becoming sharpened?

There was evidently no unanimity among the field staff as to what the changes would be like. Some believed that the entrenched habits of thought and sentiment would have absorbed the shock of the depression. Others believed that the shock had been so profound and so widespread that it had brought about fundamental and permanent changes. Others, probably including Lynd himself, expected a very uneven effect on different elements in the city or on different sectors. It was also possible that the full effects of incipient change had not yet shown themselves.

But if Middletown had changed, it is also necessary to substantiate the claim, already made, that there had been a profound development in the thinking of the Lynds. It is not difficult to demonstrate this development, but nowhere is it better epitomized than in the discovery of the X family.

Since *Middletown* was published, some local people have criticized it for underplaying the role of the X family in the city's life. This group of wealthy families . . . was not characterized as an "upper class" in 1925, because "these families are not a group apart but are merged in the life of the mass of the businessfolk." Whether or not the earlier study was entirely right in so largely grouping them with the rest of the business class, certainly no local prompting was necessary in 1935 to call attention to their overshadowing position. For, after ten years' absence from the city, one thing struck the returning observer again and again: the increasingly large public benefactions and the increasing pervasiveness of the power of this wealthy family of manufacturers, whose local position since 1925 is becoming hereditary with the emergence of a second generation of sons.[30]

From the authors' own evidence, their failure to take account of the X family in the 1924–25 survey was due as much to an observational blind spot in the field team as to the invisibility of this ubiquitous family.

The X family was a very wealthy clan of five brothers who had arrived in Middletown in the 1880's after a source of natural gas had been discovered in the city. On the basis of this cheap fuel they had sunk a $7,000 investment in a plant manufacturing glass fruit jars. The enterprise had been enormously successful, becoming the world's largest producer of fruit jars. The millionaire brothers, all of whom lived in Middletown, "had ever since held an un-ostentatious but increasingly influential place in the city's life. . . . Of the original five brothers, four remained in 1924; and when shortly thereafter another died, the entire business of the city stopped during his funeral."[31] So much for the invisibility of the X family in the mid-1920's.

At the time of the second survey, in 1935, there were still two elder brothers, both in their seventies, but by this date a second

X generation was taking over; four of the sons and two of the sons-in-law "of the family" had entered into their inheritance, and Middletown then had what amounted to a reigning royal family. The position was summarized by one of the informants there, who said, "The one big point about this town . . . [is] that the X's dominate the whole town, *are* the town, in fact."[32] Business ran Middletown, and the X family dominated business.

The Lynds neatly illustrate the pervasiveness of the X control by a reapplication of the six-way analysis of activities which they had devised for their first report. This started with the basic activity of "Getting a Living." Banking occupies a key role in industry, and there had been five banking houses in 1925, and the X family had had an interest in the three most important of these five. Even the remaining two small banks could not survive the depression. The X family, by a certain amount of manipulation, had come out of the depression with a single bank under their complete control, and this was the only bank left in Middletown by 1935.

Legal talent was similarly monopolized by 1935. At that date all the best lawyers in the town were retained in one or another of the X family interests. A local paper commented: "Lawyers and banks get along here. They maintain a happy relationship here as compared with their conflict in other cities."[33] With their common dependence on the X family they had no alternative. In industry the X influence was not always direct. Ownership was confined to the glassworks, the paperboard works, and the interurban railroad. But through the Chamber of Commerce, which they dominated to such an extent that no official there could hold his position against X opposition, they retained a powerful influence over many of the other industries in the city. While regarding themselves as scrupulous, they had been known to use their power to further their own interests; for example, they succeeded in keeping pay rates remarkably low. Apparently the rate at that time was 42 cents an hour in the glassworks, whereas the Federal Employment Relief Agency (an instrument of the New Deal), which came in to provide relief work, offered 45 cents an hour, a fact that must have annoyed the X family.

On an earlier occasion when there was too little work for machinists in Middletown some firms in a nearby city had put "want ads" in a Middletown paper. These advertisements were suppressed because local industry persuaded the Middletown Advertising Club "that it was important that plenty of skilled workers be kept in town." This event is recorded in *Middletown*[34] without mention of the X family, but in the second report reference is made to the repeated rumor in 1925 and again in 1935 that the X influence had at one time blocked the entry of a Ford plant into Middletown in order to avoid the competition of the higher Ford wage scale.

The X family had also become involved in retailing. A large retail store in the city failed during the depression. It happened to be located in a building owned by the X family, and the X family took it over when it failed and reopened it as the "X Store."

The Lynds make the point that the hegemony of the X family was not only benevolent but also a force making for efficiency in the community. The X family sincerely regarded itself as unusually scrupulous in looking out for its workers. They had saved Middletown from the banking crisis in February, 1933; the X Store became a far better store than it had formerly been; another incursion into the city's retail trade, which culminated in squeezing out a large independent dairy, gave the trade to an X subsidiary and greatly improved the quality of local milk. The X family seemed to have found a formula for helping others while they helped themselves.

The next group of X activities were those concerned with "Making a Home." This raised the issue of urban replanning, reminding the reader how very little ecological analysis there had been in *Middletown*. This was in striking contrast to the reports from Chicago, which, with their innumerable maps, provided a concrete view of what the place was like. The only exception to the neglect of ecology is the highly diagrammatic end paper in *Middletown in Transition*, which gives some impression of the city. The Lynds might have argued that they did not want to publish maps of Middletown because that would have disclosed its identity, but that had never been a deep secret. Certainly by the time of the second volume everybody knew the identity of the city in question.

In this context the achievement of the X family was their success in moving the residential heart of the city for their own benefit.

This shift has been carefully engineered by members of the X family. As a result, the aristocratic old East End, the fine residential section in the pre-motor period when it was an asset to live "close in" . . . runs a lame second to the two new X subdivisions in the West End to which the ambitious matrons of the city are removing their families.[35]

It appears that in the middle of the rather depressed East End was a dilapidated school, and that the X family made a deal with the Board of Education, providing the funds to have this school turned into the cluster of beautiful buildings which became X State Teachers College. Next to the new college they built, as an outright gift, the X Hospital. Then—this is the rather unbelievable story of one informant—their agent bought at least one neighboring property by hinting that a pesthouse was to be built in the area. Whatever the methods used, all the land around X Hospital and X State Teachers College was bought by the X family and redeveloped as the new upper-class section of the city. They apparently made an enormous profit. One local man commented, "The X's are about the only people I know of who have managed to augment their fortune by the art of philanthropy."

Here again the authors convey the impression that, although the X family were responsible for all the acts imputed to them, they did not behave in a vicious way and not even in a systematic fashion. Rather, it was just that they were so powerful and had so much money in circulation that they could hardly avoid influencing the lives of others. But certainly Lynd was not so popular with the X family after this second book. If he had said as much about them in the first book as he did in the second, perhaps he would not have gone back.

The next field was "Training the Young." Here again the X hegemony was in evidence. One of the X family was president of the School Board, and a prominent X attorney was school attorney. The authors quote a rather nice editorial comment of June, 1936, when the question of the school board came up.

There is still a feeling among women's organizations that there should be one woman on the [school] board, but that is not likely to come about until a year hence, if then, or ever. Mr. X's term will expire a year hence, *and there is no likelihood of replacing him if he still wants the job.* . . .[36]

Middletown felt comfortable with a member of this family at the head of its schools. There was also evidence that one of the X's had an influence on the College Library Committee and was able to have certain books removed from the library, for example, Bertrand Russell's *Marriage and Morals* and John Dos Passos' *1919*. The list of outside speakers invited by the student body was said to be scrutinized by the X family, and they were also reported to make it difficult for radical students to find appropriate local jobs after graduation.

The next category was "Spending Leisure." Both the Y.M.C.A. and the Y.W.C.A. in Middletown were X philanthropies. The only trouble was in the finding of suitable personnel to run them. City-trained officials were liable to have been exposed to the excessively progressive thinking of the national offices in New York, and the X family were therefore careful to avoid them in favor of locally trained officials.

In other respects—and there was nothing sinister about this—the X family enormously improved the leisure facilities of the city. The Teachers College had a large gymnasium suitable for local gatherings, and the Arts Building offered accommodation for public lectures, recitals, and art exhibitions.

In addition, the X's financed two riding clubs, they made possible the building of a huge temple for the Masons, they built a municipal airport, they built a county fairground, they provided a headquarters for the American Legion, sports grounds, a golf course, a children's recreation center, parks, and other things. Everywhere in the city you were confronted with the name X.

As far as "Religion" was concerned they made generous grants toward the rebuilding of churches, without unduly favoring any one denomination. Their influence was remote, undogmatic, and unobtrusive. But when one minister became rather liberal in his teaching, he was spontaneously flayed by another minister who was more responsive to the subtle influences of the business-class control system. Lynd says that it was most unlikely that the latter acted under orders, but at least it would be clear to such a minister that in defending the *status quo* he would do his reputation no harm. There was a rather charming illustration of the earnest and conservative temper of the older generation of X's. This story was picked up in 1924 but, characteristically, was not included in the first volume. A member of Rotary reports:

Ed X was just talking to me at Rotary about his worry over this jazzy age. "Where are we going to go to get worth-while young men?" he asked. He then told me how, missing the old Gospel songs he used to sing as a boy, he hunted up the hymnal, bought 200 copies, and sent them to his Sunday School. The Sunday School tried them two or three weeks and then discarded them as too antiquated. Ed jumped on the preacher and told him if those books were too old-fashioned, he guessed he, too, was too old-fashioned for that church.[37]

That would have meant, of course, that he would no longer be helping them.

Next came "Government." One of the peculiarities of *Middletown* is the brevity of the chapter on government and law enforcement. It is only about twenty pages long, and one quarter of it is devoted to law enforcement. In contrast to this, in *Middletown in Transition* much attention is paid to the system of government and to the examination of who rules whom and how interests create pressure groups. In the chapter on the X family the section devoted to government was given some prominence. It was reported that, although the X family had always been Republican, a time came when the Democrats seemed to be in for a long run and at this juncture one of the X's suddenly bobbed up as an influential local Democratic leader. And by virtue of his wealth and family standing he seems to have stepped straight into a Democratic seat on the school board, to have taken over control of the Democratic mayor and county chairman, and generally to have become the acknowledged boss of the Democratic machine in the area.

The Lynds examined briefly what the people of Middletown thought of this domination by one family. They drew the conclusion that there was a difference in attitude between the business class and the working class. The suggestion was that the working class were resentful of particular incidents—antilabor wage policies and unfair taxation to pay for urban developments designed to favor the rich—while the business class supported X family rule because they felt that it promoted their interests. The authors admitted that this distinction was based on impressions that were difficult to prove. In a highly complex situation certain other equally intangible impressions stood out. The lines of leadership and related controls were highly concentrated at that time in Middletown. This control net had tightened decidedly since 1925 and notably with the depression. The control was at very many points unconscious and, where conscious, well-meaning and "public-spirited," as businessmen interpret that concept. The control system operated at many points to identify public welfare with business-class welfare. There was little deliberate attempt from above to organize a self-conscious "we" pressure group, but in the propitious atmosphere of Middletown the solidary tendency of businessmen would automatically assert itself. So long as the owners of such vast personal resources as the X family exhibited a public-spirited willingness to help with local problems, leadership and control would be forced upon them by circumstances, and their patterns would tend to become the official guiding patterns. In such a situation an independent outlook would be interpreted as "cussedness."

It is clear from this formulation that the authors were not indulging in an all-out attack on the X family. In fact they produced another family, the Y family, who, though not quite so rich as the X's, were rich enough and had at least one big interest in the city. But these were curious people who kept to themselves and did not contribute to public affairs. There was a suggestion that the business circle in Middletown—and perhaps the Lynds themselves—rather regretted this fact. A family possessing such great wealth might be expected to exert it in some way in the city.

To use the chapter on the X family as an illustration of the whole of *Middletown in Transition* may perhaps convey the impression that the authors had become obsessed with this particular small group of people. Such an impression would be entirely false. And yet, the internal tensions and conflicts of Middletown society were much more sharply perceived in the second volume than in the first. In the mid-1930's the class struggle was a reality to tens of millions of Americans in a sense that has long since lost its meaning, and *Middletown in Transition* explicitly accepted this reality, in its description of the struggle for union organization or in the disputes on the New Deal relief agencies. Even in areas in which class conflict was not prominent, stress was laid on the inherent differences in ideology and behavior that distinguished the business class from the working class. It is not easy to discern how much of this reiterated contrast stemmed from the changed climate of Middletown and how much derived from a changed focus in the Lynds' interests.

THE MIDDLETOWN SPIRIT

We conclude with a brief examination of one of the most interesting chapters in *Middletown in Transition* titled "The Middletown Spirit." This was an attempt to summarize the ideology of Middletown both in its universal features, which are shared by all its citizens, and in its dichotomies—between racial groups, between the classes, between the sexes.

The first step was to set down the rough pattern of things that Middletown was *for* and *against.* Middletown was uncritically in favor of being honest, kind, friendly, loyal, successful, average, simple, sound, traditional, and courageous and of valuing "character" above "brains." Middletown believed in progress but not too fast; believed that the individual must fend for himself and would in the long run get what he deserved; that society should favor the strong; that American ways were best, and that American business was the mainstay of society; that the family was its fundamental institution; that schools should stick to teaching the facts; that leisure was a fine thing, but that work came first; that American democracy was the final and ideal form of government; that charity was good, but that those who accepted it were inferior; that Christianity was the final form of religion.

Conversely, Middletown was against the opposite of these things, and was suspicious of any strikingly divergent type of personality, any striking innovation in ideas, art or literature, government, religion, education, the family; was against centralized government and planning, against anything that curtailed money-making, against foreigners, minorities, deviants, frills; despised the weak.

This system of beliefs favored the contribution of the businessman in the community.

As . . . the chief contributor to the community's welfare, the successful businessman in Middletown elicits from his fellow citizens wholehearted praise, as well as envy and emulation. Since Middletown's values are regarded as leading to "success," it follows easily that those who are successful must obviously have these values to have become successful. So, by this subtle and largely unconscious process, Middletown imputes to the successful businessman the possession . . . of the qualities of . . . the city's other values.[38]

If he was sufficiently successful, he could afford to ignore some of the community's other virtues.

He may be more socially exclusive, cold, abrupt, dictatorial, or cynical than a less successful person can afford to be—and still meet with a large measure of community tolerance and even active approval.[39]

The triumph of the Middletown ideology lay in its ability to reconcile the apparently contradictory qualities of ruthlessness on the one hand and considerateness on the other. The successful businessman was licensed to be harshly enterprising in his strictly business relations in order that he might enjoy the luxury of friendliness out of business hours.

The Lynds were greatly interested in the shifts in values that had occurred in the ten years between the two surveys. Their impression was that tolerance had increased in many directions—in relation to religious beliefs and in relation to other previously unfamiliar types of people and manners—"movie actresses, wealthy people who live expensively, freer sex ideas, women who paint their faces, modern art, the bachelor girl, and so on."[40] At the same time economic and political tolerance was felt to have declined; there seemed to have been a hardening of the attitude against labor organization or social innovation and an increasing deference toward "the single, peremptory point of view represented by its business world."[41] Echoing the four wishes of W. I. Thomas, the authors comment: "In crisis situations, security is more valued by Middletown than new experience."[42]

Despite itself and its traditions, Middletown is slowly moving, under pressure from the competitive world around it, towards the liquidation of the traditional right to "go as you please" in matters importantly affecting the public interest; and toward the closer coordination of city government, civic clubs, and other value-carrying and -forming agencies under its business agencies to present a united front to the world.[43]

As the authors shrewdly commented, this identification of "business enterprise" and "loyalty" operated to retard the widening of the gap between Middletown's "power" values and its "lovable" values, just as the Puritan ethic had found a formula which reconciled the service of God with the profitable pursuit of mercantilism.

While recognizing that the businessman's ideology dominates Middletown, the Lynds were preoccupied with the question whether the differences in behavior and attitude between business class and working class which they had noted in the previous survey had become more or less marked in the ten intervening years. It became apparent that the formal answer was that there were no class differences in Middletown society, that "the sovereign authority rested with a great middle class, whom we like to term the typical Americans."[44] Interchangeably, nearly all were in the "working class." "Work has never been looked upon in America as degrading, but as the means to better things for the individual and his family. . . ."[45]

The Lynds were satisfied that this formal denial of class differences was subscribed to by the working class, who regarded the business class as their reference group, and by taking advantage of the rising standard of living and the bountiful supply of substandard goods achieved a shoddily satisfying imitation of middle-class life. There was an almost complete absence of working-class leadership which could offer a distinctive alternative to the largely symbolic "ladder of success."

And yet the formal denials of the separate existence of a working class were not always consistently maintained. Businessmen did seem to recognize a group apart, of people who were "different from us," "intellectually inferior," incapable of aesthetic appreciation or cultural behavior. "Why, give 'em a brand-new house, and in a few months it'll look like a pigsty."[46] These distinctions were expressed even in 1925, but "the impression was clear in the investigator's mind at the end of the field work in 1935 that the line between working class and business class, though vague and blurred still, is more apparent than it was ten years before."[47]

This consciousness of divergent class interests, now again submerged by a quarter-century of growing prosperity, was an obvious consequence of the depression. But the authors, who in their second volume were clearly preoccupied with the question why Middletown labor would not organize, may not have foreseen the businesslike form in which American labor organization has finally asserted itself, so that the two sides in an industrial dispute, as they haggle over terms, are not always readily distinguishable from any other pair of business negotiators.

Apart from this belief in a sharpening of the distinction between their original two classes, the Lynds began to discern perceptible differences within the two. This they presented in the form of a sixfold classification, which is inevitably reminiscent of W. L. Warner's typology, though based on the concept of social change and perhaps both more objective and more subtle in its distinctions.* Unlike Warner, however, the authors of *Middletown in Transition* made no discriminatory use of their elaborated classification.

The other cleavage to which they paid substantial attention was that between the white and the Negro populations, which they stigmatized as "the deepest and most blindly followed line of division in the community."[49] Active resentment of Negroes was found to be confined largely to the working class, who felt most directly threatened, whereas Middletown's businessmen appreciated having a ready pool of cheap labor available for dirty jobs. Both the business class and the working class were satisfied that the lowly position of Negroes was due to their natural inferiority. Their greater criminality and immorality was taken for granted. White business-class Middletown encouraged "good works" among the dependent colored population, and some advances in the collective standing of Negroes were marked up in the ten-year interval between the surveys, but the authors were of the opinion that in spite of bettered leadership and organization Negroes were more exposed in 1935 than before the depression.

The depression was not the only great upheaval experienced by Middletown during the ten years. The city had been rapidly expanding and changing its economic basis "from a drowsy county-seat town to a city of nearly 50,000, 'the metropolis' of the eastern section of its state."[50] This, too, reinforced the Middletown image

---

* E. Digby Baltzell has contrasted the approaches of the Lynds and of W. Lloyd Warner, pointing out that the Lynds stress the dynamics of a changing society, while Warner emphasizes the differences in ritual and style of life within a relatively static community; the Lynds employ an objective definition of social class, while Warner defines a class system in subjective terms. Baltzell attributes these differences in approach partly to the differences in the communities being studied.[48]

of self-growth. As America emerged from the depression the symbols of "progress," "improvement," "bigger and better" everything were more nearly in correspondence with reality. In spite of the sharp lessons of the crisis years the investigators were bound to conclude that basically the texture of Middletown's culture had not changed.[51] Middletown was overwhelmingly living by the values by which it lived in 1925, and no major new symbols or ideologies of a positive sort had developed as conspicuous rallying points. The depression had been surmounted by temporary expediencies designed to care for the unemployed, and by 1936 these were already being discarded.

In all this discussion the authors hardly concealed their regret that Middletown appeared to have learned nothing from their depression experiences. Leadership in the community had not changed but had merely become concentrated in fewer hands. Even this fact was felt to contain a threat. If Middletown was too busy to understand the meaning of dictatorship in Europe, and was unwilling to take a firm stand against the curtailment of civic liberties at home, might this not mean that they would be susceptible to a native American form of fascism such as Father Coughlin and Huey Long were then constantly preaching over the radio?

While *Middletown in Transition* was going to press, the 1936 Presidential election, with President Roosevelt's triumphant return, caused the authors somewhat to rethink their appraisal of the dominant views of the city. The business class had predicted disaster if Roosevelt was returned, but the electorate, perhaps groping for the security of the New Deal, overwhelmingly rejected this interpretation of a Democratic victory. The immediate threat was averted, but the authors still perceived hidden depths of self-doubt in the Middletown culture and saw the possibility that, if the returning tide of business turned sour, there would be a strong call for a "strong man" of the "right sort" and even conceivably "of a seizure of power carefully engineered as *by* the business class and *for* the business class and publicized in the name of Americanism and prosperity."[52] This remained a contingency even though, swayed perhaps by the 1936 Presidential result, on balance they predicted a period of political empiricism marked by a gradual shift somewhat toward the political left.

This was the authors' last word on Middletown, and it epitomizes the strengths and weaknesses of their approach. The great contribution in both *Middletown* and *Middletown in Transition* is their writing meaningfully about significant issues. The city laid out before us was not a desiccated model but a fascinating tracery of living people struggling, as men do, in a morass of social, economic, and political pressures. For this portraiture it was an enormous asset that the Lynds themselves were deeply involved in the political dilemmas of the time.

But involvement is only one requisite, and as the Lynds' thoughts swung increasingly to a political interpretation of the city's inter-relationships the reader, however much he might sympathize with their declared political stand, is confronted with a certain atomistic quality in their empirical theory. Even today it may be fair to assert that the policy sciences are the least firm of all the social sciences in their capacity to assimilate into their theory, and to predict, the unwinding of political events. Probably in none of the books under discussion have more far-reaching forecasts been made about the future of society, and, perhaps also for this reason, in no other book have the forecasts, and the premises on which they were based, been so completely overtaken by events.

PIONEERS IN INDUS-
TRIAL SOCIOLOGY

The subject of this chapter is *Management and the Worker*, by Fritz J. Roethlisberger and William J. Dickson.[1] The program of research described in this book has an interesting background, which will first be described.[2]

It was generally believed in the nineteenth century that the way to get more output from workpeople was to drive then harder, and any reduction in working hours was regarded more as a concession to the workers than as a form of benevolent self-interest. But as early as 1893 the Englishman Sir William Mather, managing director of the engineering firm of Mather and Platt in Manchester, decided to reduce the work week from fifty-four to forty-eight hours, and after two years' experience he was able to show that there had been a total absolute increase in production and a decrease in the amount of lost time. This was a somewhat local trial and did not have very much influence elsewhere at first; but in due course the British Government's Ordnance factories, arsenals, and dockyards followed the lead and introduced a forty-eight-hour week. Even after that there was very little response from industry in general until 1914.

Soon after World War I started in 1914 the Government set up a body called the Health of Munitions Workers Committee, and one of the first acts of this committee was to persuade the Ministry of Munitions to reduce the working hours of women who had been called into munition making. In one munition factory the reduction was from twelve hours to ten hours a day, with the result that the incidence of industrial accidents was halved. This striking improvement was taken note of, and in 1917 a permanent research unit called the Industrial Fatigue Research Board (later the Industrial Health Research Board) was set up. Meanwhile, in 1921, one of the top experimental psychologists in England, Dr. Myers, resigned from his post as director of the Experimental Psychology Laboratory at Cambridge University to become the first director of another new body, the National Institute of Industrial Psychology, which undertook, on a contract basis, to help industry solve its personnel problems.

At that date current thinking was based on the belief that fatigue was a purely physiological effect, probably due to the oversecretion of lactic acid in the muscles; there was even a time when the scientists were so optimistic as to think that it should be possible to give doses of an antidote chemical, such as acid sodium phosphate, to neutralize the lactic acid, and that fatigue would thus be removed with very little trouble or expense. But as time went on and all these experiments multiplied, they realized that the question was very much more complicated than had been thought. They began to distinguish two kinds of fatigue—direct fatigue, such as an athlete suffers when he is running very fast and lactic acid really is building up in his muscles, and the slower-developing fatigue which is brought on, for example, by a long walk, when explanations in terms of the overproduction of lactic acid cannot be shown to apply.

In the national emergency of World War I, workers were expected to carry out heavy manual operations for up to twelve hours a day, and never less than forty-eight hours a week, so physiological fatigue was a real possibility. But the more they looked into the problem the more pessimistic the English scientists became about the usefulness of the fatigue concept as a means of describing all kinds of tiredness; the more they looked at the facts the more complex the explanations seemed to be.

While this was happening in England similar developments were taking place in the United States. In 1917 the United States Public Health Service instituted a large inquiry designed to compare performance and fatigue in an "eight-hour" plant (Ford's) and a "ten-hour" plant (Scovill's, a large and efficient metalworking plant). The investigation was carried out by Philip Sargant Florence, later professor of commerce at Birmingham University, in England, and the report, published in 1920, was prepared by Josephine Goldmark, special expert of the United States Public Health Service.[3] In this report were ventilated many of the issues that will be discussed later in the present chapter. In the chapter on "Rhythm in Industry" it is shown that certain operations, such as lathe work, lend themselves to rhythmic work, so that output is maintained to the end of the day. Another chapter deals with "The Effects of Rest" and shows that rest periods increased the total output and greatly boosted morale in the ten-hour plant but had no marked effect in the eight-hour plant where hours and conditions were already much more tolerable. A third chapter, "Stereotyped or Restricted Output," shows that artificial limitation of output was prevalent in the ten-hour plant but only sporadic in the eight-hour plant; the output norm which, as will be shown, loomed so large in the Bank Wiring Room at the Hawthorne Works, was already largely understood in 1918:

The workers have their stint clearly in mind and, if they find their output progressing fast, they may deliberately slow down. . . . On the other hand, if the workers find they are getting behind they will urge themselves on by a series of spurts and thus tire themselves out for the next working period.[4]

In 1926 Dr. L. J. Henderson was given the assignment of starting the Harvard Fatigue Laboratory. From the beginning this laboratory worked in close parallel with the English scientists, and Henderson soon reached the same conclusion that fatigue, which at first seemed to be a simple problem, was really very complicated. He and his colleagues, Dr. Dill in particular, undertook a series of studies on athletes. They found some very interesting facts: for example, that athletes as a group are especially skilled at maintaining in their muscles a proper balance between the production and the reduction of lactic acid, which is brought about by getting plenty of oxygen in the right place. In fact, it is possible to tell whether an athlete is in good training by his capacity to achieve this balance. When athletes have been out of training for a time their efficiency in this respect declines.

But this, however interesting, did not seem to have great reference to industrial fatigue because other factors appeared to be operating which had nothing to do with physiological fatigue. The search for more adequate explanations led, both in England and in America, to fresh lines of inquiry into another effect which the investigators called "monotony." "Fatigue" itself is rather a vague word that covers a variety of effects; similarly, monotony, although easy to understand in broad terms, is rather hard to define with precision.

It was becoming apparent, however, that there might be some connection between monotony and fatigue, and the Industrial Fatigue Research Board consequently set some of its workers on to the study of what caused monotony and of how monotony could be reduced. From 1924 these scientists in England began to experiment with rest pauses in the course of the working day, and they found that the rest pauses were fulfilling two distinct functions. One was to relieve muscular fatigue, if that type of fatigue occurred, and the other was to relieve boredom and monotony, to protect workers from having to go on working too steadily for too long. As it happens, muscular fatigue can very seldom be shown to occur in ordinary work. Only in certain types of very heavy manual labor can muscular fatigue be detected, and the types of labor found in an ordinary factory are not heavy enough to lead to muscular fatigue.

In 1924 Dr. H. M. Vernon in England launched two studies based on as precise a definition of monotony as could be achieved at that date. One was an experimental study, the other an industrial study. These studies showed that lowering of output is related to monotony and can be reduced by rest pauses. In a subsequent study in 1928 he found that the simple introduction of rest pauses could also reduce the rate of labor turnover. It was found in 1929 by two other British scientists, Wyatt and Fraser, that either of two extreme conditions in the factory seems to minimize boredom. One extreme is when the work is highly mechanized. Under these conditions operators can think about something else, so that they live a separate life, and carrying out the same mechanical job does not disturb their train of thought. The other extreme occurs when the task is very exacting and occupies a great deal of the workers' attention; it is then impossible for them to be bored, as they have to concentrate steadily on the work in hand. It is between these two extremes, when there is a slight and intermittent demand on attention, that the worst sense of monotony seems to develop.

Wyatt and Fraser summarized their conclusions in terms of five means by which boredom can be minimized. The first safeguard against boredom is to change the form of activity from time to time within the spell of work, so that there is not too much continuity in doing the same piece of work. The second way of reducing boredom is to pay operators according to output instead of according to the time worked, as there is then an incentive to get on with the job all the time. The third way is to ensure that the work is conceived by the worker as a series of self-contained tasks rather than as an indefinite and apparently interminable activity. If the worker feels that he is merely keeping up with some process, without producing something which can be seen as a distinct product, he is more likely to become bored. The fourth way of minimizing boredom is to allow the operatives to work in compact social groups rather than as individuals or in isolated units. The fifth is to introduce suitable rest periods within the spell of work.

These studies are interesting not only in their own right but also because their findings agree closely with a quite independent piece of research which was started in 1923 by Elton Mayo and his colleagues at Harvard. These people were called in to study the mule-spinning department of a textile mill near Philadelphia because in this department there was a very high labor turnover. There had to be 40 piecers working in this mule-spinning department, and in order to keep 40 piecers working, the company had to recruit 100 piecers a year. This gave an annual turnover of 250 per cent, whereas in the other departments of the mill the turnover was only between 5 and 6 per cent. So something seemed to be seriously wrong. The executives of the company had called in a succession of efficiency experts—industrial psychologists and incentive-scheme promoters —but all their changes had been completely ineffective in bringing about any improvement in the rate of turnover.

Mayo, already a psychologist with a rather broad understanding of human and social problems, was summoned in the hope that he might detect some feature in the mule-spinning department that would explain the trouble. At first sight the conditions in this department seemed to be fairly good. The work was not exceedingly hard; there was a fifty-hour week, made up of five ten-hour days with three-quarter-hour lunch breaks. The work of the piecers consisted of walking up and down an alley 30 to 40 yards long and piecing together the threads where they had broken. In each alley there were perhaps two or three piecers. The physical environment and the physical working conditions were not bad.

On the other hand, comparison of the social and managerial conditions with Wyatt and Fraser's criteria shows that practically each one of the criteria was being disregarded in the mule-spinning department. First, the form of activity was scarcely varied at all during the working day. There were only the few occasions when a piecer had to change a spool, a procedure known as "dotting," which gave a slight break, and occasionally the machinery broke down, which gave all the piecers some relief. Apart from these interruptions the workers faced the continuous task of piecing together the broken thread.

As a second point, the method of payment was not calculated according to output, as this had been thought to be too difficult; the piecers were paid on a time basis. It was a matter of chance how many breaks there were, and breaks had nothing to do with the skill of the worker. There was a piece group bonus, but this was fixed so high that it was never earned.

The third fault was that the workers could see no beginning and no end to the job; the piecers merely had to spend their time keeping up with the breaks. Thus the third criterion, a succession of self-contained tasks, was not followed at all.

Fourth, there was no social life because, although other piecers were present in the room, they had to walk up and down independently and could find very few legitimate occasions to get together.

Fifth, when the investigation started, there were no official rest breaks.

The management at this mill was very co-operative and let Mayo do anything he wanted. Mayo's first change was to introduce a rest break; furthermore, he allowed the piecers in each alley to decide for themselves the hours at which the machines were to be stopped. This gave them the basis for some sort of social grouping, and apparently these two changes worked quite successfully. They constitute a very early example of remedial treatment, but Mayo's simple innovations were certainly more effective than the changes suggested by the efficiency experts had been.

Another of Mayo's suggestions was that a nurse be introduced into the factory on the grounds that it was useful to have someone available to look after minor accidents. This nurse was also an interviewer, and she spent much of her time receiving the confidences of the workers. In this she acted as a sounding board for their troubles, and her appointment was an early example of the use of counseling, not so much for fact gathering as for the distinct function of providing an outlet for personal anxieties.

The effects of these changes were satisfactory. Production rose sufficiently for the piecers to begin to earn some of their group incentive bonus. Although, taken as a whole, this was an inconclusive and quite small experiment, it augured well for the future.

At the same time in England the Industrial Fatigue Research Board had been trying to discover the reasons why people found certain kinds of jobs monotonous. Two research workers, Culpin and Smith, joined with Eric Farmer, who was later for many years reader in industrial psychology at Cambridge. This team made a special study of telegraphist's cramp, which at that date was apparently a rather serious occupational disease in England; this form of cramp affected the fingers of telegraphists when they had been tapping out messages, and forced them to stop work. Oddly enough this occupational disease was common in England but rare in America, probably because telegraphists in England trained for the job at an early age and remained telegraphists all their lives, whereas in America there was more occupational mobility.

It was decided to study the problem of telegraphist's cramp by means of interviewing. First the investigators used the ordinary superficial interviews, putting down their own ideas and trying out the telegraphists' responses. They found that this did not work at all well, and so they instituted what they called a "clinical" interview, which is what today we would call a "nondirective" interview. The telegraphists were encouraged to pour out their problems to the interviewers, whether or not these problems seemed immediately relevant to the inquiry, and this type of interviewing proved much more successful. Thus it was that by the early 1920's psychologists, both in the United States and in Britain, had already discovered the virtues of the nondirective interview, both for the purposes of catharsis and also because this type of interview enables the investigator to comprehend the informant more completely.

In 1926, when the Harvard Fatigue Laboratory was set up, the

Harvard Department of Industrial Research was also opened. These two departments were started with the help of funds provided by what has since become the Rockefeller Foundation, and together they were responsible for all the major early research undertaken in the Graduate School of Business Administration, the Harvard department in which they were located.

There were a few small studies in 1926, but the first major study undertaken by the Department of Industrial Research was the famous Hawthorne Experiment, which is the main concern of the present chapter. The research started in April, 1927, and continued for five years, but there was a pause of six or seven years before *Management and the Worker* was published in 1939. Before that there had been Elton Mayo's *The Human Problems of an Industrial Civilization,*[5] published in 1933, and T. N. Whitehead's *The Industrial Worker,*[6] an elaborate statistical examination of the data collected in the Hawthorne Experiment, published in 1938. The latter work gives an exhaustive analysis of the test records, but it does not concern itself with the psychological or social meanings of the results.

The investigation is known as the Hawthorne Experiment because it took place at the Hawthorne Works of the Western Electric Company, which is located at Cicero, on the outskirts of Chicago.

Before Harvard was called in, the Hawthorne Works had already started their own program of investigation. We must take a quick look at this earlier program because the Hawthorne Experiment, in a sense, grew out of what had gone before. It is clear that the Hawthorne management were very much alive to the growing science of industrial psychology and wished to utilize it by collecting some facts for themselves. In November, 1924, the Hawthorne management consequently started on a series of illumination studies in order to find out how different levels of illumination affected the worker and the efficiency of his work. Their researches passed through four stages. The first experiment was conducted in three shops at the Hawthorne Works, one for small-piece inspection, one for relay assembly, and one for coil winding. The investigators first found out the average production in these three shops, under steady conditions, and then progressively raised the level of illumination. They found that the output rose as they raised the level of illumination. However, when the illumination was restored to the previous level, output did not fall back as far as the original rate.

One technical fault was that there was no control in that experiment; the test was merely applied to these three groups, and the investigators attributed their strange result to this fact. In the second experiment they therefore decided to adopt the more normal design; then took only one shop, divided it into two physically separate halves, raised the level of lighting in one half and kept it constant in the other. Naturally, the experiment was being both officially and unofficially observed, and much interest was being centered on these two shops. In any case, in both shops, quite irrespective of the lighting, output went up. There was no significant difference between the output of the shop that had had the illumination raised and the output of the shop that had not.

In this second experiment the shops had had windows, and the measurements were somewhat complicated by the fact that quite a proportion of the light came from outside. So in their third experiment the investigators allowed no light through windows, and in this case they progressively reduced the illumination, starting at the not very high level of 10 foot-candles, and reducing it gradually to 3 foot-candles, which is extremely low. At that point they began to receive protests from the workers that they could not see very well, but up to that level there had been no fall-off in efficiency or in speed of production.

The fourth experiment was a small supplement to the previous one and was carried out on only two workers under laboratory conditions. With them the investigators continued the process of reducing the illumination until it was 0.06 foot-candle, which is about the brightness on an ordinary moonlit night, and even at this level of illumination the efficiency of production was maintained. These two operators felt that they were doing something very special and were determined not to be beaten simply by the lack of light, so they managed to carry on as though nothing had happened. In order to see how the operators responded, the investigators started to increase the light again. After a while they merely pretended to continue increasing the light. Each day an electrician put in new bulbs. The operators were not told that the replacement bulbs were of exactly the same intensity as the bulbs taken out, yet these two operators continued to comment favorably about the increase of light.

Next the investigators reversed the process. They started reducing the light again, but after a while they only pretended to reduce it. This time the workers bravely said that it was getting rather dark but that they would manage somehow. During all these operations there was a regular level of production irrespective of the intensity of the lighting.

By this time the company had realized that there was some effect operating that had little to do with the physiology of lighting. They therefore concluded that they needed more understanding of the psychology of productive efficiency, and it was at this stage that they called in Elton Mayo and his colleagues.

The active investigator from the Harvard department was Fritz Roethlisberger, who was then an assistant professor, and he collaborated very closely throughout with William J. Dickson, who was chief of the Western Electric Company's Employee Relations Research Department. This was therefore an example of close collaboration between industrial and academic research. Throughout, the investigators worked side by side, and there is no hint that this relationship led to any great difficulties.

Management and the Worker reports on three main studies conducted at the Hawthorne Works. The first is the series of investigations in the Relay Assembly Test Room and one or two smaller ancillary studies attached to that series. The second phase was the interviewing program, which developed ultimately into a permanent counseling program for the Works; the third phase centered on the Bank Wiring Observation Room. These are given in the chronological order in which they were undertaken, and there is, in fact, a development of skill and understanding as the program proceeds. In each of these phases certain ideas and truths were taken over from what had been learned in the preceding studies.

THE RELAY ASSEMBLY TEST ROOM

Although this was directly stimulated by the company's own investigations, it was not to be concerned with lighting but with fatigue and monotony and with how output could be affected by changes in working hours, by the introduction of rest pauses, and by other variations in the working conditions. For this purpose the investigators decided to make a small study of a process which was in various ways typical of the kind of work done in the whole factory. They chose the relay assembly process because it satisfied a number of predetermined criteria. The first point was that the process was typically mechanized and repetitive—the relay which had to be assembled was a fairly small unit, and each unit could be put together quite quickly. When the experiment started, assembly took about a minute, and by the finish, it took rather less than a minute. About thirty-five parts had to be placed in position in an "assembly fixture" and then screwed together with four screws; that is all there was to it. Although all together in the Works several hundred varieties of relay were made, it was possible to arrange that in the test room all the members of the experimental group were doing the same job by selecting types for assembly which were constant in all essential characteristics. Again, this job could be carried on for years if necessary because the relay as a product was in constant demand. The program was therefore not likely to be interrupted. Finally, the speed of assembly was controlled by the operator and not by a belt or another external regulator, so that variations in speed of output could be attributed directly to each operator.

The test room was designed as a small production unit of five *operators* and one *layout operator* who had minor supervisory duties. These six operators were all girls. They were chosen not at random but purposefully. The first choice was of two girls who were known to be friendly with each other as well as being fairly experienced workers, and they were asked to select four other friends who they thought would be co-operative. It is worth stressing this point that from the beginning the relay-assembly tests were made on a group of carefully selected and trained girls who were believed in advance to be willing and co-operative workers.

In the test room a variety of observations and measurements were to be taken. Of these, the first was the measurement of output, which was done quite neatly: each girl sat at a desk while she was assembling the relays, and each desk had a small hole. When a girl completed a relay she dropped it through the hole, and this actuated a simple electrical device that punched a hole in a moving strip of paper. This strip of paper was moving along at the steady rate of ¼ inch a minute, so that the record of the relays assembled by each operator in a day's work was contained on a strip of paper only 10 feet long. The investigators could read from this tape not only the total number of relays assembled but also the time intervals between the completions of relays at different times of the day and under different conditions.

A second set of observations was made by introducing into the test room a member of the research staff called the *test room observer*. He had a log sheet on which he kept a running record of general activities and of each worker's productive and unproductive time, and of other details such as changes from one type of relay to another. There was some difficulty on this point because some of the relays were slightly different from others in design and in the time it took to assemble them, and so any switch to another type had to be recorded so as to make the necessary correction afterward. The test-room observer also took a check reading of the moving strip every half-hour for comparison purposes, and he noted any incidents that occurred, such as conversations on particular topics. Besides being well experienced in shop practices he had another function, which was recognized from the beginning, of building up and maintaining a friendly atmosphere. This again illustrates the fact that the test room was designed as a place in which cooperation was to be promoted.

The third type of record was known as the Operators' Performance Record and was regularly used throughout the factory for calculating wages and bonuses. There were also records of quality output showing, first, the number of relays assembled that subsequently had to be scrapped because they were defective, and, second, the number of parts that were rejected by the operator. From time to time a piece of mica was too thick to use or the wrong part got into the bin, and the operator had to waste her time in rejecting such pieces. Corrections were made to allow for these occasions as well as to bring all assembly onto the basis of a "standard relay." Furthermore, hourly readings were taken from dry-bulb and wet-bulb thermometers so as to have a complete record of temperature and humidity conditions. There were also physical examinations of the girls, both before they started to work and throughout the program at about six-week intervals.

This first setup of observations illustrates the extent to which the investigators were originally concerned with the question of physical fatigue, and they give the impression that the problem was being approached primarily from a physiological angle. The initial questions asked were:

1. Do employees actually get tired out?
2. Are rest pauses desirable?
3. Is a shorter working day desirable?
4. What are the attitudes of employees toward their work and toward the company?
5. What is the effect of changing the type of working equipment?
6. Why does production fall off in the afternoon?

It will be seen that these questions were already slightly socially oriented, but on the whole, as the authors themselves assert, they follow fairly closely the questions that would be raised at that date by production and efficiency experts. The possibility must be mentioned that the apparent lack of sophistication was due to tactics rather than to ignorance. There is perhaps too great a contrast between Elton Mayo's already demonstrated knowledge and interest in such psychologists as Pierre Janet and Jean Piaget and the apparent belief of the investigators that the problem of fatigue was principally a physiological one. The presentation of how they learned by their experiences is perhaps a little overdone; they may have had to give the impression of physiological bias in order to take the company along with them, but they must have known the direction in which they were heading rather better than they admit in their report.

The measurements and other records that will now be discussed continued in the Relay Assembly Test Room for five years, but the material used in *Management and the Worker* covers only the first two years' work, which can be divided into three recognizably different phases.

The *first phase* contains three short periods which were devoted to settling down. During this time, which occupied fifteen weeks, the output of the girls was measured, first, on the ordinary shop floor, second, after transfer to the Relay Assembly Test Room, and, third, after changes in the basis of wage calculation designed to ensure that the girls in the test room would benefit from their own increased output. During this phase the investigators were also arranging the medical checks already mentioned, perfecting their apparatus, making sure that the records provided the data they wanted, introducing the girls to the purposes of the experiment, and completing the rather elaborate groundwork that is needed before one can launch a social experiment. During this phase there was also a manifest growth in the rapport between the test-room observer and the girls. He was getting to know them, and they were learning to trust him.

The changes that took place in that phase, even before the investigators had started altering the working conditions, are mostly the sort of change that they could understand and in fact had engineered. But there were one or two other trends of which they only gradually became aware. It seemed that the girls, not only for the purposes of wage calculation but also as a sociological entity were developing the character of a small group rather than remaining as individual members of a large unit. It also became clear that the test-room observer was falling into a supervisory position in which he attained a dual role and was responsible for the output of the test room as well as for the research. Again, the fact that the girls had had the periodic physical examinations and other attentions which had brought them into touch with the superintendent made them begin to feel more important. Finally, the working conditions in the test room were much freer than those on the regular shop floor—the girls were allowed to talk more and were in general treated more permissively.

The *second phase* in the series of studies began when the investigators started to experiment with rest periods, first introducing two short rests and then altering their lengths and times. There were four variations in the rest periods. First there were two five-minute rests, one in the middle of the morning and one in the middle of the afternoon; then these were extended to ten minutes each; next they tried six five-minute rests, three in the morning and three in the afternoon, making thirty minutes rest during each day; finally they had a fifteen-minute morning break at which the company supplied lunch and a ten-minute afternoon break when the girls were expected to rest. These four experiments all together went on for twenty-four weeks and constituted what can be called the first experimental phase.

During this phase various incidents were noted. One was that two of the girls became rather restive and difficult and did not seem to want to co-operate, and so they were replaced by two other more co-operative girls. In their description of this incident the authors make a rather interesting comment. They say:

Had the investigators possessed at that time the technique developed later, their interest would have been directed towards inquiring into the causes of this problem. . . . But it was, as yet, too early for improved techniques, and the consequent result was to label the talking and antagonism "poor co-operation" and to try to remedy the situation.[7]

This comment foreshadows the approach for which, as we shall see the Mayo school has been much criticized. It suggests that social skill is a means of manipulating people, persuading them to work harder under the thinly disguised pretext of making them happy.

On the whole the investigators found, on looking back at the first two phases (Periods I–VII) of their studies, that, although the experimental changes they had introduced were very well documented, there was an inadequate record of the changes in the social interrelations among the operators themselves, and of the growth of what they later called the group loyalties and solidarities; there was also an insufficient record of the change in the relation between the operators and their supervisors. This was epitomized by the experience of the test-room observer, who was responsible for looking after the girls and also for recording what was happening in the test room. One of the rather fascinating results of the whole experiment was that the test-room observer became attached to this group of girls and they became attached to him, which led to certain conflicts in his loyalty. He was not quite sure whether he was looking after them, or trying to increase their output, or trying to observe them scientifically, or what he was doing.

The experiment then entered its *third phase*. This was devoted to the question whether it would be as effective to reduce the total number of hours by shortening the day as it had been to introduce rest pauses. The third phase was consequently divided into six experimental periods concerned with this question. First, in Period VIII the investigators carried on as in the last experiment (that is, a fifteen-minute midmorning break with lunch supplied by the company and a ten-minute midafternoon break, making twenty-five minutes all together), but, in addition, work ceased at 4:30 instead of at 5 o'clock. Next, in Period IX, they brought the finishing time back to 4 o'clock. Then for the twelve weeks of Period X they went back to the 5 o'clock closing. In Period XI the girls worked a five-day week, continuing until 5 o'clock for five days and not working on Saturday. In Period XII the hours reverted to those in Period III with no breaks at all, work until 5 o'clock and on Saturday mornings. The girls were warned that this period was going to take place and that it would last only three months.

Finally, for a thirty-one-week run they went back to the conditions of Period VII, with a fifteen-minute morning break and a ten-minute afternoon break, with the one small change that the company no longer supplied the morning lunch—it supplied the beverages and the girls brought their own food.

The effects of these variations were evaluated in a number of ways. The first evaluation was in terms of changes in output. It was found that in Period VIII, when the 4:30 finishing time was introduced, work became steadier and faster and the change had a good total effect on output; hourly output increased enough to absorb the loss of a half-hour's working time. The loss of a whole hour of working time each day, as in Period IX, was, however, too much of a reduction; though the girls worked hard, they could not catch up with the lost time. In Period X, which went back to the 5 o'clock closing, the output was good but there was considerable complaint from the girls who had become accustomed to the earlier closing. Period XI, which introduced the five-day week, was very popular indeed. It should perhaps be mentioned, however, that although the girls were not working Saturday morning, they were being paid for it, and this unearned bonus obviously colored their preference for the five-day week. It is not possible to be sure that it would have been equally popular if the operators had dropped those three or four hours' pay in terms of output, as the loss of time was too great to be compensated for by the generally satisfactory hourly rate.

Period XII, the three-month reversion to work without rests, was naturally unpopular, but the output stayed up well, perhaps because the girls had been forewarned. In any case their working hours were no worse than those in the main Relay Assembly Department. The final return to Period XIII, with rest periods midmorning and midafternoon, was a great relief, and output both on an hourly and on a weekly basis was higher than at any time during the experiment. The facts relating to the hourly and weekly outputs of individual girls are beautifully summarized in the charts which are reproduced in Figures 1 and 2.* The authors note five conclusions which can readily be confirmed by examination of the charts:

1. Except for Periods X, XI, and XII the hourly output rate of

* Reprinted by permission of the publishers from F. J. Roethlisberger and William J. Dickson, *Management and the Worker*. Cambridge, Mass.: Harvard University Press, Copyright, 1939, by The President and Fellows of Harvard College.

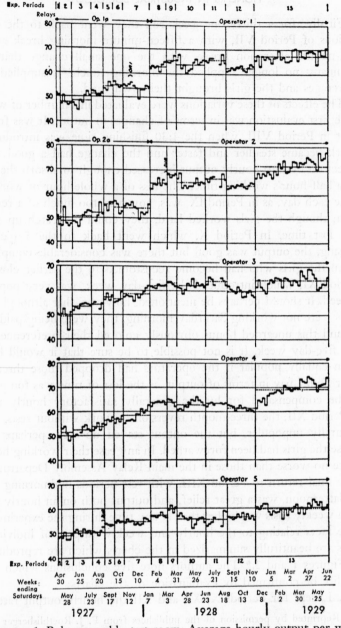

FIGURE 1. Relay assembly test room. Average hourly output per week, experimental periods I–XIII.

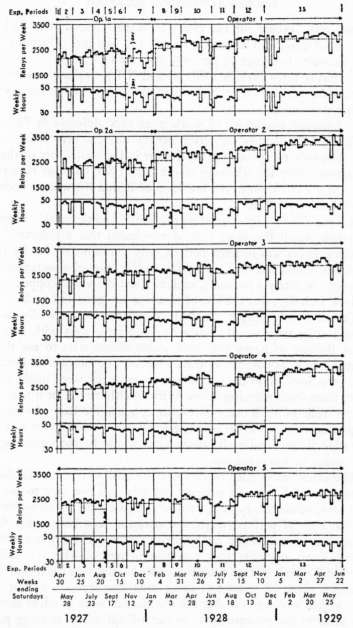

FIGURE 2. Relay assembly test room. Total weekly output, experimental periods I–XIII.

all the girls (except for the two who were replaced after Period VII) rose steadily. The output rate of the best girl (Operator 4) had increased by about 40 per cent over the two years.

2. During three periods (VII, X, and XIII) working conditions were identical, but on each occasion the hourly output rate was higher than before.

3. Although conditions of work were very different in Periods X, XI, and XII, hourly outputs in general changed very little.

4. The only exception was the decline in the hourly rate of three operators during the relatively severe Period XII, but even then the rate did not fall again to the low level of Period III, when working conditions were identical.

It is possible also, by comparing the hourly and the weekly output charts, to reach the more general conclusion that a reduction in working hours was in most periods fully compensated for by the increases in hourly rates, so that the weekly rates also increased. It was only in extreme instances, such as when the work stopped at 4 o'clock each day, that the loss of time was too great to be offset by additional hourly output. Probably companies are generally concerned more with weekly output per operator than with hourly rates. Because of heavy overhead, managements wish to use their plants as fully as possible, so that, whatever the increases in hourly rates, a serious fall in the output per operator per week might well deter them from reducing hours. With an elaborate plant it may be worth while to work out a shift scheme, but in the Relay Assembly Department there was no machinery beyond a screwdriver and an assembly fixture, and high hourly rates would be correspondingly interesting to managements.

The investigators tried to compare the quality of the work done during the different test periods, but that was not easy to do. It will be remembered, however, that the output rates were calculated on the basis of perfect relays, and it can at least be asserted that there was no measurable falling-off in quality. There was another check. Every operative took a certain amount of what was called "personal time," that is, time for going to the washroom and for having a drink of water and other such interruptions. One question looked into was whether the rest periods were in effect taking the place of the personal time, so that official time was being provided for what had previously been unofficial breaks. It was found in fact that the personal time was halved by introducing the rest periods, but this diminution was less than the increase in resting time.

The health of the operators seems to have been unaffected by the experiments, according to the six-week checks. Irregularity in attendance, consisting not only of missing whole days but also of arriving late, was very greatly reduced for the five girls. The average number of days lost a year for the girls before entering the test room was 15.2, whereas the rate in the test room was the very low figure of 3.5 lost days a year.

Finally there was the question of the operators' preferences among the different periods. Mention has been made in passing of the girls' comments during the course of each period. One fact that emerged was that the periods with six five-minute breaks were disliked because they interrupted the flow of work too much, and that the period with the 4 o'clock closing was disliked because it cut earnings too much.

In the middle of Period XII a vote was taken in which each girl was asked to list in order her preferences among the previous periods. The result was unanimous: all the operators preferred the five-day week. For second choice three out of six (the layout operator also voted) voted for the 4:30 closing with the two rest periods.

EXPLANATORY HYPOTHESES

These, then, were the results of the experiments, and the next step was to test the hypotheses by which the improved output in the test room could be explained.

The *first hypothesis* aimed to account for the higher output was that the material conditions and methods of work had been improved. This was never regarded by the authors as very plausible because the physical conditions—for example, lighting, heating, and ventilation—were not very much better than in the main factory. In some ways they were slightly worse than on the shop floor, and very little special provision had been made. Furthermore, improved material conditions could not be made to account for the steady rise in productivity over the two-year period.

The *second hypothesis* was that the girls were responding to relief from cumulative fatigue. According to this hypothesis, the ordinary working conditions had been leading to cumulative fatigue, whereas this tendency was reversed by easier conditions in the test room.

The *third hypothesis* was that the improvement was due to relief from monotony; the *fourth hypothesis* was that it was due to increased wage incentives; and the *fifth* was that certain social factors were operating to make the girls produce more.

It was not found possible to test very satisfactorily the influence of material conditions, and the investigators were in any case skeptical about the first hypothesis. On the other hand, they went very carefully and very rigorously into the possible effects of fatigue and monotony. It is an important feature of the report that the authors did not jump to conclusions, however plausible they might appear, but closely examined every possible hypothesis. This gave to their conclusions an added authority, just as a psychoanalyst may benefit indirectly from the possession of medical qualifications, which enable him to consider organic as well as psychogenic explanations. The investigators set out to apply existing knowledge of the meaning and measurement of fatigue, monotony, and boredom, and existing understanding of how these complaints could be affected by working conditions. With the findings already cited, they did not have to start from the beginning, but could call on a satisfactory battery of analytical techniques to apply to the performance figures of the test-room girls.

In the British investigations mentioned earlier Dr. H. M. Vernon had already demonstrated typical work curves. Vernon's curves were based on the premise that two factors, practice and fatigue, are at odds with each other. At the beginning of a work spell the worker is not "warmed up" to his job, and toward the end of a period he is slowed down by fatigue. Between these phases of reduced efficiency one can expect a peak in the middle of the morning and a second, lower peak in the middle of the afternoon, after which output begins to drop away seriously (Figure 3).

In another study Wyatt, Fraser, and Stock had shown that the typical monotony curve was very different, showing a high rate of output at both ends of the working period and a trough in the middle.[8] Monotony takes some time to build up after work starts, and boredom also evaporates when the prospect of finishing work looms up. The curves shown (Figure 4) are based on actual experience, not merely worked out theoretically.

One important feature of these two curves is that they both reflect an anticipatory function: on the fatigue curve there is a slowing-down because the operator knows that it is getting near to the end of the day, so that the effect of shortening the day is to make the curve start to drop a little earlier. Where there is genuine physical fatigue some fall in output is inevitable. But, as has been mentioned, in the Hawthorne Works, indeed in most modern factories, physical fatigue of that kind is seldom allowed to occur. It is rare nowadays to find a job which is heavy enough to induce physical fatigue, if only because it is normally cheaper and more efficient to install a machine that does not get tired toward the end of the afternoon.

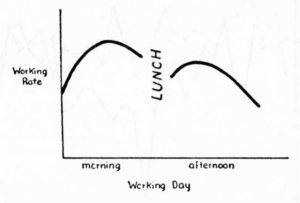

FIGURE 3. "Typical" daily work curve.

Reprinted by permission of the publishers from F. J. Roethlisberger and William J. Dickson, *Management and the Worker*. Cambridge, Mass.: Harvard University Press, Copyright, 1939, by The President and Fellows of Harvard College.

In terms of physical fatigue the argument for providing rest pauses is that, while the workers may restart after a rest at a somewhat slower pace, they will speed up afterward; it clearly takes considerable skill and luck to achieve the right relationships between work and rest.

When the authors made a detailed examination of the output in the test room they found that it did not fit the typical fatigue curve.

In particular, the afternoon output rate tended to be somewhat higher (by about 1.6 per cent) than the morning rate, a fact which was difficult to reconcile with the fatigue hypothesis. As a further check they made some direct physiological tests. First they measured the girls' blood pressure and calculated an index called the "pulse product," which was regarded by physiologists as a suitable measure of muscular efficiency. The results showed that the operatives were all working comfortably within their fatigue limits and were not exhibiting physical fatigue at any stage.

Another physiological test, which they helped to elaborate, was

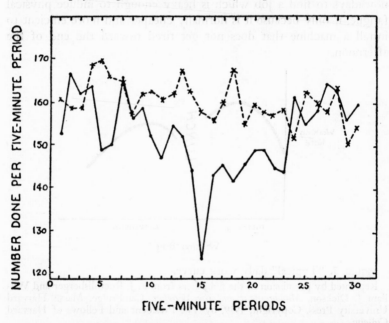

FIGURE 4. Monotony and work rate. "Curves showing rate of working when (a) boredom was prominent and mind-wandering almost absent (continuous line), and (b) boredom was slight and mind-wandering prominent (broken line)." Reproduced with the permission of the Controller of Britannic Majesty's Stationery Office, London, England, from Wyatt, Fraser, and Stock, op. cit., p. 37.

Reprinted by permission of the publishers from F. J. Roethlisberger and William J. Dickson, Management and the Worker. Cambridge, Mass.: Harvard University Press, Copyright, 1939, by The President and Fellows of Harvard College.

called the "vascular skin reaction test." Professor C. E. Turner, of Massachusetts Institute of Technology, one of their chief advisers, devised an instrument for this purpose. It consisted of a weight of known mass on the end of a rod. When the device is dropped onto the wrist and then removed, a white line appears. The speed at which this line disappears indicates the fatigue of the wrist. If it disappears quickly, the wrist is fatigued. By this test the amount of fatigue induced by the girls' work was again shown to be negligible. It was found that if the subjects clenched their fists for a second or two before the test, this fatigued the wrist more than all the relay assembling they had done all day.

Tests were also used to determine if the actual speed of an opera- tion was slower in the afternoon than in the morning. Although the results of this test were inconclusive, the authors reached the con- clusion that the fatigue hypothesis could not be upheld.

The output figures were rather more compatible with the mo- notony hypothesis. By that stage this did not surprise the authors for the reason that, as they pointed out, monotony is at least partly a state of mind. So this tentative acceptance of the monotony hypothesis was not in conflict with their growing belief that the change in output was somehow related to the attitudes of the operators.

They proceeded to test the hypothesis that the bonus incentive was the operative factor by setting up a second test group of five girls who were not subjected to elaborate observations. These girls were to some extent isolated from the shop floor and were paid a group bonus on the output of the five rather than on the output of the whole shop. It was found that their output rose substantially, that is, by about 15 per cent compared with the 30 per cent increase in the test room.[9] It seemed, therefore, that some of the increased output could be accounted for in terms of wage incentive, but that there was still a residual effect to be accounted for in some other way.

As a further study of the contribution of wage incentives to the hoisting of output, the investigators undertook a rather unsuccessful subsidiary experiment. This involved setting up a second test room in which five girls were given the highly skilled job of mica splitting; this was an individual piecework job, and payment was made to each girl according to the number of pieces of mica she split. The idea was to ascertain whether this was a more effective incentive than the group-bonus scheme. Actually various mishaps spoiled this experiment. One unforeseeable difficulty was that the 1931 recession was just beginning, so that the demand for split mica fell off and hours were cut, not for experimental reasons but in order to curtail production. So in this case the pressure to produce, which in the Relay Assembly Test Room had stimulated a steady rise in output, was replaced in the later stages of the experiment by a policy of retrenchment. The failure of the girls to increase their output is entirely explained by the investigators in these terms: "The cause of the decline in output during the second year was not difficult to locate. Everything pointed to its relation to the operators' anxieties over the uncertain future of the mica splitting job."[10] Although each girl could raise her immediate earnings by working harder, each appeared to restrict her output in order to postpone the day when she would be transferred or laid off.

A second conclusion, which was very interesting, was that, though the incentive was more direct than in the Relay Assembly Test Room, this mica-splitting group did not develop group solidarity. The girls remained individuals who happened to be working side by side. The contrast between the two experiments is so great that one wishes that greater use had been made of the mica-splitting test to specify more precisely the conditions under which the relay-assembly generalizations would operate.

But in fact the authors revert at the earliest decent moment to an analysis of the Relay Assembly Test Room. This time they are concerned with the individual outputs of the relay-assembly operators. As a supplement to the analysis of the output records the investigating her home circumstances, they found that there was test their dexterity, attention, visual perception, and intelligence. They found that, although the relay-assembly test girls were somewhat above the works average on manual dexterity, they were definitely rather low on intelligence, as measured by the Otis Examination. The tests also showed, however, that the test-room girls with the highest native skill and intelligence (Operators 2, 1, and 4) were also the girls with the highest output rate.

At this stage of their narrative, the authors include some rather good thumbnail sketches of the operatives, and the girls come very much alive in the telling. One of these sketches was particularly interesting because it echoes the *Polish Peasant* material. The girl in question was a young Polish immigrant whose parents had brought her to the United States as a child. She seemed to play the part of the test-room "jester," continually making witty remarks for the benefit of the group. She did this to such an extent that the other girls became rather bored; they found her witty remarks not very funny, and they wanted to be quiet.

But, although she always gave the impression of being frivolous and lighthearted, the investigators suspected that behind this façade she was sensitive and unhappy. At a later stage, when they were investigating her home circumstances, they found that there was indeed a cheerless background. Her family consisted of her parents, who had been born in Poland, and five other children. The father had a minor clerical job and was very withdrawn from the rest of his family, seldom speaking to his wife or children. The mother dominated the family, managing the finances and demanding strict obedience from the children. She was trying to bring them up in the strict Polish peasant tradition.

This operator, who had been Americanized to some extent, enjoyed pretty clothes and dating but was frustrated in these interests. She had little money for clothes, as she had to turn her pay check over to her mother. Her dates were a constant failure because her demands on men were highly romantic; she was always discovering new boy friends and being disappointed because they did not live up to her hopes. So her health broke down to some extent—she became rather hypochondriac, worrying over her eyes and her weight.

Here was an example of the social disorganization discussed by Thomas and Znaniecki[11] of a family which had lost touch with its ancestral ties before it had become adjusted to or assimilated by the new country. The result was a withdrawn father, a punitive and disturbed mother, a family of children who were trying to go their own ways—a disintegrating group sustained neither by the traditions and customs of the foreign society to which it had belonged nor by the new society in which it was living.

The authors close their description of the Relay Assembly Test Room with a discussion of the role of the test-room observer. Some mention has already been made of the difficulty he had in maintaining the conditions of a controlled experiment while gaining the utmost co-operation of the girls in a human situation. As the research continued it was increasingly realized that this was an inevitable problem in this kind of work. In *The Tools of Social Science* I have discussed, more fully than would be appropriate here, the ideas behind action research and the extent to which in sociological research it is possible simultaneously to gather the facts needed for theoretical understanding and to influence the chances of a favorable outcome to the immediate situation.[12] These two activities can very well go along together, and the Hawthorne Experiment was one of the first examples of an integration of the two. As the authors say, echoing the words of W. I. Thomas, with the realization of this dual function of their work the inquiry changed its character.

No longer were the investigators interested in testing for the effects of single variables. In the place of a controlled experiment, they substituted the notion of a social situation which needed to be described and understood as a system of interdependent elements. The situation included not only the external events but the meanings which individuals assigned to them: their attitudes toward them and their preoccupations about them. Rather than trying to keep these "psychological factors" constant, the investigators had to regard them as important variables in the situation. As much attention had to be given to these psychological factors as to output in assessing the external changes which took place.[13]

To sum up the results of their first two years' experimentation in the test room, the authors had to admit that there was only one indisputable positive result—the demonstration of the importance of employee attitudes and preoccupations. The facts that they had somewhat naïvely entered the plant to discover had rather escaped them. What they had discovered, and what they successfully transmitted to the management of the Hawthorne Works, was that a happy and productively efficient factory was one in which the attitudes and preoccupations of the employees were well directed toward the productive aims of the factory and were correspondingly freed from the traditional "apprehension of authority."

Although the introduction of rest pauses was one of the most practical results of the experiments, unquestionably the most important outcome was management's improved understanding of many of its problems and of the stores of latent energy and productive co-operation that could be obtained under the right conditions from its working force. The management decided, therefore, that everything pointed to the need for more research on employee attitudes and the factors to which they could be related, so that a climate favorable to high output could be established throughout the works.

This seemingly inadequate conclusion that more research is needed has a very familiar ring in the social sciences, to the extent that it is on the way to becoming a stock joke. The commonest reason is that a problem has initially been conceived in the wrong terms and, these terms regulating the method of investigation, has led the research in a false direction. Some investigators have failed to notice this fact even at the end of their journey, and it is an important merit of *Management and the Worker* that the authors did reorient their concepts and their methods of inquiry in a direction that offered a way forward.

THE INTERVIEWING PROGRAM

Thus it was that they came on to their next program, described in the book as "A Plan for the Improvement of Employee Relations," and notable for the development of counseling procedures. Having recognized the close dependence of employee morale upon supervision, the investigators and the company felt that they must address themselves energetically to the improvement of standards of supervision. With this object the company had instituted conferences to train the supervisors. They found, however, that the organizers of these conferences did not have enough factual data to use for training. Too much of the material available consisted of the personal observations of certain executives, and much of it was contradictory. An interview study was therefore planned in the Inspection Branch, covering 1,600 skilled and unskilled employees, with the intention of collecting results that could be used both for the training of supervisors and for the direct improvement of working conditions.

The first part of the interview program continued for about six months, during which interviews were conducted by a staff of five, three men and two women. One qualification required for these interviewers was that they already possess a thorough knowledge of shop conditions, so that they would be able to know the truth of comments made to them, and so that the informants would feel that they were being understood. Each interviewer was given a territory consisting of part of the Inspection Branch, and worked in close collaboration with the local supervisors, selecting subjects so as to minimize interference with the work of the branch. Rules of procedure covering the approach to the employee were carefully laid down to ensure a satisfactory relationship between interviewer and informant.

The operators found quite early that being interviewed was a pleasant experience; they liked having time off for that purpose (for which they did not lose pay), and they appreciated the opportunity to express themselves. From the beginning there were many favorable remarks, such as "It's pretty good of the company to have this interviewing. If things don't go all right, we have someone to tell them to."[14] The supervisors also liked the program, in spite of being fairly severely criticized in some of the interviews, because they found that it gave them knowledge about their own people which they would not otherwise have had. All in all, the pilot stage was so successful that on its completion the company set up an Industrial Research Division, one of the main functions of which was to extend the interview program to all eight branches of the factory. For this purpose they hired many more interviewers, and the program developed into a somewhat massive and supposedly permanent undertaking.

At the pilot stage the interviewing procedure was substantially formalized. Each interviewer had a check list of the subjects to be discussed, such as the lighting system, heat, ventilation, drinking water, toilets, lockers, and so on. The wording was not standardized, and interviewers had considerable discretion. There were also leading questions, such as "What do you think of the company as a place to work?" Those responsible thought at this stage that they were becoming very thorough and scientific. But quite soon one of the interviewers, who happened to be more aware or more honest than the others, confessed at a meeting of the interviewing staff that he must be no good at his job because he had been unable to keep one informant on the specified topics. The worker had tended to wander and to talk about his personal life, his experiences, and other "irrelevant" topics. When the ice was thus broken, the other interviewers admitted similar experiences. And this became an important issue the implications of which were carefully considered by the investigators, who realized that the questions being asked were not necessarily the questions the operators wished to discuss.

So it was that, after five months of the initial system, the program was switched officially to what we now call "nondirective interviewing." This had certain practical consequences. One was that the length of each interview increased from about thirty minutes to about ninety minutes, and another was that the length of the report increased from about two and a half pages of relatively easily processed material to about ten pages of almost unanalyzable material. But everyone was happy about the change because it was much more fun both for the interviewers and for the informants. Unfortunately, here again the onset of the depression led to a decision in 1931 to suspend the general interviewing program until the business outlook became more favorable. This opportunity did not occur until 1936, when a new program was started. This time the fact-finding function was minimized, and the new plan was overtly a program of "personnel counseling" designed specifically to sustain morale by providing a safety valve for otherwise suppressed complaints.

In spite of the development of their thinking about the interview which progressively changed its function from fact finding to counseling, the team did not ignore or discount the objective reality behind at least some of the complaints registered in the pilot stages in the Inspection Branch. Analysis took in the factual results, and some ingenuity was devoted to the task of systematizing results at this level, so that they could be used as planned for supervisor training and for the improvement of working conditions.

The analysis covered the first 1,600 interviews conducted in the Inspection Branch. It was found that of these, 321 contained adverse comments of some kind—criticisms or complaints—providing a total of 471 complaints. Nearly one-quarter of the complaints were too vague for the company to act upon, and nearly one-third of the others were, according to the company's standards, found by investigation not to be objectively justified. Thus nearly half of all the complaints originally voiced revealed a worker who was dissatisfied in an intangible way that could not be attributed to any material deficiency, such as the state of the lockers or inadequate provision of drinking water. On the other hand, as has already been mentioned, this part of the interview program did have some good side effects. Over and above its contribution to supervisors' conferences, it introduced a new and favorable atmosphere into supervision; it gave the interviewers, many of whom were supervisors, fresh insight into the human problems of their subjects; and finally it was valuable for the operatives, providing them with a means of improving their material conditions and giving them what the authors call a certain "lift" as a result of being permitted to express freely their feelings and emotions.

When the investigators came to analyze the main body of interviews, which totaled 10,300, they made use of a breakdown of topics into 37 headings that they had previously devised. They had amassed all together 80,000 comments which could be placed under one or another of these headings, and a very elaborate analysis was undertaken, in the course of which two interesting concepts were developed. One is an index named the *urgency factor* of a topic, which is the percentage of the total number of interviews containing a comment on the topic in question. For example, of the 10,000 interviews, 6,500 contained a mention of the subject job placement. This topic (the most frequently mentioned) was therefore assigned an urgency factor of 65. The authors comment, however: "No particular importance can be attached to the great frequency with which *job placement* was discussed, because some conversational remark about the job was a likely starting point for the interview."[15]

The other concept was what they called *tone*. The proportion of favorable comments to all comments on a given topic was called the *favorable ratio* or *index of satisfaction*, and the proportion of unfavorable comments similarly gave the *unfavorable ratio* or *index of dissatisfaction*. A percentage of favorable comments higher than 67 was called a *favorable tone* to that topic, and one lower than 33 was called an *unfavorable tone*.

The concepts of urgency and tone and the simple definitions arrived at are interesting because they provide an early example of what is now known as *content analysis*. It is a direct and systematic way of sorting out what would otherwise be a tremendously awkward mass of material. The details of the authors' definitions are perhaps of less lasting importance than the fact that they pioneered this type of analysis.

A detail of interest is that the investigators accepted as a neutral position a point at which two-thirds of the informants gave apparently favorable replies. This reflects the well-established fact that informants tend to give replies which are rather more favorable than their "true" position.

A full report is given on the complaints shown to have had a high urgency and a favorable tone and of those shown to have had a high urgency and an unfavorable tone, the breakdown being shown separately for men and women. The results on the whole are perhaps rather dull. There was found to be quite a volume of complaint about the lockers, but almost certainly the management already knew that the lockers were bad and were probably due to be replaced. On the whole it cannot be said that at the objective, factual level very many interesting results emerged. The interviews did confirm that the job-placement scheme was felt to be well organized, that the stock-purchase scheme was popular with the workers, and provided a few other hints of that kind. The favorable comments mostly concerned employee relations, the unfavorable ones plant conditions. But in general the facts elicited from the elaborate interview program were disappointingly elementary and pedestrian.

The authors then began to consider the more interesting part, which concerned complaints that had a less factual basis. They worked out a classification of the remarks made, again on a simple empirical plan, dividing the remarks into three classes. *Class A* comprised complaints that could be directly confirmed or confuted by reference to sight or touch; for example, the statement "The doorknob is broken" can readily be tested by simple observation. *Class B* was used for complaints consisting mainly of sensory experience of the subject but not readily seen or touched by the interviewer; for example, the statements "I get very thirsty," "It is very dirty work in this department," or "The lockers are insanitary" would be placed in Class B. Evaluations are here beginning to intrude. The third group, *Class C*, was used for statements in which the subject's own evaluation was the most important element and in which sensory experience plays a small role; an example would be: "The wage rates are too low." This was not a very rigorous type of classification, but it was found easy to apply. In retrospect, its interest is that the authors were beginning to make allowance for the fact that every comment of this sort contains two elements —what they call the *manifest content* and what they call the *latent content*. This is the important and celebrated dichotomy which was popularized by the publication of *Management and the Worker*.

The authors do not acknowledge the source of the manifest and latent content concepts, but presumably they were drawn from Freud's *Introductory Lectures in Psychoanalysis*, the English translation of which was published in the early 1920's. In his section on the interpretation of dreams Freud wrote:

This seems to me a good point at which to introduce two new terms which we might have used already. Let us call the dream as related *the manifest dream-content*, and the hidden meaning, which we should come by in following out the associations, *the latent dream-thoughts*.[16]

Roethlisberger and Dickson give examples of ways in which different states of mind of the respondent may have to be interpreted for latent as well as for manifest content. This discussion covers ground familiar today, but it was still fresh when the authors were writing. They instance the case of the man who, having quarreled with his wife, goes to work ready to "explode" at everything he notices—the temperature of the room, the condition in which his tools have been left, the "silly grin" of the boss. Another person might have a longer-lasting worry—a wife in the hospital and heavy doctor bills not yet paid. He is worried over his situation, and this constitutes the latent content of his complaint that the wage rates are too low in his factory. They give as a third example the much more deep-seated trouble of a man who complains that the supervisor is a bully; when the interviewer lets him talk he discovers that the informant had a domineering father and that he is projecting his feelings about his father onto his supervisor.

In the light of the experience gained in this program the authors laid down for the first time some orientation and procedural rules for persons undertaking the nondirective type of interviewing here developed. These are very good indeed. The presentation is slightly hard to grasp at first, as it comprises two sets of rules which have a similar flavor but are different in content. The *practical rules* are discussed in detail in *The Tools of Social Science*[17] and need not be re-examined here. It will suffice to repeat Elton Mayo's words:

It must not be thought that this type of interviewing is easily learned. It is true that some persons, men and women alike, have a natural flair for the work, but, even with them, there tends to be an early period of discouragement, a feeling of futility, through which the experience and coaching of a senior interviewer must carry them.[18]

In the present context the rules of orientation are perhaps more relevant. It is of great interest that at this point in their book the authors devote a long footnote to acknowledging their debt to their forerunners—Janet, Freud, Jung, Piaget from psychology; Durkheim, Lévy-Brhul, and Pareto from sociology; Malinowski, Radcliffe-Brown, Pitt-Rivers from social anthropology. What they do not make clear is whether their supposedly laborious attainment of the summit of understanding was achieved with the aid of these masters, or whether the significance of what had been done before became clear to them only as their own experiences accumulated. Only in one case, and then only in Elton Mayo's independent outline of the Hawthorne experiments, is the specific source given. This is the quotation from Piaget which is reproduced a little later in this chapter.

The *rules of orientation* stress that the interviewer should treat what is said in an interview as an item in a context, with the corollary that he should not pay exclusive attention to the manifest content of the intercourse but should look for the hidden meanings behind it. The authors give the example of a woman at an afternoon tea in New England who was complaining that the English public-school system tended to make men brutal. This remark was taken at its face value and led to a lively discussion. Apparently no one present took account of the fact that she was just divorcing her husband who had been to an English public school.

Another corollary is that the interviewer should not treat everything that is said as either fact or error. This is obviously of very great importance; certain statements are more like facts than others because they can be confirmed, as was recognized in the classification of comments into Classes A, B, and C, already discussed. A statement on rate of pay is a reliable fact in a factory because confirmation or correction can probably be obtained from the accounts department. If, however, at least in England, a woman is asked how much her husband earns, her answer may be unreliable. Sometimes she does not know, sometimes she thinks she knows and is wrong, sometimes she exaggerates, and sometimes she plays it down. Other statements which are made to look like statements, such as "Work in this company is like working in a jail," although expressed as facts, even more obviously contain a large element of evaluation.

The next rule is that the interviewer should not treat everything that is said as being at the same psychological level. Actually even in one interview the remarks will be at a variety of psychological levels. Some of the time the subject may be bored and may just be making conversation. Sometimes he is poking fun at the interviewer. Sometimes he is nervous and apprehensive and therefore guarded in his statements. Sometimes he wishes to please the interviewer. Sometimes he is genuinely searching for the truth. It is part of the interviewer's task to interpret the subject's mood and to gauge the level at which he is responding. How to do this, and many other questions raised by nondirective interviewing, are elaborated most usefully in Merton, Fiske, and Kendall's *The Focused Interview*, based on part of the program of Stouffer's wartime Research Branch of the Information and Education Division of the United States War Department.[19]

The next rule of orientation is that the interviewer should listen not only to what a person wants to say but also to what he does not want to say or cannot say without help. It must always be remembered that silence may mean indifference, but it may equally stem from the desire to avoid a painful topic.

As the authors point out, the preceding rules make a number of assumptions about the subject and his mental processes. In particular it follows from them that "blind thinking," concerned with satisfying rather than communicating desires, makes up much of a person's mental activity. There is no simple and direct relation between what a person thinks and what he says, and the skill of the nondirective interviewer lies in his capacity to treat the subject's individual responses not as facts but as symptoms which gradually enable the interviewer to build up a picture of the subject's personal situation. This point also is very well followed up in *The Focused*

Interview, which gives guidance on how to pick up the meaning of what someone is trying to say and to lead him on, rather than to divert him onto a topic that the interviewer may find more relevant or interesting. There is one case in *The Focused Interview* in which some soldiers were shown a short film sequence of the German *Luftwaffe*. In the subsequent interview one soldier commented that their equipment looked cheap. This subjective response was picked up quite wrongly by the interviewer, who began to treat the informants as a group of experts, asking further technical questions about the items of German equipment shown, whereas obviously he should have picked up the underlying meaning of the soldier's initial comment, which was that he was seeking some kind of assurance against his fears about going into combat.[20]

Another rule first propounded systematically by Roethlisberger and Dickson is that the interviewer should keep the personal reference in its social context. In his social past the individual has some idiosyncratic and some universal features, both of which will be reflected in his responses. There is also the social present; the interview is itself a social situation, and there will always be some interaction between the interviewer and the informant.

Some of these rules may seem familiar today, but they constitute the most detailed early formulations of the role that the interviewer should play and the way in which he should manipulate the situation in a nondirective interview in order to arrive at the richest and most reliable material. But while the presentation is exceptionally systematic, its contribution is that of a synthesis rather than that of a discovery. In *The Human Problems of Industrial Civilization*, first published in 1933, Mayo had given a quotation from Piaget that is specifically concerned with the aims of nondirective interviewing. Piaget had written in 1926:

The art of the clinician [interviewer] consists not in getting the subject to answer questions but in inducing him to talk freely and display his spontaneous tendencies in place of cramping them within imposed limits [i.e., the limits of a question]. It consists in placing every symptom in a mental context, in place of abstracting it from such a context.[21]

Thus from the clinical world there was an invaluable starting point which, according to Mayo, led to an eager search of Piaget's works for further help and direction.

THE BANK WIRING OBSERVATION ROOM

The third phase of the Hawthorne Experiment described in full in *Management and the Worker* consisted of the observations carried out in the so-called Bank Wiring Observation Room. The purpose of this undertaking was to make a purely sociological study of what goes on in a factory situation, both as an illustration of the conceptual scheme that had been arrived at as a result of the previously reported researches and also to obtain a picture of a spontaneous, informal social organization functioning within the formal framework of the company's structure.

The story of how this phase of the program was stimulated is related elsewhere by Mayo. He describes how a foreman, remembering the investigators' initial interest in fatigue, asked for an inquiry in his department to discover why the output of his girls fell off seriously by evening. The investigators happened to know from their interviewing program that these particular girls had an informal rule among themselves that they would do most of their work in the morning and take things easy during the afternoon. Here, then, were two clear-cut alternative explanations. By unostentatiously arranging to have the electric current measured, the fact was established that work slackened off each afternoon.

And the attention of the research group was, by this and other incidents, thus redirected to a fact already known to them, namely, that the working group as a whole actually determined the output of individual workers by reference to a standard, pre-determined but never clearly stated, that represented the group conception of a fair day's work. This standard was rarely, if ever, in accordance with the standards of the efficiency engineers.[22]

The description in *Management and the Worker* begins with extensive quotations from interview material that illustrates the extent to which operators were fixing informal norms. In planning a study to extend and confirm these observations the investigators decided that the best research procedure would be to take a vertical section through a normal manufacturing process by setting up a small-scale observation room. In this room they would not manipulate anything but would have observers and interviewers present over a long period and thus build up a picture of how the operators behaved.

It is interesting to record that the setup of this observation room was to some extent devised under the guidance of Lloyd Warner, who had arrived on the scene a little earlier. Warner had himself recently started his Yankee City series, which was to constitute a set of reports on different aspects of life in the city of Newburyport. Owing to the fact that when Warner and his associates arrived in Newburyport there was a strike in the most important factory there, the investigators initially concentrated attention on the strike and on the social structure of the factory. This experience had taken Warner away from the Australian aborigines, which had previously been his field of study, and had steered him onto industrial problems. Warner's orientation was on the boundary between anthropology and sociology. He advised the investigators who were setting up the Bank Wiring Observation Room as a sociological-anthropological study to look at the observation room first in terms of its formal and technical organization, on the grounds that you cannot understand what actually happens without first knowing how it is officially intended to operate in the eyes of management. The second observational task was to look for evidence of an informal organization consciously or unconsciously created by the employees, as revealed by what they say and by how they combine in groups and by how they act together in a manner that indicates group solidarity. The third task is to try to understand the function of the informal organization and its relationship to the formal company organization.

This dichotomy of the formal and the informal organization is the frame by which the authors structured the whole of the work in the observation room. It differs from the earlier stages of investigation in that the model was built in from the beginning and did not merely emerge in the course of the work.

From the nature of the approach chosen it was not possible to separate the functions of observing and of evaluating and conceptualizing the results. The three tasks just described had therefore to be entrusted to the field investigators and could not be distilled later by the authors from the field material.

The investigating work was functionally divided between an observer and an interviewer. The observer was stationed with the experimental group and given the role of a disinterested and fairly unobtrusive spectator. It was important for him to be on friendly terms with everyone in the observation room, and at the same time he was expected to keep performance records and to report all events and conversations which he considered significant in relation to the hypotheses already described. He was deliberately given no formal authority in the observation room and, unlike a schoolteacher, was placed at a desk at the back facing the side wall. He was asked not to take sides in any argument nor to intrude himself either by joining conversations or by appearing eager to overhear remarks. Under no circumstances was he to violate confidences or give any information to supervisors, whatever their rank, and he should in no way by his behavior or manner of speech set himself off from the group.

Whereas the observer's role was thus to be that of a passive member of the group, the interviewer was to remain an outsider to the group as much as possible. He was to enter the observation room only when it was essential. The intention here was to keep the interviewer virtually independent, in the belief that this would make the workers less reticent and would not make them feel that what they were recounting was already common knowledge. The interviews were to be held by appointment and conducted in private. While the observer was to record the verbal and overt behavior of the operatives, the interviewer was to probe into their attitudes, thoughts, and feelings, and also to learn about their personal backgrounds and social life outside the plant.

The department used for study was chosen by applying a number of practical criteria similar to those which determined the choice of the relay assembly process in the test room. It was necessary that the operators should remain on the same task, that the output of each operator could be exactly determined, that the completion of each unit should take a comparatively short time, that the operator could set his own pace, that there should be the assurance of a reasonable continuity of employment, that the group could be isolated from the main department without inconvenience and without moving bulky or costly equipment, and that the operators should be experienced at this work. The great depression prevailed by this time, and the most difficult condition to fulfill was continuance of employment. Finally it was decided to select the operation of bank wiring, which consisted of the wiring of fairly complicated telephone switchboards known as "connectors" and "selectors" or, collectively, as "equipments."

The observation room had fourteen operators, all men, including nine wiremen, three soldermen, and two inspectors. Each of these types of operator had a specific task to perform, and each depended on operators of the other two types for the completion of each unit of equipment, so that the work rate of each worker was regulated by the rates of two other workers. On the whole the wiremen set the pace, but it was quite possible for soldermen or inspectors to limit the completion of units by refusing to work fast.

The information obtained was recorded along lines similar to those in the Relay Assembly Test Room. Records were kept of output at the end of each day by counting the number of equipments assembled, and the quality of output was extracted by analysis of the inspectors' ratings. The observer produced a daily record of outstanding events, conversations, and so on, which for the period of the inquiry provided three hundred single-space typewritten sheets of information. Each operator was, in addition, interviewed before the study began and two or three times during the study; verbatim transcripts of these interviews produced another three hundred pages of material. There were also records of physical examinations, which showed that all the operators were in good health and without disabilities. Finally, certain mental and dexterity tests were administered on each operator by an experienced psychologist.

One of the most interesting issues was the question of how to enlist the co-operation of the operators in the observation room. The investigators were aware that they had been favored in this respect in the Relay Assembly Test Room by four facts, namely, the attention paid to the operatives by supervisors of high rank, the improved incentive bonus accorded to them as a small group, the fact that the research observer took over many of the normal supervisory duties, and the fact that the experimental changes themselves—rest periods, lunches, shorter hours—were special privileges.

These favorable features did not figure in the Bank Wiring Observation Room; nevertheless co-operation was good. In any case, as the investigators came to realize, the co-operation sought was of a different kind, for in this second study the operators were not expected to work harder or to do anything to which they were unaccustomed. The main exception was that here, as in the Relay Assembly Test Room, there was an atmosphere of abnormal freedom and a great deal more horseplay and jollification generally than was customary on the shop floor. As in this instance the formal supervisory arrangements were unaltered, this effect may perhaps be attributed as much to the greater difficulties of supervision in a secluded room as to the greater interaction of a specially selected small group.

One of the main points to be studied in the Bank Wiring Observation Room was the wage-incentive system that applied to the operators in the whole department. This was based on achieving a "bogey" of 914 connections an hour, which meant slightly over 7,200 a day. It happened that the equipments mainly being assembled had 3,300 connections on each, and the operators had convinced themselves that the daily norm was two of these equipments, or 6,600 connections, so that it was almost impossible to shift them from their belief that this was the official norm. It was found that they not only worked extremely carefully to regulate their own output in order to maintain this self-imposed norm, but also exercised social control, by means of ridicule and the use of caustic nicknames, such as "Shrimp," "Slave," or "Speed King," over operators who worked too fast, in order to bring such operators into line so that the group as a whole could keep up this general "norm" of 6,600 connections a day. Their method was almost entirely successful. Only one man did not fit in with the group norm; he regularly made more than 7,000 connections a day and was thoroughly disliked and isolated.

It became quite clear that all the men were working less hard than they were able to work. Dexterity tests and all other detailed tests showed that they were nowhere near to their full capacity. If an operator did produce more than the informal norm, he was likely to distort the record, purporting to have produced less than he actually had. By this means he piled up a reserve during the week and worked very little on the last day. The operators used many other tricks, such as incorrect reporting and exaggerating the time lost when there was a breakdown. In all, they had a complete system of running their own affairs which bore little relation to the beautifully worked-out production norms sent down from the calculators' offices.

Four main group sentiments regulated the actions of the informal group. The authors summarized them as follows:

1. You should not turn out too much work. If you do, you are a "rate-buster."

2. You should not turn out too little work. If you do, you are a "chiseler."

3. You should not tell a supervisor anything that will react to the detriment of an associate. If you do, you are a "squealer."

4. You should not attempt to maintain social distance or act officious. If you are an inspector, for example, you should not act like one.

These rules of conduct were enforced by the giving or withholding of approval by the fellow members of the group. In the authors' words: "The individual's position in the group was in large part determined by the extent to which his behavior was in accord with these sentiments." But this assertion was reinforced by a detailed examination of the relationships. This was carried out by making use of the sociomatic diagram, one of the first occasions on which it was thus employed.[23] The authors give a series of sociomatic diagrams showing which members of the group participated with one another in games during work breaks, which took part in arguments about opening and shutting windows, which operators traded jobs with or helped which other operators, thus revealing the over-all pattern of friendships and antagonisms. Their analysis showed that the group was in some respects structured in a regular and consistent manner. There were actually two main cliques. One clique had as its members the people who held the most favored position in the group, and this high regard was connected with the fact that they conformed closely with the four group sentiments listed above; the other clique was less highly regarded by the group, mainly because their outputs were smaller, so that they had to some extent to be carried by the higher-status clique. Within these cliques there was noticeable stratification—for example, the "connector" wiremen were of higher status than the "selector" wiremen —partly, it is suggested, because they sat in front of them in the main department, whereas novices started "in back." Wiremen as a group were regarded as somewhat superior to soldermen, but a solderman who served a connector wireman tended to derive some enhanced status from this fact.

In the formal organization, the inspector possessed higher status and on the whole had had more education. Inspectors reflected their supposed superiority by coming to be interviewed in coats and vests, while wiremen and soldermen came in shirts and sweaters, but this assumption of higher status was not accepted by the informal group, who resented their behavior; the inspectors were considered outsiders and had little positive interaction with other members of the group. One inspector was consistently a sociometric isolate and appeared in interaction only through his mutual antagonisms with seven other members of the observation room.

The other isolate was a deviant wireman who was a fast worker but had no regard for group sentiments.

He was hard, enigmatic, self-reliant, and entered very little into relations with other people. In the observation room he tended to isolate himself, and his attitude towards his associates was one of mild contempt. . . . By keeping his output high, he was expressing his disregard for the sentiments of the group. . . . They reciprocated by excluding him from [the clique].[24]

Oddly enough, he felt the need to justify himself before some tribunal, and although he had an exceptionally high output, he reported an even greater output than he produced and claimed a good deal of day work.

Finally we have the case of the most isolated and most disliked of all the wiremen. He followed three of the group sentiments, but he committed the heinous offense of "squealing." In an informal group, most of whose social activities were "wrong" according to the rules of management, this was the most fatal violation of all.

SOCIAL THEORY

Their careful study led the authors to their first full-dress attempt at describing the factory as they found it in terms of a theoretical sociological model. It had become clear to them that nearly all the activities of the observation-room group could be regarded as methods of social control to protect the group from internal indiscretions and from outside interference. It served the latter object by manifesting a strong resistance to change, or threat of change, in working conditions and personal relations. The investigators believed that this protective informal organization was unaffected by the introduction of an observer and an interviewer—they were not observing a situation of their own making. On the other hand, they thought it possible that the situation was being exaggerated by the external fact of the business depression, which the operators might be trying to ward off from themselves. But, while this was true, fear of unemployment was believed to be only one among many factors that led employees everywhere to set up an informal organization as a counter to the formal organization of management.

The conclusion therefore was that to grasp an industrial organization as a whole it is necessary to treat it as a social system. L. J. Henderson's publication in 1935 of Pareto's *General Sociology* had discovered Pareto for the United States. With Durkheim and Simmel, Pareto was undoubtedly one of the main final influences on the Hawthorne experimenters.[25] With this insight of the interdependence of the parts, they aimed to integrate the traditional capitalist theme, namely, that the function of industry is to produce so as to minimize cost and maximize technical efficiency and profits, with the neo-managerial theme that "the enterprise exists for its members, members do not exist for the enterprise."[26] Roethlisberger and Dickson recognize both the economic function and what "is variously described as maintaining employee relations, employee goodwill, co-operation, etc."[27] Thus it is that the industrial concern is confronted simultaneously with problems of external balance and problems of internal equilibrium.

The individual in a social system is constantly engaged in protecting his status in the prestige scale and constantly on his guard against any external change which may threaten the existing social equilibrium. In this situation no item or event can be independent of the prevailing system of sentiments. Thus in the industrial milieu material objects, physical events, wages, and hours of work are not only things in themselves but are also carriers of social value, with socially determined meanings. "If people with double-pedestal desks supervise people with single-pedestal desks, then double-pedestal desks become symbols of status or prestige in the organization."[28] Furthermore, the behavior of no one person in an industrial organization, from the very top to the very bottom, can be regarded as motivated by strictly economic or logical considerations. . . . It is likely that sometimes the behavior of many staff specialists which goes under the name of "efficiency" is as much a manifestation of a very strong sentiment—the sentiment or desire to originate new combinations—as it is of anything strictly logical.[29]

For these reasons, every formal organization, which inadequately represents the real patterns of human interaction, must be supplemented by an informal organization that fills this gap. Thus informal organizations are necessary and are not "bad," as they are sometimes assumed to be. What matters is that there should be a satisfactory relation between the formal and the informal organization, so that the functioning of the formal organization is facilitated.

In this sophisticated presentation we have come a long way from the physiological experiments which initiated the investigations at the Hawthorne Works. This is what provided Elton Mayo with the material for his extremely influential thesis on the functions of human relations skills. But it is only fair to add that in the decades following the publication of *Management and the Worker* there has been strong criticism of the Mayo school on various grounds. The objections are not normally based on disagreements with the methods of investigation or even with the detailed conclusions, but are concerned with the premises and the managerial philosophy they promote.[30]

Mayo's image is of the *adaptive society*, which lacks the consensus of an *established society* and therefore requires deliberate and skillful application if it is to head off or resolve social conflict; this task is to be entrusted to the company, which by the development of managerial skills and by the improvement of communication between managers and employees will dissipate all grievances. It has been noted that the Mayo philosophy leaves no place for the possibility of a basic conflict of interest between management and men, and consequently leaves no role for unions which are prepared to do more than negotiate mutually beneficial contracts with big business. Alternatively, there appears to be no convergence onto the genuine practice of copartnership and joint consultation.

One of the most interesting discussions of these points is contributed by Jeanne Wilensky and her husband.[31] Jeanne Wilensky had previously been a counselor at the Hawthorne works. She speaks with knowledge but not, apparently, with the authorization of the Western Electric Company, and her paper has a nice sense of perspective. As the counseling program was the main practical outcome of the Hawthorne experiments, it is fair to take personnel counseling as a major product of the Mayo philosophy.

The Wilensky paper gives frank consideration to the points raised above. It is pointed out that in the twenties unionism was at a low ebb anyway and, while it is true that the counseling program was launched at a time (1936) of a resurgent labor movement, there is no evidence to connect the two facts. On the other hand, Peter Drucker is quoted as saying: "Most of us in management . . . have instituted [human relations policies] as a means of busting the unions," and it was a fact that "outside" unions had not succeeded in penetrating Hawthorne Works. It is pointed out that in modern society many institutions compete for the worker's allegiance, and the unions, like Mayo's ideal management, move to expand hegemony over more and more areas of the member's life.

The counseling operation at Hawthorne must be seen as part of management's search for tools to cope with the challenge to its power and functions that comes from government, unions, and the recurrent minor crises attendant upon the constant changes in its own internal requirements.[32]

At a different level of abstraction, Arensberg[33] counts himself as one of Mayo's disciples. He sees a certain dissipation of the current which stemmed from Mayo but, in spite of this latter-day divergence,

what unites the [human relations] subschools is their theoretical debt to social anthropology and the formal sociologies of Durkheim, Simmel and Pareto, and their common use of participant observation, free-association interviewing, and techniques of observation derived from anthropological fieldwork. They conceive interviewing not merely as a sounding of individual minds as with workers with attitudes coming from psychology; they use it as a supplement to direct observation in a search, like that of the seeker of culture patterns, for the regularities of actual social behavior. They all agree, with other naturalists, that one gets primary data about behavior of even so talkative an animal as man from what one sees men do; they do not feel happy with those psychologists of social science who seem to be interested only in what men say. They concede meanings to be important, but they insist meanings are interpretable only against the background of behavior.[34]

An important supplement to the discussion appeared in 1958, in the form of a book with the title *Hawthorne Revisited* by Henry A. Landsberger.[35] According to his judgment, the authors of *Management and the Worker* could not be accused of being biased in management's favor, of regarding workers as being spurred on by irrational motives, or of regarding the factory as a suitable replacement for a vanished primitive society. He also absolved them from imagining that the formation of groups is simply instinctive; he believed that the authors correctly saw the informal grouping of workers as their reaction to threats by management.

On the positive side, Landsberger noted that *Management and the Worker*, by focusing on the individual's definition of actual situations and reactions to them, was likely to yield much rich data that could be used for a complete understanding of social action in general and social conflict in particular. Furthermore, the book not only showed that empirical research within industry was possible, but also pointed the way to profound advances in industrial psychology and in the whole field of human relations in industry. The author could not be blamed for the fact that the lessons of the book were in some respects misread at first, and in his opinion the book should now be accepted as a classic starting point from which a new and ultimately sober branch of the social sciences had established itself.

In the context of the present volume some final observations are necessary. The Hawthorne inquiries are in various respects far superior in method to any of the studies previously reported in this book. It is true that the investigators' task was easier because the inquiries were concentrated in one factory and because it was possible for them to use an experimental design, but even when allowance is made for these advantages, it is clear that the techniques both of observation and of interviewing represent a notable advance.

Conceptually also, the convergence onto the industrial situation from three major social sciences—social psychology, social anthropology, sociology—was remarkably fruitful. Several concepts, commonplace today, were first promulgated in the pages of *Management and the Worker* and in Mayo's generalizing volumes. The idea of manifest and latent content, the counterpoint of formal and informal organization, the call for social skills—these and other ideas have left a permanent mark on the thinking of social scientists. It is no coincidence that Homans is a Harvard man or that he used the Bank Wiring Observation Room as one major empirical source in *The Human Group*.[36]

On the whole, therefore, it is right to conclude that *Management and the Worker* is still one of the most important sociological researches ever done. Arensberg lists the considerable literature of research that has grown up as a sequel to *Management and the Worker*, but it is a most peculiar fact that the pioneer research has never been replicated. The pioneers themselves are still in office, but the research momentum seems to be exhausted. This is a familiar story, a great flash of truth and a slow dispersal. The building-up of knowledge, and not least of the knowledge how to carry out research, is an erratic and unpredictable process. Everybody knows of the Hawthorne experiments, though few have mastered them. It is worth while to try, for *Management and the Worker* is a very interesting book and a very rewarding one as well.

7

THE STUDY OF SUBCULTURES

The subject of this chapter is *Street Corner Society*, by William Foote Whyte, first published in 1943.[1] This is a deceptively simple book presented with great charm and modesty, but it is also a book that provides the raw material for an important advance in sociological understanding. It is elegantly written and stylishly put together, and the author himself appears in a very interesting light. As with Lynd, one is aware of the author's development of thought, but Whyte's metamorphosis was more sudden and is more dramatically told. He seems to have had an extraordinarily uncluttered mind when he started his work, and perhaps for this reason he was able to look at small groups from what was then an unusual viewpoint.

In the first edition of *Street Corner Society* Whyte confined himself to a description of his research findings. By 1955, however, when the second edition was published, he added a long and detailed appendix on his research procedures. He explained that in the intervening years he had had to teach the methods he had used in his research, and had found it difficult to describe how and why he had conducted his investigation in the way he had. For this reason, in this second edition he had resolved to describe his procedures. The result is a remarkably revealing, honest account of how Whyte set about his work and of some of the problems he encountered. His presentation is quite different from the rather formal statements in which some other authors have tried to present in a scientific way their techniques and their methodology. This is Whyte's personal statement of how he found himself in Cornerville and how he oriented himself toward his work, and it provides a very useful résumé of this side of his work.

Whyte starts by describing his personal background. He stemmed from a long-established upper-middle-class family. His grandfather had been a professional man, his father a college professor. Whyte himself attended Swarthmore College, where his interests were focused on economics with a special leaning toward social and other reforms and where he also cultivated his flair for writing.

When he graduated from Swarthmore his feeling for social reform was strong, but he had had no contacts outside his own social class. All his friends were solid middle-class professors and students, and, as he says, he knew nothing of the slums, nor of the "gold coast" for that matter. He was experienced solely in his own section of the community and wanted to see firsthand how the less reputable side of society lived. He had already been rather fascinated by rackets and racketeers, for reasons of curiosity rather than of reformism, and he felt a little frustrated that he did not know how racketeers go about their work.

METHOD OF INVESTIGATION

When Whyte graduated from Swarthmore in 1936, he was awarded a three-year Junior Fellowship by the Society of Fellows at Harvard. This appointment allows the Fellow great freedom to do what he wishes, but with the stipulation that he cannot use his research to earn a Ph.D., a provision that may have a rather healthy effect on the type of work done, since the Junior Fellow chooses his research topic for its own sake, rather than for the sake of the Ph.D. that might come out of it.

Whyte felt from the beginning that he wanted to study a slum district because it was there that racketeering supposedly was to be found. In an innocent way, according to his own description, he strolled around Boston (he does not specify the city in his book) and found the section of the city that he calls "Cornerville." To Whyte Cornerville looked just like what a slum should look like. It was typically run down and derelict, and he felt that it was obviously the right place to study. He admits that this was not a scientific method of choosing his study area, but it seems to have been quite successful.

It will be remembered that Whyte was an economist, and he started to plan his inquiry in terms of the features of a slum that would interest an economist. He worked out a rather elaborate program according to which he would investigate such aspects as living standards, housing, marketing, and the distribution and employment pattern of the district. He also took in the political aspects, such as the political structure and its relation to the local rackets and the local police force. He realized that he had to look at patterns of education and recreation, the church and public health, and—of all things, as he himself later comments—social attitudes. He had been doing a little sociological reading which had led him to feel that he ought to study social attitudes.

This constituted an impressive and elaborate program, and Whyte submitted the project to the Society of Fellows at Harvard with a request for ten assistants to carry out the work, with himself as director of research. L. J. Henderson, head of the Fatigue Laboratory at Harvard, who has been mentioned in connection with the Hawthorne studies and who was secretary of the Society of Fellows, called Whyte in and gave the young man a talking to. He reminded Whyte that he knew nothing about research, and that if Harvard should finance a study on this scale, Whyte would become an administrator of the project and would learn very little about how to conduct research. He strongly advised him to withdraw the application and submit instead a modest project for a piece of work that he could do himself. Whyte went away chastened and resentful toward Henderson, but when he had simmered down, he realized that Henderson was right. To learn research, he would have to get his own hands dirty. It would be much better both for himself and for the project if he took on something that he could manage without assistance, and so during the next two months— over the winter of 1936–37—he worked through successive drafts of a scheme for a much more limited study of Cornerville.

He found that these drafts were becoming more and more sociological. In spite of his grounding in economics he was in danger of becoming a sociologist or social anthropologist. In each fresh draft he devoted more attention to local attitudes and displayed more interest in the patterns of friendship between the families in Cornerville. He worked out schemes whereby he would ask a large number of families who their friends were and toward whom they were hostile, in the hope that this would enable him to develop a rigorous sociometric system of analysis of the local society.

He found that in 1936 he could obtain little help from the existing literature. Lloyd Warner's *Yankee City* series[2] had not yet begun to appear, although work in Newburyport had started. There were only two books that seemed relevant. One was Carolyn Ware's *Greenwich Village*,[3] and the other was the Lynds' *Middletown*.[4] He was somewhat disappointed in both of these because they seemed to be rooted in social problems, whereas Whyte was more concerned in the first instance to study the social system. He wanted to see how a local community worked rather than to study its particular social difficulties. He had been reading Durkheim and Pareto. Pareto's *Mind and Society* was the subject of a seminar conducted by L. J. Henderson obviously a very talented man with a great depth of vision that was in no way limited to his own specialty, hematology.

Conrad Arensberg was another junior fellow at Harvard at that time. He had just come back from Ireland, where he had been conducting his fieldwork for the book which he and Solon Kimball subsequently published as *Family and Community in Ireland*.[5] Arensberg had a great influence on Whyte, not only by instructing him in the methods of investigation he had used on the Irish peasant families, but also as a theoretician and as an analyst of social organization. On both these grounds—methodological and theoretical—Arensberg's guidance was of great value to him. Another influence was Elton Mayo, who was conducting a seminar on Pierre Janet. By this means Whyte was introduced to a most influential stream of psychiatric thought. As a subsidiary and practical training Whyte was able to do some interviewing of psychoneurotic patients in a Boston hospital. This was his first experience of how to handle interview situations.

Feeling that he should know more about the social welfare problems he would encounter in Cornerville, Whyte took a course called "Slums and Housing." In connection with this course he did a term study which consisted of a little inquiry, in collaboration with a private agency, aimed at finding out some of the housing problems of the district. Whyte was sent round ringing doorbells and asking the prescribed questions, and he hated this. He felt thoroughly embarrassed at intruding into people's homes; he had very little confidence in the answers he obtained, and he wrote his report perfunctorily, feeling very glad to see the end of that experience. In this way he discovered that this was not the kind of investigation he wanted to make.

His next experience proved a second false start. A young instructor in economics at Harvard told him how he had developed a successful research technique: he went into saloons and engaged in conversation with girls, bought them drinks, and then invited them to tell him their life histories, just as Henry Mayhew had done in England in the nineteenth century. This sounded like a very easy and pleasant procedure, and the young instructor assured Whyte that there were no aftereffects or subsequent obligations. Whyte thought this sounded like a possible method, so he visited a certain Regal Hotel in the district and went into the area where people were sitting around sipping drinks. He soon realized that there were no people sitting by themselves—they were all in twos and threes and parties. This presented a problem, but he noticed one party of two girls and one young man at a table for four, so that there was one empty seat. When he asked, "Do you mind if I sit down here too?" they were ready to throw him out, so he knew that he would have to abandon this procedure.

Next Whyte decided to try an entirely different approach. He went to the settlement house on Norton Street, in the heart of Cornerville. Here he had his first important break. He told the settlement workers what he was looking for, and one of them told him about a man known as "Doc," who had at one time worked in the settlement house. He was a native of Cornerville, knew everybody, and at that time was at a loose end. From her description Doc seemed a highly intelligent man who could be helpful in showing Whyte many of Cornerville's institutions from the inside.

A meeting was arranged with Doc early in 1937. Whyte was immediately impressed by this young man, who was then twenty-nine. He described their meeting as follows:

Doc waited quietly for me to begin as he sank down into a chair. I found him a man of medium height and spare build. His hair was a light brown, quite a contrast to the more typical black Italian hair. It was thinning around the temples. His cheeks were sunken. His eyes were a light blue and seemed to have a penetrating gaze. I began by asking him if the social worker had told him what I was trying to do. "No, she just told me that you wanted to meet me and that I should like to meet you."[6]

Then Whyte launched into a long explanation of what he was doing. Doc didn't seem to worry much about this, but at the end he asked, "Do you want to see the high life or the low life?" Bill Whyte said, "I want to see all that I can. I want to get as complete a picture of the community as possible." Doc answered that he would take Whyte to any place he liked any time. He said, "You won't have to say why you're there. Just say you're my friend, or I'll introduce you as my friend, and all will be well." This proposal seemed so nearly perfect that Whyte could hardly take it in. When Whyte asked if Doc expected any difficulties, Doc said that difficulties would arise only if they went to a gambling den and were arrested. That would be a bit embarrassing, but Whyte could buy himself out for a $5 fine and could give a false name so that he would not get his name in the papers. Doc did not seem to feel that he was doing Whyte any particular favor, but Whyte was thrilled and felt that he was on his way at last, as indeed he was. This was the beginning of his penetration into Cornerville society. In these early months, before he was accepted by the society, he found that all he had to do was to go with Doc. Doc would introduce him, "This is my friend," and Doc, as we shall see, was accepted in a great variety of the Cornerville social groups. Whyte too was an easy mixer, so he was established in no time.

His next problem was to find a place to live. He decided that he ought to live in Cornerville, but he had difficulty in finding suitable accommodations. Finally the editor of an English-language Italian-American weekly newspaper advised him to look up the Martini Restaurant, which sometimes rented rooms upstairs. Whyte found the restaurant, but the proprietor said there were no vacancies. A week or so later, however, when Whyte was having a meal there, he met the editor, who was also eating there. The editor called over the young Martini boy, introduced Whyte as his friend, and the Martinis found a place for him at once. Very soon Whyte became one of the Martini family, even though at that time he spoke no Italian and the Martini parents spoke virtually no English. This was his second experience of the force of a personal introduction.

Cornerville was an almost entirely Italian community, and Whyte started to learn Italian. Although most of the second-generation immigrants, the younger men whom he was hoping to study, spoke English as well as Italian, the recognition that he was taking the trouble to learn Italian was definitely a help with many contacts.

Whyte found that having the Martini household to go back to afforded him great personal relief. He mentions a fact well known to professionals, that conducting social investigations can be a great strain, particularly because in approaching strangers you never know quite how you are going to be received. If you spend your time visiting homes, seeing people who are not dependent on you in any way, you can be fairly sure that, while not many will slam the door in your face, quite a few will be unco-operative, at least until they are won over. And this constant courtship can be exhausting. Bill Whyte soon found that he could go back to the Martini household and relax because he was fully accepted. The restaurant closed at two o'clock on Sunday afternoon, and then the Martini family would have a big, long-drawn-out meal. At these Sunday lunches Whyte was a guest of the family and was not allowed to pay; he drank their wines, and there was a wonderfully relaxed atmosphere.

There was an occasion when he developed a cold that became worse while he was on a visit to Harvard. As he still had a room at Harvard, he decided to stay the night there. When he returned to the Martinis the next day, he found them in a terrible state. "You ought to have told us," they cried. "We were very worried and didn't know what to do." Again he felt that he was being treated like a member of the family.

Thus, with the help of Doc and the Martinis Whyte established himself in Cornerville. He had his first ways into local society, and he had a place to live. Furthermore, he even had some idea of what he was going to study. He was aiming to study ordinary people as they came, focusing his attention not on communities but on people.

The next question was how to set about his task. Whether he knew it or not, the method he was adopting was the method that had already been labeled "participant observation" by Eduard C. Lindeman, a man of genius who wrote brilliantly but left, on the whole, very little impact on the social sciences. Lindeman is remembered for two books. The first was *Social Discovery*, published in 1924, which had no great circulation. Ten years later, in 1933, he wrote, with John J. Hader, a book called *Dynamic Social Research*. His work is eccentric, highly original, but remarkably well vindicated by subsequent events. As has been mentioned earlier,[7] Lindeman was the first to make a clear distinction between objective observation and participant observation. The practice of participant observation was not new. Le Play had lodged with European workers in the mid-nineteenth century, Malinowski had moved in with the Trobriand Islanders, Anderson had experienced hobohemia from within. Each had realized that he had to become part of the community to understand it fully, and Whyte was reaching the same conclusion in Cornerville.

Whyte probably knew something about earlier participant observation, and he would soon be facing its disadvantages as a research technique, namely, that it is so time-consuming and so unsuited for collecting quantitative data. It has never been easy to induce people to become participant observers. They must be dedicated to research, free from domestic ties or other responsibilities. With the lowering of the marriage age it is increasingly difficult to persuade people to desert their routine pattern of life and work long enough to complete a useful study. Students otherwise qualified are probably working for their doctor's degree and have a number of other scholarly duties to attend to. So for various reasons the number of studies done by genuine participant observers is lamentably small and may, unfortunately, remain so.

It may be useful to note certain practical points of technique discovered by Whyte in the course of his work. As has been mentioned, one early discovery was the fact that acceptance by any social group in the district depended far more on the personal relationships he was able to develop than on any rational or logical explanation of what he was doing. As long as he could win the support of key individuals he was fairly sure to be able to obtain what he wanted from other members of the groups he approached. Whyte arrived at this conclusion through his own experience, but he happened upon an important principle that can be applied in a great variety of contexts. A similar conclusion was one of the main findings in a recent study by Katz and Lazarsfeld published as *Personal*

Influence; as the title implies, the importance of the key member of any group is here rather more elaborately studied. The main theme of Katz and Lazarsfeld is that the relevance to the social sciences of the primary group is constantly being rediscovered. Whyte's Norton Street gang is a classical primary group, characterized, in Cooley's definition, by "small size, relative durability, informality, face-to-face contact and manifold, or more or less unspecialized, purpose."[8] As Lewin has shown,[9] a primary group typically includes a gatekeeper, normally the leader of the group, one of whose functions is to monitor the admission of outsiders into the group. When Whyte had satisfied Doc, the gatekeeper of the Norton Street gang, that his intentions were reputable, he did not need to explain to other members of the group exactly what he was proposing to do. The fact that Doc had vouched for him was sufficient.

Instead of trying to explain myself to everyone, I found I was providing far more information about myself and my study to leaders such as Doc than I volunteered to the average corner boy. I always tried to give the impression that I was willing and eager to tell just as much about my study as anyone wished to know, but it was only with group leaders that I made a particular effort to provide really full information.[10]

During this period Whyte found that his relationship with Doc was changing rapidly. Doc was not merely a key informant and a sponsor who arranged introductions for him, he was becoming more and more indispensable to him as a confidant and adviser. This, interestingly, was operating both ways; Whyte was at the same time making Doc rather self-conscious about himself and his place in Cornerville. One day Doc said to him, with complaint in his voice: "You've slowed me up plenty since you've been down here. Now, when I do something, I have to think what Bill Whyte would want to know about it and how I can explain it. Before, I used to do things by instinct."[11] Even though he was doing much the same things as before he was doing them in a much more self-conscious way.

Whyte soon learned how to join in the ordinary street-corner conversations; he was relieved to discover that baseball and sex were the topics of discussion in Cornerville just as they had been in the other societies in which he had lived, and he found no difficulty in joining in such discussions. He knew less about horse racing, and he later regretted that he had not spent more time learning about it. But he sometimes wondered whether the kind of life he was leading, hanging around street corners with Doc and his friends, was an active enough process to be labeled "research." He felt a bit guilty sometimes that he was not filling up schedules and seemed mainly to be concerning himself with rather trivial items; perhaps he ought at least to be asking questions and probing a little deeper so as to speed up his accumulation of data.

One night he did try to probe more deeply, with disastrous results. He happened to be present at a meeting where a man was entertaining the company by retailing marvelous reminiscences of his life as a gambling operator. People were making comments and asking questions, and finally Bill Whyte entered in by saying, "I suppose the cops were all paid off?" The gambler's jaw dropped. Glaring at Whyte, he stated vehemently that no policemen had been paid off. The subject was dropped immediately. When they were alone the next day, Doc said to Whyte: "Go easy on that 'who,' 'what,' 'why,' 'when,' 'where,' stuff, Bill. You ask these questions and people will clam up on you. If people accept you, you can just hang around and you'll learn the answers in the long run without even having to ask the questions."[12] It is, of course, this feature that distinguishes participant observation from more active intervention —hanging around so that you become, in a sense, part of the furniture. As a matter of fact, after Whyte had been in Cornerville only a few weeks, he was greatly flattered when Doc said: "You're just as much of a fixture around this street corner as that lamppost."[13] Whyte knew then that he had arrived and that he was accepted.

He found, however, that the role of the participant observer entails many delicate dilemmas. It is one thing to be accepted, but, as Whyte soon realized, this did not mean that he had to play their game all the way; a participant observer does not have to pretend to be exactly like the subjects he is studying. One day Whyte thought he would enter into the spirit of the small talk by letting forth a stream of obscenities and profanities. "The talk came to a momentary halt as they all stopped to look at me in surprise. Doc shook his head and said: 'Bill, you're not supposed to talk like that. That doesn't sound like you.' "[14]

Another time Whyte was involved in a political compaign in Cornerville. On Election Day he voted when the polls opened and then reported for duty at the candidate's headquarters. In the morning he was assigned to another ward, but in the afternoon he was sent back to Cornerville, where he began hearing alarming reports that his candidate was losing rather badly because the opponent was organizing an efficient system of repeaters. "He was said to have a fleet of taxicabs cruising about his ward so that each of his repeaters would be able to vote in every precinct of the ward. It became clear that, if we did not steal the election ourselves, this low character would steal it from us."[15] So Whyte was told to become a repeater; he did this with considerable qualms but conscientiously, voting three more times for his candidate. He was nearly caught, but luckily the polling office at which his vote was challenged was one in which his side could fix irregularities and he was all right. But there again, although he avoided a dramatic scandal, becoming a repeater did not help him; he could have accomplished just as much as a participant observer if he had not tried to play the game of the local politicians. The politicians would not have withheld facts from him, because his role was independent of theirs.

On the other hand, the participant observer is not invisible. Occasionally he will be fairly insignificant; Lasswell's[16] example is being present at a spectacle, where the observer is one of a hundred thousand spectators, so that any one individual counts for little. In many other situations, however, to become a participant means taking a role in an organization. For example, Whyte was asked at one time to become secretary of the Italian Community Club in Cornerville. His first impulse was to decline, for he thought it would be inconsistent with his observing role to be so active a participant. On reflection, however, he realized that this post would give him an opportunity to handle all the club documents and to make copies for himself; he therefore accepted nomination. On various other occasions Whyte reveals a certain commitment to groups in Cornerville, so that he cares about his performance and is proud of his achievements. This reveals a healthy, human side to his character. On one occasion, when he was bowling, it became very important to him that he win; when he did win, he was very much pleased with himself.

It is also clear that in various episodes Whyte was regarded by the corner boys as one of the group, someone whom they knew to be different from themselves but whom they accepted for the most part as an ally because he was interested in the same objectives. This went so far that he applies to himself a quip borrowed from another sociologist, remarking that he was turning from a non-participant observer to a nonobserving participant.[17]

At this stage in his narrative Whyte interjects a brief account of how he organized his notes. It is not particularly profound, but it is quite interesting. It is clear that he kept copious notes. Though he was just hanging about street corners much of the time, he would go to his room intermittently to write up what had been happening. He spent most mornings, when not much was going on outside, recording what had happened the day before. At first he kept these notes chronologically, but they soon became unmanageable in this form. Then he had an interesting choice: whether to file his material under topics (politics, the church, rackets, the family, and so on), or to file it according to the group he was with at the time referred to. By this stage in his research it had begun to be clear to him that the groups were crucial to his conceptualization, and he therefore decided to file his data by social groups. This decision undoubtedly had a considerable effect on his thinking, for, although he had already begun to contemplate an analysis in terms of the Norton Boys and the Italian Community Club and the other Cornerville groups, the fact that he filed his material according to that classification would have made it difficult for him subsequently to rethink his analysis along other lines. He did, however, supplement his classification by a cross-indexing system, and he had the advantage that the material recorded had been collected mainly by himself.

After two years in Cornerville, Whyte married, and marriage changed his life in various ways. He left the Martini household, but as his wife was also eager to live in Cornerville, the couple found an apartment in a Sicilian section not very far from Norton Street. The only stipulation the bride had made was that there be a bathtub and a toilet in their apartment. Before his marriage Whyte had had to go back to Harvard to have a bath from time to time, but this arrangement would not suffice from then on.

Another of Whyte's preoccupations at this time was that the end of his three-year Harvard fellowship was in sight, and he had to prepare an application for the next period. This was quite good for him because it forced him to organize the mass of material he had been collecting. This period of stocktaking seemed to him to be tremendously hurried, since he had only nine months in which to do it.

Faced with the sudden task of having to organize his material, he began to realize more clearly that what he had been trying to do was something entirely different from that attempted in previous community studies such as *Middletown*. For one thing, his data collection was extremely uneven. There was, for example, very little information about the church. Even his knowledge of racketeering—the subject that had always interested him—was quite inadequate. On the other hand, his material was often much more intimate than that of *Middletown*. *Middletown* was written about people in general in that community. It was at a high level of generalization and was little concerned with particular individuals or groups. The X family are the only individuals whose activities and characteristics were described at length, and then in the second volume. From Whyte's observations it would have been impossible to write a section on "building a home" or "getting a living." And he realized that it was not his aim to give a generalized description of any aspect of Cornerville life. He was interested in the social system, particularly in the small local social system—how small groups of people structured themselves, what leadership consisted of, and how leaders emerged. He also felt that previous investigators had paid inadequate attention to the process of change. It was true that the two *Middletowns* had spanned the years and had provided some indication of the changes that had taken place, but Whyte was interested in the week-by-week dynamics of the growth and the disintegration of small societies. He realized that time was one of the key elements in his study.

It will be remembered that one criterion for any valid sociological research laid down by the authors of *The Polish Peasant* was that it must embrace as one of its central themes the idea of change. Although he does not say so, Whyte would undoubtedly have supported that viewpoint.

Whyte applied for an extension of his fellowship and was given one extra year, not the three years he had asked for. Characteristically he feels that perhaps it was a good thing that he was not enabled to carry on for the three years. He could have made his study more elaborate and detailed, but it would have been just a fuller version of the same analysis.

In the second phase of his study he concentrated on certain points which his stocktaking had shown had been rather lacking in the first study, though they had been mentioned in his original application. He made a special point of studying racketeering, thus finally satisfying his interest in the subject. It was undoubtedly an advantage that he had meanwhile clarified his ideas on group structure and leadership function, as he was thus able to apply them to the social structure of racketeering.

Whyte also developed an interesting technique in his studies of the Cornerville Social and Athletic Club. The club was one hangout for Tony Cataldo, a local boss racketeer, and Whyte joined it as a means of getting to know Cataldo. This object failed, as Tony did not frequent the club. But Whyte hung on, and happened upon the quite simple technique which he called "positional map-making." There were about fifty members in the club, and Whyte's informal methods of analyzing the interactions within the much smaller Norton Street gang were not applicable. He regarded this much larger group as a methodological challenge. The assumption on which he operated was the behaviorist one that members who consorted together would line up on the same side when decisions were taken. He therefore undertook to record the groupings of members.

This idea may have suggested itself to Whyte in the first instance because he could see into the club from the front window of his apartment, which was across the street. Unfortunately, however, his apartment was two flights up and he could see only half the room. So he went to the club continually in order to memorize where each person was and whom he was talking to, playing cards with, or otherwise interacting with; after a while Whyte would go to the washroom and write in his notebook what he had observed. In this way he prepared 106 complete maps of the grouping of people in the club.

At that time a situation in the club was producing considerable tension; two factions were not on good terms with each other. Whyte wanted to see how far this factionalism was reproduced in the groupings, and he found good behavioral confirmation of the split. Only 40 of the 106 positional maps he had recorded showed groupings containing members of both factions, and only 10 of the 106 contained two or more members of each faction. In some groups there might be one man with the rival faction; more than one outsider was extremely rare. Thus, Whyte's simple technique stems from objective rather than participant observation. In its theoretical implications it conforms closely to his thinking on clique formation, which will be discussed later.

Whyte used this club for another set of objective observations. This time the focus was on influentials. He set out to record "events in which one individual originated activity for one or more others —where a proposal, suggestion or request was followed by a positive response."[18] His results for dyads were negative, in that the member of the pair who was believed by the observer to be the subordinate partner in the relationship was found to originate activity approximately as often as the superordinate member. With triads and larger groups, however, the hierarchical structure of the organization (in terms of activity origination) clearly emerged.

This, then, is a brief résumé of Whyte's field and his analytical methods during his active period in Cornerville. When, many years later, he looked back on this period, he felt that he had learned a great deal about conducting field research, and that the approach he evolved had proved worth while though expensive. In the first place, the study took a long time because of Whyte's lack of field experience or even of relevant educational background. But it took a long time also because he believed in acquiring an intimate familiarity with people and situations. Furthermore, he was concerned to study a group through time. He felt that this had been useful not only because it allowed for changes to develop in the situation, but also because it allowed his own thoughts and theoretical understanding to mature gradually.

It is of course clear, to author and to reader, that between Whyte's starting point and his end result there is a drastic change of direction in his research orientation. He justifies this on the grounds that he was engaged in an exploration into territory that nobody else had fully explored before. But he does add a point that has already been made in this book, that although it is right to ask research workers to decide as carefully as possible what they intend to do before starting work, it does not necessarily follow that those who do precisely what they set out to do are the best research workers. It might mean that there has been little development of thought in the course of the work. It does not, of course, follow that there is any excuse for slovenly thinking at the start or at any other stage, but flexibility, alertness for the unexpected observation, and the exploitation of unforeseen opportunities—these are the signs of a good researcher and not merely of an erratic one.

Whyte's concluding paragraph states:

Although I could not cover all Cornerville, I was building up the structure and functioning of the community through intensive examination of some of its parts—*in action*. I was relating the parts together by observing events between groups and between group leaders and the members of the larger institutional structures (of politics and the rackets). I was seeking to build a sociology based upon observed interpersonal events. That, to me, is the chief methodological and theoretical meaning of *Street Corner Society*.[19]

SUBSTANTIVE RESULTS

These rather large claims can be tested only by an examination of the substantive results and conceptual advances achieved by the author. We shall therefore proceed next to a study of the substance of his book.

Cornerville, the slum district in which this study was located, was inhabited almost exclusively by Italian immigrants and their children. To the rest of the city it remained dangerous, depressing, and remote even though geographically it was only a few minutes' walk from the fashionable central areas of Boston. During World War II outsiders feared that the Italians would be susceptible to fascism just as they had traditionally been at odds with the rest of the community, making Cornerville the home of racketeers and corrupt politicians, an area of poverty and crime, a center of subversive beliefs and practices.

While these stereotyped impressions of Cornerville society could be confirmed by appropriate social and criminal statistics, they do not give the whole story. The news that filters from Cornerville is built of moments of crisis and suggests congenital disorganization, whereas the insider finds in Cornerville a highly organized and integrated social system.

While the first-generation immigrants continued to organize themselves along the lines of *paesani*, people from the same Italian town, this division was fading as the second generation grew up. Within the ranks of the younger men Whyte detected two main divisions—the corner boys and the college boys.

Corner boys are groups of men who center their social activities upon particular street corners, with their adjoining barbershops, lunchrooms, poolrooms or clubrooms. They constitute the bottom level of society within their age group, and at the same time they make up the great majority of the young men of Cornerville. During the depression most of them were unemployed or had only irregular employment. Few had completed high school, and many of them had left school before finishing the eighth grade. The college boys are a small group of young men who have risen above the corner-boy level through higher education. As they try to make plans for themselves as professional men, they are still moving socially upward.[20]

Both corner boys and college boys were "little guys" even in Cornerville. Behind them lay the "big shots," the racketeers and politicians who dominated the activities of the district. To understand Cornerville it was necessary to observe both the little guys and the big shots.

Typical of the corner boys were the Nortons. They were Doc's gang, and the gang was built around Doc. When Whyte went to Cornerville, Doc was twenty-nine. He had lived in Cornerville all his life, and in his childhood there had been a kids' gang in Norton Street for every significant difference in age. Doc's gang had included Nutsy, Danny, and a number of others. Doc had been a puny child, his left arm shriveled by polio, but he had always wanted to assert himself. The kids established the hierarchy by fighting. Thus by beating up Nutsy, Doc became head of his gang. Nutsy had been the leader, but after the fight he was content to be Doc's lieutenant. Although Doc won the leadership by physical prowess, both within the gang and during the "rallies" when his boys were clashing with another gang, according to the narrative he was not interested in hurting others for the sake of hurting them.

The childhood gang had broken up as its members settled down to school. Doc did well at school, and after the third year of high school took a job with a stained-glass firm. He was promised rapid advancement until the depression hit the firm. It was because Doc thus became unemployed that he fell back on the habit of spending nearly all his time on the street corner. This was in the early spring of 1937. The implication is that if it had not been for the depression this street-corner society of grown men would not have constituted itself.

After Doc had started frequenting the corner he was soon joined by others who had great respect for him. There was Nutsy, his childhood rival and in 1937 a part-time postal employee. There was Danny, another childhood friend, and his companion Mike, who were partners in a crap game and operated a small speakeasy next to "the corner." There was Long John, a rather dull young man with a criminal record who was being "reformed" by Danny and Mike in return for small services in their crap game. There was Angelo, a shy youth with few friends, a keen violinist, who was directly befriended by Doc and introduced by him into the gang; and there were about seven others who joined the gang in various ways.

These thirteen men became accustomed to acting together, and a strong system of group loyalties grew up on the basis of obligations to help one another. Within the group there were distinctions in rank. Doc, Danny, and Mike held the top positions. They were older than most of the others, but Whyte attributed their ascendancy to their "greater capacity for social movement." While the followers were restricted to the narrow sphere of one corner, Doc, Danny, and Mike had friends in many other groups and were well known and respected throughout a large part of Cornerville.[21] They were called upon to protect their followers in encounters outside their ordinary circle. Furthermore, these three were respected for their intelligence and powers of self-expression. In this adult group these capacities had supplanted the fighting prowess on which the kids' hierarchy had been based, but their past fighting reputations might have sustained their positions.

Of the three, Doc was the undisputed leader. The Nortons had always been Doc's gang, and his position was fortified because he could spend more time with the gang while Danny and Mike were running their crap game. This enterprise earned them status as businessmen, whereas their clients the crapshooters were held to be suckers of very low status. Long John was unable to stay away from the game, on which he regularly lost his week's earnings, and this told against him in the group. He had little authority over the followers, but his position near the head of the hierarchy was artificially kept by the patronage of the three leaders (Figure 5).

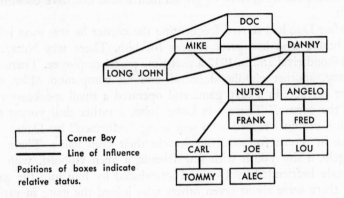

FIGURE 5. The Nortons, spring and summer, 1937.

Adapted from William F. Whyte, *Street Corner Society*, by permission of the University of Chicago Press. Copyright 1943, 1955 by the University of Chicago.

The case of Nutsy illustrates another interesting feature of the status system of the Nortons. As has been mentioned, historically Nutsy was the first leader of the Nortons, and in 1937 he was still a man of moderate importance. He was beginning to lose standing, however, because he was going steadily with a "no good" girl. A corner boy is not expected to be chaste, but in this case there was a distinct danger that he might marry the girl. This was much criticized, and he was consequently tending to withdraw from the gang.

There follow in the book a number of stories that illustrate how quite straightforward incidents could be made to reveal important features of the social system of the Nortons. The first of these stories concerns various bowling matches. The Nortons did not normally participate in a systematic way in team games, but occasionally they did field a team. Once only, a match was arranged between the Nortons and the Italian Community Club, the organ of the college boys led by Chick Morelli, of which more will be told later. Although Doc was a member of the Italian Community Club and three other Nortons had been voted into the club on his recommendation, to the corner boys as a whole this club was regarded as "high-toned" and a home of snobbery and conceit. It therefore became a point of high principle to show that the Nortons could beat the club.

Feeling ran high. The Nortons shouted at the club bowlers and made all sorts of noises to upset their concentration. The club members were in high spirits when they gained an early lead but had little to say as the Nortons pulled ahead to win by a wide margin.[22]

Quite openly this victory was regarded as satisfying because it put Chick Morelli and his lieutenant Tony Cardio "in their places." Equally clearly it was not their specific skills at bowling that was under attack but their social positions and ambitions.

Whyte goes on to suggest that a player's scores are determined largely by the confidence his fellows have in him. "If they do not believe in him, the bowler has their adverse opinion as well as his own uncertainty to fight against. When that is said, it becomes necessary to consider a man's relation to his fellows in examining his bowling record."[23] This point is illustrated by the cases of Frank and Alec. Frank had been a semiprofessional ballplayer, but he had become unemployed and had gradually drifted down in the group. He came to depend on Alec for money, and this preyed upon his mind, for, although he bowled as frequently as anyone else, he was never a serious contender for the first team.

Alec, on the other hand, was bowling very well and boasted that he could beat any man on the first team. Nevertheless, although he made the highest single score of the season, he could never do well under pressure, when the whole group was assembled. For example, Doc decided to climax the season with an individual competition among the members of the clique.

Alec let it be known that he intended to show the boys something. . . . After the first four boxes, Alec was leading by several pins. He turned to Doc and said, "I'm out to get you boys tonight." But then he began to miss, and, as mistake followed mistake, he stopped trying. Between turns, he went out for drinks, so that he became flushed and unsteady on his feet. He threw the ball carelessly, pretending that he was not interested in the competition. His collapse was sudden and complete; in the space of a few boxes he dropped from first to last place.[24]

The group was accustomed to apply sanctions to ensure that the performance of the individual was congruent with his status.

I asked Doc what would have happened if Alec or Joe had won. "They wouldn't have known how to take it. That's why we were out to beat them. If they had won, there would have been a lot of noise. Plenty of arguments. We would have called it lucky—things like that. We would have tried to get them in another match and then ruin them. We would have to put them in their places."[25]

Bill Whyte joined in the bowling, and partly because he was a semi-outsider and partly because of the high status conferred on him by his friendship with Doc, no one jeered at him. He was permitted to win on occasion and was subjected only to good-natured kidding, being hailed jocularly as "the Champ" or even as "the Cheese Champ."

Although there was undoubtedly a measure of social control of bowling performance, Whyte might well have examined more carefully the alternative hypothesis (which he does mention later)[26] that bowling prowess was one of the requisites of the leadership role among the Nortons. Otherwise it is a little hard to credit the fact that the four leaders—Doc, Danny, Mike, and Long John—were also the Nortons' four best bowlers on critical occasions.

The next narrative concerns the Nortons' relationship with the Aphrodite Club. This club consisted of a dozen girls, most of them attractive and all well dressed, who met once a week in the Norton Street Settlement House, and went to plays, held social events, and organized trips to places of interest. The girls, who "had a great respect for education," had originally become very friendly with the members of the Italian Community Club. The men found the girls attractive, but their real aim was to make contacts outside Cornerville, and the two clubs were slowly drifting apart.

At this point the Nortons came on the scene. Doc and three other Nortons who were also members of the Italian Community Club already knew the girls, but the Nortons as a whole still professed hostility toward them, finding them "high-toned" and conceited. In June, 1937, Whyte heard them discussing Carrie, one of the most attractive Aphrodite girls.

Nutsy: She's a good-looking girl, but I don't like her.
Frank: If you took three hours to make up your face, you'd be good-looking too.
Long John: She has tough pins [legs]. Did you ever notice the pins on her? That's why she always wears such low dresses.

Joe Dodge: She goes for anybody with a little money. She likes you if you have a car. I like to drive by her in my car and stick my nose in the air. . . . She's just an alley cat.[27]

Finally Doc was persuaded to arrange a meeting with them. By a ruse he arranged a bowling match, the girls probably believing that they were to bowl with the Community Club rather than with the "tougher bunch" of Nortons. They do not seem to have resented this deception, however, and the evening was a great success. For several weeks members of the two groups saw one another almost every night.

This had some important consequences for the Nortons. For one thing, they began the habit of using the settlement house regularly, either with the girls or in the hope of meeting them. This was not encouraged by the social workers, who regarded them as undesirable roughnecks and tried to patronize them. Long John, who had traveled the greatest social distance to go into the house, was the first one to drop out, but two weeks after their first evening in the game room all the Nortons had deserted the settlement.

Nevertheless, they took their activities with the girls very seriously. Undoubtedly one motive was to draw the girls away from the Community Club. In this they were soon successful, but their victory was due to the Community Club's fading interest in the girls.

The only exception was Helen, the most attractive of the girls, made particularly desirable because Tony Cardio, Chick's lieutenant in the Community Club, was infatuated with her. Later on,

Alec was always boasting about his prowess with the women. Doc paid little attention to him, but the other boys felt that something should be done to put him in his place. One night in April they were kidding Alec, when, as Doc says, Alec challenged him. "If you're such a great lover, I challenge you to show your stuff."

I said, "Alec, I might not be as handsome as you are, and I don't have all the hair that you have, but I can outbull you any day."

Alec says, "No! No!"

"Well," I said, "I'm older now and I don't want to take a girl away from a man just to show I can do it."

But then Danny says, "Doc, I think you're slipping."

Maron! When Danny says that, I must do something. He only said it to steam me up, but I said, "All right, Danny, I pick Helen. Saturday night. You watch. . . ."

Alec wasn't there to see it Saturday night. That was too bad. We were bowling one floor below the girls. I went up to see Helen, and I asked her to come down. I had something to tell her. In a few minutes she came down—by herself. She sat next to me all the evening, the only girl among all those fellows. Danny was impressed. Later he told me, "Doc, you're still the great lover."[28]

Unfortunately Alec, not being there, remained unimpressed and continued to boast. First Doc lectured him, and when this failed, he issued a challenge. He asked Alec to name the girl that he fitted best with. Alec named Mildred, and Doc told him to take her out twice more and after that he, Doc, would take her away from him. Alec protested that it could not be done, but when Doc persisted, Alec took Doc aside and said that he loved Mildred and wanted to marry her. Doc did not really believe him but "that's the screwy code around here. If he says he loves her, I have to leave her alone."[29] Later Alec proposed to Mildred, and when she refused him he lost interest in the Aphrodite girls.

Meanwhile Doc's courtship of Helen continued. When he took up Alec's first challenge and began to "bull" her, he realized that he was running some risks. It would have been easy to fall in love with her, but he could not afford to get married. The other girls encouraged the romance. In April, Helen was ill. Another girl tried to persuade Doc to send her flowers. He could not afford to do this, but Danny and Long John clubbed together and paid $5 for a dozen tea roses, which they sent to Helen in Doc's name. To Doc it seemed a great deal of money, and he had mixed feelings about it. It helped his standing with Helen, but it would make her think that he was serious, so he told her that the boys had done it on his behalf. She continued to pursue him, but she classed him with the Community Club boys, Chick Morelli and Tony Cardio, and she tactlessly snubbed his corner boys. It was Doc who had brought the Nortons and the Aphrodite girls together, and now in various ways the girls were tending to split the Nortons. So Danny and Mike acted upon Doc, forcing him to choose between them and the girls. He responded, and by fall the two groups had drifted apart back to their former distant relationship.

Viewed in this light, it is clear that the girls were a means to an end of gaining or maintaining prestige in the group. Alec had acted out of turn to claim more than his due, and, just as when he had challenged the leaders at bowling, he had to be kept in his place. Doc's leadership was recognized and reinforced by his association with Helen, but it must not be allowed to undermine the unity of the group.

The third episode relating to the Nortons centered on Doc's political campaign. Doc was now thirty and had to make a decision about his future. Apart from the skill he had acquired in the stained-glass plant, he had no training, but his intelligence, popularity, and qualities of leadership seemed to fit him for a political career, and many of his friends had encouraged him to run. Finally he yielded and agreed to run for representative in the state legislature. But his decision to do this only increased his personal problems. First, he felt that he must get a job, not only to raise money for his campaign but also to give himself some standing. He had to find a job in Cornerville, as otherwise he would not be eligible to campaign in the ward. He was helped by a vocational-guidance worker at the settlement house to get a month's job in a stained-glass concern. He did well but failed to win a definite promise of a permanent job, so the net result was bitter disappointment. He was fast losing self-confidence and began having dizzy spells.

Therefore, when Doc's political campaign got under way, he was still without a job. Mike did wonders in enlisting help for him, but Doc did nothing to help himself, even though he was constantly being pressed to go into action, to "form a committee, draw up a platform, organize a dance to raise some money, get things rolling."[30] Nevertheless, he was still considered a powerful candidate until suddenly in July, without consulting anybody, he withdrew from the contest.

Doc saw this failure as the logical consequence of his years of unemployment, which had sapped his confidence and had circumscribed his social activities. A successful politician must constantly widen his sphere of social influence, meeting new groups and participating in their activities. Doc's circle was not widening but narrowing, and he realized it.

The news of his withdrawal hit the Nortons with devastating effect. Doc had not even capitalized on his withdrawal, as he could have done, by demanding concessions from his rivals. To his gang, he had failed them as a leader, and other corner-boy leaders who had supported him as candidate also suffered a loss of prestige.

A general realignment was necessitated. The corners where he had been strong turned to other candidates, and even his own boys switched their support. For the first time in years Doc did not even lead them in these decisions. He withdrew entirely and for hours at a time sat alone in the back of Stefani's dimly lighted barbershop.

Years later Whyte decided to seek out his characters. Among these was Doc, and on several occasions the two men met again. This sequel showed clearly the extent to which Doc's decline had been a consequence of the depression of the 1930's. He was drawn into the war boom and did very well until the postwar cutback. Later he found his feet in an electronics plant, where by the end of 1953 he had progressed to a supervisory position. Although his lack of technical skill set a limit to his advancement, he was able to apply in the factory some of the social skill he had acquired in Cornerville. He explained: "On the technical side, I stink. The only place I really shine is where I have to go around and talk the foreman into running a new order ahead of the one he was planning to run. I can do that without getting him upset."[31]

Some mention has already been made of Chick Morelli, the leader of the Italian Community Club. A whole chapter is devoted to Chick and his club presenting Chick as exercising a type of leadership radically different from that displayed by Doc.

Chick Morelli gave his own account of his early days. He was born in Italy near Naples and came to the United States at the age of eight. His father had immigrated several years before and had established himself as a small storekeeper. Soon afterward he died, leaving Chick with his mother and elder sister to face a period of struggle.

Chick appears to have worked hard and played hard. He soon found ways of earning good money, which he spent on dances and parties, but he always studied keenly as well. He took an academic course in high school, for he soon realized that learning was a gateway to personal advancement. He was also very sensitive about his Italian accent and about his ignorance of correct behavior. Fortunately he had a great talent for imitation, and as he was attracted to people of a higher social and educational level than his own, he had opportunities to learn from them how to conduct himself. Soon he was able to observe lapses in the behavior of others.

After a while, I began to notice that there were other people that didn't know as much as I did. I would be in an elevator with some fellows and girls in a hotel, and I would notice that the other fellows didn't have their hats off. Or I would be sitting at a table with another fellow when a girl came up. I would get up, and he wouldn't. I began to think I wasn't so bad off. . . .[32]

The other feature in Chick's career was his capacity for seizing opportunities. His mother's encouragement and his own endeavors helped him into college. At St. Patrick's College the Italians constituted a small minority, and the college taught Spanish but not Italian. Chick organized an Italian Academy at the college, becoming its first president, and he persuaded the dean of the college to start a course in Italian.

Chick himself was taking a law course. He expected to go on to St. Patrick's Law School, but a lawyer suggested that he try for Ivy Law School.

"I said: 'I know my own limitations. I couldn't get into a place like that. I'll be content to stay in my own station.' He told me: 'Chick, don't be a jackass. If you've got the marks, you can get into Ivy, and a degree from Ivy will mean much more to you than one from St. Patrick's' "[33]

So he decided, again being helped by his mother, and in spite of financial strain he stuck to it, thus consolidating his early social and professional advance.

The roots of Chick's Italian Community Club can be traced as far back as junior high school. When he was in the ninth grade his home-room teacher had a system of choosing her best students and making them sit together. Chick, who was naturally one of these, immediately perceived that his clique was the nucleus of a group of self-improving youngsters who could help one another. Eight and a half years later Chick called on these men to organize the Italian Community Club. The first meeting of the club took place at the Norton Street Settlement House in January, 1937. Chick was elected president, and he outlined his grandiose aims for the club. These are described in the minutes of the first meeting.

Mr. Morelli roughly outlined to the assembled group the purpose of the assembly. He stated that Italians have made a brilliant reputation in the civilization of the world; hence we should consider ourselves a vital element of the American race.

We must create social bonds, principally with our intellectual equals, for chiefly among these can the influence of the Italian mind in the fields of Arts and Sciences be fully realized.

Our next aim is to instruct our community as to their duty concerning amelioration of their own educational and sectional interests.

The president [in the second meeting] presented his outline of the year's activities. The outline proposed points that were social as well as intellectual in nature:

1. Weekly talks by the members in their respective fields preferably.
2. Monthly articles for the [local newspapers], one article a month by every individual member.
3. A monthly forum for Italian parents.
4. Production of a play.
5. A debate.
6. Oratorical contests for nonmembers.

Social program:

1. Monthly socials for the members.
2. Smokers for intellectuals of Italian extraction.
3. Dance for benefit of Italian Orphans' Home.
4. Bi-monthly stag parties.
5. Fraternity pin.[34]

It will be observed that this program ranges from the sublime to the ridiculous, but its general level appears almost absurdly ambitious. However, the club had realistic aims as well, and it appears that Morelli was aware from the beginning that his real objective was the social betterment of the members. By this means Chick and his friends would be able to improve their social status, and the improvement of Cornerville could be regarded as a subsidiary practical aim. The members debated for some time whether to limit their club to college boys or to admit outsiders. It was finally decided to leave this question open so that at their discretion they could accept noncollege boys, and it was on these grounds that Doc and one or two other corner boys were admitted.

At this age Chick was never the kind of leader his group enjoyed following. His strength was that he was very fertile with new ideas, but he was anything but tactful. In fact, he did not approve of tact and was therefore always running into difficulty with the other members. On a number of occasions there were challenges to his authority and even motions to impeach him, and all round he had a checkered career as president. It is significant that Doc, who

could have swung his noncollege men against Chick, always supported him in times of crisis. He said that, while he had no love
for Chick Morelli, he was unwilling to subject him to humiliation.

The Italian Community Club carried on with its original program
for the first season and then closed down for the summer; it was
a rather reduced membership that reappeared in September at the
beginning of the second season. Chick looked around the assembly
at the first meeting and announced:

"I know I am not diplomatic all the time, I know I have lots of
enemies in the club."

[One member] said . . . under his breath, "They are legion."

"I'm glad," continued Chick, "that I have enemies in the club; it
makes it more interesting. . . . Even the greatest diplomats have enemies.
Who am I to be without enemies? . . . But one thing I want to tell you
fellows, my interests are always for the good of the Italian Community
Club. I don't want you to forget that."[35]

On the strength of this he produced from his fertile store the
idea that the Club should sponsor an oratorical test for high-school
students and offer a prize for the winner. The orators had to speak
on subjects like "The Rise of the Italian-American Youth," "The
Italian Contribution to American Civic Life," or "A Famous Italian-
American." As there were no other proposals, this suggestion was
accepted, but enthusiasm was lacking, and the idea petered out and
was finally called off. Characteristically, Chick blamed the tepid
response on the lack of spirit and the unco-operative attitude of his
fellow members. But when he launched a tirade to this effect, another
member of the club "interrupted to charge that Chick himself was
responsible for the failure of the contest, since he tried to be a
dictator instead of a leader."[36]

But Chick soon recovered his poise. Whenever he seemed to be
slipping he came forward with a brilliant new idea. In spite of his
cavalier behavior Chick had a great sense of dedication. This was
illustrated in the complicated maneuvers that took place during the
October election. At that time hostility between two cliques in the
club was openly displayed, but Chick made a deal with Doc, who
led the noncollege clique, that a certain Joe Gennusi, a budding
politician, should be president and that Art Tester, Doc's nominee,
should be vice-president. Joe Gennusi was unanimously elected

president, but when the nominations for vice-president were called, Tony Cardio was nominated as well as the "deal" candidate, Art Tester. The ballots were passed out, marked, and collected, and the vote was announced as a tie between Art Tester and Tony Cardio. As president, Chick Morelli was required to cast the deciding vote. To everyone's surprise, in spite of his prior agreement with Doc and in spite of his running fight with Tony Cardio, who had earlier tried to impeach him, President Morelli cast his vote for Tony Cardio. Everyone regarded this as a great double cross, but when Doc challenged him with this afterward, Chick merely said that when the time came to nominate he felt that Tony was the more capable and intelligent man and was better able to serve the interests of the club.

It could have been that Chick was swayed by the fact that Tony Cardio was a college boy and Art Tester was not, so somehow he could not help voting for the person who seemed to him to have the highest qualifications. But under Tony Cardio disintegration set in. Chick Morelli pulled out in good time and started a more or less regular political career, working as an agent for the attorney general. He was gradually finding his feet in the larger world, and his early endeavors were ready for the payoff.

SOCIAL THEORY

These narratives can be taken as illustrating the interwoven but distinctive lives of Doc and his corner boys, on the one hand, and Chick and his college boys, on the other. It is clearly a matter of great practical and theoretical importance to account for the differences between them.* Whyte's analysis of this central question starts with the supposition that the differences in structure between the "corner boys" and the "college boys" is due to the different social levels from which the members of the two groups were drawn. He detected three social levels, the corner boys at the bottom, the college boys at the top, and the "intermediaries," who were not only intermediate in social level but were also the means of communica-

* I am indebted to Sidney Aronsen, of Brooklyn College, for his stimulating contribution to the following discussion.

tion between the top and bottom levels. He describes a "typical" incident on Norton Street one evening when two college boys, two corner boys, and two intermediaries happened to meet. The intermediaries were noncollege men who had nevertheless been voted into the Italian Community Club. There was no general communication, and a college boy spoke to a corner boy never directly but always through one of the intermediaries. According to Whyte, even this communication could occur only when the gap separating the two groups was sufficiently narrow.

Whyte lists some of the differences between the corner-boy group and the college-boy group. Corner boys judged each member according to his personal relations with other members, whereas college boys judged one another by their intellectual accomplishments and by their ability to please outside authorities. Corner boys came together informally on Norton Street, with only rudimentary constitutions or bylaws. Decisions were taken through informal association.

Doc commented: It's better not to have a constitution and vote on all these things. As soon as you begin deciding questions by taking a vote, you'll see that some fellows are for you and some are against you, and in that way factions develop. It's best to get everybody to agree first, and then you don't have to vote.[37]

On the other hand, the college boys' organization was rigidly parliamentarian.

In settling controversial issues, [Chick] first argued and then called for a vote. When the vote went his way, he felt that he had won his objective. If the members failed to carry out the mandate of the vote, he chided them for their unco-operative attitude.[38]

Again, whereas the corner boys forgathered because they enjoyed one another's company, members of the Italian Community Club seldom associated together away from the club except in pairs.

Whyte also discusses, in a somewhat inconclusive way, the reason that the corner boys and the college boys had thrown up two leaders so very different as Doc and Chick. He is inclined to describe leadership mainly as the reward for the possession of certain personal qualities.

The leader is the man who acts when the situation requires action. He is more resourceful than his followers. . . . He is the most independent in judgment. . . . When he gives his word to one of his boys, he keeps it. The followers look to him for advice and encouragement, and he receives more of their confidences than any other man. Consequently, he knows more about what is going on in the group than anyone else. . . .

The leader is respected for his fair-mindedness. Whereas there may be hard feelings among some of the followers, the leader cannot bear a grudge against any man in the group . . .

The leader need not be the best baseball player, bowler or fighter, but he must have some skill in whatever pursuits are of particular interest to the group. It is natural for him to promote activities in which he excels . . .

The leader is better known and more respected outside his group than are any of his followers. His capacity for social movement is greater . . .

The leader does not deal with his followers as an undifferentiated group. . . . [He] mobilizes the group by dealing first with his lieutenants.[39]

"The leader spends more money on his followers than they on him . . . he must always be a free spender."[40]

It is apparent that in listing these qualities of leadership Whyte was thinking of Doc and not of Chick. It is contrary to the picture that has been built up to suppose that Chick was notable for his loyalty, fighting abilities, generosity, or his capacity to inspire devotion in lieutenants. He broke his word by voting for Tony Cardio for vice-president;[41] he was no good as a fighter;[42] he was mean with his money;[43] he antagonized his supporters to the point of impeachment.[44] In spite of his lack of these personal qualities he was for most of the time the undisputed leader of the college boys. On the other hand, Doc, in spite of his possession of these qualities, forfeited his position as leader of the Nortons when he withdrew from his campaign for representative in the state legislature.

It is not fair to blame Whyte for his failure to marry his explanations with the more sophisticated sociological theory that has grown up since he worked in Cornerville. On the contrary, his empirical material has been a source of illumination to later theoreticians. Homans, in *The Human Group*, makes explicit use of *Street Corner Society* for his exposition.

Homans' own theories owe much to the "idea of function," and one of the functionalists to whom he acknowledges his debt[45] is Talcott Parsons. On this point the conceptual schemes of Homans and Parsons are quite closely related, and are of great assistance when applied to the data in *Street Corner Society*, in accounting for the otherwise puzzling features of the groups described, namely, the conditions for the survival and even the success of such different organizations as the Norton Street Gang and the Italian Community Club, and the reason why the role of leader fell to Doc and Chick respectively.

The most famous and elaborated statement on this question made by Talcott Parsons occurs in his paper "A Revised Analytical Approach to the Theory of Social Stratification" written especially for *Class, Status and Power*,[46] and later reprinted in the revised edition of Parsons' *Essays in Sociological Theory*.

One starting point of Parsons' argument is that action is orientated to the attainment of goals, and systems of action are therefore evaluated by the individual, who judges each such system to be desirable or undesirable, useful or useless, gratifying or noxious, and in fact ranks all such systems of action according to their value to him in attaining his goals.

The second starting point is that it is a condition of the stability of social systems (such as the groups in question) that there should be an integration of the value standards of the component members so that they constitute a "common value system."[47]

Derived from these two starting points are two very practical and easily tested conclusions. The first is that the *function* of the group is to serve and to reinforce the common value system of its members; the second is that the *status* of each member within the group is determined by the extent to which he is identified with the common value system and helps to implement it.

In Parsons' analysis any given social system will have a "paramount" value pattern. In his ideal-type classification there are four major categories, of which two concern us here: the values which "emphasize a paramount system goal as the focus of valuation," and the values which "emphasize the integration of the system, the relations of solidarity of the units with each other."[48]

Arising out of these distinctive emphases, two different kinds of leadership will be called for.

In the one case, the focus of the need for authority is the need to coordinate the contributions of the various units of the system [i.e., members of the group] to the goal. Authority will tend to be a function of the urgency of "getting things done." The system-integrative case presumably gives a somewhat lesser emphasis on authority based mainly on the negative need to *prevent* units from disturbing the integration of the system, the need to keep them "in line."[49]

Parsons gives some examples, drawn from our actual social structure, of three major types of collectivities. The first is the organization—the business firm, the school, the hospital—which is normally the source of the individual's income. The second type, such as political units or churches, are associations with less specific but still recognizable aims. The third are what he calls "the diffuse solidarities" in which individuals are embedded, of which local community, kinship, and ethnic group are the most important for our purposes.[50] In practice the normal individual is affiliated with at least two of these three types of collectivity, and an adult male is almost necessarily also a member of an occupational system. His status determination based on these roles will thus be exceedingly complex; although the occupational role is highly valued in modern society and may dominate his status determination, he is not completely dependent on this or any other single role.

We may now apply these theorems to the circumstances of the Norton Street Gang and the Italian Community Club.

It is immediately clear that each of the groups in question had the opportunity of achieving stability through integrating the value standards of its component members. In the case of the Nortons, the form of integration was that characteristic of the "primary group," one of Parsons' diffuse solidarities.

The men became accustomed to acting together. They were also tied to one another by mutual obligations. In their experiences together there were innumerable occasions when one man would feel called upon to help another, and the man who was aided would want to return the favor. Strong group loyalties were supported by these reciprocal activities.[51]

The corner gang structure arises out of the habitual association of the members over a long period of time. The nuclei of most gangs can be traced back to early boyhood, when living close together provided the first opportunities for social contacts.[52]

The benefits which the Nortons derived from one another's company were those of friendship and solidarity rather than material gain or advancement. In Parsons' terminology, their paramount value pattern was system-integrative, and few of their activities had any recognizable motive in relation to the world outside their own group. The rewards and satisfactions that the members of the gang, during its heyday, derived from their membership were such that the gang seems to have dominated their lives. As has been mentioned, most of the Nortons, including Doc, were either unemployed or had casual and irregular employment, so that their occupational role was practically atrophied. Their pursuit of present pleasures left little time for Parsons' second type of collectivity, the goal-oriented association. Even the normal kinship solidarities of the corner boys were muted.

Home plays a very small role in the group activities of the corner boy. Except when he eats, sleeps or is sick, he is rarely at home, and his friends always go to his corner first when they want to find him. Even the corner boy's name indicates the dominant importance of the gang in his activities. It is possible to associate with a group of men for months and never discover the family names of more than a few of them. Most are known by nicknames attached to them by the group. Furthermore, it is easy to overlook the distinction between married and single men. The married man sets aside one evening a week to take out his wife. There are other occasions when they go out together and entertain together, and some corner boys devote more attention to their wives than others, but, married or single, the corner boy can be found on his corner almost every night of the week.[53]

Similarly, as soon as it was realized that association with the Aphrodite Club was tending to split the Nortons, the decision was taken to cut adrift from the girls. Only three low-status Nortons chose to stay with them, and this gradually dissolved their relationship with the gang.

When we examine the function of the Italian Community Club we find a completely different orientation. In spite of some confusion as to aims, which led to the inclusion of "the improvement of Cornerville" as a secondary purpose of the club and to the admission of certain selected noncollege boys, it was understood from its inauguration "that the club was to be made up of a superior class of young men,"[54] and that its primary purpose was to be the social betterment of its members. At least in the mind of Chick Morelli, every activity was geared to the promotion of upward social mobility.

The importance of social advancement in the dominant value system of the college boys is revealed by actions other than, and additional to, the formation of the club. It was, for example, characteristic of the college boys that they were careful spenders, constantly foregoing current pleasures in order to meet the costs of college and professional schools; this sharply distinguishes them from corner boys and lower-class boys everywhere for whom money in the pocket demands to be spent.

During the time that I knew a corner gang called the Millers, Sam Franco, the leader, was out of work except for an occasional odd job; yet, whenever he had a little money, he spent it on Joe and Chichi, his closest friends, who were next to him in the structure of the group. When Joe or Chichi had money, which was less frequent, they reciprocated.[55]

Contrast this with Chick Morelli, the epitome of upwardly mobile college boys.

"When my mother told me that I was going to college, I was surprised. But she had some money saved, and I always worked summers. A couple of summers I couldn't find a job, so I set up a pushcart with Lou Danaro. Once a friend of mine asked me if I wasn't ashamed to be working on a pushcart. I told him, 'Why should I be? This is my bread and butter.' "[56]

Another characteristic of the college boys was that they spent a great part of their time and energies in efforts to make contacts with members of higher-ranking groups. This is illustrated by their pursuit of the Italian Junior League, a superior girls' organization to whom the Italian Community Club transferred their attentions when they had exhausted the social possibilities of the Aphrodite Club. To the college boys the great attraction of the Italian Junior League was that its members came from beyond Cornerville, and it was on this very point that Chick and the other college boys clashed with Doc and the few corner boys who had been admitted to the Italian Community Club. The occasion of the clash was the production of a play called *Night of Horror*, which, Chick explained, was amusing and exciting and had the additional advantage that it could be had for a ten-dollar royalty. . . . There were four feminine roles to be filled. Doc told me that there was a great interest in dramatics in Cornerville, and he felt that giving Cornerville girls the opportunity of learning how to express themselves on the stage was in accord with the local improvement aim of the club. Chick felt that this was an opportunity for the club to make beneficial social contacts. He proposed that he get in touch with the president of the Italian Junior League . . . to see if they could provide the necessary actresses. This was agreed upon.[57]

Chick arranged to have some of the Junior League girls act as ushers. Too late it occurred to him that he should have invited girls from the Clarion Club, another exclusive Italian organization, so that his club could make contacts with both groups of girls.[58]

Although obviously the sexual attraction of the girls was a material factor, their natural charms were undoubtedly enhanced in the eyes of the college boys by the fact that, unlike most Cornerville girls, they held white-collar jobs and radiated social standing.

According to Whyte's narrative, these benefits of association with the Junior League girls had palled by the start of the second season, and there were signs that the club was due for a fresh turn. Lou Danaro, a noncollege member of the Italian Community Club, "predicted that the club would turn into a political organization when one of the young lawyer-members wanted to run for public office. Fred (his close friend) said: 'As long as the club has strictly a charitable purpose, it will be a good club. I don't like this mercenary stuff.' "[59] As they predicted, shortly afterward Chick proposed that the club discuss the qualifications of the candidates for city and state office, to ensure that Cornerville was well represented. He "suggested that they should write open letters to the candidates, demanding that they take a stand on certain issues. The club could put pressure upon politicians to obtain a new public bathhouse and improved park facilities for the district."[60]

Actually, in spite of some support, the club did not veer in this direction, but several of the most active members, including Chick, did move toward political careers. The club became hopelessly split and rapidly disintegrated. The second and last president, Joe Gennusi, himself a conciliatory college boy, delivered his diagnosis:

I think we had the wrong men in it. . . . In the beginning, I fought against having only college men. I hate discrimination of any kind. But maybe I was wrong. I think that the trouble with that club was that we had two kinds of members. There was one group that was aggressive and always wanted to do things. There was the other group that was always hanging back and never seemed to have the ambition. . . .[61]

This diagnosis illustrates, as revealingly as one might hope, the thesis that in order to survive a group must integrate the value standards of its members. Clearly when, as with the Italian Community Club, a common value system is absent the group remains unstable.

The corollary which Whyte discussed not altogether satisfactorily, as we have seen, was the determination of status within the group, and specifically the choice by the group of its leader. While recognizing[62] that it is misleading to contrast Chick with Doc in terms of egotism versus altruism, Whyte had no entirely satisfactory conceptual framework with which to handle the simultaneous appearance of such very different leaders.

In the boys' gang the decision had rested on the simple pecking order test of fighting prowess.[63] When the Nortons reassembled as grown men, the positions of leadership fell, according to Whyte, to the three members, and pre-eminently to Doc himself, who had not only wider contacts with outside groups but also superior intelligence and powers of self-expression. As we have seen, Whyte expanded his list of the personal qualities of leadership in a way that fitted Doc's qualities but failed to account for Chick's leadership of the college boys.

About the same time that Whyte was making his study of Cornerville, Helen Hall Jennings was working on her sociometric study of leadership, for which her subjects were the 450 inmates of the New York State Training School for Girls. Sociometric tests were given in December, 1937, and in September, 1938, and the data were used to pick out the girls who were exceptionally often or the ones who were exceptionally seldom the sociometric choice of the other girls in the institution. Out of 133 eligible subjects (present on both test occasions) 41 were distinguished as *over-chosen* and 43 as *under-chosen*.

The over-chosen group constituted the high-status individuals in the community, and observations were made to determine their personality and behavioral characteristics. This revealed that each over-chosen subject, to a greater or less extent—

enlarges her social space, for interchange of ideas and activities;

secures more and more responsibilities to be held by members in her work groups, her housing unit, and in the community as a whole;

takes definite stands on what she considers right, and will "fight for it";

aids the average-chosen individuals to broaden their conceptions of their potential capacities; . . .

shows ability to establish rapport quickly and effectively with a wide range of other personalities . . .;

insists on an impersonal fairness, and succeeds in gaining respect for this level of interaction between members;

and so on.[64]

In spite of certain apparent regularities in these behavioral features, Jennings concludes that the "why" of leadership cannot be explained by any personality quality or constellation of traits. This conclusion is based on her observation that some equally mature and creative individuals are not allowed a role of leadership. She suggests that to be chosen for a leadership role the individual must possess a special kind of sensitivity that enables him to develop a *manner of interacting with others* which wins their confidence and support—

a manner which moves others in directions apparently desired by the latter, even though they may be doing little themselves towards attaining such directions. It is as if these individuals recognize and think more of the needs of others than others think of their own needs. The leader-individuals often take actions in behalf of others whom they do not choose and who do not know of the effort made for them. . . .

While the varieties of styles of leadership . . . are many, nevertheless, a number of characteristics of leader-individuals stand out as common attributes. The social milieu is "improved" from the point of view of the membership through the efforts of each leader. Each widens the area of social participation for others (and indirectly his own social space) by his unique contribution to this milieu. Each leader seems to sense spontaneously when to censure and when to praise, apparently is intellectually and emotionally uncomfortable when others are "left out," and acts to foster tolerance on the part of one member towards another. At the same time, they may give little quarter to other leaders. . . .

The leadership thus exhibited in the community by various members appears, in each instance, to reflect a "style" of leadership—a particularized way of behaving, derived from the personality attributes of the individual in an over-chosen position. Actually, however, . . . no one personality has a constellation of attributes necessary to win an exclusive position in esteem and influence necessary to a role of exclusive leadership. Each leader makes a contribution *to some parts* of the membership which all members do not equally want or need.[65]

As we shall see in a later chapter, more recent theory by Bales and his associates supports the view that the typical group requires and receives not one but two simultaneous forms of leadership. However, instead of depending on the complex variations in personality components of the individuals concerned, the Bales theory and its supporting experiments are derived from Parsons' already quoted recognition of the variety in paramount value patterns. Small-group analysis has disclosed that problem-solving groups tend to throw up an "instrumental" leader who emphasizes the group goals and an "expressive" leader who emphasizes the integration and solidarity of the group.

The unifying consideration in all such typologies of leadership is one of function rather than of personality. In Homans' words,

The leader is the man who comes closest to realizing the norms the group values highest. The norms may be queer ones, but so long as they are genuinely accepted by the group, the leader, in that group, must embody them. His embodiment of the norms gives him his high rank, and his rank attracts people: the leader is the man people come to; the scheme of interaction focuses on him. At the same time, his high rank carries with it the implied right to assume control of the group, and the exercise of control itself helps maintain the leader's prestige. This control he is particularly well equipped to wield by reason of his position at the top of the pyramid of interaction. He is better informed than other men, and he has more channels for the issuing of orders. He controls the group, yet he is in a sense more controlled by it than others are, since it is a condition of his leadership that his actions and decisions shall conform more closely than those of others to an abstract norm.[66]

This quotation begins and ends with the recognition of the obligations of leadership, of which Whyte had showed himself to be very much aware.

Not all the corner boys live up to their obligations equally well, and this factor partly accounts for the differentiation in status among them. The man with a low status may violate his obligations without much change in his position. His fellows know that he has failed to discharge certain obligations in the past, and his position reflects his past performances. On the other hand, the leader is depended upon by all the members to meet his personal obligations. He cannot fail to do so without causing confusion and endangering his position.[67]

Nothing in the functional theory diminishes the expectation that a great variety of leadership forms will be observed, but it transfers the explanation from the qualities of the individual to the nature and situation of the group. In particular, the degree of authority that must be vested in the leader can show wide variations. Homans describes this in terms of a spectrum, at one end of which is the sea captain. If his ship

is to accomplish its purposes in a dangerous and capricious environment, a number of complex activities must be carefully co-ordinated, and the authority of the captain must be unquestioned, especially in the emergencies that may arise at any time. The authority of the captain extends, or did extend in the old days, to every aspect of the seamen's lives; while at sea they cannot escape from it. And they certainly do not choose their commander: democracy ends when the last line is cast off the pier.[68]

The relationship between Doc and the rest of the Nortons lies close to the other end of the spectrum. This group was certainly not carrying out complex activities in a dangerous environment; the men could escape from the group if they found Doc's authority intolerable, and Doc was in effect, if not by formally democratic procedures, chosen by the members of the group to be their leader.[69]

At this end of the scale the relationship between leader and led could be a relaxed one. The Italian Community Club, with its recognizable goals, was nearer to the middle of the spectrum, and there, as Homans points out, although the leader is potentially the object of greater respect, he is also, in unfavorable circumstances, the object of hostility. There was indeed a move at one time to impeach Chick Morelli, but a similar move against Doc is unthinkable.

In addition to the data in *Street Corner Society* relating to group cohesion and to leadership, there is rich material relating to social mobility. As Whyte states in his Introduction, "it is important to discover who the people are who are advancing and how they are doing it."[70]

If we again contrast Chick with Doc, we may ask why it was

Chick rather than Doc that moved into higher-status groups outside Cornerville. Both were highly intelligent, but Chick made
great sacrifices to work his way through Ivy Law School, whereas
there is no indication at any point that Doc was prepared to forego
present pleasures for the sake of a future goal. Doc was a free
spender not merely because, as Whyte suggests, this is demanded
of a leader but because "the college boys fit in with an economy
of savings and investment. The corner boys fit in with a spending
economy. The college boy must save his money in order to finance
his education and launch his business or professional career. He
therefore cultivates the middle class virtue of thrift."[71]

According to Whyte, both the college boy and the corner boy
want to get ahead, but the college boy is much more ready to
sacrifice his current friendships if his friends do not advance as
fast as he does.

In a later chapter of this book which is concerned with *The
American Soldier* a rather similar problem is described. The question arose as to which enlisted men were the most likely to win
promotion. The commanding officer was largely responsible for
promotions, and the researchers therefore advanced the hypothesis
that conformity to the officially approved military mores would improve a man's chances of promotion. This hypothesis was abundantly confirmed by a series of studies.[72]

In their re-examination of the *American Soldier* data Merton and
Kitt use this result for a highly stimulating illustration of reference-
group theory. The significant point was that the soldiers who were
heading for promotion were showing conformity not with the
norms of their current membership group of other enlisted men
but with the quite different norms contained in the official military
mores. Their positive orientation to the army mores had two consequences: on the one hand, it won them promotion and eased their
subsequent adjustment to their new role; on the other hand, it involved alienation from their present membership group, who accused them of "brown-nosing," bucking for promotion, or sucking
up. and thereby increased their desire to move out into their new
reference group.

This example may illuminate the question of Chick's behavior.
Like the promotion seekers in the army, Chick was obliged and able
to make use of a variety of higher-status reference groups to which

he aspired. His own story of his early years is full of examples. For instance, he tells the story of his relationship with a girl called Edith, whom he met at a dance and subsequently saw regularly.

"I was seeing her about every other night for almost two years. She lived with a woman named Mrs. Burroughs. Mrs. Burroughs took a liking to me from the beginning. She would introduce me to people before her own sons. I learned a lot of things from her and from Edith. I began mingling in with different people. Wherever I went with Edith, I would do what she did, and I would act the same way. Sometimes I noticed that she didn't do things just right according to the book of etiquette, but, of course, I didn't say anything. I learned a lot from her. "Bill, if . . . I have a talent for anything, it is a talent for imitation."[73]

One striking fact about this passage is that Chick gives no hint that he had any feelings toward Edith or toward Mrs. Burroughs, who treated him like a son. As in money matters, so also with his affections he presents himself as having been thrifty indeed, regarding his personal relations solely for their instrumental value to him in his struggle for self-improvement. Similarly he took it for granted that his talent for mimicry would be turned to account for the same purpose.

In American society, college education is practically indispensable for high-status achievement. There is not only book learning to imbibe but also the mode of behavior suitable in professional circles. "When I was in college, I used to pay attention to everything the professor said so that I could learn from the way he said things."[74] "Chick told me that he valued especially his friendship with Thomas L. Brown, a prominent Eastern City Lawyer. He said that Brown had a strong influence on him, often correcting his mistakes and giving him advice."[75]

Finally, when Chick launched his political career he did not identify with the Democratic party, which was overwhelmingly strong in Cornerville, but with the higher-status Republican party. At the end of Whyte's narrative Chick had been rewarded with a job on the Republican attorney-general's staff. "It was a small position, but it was a start in politics. Chick had come a long way since he had first organized the Italian Community Club."[76]

Many years later, before preparing the second edition of *Street Corner Society*, Whyte made contact with Chick—as he had with

Doc—to find out what the book had done to him. Chick received him cordially, introduced him to his wife, an attractive and pleasant girl who neither came from Cornerville nor was of Italian extraction. He seemed quite relaxed about the book, being anxious only that the brash impression of himself and his circle had caught them with their hair down. He had done well, but he was still mystified that he was not loved in Cornerville, a disadvantage which had not speeded his political career.

"You know, the funny thing is, Bill, I didn't get many votes from Cornerville. The people that you grow up with, it seems, are jealous of anybody that is getting ahead. Where I got my support was right round here where I live now [a middle-class part of the ward]. I know these fellows on the street-corner and I really fit with them."[77]

The question that is left unanswered in all this is why Chick became oriented toward higher-status groups whereas Doc did not. Doc's explanation was that he was not willing to pay the price of broken friendships. Doc commented on Chick in these words:

"Chick says that self-preservation is the first law of nature. Now that's right to a certain extent. You have to look out for yourself first. But Chick would step on the neck of his best friend if he could get a better job by doing it. . . . We were talking one night on the corner about that, and I was sucking him in. I got him to admit it—that he would turn against his best friend if he could profit by it. . . . I would never do that, Bill. I would never step on Danny even if I could get myself a $50-a-week job by doing it. None of my boys would do that."[78]

Not surprisingly, there is some evidence that an individual exposed to a higher-ranking group is more likely to adopt the norms of that group. In this context we must not neglect the existence of the settlement houses, Norton Street House and Cornerville House, which were in the heart of the section. The welfare workers at these settlements were middle-class people of non-Italian (largely Yankee) stock. The boards of directors were upper-middle-class and upper-class people of Yankee stock, including many of the socially elite of Boston. The only Italians were in subordinate positions, teaching special classes or doing clerical or janitorial work.

The welfare workers might have been expected to constitute a useful higher-ranking group to whom the poor Italians might orient as a reference group. It is clear that they expected to fill this role.

None could speak Italian, they made little effort to familiarize themselves with the local social structure, and they conceived their function to be the promotion of one-way adaptation from slum dweller to middle-class shadow.

This role of the settlements in promoting upward mobility was made explicit on one occasion by Mr. Ramsay, head of boys' work at Norton Street House. He said:

"There's one thing about this house that no one can deny. We have always done all we could to inspire you boys that were ambitious to make your way in life. I remember when Jerry, here, wanted to be a doctor. At that time it seemed out of his reach, but I said to him, 'Jerry, others have done it; why shouldn't you be able to do it too?' And now Jerry is well on his way to achieving his ambition.

"Some people think we should make an effort to get the roughnecks from the street corners to come in here. Well, I wonder about that. How would you men like it if you had to associate with those fellows?"[79]

The men who were present on that occasion were college men, and they agreed that they would not like it.

In general, the result of the settlement policies was that they became almost entirely isolated from the corner boys, Mr. Ramsay's "roughnecks," who constituted the overwhelming majority of the Cornerville male population.

Occasionally a corner boy, Lou Danaro or Doc, was pressed by the social workers to forsake the corner and join the settlement. Lou was lured away by Mr. Bacon and then suddenly dropped. Doc steadfastly resisted. Those that did associate closely with the settlement were labeled "stooges" or "flunkies," just as aspirants for army promotion were attacked for "brown-nosing," bucking for promotion, or sucking up.

Corner boys came to display open hostility to the settlement workers. They used obscene language in the hearing of the workers, not because it was their natural language but as a form of hostile expression. The social workers were completely unable and unwilling to deal with corner boys. Instead, they bent their energies to stimulating social mobility, extending middle-class standards and middle-class rewards to lower-class natives who were maladjusted in terms of the local society.

On this question Doc, who was generally so tolerant, could see no use for a Yankee-dominated settlement house. He described graphically how it felt to pass through life dependent on institutions dominated by other races, and added:

"If I had my way, I would have half the schoolteachers Italians, and three-quarters of the people in the settlement. Let the other people be there just to show that we're in America.

"Bill, those settlement houses were necessary at first. When our parents landed here, they didn't know where to go or what to do. They needed the social workers for intermediaries. They did a fine job then, but now the second generation is growing up, and we're beginning to sprout wings. They should take that net off and let us fly."[80]

Whyte himself abandons his customary detachment and comes out strongly against the settlements. He accuses them of increasing friction between corner boys and college boys, of suppressing the natural leadership of Cornerville and attempting to substitute alien leaders, of forcing the individual to subordinate himself to people that he recognizes are different from his own. If it is a bad thing to break up a traditional working-class community, the facts of his case can be taken as proven.

RACE AND COLOR

We now turn to *An American Dilemma* by Dr. Gunnar Myrdal,[1] the internationally distinguished economist. This massive and substantial book first appeared in 1944 in two volumes and is now published in one volume of nearly 1,500 pages.

The story behind Dr. Myrdal's program can be briefly told. The initiative came from the Carnegie Corporation of New York, which normally had two aims in supporting this kind of research. One was to contribute to the "advancement and diffusion of knowledge and understanding as specified in the Charter of the Carnegie Corporation"; the other was for their own direct purposes, so that they could, with fuller information, use their funds as economically and efficiently as possible.

In 1931 the late Newton D. Baker joined the Corporation board. He had been at different times Mayor of Cleveland and Secretary of War, and in both capacities he had faced the special problems associated with the presence of the Negro element in the American population. He therefore spoke with authority in asserting that better organized and interrelated knowledge of the Negro problem was needed before the Corporation could intelligently distribute its own funds in this direction. He also felt, and the Corporation agreed with him, that the gathering and digestion of material in the field of race relations might well also serve a larger purpose.

There was an initial difficulty. There was no lack of American scholars deeply interested in the Negro problem in the United States, but the subject was so emotionally charged that the Corpora-

tion felt that the director of this important project should be someone who could approach his task with a fresh mind. They therefore
decided to try to "import" a disinterested man from one of the
countries that have never been colonial exploiters nor experienced
any severe ethnic problem. Sweden was one obvious choice among
such countries, and it was there that they found Dr. Myrdal, who
was then professor of social economics at Stockholm.

The idea was that he should come to America to assemble and
organize a full-time paid staff, and that he should also be given funds
with which he could call on the experience of other scholars and
experts in a less formal fashion. It was made clear from the beginning that any reports finally presented would be Dr. Myrdal's sole
responsibility, so that there could be no dispute as to what the report
should contain.

That, then, is how the project started, and Dr. Myrdal arrived
in the United States in September, 1938. With him came a fellow-
countryman, Richard Sterner, who had been in the Royal Social
Board, Stockholm. Straightway the two men, accompanied by a
guide, set out for two months on what they called "exploration" of
the Southern states. They were clear at this stage that they were
only gathering impressions, talking to people of all kinds but in a
quite unsystematic way, learning for themselves about the extent of
the problem. Myrdal states quite openly and proudly that he had
never concerned himself with this particular field or problem before,
and this fact was an asset that made him particularly acceptable for
the job.

After this stage the procedure was characteristically elaborate and
high-powered. In January, 1939, Myrdal submitted a memorandum
on the planning of the research to be undertaken. Mimeographed
copies were submitted to more than fifty of the top experts and
scholars who had studied racial problems or had other relevant
expertise. In his Preface, Myrdal lists the names of such distinguished persons as Ruth Benedict, Franz Boas, Ralph J. Bunche,
Allison Davis, John Dollard, W. E. B. Du Bois, E. Franklin Frazier,
Melville J. Herskovits, Otto Klineberg, Ralph Linton, George
Lundberg, Frank Notestein, Robert E. Park, Hortense Powder-
maker, Dorothy Swain Thomas, W. I. Thomas, Louis Wirth, and
Donald R. Young. These and many other almost equally well-known
people made criticisms of his memorandum and offered suggestions

as to how the work should be planned. Some comments were written, but since there were ample funds, conferences were held to sort out the program. By the end of April, 1939, just six months after he had started, Myrdal prepared a more definite plan, which for the first time contained some general terms of reference, stating that the study

should aim at determining the social, political, educational and economic status of the Negro in the United States as well as defining opinions held by different groups of Negroes and whites as to his "right" status. It must, further, be concerned with recent changes and trends with respect to the Negro's position in American society. Attention must also be given to the total American picture with particular emphasis on relations between the two races. Finally, it must consider what changes are being or can be induced by education, legislation, interracial efforts, concerted action by Negro groups, etc.[2]

During the summer and fall of 1939 Myrdal and Sterner, together with Dr. Stouffer, who was coming into the picture at this date, were gradually setting the research in motion. There was a fairly long list of research assistants, and consultants were brought in who were usually given a block grant to prepare a paper on some particular aspect. These would be somewhat more senior people, such as Ashley Montagu, Eugene L. Horowitz, Otto Klineberg, Edward Shils, and Louis Wirth. Outstanding among the younger generation of research assistants was Arnold Rose, who became closely identified at the later stages of the program and with the preparation of the book. Later he prepared his own book, *The Negro in America*, which is basically an abbreviated version of the main work.

The feature that distinguishes this program from the previously described projects is that it represents one of the first examples of really heavily financed and institutionalized research in the social sciences. It is always difficult under those circumstances to keep the work under control. Myrdal was spending what time he could spare paying visits to the field, but with so many committee meetings and other administrative obligations he probably found it very difficult to give much attention to the details. In September, 1939, the Germans invaded Poland, and in April, 1940, they moved into Norway and Denmark. At this point Myrdal felt that he should go back to

Sweden. So he and Sterner returned to Stockholm, leaving Samuel Stouffer in charge of the research. After the tremendous build-up until spring, 1940, it was most unfortunate that at the crucial moment Myrdal himself was forced to disappear temporarily from the scene. Stouffer made and fulfilled an undertaking to have the research completed by September, 1940, only six months later.

The fact that this research could so rapidly be completed emphasizes the point that it was different in nature from the research for the other studies described in this book. Typically, the research for such studies occupies several years. The difference was not accidental or unplanned. The Carnegie Corporation asked for a comprehensive study comprising "the collection, analysis and interpretation of existing knowledge,"[3] and this is what they received. There was no intention of promoting any considerable amount of fresh fieldwork. In consequence the whole project consists of a highly organized compilation and secondary use of the tremendous amount of material on the Negro problem that had been accumulating before Dr. Myrdal and his colleagues started working.

When Stouffer completed his phase of the project in September, 1940, Myrdal's absence in Europe made the future program somewhat uncertain. It was therefore decided, in order to have something to show, that a number of volumes should be prepared by some of the major collaborators. These co-workers could not cover the whole field but could at least describe some of the specialist inquiries that had been made. Following this decision Melville J. Herskovits produced a book called *The Myth of the Negro Past;* Charles S. Johnson, *Patterns of Negro Segregation;* Richard Sterner completed *The Negro's Share,* which is an economic study of the financial contributions made by Negroes and their share of relief; Otto Klineberg edited *Characteristics of the American Negro,* which contains a number of research memoranda. Other manuscripts, consisting either of fragments (as they are sometimes called) prepared by the senior consultants or of fairly elaborate monographs prepared by the full-time members of the staff, were not published, but copies were deposited in the Schomburg Collection of the New York Public Library, where they still are. Also deposited in the collection were copies of the administrative and programing memoranda prepared by Myrdal at various stages in the launching of the project.

In addition, the Advisory Committee of the Carnegie Corporation went through the published and unpublished memoranda and, as Myrdal says,

coming to the material from outside and viewing it with fresh eyes, the Committee felt justified in giving the following appraisal: "The Committee found that every manuscript submitted offered significant contributions. In serving the purposes of the Study so well, the contributors necessarily subordinated their individual publication interests to the interests of the central project. This is evidence of unselfish team-play which deserves respect and commendation."[4]

One can sympathize with the Committee's dilemma, but this statement is not very realistic. It is obviously unlikely that every manuscript offered significant contributions, and some manuscripts must have been more significant than others. Altogether, the tone is a little unctuous, but perhaps in such circumstances, an administrator has to be suave and perhaps it is the price to be paid for this type of big-business research. The material the Committee had read through in reaching their conclusion consisted of 15,000 typewritten pages, so one may hope that they read it well!

Fortunately the uncertainty was ended in March, 1941, when Myrdal found it possible to return and start work on his final report. He worked in various college and other libraries throughout the summer of 1941—at first mainly at Dartmouth College, but also at Columbia University, the New York Public Library, Princeton University Library, and the Library of the Russell Sage Foundation. Most of *An American Dilemma* was written at Princeton.

In September, 1941, Myrdal was joined by Richard Sterner, his earliest associate, and by Arnold Rose. These two were conspicuously active at this stage, themselves drafting and preparing a number of the chapters, and the preparation became a collaborative effort of the three of them. This stage lasted about eighteen months; in the last few months of 1942 Myrdal and Sterner returned to Sweden, leaving to various people, including Arnold Rose, the hectic job of completing the final touches. The manuscript was checked through by Professors E. Franklin Frazier and Louis Wirth. The report came out in 1944 and was immediately received with acclaim. Happily it was well timed, for the acceleration of events caused by the war had greatly heightened American interest in the Negro problem, and the report was able to make a substantial contribution to public understanding.

AN AMERICAN DILEMMA

The book, as was intended, is extraordinarily comprehensive. It is unified by a sense of perspective that is unusual but is undoubtedly what the sponsors were hoping for when they appointed a foreigner as director of the program.

The tone of the book is set in an Introduction which immediately presents the Negro problem as a moral issue. It is suggested that to the great majority of white Americans the Negro problem is nothing but an embarrassment—difficult to settle and difficult to neglect. American society is burdened by what Myrdal calls the awkward anomaly of the presence of the Negro in America, which arouses anxiety because the Negroes are present and a sense of guilt because they were forcibly transplanted. Because American culture is so highly moralistic, so very conscious of moral questions, and not at all cynical, feelings of guilt and anxiety are particularly prominent. Myrdal therefore concludes that in order to illuminate the Negro problem it is necessary to examine the essentials of the vital and youthful amalgam of moralism, rationalism, and fatalism that he labels the "American Creed."

His title, An American Dilemma, thus refers to the ever-raging conflict in the heart of the American between, on the one hand, the American Creed—the valuations preserved on the general plane which derive from high national and Christian precepts—and, on the other hand, the valuations on specific planes of individual and group living, where the outlook of the individual American is dominated by personal local interests; by economic, social, and sexual jealousies; by consideration for community prestige and conformity; by group prejudice against particular persons or types of people; and by a great variety of wants, impulses, and habits. Thus the Negro problem is not what to do with the Negroes but rather how to guide the individual American in his personal task of reconciling the high Christian principles in which he earnestly and completely believes with his behavior and attitudes in his specific dealings with Negroes.

Myrdal's contribution, as he saw it, was to make it no longer possible for Americans to sustain the twisted and mutilated beliefs concerning the Negro that had allowed them to rationalize their otherwise indefensible attitude toward Negroes. He quotes with approval a passage from John Dewey's *Freedom and Culture:*

Anything that obscures the fundamentally moral nature of the social problem is harmful, no matter whether it proceeds from the side of physical or of psychological theory. Any doctrine that eliminates or even obscures the function of choice of values and enlistment of desires and emotions in behalf of those chosen weakens personal responsibility for judgment and for action. It thus helps create the attitudes that welcome and support the totalitarian state.[5]

To avoid this slurring of the moral issues Myrdal would set out to ascertain what the social reality in relation to Negroes in America really was. The first step would be to discover who the American Negro is and how he fares. This had to be attempted on two levels. There were the quantitative and objective indices in respect of the material conditions for his existence; this economic approach was a straightforward job for Myrdal, the social economist. But this was only a beginning, perhaps not even the most important part; beyond the material side of the problem were the doctrines and ideologies, the valuations and beliefs, embedded in the minds of white and Negro Americans. Myrdal intended to follow through W. I. Thomas' theme that when people define situations as real, they *are* real, and he planned to determine the "definition of the situation" for whites and for Negroes.

He makes the point that the Negro problem is primarily a problem for the whites in America. This is because the white American is the dominant partner, the one who determines the direction of American development and the "place" of the Negro in American society. The Negro was brought to America for the white man's profit. He was kept in slavery for generations in the same interest. If today the Negro's place in American society has become precarious, uncertain, and changing, it is because the Negro is no longer so necessary and profitable to the white man. The Negro problem is not something that can be detached from the whole problem of the direction of American civilization. It is a feature of American civilization and cannot be considered in isolation.

The American Dilemma is submitted, Myrdal states, as an analysis, not a description. By this he means that the facts—and there is a vast accumulation of facts—are presented only for the sake of their meaning in the interpretation. The book has certain theoretical aims, concerned with determining causes and effects, which are presented as tentative generalizations on the basis of known facts. It also has certain practical aims, concerned with means and ends, designed to construct, in a preliminary way, bases for rational policy. Throughout the book and his methodological appendix Myrdal makes it clear that he attaches greater value to the practical than to the theoretical aspects of his studies.

Myrdal also states that he will make his value premises explicit, for three very acceptable reasons. The first is to minimize distorting biases, the second is to determine in a rational way the statement of problems and the definition of terms for the theoretical analysis, and the third is to lay a logical basis for his practical and political conclusions. He ends the Introduction by warning his readers not to conclude that because there is much to be criticized in America's handling of the Negro problem America as a civilization is being condemned. Anyone who uses the facts beyond their immediate context is misusing them.

The first chapters of the book are designed to give an outline of the American Creed. Chapter 1 has as its title "American Ideals and the American Conscience." It demonstrates that the American system of general ideals in reference to human interrelations is explicitly expressed. Compared with every other country in Western civilization, large or small, America is continually struggling for its soul. The ideals of the essential dignity of the individual human being, of the fundamental equality of all men, and of certain inalienable rights to freedom, justice, and a fair opportunity, were written into the Declaration of Independence, the Preamble of the Constitution, the Bill of Rights. The ideals of the American Creed have thus become the highest law of the land. The only disappointment is the constant gap between such ideals and the realities of public and interpersonal behavior. It is easier for a foreigner than for a native American to realize that the high-sounding generalities demanded of all public speakers in the United States are a contribution to uplift rather than a mirror to life.

Such perorations are accepted uncritically by native Americans, and the Negro people in America, who have opportunities to check their truth, are no exception to the national pattern. In his memorandum for the project Ralph Bunche, now the distinguished Negro statesman, observed:

Every man in the street, white, black, red or yellow, knows that this is "the land of the free," the "land of opportunity," the "cradle of liberty," the "home of democracy," that the American flag symbolizes the "equality of all men" and guarantees to us all "the protection of life, liberty and property," freedom of speech, freedom of religion and racial tolerance.[6]

Myrdal adds that the Negroes, "like the whites, are under the spell of the great national suggestion."[7] This, in his view, is what has minimized the attachment of the Negro to communism and other revolutionary creeds. It is because the Negro is always waiting and hoping for American society to live up to its ideals that he has not been lured away after any external ideals, such as communism.

This is perhaps a little vague so far, but Myrdal quotes a series of slightly more specific versions of the component items in the American Creed. He includes, for example, one contemporary exegesis by Charles Merriam.

Democracy is a form of political association in which the general control and direction of the commonwealth is habitually determined by the bulk of the community in accordance with understandings and procedures providing for popular participation and consent. Its postulates are:

1. The essential dignity of man, the importance of protecting and cultivating his personality on a fraternal rather than upon a differential basis, of reconciling the needs of the personality within the framework of the common good in a formula of liberty, justice, welfare.

2. The perfectibility of man: confidence in the possibilities of the human personality, as over against the doctrines of caste, class and slavery.

3. That the gains of commonwealths are essentially mass gains rather than the efforts of the few and should be diffused as promptly as possible throughout the community without too great delay or too wide a spread in differentials.

4. Confidence in the value of the consent of the governed expressed in institutions, understandings and practices as a basis of order, liberty, justice.

5. The value of decisions arrived at by common counsel rather than by violence and brutality.[8]

Of course there have been many other formulations of the American Creed, but this quotation is more explicit than slogans such as "land of the free."

According to Myrdal, these ideas can be traced back to three European origins: the humanistic liberal philosophy of Enlightenment, the democratic teaching of Protestant Christianity, and lastly the English legal system, from which American law is derived. He contrasts these sources of flexibility and forward-looking with what he calls the conservative and almost fetishistic cult of the Constitution. The Constitution, 150 years old and in many respects impractical and ill suited to modern conditions, was made technically difficult to change, and is rescued only by a traditionally flexible and empirical executive that can absorb new problems as they arise. Correspondingly, the American conception of law and order is seen to differ from the European conception. Myrdal points out that American laws are prone to incorporate ideals as well as realistically enforceable rules, and that many of the rules written into the laws are not intended to be taken at their face value. He draws from this the highly controversial conclusion that the American, and even the American political scientist, does not ultimately believe that legislation can change anything. American laws are framed at the level of moral aspiration, and "America believes in and aspires to something much higher than its plane of actual life."[9]

The *popular* explanation of the disparity between ideals and actual behavior is that Americans act hypocritically, paying lip service to the American Creed while they get on with their graft and tolerance of political imperfections. One can imagine some societies in which this behavior would be due to hypocrisy, but in the United States the distinction is not blurred over at all, and the gap between the ideal and the real are constantly made clear. Violations of the American Creed are subjected to a barrage of publicity and public inquiry. "The American . . . is strongly and sincerely 'against sin,' even, and not least, his own sins."[10] There is a steady pressure on society to live up to its ideals and its laws; and yet it must be admitted that there is also something in the American culture which makes Americans not altogether surprised at the gap between their laws and the actual life that they see being lived round them.

Myrdal next turns to the specific subject of his inquiry. He says, first, that, at some level, the Negro problem is constantly on the minds of the whites. This is because a contented Negro is rare, and white Americans, even in non-Negro areas, are continually reminded of the Negro problem by the press and by public discussion of such matters as lynching and Negro criminality. When Myrdal was writing, the Negro problem was not a dominant issue, but even then there were signs that its importance would increase, not because the position of Negroes was deteriorating, but because developments were increasing the possibility of Negro advance. This, incidentally, is a typical application of the reference-group concept: a rise in status need not mean that the Negroes would feel less deprived, but might, by allowing them to look realistically at a higher reference group, increase their sense of relative deprivation. In other words, it is not the absolute position, not absolute depression, that causes discontent but rather the recognition of the possibility of equality.

Second, Myrdal points out that a distinction must be made between the salience of the color question to the white American and to the Negro; while some white Americans are brought more into contact with the Negro problem than others, it does not constitute a dominant issue for many of them. But to the Negroes themselves the problem of their relations with American society is all-important because they are constantly being reminded of their minority status. There are plenty of racial minorities in America whose members are allowed to think of themselves as Americans, whereas the Negro is expected to, and in fact does, concentrate his attention on Negro, and not on all-American, affairs. If he is an economist, he is expected to specialize in the economics of the Negro section of the population rather than in economics generally —there are many pressures on him to concern himself not with the whole society but with "his own" section of society.

In this respect, Myrdal reminds us, there is a parallel between the position of the Negro and the position of women. Women have won their way into many professions and positions of authority, but they are still encouraged to confine their attentions to the more feminine aspects of their field, and the word "women" will be incorporated in the titles of their professional associations not so much in order to exclude men as to assert that women have at least a sectional interest in the subject at issue.[11] It seems that there are, or were, very similar pressures working on Negroes to create their own organizations in order to talk about their own problems rather than about the problems of America as a whole.

Typically, as Myrdal points out, in addition to the American Bar Association there is a National Bar Association, which is an association of American Negro lawyers. It has to be a separate, and not always an equal, echo of the main body.

Although this is the factual situation, at the same time very many people, especially white Americans, are unwilling to accept the facts even at this level. This is Myrdal's third main point. Particularly in the Southern states, he claimed, many people would deny that there was a Negro problem, and would produce anecdotes and examples to support their denials. In his explorations of the Deep South, Myrdal seems to have had a rather effective, though perhaps embarrassing technique for dealing with this refusal to face facts. He was continually being invited to meetings and social luncheons. After much general conversation, sooner or later the question of his investigation was bound to arise. There might first be an awkward silence, then some of the guests would start explaining the local situation, claiming that they really had no problem in their area— the two races had come to terms exactly, and the Negroes did not want anything different from what they had. After listening carefully Myrdal would suggest that perhaps the situation was more fluid than was suggested: for example, advances in education would eliminate the principal argument for disfranchising the Negro, namely, his illiteracy. This set the assembly arguing among themselves, extremely vociferously for the next hour or two, while Myrdal "could lean back and listen to one of the most revealing and most ably performed, though sometimes heated, intellectual debates on the Negro problem in America I had up till then, and even thereafter, heard."[12]

Myrdal visited an art exhibition somewhere in the Old South at which one of the important exhibits was a man-sized sculpture called "Soldier in Rain." It represented a Negro man lynched by hanging. Myrdal was being conducted round the exhibition by two local ladies who were keen amateur artists, experts in art appreciation. He took a special look at this sculpture and unintentionally referred to it as representing a lynching, which it quite obviously did. His hostesses were shocked and replied: "This is not a lynching at all; it is just any soldier being hanged, probably behind the front for some offense. It has nothing to do with the Negro problem." Myrdal pointed out that no armies used hanging as a method of execution, and asked whether it was of no significance that the man's features and figure showed him to be a Negro.

Myrdal had become interested in this incident and therefore sought out the sculptor who had made the work in question; he recounted his experience at the exhibition and asked the sculptor to clear the matter up. The artist at first denied that his sculpture represented a lynching; it represented "any soldier" being hanged. Myrdal became rather angry at this point and said: "If you, the artist, do not know what you have created, I know it as an art spectator. You have depicted a lynching, and, more particularly, a lynching of a Negro." The sculptor suddenly changed personality, became intimate and open, and said: "I believe you are right. I must have intended it all the time." When Myrdal asked, "Don't you think everyone must know it?" the sculptor said, "Yes, in a way, but they don't want to know it." This was the crux of the matter; the Southerners were so determined not to let this painful incident intrude in their art appreciation that they were willing to falsify the whole situation. As Myrdal concludes, it was a "beautiful crystallization of moral escape."[13]

Myrdal found a similarly widespread tendency to ignore the scientific facts about race that had accumulated during the present century. People quite capable of appraising the truth will pretend to themselves that the old myths of race are still scientifically tenable. Myrdal met physicians who held absurd ideas about the anatomical characteristics of the Negro or about the frequency of disease among the Negroes in their own community; educators who had succeeded in remaining wholly unaware of the results of modern intelligence research; lawyers who believed that nearly all the lynchings were reprisals for rape; ministers of the gospel who knew practically nothing about Negro churches in their own town. He believed this deliberate ignorance about Negroes to be extraordinarily prevalent, both in the North, where the Yankee is permitted to know nothing about the subject, and in the South, where the whites foster the illusion that they "know the Negro."

Myrdal saw the grounds for personal ignorance increasing with the decline in institutionalized contacts between whites and Negroes. In some Northern cities into which the Negroes were immigrating, institutionalized contacts had been minimized; for many Northerners the only contacts with Negroes would be in subways or in other impersonal situations; owing to residential segregation the opportunities for wider forms of social interaction had been reduced to a minimum. Myrdal saw the same tendency increasing in the South without the Southerners' being aware of it.

Today the average Southerner of middle or upper class status seems to be just as likely as the typical Northerner to judge all Negroes by his cook, and he is definitely more disposed than the Northerner to draw the widest conclusions from this restricted source of information.[14]

One big difference between immigrant minorities of most kinds and the Negroes is that almost all immigrant minorities from Europe and from Latin America have been able and allowed to forget their origin. It has been characteristic that in two or three generations they will have lost their visibility and become absorbed into American culture. In great contrast to this, although the Negroes were almost the earliest immigrants into the United States, they are still in many respects outcasts. Unlike almost all other minorities, Negroes have been regarded as unassimilable.

All this material brought together by Myrdal is now fairly familiar, and it was not startlingly original even when *An American Dilemma* was published. It had been rather fully treated in other well-known books dealing with the color problem. For example, a discussion of the inconsistencies in the white American attitudes to sexual relations between whites and Negroes—what the prejudiced call "miscegenation"—had already been systematically treated by Dollard, by Allison Davis, and by the Gardners,[15] as well as in other well-known sociological textbooks. These texts were available to Myrdal, but it may be that he did not make the best advantage of them. He quotes Dollard from time to time, but Dollard's analysis is so penetrating and so understanding that some of Myrdal's presentation at this point is less impressive than it could be.

And yet there is a genuine attempt in *The American Dilemma* to present the problem in a sociological frame of reference. Myrdal gives a rank order of discrimination, which was, I believe, an original use of the approach pioneered by Emory Bogardus. The relationship that has the highest rank of discrimination—the most unattainable of all—is intermarriage and sexual intercourse involving white women. The second rank includes "the several etiquettes and discriminations which specifically concern behavior in personal relations." These include barriers against dancing, bathing, drinking, eating together, and social intercourse generally in a manner which would admit "social equality." Next come the segregations and discriminations in the use of public facilities, such as schools, churches, and means of conveyance; next, political disfranchisement. Even lower come discriminations in law courts, by the police, and by other public servants; and finally "discriminations in securing land, credit, jobs, or other means of earning a living, and discriminations in public relief and other social welfare activities."[16]

Myrdal claims that this rank order existed almost universally, but he does not explain the empirical procedures on which it was based. It may obtain in the Southern states with which he was primarily concerned, but he puts it forward as true for all parts of the United States. Its universality can be questioned; in the North, for example, political disfranchisement is not applied, nor are segregation and discrimination in the use of public facilities. But forms of discrimination in the law courts, by police, and so on, definitely persist, in the North as well as in the South. It may be felt that this rank order would not be very easily sustained against new empirical studies, and even theoretically it does not seem to be tremendously illuminating or useful as it stands.

The next topic discussed by Myrdal is the important question as to what holds Negroes down. He states—and he is again seemingly talking mainly about the South—that the Negroes behave in such a way that they hold themselves and one another down. This is put forward as a special case of the more general hypothesis that in a modern industrial society "the lower class groups will, to a great extent, take care of keeping each other subdued." For the same reason poor whites and Negroes, both groups suffering from poverty, depressed status, and insecurity, will not display proletarian solidarity toward each other, as the Marxian theory of class society would have us expect, but will expend their energies in holding each other down.

This interesting hypothesis is supported by other sociological and psychological studies, some of which are described or mentioned in Chapter 13. There is accumulated evidence that low-status groups take on the value premises of dominant groups, and accept as true the low-status evaluations of them made by dominant groups, turning their aggressions onto groups or individuals of similar status to their own.

The fact that Negroes and poor whites vie with each other in perpetuating their subordinate positions is treated by Myrdal as one facet of his general *principle of cumulation,* which is the subject of an appendix.[17] This principle calls attention to the fact that most normative notions of equilibrium have been concerned with *stable equilibrium,* whereas in the social sciences a more appropriate model is *dynamic equilibrium,* which takes change for granted. The lesson of this principle is that if a group is low in standards of living, health, education, manners, and morals, this depressed status will support the prejudices of dominant groups and will drive the low-status groups lower still. This is the operation of the "vicious circle," but Myrdal is careful to point out that the effect can also serve to reinforce the status of those of high or of rising standards. Where there is no natural status hierarchy there is also no permanent and immutable barrier to an equalization of status.

Myrdal next considers in greater detail the beliefs about racial differences. He takes some of the ancient myths, such as that of the biological inferiority of Negroes, and shows how, in spite of their scientific naïveté, these illusions manage to survive, essentially because they provide useful rationalizations for specific attitudes toward Negroes. For example, the belief that Negroes become sleepy when working with machines and lack mechanical aptitudes was long used to keep them out of industry. That particular prejudice was swept away by economic pressures, but many less specific race myths survive. There is the old, completely unsupported suggestion that Negroes have a smaller cranial capacity and hence lower intelligence and reasoning power. They are thought by some to be inherently lazy, thriftless, happy-go-lucky, amoral, criminalistic, and so on. Others suggest that Negroes are especially susceptible to disease, and this argument is still being used as a reason for discrimination.

Even if specific prejudices are tumbled, the idea of the inferiority of the Negro "race" is so deeply embedded in the minds of Americans that it is very hard to remove them. A very depressing account is given of one of Professor Donald Young's courses in race relations; at the end of the course he asked his students to rank different "races" (as he called them for the purpose), and more than five hundred students continued to rank the "American" as the superior "race," even after he had spent a semester trying to explode racial fallacies.

But to counter prejudices it is never enough merely to show that the ideas behind them are nonsensical. When the ideas exist and are currently accepted, they are, in Durkheim's words, "social facts" with which any politician or social scientist has to reckon. What the social scientist can do is to penetrate a little deeper and attempt to discover the reasons for the persistence of such beliefs and the function they are serving. Often the answer is quite easy to discern. Sometimes the cause is direct, as with the poor whites who felt that their security of employment was threatened by competition from Negro industrial workers. In other cases there is a general sense of threat, of anxiety aroused by the fact that a process of leveling is taking place.

The foregoing pages have been designed to give a taste of the contents of *The American Dilemma*. They have been taken from the first four chapters, substantially less than one-tenth of the book, which proceeds to a more detailed examination of these and other similar topics backed by a thorough demographic and economic analysis. Myrdal shows the trend of northward migration and the gradual economic emancipation that departure from the South has offered. At the same time he shows the perpetuation of various forms of discrimination.

In the realm of politics he demonstrates the two simultaneous issues—the role played by the Negro in American politics and the Negro as an American political issue. He examines the extent to which democracy operates and fails to operate; the differences between the North and the South and the elaborate ideology which the South has erected in defense against equality. He examines the relation between Southern conservatism and Southern liberalism, and exposes the techniques by which disfranchisement is carried out. This political analysis is a thorough and conscientious piece of work, and at the date of publication it was attacked less on grounds of fact than on grounds of valuation.

Today it is a fair comment that a piece of research which is concerned with factual description is particularly liable to become dated. Theories can survive changes in facts. These last twenty

years have seen tempestuous changes, and the facts are quite
evidently in need of revision. One is reminded of President Hoover's
famous investigation into "recent social trends." It was a very good
idea in the first instance; but if a job like that is worth doing at all,
it is even more worth repeating on a regular and consistent basis,
so that one is able to build up a picture of contemporary historical
change. Similarly, it would be invaluable to have an authoritative
descriptive review of what has been happening, decade by decade,
in all the fields covered by Myrdal in relation to the Negro
problem.

Some people in close touch with the problem would know how
many of the facts in Myrdal's book still apply and how many have
changed. Perhaps in general the situation has not changed radically,
and many of the discriminations which then existed may still be
found today. It would be interesting to know whether Myrdal's
work now belongs to history or to contemporary politics, and
whether Myrdal was right in thinking that improved standards of
education would disperse ignorance and the forms of racial discrimination based on ignorance.

One other point deserves comment. Myrdal starts certain of his
chapters with what he calls an "overview." His idea was that he
should make his personal stand clear on each of these issues, and in
his overview he allows himself considerable latitude in expressing
what he thinks is the correct line of development on each issue, such
as, for example, educational policy. (This particular issue was one
on which he was rather cautious; he suggested not integration but
separate, though genuinely equal, education.)

At the level of social administration the value judgments Myrdal
expresses are quite predictable. One knows what he is and was—a
good Scandinavian who had come to the United States—and one
knows that he would have a rational and solid approach to the
American dilemma. Most of his attitudes are unexceptionable, but
occasionally he makes statements that may be found rather shocking.
For some reason Scandinavians are enthusiasts for sterilization—they
sterilize some criminals, for instance—and Myrdal concludes rather
regretfully that the American Creed would not tolerate this rational
solution to overpopulation in the Southern states.

It will be remembered that Myrdal promised that his book would
be analytical rather than descriptive. It is difficult to agree that the

book is an analytic treatment, because in order to analyze efficiently a rather more sophisticated conceptual framework is called for. It is partly a reflection of the date at which Myrdal was writing, partly perhaps that his background was in economics rather than in sociology or social psychology. Be that as it may, his formulation has since been greatly improved upon. For example, in a study of West Indians working at Liverpool, England, Anthony Richmond advances a considerably more highly developed theory of racial prejudice. After an excellent brief review of the findings of sociologists and social psychologists as they relate to the tensions of intergroup relations, Richmond summarizes his theory in terms of three hypotheses.[18]

The first is the *In-group/Out-group Hypothesis,* which states that where two or more groups of different ethnic composition come into contact and communication with each other, there will be a tendency for the members of the same ethnic group to identify closely with one another to the exclusion of the members of other groups to whom derogatory characteristics and hostile intentions may be attributed. This hypothesis could clearly have been generalized beyond the discussion of relations between different ethnic groups.

Richmond's second hypothesis, the *Status/Security Hypothesis,* states that an individual's sense of status and security is derived from his group membership and through receiving expressions of love, approval, and esteem from those with whom he identifies. Insecure group membership or fear of losing status is a source of anxiety and may result in the direction of hostility upon out-group members and others.

Third is the *Frames of Reference/Communication Hypothesis,* which reads:

The attitude of a person towards members of out-groups is the product of a frame of reference largely derived from the individual's own group membership. Subjective and institutionalised barriers to communication re-enforce stereotyped beliefs and hostile attitudes which are only effectively modified when the individual has the shared support of the members of his own group.

It would be equally possible to apply Homans' system, which postulates a mutual dependence of sentiment, activity, and interaction. According to this system, sentiments of liking will be expressed in the pursuit of common activities, and the groups thus crystallized will increasingly differentiate their activities from those of other subgroups.[19]

There is at least a level of generality about these theorems that is somehow lacking in Myrdal's approach. The only general principle that he adduces at this point is the *principle of cumulation*, which is essentially applied to economic status. It is as though he had treated the Negro problem—the "American dilemma"—as a local and to some extent a unique problem, when in fact the problem of intergroup relations can be broken down into components that are very general in their applicability. To take one example, Myrdal dismisses in one paragraph[20] the suggestion that the problem of Jews or other racial minorities is comparable with the Negro problem; his nearest approach to a generalization is in Appendix 5, when he compares the status of Negroes with the status of women and children. And although by his whole outlook he recognizes that this American dilemma is a problem in the minds of white Americans, he does not proceed from this to make any study of the roots of prejudice as such, irrespective of the group on which the prejudices may be focused. He studies prejudices in considerable detail, but he does not study prejudice. This cannot be explained by the fact that the study of the *Authoritarian Personality* (see Chapter 11) had still to be undertaken. After all, Myrdal enjoyed the incomparable support and help from an extremely strong cast of social scientists, and he could have leaned quite heavily on work that they had already produced. The difficulty perhaps is that Myrdal is primarily a social economist, a sociologist at one remove, and a psychologist not at all. Though *An American Dilemma* is an extremely courageous book and a mine of information about the past, present, and possible futures of the American Negro, it does not at the substantive or theoretical level provide any important increment to the general corpus of the social sciences.

METHODOLOGY

We can next turn to the methodological appendices. These are the most famous, and perhaps the most lasting, contribution of the book. They are rather carefully worked out and, although not always easy to follow, do materially advance the methodology of the social sciences.

The first appendix is called "Note on Valuations and Beliefs."[21] It starts by distinguishing *beliefs, valuations,* and *opinions.* Beliefs can be shown to be true or false and more complete or less complete. Valuations, in the absence of a science of ethology, cannot be judged by similar objective standards. Opinions are an amalgam of the two, containing assertions as to what is believed by the speaker to be true or false and also as to what is valued by the speaker as good or bad. Often people do not distinguish what they think they know from what they like or dislike, but it is much safer to separate the two to make it clear what is being discussed.

People in our civilization desire to be rational and objective in their beliefs. We have faith in science and are, in principle, prepared to change our beliefs according to scientific findings. People also like to have "reasons" for the valuations they hold, and they usually express only the valuations for which they think they have reasons. With the help of certain beliefs about reality, a general value order is assumed and the specific valuations are derived as logical inferences from this general value order.

The difficulty in which the ordinary individual finds himself is due to the fact that many of his specific valuations are in conflict with one another; consequently there is no logical and coherent general value order from which all such valuations could have been derived.

In view of these inconsistencies it becomes important to recognize that the specific valuations occupy very different levels of generality.

Some concern human beings in general; others concern Negroes or women or foreigners; still others concern a particular group of Negroes or an individual Negro. Some valuations have general and eternal validity: others have validity only for certain situations.[22]

Now it is an abstract proposition, in Western society at least, that the more general and timeless valuations, the eternal verities, are morally higher and more desirable than transient valuations, and it is therefore always found more acceptable to deduce one's more specific valuations from the more general ones, as they will then have the credit attached to the general ones. Valuations used to defend specific actions (or inactions) are often opportunistic, and people find it possible in the short run to keep their higher moral valuations in the shadows. But such valuations cannot be permanently silenced, and, as Myrdal points out, it is one of the functions of the ordinary democratic way of life that if certain public actions imply moral valuations that are not shared by all of society, then those sections of society that do not share these valuations will, by public discussion, make them explicit and will demand justification for them.

The temptation will be strong to deny the existence of a conflict in valuations. This is often done by denying the existence of the fact to which the valuation relates. If you can say that the Negro problem does not exist, and can persuade yourself and others that this assertion is true, you are thereby absolved from making any valuation about behavior which is prejudicial to Negroes. This refusal to recognize facts is, however, becoming increasingly difficult. Society is steadily moving toward more general and more all-embracing valuations, and under these conditions the possibility of suppressing inconvenient valuations is being reduced. It is on these grounds that Myrdal expresses a deep-seated and quite explicit belief in social progress. Social amelioration is to him made inevitable by the fact that inconvenient valuations are constantly being exposed and thus made untenable. Education and the free dissemination of knowledge appear to him the ultimate safeguards against crude ideologies and irrational beliefs.

The next section of the appendix is devoted to a theoretical critique of the concept "mores." Myrdal was a fierce opponent of William Graham Sumner, principally on the grounds that Sumner's emphasis on "folkways" seems to suggest that there is something unchangeable about society or that changes must be slow. It is true that Sumner was conservative in his approach to political and social changes, whereas Myrdal, who believes social change to be necessary and desirable, is unwilling to agree that the existence of mores will hold out against social changes induced by legislation. Myrdal's belief is that, while it may have been true in primitive societies, and even in the static periods of civilization—such as classical Egypt or to some extent eighteenth-century Europe—it is not true at all that folkways and mores can prevent change in a modern adaptive society, because modern society is not a "homogeneous, unproblematic, fairly static, social entity."[23] In modern society valuation conflicts are typical, and moral compromises unavoidable.

If conflict is indigenous, we have to accept the fact that there will be "valuation explosions," that is, occasions when inconsistent valuations collide with each other in a fashion that cannot be ignored. Change is therefore normal, and static equilibrium, or "stability," is abnormal. Myrdal links Marx and Sumner in his criticism that both took an essentially static and fatalistic view of history, not realizing that opinions themselves are an active ingredient in social change. They were both too busy with the external material forces making for social change to pay attention to the way in which opinions themselves help to mediate social change. Thus Myrdal came to believe that the spread of social democracy is an inevitable consequence of popular education and of the decreasing inconsistency in valuations. The alternative, which is a very serious and constant threat, is what he calls "moral cynicism," the permanent and growing acceptance of inconsistencies in valuation; if these gain the upper hand, there may be a reversion to fascism and pagan gods. Even if this disastrous eventuality is avoided, the danger remains that at times of change ideologies thrive, and leaders have great power for good or evil. In the unstable modern world "there is continuously the possibility of rapid, and even induced, change, the direction of which is not altogether predetermined by trends and natural forces."[24]

This is a highly coherent presentation of an idea which is very clearly related to the possibilities of amelioration and social progress. On the other hand, the universality of conflict in modern society must also be accepted, and Myrdal is undoubtedly right in his criticism that Sumner does not take enough account of the complexities of a modern civilization.

Myrdal devotes his next appendix[25] to the biases and valuations to which social scientists themselves are prone.

Full objectivity . . . is an ideal to which we are constantly striving, but which we can never reach. The social scientist, too, is part of the culture in which he lives, and he never succeeds in freeing himself entirely from dependence on the dominant preconceptions and biases of his environment.[26]

All scientists have biases and seek rationalizations, but these are more prominent and serious in the case of social scientists than in the case of natural scientists. The remedy, according to Myrdal, is to apply scientific methods: by stating all premises explicitly, to eliminate inconclusive inferences; by repeating observations, to ensure that observed data are correctly perceived and recorded; by applying alternative hypotheses to the data and by widening the field of the study, to ensure that the conclusions are not predetermined by the choice of data.

In particular relation to the research on the Negro problem he lists the tendencies toward scientific bias that he has detected in various authors. There are laid out along six different scales, on each of which an author may conceal a bias which works either for or against a disfavored group such as the American Negroes.

He calls the first the scale of *"friendliness"* to the Negro. It is not so long ago that white scholars seemed to work more or less consistently in the interests of the dominant white ideology, justifying the traditional treatment of Negroes in America or explaining the subordinate position of Negroes in terms of biological or racial traits. More recently the scientific treatment of the Negro problem had become vastly more friendly to the Negroes, partly as a reaction, a feeling for "fair play," and for consideration toward the "underdog." Negro social scientists might be assumed to be pro-Negro, but, on the other hand, the desire to be objective causes at least some of them to lean over backward in the interests of science, so that they interpret the facts in a way which is actually biased against their own people.

The second source of bias is expressed in the scale of *"friendliness"* to the South. This can represent the stand of a Southern writer or the defense mechanism of a Northern writer to atone for the Civil War; in this case a bias toward the South will mean a bias toward the Southern whites and hence a bias against the Negroes.

The third scale is that of *radicalism-conservatism*. In a sense this is the master scale of biases in the social sciences. At the time of Myrdal's writing there had been a general tendency over several decades, in American society and its social science, toward greater liberalism. This cumulative liberal-radicalism would favor a pro-Negro attitude.

The fourth scale relates to *optimism-pessimism*. An optimistic attitude is liable to discourage the exposure of bad features of society and will generally lead to a soft-pedaling of such adverse facts in the interracial situation as are likely to persist.

Fifth, the increasing generality of valuation already referred to favors *incorporation of the Negro problem* in the total social, economic, and political statement. One cannot be sure how this will affect results, but greater integration of the Negro problem in the total statement should decrease bias.

Sixth, increasing scientific status is likely to increase the scientist's fearless *exposure of anti-Negro excesses*. Certainly on the whole the advances of sciences to date have helped to silence those who voiced some of the worst racist absurdities.

Now comes the question of how we may set about mitigating bias in the social sciences. As Myrdal reminds us, facts are necessary in exposing ideologies, but they are not sufficient; there must also be hypotheses which are related to significant issues. There must also be practical conclusions. This is a point on which Myrdal is quite explicit. He is opposed to those who feel that social science should be value-free. He comments: "Science becomes no better protected against biases by the entirely negative device of refusing to arrange its result for practical and political utilization."[27] In fact, the opposite is true. It is thus part of the social scientist's task not only to expose the facts but also to show the implications of these facts for practical action, and in Myrdal's opinion it is largely a historical accident that American social scientists are so reluctant to commit themselves to the practical implications of their findings.

It is impossible to find any piece of research in which facts are not permeated with valuations. This applies even to the most ostentatiously "pure" fact-finding research, which differs only in concealing the implicit value premises. Again, the only safeguard is to make the premises explicit. Sometimes the bias is more subtle, as when the social scientist is so determined to be open-minded and balanced in his judgment that he inevitably adopts a compromise position that will offend nobody; every unfavorable statement is balanced against a favorable one. Another offender is the social scientist who will always try to protect himself from the need to take decisions on the grounds that not enough is known and that further research is needed.

It must be remembered that even in the early 1940's some soci-

ologists were articulately promoting the philosophy of the pure
accumulation of knowledge. George Lundberg, one of the protago-
nists of this viewpoint, was himself a consultant with Myrdal's
project, but he is not of course named in this context. Myrdal was
explicitly against Sumner's position, for reasons already given. He
was against Park's work because he found Park too much of a
natural historian who merely described the nature of society—pas-
sionately curious about society without passion for changing it—
whereas Myrdal favored "social engineering," a phrase of his own
coinage. He was against Ogburn's influence because in his opinion
Ogburn was too much devoted to science, had a scientistic deviation.
He was against Giddings because Giddings was a prophet of laissez
faire. He was against the static and fatalistic valuations that so many
sociologists adopt, and transmit through the hidden ethos of a natural
order of things which is contained in words like "balance," "harmony," "equilibrium," "adjustment," "accommodation," "function,"
"disorganization," and so on.

However, not all American sociologists came under his lash. He
was in favor of the reformism of Lester F. Ward; he was in favor
of Louis Wirth, who had expressed opinions in fundamental agreement with his own. He praised John Dollard, Robert MacIver, and
the later (*Knowledge for What?*) Robert Lynd. He did not mention
Elton Mayo, but Elton Mayo was the prophet of "social skills" as
opposed to "social philosophy," and their views on this point certainly had much in common.

The conclusions of this methodological note are elaborately and
cogently summarized. First Myrdal stresses the importance of the
distinction between *theoretical* research, aimed at ascertaining facts
and causal relations between facts, and *practical* research ("social
engineering") concerned with ends and means. Theoretical research
tries to establish the facts about past and present and a prognosis of
the future: practical research, which is oriented to the future, has
as its final goal the scientific planning of "induced changes." As has
been mentioned, Myrdal's explicit valuation is that, although practical research needs sound theoretical analysis of actual facts and
their causal interrelations, this is not enough. Practical conclusions
are, by logical necessity, inferences from value premises as well as
from factual premises.

As practical problems were to be central in his work, it was therefore necessary to devote the closest attention to value premises. For research, value premises are required to satisfy the following criteria: they must be *explicitly stated* and not hidden as tacit assumptions; they must be *specific* and *concretized;* they must be *purposively selected* with reference to the aims of the practical research; they must be recognized as *hypothetical* rather than as self-evident or generally valid; because society admits incompatible valuations *alternative* value premises should be tried; the first principle of selection should be *relevance;* the second principle of selection should be *significance,* that is, valuations held by large or powerful groups, and therefore politically realistic; the goals set by value premises must also be *feasible* (indeed one of the most important tasks of social science is to criticize people's actual valuations in terms of feasibility); finally, the set of value premises selected for practical research must be *internally consistent.*

In summary, "the aim of practical research . . . is . . . to show precisely what should be the practical and political opinions and plans for action from the point of view of the various valuations if their holders also had the more correct and comprehensive factual knowledge which science provides."[28] That quotation is slightly obscure in its wording, but it is a carefully formulated answer to a recurring question. Max Weber, for example, was worried during World War I what his function should be as a man in authority in the university, as a potential professorial prophet; he had to search his own integrity to see what role he should play. Should he tell people what to do or help them to analyze for themselves what the consequences would be of taking different courses? "In theory," as Gerth and Mills delicately put it, "he rigidly segregated his role as a professor and scientist from that of a publicist."[29] Max Weber inscribed his own position in *Science as a Vocation* (*Wissenschaft als Beruf*):

To take a practical political stand is one thing, and to analyze political structures and party positions is another. When speaking in a political meeting about democracy, one does not hide one's personal standpoint; indeed to come out clearly and take a stand is one's damned duty. . . . It would be an outrage, however, to use words in this fashion in a lecture or in the lecture-room. If, for instance, "democracy" is under discussion . . . one confronts the forms of democracy with non-democratic forms of political order and endeavors to come to a position

where the student may find the point from which, in terms of his ultimate ideals, he can take a stand. . . . One can only demand of the teacher
that he have the intellectual integrity to see that it is one thing to state
facts, to determine mathematical or logical relations or the internal
structure of cultural values, while it is another thing to answer questions
of the *value* of culture and its individual contents and the question of
how one should act in the cultural community and in political associations.[30]

It is clear that this is very much in line with what Myrdal is
proposing here. To Weber the function of the social scientist as
a scientist is to give people an opportunity to choose rationally
between alternative courses of action by providing them with
scientific predictions of what the results of alternative courses of
action will be. Myrdal wishes to go further than this. He sees
himself not merely as a provider of prognoses but as actually
involved in policy making, taking into account the political prac-
ticability of alternative aims. This means that the appropriate practical research becomes rather closely identified with the programs
themselves. To him, it is not enough to be a spectator of these
alternative programs; it is necessary to work through policy makers
to rationalize existing programs.

Theoretical analysis reveals that there is actual struggle and competition
between individuals and between groups, and that social trends take their
form as an outcome of this struggle and competition. For practical
analysis, therefore, there must be alternative programs.[31]

Up to this point the principles described for selecting value
premises and introducing them into scientific research have been
idealized, untrammeled by practical difficulties. In reality, however,
the choice of value premises is greatly restricted. The first restriction
is lack of knowledge; for example, in the case of the Negro problem
public attitudes have been inadequately studied. Moreover, as has
been shown, the Negro problem is not a problem in isolation, and
valuations with respect to the Negro cannot be isolated. Again,
popular valuations do not distinguish between "ends" or goals and
"means" or side effects. Another difficulty is that conflicts of valuation occur not only between individuals or groups but also within
single individuals, who may be blind to the inconsistencies in their
position or to the extent to which their beliefs and valuations are

interwoven. Finally, there is the practical operational problem in this kind of research that sets of valuations cannot easily be sorted out into neat and manageable categories.

It is clear that a research worker confronted with a tangle of popular valuations will find it impracticable to follow them all up simultaneously. Myrdal therefore suggests the following practical solution:

> That one single set of relevant and significant value premises be selected for utilization in a preliminary analysis and that other significant sets of value premises be introduced at a later stage of the investigation to make possible judgments in terms of alternative valuations and policies.[32]

But—and this is his caveat, one almost impossible for a human being to follow—you must constantly bear in mind the provisional nature of your choice of value premises, which has been made purely for technical and instrumental reasons. In practice, as Myrdal fully recognizes, the one set of value premises that you choose is given a strategically favorable position in the study. The whole direction of the subsequent theoretical research becomes determined by this norm, and with the typical limitations on research resources there is seldom time or money left to rework the material in the light of alternative sets of value premises. Even this neglects the observable fact that the research worker probably does as Myrdal has done and initially selects for his study the value premises most congenial to himself; after working with them for a few years, he is so identified with his premises that he would find it very hard to abandon them or to work equally sympathetically with other premises. The "instrumental norm" is destined to become the final norm of the scientist.

The last practical difficulty discussed by Myrdal concerns the inevitable introduction into scientific research of the "value-loaded term." In the case of the Negro problem, terms such as "disfranchisement" or "discrimination" determine the lines that the subsequent research will take. Many scientists, like many administrators, attempt to avoid the biases attached to these words by choosing new terms that do not yet have evaluatory associations. Myrdal regards this attempt as misdirected. The terms themselves are naturally evaluative as well as descriptive because they are defined in relation to the ethos of a society. He quotes a letter from Louis

Wirth: "Without valuations, we have no interest, no sense of relevance or of significance, and, consequently, no object."[33] A "disinterested social science" is pure nonsense. It never existed and it never will exist. We can make our thinking strictly rational in spite of this, but only by facing the valuations, not by evading them. I do not propose to comment in general on Myrdal's methodology, except to say that it is taken rather seriously. In detail, perhaps one of the weakest links is the assumption that the individual can be explicit about his own valuations. Since the Greek philosophers the suggestion has constantly been made that the scientist (or philosopher) should take thought and get to know himself. This implies that, if by a process of self-analysis you make your own assumptions explicit, you will find it easier to discard them and try another set. Since Freud's demonstration of the role of the unconscious in determining attitudes and behavior it has become clear that the possibilities of this kind of self-analysis are somewhat restricted. The things that you can externalize are the things that do not matter so much to you, whereas to expose the attitudes that are based on deep-seated mental experiences may require prolonged help from a qualified psychoanalyst. Many social scientists have undergone psychoanalytic courses, but it is perhaps not entirely proved that they are more emancipated from social prejudices than those who have not had this experience.

On the general relation between a social scientist's professional work and his personal social and political inclinations one may be allowed to doubt whether Myrdal had at the date of writing completely resolved his own position. Essentially *An American Dilemma* leads to a program based on liberal-democratic ideology. Like the program presented by Lynd in *Knowledge for What?* and discussed in an earlier chapter, it offers a course of action which most men of good will and of progressive persuasion would happily endorse. But we cannot forget that Myrdal laid down for us a different criterion for social research in which, starting with alternative sets of value premises, different courses of action would be worked through to their consequences. To the best of my knowledge this exercise has never been undertaken, and Myrdal hardly attempted it in this study. Could the reason for this failure be that the aim is unrealizable? May it not be that the social scientist engaged in what Myrdal calls "practical research" must be committed to an objective in which he truly believes, and that the exclusive study of causal relationships requires the detachment of what he calls "theoretical research" in which, ideally, "facts" predominate and "valuations" can be minimized?

SOCIAL THEORY

Finally, there is the question of what is normally regarded as theoretical sociology. Granted that Myrdal is no social theorist, what contribution did *An American Dilemma* make to the development of theory? Perhaps the first answer is that it constitutes a massive and careful compilation of information on Negroes and their interrelationships with American whites that can be worked over by secondary analysis. Throughout this chapter I have attributed all statements to Myrdal, but it should be remembered that there were two main collaborators, namely, Richard Sterner, the Swedish economist, and Arnold M. Rose, then a very young man but now a distinguished sociologist, for many years a professor of sociology at the University of Minnesota. Since he collaborated in the writing of *An American Dilemma*, Rose's interests have inclined toward sociological theory in its orthodox sense. Soon after the publication of *An American Dilemma* and of his own book, *The American Negro*, Rose produced *Studies in Reduction of Prejudice*, asserting his recognition that prejudice is a subject in itself.

By 1953 Rose contributed to a conference on behavioral research a paper entitled *Some Suggestions for Research on Race or Culture Conflict*. The focus has significantly altered, away from such practical questions as "What shall we do about the Negroes and our attitude to the Negroes?" to such theoretically phrased questions as "What are the determinants of inter-group conflict?," "What is the effect on prejudice of certain planned actions intended to reduce prejudice?," or "What personality disturbances, if any, accompany group self-hatred?" In the same paper he declares:

Lasting and fruitful theory builds up slowly, in intimate contact with empirical research. After decades of research we are just now becoming able to formulate soundly based theory. . . . The earlier essays, that have passed for theory, were in the nature of intelligent guesses and have had the function of provoking research. Unfortunately, not all of these ideas have been tested empirically, and most of them deserve to be. So many of the researches in the field of race and culture conflict have consisted of pointless description or of description to refute stereotypes and other false popular ideas that there has not been enough time available to specialists to test many of the seminal ideas that could lead to the development of real theory. Perhaps the changing popular attitudes towards minority groups and the new opportunities for conducting research in the social sciences will allow an increased emphasis on research with broader theoretical implications.[34]

Also in 1953, Gunnar Myrdal, by then the executive secretary of the Economic Commission for Europe, was called upon to address the first conference of the British Sociological Association on the subject of "Social Theory and Social Policy." A major theme of his address was that the social sciences have had a very great influence on social policy, but that this influence was indirect, being "due in the main to their exposition and propagation of certain general thoughts and theories."[35]

As specific instances Myrdal cites Malthus, Ricardo, Marx, Darwin, Spencer, and Keynes. He continues:

It is also my considered opinion, reached after careful study, that the important changes in race relations now slowly taking place in America are to a considerable extent the result of the sociologists' exposure of the stereotyped superstitions present about the Negro in the popular mind.[36]

This statement may well be contrasted with that of Rose. But Myrdal is not defensive. He makes it clear that to him theories are general ideas that can influence social policy.

I do not, of course, want to deprecate penetrating theoretical thinking and the collection and analysis of facts. The progress of science is attained only by hard work. Even general ideas of the type which I have mentioned have often developed and have always been modified as a result of involved thinking and intensive research. But it is only natural that public interest should be focused rather on the general conclusions we reach as the result of our work.[37]

It may be felt that this statement leaves the relation between ideas and theories still unclarified.

9

SOCIAL SCIENCE AND THE SOLDIER

The subject of this chapter is the series, "Studies in Social Psychology in World War II," which was published in four volumes in 1949 and 1950. The first two volumes are titled *The American Soldier*, Volume I being subtitled *Adjustment during Army Life* and Volume II, *Combat and Its Aftermath*. They describe the substantive results relating to these two subjects which were obtained in the course of the research program. Volume III, *Experiments on Mass Communications*, describes the work done in appraising the effectiveness of films and other mass-communication devices. Volume IV, with which we shall primarily be concerned, is the methodological report, *Measurement and Prediction*. Also to be discussed in this chapter is the companion volume, *Continuities in Social Research: Studies in the Scope and Method of* "The American Soldier," edited by Merton and Lazarsfeld.[1]

The research effort reported in these four volumes is very impressive. The researches previously described in this book have mainly been either academic or sponsored on a small scale. The one exception was *An American Dilemma*, sponsored by the Carnegie Corporation, which, as we have seen, was primarily a policy statement on a major public issue rather than a supply of fresh empirical data. The research program reported in *The American Soldier* was an official program of the Information and Education Division of the Army. This very fact demonstrated how rapidly the social sciences were becoming respectable in the United States. Since then not only the Pentagon but many other departments of the Federal and state governments in the United States have been spending large sums in sponsoring sociological inquiries of different kinds.

Thus, the initial surprise is that this program ever started. The fact that it did start and on the whole was a great success—an administrative success and also a scientific success—has undoubtedly set the pace for later developments.

The origins of the project were quite insecure. As recently as May, 1941, only about five months before the Research Branch was set up, the then Secretary of War issued a special directive aimed against all polling of the armed forces.

Our army must be a cohesive unit, with a definite purpose shared by all. Such an army can be built only by the responsible effort of all of its members, commissioned and enlisted. Anonymous opinion or criticism, good or bad, is destructive in its effect on a military organization where accepted responsibility on the part of every individual is fundamental. It is therefore directed that because of their anonymous nature, polls will not be permitted among the personnel of the Army of the United States.[2]

This very definite instruction looked as though it would not easily be overthrown. But quite soon thereafter, and some time before the United States entered the war, Henry L. Stimson became Secretary of War, and General Frederick H. Osborn, businessman and personal friend of both President Roosevelt and Mr. Stimson, was appointed Director of the Morale Division (as it was then called) of the Army. This division had been set up to look after all questions of morale among the armed forces; it later became the Special Services Division and finally took on the title that it kept for the rest of the war, namely, the Information and Education Division.

Quite soon after he was appointed, General Osborn saw that he would be handicapped in his attempts to deal with questions of morale if he had no means of discovering what the morale level was. So on these grounds he asked for a reversal of the directive against polling. In this he was supported by General George C. Marshall and also by another Army Division, G2 (Intelligence Division). G2 had in fact themselves taken the preliminary steps toward setting up their own polling unit, but they generously withdrew their interest in favor of General Osborn's project.

So as little as five months after the original directive, the staff for the Research Branch began to be assembled, it being clearly understood that their research would entail the polling of the members of the armed forces. By chance, the first actual survey was launched on December 8, 1941, one day after the bombing of Pearl Harbor.

Initially the Research Branch was manned mainly by Army personnel, but some civilian advisers were brought in from the early stages. The advisers included Samuel A. Stouffer, of Harvard University, Rensis Likert, of the Department of Agriculture (the originator of the Likert Scale in the thirties and forties), and Quinn McNemar, of Stamford. An advisory committee was formally constituted and tried to inculcate some respect for research procedures into what was still primarily a military unit.

Although the Research Branch was launched, there were at first many frustrations. The program was a long time taking shape, and the personnel did not have any great standing with the Army. It was only by June, 1942, that a satisfactory administrative pattern for the unit began to emerge. By then, while the administrative direction was still entirely military, Stouffer had become technical director. All the decisions concerning technical questions were referred to Stouffer, who remained director throughout the war.

In June, 1942, he prepared a memorandum for General Osborn describing the current difficulties and proposing remedies. He had the advantage of having had previous experience of a similar problem. As early as 1937 he had been asked by the National Resources Planning Board to make a study of research agencies in Washington; he had then reached the conclusion that such research agencies could succeed only if two conditions were satisfied, and he put these forward again in the present context. The first condition was that there should be really good and continual touch between the administration and the research direction, so that administrative policies needing research for clarification or decision could be brought to light at the earliest moment. The second condition was that the research unit itself should have the power to look ahead, so that their research program would enable them to anticipate problems and thus to have ready answers. Otherwise—and this is a typical experience—an administrative body with a docile research unit suddenly runs up against a difficulty and calls in the research unit to supply an answer. The research unit will ask for six months to find an answer, and the administrators will retort that this would be too late. Such a relationship is obviously unsatisfactory. Most people who have been connected with research in this or similar fields will have had the same experience of being asked too late to tackle an urgent problem. Stouffer pointed out that a better arrangement is to entrust the research unit itself with the responsibility for anticipating problems so that they may undertake research in advance of requests from the administrators.

Stouffer suggested that contact with administrative policy be maintained on several levels. *First*, there should be regular conferences of the research team with the chief, assistant chief, and other top administrators in the division, who were military men. This meant not simply sitting around in a formal situation but what he calls "occasional relaxed free-flowing bull sessions in which broad policies are talked over and in which the mutual give and take of leisurely discussion encourages new ideas to be bandied about."[3] One may comment that this is a very demanding suggestion to make of a military organization. Not that military personnel object to relaxed and free-flowing discussion, but they may well be found to object to civilians', however expert, coming in and offering free-flowing suggestions. In particular, they may object to groups that break away from the hierarchical system, and in which quite expert but rather young scientists might deliver a lecture to the general on the rights and wrongs of policy. Even more irritating, the young scientist would quite possibly be the very man who has at his disposal the facts that justify him in lecturing the general.

In practice, perhaps because Stouffer was clear about his objective from the start, the relationship between the civilian and military personnel appears to have worked smoothly. Moreover, the fact that the Research Branch was prepared to advise on policy questions that might concern the whole Army came to be recognized, and as time went on and their status was consolidated, they did in fact make direct and positive suggestions on policy matters; for example, it was the Research Branch that recommended the points system for demobilization, basing this advice on their polls of army units.

As a *second* point Stouffer asked for personal contacts between his research team and senior officers in other units. He went so far as to suggest that they have at least one reliable and influential contact in every key office in the Army and War Department; this officer would be not just a postal contact but somebody well informed about the research program who would be able to "sell" the Research Branch to his division and could also filter back any problems or ideas for research from the division.

The *third* stipulation, which must also have been rather hard for the Army hierarchy to accept, was that the research team should have personal contacts with enlisted men, in the sense that they should be free—not only subject to specific authorization, but in a general way, as and when they felt it necessary—to scout around and ask enlisted men to state their gripes. Stouffer's irrefutable argument was that, unless his team were permitted to get the feel of the problem on the ground in that way, all their questions would be too formalized.

Fourth—and there would have been less difficulty about this—he asked for free and personal contacts with research men in other agencies and outside the government.

The memorandum also contains an idea of the sort of program Stouffer had in mind. Items of the first type consisted of what he called "planning surveys," which were the ones already mentioned, designed to anticipate future inquiries. He cited as examples the problem of troops that were vegetating in countries, such as Newfoundland and Trinidad, away from the main theaters and likely to suffer a fall in morale for that reason; attitudes of troops that were soon going overseas; attitudes of Negroes; attitudes in special branches, such as the air corps, as compared with those in the rest of the army; and attitudes of troops fighting under special conditions, such as the desert army. Planning surveys would provide a steady routine buildup of knowledge of the attitudes of different units which would be worked out and confirmed well ahead of immediate problems. Second, he put forward another long-range proposal that wherever possible experimental programs should be developed. He pointed out that experimentation was not a novelty to the Army. For example, the introduction of a new type of boots was preceded by a scientifically controlled experiment, and there seemed to be no reason why a similar procedure could not be extended to other fields. Third, he recognized that, in spite of the most careful long-term planning, there would very often be quite small and not necessarily very interesting problems that would arise and would require an immediate answer. He therefore suggested that provision be made for these eventualities by building up an organization designed for rapid results. At any hour of the day or night a couple of men could be sent to any camp and, with local help, could run off an investigation, airmail it back to headquarters for processing, and the answer could be ready in a few days. Fourth, he put forward the suggestion that without delay the research team begin to work on what he called "indices of morale," which would determine by some routine measurements how morale in different places was developing.

This memorandum is of great interest. It sets the pace for the later development of the Research Branch, and it shows what was perhaps Stouffer's outstanding asset, namely, his great sensitivity to administrative need. He showed himself to be a practical man who got on well with generals and knew how to speak their language, and his memorandum was calculated to be a realistic and reasonable document that it would be captious to object to. With typical skill he closed his memorandum with the words "We want our Branch to be a model in Washington for its marriage of honest competent research to statesmanlike policy."[4]

It happened that June, 1942, the month in which this memorandum was submitted, was probably the low point in the history of the Research Branch. It must have seemed as though no progress was being made, but, in point of fact, things began to move quite soon afterward. A month or two later they were able to start their first full-scale study in the Air Force. In the fall of 1942 General Eisenhower in London had a talk with Elmo Roper, of the *Fortune* poll, which led to the setting-up in London of an ETO section of the Research Branch. In 1943 and 1944 other overseas theaters were opened up in the same way. So this unit, which had for a time looked as though it might be stillborn, began to gather strength. This was of course a period in the war in which the United States effort was building up very fast.

With this rapid expansion of the Research Branch the decision was taken that wherever possible there should be administrative devolution to the separate theaters. The Central Office in Washington was maintained for dealing with all domestic surveys, but a large proportion of the surveys were run entirely by teams attached to the theaters, who were in contact only by remote control and who undertook all their own investigation and their own analysis. By this method the Washington component was kept quite small; at its peak, in the spring of 1945, it consisted of ten officers, nine enlisted men, twenty-four professional civil servants up to the level of P-2., and fifty clerks. That was small as such organizations go.

Besides having a good statesmanlike, honest, competent approach to their task, the Research Branch worked out a smoothly operating "research pattern," a routine procedure for dealing with their surveys. This was typically straightforward. First, a request would come in; dependence on requests from outside remained the normal starting point in spite of Stouffer's case for "planning surveys." The Medical Division, for example, would ask for an inquiry into the men's attitudes toward the medical services. At the first convenient moment the Research Branch would fit this item into their program, and the scientist in charge would then begin discussions with the Surgeon General's staff to decide on the questions to be examined. The Research Branch would then start scouting; enlisted men from the unit would enter into informal discussions with enlisted men in selected camps, and, insofar as attitudes of officers were also being canvassed, officers from the unit would converse with officers. The enlisted men employed in this work were normally selected because they had had some experience of interviewing and analysis of interview material, and after further training with the Research Branch they became highly skilled interviewers. After the scouting stage they would return to the unit, and following lengthy discussions a questionnaire would be drafted. This would next be pretested—an indispensable preliminary to any serious interview survey. The results of the pretest would be examined to detect and eliminate obscurities and ambiguities, and the final schedule would be taken back to the client—in the example chosen the Surgeon General's Department—so that a final version could be hammered out with them. Only after all these preliminaries would the survey be put into the field. Today these stages would be regarded as constituting a routine procedure for any organization of high standing that conducts this type of inquiry.

In England the Government Social Survey has a function which in many ways corresponds with that of the wartime Research

Branch. The Social Survey, which is a permanent government unit under the direction of Louis Moss, undertakes surveys at the request of British Government departments and other official bodies in England. Their mode of procedure corresponds very closely with that of the Research Branch, and they have undertaken surveys on an astonishing range of subjects. Many of the results have been published or have at least been made available to research workers, but unfortunately there has as yet been no secondary analysis or integration of their work at all corresponding with that accomplished for the Research Branch in the four volumes.

In important respects the methods of the Research Branch, though extremely rigorous, were realistic. Frederick Mosteller, the distinguished statistician, had been an adviser on sampling at a critical period; and all the sampling was done as centrally as could be arranged, which meant that the domestic surveys were sampled in Washington and others at the theater headquarters. The fieldwork was undertaken by sending out a nucleus of staff, perhaps one officer and one enlisted man, and the other research staff would be attached to the survey from the local unit. By this method high technical standards were married with thorough local knowledge. From the beginning Stouffer's request for close contact with civilian authorities was granted, and a number of eminent sociologists and social psychologists—John Dollard, Louis Guttman, Hadley Cantril, and others—were associated as advisers in the work of the Research Branch throughout its existence.

The surveys completed in the four or five years' life of the Research Branch numbered between two hundred and three hundred. They are listed in an appendix to Volume II of *The American Soldier*. There were naturally considerable repetition and replication in different contexts, but a quite clear pattern emerges. This can be illustrated by citing a few examples (size of sample in brackets):

Attitudes of soldiers stationed in Bermuda
　(a small survey with a sample of 300)
Attitudes toward the war (2,900)
Attitudes toward civilians (3,500)
Leisure-time activities (2,400)
Attitudes toward army jobs, etc. (3,000)
Attitudes of and toward Negroes (12,200)

Attitudes of WAC recruits (100)
Leisure-time activities (again) (4,300)

It appears that rather more than half of the surveys were undertaken in the United States, but almost all the theaters of operation were quite well represented. It will also be seen what an important part the study of attitudes took in the series.

Each one of these numerous surveys was concluded by an individual report sent to the appropriate authorities, and it may be presumed that the authorities at least sometimes acted on the results. But at the end of the war it was suggested that there be an attempt to make more permanent use of these inevitably ephemeral reports. It was proposed that the material be worked over and in some form be released to the public. The Army seems to have taken a very liberal attitude toward this suggestion and to have put very few restrictions on the reuse of their data for publication in the proposed volumes. The Army could not allocate money to have the work done, but happily the Carnegie Corporation made to the Social Science Research Council in 1946 a grant which was generous enough to collect a very strong team to work through the material for publication. The team was headed by Dr. Stouffer, and it included Edward Suchman and Robin Williams (both from Cornell), Leonard Cottrell (Russell Sage Foundation), Louis Guttmann (previously at Cornell and now in Israel), and Paul Lazarsfeld (Columbia), all social scientists who had already had connections with the surveys. They set to work milling over the material, having it reanalyzed and retabulated in a variety of ways, so that the dispersed results of these rather repetitive surveys could be brought together for the purpose of generalization.

The four volumes of "Studies in Social Psychology in World War II" are based on the original survey. No fresh fieldwork was undertaken for the preparation of the Social Science Research Council report, but what was new was the reconceptualization of the original field material in a more explicit and more organized theoretical setting. This task was much aided by the interaction of the original research team, whose major orientation was perhaps methodological, and the newcomers who were drawn somewhat eclectically from a number of related disciplines, each with a very distinctive theoretical slant: dynamic psychology and psychoanalysis; learning theory and experimental psychology; social anthropology and sociology, with its emphasis on social roles, social mobility, social institutions, social control, and social change. This acted as an amalgam. It began to be realized that, just as an understanding of *aptitudes* had been one of the by-products of World War I, so the work of the Research Branch had thrown fresh light on *attitudes*. Just as World War I had led to extensions in the use of *factor analysis*, they had evolved and elaborated *scale analysis*, and could put this forward as a substantial technical contribution to the social sciences.

TECHNIQUES OF INVESTIGATION

Reviewing their work in perspective, Stouffer points out that one method of learning what people are feeling is the method of serious journalism; up to a point the Research Branch could have proceeded by some inspired variety of systematic journalism, with suitable personnel circulating freely and reporting what they encountered. A second possible method would have been to lean on the techniques that had been developed in the 1930's for market research, by which fairly simple sets of questions could have been used as indicators of morale. Yet a third method would have been to rely almost entirely on the analysis of available objective data, such as sickness rates, AWOL rate, and so on, and to derive from them some indices of morale. In practice, to a slight extent they made use of all three methods; for instance, many of their hypotheses came from scouting, which is what journalists do. But the Research Branch was determined to quantify its results, and the decision was therefore taken to develop simple types of questionnaire which could, as a general rule, be filled in by the soldiers themselves. Thus the self-administered questionnaire became the primary tool used in the inquiries.

There were exceptions to the general adoption of this method. A special program that was undertaken for the purpose of evaluating a series of orientation films, *Why We Fight*, prepared to explain the background of the war, had led to the development of the focused interview, which was later elaborated and described by Merton, Fiske, and Kendall.[5] Other studies, described in Volume IV,

Measurement and Prediction, examined the uses of filmstrip with audience participation and compared live talks with documentary films. But these were essentially subsidiary inquiries.

Even in the main program the team was not doctrinaire. For example, a proportion of the troops studied were unable to complete the questionnaires without help, normally because they were not sufficiently literate. In such cases a routine was followed whereby the investigator invited the soldier outside so that he could read the questions to him in privacy and could fill in the form on his behalf. Naturally the soldier would feel at a disadvantage at that moment, and it called for tactful handling not to embarrass him. It was also confirmed in practice that it was particularly important on such occasions that the interviewer be as similar as possible to the soldier being questioned; for example, if the soldier was a Negro, the interviewer too should be a Negro.

In spite of these minor irregularities the self-administered questionnaire had the great advantage of practical economy, which made it possible for a relatively small staff to carry out a very large program. While, however, the method of approach most closely resembled the techniques of market research, at a very early stage the investigators became disturbed by a weakness in current market-research practice which ultimately led them to the refined forms of scale analysis that will later be described. Market researchers, at least in the 1930's, were accustomed to assess attitudes by relying on one answer to one question, and did not bother to discover how well this one question and answer fitted into the spectrum of possible approaches to the same topic.

This may be illustrated by an actual instance taken from a study in progress in November, 1943, which was concerned with the attitude of enlisted men to the WACs. In this study the schedule contained five questions which, though different, were obviously related to the same topic, namely, the attitude of soldiers toward the WACs. There was a remarkable variation in the percentage of pro-WAC replies. The five questions were:

1. In your opinion how necessary is it for the war effort to have women in the Army?

   39 per cent of respondents checked "not so necessary" or "not necessary at all."

2. Do you agree or disagree with this statement: "Being a WAC is bad for a girl's reputation"?

43 per cent agreed with this.

3. Suppose a girl friend of yours was considering joining the WACs, would you advise her to join or not to join?

50 per cent checked "I would advise her not to join."

4. If you had a sister, twenty-one years or older, would you like to see her join the WACs or not?

70 per cent checked "I would not like to see her join."

5. Do you agree or disagree with this statement: "A woman can do more for her country in the WAC than she can by working in a war industry"?

77 per cent disagreed with the statement.

This shows the fallacy underlying the still prevalent practice of using polling results as the basis of statements such as: "Soldiers were 77 per cent against having WACs." Such remarks will probably be found to be based on one particular answer to one particular question. Herbert Hyman's *Interviewing in Social Research* and Payne's *The Art of Asking Questions*[6] give a number of examples of very large differences in responses obtained according to the interviewer employed or the way in which the question is framed.

There are, of course, valid ways in which sets of answers to single questions may be used. As an imaginary example, the researchers might have divided their respondents by age and found that the older enlisted men gave a 62 per cent anti-WAC response to one particular question, whereas the younger enlisted men gave only a 46 per cent anti-WAC response, and it would be justifiable up to a point to infer that attitudes to WACs varied with age. But, as will be shown, the development of scalogram analysis greatly increased the reliability with which such results based on batteries of questions could be interpreted.

Another conclusion that did become very clear was that it is imperative to replicate. As has been mentioned, many of the surveys undertaken were on very similar lines, distinguished mainly by having taken place in different theaters. In these circumstances it enormously enhances confidence in the conclusions if there are regularities in the results obtained from different places. In all surveys of this kind there must be a lingering doubt that results are the consequences of some local irregularity, and the only way to dispel this doubt is to obtain a similar figure from different places. This point is examined by Kendall and Lazarsfeld in the *Continuities* volume; they cite a case where the question of the relationship between overseas service and high spirits is answered by examining the *consistency* with which differences in attitudes between soldiers at home and overseas occur in a large number of small samples. Of 138 such comparisons, 113 showed the subgroup overseas to be in less good spirits than the subgroup in the United States, which supports the presumption that overseas service leads to a deterioration in morale.[7]

An awkward situation arises when the results of a second survey conflict with those of the first. It is a very challenging and not very rare event, and it was then, as the authors comment, that their IBM machines ran overtime. The first response to an astonishing result is to check your arithmetic. Only later do you begin to devise explanations.

Of course, the description of a result as "astonishing" presupposes that another result would have been the expected one, and this in turn implies that some theory, at least of limited generality, is in existence. On the other hand, disagreement may be very fruitful if it shows the need for a higher-level generalization.

The authors stress the point that social science requires theories which can be operationally formulated so that verification is possible and from which predictions can be arrived at to apply successfully to new specific instances.[8] It is useless merely to throw out results with the comment: "Isn't that interesting!" It is necessary also to have at least some provisional explanation in theoretical terms, and hence some expectations that can be falsified. Moreover, in the authors' opinion, before any such theory can validly be tested, the objects of study must be capable of isolation and accurate description, preferably by measurement. Finally, they stipulate that, once the variables are identified, the test of the adequacy of the theory, in comparison with alternative theories, must be rigorous, preferably evidenced by controlled experiment and preferably replicated. These are all unexceptionable statements about what science consists of, even if it is not always easy for social scientists to live up to them.

SUBSTANTIVE RESULTS

We shall next examine some typical results. These are of various kinds, but basically, as always, they break down into the two categories of *descriptive* results and *explanatory* results, as they have been labeled by Herbert Hyman.[9]

The *descriptive* material comes close at some points to providing sample census data about the Army, and offers information that would otherwise be quite unobtainable. As the authors point out, if some results pertaining even to one hundred of Stonewall Jackson's soldiers were suddenly to be discovered giving information about them that was comparable with a questionnaire protocol, historians would become tremendously excited to have such a magnificent source of data. Here there is a total of half a million American soldiers who have been canvassed on one question or another—and very carefully and scientifically canvassed.

As an example of information not available from any other source we may take the question of what proportion of soldiers had been in combat. While it was true that some estimate of this could be derived from the individual soldiers' records, nobody had actually ever attempted to do this, perhaps because it would have involved a very tedious search even on a sample basis. And yet, merely as a by-product of another survey the Research Branch was able to show how many soldiers in each theater of operations had been in actual combat. Even though a fresh survey was simpler than the search of existing records, the investigators encountered certain technical difficulties when asking the questions. They found that if you ask soldiers, "Have you been under combat conditions?" without being more specific, the soldiers will naturally make the most of what they have been through, and too large a proportion will reply that they have been in combat. After some trial they overcame this problem very neatly by including an escape answer as a third alternative. In addition to (1) "No, I have not been under combat" and (2) "Yes, I have been in actual combat," they provided a third choice, (3) "Yes, I have been under enemy fire but not in actual combat." So the soldiers that had not been particularly close to the fighting could save their face by checking number 3, which could mean that they had been in a city during an air raid, or something of that kind.

The authors make quite a point of the value of descriptive material, perhaps because certain historians and other academics had been criticizing the waste of effort going into the preparation of these four volumes, suggesting instead that the best way to understand the soldier was to read Ernie Pyle or to look at topical cartoons. The authors remind us that these popular versions convey the impression that all airmen were constantly flying in the substratosphere through heavy enemy fighter opposition, and that all soldiers were in the middle of battle all the time, whereas the facts showed that, taking the Army as a whole, not more than 27 per cent of either officers or enlisted men had ever been in actual combat, the rest being occupied in keeping the front-line soldier supplied and organized. If you wish to speak about "the soldier," it is necessary to have this factual corrective to counteract the Ernie Pyle stereotype.

When the first two volumes, *The American Soldier*, were published, A. M. Schlesinger, Jr., actually delivered a slashing attack on them that contained the following sentences:

The American Soldier is an entirely harmless book. . . . "Social Science" as a whole is perhaps doing no present harm, *except as it engrosses money and energy which might be put more wisely to other uses*. But it might eventually do great harm in obscuring from ourselves the ancient truths concerning the vanity of human wishes, and the distortions worked by that vanity upon the human performance.[10]

It seems likely that the authors had a foretaste of what Schlesinger was going to say, and for that reason wrote their answer in advance.

In point of fact, there is often great value in fresh descriptive material, particularly, of course, when it genuinely extends our knowledge of the world. But this does not obscure the far greater importance of explanatory surveys, on which generalized understanding of causes depends. In the social sciences the explanatory survey is often the nearest possible approximation to an experiment. This requires care in survey design. As Hyman puts it,

The explanatory survey follows the model of the laboratory experiment with the fundamental difference that it attempts to represent this design in a *natural setting*. Instead of *creating* and manipulating the independent variables whose effect is to be traced the survey analyst must find in the natural setting instances of these factors. By measuring their presence and magnitude, their relationship to the phenomenon can be established in the course of the analysis. But since these variables are not created, but merely found in the natural setting, there is the great danger that a variety of other factors accompany them, and that respondents characterized by particular attributes may vary in other important respects. The influence of these other sources of variability must somehow be reduced. Otherwise any inference about the hypothesized cause may be shaky.[11]

In the present context the variables most regularly used for contrasting different groups of soldiers included educational level, marital status, age, and color. Many of the most interesting studies are, however, concerned with highly specific problems.

One problem that the Research Branch was asked by the Medical Department to study was the relatively high incidence of venereal disease among Negroes. For this purpose they took two accurately constructed samples, one consisting of 863 representative Negro enlisted men and the other of 1,866 representative white enlisted men. Negro enlisted men were specially trained on this occasion to interview the Negroes that needed help with their questionnaires. A check on sample reliability was made by comparing the venereal-disease rates reported by the sample with the rates for the soldier populations already established by the Medical Department, and the two sources agreed quite well.

Among the Negroes, 54 per cent had had venereal disease at some time in their lives, and 21 per cent had contracted venereal disease since going overseas; among the white troops, 15 per cent had had venereal disease some time in their life, and 8 per cent had contracted the disease since going overseas. This discrepancy was partly explained by the fact that the average educational level of the Negro troops was lower than that of the white troops, and venereal disease rates varied inversely with educational level, but this variable accounted for only a very small proportion of the total difference, and an additional explanation had to be found. First they found that the Negroes reported having had more frequent intercourse, two or three times a month compared with once or twice a month for the white enlisted men; but even this was not enough to account for the whole discrepancy. Other data showed that, out of every thousand sexual contacts, seven in the case of Negroes but only four in the case of white troops led to venereal disease. This furnished a lead, and the next question studied was whether Negroes took fewer precautions against venereal disease than did the white men. This was shown not to be the case; if anything, the Negroes seemed to use prophylactic measures more than did the white men, and, furthermore, because the Negroes were granted fewer overnight passes, their potential exposure to infection was less. Again, in a quiz on the facts about venereal disease it was found that the Negroes knew quite as much as, even a little more than, the white enlisted men about the medical aspects. The only residual reason seemed to be that the women available to Negroes were more infected and that this greater infection among the women available to Negroes and consequently among the Negroes themselves tended to perpetuate the higher Negro infection rate.

This seemed a fairly plausible explanation, particularly when it was supplemented by full written comments by the Negroes which showed that the Army policy tended to reinforce the discrimination against Negro opportunities; if a girl was seen walking out with a Negro, she was promptly classified as a prostitute. Obviously, measures of this kind helped to reduce the availability of decent women for the Negroes. So the Research Branch reached the conclusion that the policy of the Army authorities must take a share of the blame for the high incidence of venereal disease among their Negro enlisted men. Unfortunately, the same consequences of the same social attitudes are found outside the Army and also outside the United States.*

The process of successive elimination of causes here described is reminiscent of the process used by Durkheim in *Suicide* and that

* Richmond quotes a similar attitude in Great Britain: "Some girls are quite friendly towards the West Indians inside the factory but cut them dead on the street. This is naturally resented by the men, who found it difficult to understand at first and took it to be nothing but very bad manners; later they may have realized that for a girl to acknowledge a Negro in the street, while with a friend or member of her family, is to label her as little better than a prostitute in their eyes."[12]

used by the authors of *Management and the Worker* to account for the increased rates of output in the Relay Assembly Test Room.

Another large question with which the Research Branch was concerned was the extent to which attitudes of soldiers under training could be used to predict how they would perform in combat. Volume II of *The American Soldier* is concerned with combat performance, with ways to predict combat performance and ways to account for anomalies in combat performance. Two of the studies on this subject will be taken as further examples of the substantive results obtained.

The first major inquiry was concerned with the possibility of predicting which companies would perform best in combat. This was on a rather large scale and was conducted among units that had been in training for D day and the liberation of Europe. The fieldwork took place between January and April, 1944. For this purpose four divisions stationed in England were interrogated on their attitudes to combat. The intention of the investigators was to compare two sets of data. One set of data consisted of the soldiers' subjective responses to test questions about their attitudes toward combat; the other set consisted of the objective facts of how the same units stood up to combat during their first engagements in France. The objective index employed to establish the combat performance was what was called the *nonbattle-casualty ratio*, which was based on the number of soldiers that reported sick for reasons other than having been wounded; the nonbattle-casualty ratio was calculated by dividing the number of nonbattle casualties by the average number of men available for combat on the day in question. (There is a full description in Volume II of how this ratio was computed and checked.) A daily return was completed at company level, and from this it was possible to calculate the nonbattle-casualty rate for each company.

The subjective responses were also calculated on a company basis. Attitudes were assessed by asking questions relating to three issues concerned with combat readiness. The first issue was *readiness for combat;* this was probed by two multiple-response questions: "Which of the following best tells how you feel about getting into an actual battle zone?" and "Which of the following best describes your own feeling about getting into combat with the Germans?" In each case the soldier had to check one of several provided answers as best representing his attitude. The answers to these two questions were combined to indicate each respondent's actual readiness for combat. In the case of the first of these two questions, seven options were available:

1. "I want very much to get in to it just as soon as possible."
2. "I am ready to go any time."
3. "I would like to go before it is over, but I don't think I'm ready yet."
4. "I hope I won't have to go, but if I do, I think I'll do all right."
5. "I hope I won't have to go because I don't think I would do very well."
6. No opinion.
7. No answer.

For aprioristic and slightly arbitrary reasons the investigators scored these on a constructed scale corresponding with the supposed order of favorable attitude to combat. Thus the first two answers scored two points, the next two scored one point, and the other three scored zero. Similarly, in the case of the second of these two questions five options were available:

1. "I would like to get into the fight as soon as I can," scored two points.
2. "I am ready to go when my turn comes," scored one point.
3. "I would just as soon stay out of combat if possible," scored one point.
4. "I don't want to get into combat at all," scored zero.
5. "No answer," scored zero.

It will be noted that to each of the two questions the respondents had a chance of scoring two, one, or zero points. The investigators next combined each respondent's two scores by simple addition, and so each respondent could have a total score, for that issue, of any value between four and zero. The number of respondents with each of these scores was counted and this count became the predictive indicator as far as the first issue was concerned.

The second issue was on *confidence in their stamina for combat*. This was approached in a similar way by asking three questions:

"Do you feel that you are in tough enough physical condition for going into combat?"

"If and when you get into combat, how well do you think you will stand up under battle conditions?"

"Do you think that you are in good physical condition?"

The third issue was concerned with the question of *confidence in combat skill*, and the questions asked were:

"Do you feel that you are now trained and ready for combat, or do you feel that you need more training?"

"If you were given a group of men and told to take charge of them all by yourself on a mission under enemy fire, how well do you think you would do?"

"Do you think that you have been given enough training and experience so that you think you could do a good job in taking charge of a group of men on your own in combat?"

These issues were set up as three separate indicators of attitude toward combat, and the survey did show a satisfactory correlation between the precombat attitudes and the combat performance in terms of nonbattle-casualty rates when they had actually gone into battle.

The conclusion was that it would be useful if similar surveys were conducted as a matter of routine and completed early enough to enable army commanders to pick out the companies for the missions that were crucial to their plans. In this way they could ensure that they chose the companies with the highest morale for the most difficult and important tasks. The claim was made that the choice of companies with potentially high combat performance could be made twice as well as if selection were carried out at random. For example, if one-third of all companies had above-average combat performance, a random selection of thirty-six companies would include twelve above-average companies, whereas using the predictive method described it would be possible to include twenty-four companies above average in combat performance among the thirty-six companies selected.

Clearly, the usefulness of the social sciences depends greatly on their capacity to make predictions, even if these are not infallible, and this particular study seemed quite promising. On the other hand, one thing that a good commander should be able to do is to pick out his better companies. It is ridiculous to assume that commanders choose their companies for special tasks by random selection. In a prediction study it is necessary to prove that the predictive instrument can improve upon choices that are purposive and not merely upon random choices.

This is not to minimize the difficulties of systematic prediction. One restriction in a real-life situation is that the data available for constructing the prediction table are generally data collected for quite different administrative purposes and may not be what the investigator would choose if he had a free hand. In this instance the nonbattle-casualty rate was not a very satisfactory index because on any given day some companies would naturally be much more exposed to the rigors of combat than others, and there are obvious psychosomatic and other reasons why sickness would show more at one time than at another. In any case it is not entirely clear what theory underlies the suggestion that performance in battle bears a close relation to low sickness rate.

It is interesting to compare this study with another investigation undertaken about the same time but run on different and more effective lines. In the fall and winter of 1943 a team was sent to Camp Adair in Oregon to administer a schedule of questions relating to attitudes to combat. The sample was drawn from a newly activated regiment that was there in training. In this case the investigators were concerned with the performance of individuals, and not merely with companies as in the other study. Here again the question at issue was the relationship between actual performance in battle and information that could be collected during precombat training. This precombat information about each individual consisted of factual data—data of induction, age, state of birth, and certain other details taken from his personnel card—and also the answers to various subjective questions.

Four of these questions were:

1. "If you were sent to actual fighting after finishing one year of training, how do you think you would do?"
2. "Do you ever worry about whether you will be injured in combat before the war is over?"
3. "How do you think you would feel about killing a Japanese soldier?"
4. "How do you think you would feel about killing a German soldier?"

These soldiers were subsequently sent over as reserves to replace casualties in the fighting in France, and after they had been in battle for a while, they were rated for individual performance under combat conditions by people in their own battle formations—at least two independent raters, normally of their own rank. The raters classified each individual in the sample into one of three groups: either below average combat performance, or average, or above average. These assessments were correlated with the replies the soldiers had given some months before in Oregon. In replies to three of the questions (1, 3, and 4) there was a statistically significant correlation between promise and performance; for some reason, however, willingness to kill Japanese did not prove so efficient a predictor of combat performance as the other three questions quoted.

This was a particularly strict test because the sample had already been matched for such characteristics as age, educational level, and marital condition, so that those who gave the "good" replies to the four questions cited would be compared with other soldiers whose backgrounds would make them also probable "good" combat performers, being drawn from the better-educated, the older, and the married, all features that make for better fighters. The authors claim that if they had taken a random rather than a matched sample, the predictive value of all four questions would probably have been "significant." In any case it encouraged the research workers that the answers to these four questions correlated better than answers to any of the other questions asked in the original test battery. Of the various other questions, which were not so directly related to combat attitudes, the only one that correlated well with combat performance was one on the subject of going AWOL, which revealed that the best fighters were the ones who had thought that going AWOL was a very serious offense. Taken all in all, this second predictive study of the combat performance of individuals showed considerable promise as an administrative tool.

ANALYSIS

One highly important sequel to these and similar studies was that the strong team of social-science methodologists gathered together in the Research Branch resolved to take steps to improve their scaling methods. The procedures used in combining answers to different questions on the same issue were so difficult to justify logically that they constituted a personal challenge to methodologists on the team. Louis Guttman had for many years worked on questions of scaling, and the team were well aware of the arbitrariness of commercial and other attitude-survey results. They determined to tackle the fundamental problem in all scaling based on asking one question, which is that one can only guess how the single answer relates to the general attitude of the individual on that issue.

There is a second problem, which is that respondents vary in the degree of their commitment to the issue. To one respondent an attitude on a particular issue may be very strongly held, whereas another respondent may give the same reply but be essentially uncommitted and indifferent on that issue. As has been mentioned, one of the original civilian advisers had been Rensis Likert, formerly of the Department of Agriculture, who had done important pioneer work in the 1930's in perfecting the "Likert Scale" technique which takes account both of the direction and of the intensity of an attitude.

The first step, therefore, is to replace the simple question by a battery of questions; but as soon as you introduce multiple questioning, you face the problem of which answer to believe and how much faith to place in it. Until this is decided, it is not possible logically to combine questions so as to obtain one composite answer that "represents" the attitude of the person toward the issue.

Thus, it is necessary by some means or other to examine how far the answers relate to one universe, or, in the Research Branch language, how far they are unidimensional. The essential function of the scalogram is to discover how a number of different answers relate to one another, and whether within all of these there is some continuous underlying theme that can be isolated from the totality of individual replies so that all the separate questions and answers can be utilized in giving precision to this underlying attitude.

Louis Guttman contributes the key chapter on the methodological basis of scalogram analysis.[13] He points out how crucial the problem of consistency is in the social and psychological sciences, in many of which some parameter, such as "marital adjustment," "scholastic achievement," or "social status," is sought by a process which involves the assigning of numerical values to qualitative observations in an attempt to evolve a single rank order, so that a drastic condensation of data can be undertaken. The desired end product is a simplified statement such as that one couple is better adjusted than another or that one student has a greater knowledge of arithmetic than another.

Guttman quotes Murphy, Murphy, and Newcomb in reminding us of the essential feature of a true scale, which is that an individual's response to a given item enables us to predict successfully his response to all other items.* Another statement of the same condition is that, if each respondent is assigned a rank position according to his responses, the process can be reversed and his responses can be deduced from his rank.

Clearly, when a dimension is fully understood, as in determining the height of a man, no difficulty occurs in selecting suitable questions. Unfortunately, this certainty is generally lacking in the case of problems in the human sciences, and the investigator has to feel his way toward the selection of a suitable set of questions. With ordinary bivariate techniques the relationship between different items can be examined, but the relationship of the items as a whole with the universe at which the items are directed is left undetermined. This is a basic point in the theory behind scalogram analysis.

An important consideration of the present theory of scales becomes that of the sampling of items. In studying any attitude or opinion, there is an unlimited number of questions or question wordings which could be used. Any question used in an attitude or opinion survey is ordinarily but a single sample of indefinitely many ways the question could be put. It is well known that changing the wording of the questions, changing the order of presentation of questions, changing order of check lists of answers, etc., can yield apparently different results in the responses. Conceivably, one could ask questions which would secure "favorable" replies ranging from 0 to 100 per cent, depending upon the extremeness of the statement that the respondents are asked to approve or disapprove. It is, therefore, essential to inquire into the nature of the *universe of all possible questions of the same content*, and to determine what inferences can be made about that universe that will not depend on the particular sample of questions used.[15]

The essential operational feature of scalogram analysis is the ordering of results simultaneously in two directions. In one direction, the

---

* If, as Stouffer illustrates this elsewhere,[14] a man replies that he is over 5 feet 6 inches tall, you can be sure that he will also reply that he is over 5 feet tall, whereas if he replies that he is not over 5 feet 6 inches tall, you can be equally sure that he will not reply that he is over 6 feet tall.

question-and-answer categories are ranked in order of "extreme-ness"; the degree of extremeness is determined empirically, the most extreme category being the one that is endorsed by the fewest people. There will, however, be an extreme at each end, more precisely when the analysis is based on dichotomous (that is, either yes or no) answers; under these circumstances the question which is least extreme in terms of "yes" answers will automatically be the most extreme in terms of "no" answers.

In the other direction, the respondents are ranked in order of "favorableness," the persons giving the largest number of favorable answers being placed first and the persons giving the smallest number of favorable answers (which in a dichotomous analysis will mean the persons giving the largest number of unfavorable answers) being placed last.

If these results are brought together on a chart, the visual effect is a parallelogram. This effect is illustrated by Guttman with the example of a group of people who attempt to answer three questions of varying difficulty, such that 10 per cent get the first question right, 40 per cent get the second question right, and 80 per cent get the third question right. This result can be represented in a bar chart (Figure 6).

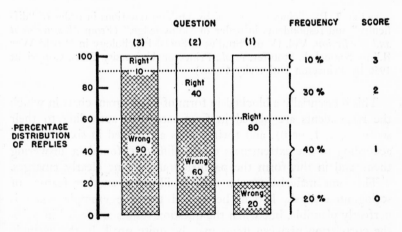

FIGURE 6. Bar chart illustrating comparative hardness of three questions. (From *Measurement and Prediction*, Vol. IV of "Studies in Social Psychology in World War II," by Samuel A. Stouffer, *et al.*, Princeton University Press. Copyright 1950 by Princeton University Press.)

Now, if all those who answered question 1 correctly also answered questions 2 and 3 correctly, and so on, and if all those who answered question 3 wrongly also answered questions 2 and 1 wrongly, and so on, this material has the properties that will allow it to be expressed as a scale. It can then be redrawn in a slightly more elaborate bar chart (Figure 7).

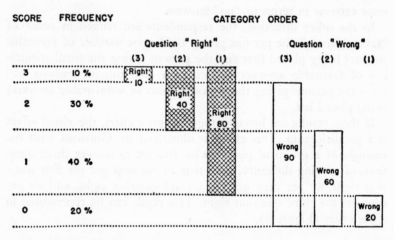

FIGURE 7. Parallelogram formed by ranking questions in order of "difficulty" and respondents in order of "knowledge." (From *Measurement and Prediction*, Vol. IV of "Studies in Social Psychology in World War II," by Samuel A. Stouffer, *et al.*, Princeton University Press. Copyright 1950 by Princeton University Press.)

This is essentially a blocked-in form of a scalogram chart in which the respondents are placed in four categories according to their score (3, 2, 1, or 0), and their replies are placed in six categories according to the extremeness of the difficulty found in answering them, and in this form the parallelogram outline clearly emerges.

The same material can be used to illustrate another feature of scalogram analysis. It will be agreed that the example taken is perfectly plausible, but when the question results are tested in pairs, the correlation between items may be quite small. In the example given in Figure 7, the point correlation between questions 2 and 3 is 0.41. Guttman adds, "As a matter of fact, the point correlation between two dichotomous items may be anything from practically zero to unity, and yet they may both be perfect simple functions of the same quantitative variable."[16]

It may also be noted that the presence of a zero cell in the proper place (in this case indicating that nobody who correctly answered the more difficult question answered the easier question incorrectly) is a necessary condition for the existence of a perfect scale. It is clearly not sufficient proof, however, as it might be due to chance in such a small sample, and the existence of a perfect scale can be accepted only if zero cells recur in their proper positions in the multivariate distribution of several questions, and, furthermore, if there are some theoretical grounds for assuming that the questions belong to the same content universe by virtue of their content.

Following up this last point, scalogram analysis may also be used in the reverse direction, for testing the validity of a concept. One interesting example of this relates to the question of morale. It has already been mentioned that one of Stouffer's original ambitions was to set up an index of morale which could be applied as a routine test to groups of soldiers in particular circumstances. The word "morale" has an honored place in the theory of warfare, and it was to be assumed that it would not be overly difficult to find a sample of questions suitable for detecting variations in morale. But in spite of all their efforts the Research Branch found it impossible to devise questions relating to what they thought of as morale and which also satisfied their criteria of scalability. On the other hand, they found that their questions could be grouped around certain components or subuniverses of what is normally known as morale, and that these subuniverses were independently scalable. Thus they had to content themselves with setting up several tests which, though independent of one another in terms of the abstract state of morale, might separately influence the actions and attitudes of different outfits. Three major scalable components were (*a*) pride in one's outfit, (*b*) satisfaction with one's job, (*c*) confidence in one's leaders; the empirical conclusion that they were forced to draw was that knowledge of a man's feelings of pride in his outfit gave no indication of how much confidence he had in his leaders, and so on.

This was a very interesting result. On the one hand, it vindicated the claim that scalogram analysis can discriminate between good and bad questions in any given context; on the other, it perhaps suggests that the technology of the Research Branch had somewhat out-stripped their theoretical understanding of the issues involved.

Before leaving the question of scalability, we must consider a little further what is meant in scalogram analysis by the statement that the different test items mentioned did not form a scale. It will be appreciated that in practice perfect scales do not exist, and a measure known as the *coefficient of reproducibility* is used as the first test of whether an efficient approximation to a perfect scale has been obtained. This coefficient is based on the proportion of results which fall inside the solid parallelogram on the scalogram chart. In practice a coefficient of reproducibility of 90 per cent is taken as an efficient approximation. The remaining 10 per cent which fall outside the parallelogram are known as errors.

For technical reasons a more rigorous test of scalability is given if some of the test items are trichotomous (that is, the answers to questions are classified in three categories rather than merely as yes or no), and obviously the number of questions and of respondents affects the sampling error to which the coefficient of reproducibility is subject.

Two other features of the test results must also be taken into account. One is the distribution of answers to each item; this should be well spread, so that questions are not bunched in respect of "extremeness," and specifically items should be included which evoke more or less equal "favorable" and "unfavorable" responses.

The other characteristic to be examined is the pattern of errors, which may be important even if they do not constitute 10 per cent of results. This pattern provides a test of what has gone wrong with the scale. With a scalogram chart or board the distribution of errors can be examined by eye. In some instances the errors will be concentrated in one or two solid streaks; this suggests the presence of one or two additional variables which do not fit into the prevailing universe of content. The presence of *nonscale* material somewhat impairs the value of the result. In other cases the errors are distributed at random, and this is a more satisfactory result in terms of reproducibility. In fact, in these cases use can be made of the material even if the coefficient of reproducibility is less than 90 per cent. The explanation in these cases is that, although there is one dominant variable, there are "infinitely many small random factors"[17] and the dominant factor can still be used to predict an external variable; these are described as *quasi-scales*.

One task which the authors set themselves was to analyze and describe the differences between scalogram analysis and other available techniques. Naturally one of the techniques examined was factor analysis. As they were interested in distinguishing a single dimension from their data, this entailed comparison with Spearman's original single-factor analysis. The basic difference between the two techniques was that factor analysis was specifically designed to treat quantitative data, whereas the responses collected by the Research Branch were essentially nonmetric and therefore expressible only in qualitative or rank-order terms. You can say that one man is more favorable to something than another man but not that he is twice as favorable.

On the other hand, when material has been combined into subuniverses, each of which is separately scalable by scalogram techniques, it is possible to test these subuniverses by Spearman single-factor analysis because each subuniverse can now be treated as a quantitative variable. If in fact one item is selected from each scalable subuniverse as the "spokesman" for that subuniverse, these items can be used to form a quasi-scale, and the quasi-scale score will be essentially the score on the Spearman common factor.[18]

This procedure was carried out in the case of the morale subuniverses already mentioned, and it was found that the intercorrelations of scale scores did not conform to the Spearman structure. It could thus be inferred that there was no common factor linking the morale subuniverses. The morale material was not only nonscale but was not even quasi-scale. Morale, as operationally defined by the Research Branch, did not even consist of one dominant variable and a number of lesser variables, but comprised a number of independent variables of roughly the same order of importance.

This use of factor analysis is of interest, but, as has been shown, the absence of even quasi-scales could be demonstrated by examination of the scalogram-board pattern. Louis Guttman summarizes his views on the relationship between scalogram analysis and factor analysis in the following passage:

A factor analysis in the Spearman-Thurstone sense will fail to test adequately the scalability of qualitative data, because it was not designed for that problem. Scale analysis is designed as a single-factor theory for qualitative data. *From a scale analysis it can be known what a factor analysis will show.* The converse is not true; from a factor analysis it will usually be difficult, if not impossible, to know what a scale analysis will show. Scale analysis . . . makes a complete analysis of qualitative data, using no extraneous assumptions, and using only techniques appropriate to qualitative data. A factor analysis in the sense of Spearman and Thurstone was not designed for qualitative data and will not make a complete analysis of qualitative data; it will ordinarily use extraneous and often misleading assumptions, will not use techniques appropriate for qualitative data, and can lead to quite erroneous interpretations.[19]

There are obviously many problems for which scale analysis is not appropriate, and the Research Branch did not then hesitate to use other methods, such as the method of *paired comparisons,* which was used to determine what would be the least unpopular application of a point system in determining the order of demobilization. After ten years the method has naturally developed considerably in various directions and has become part of normal testing procedure in a wide variety of contexts.

One important feature of the scalogram method was that the analytical procedure was matched by a highly original operational procedure that greatly simplified the task of placing both respondents and responses in the required rank order. The scalogram equipment consists of two identical wooden boards. Each of these comprises a board within which 100 removable wooden slats are held in place by a frame attached to the base. When the clamps are released, the slats can be removed and replaced in any desired order. Each slat has 100 holes bored at equal distances along its length at intervals exactly equal to the thickness of one slat, so that with all the slats in position each board has a completely regular pattern of 100×100 holes. The holes are big enough to take plated balls (for example, silver-coated 118-caliber shot or small ball-bearings). These balls are dropped into the holes of one board to represent the responses of the subjects being tested. The slats are next shifted in order to place the individuals in rank order; then the second board is placed on top of the first board and at right angles to it and the whole assembly is turned upside down, so that the balls fall into the corresponding holes in the second board. Finally, the slats in the second board are shifted in order to place the response categories in rank order; if the material is scalable, a satisfactory parallelogram of balls will appear at this point.

Those who have used the scalogram board will agree that considerable judgment is required of the operator to achieve the highest possible coefficient of reproducibility while at the same time satisfying the other criteria. Interpretation of the board pattern also requires craftsmanship. The exercise of personal skill can now be minimized by the use of a systematic *coefficient of scalability*[20] and also by the substitution of electronic data processing for the scalogram board. In essence this tests all possible orders to discover the order giving the smallest number of errors, and it can be done on a quite small installation provided it includes a reproducer as well as a tabulator and a sorter.

In the last years of the war Paul F. Lazarsfeld, perhaps the most resourceful and versatile of all social-science methodologists, was a consultant in the Research Branch, and he became particularly interested in the problem of quasi-scales. His approach to scaling was different from that of Guttman; while the latter dealt only with manifest relationships between expressed attitudes, Lazarsfeld thought it better to return to an earlier idea (which, incidentally, Guttman had at first pursued and finally rejected) that statements made by subjects should be treated not at their face value but as indicators of certain latent attitudes held by the subject. This starting point leads to the method known as *latent-structure analysis*, which provides a model of greater generality than scalogram analysis, such that the scalogram quasi-scale becomes merely a special case in latent-structure analysis and the perfect scale becomes a limiting case of the quasi-scale.

The basic postulate of latent-structure analysis "is that there exists *a set of latent classes, such that the manifest relationship between any two or more items on a questionnaire can be accounted for by the existence of these latent classes and by these alone.*"[21] All other components of the responses of individuals or of the responses to items will be specific and independent of the residual components of other responses. It will be seen that this bears a close relation to the basic postulate of factor analysis.

In the simplest case, known as *latent-dichotomy analysis*, the task of the analyst is to partition the sample into two classes of respondents—those who possess the latent character and those who do not.

As the latent character can only be inferred from the manifest data —that is, responses to questions—the principal task is the methodological one of carrying out this inference in a rigorous manner.

Lazarsfeld[22] and Stouffer[23] take a concrete example to illustrate a simple case of the procedure evolved. The starting point is a batch of four sets of answers given by a sample of 1,000 noncoms. The answers are dichotomized, on a priori grounds, between those respondents who seem favorable and those who seem unfavorable, and the proportions of favorable responses are noted.

1. Do you think the Army has tried its best to look out for the welfare of enlisted men?

Proportion saying "Yes, it has tried its best": 0.254

2. In general, do you think that you yourself have gotten a square deal in the Army?

Proportion saying "Yes, in most ways I have": 0.300

3. Do you think when you are discharged you will go back to civilian life with a favorable or unfavorable attitude toward the Army?

Proportion saying "Very favorable" or "Fairly favorable": 0.374

4. In general, how well do you think the Army is run?

Proportion saying "It is run very well" or "It is run pretty well": 0.641

To the four dichotomized questions there are 16 (i.e., 2^4) possible response patterns. Of these, five would constitute perfect scale types ($++++$, $-+++$, $--++$, $---+$, $----$) and the other eleven (e.g., $+-++$, $-++-$) would in scalogram analysis have been classed as errors. Even if we bear in mind that the cutting point is here chosen aprioristically, it is still of interest that in 67 per cent of the cases the response patterns fitted into one or other of the perfect-scale types.

It is of course purely a matter of arithmetic to determine the actual frequencies of occurrence of each response pattern, but before they can be used these have to be adjusted so that the division into latent groups can be performed with precision. The amount of adjustment needed is a measure of the adequacy of the latent-dichotomy model being used. The next step is to calculate for each response pattern the proportion of respondents who possess the postulated latent character, and finally these response patterns are ordered so that those containing the highest proportion with the latent character are at the top and those containing the lowest proportion are at the bottom. It is thus possible to pick out from their response pattern the respondents most likely or least likely to possess the latent character.

The application of this procedure is clearly somewhat different from that of scalogram analysis, but it does provide a rigorous method of extracting special groups for intensive study or for correlating possession of a given latent character with an outside criterion. Against this is the fact that the description here given glosses over the considerable amount of computation needed to derive an adjusted response pattern from the observed response pattern, and to calculate the proportion of respondents who possess the latent character. There are also certain problems of reliability that had not been completely solved in 1950, when *Measurement and Prediction* was published.

This very brief account of scalogram analysis and the even briefer reference to latent-structure analysis, may have demonstrated sufficiently that the work of the Research Branch stimulated some very hard thinking and led to some rather practical results in mathematical analysis.

Apart from these important advances in manipulative procedures one may ask what are the final and lasting results of the work of the Research Branch. The substantive results have their historical interest. Max Lerner summarizes them thus:

Attitude studies of the Army, notably Samuel Stouffer's work in *The American Soldier*, found that what the soldier wanted from the Army was: status while he was a soldier, training which would help him in his job or career after he left the Army, the minimum of exposure to the dangers that would make a casualty of him, and the kind of comfort he could not get if he was stationed at a "God-forsaken place" like the Aleutians or Tasmania. These four wishes may seem the desires of men who are not serious about the business of war, but they are characteristic of a society that values the pursuits of peace and leaves them only under pressure of necessity and not from any valuing of the martial virtues.[24]

The substance in these findings may appear relatively trivial, but it may be argued that the act of canvassing soldiers' opinions and of disclosing their hopes and fears is a more democratic mode of behavior than the use of traditional disciplinarian methods. It may also be seen as a sinister development, just as Mayo's promotion of "social skills" was seen by some to be sinister. Robert S. Lynd reviewed the first two volumes, *The American Soldier*, in the *New Republic* under the heading "The Science of Inhuman Relations." An extract, quoted in *Continuities*, reads:

These volumes depict science being used with great skill to sort out and to control men for purposes not of their own willing. It is a significant measure of the impotence of liberal democracy that it must increasingly use its social sciences not directly on democracy's own problems, but tangentially and indirectly; . . . in the present case, [in] Army research on how to turn frightened draftees into tough soldiers who will fight a war whose purposes they do not understand. With such socially extraneous purposes controlling the use of social science, each advance in its use tends to make it an instrument of mass control, and thereby a further threat of democracy.[25]

Also reviewing the first two volumes in *The Annals*, Alfred M. Lee made a similar point:

If managerial problems for industry and the military are to continue to dominate the research of leading social psychologists and sociologists, the value orientation of the managerial technician rather than the value orientation of the social science educator will dominate what evolves and is called social science. The emphasis can thus shift from service to citizens in a democracy to service for those who temporarily control and who wish to continue to control segments of our society.[26]

The extension of this argument is that the social scientist should not waste his talents on what George Simpson calls "administrative research," however profitable that may be and however much it may enhance the status of social science in the dominant political structure,* but should devote himself to questions of a different kind.

---

* Samuel Stouffer was well aware of the cost of co-operation. "Most of our time was wasted, irretrievably wasted, in so far as any contribution to social science was concerned. Sometimes a study like whether men preferred Coca-Cola to Pepsi-Cola or whether they preferred nuts in their candy bars may have had a neat technical twist, but ordinarily it did not, or if it had we just did not have time to investigate." He goes on to describe his dilemma, as director of professional staff, between the need to keep his clients happy that he was concentrating on what they immediately wanted and the need to keep his best analysts from feelings of frustration at the triviality of the problems set for them.[27]

This may lead social scientists to a critical analysis of contemporary society, to posing questions such as Lynd posed in *Knowledge for What*.

Equally it may lead them to another form of higher generality, by which the empirical findings of the Research Branch are used for the reinforcement or reconsideration of growing points of social-science theory. In spite of the talent that had been recruited for the "Studies in Social Psychology in World War II," those who had to base their views on the published volumes would have been justified in feeling that the material was presented with an inexplicit and probably eclectic theoretical orientation.

CONTINUITIES

It was the function of the little book already referred to, *Continuities in Social Research: Studies in the Scope and Method of "The American Soldier,"* to dispel this criticism. Edited by Merton and Lazarsfeld, this appeared in 1950. It was prepared before Volumes III and IV of "Studies in Social Psychology in World War II" were ready and refers only to Volumes I and II. Besides a very important statement of the problems of survey analysis by Lazarsfeld and Kendall it contains three additional essays of more than ephemeral interest.

Of these three, the paper by Hans Speier on "The American Soldier and the Sociology of Military Organization" is the most critical in tone. Speier complains that the authors of *The American Soldier* appear to ignore the very extensive literature on the sociology of the Army as an institution and the social psychology of the soldier as a role player. He feels in particular that there would have been an opportunity to probe into the peculiar dilemmas of the civilian army, in which

a modern soldier may also be a husband, an engineer in civilian life, a Swedish-American, a Republican, etc. Hence, the identifications and loyalties of this man are manifold in content and intensity. As a soldier, he is expected to subordinate all other loyalties to his identification with the armed forces. Conflicts among the various demands upon life and loyalties which tie him into the larger social network are likely to arise and in serious cases to interfere with his military performance. The requirements of military discipline and the demands for readiness to face the risks of combat unswervingly, with professional *sang-froid*, and in fact with enthusiasm, are best met in closely knit military groups that have a highly developed and frequently fiercely exclusive *esprit de corps*.[28]

Readers will recall the fact, discussed by Durkheim, that professional soldiers are particularly prone to suicide, and that the diversification of roles of the modern semicivilian soldier was already modifying this tendency. (See Chapter 2, page 40.)

Speier also uses *The American Soldier* to quantify the theory associated with Mannheim's sociology of knowledge, that various social classes display "perspectival thinking" which affects their views not only as to what should be but also as to what is. Unfortunately, as Speier points out, Mannheim never succeeded in defining social class in terms that would permit a test of his theory, or in differentiating the effect of perspectival thinking in relation to the content of the question at issue. Speier ingeniously uses the *American Soldier* results to show that there is a very distinct difference in the opinions stated by officers and enlisted men, and that this difference varies with the extent of personal commitment. At one end of the scale, the difference between officers and enlisted men is minimal when the issues do not involve the Army as a whole, the respondent himself, or relations between officers and enlisted men; at the other end of the scale, the difference is maximal on issues directly connected with relations between officers and enlisted men. As a result of this analysis he concludes that the social perspective effect varies with the subject matter to which the opinion pertains, and almost disappears on matters not affecting the hierarchical relationship of the two status groups.

Another point made by Speier is that, if the responses made by the soldiers really reflected their lack of knowledge and commitment in relation to the war and the moral and political objectives of the Allies, it is very difficult to understand why the American Armed Forces fought as well as they did. He accounts for this partly in terms of the extraordinary importance of primary-group relations in sustaining morale and partly in terms of the generalized but inarticulate convictions of the American people. He reminds us, however, that these are not separate and independent factors but are closely linked together. Without strong generalized convictions about the war or a strong sense of commitment, the nature of primary-group relations would suffer; without active and healthy primary-group relations the fighting spirit of the Army would correspondingly suffer.

The whole question of primary groups in the American Army is the subject of a paper by Edward A. Shils, whose examination of the *American Soldier* material leads him to the very similar hypothesis

that primary group solidarity functions in the corporate body to strengthen the motivation for the fulfillment of substantive prescriptions and commands issued by the official agents of the corporate body, within the context of *a set of generalized moral predispositions* or *sense of obligation.* The latter need not be strongly present in consciousness but some measure of identification with the collectivity and some sense of generalized obligation and readiness to acknowledge the legitimacy of its demands in numerous particular situations must exist. . . . In other words then, it cannot be said that goals are set by membership in the primary group but only that efforts to achieve the legitimate, formally prescribed goals may be strengthened by such membership.[29]

In this paper Shils addresses himself to certain familiar aspects of primary-group theory in an attempt to extend or to clarify previous hypotheses. He examines, for example, the function of the primary group in reducing a soldier's fear of death or injury by interposing the desire to secure favorable responses from his comrades. Remarking on the widespread comment made by combat soldiers that "prayer helped a lot," and that this response was more common in replacement troops than in veterans, he speculates that resort to primary-group solidarity and to prayer may have been alternative methods of diminishing fear.

He squeezes out some quite interesting, if inconclusive, material relating to assimilation into the primary group by using the data which contrast the responses of veterans in veteran divisions, replacements in veteran divisions, and "totally green men" in inexperienced divisions. The results showed that replacements were intermediate in their self-confidence as combat leaders but most favorable in their attitudes toward noncommissioned officers and most proud of their company. Shils reconciles these positions as follows:

Except with regard to attitudes which involved direct judgments of themselves and which aroused their insecurity and pride, they sought to "prove" themselves by taking over the veterans' attitudes, e.g., conviction about the war. Accordingly in such situations, they stood between the other two groups.[30]

In a separate analysis Shils shows that replacements have less self-confidence than "primary group members," and adds:

The self-confidence and self-esteem which primary group members obtain from their membership is heightened by the confidence and esteem in which they hold their superiors in the group and in the corporate body within which the group exists.[31]

This brings him to one of the most important considerations in good combat morale, namely, the primary-group relations between officers and soldiers. He shows "the enlisted man's desire for some type of personal relationship, particularly for a protective personal relationship."[32] For any primary group to operate effectively, leadership is necessary.

It is easy to understand that soldiers who are being pressed by conscience, command and the expectations of their primary group comrades will be better able to face these dangers where they can identify with an exemplary and protective leader.[33]

Response to leadership thus takes its place beside the sense of social obligation and the desire for the approbation of comrades, but leadership has more than one component—command (which in the Army involves deprivation, if not danger) is matched by example and protection.*

Shils contrasts the relations between officers and soldiers inside and outside combat conditions. Outside combat, the exercise of high courage and the protection of his men from danger cannot be demonstrated by the officer, and the display of benevolence—the only component of the officer's contribution to primary-group formation available under these conditions—is hampered by the officers' privilege system. In combat, the opportunities for privilege are lacking, and the opportunities for exemplary and protective leadership are highlighted, so that the circumstances are propitious

---

* It is interesting to compare these factors with the three morale components differentiated by scalogram analysis.

for primary-group formation and for the growth of confidence in the immediate leader. One important hypothesis that Shils associates with this formulation

is that which asserts that the rate of assimilation of newcomers into established primary groups is accelerated by combat. There were no significant differences between the morale indices of replacements who were sent into combat nearly at once (i.e., three days or a week after attachment to the unit) and those who had longer periods of precombat association.[34]

The primary group is, of course, one of the classical concepts of American sociology, and even since Shils was writing there has been a very considerable development in both theory and research relating to this field. Much of the attention has focused on small-group analysis, and this is reflected in other chapters of this book. Against this background there is an impression that the examination of the primary group in its natural social setting—the only kind of examination that Charles H. Cooley and his contemporaries would recognize—has been submerged in what may be a disproportionate concentration on the laboratory experiment. For example, the volume *Small Groups*[35] sets out to cover the whole field, from early theory to the latest developments. One section of the book (Part II), 150 pages long, has as its title "The Individual in Social Situations." Of the fifteen items included by the editors, ten describe studies conducted in contrived situations with student volunteers and military and naval enlistees and recruits, three describe studies that took place under semicontrived conditions which depended to some extent on the subjects' already knowing one another, and the other two were based on real situations. One of these last two was a description of one of the many sociometric experiments carried out at the New York State Training School for Girls; in the other case, the author states: "The hypothesis is one that can be tested either by creating groups in the laboratory, or by obtaining the appropriate information from 'natural,' existing groups; only the latter procedure was employed in this study."[36]

This analysis is not included in order to poke fun at the items published. Indeed, there is no doubt that the minute and painstaking examination of small groups under controlled conditions is leading to a cumulative understanding of small-group interaction, of the perceptions of the individual in a social situation, and of the nature and function of leadership in the group. This high regard for the value of such an approach is reflected in the choice of Robert F. Bales' *Interaction Process Analysis* as one of the examples to which a chapter of the present book is devoted. (See Chapter 12.)

At the same time one cannot escape a certain regret that these developments appear to take place at the expense of the much more difficult examination of the primary group as a social institution with characteristics which are materially affected by specific social settings. Edward Shils found that the data and interpretations in *The American Soldier* have given rise to no fundamentally new hypotheses on the problems concerned with the establishment and disruption of primary-group morale. He attributed this in part to the fact that, in spite of the exceptionally high quality of the empirical field material, the research was tailored to the needs of administration rather than to those of science and theory. It is permissible to wonder whether perhaps there is something in the nature of the primary-group concept and its elaborations that makes it difficult to apply them to precise, operationally defined empirical data of any kind. This doubt is prompted by the very solid achievement of Merton and Kitt in their long and important paper "Contributions to the Theory of Reference Group Behavior," first published in *Continuities: The American Soldier* and later reprinted in the second edition of Merton's *Social Theory and Social Structure*.

This paper, which is dedicated to the belief that there is a two-way traffic between social theory and empirical research, is based on an internal analysis of the use of the *reference-group* concept as an interpretative variable in Volume I of *The American Soldier*. Before the appearance of this paper, use of the term *reference group* was confined mainly to certain social psychologists, and in *The American Soldier* the term is not employed. On the other hand, Stouffer and his colleagues did on various occasions have recourse to the parallel concept of *relative deprivation*.

Starting from this clue, Merton and Kitt make a compilation of all the occasions in the volume in which some version of the concept of relative deprivation is drawn upon. They quote nine items from Volume I. A typical example is No. 8:

. . . it seems likely that both Northern and Southern Negroes may have been considerably influenced in their overall adjustment by other psychological compensations in being stationed in the South, which can be understood if we look at their situation as one of *relative status*. *Relative to most Negro civilians whom he saw in Southern towns*, the Negro soldier had a position of comparative wealth and dignity.[37]

In each of the nine cases quoted, the concept of relative deprivation is used to an *interpretative intervening variable*, to account for otherwise anomalous results. For example, an older or married man is found to exhibit more resentment toward induction than a younger or unmarried man. Taking the status of the individual as the *independent variable* and his attitude as the *dependent variable*, the fact is analyzed as follows:

The married man (independent variable) more often questions the legitimacy of his induction (dependent variable), because he appraises the situation within the frame of reference (interpretative variable) yielded by comparing himself with other married men still in civilian life, who escaped the draft entirely, or with unmarried men in the Army, whose induction did not call for comparable sacrifice.[38]

Examination showed that the frames of reference for the soldiers in the cases cited were of three kinds. First were those whose reference group consisted of others with whom they were in *actual association*, in sustained social contact, such as "married civilian friends." Second were those known or unknown members of a recognizable group *of the same status*, such as "other captains." Third were those, known or unknown, who were *of different status*, such as the noncombat soldier in relation to the combat soldier.

The important general point is that in the concept of relative deprivation the emphasis is on the comparison with the subject's "pattern of expectation" or his "definition of the situation" rather than on his absolute deprivation. It is not that he is poor but rather that he is poorer than he feels he should be when he compares his lot with that of others. But this does not help to answer the crucial question, which is what *reference group* the individual selects for his comparisons. It seems from the *American Soldier* material that the groups most commonly selected are either associates of the same status or various unassociated "others" whose status is similar in

TABLE I

ATTRIBUTES OF INDIVIDUALS, SOCIAL CATEGORIES, AND GROUPS TAKEN
AS A FRAME OF COMPARATIVE REFERENCE BY INDIVIDUALS

In Sustained Social Relations with Individual	Same Status	Different Social Status		
		Higher	Lower	Unranked
Yes (membership group)	Married friends. Non-high-school acquaintances. Friends at same educational level.	Officers	Negro civilians in South	Friends, acquaintances
No (non-membership group)	Soldiers in U.S. or in active combat. Soldiers of equal longevity. Other captains	Officers	Negro civilians in South	

some respects and different in other respects. The nine cases appear
schematically in Table I.

This scheme crystallizes the distinction between membership
groups and nonmembership groups. It is the importance of the non-
membership group as a frame of reference that is the critical feature
of reference-group theory.

That men act in a social frame of reference yielded by the groups of
which they are a part is a notion undoubtedly ancient and probably
sound. Were this alone the concern of reference group theory, it would
merely be a new term for an old focus in sociology, which has always
been centered on the group determination of behavior. There is, however, the further fact that men frequently orient themselves to groups
other than their own in shaping their behavior and evaluations, and it
is the problems centered about this fact of orientation to non-membership
groups that constitute the distinctive concern of reference group theory.[39]

In some instances, however, the membership group does act as
the reference group. Merton and Kitt give one example that at first

sight is almost unbelievable. Many branches were questioned on their evaluations of promotion opportunities, and it seemed that, as a general rule, "the *less* the promotion opportunity afforded by a branch or combination of branches, the *more favorable* the opinion tends to be toward promotion opportunity."[40] Thus, though the Air Corps had a high promotion rate, Air Corps men were definitely more critical of their promotion prospects than men in the Military Police, where the objective chances for promotion were exceptionally bad. The only possible explanation suggested by the authors is that "such opinions represent a relationship between their expectations and their achievements *relative to others in the same boat with them*."[41]

This still leaves unanswered the question why the Military Police selected for reference their own branch rather than the Air Corps, whose high rate of promotion must have been known to them. Equally unpredictable were the replies of certain noncombat men overseas. Since surveys had shown that the major concern of the men overseas was to return home, it might have been expected that the percentage reporting themselves as "usually in good spirits" or holding that "the Army is run pretty well or very well" would be distinctly low. In fact, noncombat men overseas were only a little less favorable in their replies than noncoms still in the United States. This is explained by the fact that the noncombat men overseas were actually compounding their replies from two contexts of comparison operating at cross purposes; one was relative to *soldiers still at home*, while the other was relative to the *combat soldiers overseas*, with whom they were associating.

Obviously, as Merton and Kitt point out, there were other reference groups available to the individual soldier—a civilian friend in a "soft" job back home, a cousin enjoying life as a war correspondent, an undrafted movie star whom he had read about in a magazine —but the principal reference groups were *socially structured* by the common circumstance of the group (for example, noncombat men overseas) as a whole.

This effect of the social structure on the sense of deprivation is also illustrated in another case, which makes it clear that official institutional norms, such as the rules governing induction and discharge, are used by soldiers for judging the legitimacy of their own induction into the service. This leads them to adopt reference groups consisting of men with comparable official statuses, in such terms as marital condition and age.

So far the emphasis has rested on the concept of relative deprivation because this was the starting point suggested by the authors of *The American Soldier*. But this is a special case of the operation of reference-group behavior. In the first instance, the concentration on deprivation is in no way intrinsic; in other contexts, examination of relative reward, subjectively felt, or relative satisfaction is equally valid. Even this extension by no means completes the possibilities of the reference-group theory.

It is interesting that Merton and Kitt make use of some of the material Shils had cited in his analysis of the primary group. Here again we meet the veterans in veteran divisions, the replacements in veteran divisions, and the green troops in green outfits. In the reference-group framework what is most significant is the difference in response between the latter two categories, that is, those who both lacked combat experience, but differed in the kind of group in which they found themselves.

What has to be explained is why, whereas in attitude to non-coms the replacements were intermediate between veteran and green troops, when asked whether they would be able "to take charge of a group of men" the replacement troops were consistently the least confident of the three groups. Again, when asked about his own physical condition, the replacement was virtually indistinguishable from the other green troops, but he was far more likely than the veteran to consider himself 'in good physical condition."

Merton and Kitt point out that the authors of *The American Soldier* account for these three results by independent and diverse interpretations and do not examine the apparent inconsistencies between them. They contrast this with the situation in which Durkheim found himself when confronted with an immense variety of suicide rates differing according to sex, rural or urban area, military or civilian population, religious affiliation, and so on. Durkheim sought to organize these varied results under a limited set of propositions, and in this more restricted collection of diverse empirical findings Merton and Kitt set out to discover the underlying uniformities. They find their clue in the fact that "willingness for combat" constitutes an *attitude*, as defined, for example, by Allport as "a mental and neural *state of readiness*, organized through experience, exerting a directive or dynamic influence upon the individual's response to all objects and situations with which it is related,"[42] whereas "self-confidence in leadership capacities" represents a *self-image and a self-appraisal.*

Veterans, having learned by experience that "combat is hell," are least willing to enter into combat, whereas green troops are still puffed up with the conventional stereotypes of Ernie Pyle. The replacements, exposed to and eager to assimilate the tough-minded values of the veterans, had moved part of the way from the more naïve civilian-like values.

The replacements' faith in the stereotype is held not to be inconsistent with their marked lack of confidence in their own leadership capacities. This involves them in a self-appraisal, and, surrounded by experienced and prestigeful veterans, they see themselves, not surprisingly, as inadequately prepared for leadership in battle. What links the two instances is the fact that the replacements have gone far in assimilating the values of the veterans, whose acceptance they seek, but, when exposed to veterans' standards as well as veterans' values, see themselves as comparatively inadequate.

Finally, it is suggested that the same framework can accommodate the results related to physical fitness. It is postulated that the poor physical condition of veterans is a fact and not a *social value* (except as a possible rationalization for escaping further combat). Replacements are therefore absolved from the need to seek veteran recognition by asserting that they too are in poor physical shape. In fact replacements, like green soldiers in green outfits, would arrive in the combat zone in excellent physical condition, and their recognition of this would not set up a countervalue that would prejudice their acceptance by the veterans.

At a theoretical level this argument is convincing, but Merton and Kitt themselves called attention to the fact that much work remained to be done before it would be possible to establish the conditions under which values intervene to distort realistic appraisals into perspectival judgments. Equally unexplored was the context of social structure under which, and the machinery by which, members of one group identify their fate with that of another group, so that they no longer faithfully express their own distinctive interests and values.

Since the 1940's much work has gone into a study of social

mobility in an adaptive society, a development which represents a cross-fertilization between the work and insight of social psychologists and of sociologists. Here again, in this same secondary analysis of *The American Soldier,* Merton and Kitt pointed the way toward a detailed empirical examination of the processes by which individuals and groups transfer their allegiances. Discussion of later contributions will be found in Chapter 13 of this book. Enough has already been given to show that a mine of systematic data has been found in the solid volumes of "Studies in Social Psychology in World War II." Not only did the Research Branch successfully accomplish its task of keeping commanders properly informed, for the first time, of the state of mind of their troops, but long after the civilian army had gone home, their responses were providing a unique stimulus to the insights and consolidations of sociological theory.

FREE SPEECH ON SEXUAL BEHAVIOR

Sexual Behavior in the Human Male was published in 1948, and *Sexual Behavior in the Human Female* in 1953.[1] The research on which these two were based began in July, 1938. The first report thus took nearly ten years to prepare and publish. By that date Kinsey and his colleagues had succeeded in completing 12,000 interviews, counting both males and females. From the beginning they interviewed males and females concurrently, but the first book uses only a few facts from the female interviews and concentrates almost entirely on the interviews with male subjects.

The project was sponsored throughout by Indiana University. Dr. Kinsey had been on the faculty in the Department of Zoology at Indiana since 1921, and he was a senior member of the faculty when, in 1938, he decided to undertake this massive piece of research. It began as a departmental activity, but in 1941 the National Research Council's Committee for Research on Problems of Sex assumed sponsorship of the research program. A major part of the cost was contributed by the Medical Division of the Rockefeller Foundation.

In his introductions to both volumes Dr. Kinsey states his reasons for undertaking the task. He found that as chairman of his department he was constantly being asked by his students for help and advice on questions of sex, and as a biologist he did his best to advise them on many different aspects of sexual life and sexual behavior. He therefore began to read biologic, psychologic, psychiatric, and sociologic studies to obtain the answers to some of these questions, and, as a taxonomist, he was struck by the inadequacy of the samples used in these studies, feeling that they did not warrant the generalizations their authors put forward. Kinsey had other criticisms of the research techniques used in this field, and he concluded that more needed to be known about the actual behavior of people and about the interrelationships of that behavior with the biologic and social aspects of their histories.

Kinsey realized from the beginning that he would encounter strong objections to any study of sexual behavior because of the strong taboos against any open expression of interest in the subject of sex. He attributed this, very naturally, to the emotional importance of sex and to the close association in people's minds of sex, religious values, rituals, and customs. One result of this close association of sex with rituals and social mores is that society appears to regulate sexual behavior more than would seem to be justified on grounds of public interest. Whereas in most respects society is concerned only with regulating public acts that affect other people, there is always a tendency in matters of sex to go further and to wish to regulate what people do in the privacy of their homes or anywhere else. Kinsey felt, as we have all felt, that in every respect sex is less rationally treated than most other issues. So he set himself what seemed to be the fairly definite and simple task of accumulating an objectively determined body of facts about sex which would strictly avoid social or moral interpretations of the facts. His idea was to provide the data on which any reader could hang his own interpretations and moral judgments. As for himself, he set out with the intention of avoiding any moral judgment, and on the whole he succeeded. For, although his own values do emerge fairly clearly, these values are highly permissive, so that his moral judgment is in fact that any sexual activity is capable of being good. In consequence his judgment is neither restrictive nor discriminatory.

The groups included by 1948 already comprised persons classified in different ways: males and females; whites, Negroes, and other races; single, married, and previously married; ages from three to ninety; adolescents at different ages; various educational levels; various occupational classes; various social levels; urban, rural, and mixed backgrounds; various religious groups; various degrees of adherence to religious groups, including those with no religion; people of various geographic origins. The intention, at that date, was that the sample should gradually build up so that it would represent a cross section of the entire population from all parts of the United States. Kinsey did not actually state that he intended to treat the whole human species as one group, although of course this is implicit in his title, which claims to cover "the human male" and not just "the American male."

For reasons to be examined later, Kinsey decided that it was necessary to have a minimum of three hundred cases in any of the subcategories which survive after six or seven breakdowns. He calculated that in order to do this they would have to interview a sample of one hundred thousand subjects, and at that date he hopefully estimated that this could be completed in twenty years if he had a greatly expanded staff of interviewers. Unfortunately, when he tried to recruit staff he found that the qualities needed for interviewing in this project were so specialized, and so hard to come by, that in the end the main load of interviewing was borne by Kinsey, Pomeroy, and Martin.

Another indication of Kinsey's energy and dedication was the fact that as early as 1948 he had decided on the subject matter of eight future books. The second was to be *Sexual Behavior in the Human Female*, which appeared in 1953; then *Sexual Factors in Marital Adjustment*, published in 1957. Also planned were "Legal Aspects of Sex Behavior," "The Heterosexual-Homosexual Balance," "Sexual Adjustments in Institutional Populations," "Prostitution," "Sex Education," and "Other Special Problems."

Kinsey was determined to include in his survey anything that people did which came within his definition of sex. He was not at all concerned with how people should behave or with the fact that certain types of sexual behavior included in his categories would be regarded by society as neurotic, psychotic, perverted, or morally wrong. If, according to his definition, these were sexual activities, they went in. But although he did not draw the line at any form of physical activity, his orientation, insofar as he did have a psychological orientation, was strictly behaviorist, so that the manifestations with which he concerned himself had to be of a physical and directly carnal nature. This approach excludes even the physical display of parental affection; love of any kind, if not accompanied by carnality, would be excluded from his line of vision. Perhaps the one extraordinary feature of the Kinsey reports is that most of the time—not quite all of the time, because the authors are not entirely consistent—the only data discussed in detail are physical acts. The authors appear quite uninterested in the fact that humans can be sexually moved by each other without indulging in sexual relations, and there is no suggestion that a parent can love a child or that childbearing has any sexual connotation. The word "love" does not appear in the index.*

Coming into this research as a zoologist, Kinsey realized that he must make use of colleagues with special backgrounds in anthropology, biology, psychology, clinical psychology, animal behavior, and the social sciences. The specific backgrounds of his two main colleagues, Pomeroy and Martin, are not specified, but internal evidence suggests that their academic training and probably most of their postgraduate experience was on the more strictly biological side and that such particles of anthropology and the social sciences as they had accumulated were probably not at a very advanced academic level. But the team did also call in, and spend many hours in consultation with, experts from thirty-three disciplines, including anatomy, animal behavior, anthropology, astronomy (for statistical advice), biology, child development, criminal law, endocrinology, and so on. Kinsey includes sociology but mentions no particular sociologists with whom he had contact.

Kinsey was explicitly dissatisfied with the current state of research in the field of sexual behavior, and expressed the hope that publication of their first volume would at least stimulate these other specialists into doing more work on the problems of sexual life. If these

---

* A triangle situation is typically described in the following paragraph:
"Not infrequently the extra-marital activities had led to the development of emotional relationships which had interfered with the relations of the lawfully wedded spouses. This had caused neglect and disagreement which had seriously affected some of the marriages. This is the aspect of extra-marital activity which most societies, throughout the world, have been most anxious to control. We doubt whether such disturbances are inevitable, for there are cases of extra-marital relationships which do not seem to get into difficulties. There are strong-minded and determined individuals who can plan and control their extra-marital relationships in such a way that they avoid possible ill consequences. In such a case, however, the strong-minded spouse has to keep his or her activity from becoming known to the other spouse, unless the other spouse is equally strong-minded and willing to accept the extra-marital activity. Such persons do not constitute a majority in our present-day social organization."[2]

other experts objected to his method of procedure or to his conclusions or to his conceptual framework, he invited them to contribute to the knowledge of sexual behavior by doing more research themselves.

He was entirely unimpressed by the sex studies done up to that date. It appears that his primary criterion was that the study must be based on adequate numbers. As an insect taxonomist he had previously completed a major work on gall wasps, and for this study he had had 150,000 gall wasps, sufficient for him to work out some quite detailed taxonomic classifications. Therefore, when he looked at the literature on sex studies and found that the most detailed of the case-history studies had been based on only three hundred cases, he felt that the time had come to rectify the situation by a study based on adequate numbers.

After he started, it took him some time to develop a suitable method of securing subjects and a suitable interviewing technique. At the end of the first six months he had completed only 62 interviews: the next years' increment was 671; a few years later he was joined by Pomeroy and Martin, and by 1945 the total of interviews completed during the year had risen to 2,668. By that date the cumulative total just exceeded 10,000. In subsequent years the rate slowed down, presumably because the researchers were working on the results.

It should be made entirely clear that this was not the type of collaboration in which a senior professor surrounds himself with a flock of research assistants who collect data for him to write up. All the way through, Kinsey took the major load of work. Of the first 12,000 interviews completed by 1948 Kinsey personally had completed over 7,000, about 58 per cent of the total. Pomeroy, his next senior colleague, had conducted 31 per cent, and Martin, the third author of the book, had done 7 per cent. Three other assistants had done some interviewing for a short time, but they had contributed only the remaining 4 per cent. It is unquestionable that Kinsey had not only conceived and launched the program, but had also done the major part of the work; he had become the most experienced interviewer, to whom the most difficult interviewing assignments were entrusted.

It was, of course, understood from the beginning that the subject of sexual behavior would be awkward to approach by an interview survey, particularly before the study had acquired a reputation for objectivity and respectability. Some difficulties were in fact encountered. In one city the medical association tried to bring a suit on the ground that the team were practicing medicine without a license. In two or three cities there was some interference by the police, and there were a few attempts to persuade the University to stop the study, to prevent the publication of the results, or to dismiss Kinsey from his university connection. But the administration of Indiana University was solidly behind him all the way through, and the opposition soon subsided.

There were also some academic objections, mainly from other professional people who thought Kinsey was not qualified to undertake the task. Some psychologists thought that the problems were of a psychological nature and should not be touched by biologists, and some sociologists thought that the problems were of a sociological nature and that neither a biologist nor a psychologist was the right person to make a sex study. Various other scientists felt that somehow their own particular discipline was the right one to be entrusted with the job. Some people, of course, said that human sex is not a suitable subject for study by statistical methods. Others suggested that, while it was probably all right to make the study, the results should somehow be kept dark because society was not ready to face such facts. Several scientists suggested that the inquiry should be confined to what they called "normal" sexual behavior, whereas Kinsey, with his taxonomic and latitudinarian approach, was determined to keep his definition as broad as possible within his own imposed limits. He declared that the difference between normal and abnormal behavior is merely a matter of statistics. It will be recalled that Durkheim and many later authorities have tussled with the problem of normality. Kinsey was not unaware of the pitfalls of the modal norm, but as a taxonomist he naturally favored this definition.

The best objection encountered was that of the hotel manager who refused permission for interviews to take place in his hotel because, as he said, "I do not intend that anyone should have his mind undressed in my hotel."[3] But on any score, the sum total of objections was very much less than could have been anticipated. The state of Indiana, where the study started, proved surprisingly receptive. And on the positive side Kinsey does seem to have been very successful in enlisting the help of various professional groups and other institutions and universities of various kinds. The long list published includes twenty-six medical institutions and thirty-seven educational institutions, among which are most of the famous universities and liberal-arts colleges. There were also various official bodies: histories were secured from city courts in New York, Chicago, and elsewhere; some prison authorities gave permission for interviews to take place among prison populations; some mental institutions did the same. Finally, there is a miscellaneous group of organizations, such as the American Museum of Natural History and the Young Men's Christian Association, with which individual informants were associated. Even travelers on trains get into the list. It must be conceded that the sample was very well spread out as far as respectability is concerned. How far it was statistically adequate will be discussed later.

It has already been mentioned that Kinsey adopted a taxonomic approach to the problem of sexual behavior. Taxonomy is a biological method of classification which is useful in sorting out the many varieties of a particular plant, insect, or animal; the method is to choose a system of categories (for example, in botany, number of petals and color of flowers) and to examine very large samples of specimens so that a statistically valid frequency distribution of these characteristics can be established. If this distribution has more than one modal value, we can deduce that a corresponding number of major varieties are to be distinguished.

Thus the function of the taxonomic approach, as a development of systematic botany and systematic zoology, is to name, describe, and classify species and the higher categories. The size of the samples necessary to do this is determined by ordinary statistical considerations. Kinsey summarizes the task in the following sentence:

If individuals are collected in a fashion which eliminates all bias in their choosing, and in a fashion which includes material from every type of habitat and from the whole range of the species, it should be possible to secure a sample which, after measurement and classification, will indicate the frequency with which each type of variant occurs in each local population, or in the species as a whole.[4]

In the biological sciences the power to arrive at reliable generalizations depends on the size and quality of the sample. The taxonomist also, at a later stage, may proceed to analyze some of the factors which account for the differences found to exist, which he will do by comparing groups which are similar to one another in every characteristic except one; by this pseudo-experimental design he can find the explanatory variables.

This mode of procedure is contrasted with the single-case, *idiographic*, study. Kinsey does remind us that Linnaeus, the father of modern botanical classification, did at one time extol "the lone moss which was worth a life-time of study," but he regards this as an aberration comparable to Tennyson's thought that the flower in the crannied wall is the key to the secrets of the universe. To Kinsey and his colleagues

such detailed studies of single individuals have often represented a certain high degree of industry and scholarship, but they are dangerous as sources of generalizations about larger segments of the population. Like descriptive systematics at its worth, such detailed studies of individual cases are the antitheses of analyses based on large and statistically well selected samples of the sort the modern taxonomist employs.[5]

Their position is thus made quite clear. But they were also very much dissatisfied with what they regarded as the rather feeble attempts by social scientists to collect statistical information on sexual and marital behavior. They mention, for example, the study by Burgess and Cottrell, *Predicting Success or Failure in Marriage*,[6] and comment that such studies appear statistical because they carefully define the group which was studied without, however, making any effort to select a sample which would be homogeneous and representative of any larger portion of the total population.[7] Sometimes, they add,

social scientists hobnob as tourists in some social milieu sufficiently removed from their own to make it possible for them to acquire "impressions" and "hunches" about "social patterns" and "motivations of behavior" in whole cultures. This method has the merit of requiring a minimum of time—much less than the public opinion polls or the taxonomists need for arriving at their generalizations. Nevertheless, to some students the day seems overdue when scientists studying human material will forsake barbershop techniques and attempt to secure some taxonomic understanding of the human population.[8]

These remarks are simply a curtain raiser for the controversy which raged when *Sexual Behavior in the Human Male* was published. Obviously, if you attack psychologists, psychiatrists, psychoanalysts, and sociologists, you may expect that in due course, when they are reviewing your book, they are going to hit back. And so they did, in large numbers.

It is clear that Kinsey's taxonomic procedure does depend entirely on having a rigorous statistical method. One of his difficulties was that soon after his inquiry began World War II started, with the result that all the statisticians that would normally have been available for this kind of work were being called into the war effort. Presumably for that reason Kinsey had to rely on astronomers and other mathematicians whose experience in statistical techniques used in the social sciences was naturally limited.

In one section of the book Kinsey systematically examines the nineteen main studies previously undertaken that relate to this field. He is particularly critical of one of these, Hamilton's *A Research in Marriage*,[9] on the grounds that its conclusions are greatly overgeneralized. He adds:

There is no indication that it is supposed to end up as a study of the marriages of a particular group of two hundred people; but, rather, that it is a study of marriages in general, among people in general. No one would bother to study and to publish on the sexual behavior of particular persons if he did not expect that his generalizations would have some applicability to at least some other persons in the world.[10]

One cannot ignore the fact that Kinsey invited exactly the same criticism by calling his book "Sexual Behavior in *the* Human Male." He objected to the title *A Research in Marriage* because it conveyed the impression that the book related to all marriages, and he falls into the same trap by his own choice of title. As virtually all the work reported in Kinsey's first volume refers solely to a sample of Americans, the use of the word "human" appears rather insensitive —as though he did not quite realize the infinite variety of human customs. Even within the American population it appears as though quite important groups were omitted or only selectively included (for example, Negroes, prostitutes).

Kinsey was of course exposed to criticism on these grounds as soon as his book was published, and he offered what was perhaps a

rather lame defense of his choice of title; this appears at the beginning of *The Human Female*. Here he states:

This is a study of sexual behavior in (*within*) certain groups of the human species, *Homo sapiens*. It is obviously not a study of the sexual
behavior of all cultures and of all races of man. At its best, the present
volume can pretend to report behavior which may be typical of no
more than a portion, though probably not an inconsiderable portion, of
the white females living within the boundaries of the United States.
Neither the title of our first volume on the male, nor the title of this
volume on the female, should be taken to imply that the authors are
unaware of the diversity which exists in patterns of sexual behavior in
other parts of the world.

And, in a footnote:

The use of the preposition "in" is common throughout scientific writing,
including studies in biology, physiology, psychology, medicine, public
health, education and sociology. There are studies on *Finger Sucking
in Children, Sweating in Men, Blood Pressure Changes in Dogs, Academic Success in College Students, Superstition in the Pigeon*. For instance, typical pages of the *Zoological Record* may show three or four
out of every ten English titles in this form.[11]

As it happens, this particular lapse is of more than passing importance. The basic error is that Kinsey fails to distinguish between
descriptive and *explanatory* surveys. One may be sure that most, if
not all, of the examples he cites are concerned not with a census-
type survey but with relationships between, for example, finger
sucking and weaning practices. This contrasts with his declared
aim: "Descriptive taxonomy provides an over-all survey."[12] Here
the large representative sample is, as he suggests, essential. It is all
the more surprising, therefore, to read in his treatise on the "human
male" the very reasonable statement that "the Continental European
patterns of sex behavior are so distinct from the American . . . that
no additions of the European to the American data should ever
be made."[13]

The Kinsey reports provide the chief example in this book of research devoted to census-type descriptive material. The fundamental
difference between descriptive and explanatory surveys is that the
only hypotheses contained in descriptive surveys are inherent in the
definitions of things enumerated, whereas explanatory surveys con-

tain two types of hypotheses, those inherent in the definitions and those postulating relationships between the things defined. Furthermore, this last type of hypothesis is normally derived from some higher-level theory of which the hypothesis is a special case. In the Kinsey reports, while the authors state that "scientifically and socially it is of the greatest importance to understand why populations differ as much as [they do],"[14] the whole emphasis is on establishing the facts of sexual behavior and its variations, and very little space is devoted to probing the reason for such variations.

The sampling requirements of descriptive surveys are well known; in such inquiries the aim is to randomize in order to achieve a representative sample of the population. This material may also be useful in explanatory analysis, and it will often be found that higher-level theories are implicit in the definitions of the things enumerated. To take an example from the Kinsey reports, it is possible to test very fully the relationship between, on the one hand, the frequency and sources of human sexual outlet and, on the other hand, eleven factors which, on implicit theoretical grounds, the authors regarded as material in affecting sexual activity. "They are sex, race, age, age at onset of adolescence, marital status, educational level, the subject's occupational class, the parental occupational class, rural-urban backgrounds, religious affiliations, and the extent of the subject's devotion to religious affairs."[15]

In the case of explanatory surveys, however, it may often be preferable to restrict the sample to those sectors of the universe which best permit comparison between the effects of the independent variables under study. In Hyman's words:

The explanatory survey follows the model of the laboratory experiment with the fundamental difference that it attempts to represent this design in a *natural setting*. Instead of *creating* and manipulating the independent variables whose effect is to be traced the survey analyst must find in the natural setting instances of these factors. . . . But since these variables are not created, but merely found in the natural setting, there is the great danger that a variety of other factors accompany them, and that respondents characterized by particular attributes may vary in other important respects. The influence of these other sources of variability must somehow be reduced. Otherwise any inference about the hypothesized cause may be shaky. *The restriction of the universe which is covered and the design of the sample in the explanatory survey provides the basic technique by which other sources of variation in the phenomenon are excluded.* It is in relation to this problem that the descriptive and explanatory surveys lead to opposing designs.[16]

While the most caustic remarks were directed at Hamilton's *A Research in Marriage*, the authors' criticisms of other American studies of sex behavior were of the same order of severity. Before admitting a study to consideration they applied certain criteria; it had to be "(1) scientific, (2) based on more or less complete case histories, (3) based on a series of at least some size, (4) involving a systematic coverage of approximately the same items on each subject, and (5) statistical in treatment."

On this basis, 19 studies, including the one by Hamilton, are listed and examined in turn. The main results of this analysis are summarized in the following points:

1. Previous investigators of American sexual behavior have included 9 psychologists, 4 psychiatrists, 2 journalists and 2 biologists, but no sociologists. About half of the studies conclude with generalizations based on mixed or otherwise inadequate populations.

2. The preferred method has been the questionnaire, used in 10 cases. In only 8 cases has the investigator conducted a face-to-face interview with his subjects, and in only 4 of these were "pre-formed questions and stilted formalities" abandoned. Many of the questionnaires were administered under quite unsuitable conditions.

3. The studies were very unevenly distributed geographically. Seven of the 19 had been based on material from New York City, and another 5 on material from the east coast. Kinsey had found in his studies that sexual behavior in New York City differed in certain important respects from that in the United States as a whole, and so this skewed the distribution of previous studies and could lead to misleading results.

4. Of the 19, 10 had been concerned with men only, 5 with women only, and only 4 with both men and women.

5. Of the 19, 10 were based on individuals at the college level only, and 6 were mostly confined to people who had not gone beyond high school. This seriously skewed the distribution by educational groups, which, as they themselves had found, had a big bearing on modes of sexual behavior.

6. The number of questions asked was often rather small. The minimum was in Exner's study (1915), which was based on 8 questions; at the other extreme, Hamilton in the otherwise criticized *A Research on Marriage*, asked 147 questions. Ramsay, who had undertaken a study in

1943 in coordination with the Kinsey team, had asked 218 questions. These numbers can be compared with Kinsey and his associates who had included 521 questions in the full interview.

7. Kinsey found that, on the whole, these earlier studies had depended upon very small samples which were insufficient for sound and reliable generalizations. This inadequacy was often heightened by the extremely heterogeneous nature of the material and the consequent need for a particularly large sample. Kinsey and his colleagues were quite evidently certain that on these grounds the scale on which they were operating was fully justified, and made their studies definitely superior to any previous work in this field; in spite of the highly controversial nature both of his methods and of his results, this judgment will be shared by most objective critics.

RESEARCH TECHNIQUES

It was inevitable that Kinsey should attract controversy because of his dramatic and uncompromising invasion of the territory of the social sciences. A stranger from another universe of discourse, he sought to impose his own language and customs on established social scientists. His development of a new, specialized, and highly skilled method of interviewing is typical of his procedure.

The authors begin with a lament that "academic departments so often offer courses on the statistical manipulation of human material to students who have little understanding of the problems involved in securing the original data."[17] On these grounds they feel free to develop a method of interviewing suitable for eliciting data on sexual behavior. This leads them to a type of interview that is, in some ways, at the opposite pole from the nondirective interviewing that is the other specialized form thus far described. It is no less logical than other methods, but, as we shall see, the premises are entirely different.

Kinsey found, as has already been mentioned, that the special qualities needed for his kind of interviewing were so rare that it was best to concentrate the work in the hands of a small number of interviewers who had shown themselves capable of developing highly specific skills for dealing with this particular situation.

Part of the difficulty is inherent in the subject matter. Kinsey comments: "It is astounding that anyone should agree to expose himself by contributing his sex history to an interviewer whom he has never before met, and to a research project whose full significance he, in most instances, cannot begin to understand."[18] This is too strong a statement and should of course be modified in one or two respects. Those responsible for interviewing discovered long ago that informants like to talk about themselves. Furthermore, sex is a subject that interests the great majority of people, and it could be predicted that many people would be very glad to have an anonymous talk with a reliable stranger on various aspects of their personal lives, their marriages, their families, friends, or social relations.

It can therefore be said that the altruistic motive—which leads people to give information about their own sex lives in order to further scientific research—is supplemented by certain more selfish, though in no way exceptionable, motives. Those co-operating very often used the opportunity of the interview situation to ask questions concerning their own sexual behavior. A surprising number of informants at some stage in the interview would turn to the interviewer and ask such questions as "Am I normal?," "Are there any harmful effects from 'excessive' sexual activity?," or ask about the medical aspects of contraception or about the physical and social significances of petting. These questions are among those most frequently asked by the anxious informants that came to see them, and as the informants were normal individuals, Kinsey and his colleagues concluded that these and other similar items must be the everyday sexual problems of the average person.

Many psychologists critical of the Kinsey reports have pointed out that certain types of individuals will use the opportunity of an interview concerning sexual histories to be exhibitionistic; even if they do not fabricate their stories, they will in many ways embroider them. Kinsey was well aware of this risk, particularly as the informants were volunteers. In these circumstances there is inevitably some self-selection, and a consequent overrepresentation of those most eager to describe their own sexual behavior. It does not follow that the volunteers were neurotics or psychotics; if obvious psychotics did come forward, and of course a few did, they were refused. The decision to exclude them was not based on a moral judgment on the part of the interviewers but was made on the grounds that the facts provided by the psychotics would be unreliable. Their poor memories, hallucinations, and fantasies, as soon as they became recognizable, made nonsense of the whole interview program, and the session was terminated.

Kinsey examined, perhaps not quite adequately, the distortions that are liable to occur in the statements of people who wish to inflate their own egos: they may describe unusual prowess, sexual athleticism; they may claim exceptional normality; or they may understate their rates of sexual activity because they want to be pitied. The authors' feeling was that distortion was not very great and was dwarfed by the altruistic desire to further scientific knowledge.

It was found that the best way to obtain volunteers was to interest certain key individuals in appropriate communities or societies in the project and then to persuade them to draw in every member of that group for interviewing. This method leads to what is called "cluster sampling," which from a statistical point of view is not very efficient, as will be discussed later. What is interesting in the present context is that this method of winning entry through leaders is basically the same sort of approach as that used by W. F. Whyte in *Street Corner Society*. (See Chapter 7.) Whyte said that he could get in anywhere if only he could win the confidence of certain key individuals; from then on he did not have to explain anything more to the other members of their groups but was accepted simply on the grounds that the leader of the group in question vouched for him.

The number of types of people included in the interview program constitutes almost a complete list of occupations. In *Sexual Behavior in the Human Female* the list is made even longer and extends for several pages. But it is of no great interest except that it is a somewhat more informal list than the Bureau of the Census would produce. It has certain categories, such as "pimps," "male prostitutes," "female prostitutes," "ne'er-do-wells," and "persons in the social register," which would not normally be recognized in official statistics. It is evidently a conscientious attempt to cover the whole population.

The question arose regarding payment for informants, as it often does in the social sciences, and the decision was taken to make a small payment to certain groups: to the economically poorest elements; to those who were professionally involved in sexual activities (as prostitutes, pimps, exhibitionists, etc.); and to others who had spent an exceptional amount of time on behalf of the investigation. The payments were never large, perhaps a dollar or two for the couple of hours that the interview took, and Kinsey was satisfied that they did not destroy the quality of the record.

Although obviously there were anomalies in the sample, with underrepresentation of some groups, there seems little doubt that Kinsey and his colleagues were extraordinarily skillful at gaining access to different societies and at obtaining data from whole groups of people. Kinsey emerges from this test as a man of great strength of character and of complete integrity.

Once the interviewer had persuaded a person to volunteer as a subject, his first task was to establish rapport; it was found that there were only two points on which it was essential to convince the subject in order to win his full co-operation. The interviewer had first to make the subject realize that he was not exercising any moral judgment on him—that the subject could tell him anything and it would not shock him in any way, and he would not for a moment suggest, either overtly or by the slightest hint, that one form of behavior was preferable to another. The second essential was to convince the subject that the confidences of the record would be kept without question. This was not merely to quiet the fear of social ostracism if the subject's more irregular sexual activities were known but also to obviate possible legal prosecution of the subject in case of betrayal of confidences.

Apart from these two negative injunctions, not to moralize and not to tell, there was also a need to show positive qualities of warmth and understanding. This did not have to be done in a dramatic way, but the investigator had to show his sympathy by always behaving with full courtesy, by never showing surprise, disapproval, condemnation, or even disinterest in any statement made. It was found that a quiet and genuine show of warmth was highly effective. And, of course, the interview offers opportunities for human sympathy that cannot be summoned in a self-administered questionnaire; people do not complete a questionnaire feeling warmer than when they began, whereas at the end of a properly conducted interview a subject can definitely feel great relief and pleasure.

It is one thing, however, to show sympathy and another to believe everything that is told to you. Investigators, particularly in an affect-laden field such as sexual behavior, have to be constantly on their guard to detect lies. Attempting to describe how investigators do this, the authors sum it up by saying, "As well ask a horse-trader how he knows when to close a bargain."[19] It is an extra sense that a skilled interviewer develops, and he must learn to detect very slight indications of dishonesty, slight hesitations, as well as inconsistencies in the record itself. In the Kinsey studies the interviewers were exceptionally tough with informants whom they suspected of withholding information.

At the beginning of an interview the subject must be assured that he can tell all, but it is not always possible to win complete rapport at the very start. The subject will need to be reassured many times in the course of the interview, and continually convinced by the evident sympathy of the interviewer. Often the subject begins by admitting only a small part of his activity, and adds more only gradually as he becomes more certain that he can do so without disapproval—"Yes, I have been approached for such relations, but I did not pay attention."—"Yes, there were physical contacts, but they did not interest me."—"Yes, there were complete contacts—when I was asleep."—"Yes, there was one affair in which I responded, in a mild way."—"Yes, I liked it well enough, but I didn't think I wanted any more of it."—"Well, yes, I did try it again."—"Yes, since then I have become interested, and I have had a good deal of it lately."—So the history builds up.[20]

It can be quite a strain for the interviewer to avoid expressing any surprise or disapproval. Whatever his sexual background, every investigator has a limit to his personal experience and to his capacity to understand the motivations of others. "Beyond that there are always things which seem esthetically repulsive, provokingly petty, foolish, unprofitable, senseless, unintelligent, dishonorable, contemptible or socially destructive."[21] And the only way to overcome one's sense of disgust is by increasing sophistication and by reminding oneself of the immense range of possibilities in human feelings and activities, which leads to a certain necessary blunting of the interviewer's susceptibilities.

The confidence of the record was ensured by the fact that what was said was never written out in words. Each of the six interviewers learned a code for describing the responses of the informants; this code was memorized and was not committed to paper. Two interviewers learned only a part of the code, and the only persons that ever knew the whole code were the principal investigators. The code was quite professional, having been devised with the help of a cryptographer, and would have been difficult to break.

Of course, if you use a secret code, you will be constrained to do all the handling of the data. This meant that Kinsey and his three associates became computing-machine operators and did their own punching, sorting, and tabulating; to do this they equipped themselves with a complete computer outfit, demonstrating how seriously they also took this aspect of their work.

The authors resolved at the beginning of their program never to publish any case histories; and when in lectures or on other occasions they quoted from case histories they were careful to make them composite cases, even if the informant came from the other side of the United States.

They complain, probably quite justifiably, that some professional people—doctors, lawyers, academic persons—in ther own offices will tend to discuss openly among themselves cases that have come to their attention or will pass data on to their graduate students. And they are not always as careful as they might be that no secretaries, nurses, or other people are present, with the result that facts given in confidence do manifestly filter through and back to the patients themselves or to others. In the courts or in penal institutions the consequences may be serious for the prisoner whose confidences are thus betrayed. In one case a psychiatrist, examining a subject who was under criminal indictment, questioned him in a small room in which half a dozen persons were listening to the whole conversation. Kinsey and his colleagues were determined to go to any lengths, including the destruction of their data, in order to avoid revealing confidences.

Other occasions arose when they were pressed to pass on information. Often when interviewing in groups they had both husband and wife in their sample, and sometimes the husband or the wife would ask them to reveal what the spouse had told them about their sexual behavior. Though the interviewers recognized that often this would improve marital adjustment, here again they had to respect the confidence of the individual.

When they visited penal institutions they made it a prior condition that no pressure be put on them by the authorities to reveal anything they were told. They said that in fact the authorities never did attempt to use them as a source of information about the sexual behavior of their prisoners.

Twelve pages are devoted to a twenty-three-point summary of the technical devices used in their type of interviewing. Some of these devices have already been discussed or are implicit in earlier discussions. For example, the interviewer should always aim to put the subject at his or her ease, and should start by making general conversation about everyday affairs of general interest or about mutual friends. In fact, he should act like a thoughtful host.

The second point is that he should be sure that every interview takes place in privacy and without fear of interruption. Here again professionals sometimes err.

The third is that, in the establishment of rapport, the interviewer should be courteous always and show interest in the person as a person—more interest in him as a person than in his history as just another case to be recorded. Here for the first time the authors mention the importance of looking the subject squarely in the eye while giving a minimum of attention to the record that is being made. They add, "People understand each other when they look directly at each other." This advice is perhaps rather revealing, for it suggests that although the investigators ostensibly aim at a friend-to-friend relationship with their subjects, they do in fact establish a power relationship with them. Obviously the interviewer, by his superior knowledge, by his skill, and by the fact that he is acting as the host, is able to elicit more from these informants than the informants had meant to reveal.

The next point discussed is the sequence of topics. This is all fairly familiar ground; social scientists are aware that they should start from the subject that is of least emotional importance and gradually work through to the emotional subjects. In this context the investigators begin with nonsexual questions and lead through to sexual questions; from the sexual questions that are least disturbing to the ones that are most disturbing. After the ordinary classifying details of age, place of birth, educational history, recreational interests, physical health, parental background, they move on to simple sexual data, such as the subject's early sex education; this is used as a starting point on the grounds that it is something for which the informant would not feel responsible. The record of overt sexual activities begins with preadolescent sex play, which would be remote enough for the subject to discuss with detachment.

At this stage they found it necessary to vary the approach according to the social class of the subject. In the case of college boys it proved desirable to discuss sexual outlets in the following order: nocturnal emissions, masturbation, premarital petting, premarital intercourse with companions, intercourse with prostitutes, animal contacts, and last of all homosexuality. In this list the first item was regarded as least disturbing and the last item as most disturbing to college males. In contrast, in the case of those who had left school at or before the tenth grade it was found that premarital intercourse was not regarded as very serious and therefore deserved an earlier place in the list.

When interviewing prostitutes the investigators found that the prostitutes would freely discuss their professional activities but would show considerable resistance when it came to questions of their own personal sex life, with a boy friend or a husband.

The next point is that the investigator should recognize the subject's mental status. The authors make the obvious point that it is useless to try to interview a person who is intoxicated or under drugs. They also had to concede that people who are congenitally very stupid simply cannot be interviewed; an IQ of 50 was, in their opinion, the lower limit, and it proved virtually impossible to obtain coherent answers from subjects with an IQ of less than 50. They found that they could interview people with IQ's between 50 and 70 only by going very slowly, with frequent repetition and a very simple vocabulary.

The perennial question of recording is next mentioned. The investigators tried to do what many other social scientists claim to be able to do, namely, conduct the interview first and record it afterward. By this procedure they made so many mistakes that they decided to record during the interview. They claim as one of the advantages of their code notation the fact that it hardly disturbed the flow of conversation.

Since Kinsey started his fieldwork the tape recorder has become much more freely available and is an important asset to the social investigator. It is sometimes suggested that subjects will "dry up" on the introduction of a tape recorder. This objection can easily be exaggerated; often they dry up at first but quite soon pick up again. Most subjects can appreciate that the tape recording is a useful check on the written notes.

The use of tape recorders is perhaps most suitable in group interviewing because the machine is then least prominent. Even in these circumstances, however, participants undoubtedly remain aware of its presence. This is shown by the fact that when the tape is turned off, at the end, there is often much residual tension to be released. It is noticeable that, although participants seem to be talking quite freely while the machine is running, when it is turned off, they often start working off their aggressions on the interviewer, and there may be a spate of teasing and chaffing which is very different from the well-behaved discussion on the tape.

The next point discussed is what the authors call "systematic coverage." They put to every subject a minimum of 300 question items. For subjects with a full range of experiences the total might be as high as 521. Obviously a person who had never been married would not be questioned on marital history, but the basic minimum of 300 items would be covered to ensure comparability. Reference to the code sheet afforded assurance that all the questions had been asked.

This standardization of questions did not preclude supplementary exploration. Always in a sample of this kind there will be subjects who have had special experiences or who are particularly interesting for one reason or another. They might be identical twins, they might be sado-masochists, they might have lived abroad in other cultures, they might have had army sexual experiences, and so on. So always the interviewers were encouraged to extend their interviews to take in any relevant questions. Here again an addition to the schedule in this way is possible only with highly skilled and experienced interviewers who know exactly what the whole program is about. In this respect the Kinsey report was almost uniquely well served.

In the presentation of their normal set of questions the interviewers were quite clear that they must standardize what they call "the point of the question" rather than the form of the question. They were not in favor of using exactly the same wording in approaching different subjects because many words vary in meaning considerably between individuals; but the interviewers themselves must know exactly what they are concerned with in respect of each item and must vary the wording of the question to suit the informant. If, for example, it is a question about petting, they must know exactly which activities can be classified as petting. For a question about prostitutes, they must have a systematic way of deciding when a prostitute is a prostitute and when she is only a good-time girl. In their opinion it is a mistake to try to put these definitions into their questions; they prefer to ask the questions around the definitions so that they can classify subjects and their sexual behavior according to the objective rules of the investigation. Naturally, since the questions themselves were not standardized, it is not possible to list them. But the 521 items covered are listed,[22] and they are certainly comprehensive.

As the investigators concentrated on the meaning of each question and varied the phrasing, they had to become very skilled at adapting the questions to suit the vernacular. This entailed familiarizing themselves with the language customarily used by each subject. They found this knowledge very helpful; they could avoid offending a highly educated person by the use of vulgar words and could avoid confusing a less literate person having little knowledge of clinical terms. The investigators were always free to amplify their questions in order to make their meanings clear.

Responsibility for avoiding bias was placed on the interviewer, who had to prevent himself, by careful moderation of his tone of voice and his choice of words, from giving the subject any idea that a particular answer was expected. Experience shows that the average semiskilled interviewer is unable to avoid biasing the subject; therefore, if these investigators did avoid bias, they must have been exceptionally skilled interviewers. They did prompt; that is, if the subject was at a loss for an answer, they indicated the range of answers from which he might wish to choose. If, for example, it was a question of the frequency of a particular form of sexual behavior, the interviewers would give a list of possible frequencies in a scrambled order. They might say, for example, "Once a week?," "Three or four times a week?," "Once a month?," "Every day?," and so on. And informants would choose an answer from this series of possibilities. They found from regular experience that all subjects, and especially the dull-witted ones, tend to echo the last words they have heard, so it is necessary to vary the order of prompt answers or too many of those mentioned last will be given in answer. This device makes for the statistical reliability of the sample as a whole but does not eliminate the difficulty of obtaining valid relations within the answers of one respondent.

The interviewers soon learned that in dealing with such a socially involved question as sex it is important never to be squeamish. Euphemisms should not be substituted for franker terms. Within the language understood by the informant they found it best to say just what they meant. For example, in talking about masturbation, they called it masturbation; they did not say "touching yourself" or use some other polite phrase. They were highly critical of the widespread use of euphemisms by earlier research workers.

The next point to be made was the need to place the burden of denial on the subject. The interviewers always assumed that every subject had engaged in every type of sexual behavior, so that instead of asking, "Do you do so and so?" they asked, "When did you begin doing so and so?" This is somewhat more questionable advice. In view of the fact that the Kinsey reports have shown sex practices to be much commoner than was previously supposed, it must be noted that the effect of asking questions in the form used by the investigators would be, if anything, to exaggerate the number of positive answers and the apparent frequencies of activity.

They next remind us to avoid multiple questions and to ask about only one idea at a time. Do not say, "Do you feel erotically aroused by seeing nude males or females?" If one wants to ask about this, it should be put in two questions, or men will be able to evade stating the fact that they are to some degree aroused by seeing nude males.

Their celebrated advocacy of rapid-fire questioning represents a central point in their technique. One advantage claimed for this method is that it saves time; another is that it elicits more truthful data by giving the respondent no time to fabricate an answer. They say that detectives and other law-enforcement officials have learned that this is the way to arrive at the truth—just fire questions at people and they will give the correct answers.

Another technique for improving accuracy is based on the merited belief that coverup is easier than exaggeration. It follows that the best protection against coverup is the use of interlocking questions. For example, in approaching the question of homosexuality the investigators build up slowly with twelve preliminary questions before asking the direct one about homosexual activity. Another example of buildup has already been quoted. This approach ensures that people are softened up when the direct question comes. They also found it possible to some extent to defeat the coverup by slipping in a vernacular word which the subject would presumably know only if he was experienced. For example, if one asks a female subject, "How many years have you been 'in the life'?" she either displays an honest confusion or she reveals herself as understanding the phrase, which is part of the argot of the prostitute. The presumption is that if she understands the question, she identifies herself as a prostitute, however she may actually answer the direct question.

The technique of "proving the answer" refers to the additional testing of a reply. If the interviewer does not believe the answer, he is advised to ask a second time. In the case of feeble-minded or undereducated people whose replies they disbelieved the investigators found it effective sometimes to pretend that they had misunderstood the negative replies and to carry on as though the original answers had been affirmative. If one says, "How long have you been doing . . .?" and the subject says, "I haven't ever done it," the investigator may reply, "Yes, I know you have never done that, but how old were you the *first* time you did it?" They state, surprisingly enough, that this technique breaks many subjects down, but they add that one must be on guard against fictional admissions.

On the other hand, if a subject contradicted himself, they did not, as some social scientists have proposed, point out to him that he was being inconsistent. Their method was to accept the last statement the subject made, ignoring his earlier evasions and contradictions. On a few occasions when they were still convinced that the subject was lying, they would look him squarely in the eye and suggest that he "now give it to us straight."

They describe the next component of their technique as "forcing the subject." This is brought into play when the investigator suspects that one of his subjects has come to the interview out of curiosity with no intention of telling the truth. Their advice is that in such circumstances one should "denounce the subject with considerable severity" and refuse to proceed with the interview. Recognizing that this is quite contrary to the usual rules for interviewing, they adopted this practice with hesitation and confined it mainly to some older teenage males and some females from underworld groups. One motive for this severe treatment was to retain the prestige of the investigation, which would obviously decline if it were thought that the interviewers could be fobbed off with obvious falsifications. According to the authors, this drastic step lost them no histories and won a number of stanch friends who were impressed by their insistence on scientific honesty.

The authors' last points are concerned mainly with certain limitations to their inquiry which either were imposed by the exigencies of time or were voluntarily adopted. They show themselves well aware, for example, that they will be criticized by certain colleagues for their omissions; for example, by anthropologists for omitting racial ancestries, by marriage counselors for omitting non-sexual factors in marital adjustment, by psychoanalysts for their inadequate data on early childhood, by sociologists for insufficiently detailed studies of cultural and community backgrounds. They apologize for these omissions; but they remind the reader that each history covered five times as much material as in any previous study and that it does in fact take in an extraordinary range of data for what they found to be the longest feasible single interview— from one and a half to two hours. A little dramatically they claim:

The extension of each interview by even ten minutes would lower the quality of the intake and materially reduce the number of histories that could be secured in a year. To add such a thing as a good test of economic status, or a masculinity-femininity test, would nearly double the length of time needed for each individual.[23]

Quite rightly they repeat the reminder that they were conducting a taxonomic survey, and even this was scheduled to occupy the team for twenty-eight years. Any more intensive study would in any case be most suitably entrusted to specialists—in psychoanalysis, in mental measurements, in gynecology, or in other appropriate disciplines.

Another feature of their program, which some would consider a limitation, was their concentration on overt activities as opposed to attitudes, although it was decided upon entirely deliberately.

This has been because we feel that there is no better evidence of one's attitudes on sex. Specific questions have been asked about each subject's attitudes toward his parents, toward masturbation, premarital intercourse, sexual relations with prostitutes, and homosexual experience: but we do not have much confidence in verbalizations of attitudes which each subject thinks are his own, when they are, in actuality, little more than reflections of the attitudes which prevail in the particular culture in which he was raised. Often the expressed attitudes are in striking contradiction to the actual behavior, and then they are significant because they indicate the existence of psychic conflict and they throw light on the extent to which community attitudes may influence an individual.[24]

We need not here discuss the large question of the adequacy or superiority of behaviorist data, but it may be remarked that it is surely an extraordinary assertion that "verbalizations" are culturally regulated but activities, sexual or otherwise, are not.

The authors of *Sexual Behavior* may show little sociological sophistication, but they do display a spirit of inquiry and a quality of thought of a very high order. This shows itself in the originality with which they touch upon some of the age-old dilemmas of the social sciences. For instance, it has been mentioned that as taxonomists they are bound to define normality in terms of frequency of occurrence. But their adoption of the statistical norm does not confuse them into attaching an ethical value to their concept of normality. They eschew the moral judgment with remarkable thoroughness, but they do in places hint at another norm which is described as "natural behavior." Recognizing the existence of legal determinations of sexual acts as "natural" or "contrary to nature," they do not challenge the concept of naturalness, but complain instead that the concept is not based on data obtained from biologists and does not take account of modern psychological knowledge.[25] They reject the assertion of a fundamentalist professor of philosophy: "There are some things that one innately understands to be right or wrong, and about which there is no need for logical discussion."[26] They recognize the extent to which concepts of sexual normality are related to cultural influences and particularly to social level, and they strongly criticize the authorities—physicians, marriage counselors, and so on—who do not take social level into account. And yet behind it all they appear to have an image of a state of grace before the fall of man, when innocent humans practiced and tolerated behavior such as is no longer acceptable in civilized societies.

In many instances variant types of behavior represent the basic mammalian patterns which have been so effectively suppressed by human culture that they persist and reappear only among those few individuals who ignore custom and deliberately follow their preferences in sexual techniques. In some instances sexual behavior which is outside the socially accepted pattern is the more natural behavior . . . because it is less affected by social restraints.[27]

They then refer to homosexuality. In *Sexual Behavior in the Human Female* the authors elaborate this point. For example, they list the mammals in widely separated species whose males and females have been observed in homosexual contacts. They do not press the claim that such behavior is "more natural" than heterosexual contacts, but they conclude:

Psychologists and psychiatrists, reflecting the mores of the culture in which they have been raised, have spent a good deal of time trying to explain the origins of homosexual activity; but considering the physiology of sexual response and the mammalian backgrounds of human behavior, it is not so difficult to explain why a human animal does a particular thing sexually. It is more difficult to explain why each and every individual is not involved in every type of sexual activity.[28]

The first book includes a very full account of the technical and statistical details of the procedure for data recording. One feature, already mentioned, is their system of coding, which was worked out so that they could record the subject's responses without slowing down the interview. This had the added advantages that, being in code from the start, it preserved the confidentiality of the data; it facilitated the transfer of their results onto punched cards; it increased the accuracy of coding because it eliminated one stage in the procedure and, if there was any point of doubt in the response, the difficulty of coding the response was immediately apparent, so that they would ask supplementary questions for clarification. They found also that their code saved space on the sheets which the interviewers carried with them, and finally that it facilitated the coverage of all points—the investigators simply glanced down the line at the end to ensure that they had asked all the questions.

The authors do not mention any disadvantages of this type of rigid precoding. It is normally felt to be a disadvantage to have completely predetermined the data that can be recorded. Any response that does not fit into the system of recording will somehow be eliminated at that early stage of fieldwork, and there will be no further reference to it.

There is nothing very unusual about the practical details of their coding procedure. They used standard data sheets with minor modifications; the sheets were divided into blocks by heavy ruling at certain predetermined points, and each section of the interview was put in a fixed position on the block, so that the meaning of each symbol depended on its position on the block. Quite simple mathematical symbols were used. Ordinary numbers were used, wherever appropriate, to record ages, frequencies, and so on, and various mathematical signs ($+$, $-$, $\times$, etc.) made up most of the remainder.

As has been mentioned, the interviewers had to memorize the whole code in advance. This entailed considerable training, and they spent their first few months working over old coding sheets until they could read them as well as a sheet of written words. Strict precautions were taken to ensure standardization between the different interviewers.

While these standard interviews provided the main source of information, the investigators availed themselves of various supplementary sources. For example, they made participant observations in subjects' homes and in their visits to friends, night clubs, taverns, and other places of recreation.

They also collected activity records compiled by the subjects at their request; in these reports the subjects reported day-to-day facts about their activities or their thinking on various aspects of sex. Some of these documents were several hundred pages in length, and two were over a thousand pages long. It is a familiar fact that some informants are willing to write essays.

Some subjects supplied photographs and books or made available transcripts of court records and other social data.

The number of items of supplementary information was being steadily increased. By 1953, when the *Human Female* was published, the investigators had collected 377 sexual calendars (312 female, 65 male) covering periods from six months to as long as thirty-eight years. The preponderance of female cases was explained by the fact that females frequently record coital activities in relation to menstrual periods. The number of diaries, files of correspondence between sexual partners, scrapbooks, toilet-wall inscriptions, and other exhibits is not specified, but it must have been rapidly accumulating.

As time went on, increasing attention was given to clinical and mammalian studies. A total of 1,300 histories of females and males convicted of sex offenses had been collected. The Institute for Sex Research at Indiana University had by 1953 become the repository for the original data from several earlier studies on sexual behavior. The library of the Institute already had some 15,000 volumes; the subjects best represented were "Fiction, Pre-1930" (1,546 volumes); "Psychology and Psychiatry" (1,210); "Fiction, Modern" (1,140); "Poetry" (1,138); and "Art, by Artists" (1,049). Far down the list came "Woman and Love," presumably nonfiction, with 342 volumes.

ANALYSIS

The design of their analysis involved a breakdown of the interview material on the basis of twelve biological and socio-economic characteristics of their sample population. This comprised a two-way breakdown on "Sex," an eleven-way breakdown on "Race-Cultural Group," a three-way breakdown on "Marital Status," an eighteen-way breakdown on "Age," a six-way breakdown on "Age at Adolescence," a nine-way breakdown on "Educational Level," a ten-way breakdown on "Occupational Class" (based on Chapin, Lloyd Warner, and Hollingshead), a ten-way breakdown on "Occupational Class of Parents," a five-way breakdown on "Rural-Urban Background" (whether the subject was wholly urban or wholly rural, or at what age he or she moved into the city), a three-way breakdown on "Religious Group," a four-way breakdown on "Religious Adherence" (whether the subject was devout or inactive in his religious group), and finally a breakdown, not yet attempted by 1953, on "Geographic Origin."

It will be appreciated that a full examination of the influence of these factors is quite impracticable. On the first eleven factors alone there are nearly 400 million possible combinations, so that even the whole population of the United States would have provided on average less than one case in every other cell, whereas for any analysis of sampling errors quite a large number of cases are needed in each cell examined. In practice, of course, the cells are very unevenly filled, and there is also considerable interaction between factors (for example, Occupational Class of Subject is not independent of Occupational Class of Parents), with the result that it is possible to collect quite large numbers of cases with certain sets of characteristics and extremely difficult to find any cases at all with other sets of characteristics.

For instance, it would never be possible to secure a statistically good sample of Orthodox Jewish males who were Negro, single, between the ages of eighty-five and ninety, illiterate, living in rural areas, and belonging to the Social Register.[29]

For the analysis contained in the *Human Male*, only 12,000 interviews were in hand, and only 5,300 male interviews were usable, and this limited the authors to a maximum of a six- or seven-way breakdown and to much less at some points. Even so, they had to reduce the eleven race-cultural groups to two (American and Canadian white, and Negro) and the age groups from eighteen to eleven (ten to sixty years old). However, utilization of the memory of older subjects enormously supplements the number of cases in the earlier age groups, so that a quite elaborate breakdown emerges as less unrealistic than at first appears.

As was mentioned earlier, the authors reached the conclusion that 300 cases were necessary in each ultimate cell to ensure sampling reliability. The method of arriving at this figure entailed a rather curious and extremely empirical train of argument. The investigators took their actual results and then drew different sampling fractions from them, thus determining which sampling fractions produced results within 5 per cent of the total set of data. Their conclusions were in terms of the percentage of samples providing this level of accuracy. Oddly enough, according to their figures, this percentage increases as the size of sample is raised until the figure of 400 is reached and then in many instances, for some inexplicable reason, starts decreasing again. In almost every instance their samples of 1,500 cases are statistically less sound than those of 1,000. The authors comment that this seems to be contrary to statistical theory, but they do not pursue the anomaly any further. One feels that if a statistician had been on the job, he would have shown some interest in this result and would have wanted to probe deeper to find out what had been happening. He would probably have concluded that there were not enough examples of samples of 1,000 and 1,500 cases and that the apparent result was due to second-stage sampling error. But he would almost certainly also have recommended that the normal theoretically based tests of sampling error should have been used.

Curiously, this reluctance to rely on normal sampling theory had been anticipated in England some seven years earlier. The distinguished British social investigator B. Seebohm Rowntree published his first survey of the city of York, *Poverty: A Study of Town Life,* in 1901. For this he and his assistants had obtained particulars regarding nearly 50,000 inhabitants, or almost exactly two-thirds of the entire population.[30] Later British social surveys made use of the economies offered by sampling techniques; Professor Bowley was the pioneer of sampling methods in the social sciences, and his guidance was widely followed. But when, in 1935, Rowntree decided to conduct a second social survey of York, he was not yet prepared to trust to a sample. He therefore again organized a house-to-house investigation covering practically every working-class family in York.

Aware, however, that by 1941, when his report *Poverty and Progress: A Second Social Survey of York* appeared, he would be open to criticism on the grounds that he had not made use of sampling techniques, Rowntree included a supplementary chapter on "An Examination of the Reliability of Social Statistics Based on the Sampling Method." In this he simulated a sample survey by arranging his schedules in street order and then taking every tenth one, "just as I should have done if calling at every tenth house."[31] He repeated the results for samples of one in 20, one in thirty, one in forty, and one in 50. For each item analyzed he took only one sample. He then tabulated the results of this operation, marking the sample results that deviated between 10 and 15 per cent, between 15 and 20 per cent, and more than 20 per cent from the complete survey results. He reached the unexceptionable conclusion that sampling is suitable for large populations but unreliable for small populations, but obviously his method of demonstration was technically weak and contributed nothing to statistical theory or application.

The authors comment on the fact that the frequency distributions of the material reported were often irregular. They take this irregularity as typical of living structures and biological phenomena, in which normal distributions and even smooth curves are rare.

They conclude that it does not follow that the material is inferior; one might easily collect a very small sample which would appear to be homogeneous and therefore big enough, but this could be due to chance and might be falsified by taking additional cases. This is statistically a rather doubtful statement because any statistical statement of homogeneity inevitably takes account of the size of the sample.

SAMPLING

One aspect that has been much commented upon is the method of sampling. As the authors saw it, the sampling in their investigation was dominated by the need to accumulate more or less equal samples in each of the ultimate cells, and they aimed accordingly to stratify their sample by the characteristics sought. This was obviously a sound policy if they wished to secure adequate numbers for internal analysis of each cell, but great care must be taken, and was in fact taken by Kinsey and his colleagues, to reconstruct a stratified sample when it was desired to provide censuslike data relating to the population as a whole.

This difficulty is particularly acute when the selection of cases is imperfectly randomized, as unfortunately it was in the case of the Kinsey investigation. The authors appear to consider randomization impossible in the human sciences.

Unfortunately human subjects cannot be regimented as easily as cards in a deck, and the investigator of human behavior faces sampling problems which are not sufficiently allowed for by pencil and paper statisticians. . . . Neither is it feasible to stand on a street corner, tap each tenth individual on the shoulder, and command him to contribute a full and frankly honest sex history. Theoretically less satisfactory but more practical means of sampling human material must be accepted as the best that can be done.[32]

The practical means proposed and used is to safeguard representativeness by

. . . diversifying each collection which enters into the sample. . . . The cases that are used to represent each ultimate cell in a human population should be drawn from a number of groups, widely distributed geographically, and including as great a diversity as is possible within the limits of the group.[33] *

The other precaution by which the authors laid great store was their endeavor to secure 100 per cent samples of the social units approached,

One hundred per cent of the members of a family group, all the persons living in a particular apartment house, all the members of a college sorority or fraternity, all the persons in some service club, all the members of some Sunday School class or some other church organization, all the persons in a city block, all the persons in a rural township, all the inmates of some penal or other institution, all the persons in some other unit, provided that unit has not been brought together by a common sexual interest.[34]

It is not entirely clear why they believed that this sampling design was such a good substitute for randomization. Evidently the groups designated as social units varied greatly in their social integration, from the family at one end to the "persons in a city block" at the other. In practice, the 100 per cent groups included even such examples as "hitch-hikers (over a three-year period)," who could hardly be regarded as a tight-knit social unit. But even if they had all been highly integrated groups, it is difficult to see the virtue of this fact, except for the advantage that it may have been easier to enlist subjects through organizations with which the investigators already had contacts. But in fact, as Cochran, Mosteller, and Tukey have forcibly pointed out,[35] this feature in their sampling design is statistically very inefficient; it represents a type of two-stage sample in which full coverage for the second stage is attempted, so that the effective size of the sample is not the total number of informants but the number of "clusters" or first-stage units.

Actually, only about 26 per cent of the first 12,000 subjects were members of 100 per cent groups. Three-quarters of all subjects were members of partial samples or individuals. The authors were much more concerned about the representativeness of these partial samples. Experience had shown, for example, that the first volunteers from a group were exceptionally active and aggressive but responsive to a call for co-operation and less inhibited sexually. The last persons to contribute were sometimes relatively prudish, re-

* This proposal is closely related to the policy behind quota sampling.

strained, apathetic, and sexually inactive. Hence the use of partial samples would exaggerate the incidence of sexual activity.

On the other hand, the authors recognize that the 100 per cent groups were not entirely representative, giving excessive weight to college groups. They knew also of specific imbalances in the 100 per cent samples, such as the inclusion of too many freshmen and too many Jews. They concede that those who came forward last in the 100 per cent groups may have suppressed more information, being relatively unwilling to speak about their experiences.

What they do not discuss is the fairly obvious possibility that, just as the most extroverted individuals were the first to volunteer, so also the 100 per cent groups might well be more extroverted as groups than the population as a whole. It is undoubtedly a particularly acute problem to obtain a proper sample in a subject such as sexual behavior, but reliance on volunteers would seem to raise problems that cannot be neutralized by any conceivable means. Whether they come forward as individuals or as members of 100 per cent groups, the critic will be left with a lurking suspicion that the subjects are in various ways untypical.

This makes it all the more important to draw in the maximum number of reluctant volunteers. The investigators developed various procedures with this purpose in view. The first was to emphasize in the course of all general appeals for histories that they desired to obtain every kind of history, however blank or however full it might be. They found the restrained histories the more difficult to get; because the subjects felt that they had too little of interest to contribute, it was constantly necessary to assure them of the importance of their contribution.

The investigators used intermediaries to whom, at lower social levels, they made payments for the successful introduction of subjects. They explained to these contact persons "that the forty-minute history of an inexperienced teen-ager is as important as the two- or three-hour history of an older person who has been involved in every conceivable sort of sexual activity."[36]

Another device used to improve coverage was to work with groups over a protracted period. They found that after all the active individuals had volunteered, there might be a trickle of contributors over two or three years, the later volunteers becoming convinced by the reaction of the community that no harm would be done to their reputations if they co-operated.

Rather than approach new groups they would concentrate on securing an appreciable proportion of members of groups already approached. They gained the impression that the responses of from half to three-quarters of a group would not be so different from those of a 100 per cent sample.

The question of nonresponses is, of course, constantly encountered in social investigation, and it is important to be able to estimate the characteristics and probable replies of those who refuse to co-operate. As Glass has shown, this can be attempted by comparing the data from early and late volunteers.[37]

The securing of a numerically adequate sample was simplified by the Kinsey team's decision to use quota sampling; curiously, they appear to be unaware of the methodological disadvantages of this procedure. They merely state:

If one is satisfied to accept material in the order in which it appears, one sooner or later finds the particular cases which are necessary for the completion of a study. . . . At the present writing there are only two cells from which we have enough histories, and it is now a matter of avoiding cases that belong to those particular groups. In the course of time one has to go further out of his way to secure histories from certain other groups, and that will increase the cost; but the cost can always be kept relatively low if one bides his time and takes the material that is most available.[38]

As far as the statistical analysis is concerned, it may be said that the procedures are conscientiously carried out and adequately described. There is a noticeable freedom from obscured approximations or estimates, and checking is exemplary in its thoroughness. In relation to the richness of the data collected, the analysis is deliberately kept simple, "in consideration of the approximate nature of the original data."[39] But the processing itself—which, it will be recalled, was carried out by Kinsey and his colleagues themselves— was bound to be quite elaborate. Each of the histories, 12,000 in number even by 1948, was punched onto thirteen standard punch cards.

Apart from the mathematical checks incorporated into the processing of the data, there was an impressive series of substantive checks on the validity of the data. Retakes of whole histories were made on 162 subjects (108 males, 54 females), not less than eighteen months, and on average of three years, after the first history was taken. On the whole, there is a very satisfactory correspondence between the two sets of data,[40] with a slight tendency on the part of subjects to reveal more sexual activities on the second interview. Statements on sexual activities and ages at first knowledge and at first experience of sexual matters are as consistent as statements on age of parents or on own age and age of spouse at marriage. The authors were dissatisfied with the size of this sample of retakes in 1948 and proposed to extend it, and by the time of the preparation of the *Human Female* the number had risen to 319 retakes (195 males, 124 females). The extended series confirmed a high level of consistency between original interviews and retakes, with the incidence data showing more stability than the frequency data.

Another device reported in the *Human Male* was the checking of data contributed by spouses. The authors found that on questions such as

coital frequencies and details concerning the foreplay, positions, and other techniques employed in the marital coitus . . . the record shows an amazing agreement between the statements of the husbands and of the wives in each marriage, although allowance must be made for the possibility that there may have been collusion between some of the partners, and a conscious or unconscious agreement to distort the fact.[41]

Other cross-checks include analysis of the internal consistency of the histories. Under rapid-fire questioning covering three hundred or more items inconsistencies are easily detected.

It is naturally difficult to elicit admissions of criminal sexual activities, such as homosexuality. This is particularly the case in prisons, where homosexuality is widespread but is also often severely punished when detected. The collection of such data is therefore a considerable test of the ability of an interviewer, yet between 35 and 85 per cent of the inmates of every institution visited admitted to homosexual activities.

The authors record an experience at one prison. A male who was well acquainted with the institution agreed to look over the list of 350 men that had contributed histories and to indicate which of them were, to his knowledge, currently having homosexual relations. He did not know most of the men listed, but he picked out 32 with whom he claimed to have had relations or to have actually seen in such relations. Comparison showed that of these 32 men, 27 (85 per cent) had admitted their experience to the interviewers. Two others had left the institution, but the other three, when confronted with the new evidence, readily admitted its truth. In this instance the original histories may have understated by 15 per cent the incidence of homosexuality among the 32 men in question.

Comparisons were also made between data based on subjects' memories and data based on physical findings. For example, comparison of the two sources on the age at onset of growth of pubic hair shows good correspondence.

An interesting analysis was made of the results shown by the three main interviewers—Kinsey, Pomeroy, and Martin—based on histories taken during a sample of four years' research. This analysis showed that the three interviewers had obtained very similar results, particularly on incidence data, even on such a taboo item as homosexuality and even though some selection had been involved in assigning subjects to interviewers. As has been mentioned, the more difficult cases (older persons, persons with more promiscuous histories, and persons with socially unusual items in their histories), when they could be foreseen, were entrusted to Dr. Kinsey, especially during the early years.

The interviewers also looked into the *reliability* of the subjects' memories of events that in many cases dated from a very remote phase of their lives. They record on this point certain not very surprising impressions that they gained in the course of their interviewing: most recent events are in general best remembered; young children's memories are short; older persons tend to remember remote rather than recent events; memory is not directly related to intelligence or formal education; subjects may pretend to forget recent events that they still wish to conceal; some past events are minimized and some are played up, and not always the same emphasis is given on retakes.

Nobody could complain that these investigators paid insufficient attention to *validation*. One of the most striking features of their work is the fact that so much of it was directly and personally undertaken by the three men, with the result that at all points the formal analysis is reinforced by their personal experiences and knowledge. We are therefore in a receptive mood for their general conclusions concerning the validity of data obtained through personal interviewing in a case-history study. They summarize their conclusions in the following nine points:

1. The accuracy varies considerably with different individuals, due to variations in simple forgetting, deliberate or unconscious suppression, or deliberate coverup. There is no firm evidence to make possible a comparison between different methods of interviewing—from psychoanalytically derived techniques at one end to the "rapid-fire questioning" at the other. Kinsey and his colleagues would welcome joint studies on this point.

2. Validity varies with particular items and for different segments of the population, but is extremely high. Points that show low correlations are themselves revealing because they throw light on the etiology of errors and falsifications.

3. It is very difficult to identify inaccurate informants.

4. Accuracy of averages calculated for groups is definitely higher than accuracy of individual histories, as might be foreseen.

5. Incidence data are more accurate than frequency data, and are accurate to within 5 per cent on most items and to within 10 per cent on all items. There is a strong tendency to understate both incidences and frequencies.

6. The subjects' personal socio-economic data are the second most accurate. On average they are almost precise statements of fact, but they are not so dependable on individual histories.

7. Frequency data are not very reliable; on individual histories they may be removed by as much as 50 per cent from the reality, but on group data the error is unlikely to be more than ± 10 per cent.

8. The least accurate data are those concerned with an individual's first knowledge of an event. This is attributed in part to the difficulty in pinpointing a particular date as the moment at which one is conscious of knowing something. On individual histories an error of ± 2.5 years is possible, but on group data it is unlikely to be more than ± 5 per cent.

9. These calculations of validity are based on college samples, the only sufficiently large groups available for this purpose. Preliminary studies suggest that at lower social levels the variations may be greater.

In the *Human Female* the question of reliability and validity of data is again examined, with similar results. One point made is that, contrary to a common belief, the female subjects were no more prone to falsification than the males.

APPRAISAL

Few works have received more critical attention than the Kinsey reports. An admirable compilation of the comments made was edited by Himelhoch and Fava, and published in 1955. Most observers would probably agree that on the question of validation the reports have stood up well to criticism. One must conclude that the weakest link in the technical chain mail is the method of sampling, which would admit some overrepresentation of unconventional behavers, but probably few would still assert that the figures of total incidence are wildly incorrect. This conclusion is confirmed by the most authoritative of the many critiques of the Kinsey methodology, the monograph prepared at the instance of the Commission of Statistical Standards of the American Statistical Association by Cochran, Mosteller, and Tukey.[42] It should be noted that this report relates only to *Sexual Behavior in the Human Male*.

The authors of this monograph compare the first Kinsey report with eight other studies on sex and conclude that in their methodological and statistical aspects the Kinsey techniques are outstandingly superior. The principal merits of the Kinsey report lie in its systematic coverage, in the number of items included in the study, in the composition of the sample, in the number and variety of methodological checks, and in the statistical analysis. On the other hand, the authors are criticized for making some statements in the text that are not substantiated by data and for making other statements that are overprecise in view of the inadequacy of the data. Cochran *et al.* discuss the possibility of bias in the sample that cannot be determined because of the sampling method. They are doubtful about the level of accuracy because of the difficulties of recall, which would not be circumvented even by the Kinsey checks. They feel that the quality of the statistical treatment could have been improved if the availability of statisticians had not been restricted by wartime conditions, and they feel that, while a volunteer sample may have been inevitable in the early stages of the inquiry, a probability-sampling program should have been adopted at the earliest possible stage.[43]

The Kinsey assertion that probability sampling was impracticable was also questioned by other critics. Harvey J. Locke was able to cite his own experiences while undertaking a study that led to his report *Predicting Adjustment in Marriage*. Locke states[44] that, starting from courthouse records of divorced persons, he was able to obtain interviews with over 85 per cent of the more than 600 divorced persons contacted, while of over 400 married persons contacted only 5 per cent refused to participate. Furthermore, Locke argues that the group-sampling method, apart from other statistical weaknesses, is objectionable because of the likelihood of collusion between members of the groups selected.

Locke was writing after the second volume had appeared, and he pointed out that the authors had become much more cautious in claims that their sample was representative. In fact they called attention to the overrepresentation in the female sample of college students, of urban dwellers, and of single women, pointing out that this lack of balance, aggravated by the exclusion of nonwhites and of prisoners, was bound to disturb the results.

In another paper Maslow and Sakoda point out some of the experimentally determined characteristics of volunteer informants.[45] Maslow had found in an earlier study that female volunteer informants were predominantly high in self-esteem and correspondingly high in both conventional and unconventional sexual activities. In co-operation with Dr. Kinsey and his colleagues Maslow was able to repeat the self-esteem test on students from his psychology classes, some of whom had been interviewed by Kinsey or Pomeroy and some of whom had refused. It was found again that volunteers were relatively high in self-esteem. Only Dr. Kinsey had the data to determine whether these high-self-esteem volunteers again manifested abnormally active sex behavior, and, at the time of writing, the necessary analysis had not been forthcoming.

This hint of abnormal activity by certain members of the sample is supported by a secondary analysis undertaken by Landis, which shows from Kinsey's own figures that a large proportion of the premarital sexual experience reported was accounted for by a minority of the nonvirgin single women in the sample who had a very high rate of experience with a number of partners.[46]

The method of interviewing has already been quite fully discussed. One further important point was made most forcefully by Clausen, who reminds us that, although the authors are aware of the relative secretiveness of women about sexual experience, they "do not seem to have seriously considered the possibility that the use of female interviewers might have yielded a less biased sample of volunteers."[47]

In view of the militantly zoological antecedents of the Kinsey team it is natural that they should have received some counterattack from human scientists of various sorts. It will be remembered that the *Human Male* took up an explicitly behaviorist frame of reference, and accepted the minimum of theoretical entanglements, so that the end product is primarily a set of statistics of sexual performance and only fragmentarily a study of how sexual behavior relates to other forms of social behavior, still less to social attitudes. This point is made by many critics. Kuhn points out, for example, that the psychological stance of the authors is essentially that of learning theory, with its heavy reliance of physiological explanations for human (and hence for social) behavior.[48] The strict learning theory and behaviorist frame of reference was somewhat relaxed in the *Human Female*, which displays a greater interest in stated attitudes to various items of sexual behavior, such as premarital coitus, which are regulated by strong social sanctions. On the other hand, Kinsey is criticized by Gorer for failing to account in the analysis for those characteristics of informants which might well be expected to have a strong influence on their sexual behavior—for example, the effect on extramarital relations of whether or not a woman has living children.[49]

Complaints are also made that Kinsey and his colleagues wrongly claim to be able to estimate correctly the personal or social adjustment of an individual. Eisenbud writes:

It would have been much better if the incidence and frequency data on sexual behavior had been presented without any attempt to smuggle in implicit or explicit linkages to factors in adjustment. But again and again Kinsey makes passing remarks about these matters in a way to suggest that he was somehow able to evaluate such factors. He will refer to the "skilled and scholarly lawyer," who had one of the highest frequencies observed, with the implicit assumption that the fact of this designation rendered the individual in question a paragon of adjustment; or he will state explicitly that a good deal of psychiatric treatment has been wasted on individuals with low frequencies, as if a low frequency were the only complaint for which a person sought treatment and were not most often linked to other difficulties.[50]

Certain psychoanalysts have commented that Kinsey and his colleagues conducted their interviewing at altogether too literal a level, as though sexual behavior were a subject that American informants could discuss with as little affect as they would devote to their choice of breakfast cereal. Kubie, while praising the human wisdom and technical adroitness of the interviewing program, found its deficiencies also illuminating: failure to consider transference effects, failure to recognize latent as well as overt meanings, absence of concern with signs of emotion displayed by the informant during the interview, indifference to the possible therapeutic or noxious consequences of the interview.[51]

The criticisms on procedural grounds are matched by a widespread feeling of disappointment at the inadequacy of the authors' theoretical framework. Their permissive standpoint, whatever its practical consequences, was judged to have led them inevitably to a theory of normality which discriminates on no grounds other than frequency of occurrence. According to Kinsey, the normality of a particular type of sex activity was to be gauged solely by its commonness. The evident advantage of this definition of normality is that it bypasses any exercise of moralistic judgment. The disadvantage, as Kubie[52] and others have pointed out, is that it takes no account of the fact that the normality of an act can be judged in individual cases only by reference to the nature of the purposes served by the act. In the case of some individuals the practice of sexual perversions may enable them to filter off the neurotic element in their personalities so that they may lead in other respects socially useful and effective lives. Other individuals may reveal the extent of their neuroses by an exaggerated and obsessive concentration on inherently normal acts, such as hard work or hand washing.

The normal individual grows out of the polymorphous perversions of the child, and it is a sign of maturity when he puts these behind him. But if he continues intermittent perverted practices, the extent of neurosis may be revealed less by the acts themselves than by the compulsive nature of his behavior and by the guilt and anxiety generated.

Kinsey's failure to take into account the total setting of the individual's behavior also leads to an exaggerated belief that frequency of sexual activity is synonymous with psychological adjustment. Here again it is always possible that the sexual athlete is responding not to the vigor of health but to the overdrives of neurosis.

Critics cite various instances in which Kinsey reveals his innocence of any basic theory of sexuality. Since Freud we have become accustomed to recognize the sexual etiology in many activities, from stealing to painting, that, on the face of it, have nothing to do with sex. The subtle and complex mechanisms delineated by the psychoanalysts are roughly cast aside by the Kinsey team, who substitute the suggestion that, as Gorer puts it,

. . . by Dr. Kinsey's implied standards, sex becomes a quite meaningless activity, save as a device for physical relaxation—something like a good sneeze, but involving the lower rather than the higher portions of the body. If "tensions" build up, one takes either a pinch of snuff or a mistress: it doesn't much matter which, and both are equally efficacious.[53]

Kinsey was perfectly aware of the protean manifestations of sex, and yet his adoption of the orgasm as the unit of tension release led him to play down the significance of all sublimations and diversions of the primary sexual drive.

Finally, we may consider for a moment the historical significance of the Kinsey program. In spite of all criticism there is no doubt that the impact of the reports has been tremendous. The traditional gap between sanctioned and actual behavior with reference to sex has been sustained largely through suppression of the truth. Transgression of the sexual code has always carried a high emotional charge. In the days of traditional morality, shame and guilt were the lot of transgressors; in the looser sands of today, millions of persons of both sexes, young and old, have suffered the pangs of anxiety because they have felt that they were somehow failing to live up to the standards of their society. And here, in a report of scientific integrity, avoiding euphemisms or moralization, was the evidence that sexuality takes many forms and that many practices formerly only whispered were regularly indulged in by apparently good citizens.

The permissive connotations of the presentation were not lost on the millions who read the reports or the condensed versions carried in the popular press. The evidence, such as it is, does not suggest that these readers were much influenced in their behavior by what they had read, but it is certain that the reports have played an important part in the reduction of sexual anxiety and the dissemination of tolerance and understanding. Of all the works described in this book, perhaps none has had a more direct public impact, or has more demonstrated the immediate value of the study of man in society, than the *Human Male* and the *Human Female*.

THE HUMAN ROOTS OF FASCISM

The subject of this chapter, *The Authoritarian Personality*,[1] is a rather difficult book to discuss because of the tremendous amount of attention that has already been given to it. But it is undoubtedly one of the key modern works in the empirical social sciences, and many valuable lessons can be derived from examining it closely.

The history of the study is reasonably straightforward. Toward the end of World War II the American Jewish Committee decided to set up a Department of Scientific Research, feeling that there were various aspects of anti-Semitism that should be investigated. The first director of this department was Max Horkheimer. This fact is very relevant because Horkheimer had been director of the Institut für Sozialforschung in Frankfurt, Germany. This institute had been suppressed by Hitler, and Horkheimer and most of his colleagues, including Erich Fromm and T. W. Adorno, found their way to the United States via Paris, and the Institute of Social Research was eventually reconstituted in New York. It was the Institute of Social Research to which this program was entrusted, so that Horkheimer was involved in a dual capacity, both as head of the Department of Scientific Research of the Jewish Committee and also as director of the Institute of Social Research. It was because of his special position that he was able to initiate the study which led to the preparation of *The Authoritarian Personality*, and it is clear that throughout the work he retained a very direct and practical interest in its progress.

Administratively the study was a joint venture of the Institute of Social Research and the Berkeley Public Opinion Study of the University of California. For this reason there were two directors of the study—Dr. T. W. Adorno, who came in from the Institute of Social Research, and Dr. Nevitt Sanford, of the Department of Psychology of the University of California at Berkeley. These two men had as senior collaborators Dr. Else Frenkel-Brunswik and Dr. Daniel Levinson. It seems that, although the four had rather different backgrounds, the collaboration was smooth and very complete.

The idea for the study arose from a conference held by the American Jewish Committee in May, 1944, at which a group of American scholars from various disciplines were invited to discuss the question of religious and racial prejudice. This conference suggested that the subject of prejudice should be studied at two levels —at what might be called the administrative level, concerned with public reaction to current events, and at the basic level, concerned with the features in the individual personality and in the social situation that tended to foster prejudices.

This program produced a number of books, but none had as great an impact as *The Authoritarian Personality*, although several of them were also concerned with the connection between personality traits and susceptibility to prejudice.

One of the criticisms sometimes leveled at *The Authoritarian Personality* is that it concerned itself exclusively with questions of personality and neglected the social and cultural background. In his Foreword, Dr. Horkheimer sets out to forestall this criticism by explaining that the program of his Department of Scientific Research was intended to maintain a balance between sociological studies and psychological studies. He states that this particular book was one of the studies intended to be concerned solely with the psychology of the individual, and that the program would subsequently move on to the area of group pressures and the sociological determinants of roles in given social situations.

AUTHORITARIANISM

This is the position from which the investigators set out on their inquiry. At least in the telling, their purpose was exceptionally explicit:

The research to be reported in this volume was guided by the following major hypothesis: that the political, economic and social convictions of an individual often form a broad and coherent pattern, as if bound together by a "mentality" or "spirit," and that this pattern is an expression of deep-lying trends in his personality. The major concern was with the *potentially fascistic* individual, one whose structure is such as to render him particularly susceptible to anti-democratic propaganda.[2]

This hypothesis raises a question that has much troubled the critics of *The Authoritarian Personality:* they ask whether the personality syndrome finally identified as authoritarianism was in the minds of the investigators when they began to work?

It will be remembered that in the case of *Management and the Worker* there appeared to be grounds for suspicion that the authors were more sophisticated theoretically when they started than they admitted. A similar impression is conveyed by the present book. We note that the idea of the authoritarian personality is not introduced until quite near the end of the book: it is first discussed seriously in Chapter XIX, in which Adorno is comparing various different personality types and syndromes, one of which is the authoritarian syndrome. This formulation is resumed later in the Conclusions (Chapter XXIII), where it is suggested that the authoritarian syndrome slowly emerged as a result of empirical observation and statistical analysis.[3]

Some critics have accepted this statement at its face value and have repeated the assertion that the authors simply stumbled on authoritarianism as time went on. But this is confusing because, in fact, the very words "the authoritarian character" had been used and a detailed description of its features had been given long before by Erich Fromm in *Escape from Freedom*, written when Fromm was working at the Institute of Social Research in Frankfurt. Indeed, the first formulation of authoritarianism as a concept appeared even earlier, in a book called *Autorität und Familie*, published by the Institute of Social Research in 1936, when the institute was in Paris. In *Escape from Freedom* two chapters are devoted to this subject; Chapter V, "Mechanisms of Escape," contains a section on authoritarianism and deals with the whole background to the authoritarian character and its etiology. I do not doubt that Fromm's concept must have been very much in the minds of the researchers from the beginning, even though they delayed the systematic exe-

gesis of authoritarianism until the concluding chapters of the book.
Thus, while Brewster Smith may have been justified in his comment: "In no single place in the volume . . . is there to be found a concise statement of the hypotheses underlying the entire undertaking or of the integrated conclusions of the project as a whole,"[4] this fact does not warrant Richard Christie's curious assertion that "there are occasional references to 'authoritarian' and 'authoritarianism' in the text of The Authoritarian Personality but these appear to be used in a descriptive sense and not as implying that all authoritarianism is fascism—explicitly or implicitly."[5]

While, therefore, a minor mystery remains, it does not center so much on why the authors had no central hypothesis as on why they delayed for so many chapters of their book an explicit reference to the hypothesis of the authoritarian syndrome. It may also justifiably be asked why the hypothesis is at no point stated in a formal way. But when that has been said, it must also be stated that there is a fairly consistent development of the theme of authoritarianism throughout the book. The method is perhaps somewhat impressionistic, but there is considerable discussion regarding the characteristics of the high and of the low scorers on their "prejudice" scales, and these build up into a clearly recognizable and thoroughly consistent picture of the authoritarian character. For this reason the suggestion that the concept of the authoritarian personality gradually emerged from the statistical analysis is an almost incredible one.

In commenting on the character of those whose personality is dominated by sadistic and masochistic traits, Erich Fromm wrote in 1941 in Escape from Freedom:

Although the character of persons in whom sado-masochistic drives are dominant can be characterized as sado-masochistic, such persons are not necessarily neurotic. It depends to a large extent on the particular tasks people have to fulfil in their social situation and what patterns of feelings and behavior are present in their culture, whether or not a particular kind of character structure is "neurotic" or "normal." As a matter of fact, for great parts of the lower middle class in Germany and other European countries, the sado-masochistic character is typical, and . . . it is this kind of character structure to which Nazi ideology had its strongest appeal. Since the term "sado-masochistic" is associated with ideas of perversion and neurosis, I prefer to speak of the sado-masochistic character, especially when not the neurotic but the normal person is meant, as the *"authoritarian character."* This terminology is justifiable because the sado-masochistic person is always characterized by his attitude towards authority. He admires authority and tends to submit to it, but at the same time he wants to be an authority himself and have others submit to him. There is an additional reason for choosing this term. The Fascist system calls itself authoritarian because of the dominant rôle of authority in its social and political structure. By the term "authoritarian character," we imply that it represents the personality structure which is the human basis of Fascism.[6]

In the light of this quotation it is not surprising that in the F scale, which, as we shall see, is a major instrument in the technique of the *Authoritarian Personality* investigators, the letter F stands for Fascism, "to signify its concern with implicit prefascist tendencies."[7] But the profession that the authors embarked on the F scale without being aware of the connection between authoritarianism and prefascist tendencies is hardly tenable.

METHOD

Another important point is that, according to Marie Jahoda, the idea of using a questionnaire to detect authoritarian traits had already occurred to Horkheimer in 1936. In *Autorität und Familie*[8] there appeared a questionnaire containing more than seventy questions closely related in content to the questions in the PEC and F scales developed for *The Authoritarian Personality*. It would therefore appear sensible to think of *The Authoritarian Personality* as a logical extension of a program that had been launched in Frankfurt some ten years before. The main change was that in America for the first time the sophisticated psychoanalytic thinking, which derived from Central Europe, had been interwoven with the empirical skill of American social psychology. And this enmeshing of the two traditions is the tremendous contribution of *The Authoritarian Personality* as a piece of research. For the first time the rich data from depth interviews—which were very close to being full psychoanalytic interviews—were to a considerable extent integrated with test items in scales, with projective tests, and with other subsidiary empirical material. This integration of depth and superficial material was not easy. As the authors state,

. . . a particular methodological challenge was imposed by the conception of *levels* in the person; this made it necessary to devise techniques for surveying opinions, attitudes, and values that were on the surface, for revealing ideological trends that were more or less inhibited and reached the surface only in indirect manifestations, and for bringing to light personality forces that lay in the subject's unconscious.[9]

It was this simultaneous attack on the personality at several different levels which, even if not wholly successful, was the enormously ambitious characteristic of this work.

The authors' pre-eminently sensible line of approach demonstrates that the investigators knew from the start that their task was explanatory rather than descriptive. Instead of studying a whole population for possible antidemocratic tendencies, they started with the idea of using a simple method of identifying antidemocratic characters and of exposing these subjects to detailed comparison with subjects that showed exceptionally few antidemocratic tendencies. This plan was to be carried out by devising a questionnaire that would be simple and economical to administer and that could be used to select suitable subjects for depth interviewing. The results of the subsequent depth interviews could in turn be fed back to refine and improve the questionnaires. This reciprocal design is another feature that differentiates *The Authoritarian Personality* from most other studies. The investigators did not begin by preparing a list of sensible questions to which they would adhere throughout the inquiry. In practice they were constantly refining and changing their questionnaires.[10] And even after *The Authoritarian Personality* was completed, the process of refinement was continued.

The authors make for the merits of this two-way process an additional claim that is not so easy to substantiate. They state that

. . . the interview was used in part as a check upon the *validity* of the questionnaire . . . a basis for judging whether people who obtained the highest antidemocratic scores on the questionnaire were usually those who, in a confidential relationship with another person, expressed antidemocratic sentiments with the most intensity.[11]

As Hyman and Sheatsley point out,[12] the interviewers were instructed to acquaint themselves with each subject's questionnaire responses before interviewing him, for the express purpose of enabling the interviewer to structure the interview situation, with the result that the test for validation was not independent of the original data. The interviewer was exposed to the danger of prejudging the intensity of antidemocratic sentiments.* The authors might therefore have been wiser to confine themselves to the perfectly legitimate use of the depth interview and the projective tests for the purpose of devising scales which, though seemingly containing very few references to anti-Semitic or other prejudiced sentiments, could reveal deep-seated antidemocratic sentiments that people were not entirely aware they were expressing.

Each questionnaire from the beginning contained two types of question. First came factual questions, mainly concerned with past and present group membership, church preference and attendance, political party, vocation, income, and so on. The assumption was made that the answers to these broadly factual questions could be taken at their face value.

The second, and more important, group consisted of the celebrated "Opinion-Attitude" scales, used "to obtain quantitative estimates of certain surface ideological trends";[13] these were the "Anti-Semitism" (A-S) scale, the "Ethnocentric" (E) scale, the "Politico-economic Conservatism" (PEC) scale, and finally the "Fascism" (F) scale.† The scales were designed and analyzed according to the Likert method.

Since this is the first occasion in the present book that an example of Likert scaling has occurred, it may be appropriate at this point to discuss the main features of this method of scaling. It will be remembered that in *The American Soldier* the questions asked were not designed to elicit direct expressions of intensity of sentiment. This avoidance of direct expression of intensity was deliberate, being based on the difficulty found by subjects in making complex judgments. The *American Soldier* method is to make inferences about intensity of sentiment from the consistency of answers to component questions.

---

* It should be noted, however, that the questionnaire protocols were pruned of references to ethnic prejudice and political ideology before being handed to the interviewers. (See page 410.)

† At a later stage in preparing the F scale they introduced projective questions, and also developed the use of thematic Apperception Tests.[14]

The Likert scale was devised in 1932 as a successor to the Thurstone method, which, it will be remembered, was also the starting point for Lazarsfeld's *Latent Structure Analysis*.[15] The Likert method was aimed at eliminating the difficulty and the potential unreliability associated with the use of intermediary judges in the scale construction.

The items in Likert scales are similar in character to those used by Thurstone. They include statements believed to range from extremely favorable to the issue in question through moderately favorable and moderately unfavorable to extremely unfavorable. No items believed to be neutral (for example, that there is much to be said for and against) are included.

One feature of the Thurstone scale is the use of judges to place the items in a supposed order of favorableness. In the Likert scale the subjects themselves place the items in order of favorableness by recording how strongly they agree or disagree with the sentiment expressed in each item. The set of subjects' responses to each item is subsequently examined by a process called "item analysis" in order to determine how well that particular item contributes consistently to the scale. By elimination this analysis leads to a gradual reduction in the number of items used until the investigator is left with a relatively small and manageable set of items.

THE ANTI-SEMITISM SCALE

The procedure can be illustrated by taking one subscale of the "Anti-Semitism" (A-S) scale, the first scale constructed by the *Authoritarian Personality* investigators. The whole scale of fifty-two items was built up from five subscales. The "Threatening" subscale contributed ten of these items. Typical examples are:

I-2. The Jews must be considered a bad influence on Christian culture and civilization.

I-5. One trouble with Jewish businessmen is that they stick together and connive, so that a Gentile doesn't have a fair chance in competition.

I-11. There are too many Jews in the various federal agencies and bureaus in Washington, and they have too much control over our national policies.

II-2. War shows up the fact that the Jews are not patriotic or willing to make sacrifices for their country.

II-8. The Jew's first loyalty is to Jewry rather than to his country.

II-11. Jews seem to have an aversion to plain hard work; they tend to be a parasitic element in society by finding easy, nonproductive jobs.

(The items are numbered in two series, indicated by I and II, because the whole scale was administered in two twenty-six-item parts separated by an interval of one week.)

These and the other items were selected from the writings and "parlor discussions" of American and European anti-Semites, and from the literature of those trying to dispel anti-Semitism by means of rational argument. The only assumption underlying their choice is that they relate to the subject of Jews and that they are all negative (i.e., unfavorable to Jews). Nothing is initially known as to which items are more unfavorable to Jews than others. It will be seen, however, that inconsistent attitudes are allowed for; for example, a subject could agree that "Jews keep too much to themselves" (II-23) and also that "they have too much control over our national policies" (I-11).

For each of the items each subject was asked to express his extent of agreement from + 3, strongly agree, to − 3, strongly disagree. These were converted to a six-point scale, i.e., + 7, + 6, + 5, + 3, + 2, + 1. (Neutral + 4 was not allowed.) Each subject's *total score* on the fifty-two items of the whole A-S scale would then lie somewhere between 364 (i.e., 7 × 52) and 52 (i.e., 1 × 52), and his mean score per item would lie between 7 and 1.

Each subscale was then tested for its reliability and related statistical properties. In an initial test on 144 women students attending a class in introductory psychology at the University of California at Berkeley the statistical qualities seemed quite satisfactory. (Men could not be used, since there were insufficient men students because of the war.) Split-half reliability, using the Spearman-Brown correction, was 0.89 on the ten items of the "Threatening" subscale, and at the same time the mean scores per item ranged well, lying between 1.0 and 5.7.

The next operation in the Likert procedure is the application of *item analysis*. This simple operation was adopted as a timesaving alternative to the more tedious computing of correlations between item scores and scale scores, after Murphy and Likert[16] had shown that the two measures gave essentially similar results.

The procedure is as follows. The subjects are divided according to their total scores, so that "high scorers" and "low scorers" (those in the upper and lower quartiles, respectively) are distinguished. For each item the mean of the high scorers and the mean of the low scorers are calculated. The difference between these mean values for each item is known as its "discriminatory power" (D.P.), and this value is used as a criterion of the success of the item in measuring the sentiment being studied.

Table II presents the results of this operation applied to the six items from the "Threatening" subscale previously given. Each item is identified by a key phrase.

TABLE II

MEANS AND DISCRIMINATORY POWERS OF ITEMS FROM ANTI-SEMITISM SCALE. UNIVERSITY OF CALIFORNIA WOMEN

		Mean			Mean for
		High	Low		Total
No.	Item	Quartile	Quartile	D.P.	Group
I-2.	"Bad influence"	2.75	1.11	1.64	1.85
I-5.	"Businessmen"	5.86	1.38	4.48	3.45
I-11.	"Washington"	4.55	1.24	3.31	2.56
II-2.	"Unpatriotic"	2.97	1.05	1.92	1.75
II-8.	"First loyalty"	5.05	1.81	3.24	3.10
II-11.	"Parasitic"	4.36	1.27	3.09	2.19

It will be appreciated that an item mean for the total group (last column) of around 4.0 indicates a fairly even division of opinion on the issue raised in that item. Item I-5 comes closest to this criterion, but several items, including II-2 and I-2, have rather seriously low means; this feature indicates a strong tendency of the group as a whole to disagree with the item. Satisfactory items should have means near to 4.0, and it is recommended[17] that when the mean is above 5.0 or below 3.0 the items should be reworded in more generally acceptable terms so as to achieve a better balance between the number of subjects that agree and the number that disagree.

Within this middle range of means it is considered that a D.P. of over 4.0 is very superior, indicating an almost total lack of overlap between high and low scorers. A D.P. of 3.0 to 4.0 is also very satisfactory. Even with a D.P. as low as 1.0 the difference between the low mean and the high mean is often statistically significant.

Of the six items quoted, two have D.P.'s of less than 2.0. Not unnaturally, these are the two with the lowest group means, indicating that few even of the high scorers (that is, prejudiced subjects) agreed with the sentiments expressed, generally because they were couched in insufficiently pseudodemocratic terms.

Apart from the "Threatening" subscale, there were three other main subscales. The first was the "Offensive" subscale; it contained statements attributing unpleasant traits to Jews (as a racial entity). Examples are: "A major fault of the Jews is their conceit, overbearing pride and their idea that they are a chosen race" and "Jews should be more concerned with their personal appearance and not be so dirty and smelly and unkempt."

The third subscale, "Attitudes," included certain attitudes regarded as negative or hostile to Jews as a group, and suggesting actions which would implement these attitudes. Examples are: "In order to maintain a nice residential neighborhood it is best to prevent Jews from living in it" and "It would hurt the business of a large concern if it had too many Jewish employees."

As has been mentioned, allowance was made for quite contradictory attitudes held by the same person, such as that Jews are too prone to keep to themselves and simultaneously that they try too hard to break into Gentile society. These attitudes were covered in two subscales, "Seclusive" and "Intrusive." An example of the first is the statement: "One general fault of Jews is their overaggressiveness, a strong tendency always to display their Jewish looks, manners and breeding." An item from the "Intrusive" subscale is: "The trouble with letting Jews into a nice neighborhood is that they gradually give it a typical Jewish atmosphere."

These instances give an idea of the way in which the items were broken down into subscales, but it will be found that the breakdown was fairly informal, so much so that the same item sometimes occurred in at least two subscales. Also, for a reason which is not entirely clear, four items that did not belong to any of the four subscales were inserted in the total A-S scale. These are described as

"Neutral" items, but they are not less critical than the other sub-scale items. Perhaps they were afterthoughts.

Analysis showed not only that the separate subscales performed very adequately but also that intercorrelations between subscales were high and that the intercorrelation between each separate sub-scale and the total A-S scale was very high indeed, ranging from 0.92 to 0.94. The authors were naturally delighted with the perform-ance of their fifty-two items, which seemed to offer a very useful measure of anti-Semitism in many of its manifestations. They were encouraged to conclude that the higher an individual's score the more likely he would be to engage in anti-Semitic attitudes and programs.

This did not mean, however, that the scale had reached its ulti-mate form. The fault already disclosed in the "Threatening" sub-scale items which had too low a mean for the total group and too low a D.P. was found to be true also of some items included in the other subscales. It seemed to be generally true that the items were phrased in an overly critical form, so that few even of the high scorers (prejudiced subjects) could agree with their sentiments. It became clear that items required some "pseudodemocratic coloring" in order to discriminate well between the nonfanatic prejudiced and the unprejudiced. It was also found that the more successful items invited a tendency to stereotype (e.g., I-13, "Jews are all alike," or stressed the idea of Jews as an *economic threat* (e.g., I-22, one of the "Neutral" items, "Jews . . . always try for the best jobs and the most money"), or as a *moral threat* (e.g., II-7, "Jews . . . gradually give . . . a nice neighborhood . . . a typical Jewish atmosphere"). Certain items indicating restrictive attitudes (e.g., I-18, "It is best that Jews should have their own fraternities and sororities") were also found to discriminate well.

On the strength of these initial results a second and much shorter version of the A-S scale was devised. From the original fifty-two items a short list of ten items was selected, on the grounds both that each had a good D.P. and also that each was compatible with the theory as to the nature of anti-Semitism that the authors were begin-ning to formulate. From the "Threatening" subscale two items sur-vived, namely, I-5, "businessmen," and I-11, "Washington." It was found that this shortened battery was as efficient for discriminating between high and low scorers as the full battery had been.

These ten items were subsequently combined with items similarly selected from the other initial scales (designed to identify Ethnocentric, Politico-economic Conservative, and Antidemocratic ideologies) to make up a new consolidated scale of seventy-eight items. This questionnaire, identified as "Form 78," was administered in the second phase of the inquiry, starting in spring, 1945. The performance of the ten A-S items in this second stage was excellent. Split-half reliabilities of 0.89–0.94 were obtained, and the average D.P. was as high as 3.68, eight of the ten items having D.P.'s between 3.5 and 4.3.

As a subsidiary exercise the short *A-S scale* was also tried on a group of students at George Washington University. In this case the results show an interesting variation. One item in the scale asserts that "there are too many Jews in Washington agencies." In the Washington sample the D.P. on this item was significantly higher than elsewhere. This contradicted the hypothesis that living in Washington would provide a reality basis on which to respond and thus minimize the differences between those with and those without anti-Semitic prejudices. In fact, living on the spot merely intensified the saliency of the "Jewish Problem" to those prejudiced individuals in the sample. As the authors comment, "Living in Washington appears to have mainly a polarizing rather than a homogenizing effect."[18]

This provides one further illustration of the general principle that factual campaigns designed to conquer racial prejudice are unsuccessful. The anti-Semite is so receptive to negative and hostile imagery and so resistant to factual correction that the attempt to substitute facts while leaving the prejudiced ideology undisturbed is bound to failure.

So far, then, the empirical results seemed to support the authors' theory that anti-Semitic ideology is an all-inclusive standpoint that is held by a recognizable group of individuals whose prejudices reach far beyond the issue of racial minorities. Other traits appeared to be associated with anti-Semitic prejudice: the tendency to think in stereotypes, rigid adherence to middle-class values, belief in one's own group as morally pure in contrast to the immoral outgroup, opposition to and exaggeration of prying and sensuality, extreme concern with dominance and power (that is, fear of Jewish power and desire for Gentile power), fear of moral contamination, fear of being overwhelmed and victimized, and desire to erect social barriers against infiltration by outsiders. All these characteristics seemed fairly consistently to be possessed by anti-Semitic individuals.

After thus showing that many of the traits of the anti-Semite were not specifically related to the "Jewish problem," the authors naturally turned next to examine the question of anti-Semitism in the wider context of prejudice broadly conceived. Could it be shown that the same trends were present in other ideological areas, or that they were present also in nonideological thinking, relating to people and life generally, so that some individuals would consistently display general signs of prejudice, while other individuals would consistently display themselves as unprejudiced?

This question was the central issue of their next study, which was concerned with Ethnocentric ideology. The instrument developed was the "E scale," which was one of their most successful scales. The procedure was similar to that described for the A-S scale.

THE E SCALE AND THE PEC SCALE

The E scale was compounded of three subscales that dealt respectively with Negroes, with minorities generally, and with patriotism. It is noticeable that, although several anti-Negro items are couched in more aggressive terms than the anti-Semitic items had been (e.g., No. 5, "The Negroes would solve many of their social problems by not being so irresponsible, lazy and ignorant"; No. 22, "The people who raise all the talk about putting Negroes on the same level as whites and giving them the same privileges are mostly radical agitators trying to stir up conflicts"), the mean level of agreement with such sentiments was slightly higher than for the generally milder A-S items.

In the case of the "Minority" items, the aim was to select items that had nothing to do with racial minorities. In the original thirty-four-item E scale there was an item relating to women (No. 9, "Although women are necessary now in the armed forces and in industry, they should be returned to their proper place in the home as soon as the war ends") that reminds one of Myrdal's comment that the status of Negroes as a depressed minority was most closely paralleled by the minority status of women. In its first form this attracted a large measure of agreement (mean = 4.76), but its revised form ("Women, if they work at all, should take the most feminine positions, such as nursing, secretarial work, or child care") was for some reason much less acceptable. On the other hand, another item condemning "zoot-suiters" (a cultural minority of that period) performed consistently well and moved up to the highest ranking D.P. in the revised scale.

The revised scale referred to consisted of fourteen E-scale items which were incorporated in Form 78. As a later development the separate ideas of anti-Semitism and ethnocentrism were merged, and the twelve E-scale items selected for inclusion in Form 60 contained four A-S items, three Negro items, and five items dealing with other minorities (Japanese, "zoot-suiters," and "Okies" in California).

In due course the authors were led to the following statement:

Ethnocentrism is based on a pervasive and rigid ingroup-outgroup distinction; it involves stereotyped negative imagery and hostile attitudes regarding outgroups, stereotyped positive imagery and submissive attitudes regarding ingroups, and a hierarchical, authoritarian view of group interaction in which ingroups are rightly dominant, outgroups subordinate.[19]

(Note the use of the word "authoritarian.")

They next proceeded to study the Politico-Economic ideology by the development of the "PEC scale." Although their procedure proved somewhat less satisfactory, it permitted them still further to widen their horizon, so that they concluded that "ethnocentrism itself is but one aspect of a broader pattern of social thinking and group functioning."[20] This reinforced their belief that they might find an even more central ("subideological") psychological disposition from which all the observed ideologies would be found to stem.

THE F SCALE

It was from this point that they set out to construct the "F scale," the scale of the Fascist personality. In truth, this was the goal toward which they had been aiming from the start, and now at last they were ready to measure the implicit and underlying antidemocratic trends of the prejudiced personality. The F scale would be designed as a substitute for the Anti-Semitic scale and the Ethno-centric scale (not the PEC scale because it did not correlate well enough), and would be so phrased that those being tested would be unaware that their prejudices were being disclosed.

How did the team go about it? They had a number of sources from which to select suitable items, including the results of the three initial scales (A-S, E, and PEC); a number of specially prepared essays pertaining to such topics as religion, war, ideal society, and so forth; early results from Projective Questions; and, finally, the results from the depth interviews and the Thematic Apperception Tests. But these did not exhaust their sources, for they could also call on previous studies on which the authors had been engaged. Sanford and his colleagues at the University of California at Berkeley had made during the war a series of studies of war morale and ideology; on the other side there were the studies of anti-Semitism that had been conducted by the Institute of Social Research. In addition they could take advantage of the general literature on anti-Semitism and fascism.

On the basis of these sources, they set out to depart from the specific question of anti-Semitism and ethnocentrism and to find certain questions that relate to the following nine characteristics, which, according to their hypotheses, indicated the prejudiced authoritarian individual:

1. *Conventionalism: Rigid adherence to conventional, middle-class values.* The new F scale included six items that related to this feature. Typical items were: "*What* a man does is not so important so long as he does it well"; "Although leisure is a fine thing, it is good hard work that makes life interesting and worthwhile"; and "One should avoid doing things in public which appear wrong to others, even though one knows that these things are really all right."

2. *Authoritarian submission: Submissive, uncritical attitude toward idealized moral authorities of the ingroup.* This is the projection to society at large of one's submission to one's father. There were eight such items. Examples were: "He is indeed contemptible who does not feel an undying love, gratitude, and respect for his parents"; and "Obedience and respect for authority are the most important virtues children should learn."

3. *Authoritarian aggression:* (the other side of authoritarianism): *Tendency to be on the lookout for, condemn, reject, and punish*

people who violate conventional values. Two of the five such items included were: "No insult to our honor should ever go unpunished" and "It is only natural and right that women be restricted in certain ways in which men have more freedom."

4. *Anti-intraception: Opposition to the subjective, the imaginative, the tender-minded.* "Intraception" and "extraception" were two of Henry Murray's concepts. *Intraception* stands for pleasure in the emotional, sensual world, and *anti-intraception* thus stands for the rejection of such sensual pleasures, a concentration on practicality rather than an aesthetics. The schedule included six items relating to anti-intraception. Of these, two were: "There is too much emphasis in colleges on intellectual and theoretical topics, not enough emphasis on practical matters and on the homely virtues of living" and "There are some things too intimate or personal to talk about even with one's closest friends."

5. *Superstition and stereotypy: The belief in mystical determinants of the individual's fate, the disposition to think in rigid categories.* There were five items on this, of which one was: "It is more than a remarkable coincidence that Japan had an earthquake on Pearl Harbor Day, December 7, 1944."

6. *Preoccupation with power and "toughness": Concern with the dominance-submission, strong-weak, leader-follower dimension; identification with power figures; overemphasis upon the conventionalized attributes of the ego; exaggerated assertion of strength and toughness.* There were five items on this theme. Two were: "There are some activities so flagrantly un-American that, when responsible officials won't take the proper steps, the wide-awake citizen should take the law into his own hands" and "What this country needs is fewer laws and agencies, and more courageous, tireless, devoted leaders whom the people can put their faith in."

7. *Destructiveness and cynicism: Generalized hostility, vilification of the human.* There were eleven items for this trend: "Familiarity breeds contempt"; "No matter how they act on the surface, men are interested in women for only one reason"; "Human nature being what it is, there will always be war and conflict."

8. *Projectivity: The disposition to believe that wild and dangerous things go on in the world, the projection outward of unconscious emotional impulses.* There were five sinister items on this point: "The sexual orgies of the old Greeks and Romans are nursery school stuff

compared with some of the goings-on in this country today, even in circles where people might least expect it"; "To a greater extent than most people realize, our lives are governed by plots hatched in secret by politicians."

9. *Sex: Exaggerated concern with sexual "goings-on."* Two of the four items used were: "Homosexuality is a particularly rotten form of delinquency and ought to be severely punished"; "Sex crimes, such as rape and attacks on children, deserve more than mere imprisonment; such criminals ought to be publicly whipped."

It is not explained how the investigators decided on the number of items to include under each heading; presumably the numbers reflect the theoretical importance they attached to each type of prejudiced response.

It must be made clear that, taken on their own, at least some of the items which performed satisfactorily did not lack an element of objective truth. The authors recognize that a subject's response to a particular item might conceivably be determined by a recognition of its objective element. On the other hand, the fascinating part of this test is that these questions discriminate between individuals, so that a person who agrees with one such item is likely to agree also with the other items, thus revealing his prejudiced character. The meaning of an individual's responses is inferred not from his answers to individual items but from the total pattern of his response.

As in earlier scales, some items tend to recur. Of the items used, seventeen are used twice. Thus, although the number of items included under the above nine subscales totals fifty-five, there are actually only thirty-eight independent items in the scale.

It must be emphasized that the choice was determined by the attempt to develop indirect indicators of prejudice. For example, an item suggesting that "astrology can explain a lot of things" was felt to be superior to the one suggesting that we should put our faith in "courageous, tireless, devoted leaders," on the grounds that the second item is too direct in its fascist implications. Furthermore, they had to aim at the proper balance in each item between an obviously irrational statement and a pseudodemocratic one which had a glimmer of objective truth in it; this was needed in order to obtain the proper discrimination between prejudiced and unprejudiced subjects.

This F scale of thirty-eight items was included with the shortened A-S, E, and PEC scales in Form 78, of which mention has already been made, and was first administered to four groups of subjects in the spring of 1945. The formal tests showed that the avoidance of direct clues to the subjects had been bought at the cost of a much inferior performance under item analysis. The over-all split-half reliability, at 0.74, was well below that required for a truly accurate instrument. The Discriminatory Power was at least as disappointing. Of the whole set of nine subscales, only three had average D.P.'s higher than 2.0, namely, those relating to authoritarian submission, authoritarian aggression, and sex.

Of the individual items, only sixteen out of thirty-eight achieved the very low D.P. value of 2.0, and four had D.P.'s less than 1.0. The means, at 3.71, were fairly satisfactory.

Some successful items did, however, emerge. The most satisfactory item, in terms of both theory and performance, was the one suggesting that "those guilty of sex crimes should be publicly whipped." Also useful was the item stipulating obedience and respect for authority as the most important lesson in child training. A third item which performed well accepted the inevitability of war and conflict, a fourth advocated unquestioning dependence on some supernatural force, and a fifth called for undying love, gratitude, and respect for parents.

The failure of some of the other items to achieve sufficient discrimination was naturally a matter of concern. Some failures were attributed to poor formulation, some to the incorporation of too large an element of rational justification, while others erred in the opposite direction by being too crude or openly aggressive. It was not, however, felt that the underlying theory was in any way prejudiced by these failures. The development procedure thenceforward was by progressive elimination to sieve out the most discriminating items.

The resulting form became much shorter. The E-scale and PEC-scale items were most freely sacrificed, but in the last stages the F-scale items were reduced from the original number, thirty-eight (in Form 78), to thirty (in Forms 40 and 45). The natural consequence was to improve the internal consistency of the scale and correlation with the E scale. Although there was some sacrifice of breadth of coverage, the test was undoubtedly improved as a measure of prejudice.

It is an interesting fact that the D.P.'s were somewhat higher for women than for men; that is, the items discriminated better between high- and low-scoring women than between high- and low-scoring men. There is some discussion as to why this difference should exist, and the conclusion is reached that it is because of the higher general level of education of the women in the sample, which did not include groups comparable with the "San Quentin Inmates" or the "Working-Class Men."

The authors subsequently undertook a very elaborate inter-item correlation analysis using some fresh material from a psychology class at Berkeley. This showed that the E scale had a degree of unidimensionality comparable with that of an acceptable intelligence test (e.g., the 1937 Stanford-Binet Revision); the result of the same analysis applied to the F scale was considerably less satisfactory. Statistically the F scale could not be shown to be unidimensional. In spite of this the authors felt confident in claiming: "We are justified in speaking of an F pattern or syndrome, for the items do 'hang together' in the sense that each is significantly correlated with the scale as a whole."[21]

It is clearly necessary to distinguish two components in this claim. The construction of the F scale is almost diametrically opposed to the process of scalogram analysis. Few would assert that in terms of mathematical manipulation the handling of the *Authoritarian Personality* is comparable in rigor with the scalogram procedures. One must consider the extent to which the Likert scale is measuring what it sets out to measure and the extent to which it is capable of confirming or rejecting the belief that a single "dimension" (to use the *American Soldier* nomenclature) is involved. The internal consistency is to some extent safeguarded by the method of analysis, which arranges that all the individual items are examined in relation to preselected batches of high and low scorers, so that the items that fail to discriminate satisfactorily between high and low scorers are successfully eliminated; it must be assumed that the sentiment finally being canvassed is, by operational definition, the projection of the items which survive this procedure.

It has also been claimed that close examination by the Likert method can reveal the presence of more than one dimension. For example, Newcomb states:

Careful item analysis sometimes reveals that there are two or three "clusters" of items in a scale. The items in such a cluster are very closely related to one another (that is, people who respond favorably to one item are quite apt to respond favorably to each of the others) but they are less closely related to items in different clusters. The over-all consistency may nevertheless be great enough to result in satisfactory reliability. This is just what happened in one study of international attitudes.[22] Item analysis showed that the original scale, designed to measure attitudes of internationalism, was actually composed of two sub-scales.[23]

It was presumably for this reason that each scale in the *Authoritarian Personality* was originally composed of three or four sub-scales, and that part of the analysis undertaken by the investigators was a study of the intercorrelations between the subscales and the correlations of the subscales with the total scale.

It would, however, be generally agreed that the Likert method does not approach the Guttman scale in its capacity to identify the presence of more than one dimension in the scale. The great strength of the Guttman method of scalogram analysis is that by the use of the coefficient of reproducibility the material itself reveals how closely it relates to a single dimension. By contrast, in *The Authoritarian Personality* it is largely a matter of guesswork, and at best a matter of trial and error, how far each scale is limited to one universe; from time to time the authors rather hopefully state that, while they cannot be sure that they are studying one universe, they have at least taken care to include items that will cover as much as possible of the problem.

The degree to which items within a scale will "hang together" statistically, and thus give evidence that a single, unified trait is being measured, depends primarily upon the surface similarity of the items—the degree to which they all say the same thing. The present items, obviously, could not be expected to cohere in this fashion; all that could be required statistically of them was that they correlate to a reasonable degree with the total scale. . . . Concern with highly specific, statistically "pure" factors was put aside, in favor of an attempt to gain a dependable estimate of an over-all system, one which could then be related to other over-all systems in an approach to the totality of major trends within the individual.[24]

This apologia is not altogether convincing. *The American Soldier* showed that it is possible to measure a single, unified trait without relying on questions that all say the same thing. If the "over-all system" is the theoretically intelligible concept of authoritarianism, surely it is necessary to test in some way whether the questions and answers do relate to this trait. Rather disturbingly, one can imagine another study, hundreds of pages in length, devoted to a discussion of something called "morale" without an opportunity being provided to discard the unidimensional concept of morale. Contrast this with *The American Soldier;* although the latter operates at a lower theoretical level, empirically it does show quite elegantly that, at least with the set of questions used, there does not appear to be a single dimension of morale and that what is commonly thought of as morale can be treated analytically only after subdivision into components (faith in the leadership, pride in one's outfit, satisfaction with one's job, and so on).

Furthermore, it must be remembered that the Likert method, like that of Thurstone and that of latent-structure analysis, involves making inferences about *latent classes* into which the manifest data can be made to fit with greater or less success. As has already been shown (in the chapter on *The American Soldier*), this inference is not involved in the Guttman approach, which manipulates the empirical data directly for the determination of an attitude, which is given a name only for reasons of convenience.

It is clear, however, that in the case of *The Authoritarian Personality* the essentially theoretical approach of the authors made it inevitable that the manifest data be interpreted at a more profound level. Throughout the study the subjects' superficial responses were of interest to the investigators not for their own sake but for the light they could throw on fundamental differences in personality traits. For this reason questions were preferred which concealed the primary purpose of the inquiry. Believing that people are incompletely frank about their attitudes to such issues as anti-Semitism, particularly when questioned by strangers, the investigators deliberately searched for items that enabled them to discern an underlying central trend in the personalities of certain prejudiced individuals.

Thus it was that they announced themselves as conducting a "survey of opinions about various issues of the day" and tended more and more to incorporate items with no manifest relationship to racial prejudice. This explains why they gradually evolved items such as "Nowadays with so many different kinds of people moving around so much and mixing together so freely, one has to be especially careful to protect himself against infection and disease" and "Homosexuality is an especially rotten form of delinquency and ought to be severely punished." Methodologically, the inclusion of such items is of primary importance, as it illustrates one of the great advantages of the Likert method over that of Thurstone. Marie Jahoda comments,

In the Likert scale, items can be included which need not be related in an overt and logical manner to the attitude to be tested. What is finally included in a Likert scale is determined by an item's correlation with the entire scale score. In contrast, the judges in the Thurstone technique are restricted, of course, to a rational judgment about an item's relation to others; underlying psychological relationships of items are by that method excluded. The entire approach in *The Authoritarian Personality* is served much better by the greater psychological flexibility of the Likert technique. The concomitant disadvantage is this method's lack of "objectivity."[25]

Throughout the program almost all items were deliberately phrased so that agreement to an item implied some prejudice in the subject's attitude. This exclusive use of "negative" items was justified empirically; experience showed that they were more efficient at discriminating between the people who accepted such attitudes and the people who rejected them. There had been one unsuccessful attempt to introduce a positive E item in which agreement would signify lack of ethnocentrism. This read: "All forms of racial and religious discrimination should be made illegal and punishable." This had a group mean of very near 4.0, but an inadequate D.P. of only 1.51, which suggested that subjects, whatever their level of ethnocentrism, were unwilling to take a stand for the forcible control of discriminatory practices.

Another advantage claimed was that negative items could be phrased to express subtle hostility; that is, although they were anti-Semitic, they could be qualified and presented to sound fairly acceptable and familiar. The investigators found that many subjects who would agree with *pseudodemocratic* statements—"Jews have their rights, but . . ."—would reject openly hostile or violently prejudiced statements.

Even though the use of negative items is unobjectionable if such items are used solely to discriminate between prejudiced and un-prejudiced individuals, critics have pointed out that the authors are not justified in concluding on the strength of this evidence, as they in fact conclude, that the prejudiced person is the more stereotyped and rigid in his thinking. If a subject gives even slight support to a prejudiced statement such as "All Jews are self-seeking," he appears to be agreeing with a highly stereotyped racist assertion. He may want to say, "Most Jews are self-seeking," or "Middle-class Jews are self-seeking and working-class Jews are not," or to make some other statement, but this possibility is ruled out by the alternatives presented to him. The prejudiced person is thus placed in a dilemma. Either he has to give a negative answer, which frees him from appearing stereotyped in his answers and conceals some of his prejudice, or he gives the only positive answer available to him, which is then interpreted to mean that he is stereotyped in his response to that issue.

For these and other reasons, in spite of certain disadvantages, it would seem preferable to use a mixture of "negative" and "positive" items.

Another technical question is that of the sample. The initial sample consisted of college students. This familiar choice was made for the usual practical reasons: the students "were available for the asking, whether singly or in groups, they would cooperate willingly, and they could be reached for retesting without much difficulty."[26]

At various times many generalizations about the world have been based on the study of small groups of students, generally psychology students, who naturally constitute rather sophisticated and otherwise atypical subjects. In the present instance the investigators do not fall fully into this temptation. While it is true that college students were the first "guinea pigs," they were used solely in the first instance to evolve methods of operation and questioning. Unfortunately, however, the complete list of groups from whom the questionnaires were collected is not very reassuring, for college students predominate, just as in the Kinsey studies. It has not escaped the notice of critics that the great majority of the subjects were college-connected in some way, the main supplies coming from the University of California and the University of Oregon and a smaller group from George Washington University. The sample was thus skewed toward the West Coast, toward the young, and toward the middle classes. The only working-class groups that were included were not representative, being either members of militant unions or students at the California Labor School, a strongly left-wing institution. They were also very small in quantity, numbering only 114 of the total sample of 2,000. The remainder, apart from 110 inmates of San Quentin State Prison and a batch of 106 Employment Service Veterans, were in one way or another associated with colleges, with social or service clubs, or with the kind of bodies that "joiners" tend to join. As has been pointed out by Hyman and Sheatsley, a quite serious bias is introduced; a number of other inquiries have shown that those of higher levels of education and those accustomed to join societies are likely to have opinions that vary from those of the 90 per cent of adult citizens who do not belong to clubs or societies.[27]

Another source of bias relates particularly to the prevalence of volunteer subjects. It will be remembered that the Kinsey team encountered the problem of unrepresentative volunteers in a particularly acute form because of their attempts to obtain 100 per cent samples from a limited number of groups. The *Authoritarian Personality* investigators were also faced with the problem of self-selection. They found that liberal and radical organizations were more favorable to the idea of the survey than those with conservative inclinations. The results of this initial bias could be quite serious.

The primary purpose of *The Authoritarian Personality* is explanatory. For the most part the authors conduct themselves at a level of abstraction higher than the descriptive, indicating that the possession of certain characteristics is associated with the possession of certain other characteristics. Those who are rigid in their thinking or those who have had a loveless childhood, for instance, may be expected to feel prejudice toward racial minorities. Hyman and Sheatsley cite a few examples from the book on which the authors indulged in unsupported explanatory generalizations,[28] but most critics might feel that these examples are exceptional lapses rather than typical of the presentation. This feature of the book perhaps stems from the exceptionally comprehensive theoretical thinking of the authors.

It has to be conceded that in *The Authoritarian Personality* the restriction of the universe to college students, prison inmates, and joiners is a response not so much to the purposes of the survey design as to the exigencies of supply of willing subjects. If conformity to national norms is to be the criterion, it is entirely possible that a minority of this sample is more normal than the majority; what may appear to be deviant behavior among a group of college students may be conformist behavior in the population of the United States as a whole.

On the other hand, it may be that the difficulty of elaborating the authoritarian-personality hypothesis would make it more appropriate to regard this volume as a first stage in a longer process, as indeed it has historically proved to be. In this case the survey may be judged as exploratory research, and another statement by Hyman and Sheatsley may be applied:

Particularly in exploratory research, where the primary aim is to develop hypotheses and investigate ideas, the use of rigorous sampling methods is usually unjustified. More limited studies of less representative samples permit a greater concentration of research funds and effort on the questionnaire design, interviewing and analysis.[29]

There remains, however, one legitimate cause for complaint. By their concentration on the nature of the personality *in vacuo* the investigators have paid too little systematic attention to the analysis of the personalities *in vitro*, in the setting of their own membership groups. It is arguable that on any count the sampling and the analysis should be conducted in two stages, so that both conformity and deviance can be gauged in relation to local norms. The failure to do this at all consistently is a reflection of the inadequacy of the authors' sociological perspective, which has already been commented upon.

The actual administration of the questionnaires contained no outstandingly abnormal features. Groups were approached through their leaders. If the leader was liberal in outlook, the purposes and procedures of the study were explained to him fully, and he was left to enlist the support of his group. If the leader was conservative, the approach was less frank, and it was the habit "to present the whole project as a survey of general public opinion, 'like a Gallup poll,' being carried forward by a group of scientists at the University, and to count upon the variety and relative mildness of the scale items to prevent undue alarm."[30]

In the case of university classes and study groups, the class instructor normally organized the completion of the forms. Sometimes a talk by the member of the study staff on "Gauging Public Opinion" was arranged, and the administration of the questionnaire was included in the proceedings. In all cases the groups were given written instructions explaining that the form was neither an intelligence test nor a test of knowledge; hence, there were no right or wrong answers.

It is not surprising that with this careful preparation a 90 per cent response was obtained from those present at such meetings. In contrast, one attempt to use a mailed questionnaire elicited only a 20 per cent response, which was too low a rate to permit results to be used.

The choice of the subjects for intensive clinical study was based on the results from the questionnaires; with a few exceptions those chosen had all been either high scorers or low scorers on the E scale. To preserve anonymity the only identifying fact on the questionnaire form was the birth date; if a subject was wanted for further test, the instructor would at the next class ask those born on specified dates to stay behind, and an appointment would then be made. Those selected for the clinical sessions were paid $3 for the two or three hours taken by the interviews and tests.

SUBSTANTIVE RESULTS

This, then, is an outline of the field methods used, and we may now turn to the substantive results. The book begins at a discursive level, presenting the full interview records of two college men, Mack and Larry, who are used throughout the book as ideal examples of two contrasting ideologies. On each occasion that the authors discuss some particular aspect of their findings, it is their custom first to give a number of quantitative results and then to show how these results fit the cases of Mack and Larry. In doing this, it may be felt, they spent a little too much time in explaining away abnormalities or idiosyncrasies in the responses of Mack and Larry; after all, Mack and Larry are no more than single items from a statistical sample, and one would therefore not expect to find total conformity with their ideal types. It might even have been better to suppress the idiosyncrasies.

Mack was a high scorer (that is, "prejudiced") and Larry was a low scorer ("unprejudiced"). In many respects the two had rather similar backgrounds; their religious affiliation was in each case primarily Methodist with a little Catholic influence. They were both near to the center in politics—supporters of the anti-New Deal Democrats. If anything, the low scorer was somewhat the more conservative; he was officially a Republican, whereas the high scorer was officially a Democrat. It is conceivable that the authors deliberately chose these two cases because the reversal of anticipated party affiliation made it seem more convincing that the analysis was operating at a different dimension from that of the ordinary radical-conservative dichotomy.

These two interview protocols read convincingly; they give a total impression of two well-rounded characters who sound quite like real people. On first reading, without the subsequent theoretical help the authors provide in dissecting the interviews, it may not be immediately clear that Mack is revealing himself as a high scorer and Larry is revealing himself as a low scorer, but this use of case histories provides an easy introduction to the theoretical approach.

Mack, for example, accuses Jews of violating conventional values, of showing ingroup characteristics (clannish and power-seeking), and of being burdens and misfits. He does not recognize that he is inconsistent in labeling them both too powerful and clannish and too weak and helpless, so that they have to be supported by the whole community.

Mack characteristically talks about the problem of anti-Semitism in terms of what is wrong with Jews, whereas Larry, the low scorer, spends much of his time discussing what is wrong with non-Jews and with a society that cannot assimilate all its members.[31]

By these and similar contrasts the main distinctions between the attitudes of Mack and Larry are established. Mack goes in for stereotypes; he likes to think in terms of groups, such as "the Jews," and regards them as homogeneous units. He assumes that society is made up of such groups, which keep coming into conflict with one another, so that there are inherent tensions in Society. He regards the tensions as in no way the responsibility of his own ingroup, and there is no suggestion that his own ingroup might need to modify its behavior and attitudes. By contrast, Larry tends to look at the situation in terms of the failures of his own ingroup; in any case his thinking is more in terms of individuals and less in terms of stereotyped group images.

Again, Mack seems to believe in the "blood strain"; to him, the behavior of the Jews or the Irish or of any other group can be accounted for in terms of their race. He favors *either* of two radical solutions to the problem of Jews in society. One is their total assimilation, and the other is their total segregation. He regards society as built up hierarchically: it is the natural order that some people should have power over you and that you should have power over some other people. Mack regards any minority as an exploitable minority that, because of its weakness, deserves to be despised and ground under. Larry, on the other hand, feels that it is quite possible for people to get along without recourse to any of these extreme solutions: he is not willing to accept a power hierarchy, he wants full "social equality," and he is always rather disgusted at manifestations of power.

In these terms the authors present these two individuals as examples of two different types of people. The reader cannot check whether they are typical. All we know is that Mack's questionnaire score is in the top quartile and Larry's is in the bottom quartile. They could have been carefully selected to prove some point, and the presumed purpose of introducing them is to sketch the beginnings of a hypothesis. But at least they fit in and begin to make sense as two recognizably different types of person.

EXPLORATIONS OF PERSONALITY

The book then turns to a detailed description of the development of the personality scales that have already been discussed. The authors were entirely frank about the position attained up to this point. While concluding that the attempt to construct a scale that would measure prejudice without naming the object of prejudice had been "fairly successful," they also admitted that they had not succeeded in constructing an instrument that would yield an estimate of fascist receptivity at the personality level. "It remains to be shown conclusively," they add, "that the variables with which the F scale has been concerned are, in reality, variables of personality."[32] Hence they stress the importance of the more profound clinical investigations of personality to be reported in subsequent chapters of the book.

There is space in this chapter only to deal summarily with these explorations of personality. They did contain certain extensions of method, but basically, unlike the scales already described, they were derived ready-made from the direct context of personality testing.

Two of the methods used were examples of projective testing. The *Thematic Apperception Test* (TAT) was a likely choice, particularly as Sanford had been associated with the development of the TAT, which had been pioneered by Murray and Morgan in 1934 at the Harvard Psychological Clinic.

The TAT consists of a series of ambiguous pictures, often rather badly reproduced so that one cannot determine exactly what is happening, portraying generally one or two persons apparently in a somewhat emotional situation, as revealed by their stressed expressions. Each of the series of pictures is shown in turn to a subject, who is asked to describe what is happening. It has been found consistently that enormous variations occur in the answers given; undoubtedly the tests are measuring something, and the assumption behind their use in psychological testing is that they are measuring areas of the personality that may otherwise remain submerged.

The method of analysis had already become extremely elaborate. In order to construct a shorthand representation of the subject's fantasies as revealed in their stories of what the pictures show, a content analysis had been devised in terms of two major sets of variables, "need" and "press." The "need" variables correspond with the ways in which the subject acts, or imagines the characters in the pictures to be acting, in relation to the situation. The "press" variables relate to the external forces (personal or physical) supposed by the subject to be working on the characters in the pictures. It is not immediately clear why the words "need" and "press" were used to convey these concepts of activity and environment.

An example of a "need" variable is "aggression," defined as the need "To Fight. To criticize, blame, accuse or ridicule maliciously. To injure or kill. Sadism." If the hero of the subject's story displays aggression, this item is marked up in the "need"-variable table, the number of points scored varying from 1 to 5 according to the intensity of the aggression. "Aggression" is one of the variables that can also appear as a "press" variable, indicating that aggression takes place against the hero. There are other "press" variables, however, that are not contained in the list of "need" variables, and vice versa. Thus, "seclusion" is only a "need" item, and "bad luck" is only a "press" item.

The investigators also undertook a thematic analysis, which was concerned with the actual type of story that was read into the pictures by the different subjects. This was a feature of the technique that the *Authoritarian Personality* investigation developed further than had been done before.

The procedure is perhaps more straightforward than would appear from this highly condensed account. Its application in the present context was to discern differences between the high and the low scorers in terms of their responses, and the existence of such differences was in fact established. It was found, for example, that the low scorers tended to identify more closely with the hero characters in the pictures, to whom they gave the attributes that fitted in with their self-image. The heroes projected by low scorers were relatively more concerned with creative activity, with sensual enjoyment, and with congenial relationships generally. When the interaction between two people in a picture was ambiguous, the low scorers would tend more often to interpret this in terms of some pleasant experience.

Conversely, the high scorers tended to describe behavior of a less constructive nature and to linger on aggressive and compulsive acts; they were more concerned with the status relationships between the figures in the pictures, so that the parent to them was regarded as more domineering in the situation and the children more submissive. Although the distinctions were not always clear-cut, the results echo the same syndromes as those indicated by the earlier work.

In addition to the TAT, the investigators undertook a program of *Projective Questions*. These consisted of a list of eight open-ended statements to which subjects had to write a short reply. Items were: "What great people, living or dead, do you admire most?"; "What do you consider the worst crimes a person could commit?"; "If you knew you had only six months to live and could do just as you pleased during that period, how would you spend your time?" Projective Questions were included in Form 78 and subsequent F scales.

The authors claim that this represents the first systematic quantitative use of Projective Questions as a formal technique. Here again the instigator appears to have been Sanford, who had had experience of their use in the Harvard Growth Study of School Children and later in the assessment program of the O.S.S. with which he was also associated.

The Projective Question is regarded as an economical substitute for the traditional psychoanalytic session, with which it shares the capacity to penetrate to deep-lying layers of the personality in a way that leaves the subject unaware of the full implications of his responses. It differs from the psychoanalytic technique in various other respects than its simplicity of administration: the relation of subject to therapist is casual rather than intense; the materials are relatively structured; (cf. the focused interview, page 296); the purpose is to gather information rather than to treat the patient. Furthermore, the material can be analyzed in terms of variables related to selected F-scale and other scale items; in practice, the Projective Question results contributed by high and low scorers were an important source of ideas for F-scale items.

A very elaborate scoring manual was worked out. For each of the eight Projective Questions the expected responses were preclassified as high, low, or neutral. These naturally followed the theoretical approach adumbrated elsewhere in the book. For example, replies to the question how the subject would spend his last six months, replies implying conventional morality and inhibitions ("Getting my affairs in order"; "I would live with God and prepare myself to meet him") and replies implying incidental, dilute pleasures ("See interesting things, read books"; "Try to be happy") were placed in high categories, while achievement values ("Fight intolerance and social wrongs"; "Make people happy") and open sensuality and active pleasure ("Drinking and carousing around with women"; "Travel, enjoy life, take it easy with friends") are placed in low categories.

On the whole the theoretical predictions as to high and low

scorers were confirmed by replies to the Projective Questions. In view of their remoteness in subject matter from the issue of ethnocentrism, it is quite striking that 78 per cent of the anti-ethnocentric group (that is, low scorers on the E scale) and 86 per cent of the ethnocentric group would be correctly diagnosed on the basis of their replies to Projective Questions.

We now turn to the *clinical interviews*, which were a basic component of the total approach. These provided the subject with his best possible opportunity to express himself freely on whatever seemed important to him. "Thus we may learn what he thinks about himself, about his hopes, fears and goals, about his childhood and his parents, about members of the other sex, and about people in general."[33]

As every social investigator knows, however, the richness of depth-interview material is matched by a very great difficulty when it comes to using the material. Verbatim protocols may make fascinating reading, but they may also leave the onus of interpretation on the reader. For this reason the authors were determined to find some systematic procedure for breaking down their clinical-interview results so that some kind of quantification within groups could be undertaken. The analysis itself again makes use of fairly elaborate interviewing and scoring manuals.

The interviewing technique depended on assembling a team of skilled interviewers. There were nine in all, college graduates and psychologically trained, and more than half had special clinical training with emphasis on psychoanalysis. Four had undergone analysis. The interviewers had freedom to conduct their sessions as they thought fit, provided they covered the relevant issues as listed in the interview schedule.

The schedule included six broad areas: vocation, income, religion, clinical material (family background, childhood, sex, social relationships, school), politics, minorities, and "race." For each of these areas the questions were listed in the form in which the interviewer would have to answer them and not in the form in which the interviewer would put them, but some direct questions are also suggested. Thus, under Clinical Material (Family Figures) one point to be established is the Pattern of Power-Relations between Father and Mother (domination-submission, activity-passivity, etc.). This was formulated in the following Suggested Direct Questions:

How did your parents get along together?
In what ways were your parents most alike?
In what ways are they different from each other?
Who made the decisions usually? (Get specific information, e.g., re finances, recreation, discipline of children, residence, etc.)
Disagreements arise in every family from time to time; what bones of contention did your parents sometimes have?[34]

The results from the interviews were then rated according to a systematic set of classifications which, with subcategories, brought the number of items for each female subject to 90, the total being slightly less for men. These categories, like those in the whole program, were at three levels: predominantly factual material, such as family structure; data dealing with attitudes toward self and others; highly interpretative and technical dimensions assessed by the raters, such as "counter-cathectic rejection" of certain drives or "anti-intraceptiveness."

The rating procedure was carried out on 80 usable interview protocols, the raters also having access to the same subjects' questionnaire protocols, except that all explicit references in the latter to the topic of ethnic prejudice or tolerance and to political ideology had been carefully deleted. The raters knew only that, because of the method of selection of the sample for interviewing, the subjects had been either high scorers or low scorers. Rating for each of the 80–90 categories was done synoptically, taking into account all relevant references available to the rater. Each category was scored high, low, or neutral. All ratings were carried out by one of two trained psychologists, a man and a woman, and correspondence between their judgments was good.

The results of this operation appeared to reinforce the results obtained by other methods. In their attitudes toward parents, for example, the high scorers seemed to express *conventional idealization*, while low scorers made an *objective appraisal*; high scorers exhibited externalized *exploitative-manipulative* attitudes, while low scorers looked to parents for love and succor. In recalling their childhood, high scorers remembered their fathers as distant and success-seeking, their mothers as sacrificing, and both as a moral-model; whereas low scorers recalled the traits of warmth, understanding, and demonstrativeness.

The Authoritarian Personality spells out in great detail the responses that the authors believe are associated with high and low scorers. On every issue generous quotations from the protocols are used for illustration. On the question of childhood discipline, for example, a high scorer is quoted as reporting:

> My father spanked me on rare occasions, did it solemnly and it didn't hurt; and when he did everybody cried. . . . But Mother had a way of punishing me—lock me in a closet or threaten to give me to a neighborhood woman who she said was a witch. . . . I think that's why I was afraid of the dark.[35]

In contrast, a low scorer replied:

> Mother was in charge although they handled us well, I think. We were good, almost too good—and we were punished only rarely. Then it was a little spanking or scolding. There were never problems about going out. We could have had more freedom than we took.[36]

APPRAISAL

In *Studies in the Scope and Method of "The Authoritarian Personality,"* edited by Richard Christie and Marie Jahoda, to which earlier reference has been made, there appears a devastating attack on the methodology here described. The authors of the critique, Hyman and Sheatsley, are concerned to expose the methods used in arriving at the conclusions rather than the conclusions themselves. Of the authors they conclude:

One feels intuitively that they have wisdom in their views and soundness in their conclusions, and it is sad that the acumen which inspired the project, the energy in executing a research task unparalleled in scope, and the intuitive power devoted to the appraisal of the results, were not matched by equal methodological skill.[37]

These critics list eight major objections to the methods used, many of which have already been mentioned in this chapter:

1. The authors freely admit throughout the book that the sample of 2,000 subjects is unrepresentative, being drawn almost entirely from the middle socio-economic class and from younger people and excluding minority groups.[38] This does not prevent them from indulging in massive generalizations: "The imagery described above

seems to characterize the thinking of most anti-Semites."[39] "It would seem that criminals tend in general to be conservative in their politics."[40]

2. In particular, the analysis takes no account of the important variable of formal education, which has in other studies been shown to have a big influence on attitudes of the types with which the authors are concerned. Hyman and Sheatsley cite a sample inquiry which included an "abbreviated F scale" in which the results show that the less-educated consistently give a higher percentage of high-scoring responses than college-educated subjects. They also point out that the "great men" admired by high scorers are those that would be more familiar to nonintellectuals.[41]

3. A false conclusion is drawn from the stereotype responses allegedly characteristic of high scorers, revealed in the tendency to overgeneralize single traits, to base views on the knowledge of a few individuals, and to ignore the variations natural to any group of individuals.[42] The critics point out that such apparently stereotyped answers are a natural consequence of the scales used, which permitted the anti-Semite to indicate his general prejudice and dislike but gave him no way of expressing the refinements of his prejudice.[43]

4. A correlation between the E, F, and PEC scales is alleged without sufficient regard to the content of the scales, whereas comparison shows that the F scale and the PEC scale contain questions that are basically similar in content. For example, the item "Young people sometimes get rebellious ideas, but as they grow up they ought to get over them and settle down" seems to the critics more closely related to authoritarianism than to politico-economic ideology,[44] and they feel that the authors should at least have hinted at the possibility that the relationship was a spurious one owing to the overlapping content of the scales.

5. The alleged relationship between the E scale and the F scale is even more open to criticism. The F scale had two purposes: first, to test the relation of authoritarianism to prejudice and, second, to construct a disguised instrument to measure prejudice without introducing obviously racial items. The authors do not recognize the incompatibility of these two goals. The construction of a hidden test always involves the empirical procedure of adding and deleting items until a functional battery is arrived at, but obviously the items

retained as a result of this procedure are no longer a test of the relationship of the open content to the hidden criterion.

6. The claim made that the questionnaire results are validated by the interview program cannot be substantiated. This would have been true only if the two sets of results had been independently derived, a condition not met in this instance. In fact, the interviewers were frequently reminded to prepare themselves for the interview session by careful study of the questionnaire protocol.[45] It is true that the openly prejudiced responses had been deleted, but interviewers knew that all subjects had already been selected as extreme high scorers or extreme low scorers, so that the interviewers had plenty on which to base their expectations.

Obviously the supposed validation by the case studies of Mack and Larry, which occur four times in the text, has no statistical significance.

7. Apart from the differences due to variations in formal education, already mentioned, there is insufficient recognition that certain sentiments are widely distributed in the American population and that adherence to these sentiments can be traced to group membership rather than to processes in the prejudiced individual. This possibility was dismissed by the authors after the examination of one particular relationship—political-party affiliation—in the following words: "These intra- and intergroup affiliations suggest that group membership is not in itself the major determinant of ideology in the individual."[46] It has been shown, for example, by Lazarsfeld in *The People's Choice*,[47] that a close analysis of an individual's network of memberships can account for much apparent intragroup variability.

8. Hyman and Sheatsley make a fierce attack on the authors' propensity for psychodynamic explanations, which leads them to a qualitative analysis of respondents' ideology that "is almost completely unrestrained by any attachment to scientific method."[48] When the sentiments of certain ethnocentric subjects do not conform to demonstrated truths or to the superior knowledge of the researchers, the judgment is made that these sentiments are irrational, representing some distorted expression of deeper, unconscious tendencies. The critics object to this judgment on the grounds that it ignores the social conditions which define the knowledge available to any individual. They accuse the authors of taking the irrationality out

of the social order and imputing it to the subjects. Prejudice is a social norm, and prejudice against individuals or groups is determined not by contact and experience with the people concerned but by exposure to the *prevalent attitudes* to these people.

It is true that *The Authoritarian Personality* does concentrate, as it was intended to do, on the individual rather than on the group determinants of attitudes, and the analysis would undoubtedly have been more complete if factors such as educational level and group affiliation had been taken into account. At the same time Hyman and Sheatsley seem almost emotionally involved in the denial of psychodynamic factors. The battle between personality and culture has continued too long, and it is now generally recognized that few forms of deviant behavior, from delinquency to racial prejudice, can be accounted for without an understanding of all influences operating on the individual, whether internally or externally generated.

Furthermore, it is as justifiable to work for a typology of personality as it is to aim at a typology of social environment. The authors of *The Authoritarian Personality* are highly sophisticated about such typologies. In a penetrating analysis Adorno begins by showing that he is forewarned of the hazards of any doctrine of types:

Any such doctrine is subject to devastating attacks from both extremes; because it never catches the unique, and because its generalizations are not statistically valid and do not even afford productive heuristic tools. From the viewpoint of general dynamic theory of personality, it is objected that typologies tend towards pigeonholing and transform highly flexible traits into static, quasi-biological characteristics while neglecting, above all, the impact of historical and social factors. Statistically, the insufficiency of twofold typologies is particularly emphasized. As to the heuristic value of typologies, their overlapping, and the necessity of constructing "mixed types" which practically disavow the original constructs, is pointed out. At the hub of all these arguments is aversion against the application of rigid concepts to the supposedly fluid reality of psychological life.[49]

In practice, typologies may not only be scientifically useful (if they work), but may also find correspondence with the real world because social processes which determine the individual personality are themselves standardized.

There is reason to look for psychological types because the world in which we live is typed and "produces" different "types" of persons. Only by identifying stereotypical traits in modern humans, and not by denying their existence, can the pernicious tendency towards all-pervasive classification and subsumption be challenged.[50]

This passage shows Adorno's awareness that although the end product may be regarded in terms of personality, the formative influences are external as well as internal, and personal attitudes tend to be standardized because they themselves are the product of societies that enjoin conformity.

It is stated categorically that the hypothecated types are formulated according to psychoanalytic theory and the personality syndromes must be correspondingly oriented. One element in the theory is that the cluster of characteristics associated with the authoritarian character is essentially unitary, so that traits such as conventionality, authoritarian submissiveness and aggressiveness, projectivity, and manipulativeness regularly go together, whereas various other combinations of traits may be found in the unauthoritarian character.

In a detailed statement the cluster of traits associated with the high scorer are organized under six headings: surface resentment, conventionality, authoritarianism, rebel and psychopath, crank, and manipulative type.

Surface resentment relates to the more or less fully externalized attitudes that generally maintain a rational or pseudorational element. A housewife is fearful of the infiltration of her neighborhood by Jews because this may lower her economic standing, or a shopkeeper feels that his lack of success is caused by Jewish-owned chain stores. Those who feel guilty because of their failures can use the Jews as scapegoats and thus relieve their guilt. Adorno recognizes that the "blind spots" of such people are culturally acquired, "at least partly to be attributed to the narrow, petty bourgeois" limitations of experience and explanation on which they have to draw.

The *conventional* syndrome is displayed by the acceptance of prevailing standards as preferable to discontent and to an excessive deference to the mores of the ingroup. A thirty-year-old welder, "extremely charming in manner," accepts the anti-Semitic prejudices of his own group. He is concerned with his status as a skilled craftsman and regards possible alternatives, such as a while-collar job, in terms of their relative status. Characteristically, he abhors untidiness. Though disapproving of the persecution of Jews, he is in favor of complete exclusion of further Jewish immigrants and would not be sorry if Jews already in the country were to "return to Palestine."[51]

The *authoritarian* syndrome is explained psychoanalytically as sadomasochistic in character, so that the person overappeases his superego and achieves his own social adjustment only by taking pleasure in obedience and subordination. But although he is able to transform most of his frustrated hatred into love for his father and any other figure of authority, he is left with some aggressiveness that seeks an outlet in the outgroup. "The Jew frequently becomes a substitute for the hated father, often assuming, on a fantasy level, the very same qualities against which the subject revolted in the father, such as being practical, cold, domineering, and even a sexual rival."[52]

In Europe these traits are said to be found particularly in the lower middle class, whose circumstances require them to be deferential but at the same time give them some power over others, and whose way of life requires a punitive denial of material gratifications. Ambivalent attitudes are common. What is forbidden may be acceptable if it does not lead to social conflict: "Adultery, as long as never found out, is O.K.—if found out, then it's wrong—since some of the most respected people do it, it must be all right."[53] The superego remains outside the individual as a strong, helpful, but punitive father figure, and the authoritarian character will both depend on and also model himself upon such a figure.

The *rebel* and the *psychopath* are transformations of the Oedipus complex that lead not to identification with parental authority but to rebellion against all authority. They may be linked with strong destructive impulses accompanied by a secret readiness to capitulate to the hated authority. This is suggested as the mechanism exemplified by the storm-troop leader Roehm in Nazi Germany and characterized by nihilistic swashbuckling behavior. The extreme type is the psychopath, whose indulgence in persecution is crudely sadistic, directed discriminately against any helpless victim. This identification of the psychopath with the storm trooper is recognized by Lindner in his portrait of a criminal psychopath, *Rebel without a Cause.*[54]

The *crank* is the individual whose failure to accept the "reality principle" drives him into isolation based on a spurious inner world.

Cranks develop a preoccupation with their own "soul" and a paranoid suspicion of the world outside. To them prejudice is all-important; they are to be found in lunatic sects, often with some panacea of "nature," battling against imagined forces of evil with a magical belief in undigested science, and an easy prey to racialist theory.

The *manipulative* type, potentially the most dangerous, is epitomized by stereotypy: the world is viewed diagrammatically as a field for administrative manipulation. Obviously there is attachment not to persons or things but only to the technical aspects of life. The emphasis is on action, and the content of what is performed is viewed with indifference. Technology is an end in itself, and the good solution is the one that is technically efficient rather than the one that promotes human welfare. Adorno cites as a symbol of this type the cold Himmler, who with his sober intelligence and lack of human affection carried out organizationally efficient measures in the interests of National Socialism. Such a man prefers the gas chamber to the pogrom. In Freudian theory he comes close to the classical "anal" character.

These, then, are the six subsyndromes which are all recognizable types, with characteristics that might permit the prediction that they would betray an attitude of prejudice. It is somewhat harder to accept Adorno's statement that " 'the subsyndromes' . . . are not intended to *isolate* any of these traits. They are all to be understood within the general frame of reference of the high scorer."[55] While it is true that totalitarian Germany had room for both a Roehm and a Himmler, it is not so easy to accept that they, and other dedicated Nazis, shared one personality syndrome.

The same claim is not made that the five syndromes found among low scorers are all parts of an over-all low-scoring type. Otherwise, to some extent they mirror the parts of the high-scorer syndrome. The "Rigid" low scorer is characterized by strong superego tendencies, this time projected onto some collectivity or ethical dictate. The "Protesting" low scorer differs from the Authoritarian high scorer mainly in that the external authority is rejected instead of being accepted. The "Impulsive" low scorer has an under-restrained id and resembles the "Psychopathic" high scorer, but differs through freedom from destructive impulses. The "Easygoing" low scorer also possesses an unrepressed id, but in his case the impulses are

sublimated into compassion, so that the main observable characteristic is indecision. Finally, "the Genuine Liberal may be conceived
in terms of that balance between superego, ego and id which Freud
deemed ideal."[56]

The least that can be said of these low scorers is that they are all
thoroughly "nice guys," even though some of them may fail to pull
their weight in an integrated society. In fact, possibly the least en-
joyable holiday companion among them is the Genuine Liberal:

The subject in whom it is pronounced has a strong sense of personal
autonomy and independence. He cannot stand any outside interference
with his personal convictions and beliefs. . . . One of his conspicuous
features is moral courage, often far beyond his rational evaluation of a
situation. He cannot "keep silent" if something wrong is being done,
even if he seriously endangers himself. . . . He is little repressed, and
even has certain difficulties in keeping himself under "control." . . .[57]

PRACTICAL CONCLUSIONS

In completing this rapid survey of *The Authoritarian Personality*,
a thousand pages long in all, we must glance at the concise chapter
of conclusions. To the authors the most crucial result appears to be
the demonstration of the consistency of outlook on a great range of
topics exhibited by each individual investigated. The basically hierarchical, authoritarian, exploitive parent-child relationship with its
expression in the conventional and repressive personality of the
high scorer is contrasted with the affectionate, basically equalitarian,
and permissive interpersonal relationships and attitudes of the low
scorer. Although a distinction must be made between the conventional and the psychopathic high scorers, it is again claimed that the
prejudiced subjects are more alike as a group than the unprejudiced,
who are mainly linked in character by the absence of a particular
brand of hostility.

Behind the formation of the prejudiced personality the authors
see unequivocally the influence of an unsatisfactory and self-
perpetuating parent-child relationship. They recognize that characteristic family patterns are related to social and economic processes
with which they do not concern themselves, but they say relatively

little about the extent to which certain types of social structure facilitate "hierarchical, authoritarian, exploitive" behavior.

It is made clear that their examination is aimed at dynamic potentials rather than at overt behavior. They define their task as that of predicting the readiness of one individual rather than another to break into violence, but they recognize that their inquiry was intensive rather than representative, so that there is no question, from their results, of being able to appraise quantitatively "the amount of prejudice in our culture."

As to the implications of their results, they suggest that countermeasures designed to combat prejudice should take into account the whole structure of the prejudiced outlook. The major emphasis should, in their opinion, be placed "not upon discrimination against particular minority groups but upon such phenomena as stereotypy, emotional coldness, identification with power, and general destructiveness."[58] Rational arguments are understandably futile; appeals to sympathy are interpreted as weakness; as the prejudiced person is incapable of sympathy, hostility diverted from one group by closer association is very likely to descend onto another less accessible group.

The authors therefore suggest that the best way of neutralizing prejudice is to use the established characteristics of the prejudiced individual—his conventionality and his submissiveness toward authority. Legal restraints against discrimination would be interpreted as signs of strength and consequently respected.

It is recognized that these social measures may restrain the outbreak of prejudiced behavior, but they do not by themselves "cure" prejudiced attitudes. As to the disease itself, the difficulty is that prejudice is implanted in the personality at such an early age, and that the child training needed to correct such tendencies—essentially love and humanity—is particularly alien to ethnocentric parents, whose own moralistically punitive attitudes will inevitably be directed at their children, just as they are against ethnic minorities and against themselves.

Thus, potential fascists cannot be headed off by psychological means alone. What is needed is a combined effort by all social scientists, and all that the authors claim is that psychology should have a voice in the team. It is suggested that perhaps the biggest contribution would be an extension of the methods of group psychotherapy, so that the large majority of potential fascists could be saved. In fact, although the prejudiced may gain greater material rewards from present-day society, the authors believe that the tolerant receive more gratification of basic needs and are therefore basically happier than the prejudiced. Any therapy that deals with the personality limitations of the prejudiced individual can therefore have not merely a rational but also an emotional appeal.

On this fairly optimistic note the volume ends, and we must now briefly consider what has happened since in this area.

SUBSEQUENT DEVELOPMENTS

The importance and impact of the work was reflected in the publication in 1954 of the *Continuities* volume, edited by Richard Christie and Marie Jahoda, which has already been mentioned. Apart from the methodological critique by Hyman and Sheatsley, this book contained interesting papers by Edward A. Shils, Richard Christie, and others.

Shils is concerned to put the liberalistic assumptions of the authors in their proper place. He finds that the prejudiced-tolerant dichotomy is confounded with the traditional right-left dichotomy, with a consequent blindness toward the prejudices associated with left-wing ideologies. Shils believes that authoritarians of the left would have been recorded as low scorers, and he complains that there is not enough discussion of these rigid low scorers.* Furthermore, he doubts whether in the United States the typical nativist-fundamentalist movements had any of the essential characteristics of fascism in spite of the fact that their leaders were authoritarian in character. In fact, not only is the presence of a core of authoritarian personalities insufficient to create an authoritarian society, but even a liberal democratic society has need of some authoritarian personalities in certain social roles.

Christie sets out to provide an overview of the large amount of research that was either reported in or inspired by *The Authoritarian Personality*. Unlike some of the other works discussed here, *The Authoritarian Personality* was, for all its prominence, very much

---

* This follows a well-trodden path from William James, to which Eysenck's use of factor analysis has given some modern precision.

in one main stream of social psychological research. For example, there was a long history of the attempt to scale fascistic attitudes. (It will be recalled that the F scale was so called "to signify its concern with implicit prefascist tendencies."[59]) In 1936 Stagner constructed a scale of fascistic attitudes based on nationalism, racial antagonism, imperialism, militarism, antiradicalism, middle-class consciousness, and a strong-man philosophy of government; all these aspects are found in either the E scale or the F scale. H. V. Dicks, by the use of intensive psychiatric interviews, identified enthusiastic Nazis with "a tenderness taboo, sadism, homosexual trends, projection, anxiety, low identification with the mother and lack of rebellion against the father."[60] After examination of other evidence, Christie, like Shils, asserted that "the F scale does not measure authoritarianism in general but more specifically fascistic ideology."[61]

In general, Christie concluded that, on the basis of available data, "the general point of view regarding the relationship between personality characteristics and ethnic prejudice developed in *The Authoritarian Personality* has been substantiated by subsequent research."[62] In Christie's estimation the personality component captured by the F scale would account for roughly a quarter or a third of the total variance. He was unable to indicate how much of the remaining variance would fall to more refined personality measures and how much would be due to influences other than the personality.

Since the early 1950's various developments have been taking place. Professor Sanford spent most of the decade in charge of a research program at Vassar College in which he was concerned with the ostensibly different problem of personality development during the college years. In practice the method of approach evolved as a natural extension and elaboration of the method used in *The Authoritarian Personality*. Responding to the criticism that the condensed F scale was too short for rigorous mathematical analysis, Sanford and his colleagues built up by an empirical process, but based on their existing theoretical framework, a list of 677 items which subjects could judge as true or false. Of these items, 149 survived a series of validation tests and were adopted as the items of a fresh scale. It is claimed that "the 149 items have about three-fourths of their true variance in common with F."[63] These items cover familiar ground and are concerned with the traits of compulsiveness, punitive morality, authoritarian submission, conventionality, religious fundamentalism, anti-intraception, and so on. It was felt that this new instrument overcame some of the ideological difficulties of the original F scale, and in particular that it could disclose authoritarianism in political leftists.

Meanwhile the F scale had been adopted for use in two important personality tests, the MMPI (Minnesota Multiphasic Personality Inventory) and the Californian Psychological Inventory. Some critics had asserted that the authors of *The Authoritarian Personality* had attempted to brand authoritarianism as a type of psychological disorder. This assertion was not true, and the book "left the question of the relation between psychopathology and authoritarianism or ethnocentrism quite up in the air."[64] The accumulation of personality inventories allowed this deficiency to be remedied, with interesting and surprising results. The issue is discussed in terms of the three alternative methods by which the individual handles aggression. In *The Authoritarian Personality* it had been suggested at different times that all three methods—intropunitiveness, extrapunitiveness, and impunitiveness—could be associated with high authoritarianism. In the more rigorous analysis based on the personality inventories it was found that only intropunitiveness could be associated with high authoritarianism and that in fact impunitiveness is negatively related to authoritarianism.

Meanwhile the periodical examination of the mathematical basis of the F scale continues. Christie and Garcia in 1951[65] and O'Neil and Levinson in 1954[66] detected empirical clusters of personality traits that bear some relation to the theoretical structure of the F scale. Demolition also continues, as is evidenced by Camilleri (1959),[67] whose factor analysis failed to verify the theoretical basis.

Perhaps a more subversive attack comes from the accumulation of evidence relating to the class determination of authoritarianism. Because of the traditional identification of the working class with radical political views, this picks up the issue raised by Shils in the *Continuities* volume. Shils' contribution had the title *Authoritarianism: "Right" and "Left,"* and he sets out to show a strong "soft leftist" bias in the scale items that did not provide adequate openings for the display of leftist authoritarian leanings.*

More recently Lipset[68] has assembled material to demonstrate that

* The 149-item scale mentioned above was designed to overcome this difficulty.

by the nature of things the working classes have their own brand of authoritarian tendencies. By secondary analysis of material collected by Stouffer[69] he is able to show that tolerance "with respect to civil liberties issues" increases with occupational level and with educational level. The same result is inferred from a great variety of sources. It is clear that the authors of *The Authoritarian Personality* would have been prudent to standardize their sample on class and educational characteristics more carefully than they did.

In spite of all reservations, however, in spite of the subsequent demonstration that the F scale is made up of many dimensions, it remains true that no one has dented the outstanding quality, or indeed the essential truth, of this work. It is, in fact, a measure of its importance that not only Sanford and his associates but many other individuals and groups are still concerning themselves with the social problems posed by the existence of an unfortunate minority of individuals whose punitive and affectionless childhood has left them permanently warped and a potential menace to society.

12

THE DYNAMICS OF INTERACTION

In this chapter we examine *Interaction Process Analysis*[1] This book by Robert F. Bales, published in 1950, was the first full-length description of a program of work that had already been in train at Harvard for some twenty years. Bales started systematic observation of field situations in 1943, and the final stages had begun in 1946 with the completion of the observation room at Harvard. Initially it enjoyed more or less a one-way relationship with the theoretical developments in Harvard sociology, but in recent years Bales has been very closely associated with Talcott Parsons and his theory of action.

Bales is himself a theoretician, and he entered the empirical field because he was perhaps more eager than some other sociologists to test his theories in order to discover how well they stood up under practical examination. Consequently the empirical side of his work is highly simplified and stripped down so as to provide the essentials of the more theoretical situations he sought. This is a feature of the whole approach, and, as will be suggested, is a source both of strength and of weakness.

It seems appropriate to begin by giving an outline of the theoretical thinking behind the empirical work. This is not the fundamental theoretical framework—that will be discussed later—but rather the practical conceptual framework that Bales built up in the course of his observations. In his book he plunges somewhat baldly into a description of what he did and the techniques he evolved, but it may

424

perhaps be better first to provide some background of his conceptual approach.

PRACTICAL THEORY

Bales' starting point is the assertion (following Parsons) that all
empirical observations can be described under two heads, namely,
action, which includes interaction, and the *situation*, in which the
action takes place. All generalizations must identify both the concrete action and the situation of the action, whether the ultimate
concern is personality, social system, or culture. Thus, by setting
out to observe and record systematic data on action and situation
Bales aims to provide a bridge that will take in the whole of the social
sciences, from individual psychology at one end to cultural anthropology at the other end. As social scientists speak with many voices,
the units of analysis will differ from one discipline to another, but
this does not rule out the development of a method of analysis or
abstraction that applies equally well to individual personality structure and to the social structure of a group.

Bales' immediate concern in the Harvard Laboratory was the
study of small groups, and for this he needed a reasonably formal
definition of the "small group":

. . . any number of persons engaged in interaction with each other in
a single face-to-face meeting or a series of such meetings, in which each
member receives some impression or perception of each other member
distinct enough so that he can, either at the time or in later questioning,
give some reaction to each of the others as an individual person, even
though it be only to recall that the other was present.[2]

This fairly complete, if arbitrary, definition is designed to exclude
the chance meetings of people who have no interaction with one
another. For example, an audience in a lecture hall engaged in listening to the lecturer but not interacting with one another, as might
happen at an isolated attendance at a lecture, or passengers riding
together in a subway car, would not qualify as groups according to
this definition. This is, of course, an initial simplification. In practice
often one cannot state whether a collection of people constitutes a
group or not; actually people are simply more grouped or less

grouped. But a minimum level of interaction is necessary before individuals can be considered or observed as a group, and the purpose of this definition is to limit the meaning of group to collections of people who are recognizably in interaction with one another.

In the series of laboratory observations undertaken by Bales and his colleagues the investigators concentrate upon the nature of the relationship between individuals and the group rather than with the subject matter of what is being discussed or acted out by the group. For his purpose it is not felt to be of direct interest what people are talking about or what the particular situation or problem is. The concern is rather to discover how, in a problem situation, different individuals contribute to the solving of the problem and what related problems arise in the social and emotional field. This disinterest in meanings is a basic characteristic of interaction process analysis which, as various critics have pointed out, to some extent limits its usefulness and also the analyst's capacity to generalize beyond the somewhat artificial situations initially studied.

If a problem-solving session is to be observed, the investigator might reasonably be interested in the solutions arrived at and in the suggestions made in the process. It could easily be interesting to discover the provenance of the ideas thrown up, to discover whether they are external or are generated by the group situation. But although Bales arranged for the discussion to be recorded, he was not in this program addressing himself to the content; he was concerned with the formal characteristics of the interaction according to certain predetermined categories, to be described in due course, and with the roles taken up by individuals in the process of problem solving. It should be made clear that Bales has also worked actively on content analysis, but not in the program here described.

Although it has led to criticism, this restriction is a legitimate one. For purposes of observation it is necessary to omit something, and Bales was entitled to proceed as he did. It will be recognized, however, that there are important assumptions behind his decision, in particular the assumption that there are some common features in all groups that will lead to certain regular patterns of activity in the problem-solving process. The basic assumption is "that all small groups are similar in that they involve a plurality of persons who have certain common task problems arising out of their relation to an outer situation, and certain problems of social and emotional relationships arising out of their contact with each other."[3] The second assumption, which is derived from the first, "is that each act of each individual in the group can be analyzed with regard to its bearing on these problems."[4] In other words, the acts of each individual in such a group are not independent but, either by deliberation or in the nature of things, are affected by and have some effect upon the way that the group behaves. Thus, the observations must take in every observable act (that is, they must be *inclusive*), and there must be no gaps in the record (that is, observations must be *continuous*). Any omission of an observable act represents an error in the record.

As a practical consequence of this requirement, it is inevitable that the observer is always very busy, as we shall see. There is also the incidental consequence that all the inferences made by the observer in the course of recording must be very simple, for the observer has no time to pause and consider what an individual means by his contribution or what are the motivations underlying what he says. There must be a form of classification that relates directly to the overt behavior of the people under observation.

It is necessary to be clear as to the precise limitations that this procedure entails. The analyst cannot trace from the interaction data alone the origins of particular ideas or their originators because the ideas themselves are not part of the primary record. For the same reason the analyst cannot judge the relevance of each person's contribution. He will know that the person made one or more contributions, but whether the contributions were good or bad is not determined. Again, there is no evidence of how rigid or persistent a person is in his ideas because it is not known what his ideas were and hence whether he is persisting with the same ones or turning up new ones. These limitations are explicitly stated in the book.

The *act* is the unit that it is the function of the observers to record. More properly, this is the *single interaction*. As each act recorded is assumed to evoke a response in one or more other members of the group, it represents a single interaction in a succession of interactions. Such acts can be verbal or nonverbal. Bales claims that many nonverbal acts are recorded, but it seems probable that more nonverbal acts than verbal acts will be omitted from the record. Although devices are used to direct the observers' attention to nonverbal acts at regular interviews, it is more reasonable to suppose that the nonverbal acts recorded are, at best, a sample of the nonverbal acts occurring.

The experienced observer is constantly watching the group, and he records many more nonverbal acts than the inexperienced observer. Even the verbal acts recorded seem to increase considerably with experience. It has been found that inexperienced observers record only half as many acts of all kinds, verbal and nonverbal, as experienced observers. One inference from this is that the total number of acts is always greater than the number recorded.

The underlying belief is that each verbal act, and even nonverbal act, can be translated by a trained observer into a simple sentence with a subject, a verb, and a predicate. For example, if a person raises his eyebrows in a certain way, the observer translates that to mean "What do you mean?" Or if somebody asks "Why?" this can also be translated into a more complicated sentence. But beyond that, if the sentence seems to have two or more such simple ideas, then it will count as two or more acts. The analysis into acts is quite important, because certain of the results are based on the frequency of acts, so that the definition of what one act consists of is directly reflected in these results. Bales provides as an example a short sentence in which his procedure distinguishes four acts. The sentence is: "This problem which we talked about for three hours yesterday/ impresses me as very complicated/, difficult/, and perhaps beyond our power to solve." The first act ends with "for three hours yesterday," because these words convey a suggestion that yesterday's discussion was a rather slow and protracted process; "impresses me as very complicated" is the second act; "difficult" is separate again; "and perhaps beyond our power to solve," which conveys a fresh idea, is the fourth act.

The next question is how the observer determines the purpose or function of each statement. In order to do this he is trained to take what is called "the role of the generalized other." He must imagine himself by a process of empathy to be a member of the group. He has to empathize first with the actor and then with the member of the group perceiving the act while the latter is simultaneously empathizing with the initiator of the act and evaluating the content of the act. For example, if A makes a remark to B, then B tries to understand what A means by putting himself to some extent in A's place, and he is also evaluating A's remark in deciding whether he agrees with it; the function of the observer is to try to put himself in the position of B while B is doing both of these things. It is clear that several steps of inference are involved.

Various safeguards are also essential; for example, the observer must not know more about the members of the group than they know about one another. Otherwise he would obviously be able to make better evaluations and empathize more efficiently than they could. Practically all the groups studied at Harvard have been collections of people, very often students, who knew one another slightly, if at all; they were generally hired for the test and dispersed at the end of either one session or a short series of meetings. This procedure ensures that neither the members nor the observer will possess any special foreknowledge of any individual member and leaves "the content of the common culture of the small group . . . as the norm or baseline from which present interactions are to be interpreted, whenever possible."[5] This common culture will be the baseline not only for the members of the group but also for the observer.

As has been stated, the basic analysis is in terms of a succession of interactions, each involving one actor in one situation. Normally each unit is an act between individuals, in which one member speaks directly to another member or to the whole group. But theoretically the act can equally well be aimed from the person to himself. Bales includes as acts such things as being ashamed of yourself or talking to yourself. There are obvious practical difficulties in recording such acts, but it will be seen why their inclusion is necessary for his chosen type of analysis.

From this standpoint the personality is treated not as an irreducible unit but as one of a series of subparts any one of which is in action at a given time. Thus the actor is to be thought of not as synonymous with the biological individual but solely as a point of reference adopted for the analysis of a particular act. "This author or actor stands behind the overt act, persists through it, and ties the present act to acts which have gone before and to acts which are to come, but is nevertheless not identical with the more extended self seen as object by the actor."[6] This will be seen to bear out the previously mentioned point that the observation conditions do not take in the whole background of the actor but treat him merely as an object that is behaving in certain ways within the test situation. The analysis is strictly behavioral, taking in only what can be seen or directly inferred from behavioral clues while the actor is under observation. Consequently everything outside the actor, including that part of him that one cannot observe, constitutes the situation. At each stage of the analysis everything to be recorded relates either to the actor or to the situation.

The situation in turn has three major foci, or *target objects*. The inner focus is the actor's whole *self* (not just the subpart in action at the time) regarded as object. Next outside comes the *in-group*, either as a whole or one or more of its members. Outside this again is the whole situation, consisting of other people who are not present, and the whole *outer situation*, which includes the observers. The interrelation of these target objects to the actor, and his act, and to the time process are illustrated in Figure 8.*

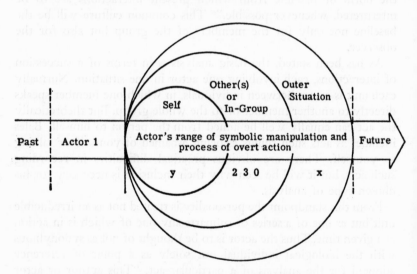

FIGURE 8. Actor and situation as a frame of reference.

There is an interesting point, in passing, about this conceptual frame. During this period Bales was deeply interested in psycho-analysis; his interest led him to suggest a relation between the three

* Figures 8 through 20 in this chapter are taken from Robert F. Bales, *Interaction Process Analysis* (Reading, Mass.: Addison-Wesley, 1951), and are used with the kind permission of Mr. Bales.

foci and the psychoanalytic concepts ego, id, and ego ideal. The actor is roughly similar to ego; the self, regarded as object, to the id; and the outer situation, to reality. This leaves the inner or social situation, which corresponds with the superego or ego ideal. In the experimental situation the only group with which the actor is concerned is the in-group, which for that period is assumed to provide the limits of his social situation, and it is to this group that he turns for sanction. The out-group, or outer situation, is imperfectly perceived as influences and events in his past and his future about which he is not worrying at the time. Bales does not claim that there is any close analogy between his concepts and those of psychoanalysis, but clearly there are stimulating points of correspondence between them.

Once the concept of process in time has been introduced, one can make use of the traditional division of modes of orientation into *cognitive* (involving "adaptive" understanding by means of the manipulation of symbols), *affective* (involving "expressive" responses, such as liking or disapproval), and *conative* (involving "instrumental" acts definitely aimed at dealing with the situation confronting the group).

The words "expressive" and "instrumental" are important to an understanding of the method of analysis here being described. "Instrumental" acts, which contribute to problem solving, are closely related to the future because the solution of any problem involves a time process, and the actor acts as he does in order to realize his objective at some future instant. But in the course of solving problems certain tensions are set up in the group—members of the group are forced to adjust their ideas, or they are shown to be wrong, or certain awkwardnesses arise through disagreements. Thus, in order to have a problem solved to the satisfaction of the group, one must have not only skill at solving the problem but also a means of reducing the tensions generated in the process. This release of tension is described as the "expressive" function, which, if positive, increases or restores the internal solidarity of the group. Unlike the progressive drive of the instrumental act, the positive expressive act is normally concerned with rectifying some tension or emotion that already exists.

An expressive act may be negative instead of positive. Sometimes an instrumental suggestion will lead to a negative reaction from another member of the group; one person makes a suggestion and the next person disagrees. This can obviously also be an expressive reaction; the second person may disagree because he does not like the first man making the suggestion rather than because the suggestion is a bad one. If the second person is concerned solely with solving the problem, then he will probably ask for further clarification, which is to be regarded as an instrumental act. But if he merely shows antagonism, making some remark such as "You are always putting forward foolish suggestions," then this is a negative reaction of an expressive kind. It appears that a negative expressive act must be followed by a positive expressive act before the integrative problem may be considered solved.

It must, of course, be appreciated that all instrumental acts have an expressive component, because it is impossible to make a suggestion without emotionally affecting other members of the group. On the other hand, it does not necessarily follow that all expressive acts have some instrumental value—they may sustain group solidarity but not otherwise promote the task in hand. This partial interweaving of the instrumental and the expressive functions of any act merely parallels the fact that every act contains some characteristics of a cognitive, of an affective, and of a conative nature.

One essential feature of the acts being considered is that they are *social* in character, involving interaction between individuals. It is not a question of an individual's sitting down and solving a problem but rather a process of arriving at a *joint* or *shared* evaluation of the situation and a joint or shared decision or consensus about the direction of instrumental activity.

We next move from consideration of the actors and their individual acts to a consideration of the problem-solving process as a system. For this purpose the empirical interaction system must naturally be idealized. In Bales' model the process is dissected into supposedly self-contained sequences, each starting with an "initial act," which may be instrumental (such as asking for information) or expressive (such as a startled or bewildered look). This creates discomfort in the group and will stimulate attempts to restore equilibrium. It will therefore lead to a "medial act," which may be expressive but more often is instrumental (such as attempting to answer the question). The original instigator of the current sequence (or another member of the group) can then terminate the sequence

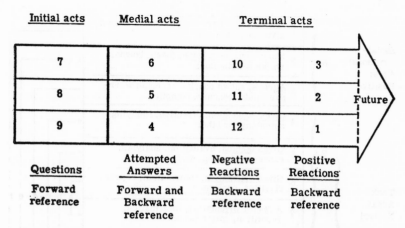

Initial acts	Medial acts	Terminal acts		
7	6	10	3	
8	5	11	2	Future
9	4	12	1	
Questions	Attempted Answers	Negative Reactions	Positive Reactions	
Forward reference	Forward and Backward reference	Backward reference	Backward reference	

FIGURE 9. The problem-solving sequence as a frame of reference.

by nodding agreement. This is regarded as a "terminal act," even if the response is a negative one, in which case another sequence is initiated. This sequence is shown in diagrammatic form as Figure 9.

The interaction system itself is put forward as a key concept which unifies the ideas of personality, social system, and culture. It leads to the set of twelve action categories which fit together so perfectly that they can be grasped as a Gestalt even without theoretical explanation. These categories are reproduced as Figure 10, and it will be seen how tidily they nest into and mirror one another.

The next step is to consider the social structure of the group as a whole. This involves a transformation of the raw data. The initial record is based entirely on the acts of individual members of the group who either speak to (or otherwise communicate with) another individual or to the group as a whole, but the analysis can bring out the characteristics of the group as a whole. The actions of the other members of the group are always relevant to the problems of tension reduction of any given individual and therefore influence the ways in which he acts. No individual desires uncertainty, and each member of the group consequently wishes to achieve a stable relationship with the group, favorable if possible but at least predictable. He wishes, as Bales puts it, "to stabilize the potential activity of others toward him"[7] because this enables him to anticipate their behavior. The group thus has a common interest in stability,

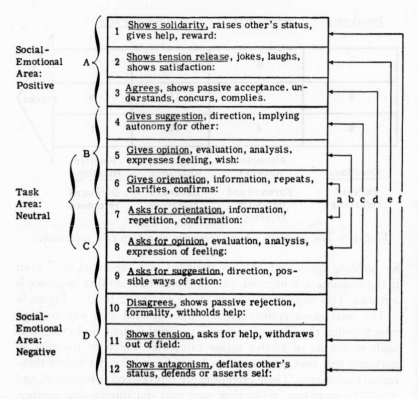

FIGURE 10. The action categories and their major relations.

and therefore develops a "social structure" that regularizes certain roles and develops certain patterns of interaction between the members and protects every member from surprises from within the group. Similarly the "culture" of groups develops to regularize the interaction of the group with its outer situation, and the "personality" of an individual is created by the crystallization of responses to regularly experienced interaction patterns.

It will be appreciated that this formal reconciliation of the interaction system with personality, social structure, and culture is an important derivative from Bales' theory, but it has relatively slight application to the particular experiments described in *Interaction Process Analysis*.

In contrast, the concept of "motivation" is an empirically useful way of describing what leads the individual to act as he does in a given structured situation. An important point to note, however, is that the motivation of the individual is not to be ascertained directly from the empirical observations but can only be reconstructed or inferred. Furthermore, motivation can be accounted for completely only if one has sufficient knowledge of the life history of the individual to determine the outer situation as it relates to him personally as well as the inner situation—facts which in these problem-solving groups were not available.

In other problems an adequate interpretation of actions is possible with some knowledge of established status relationships among people, but again the artificial problem-solving groups brought together in the Harvard laboratory have no preliminary status relationship. Any status relationship that builds up will be due to interaction within the group and not to anticipatory responses brought into the situation. Nevertheless, for purposes of analysis, one may well have to take the status relationship into account. The same behavioral acts can sometimes be fully interpreted only by foreknowledge of the status relationship. For example, if A says to B, "You did very well," various interpretations are possible; it may be that A is superior in status to B and is rewarding him for doing well, or A and B may be more or less equal in status and A is merely congratulating B, or A may be inferior to B and is expressing his admiration.

It is an interesting fact that when Bales started his experiments, he used a great many categories of interaction. Although at first sight each category seemed different, in practice it was difficult to decide which one to use to describe a given act. Bales then realized that the classification could be made not only much shorter but also much simpler to use by omitting all distinctions based on assumptions as to the social relationships of the participants. Thenceforward such different acts as "rewarding," "congratulating," and "admiring" were all subsumed in a composite Category 1—"Shows solidarity, raises others' status, jokes, gives help, rewards."

It might seem at first as though status considerations would apply only to expressive acts. This is not in fact the case. For example, questions are instrumental acts, but they may easily have status implications. For example, if a teacher in class asks one of his students a question, this has a quite different meaning from the situation when the student asks the teacher a question. Though asking the question may be common to both occasions, two separate activities may be inferred. It is convenient that, for the purposes of interaction analysis, this distinction, like the others mentioned, can be ignored at the recording stage, though it can be put in afterward, when status relationships within the group are inferred from analysis of the record of discussion and from subsidiary questions.

This inference of status relationships within the group is justified by the belief that, in order to function effectively a group normally differentiates the roles of its members. This is necessary because the members of the group are more at ease if they can predict the behavior of other members of the group. In the case of these particular experimental groups whose members were previously unknown to each other, the expectations of each member about the others must be inferred by him from behavior in the group. On the other hand, the normal ideas and stereotypes about people, their roles and relationships, will be quite familiar to members of the group. Bales identifies four dimensions of status differences likely to be generated by the group experience: differences in access to resources such as skill and knowledge; differences in control over other persons, shown in the emergence of the leadership function; differences in status independent of skill or leadership functions; differences in solidarity or identification with the group. His assumption is "that in *every act* the position of the self in these various dimensions is potentially at stake, in the sense that the act may conform with the expectations of others and reinforce or confirm the present position, or help make it, or may deviate either in a positive or negative way from expectations and lead towards a change in position."[8]

It is hoped that this somewhat condensed description will make it clear that interaction process analysis is basically aimed at studying the relational behavior within groups and the differentiation of roles within groups, and for this purpose is designed to detach these second-order data from the immediate content of the activity being pursued by the group.

Against this theoretical background it is easier to examine some of the practical and methodological corollaries of the experimental method.

METHOD OF OBSERVATION

The first item is the observation room. This was described in *Interaction Process Analysis*, and an amplified description was published in December, 1954.[9] Although observation rooms had been used by psychologists for a long time, the Harvard setup was still rather novel in 1950, when the book was published. By the end of 1954, however, Bales and Flanders reported that, apart from the observation rooms at Harvard and Minnesota, with which the authors were most familiar, similar installations already existed at eleven named institutions, and that undoubtedly there were many others. Furthermore, the paper was aimed at the many universities and other institutions which were by that time constructing facilities for the direct observation of human behavior.

Although there had been no fundamental changes, the design had been refined and elaborated by trial and error, and was more or less standard by 1954. Apart from technical developments, perhaps the major change in accommodation required was the provision for the stream of spectators who became an important concern as the fame of the group laboratory increased and who might prove a distraction unless special arrangements for them were incorporated.

The layout consists basically of two rooms. One is the *meeting room* of, say, 400 square feet, with the character of a well-appointed conference room or classroom, arranged for the most convenient conduct of the group meeting. The other is the *observation room*, slightly raised, which is like the engineer's booth in a television studio or like the special observation room in a modern surgical operating theater, and accommodates the observers, technicians, students and trainees, and spectators. Between these two rooms there is a row of *one-way mirrors* that look more or less like ordinary mirrors from the meeting room (provided the light in the observation room is subdued and no lighted matches or other light sources are visible) but give a direct view of the test group from the observation room.

Normally the subjects are told in a matter-of-fact way that they are under observation, but, it is believed, the fact that the observers are invisible and inaudible minimizes the distraction they cause. Bales claims that the groups are not made to act artificially by the knowledge that they are being observed, "possibly because we are all used to being observed in social situations, at least in an informal sense."[10] But, as is well known, it has been found difficult to test how far knowledge of being observed further distorts an already highly artificial situation.

Occasionally the arrangements require that subjects learn only after the session that they have been observed. On such occasions they are taken into the observation room after the meeting and the recording is played back to them. They are also asked whether they have any objections to the specific use of the data intended. Few refusals are encountered.

This secrecy is employed only if it is necessitated by the study design. An example will make this clear. In 1951 Strodtbeck[11] was studying the extent to which the views of one marital partner were affected by the views of the other partner, and particularly which partner tended to prevail when a disagreement arose. Results were to be compared in three distinctive cultures: the culture of Navajo Indians, that of dry farmers from Texas, and that of Mormon settlers. In the Navajo, the husband leaves his family of orientation to live with that of his wife and in various ways is economically and ideologically dependent on his wife. Among the Texan group, although the men dominate the home, the wives have some economic independence. The Mormons still live according to the doctrine that the home is presided over by the father, whose authority derives from the church. It was therefore predicted that the views of the wife would prevail among the Navajo and that those of the husband would prevail among the Mormon group, with the Texan farmers occupying an intermediate position. In a primitive laboratory, with portable sound equipment powered from a truck, Strodtbeck tested this hypothesis using ten couples from each of the three cultures. In each case husband and wife were first asked individually questions about three families well known to them. Typical questions were "Which family has the happiest children?"; "Which family is the most religious?"; "Which family is most ambitious?" These choices were unobtrusively recorded, and then each pair of spouses was asked to reconsider the questions together, supposedly in private. Results showed that, as expected, the views of Navajo wives and of Mormon husbands were most likely to prevail. It was also found that there was a very strong relationship between the amount of talking and the number of decisions won; the most talkative spouse tended most frequently to *ask questions*, carry out *opinion and analysis*, and make *rewarding remarks*.

It will be noted that these categories, like the rest of the analysis, are based on the Bales method. It is clear that the study could have been conducted without using his method, but it is an interesting instance of the wide applicability of the technique. In this case it was felt that, if the spouses had known that their discussions were being observed and their voices recorded, they might either have produced "polite" interaction or overstructured the task so that they would not have interacted in their normal way.

Next to the one-way mirrors the most important equipment is the speaker and recorder system. Originally two microphones were strung up in the ceiling in the meeting room. These were fed to speakers, so that the observers could hear what was going on, and were also recorded for future reference. At the time when his book appeared, Bales was using wire recorders for high fidelity and plastic disks for low fidelity. By 1954 a sophisticated installation was in use, with three microphones to provide audio balance for a stereophonic sound output and with both tape and dictation disks. There is good soundproofing between the two rooms so that observers can talk quietly to one another and compare notes during the session without being heard. Soundproofing is essential for training purposes, to enable the observers to explain to the trainees what they are doing, and is also necessary for coping with visitors.

The third device needed is an interaction recorder. In 1950 this instrument was a simple, slightly mechanized device for keeping a rapid record of interaction. It consisted of a deck with a wide paper tape that slowly moved across from right to left while the observer marked up, according to the twelve categories, the actions of the members of the group being observed. Inside the case a marker drew an inked line across the record at the end of each minute. There was also a light that flashed once a minute to remind the observers to observe the nonverbal behavior. This interaction recorder was described as a convenience but not a necessity, its main function being to help the observer record faster. Students learned on pads. By 1954 use was being made at Minnesota of inking galvanometer units operated by levers.

There is an obvious temptation to use elaborate recording apparatus, ideally even a sound film. The difficulty with all such records, apart from the cost, is that they merely delay the need to simplify the data. Transcribing the sound track may take from six to ten hours of secretarial time for every hour of record, and the transcription in any case lacks voice inflections, speeds of interaction, and other relevant features. Records of this kind are a safeguard against the breaking-down of the other recording instruments, and are useful for playing back to a panel of judges, and for certain "stimulated-recall" sessions in which the original subjects are helped to re-create the feelings they had in the original group situation; but they should not be passed for transcription unless the investigator is very certain that the transcription will be definitely needed.

One development since the publication of *Interaction Process Analysis* is the recording of synchronized reactions. According to Bales and Flanders,

. . . subjects, in a relatively short time, can be trained to indicate simple introspective reactions at the same time they are participating in a group discussion. Dichotomous continua such as "like-dislike," "agree-disagree," set up either on a five-point or three-point scale, can be recorded and mechanically synchronized with a voice recording of the total group discussion. . . . Systematic analysis of such lever reaction-data provides additional non-verbal data.[12]

This approach has interesting possibilities, limited only by the rather high initial cost of the mechanical electrical equipment required.

It remains to be mentioned that from early days IBM cards were used for processing the results. A separate card was used for each unit of action, each card being punched for three items of information, namely, the number of the category in which the act was classified, the number of the person in the group initiating the act, and the number of the person who was the object, or target, of the act. The in-group as a whole was designated by a zero. Tabulations could be concentrated either on the group as a whole, on an individual member, or on act-to-act sequences. More elaborate computers are now used, and a number of scores are entered on each card.

So much for the machines. We now turn to the question of the role and techniques of the observer. The observer has a double task.

He must see what the subjects are doing and he must also interpret their actions. As has already been explained from the theoretical point of view, this requires that he see the situation through the eyes of the members of the group and that he simultaneously evaluate the acts of members of the group. As far as possible he must put himself in the position of the man speaking and of the man being spoken to. The fact that the observer must interpret as well as record is what distinguishes this method from most other observation-recording methods. Most other techniques are concerned more with categories of behavior and less with categories interpretative of behavior than in Bales' method. What is asked of the observer in Bales' method is more exacting than in other methods, but it has the advantage that the data are immediately placed in the analytical categories required.

In practice the observer must be versatile. He must possess not only the stenographic skill required for systematic recording but also the analytical skill required for interpretative classifying. He also must be entirely familiar with the twelve categories, not only as to their definitions but also as to their theoretical significance and how they hang together. He must be very quick in deciding into which category to place each act that occurs, because these acts are accumulating at an average rate of as much as one act every three seconds.

Furthermore, the observer must learn to work a few seconds behind what is currently taking place, as this will be necessary whenever there is a burst of interaction. This skill, which depends on picking up the sequential rhythm of the acts, is rather like the task of the simultaneous translator at any international conference. He interprets a speech about one sentence behind what is being said; he must be able to listen with one ear while interpreting with the other. In the same way the observer of interaction must be able to listen and observe what is going on while he is recording what happened an act or two before.

We may thus summarize what the observer must do: first, he must determine who is speaking and to whom he is speaking; second, he must distinguish the beginning and the end of each individual act, so that no separate act is omitted from the record; and, third, he must decide where within the twelve categories the act in question belongs.

The process is fairly simple. On the interaction recorder the moving pad is divided by horizontal lines into twelve bands. Each band corresponds with one of the twelve categories, and for each act in this category the observer merely records the actor and the recipient; each participant is designated by a number. If, for example, Ed (number 3) makes a suggestion to Joe (number 5), the observer will record 3–5 in the band for category 4 (gives suggestion, direction, etc.). If the remark is addressed to the group at large, the recipient is coded 0, if to the self, is coded X, and if to anyone outside the group (for example, an observer), the code is Y. These three numbers, for example, [(4) 3–5], summarize the information about that particular act.

In the original setup the two observers sat side by side, each with his own interaction recorder. At the end of the session they drew a line between successive acts and then ran the two tapes along side by side so as to determine visually whether the two records looked more or less the same. Some differences were to be expected, but a reasonable similarity provided the first check that nothing had gone seriously wrong.

We have already looked briefly at the twelve categories from the theoretical point of view, and we are now ready to look at them from the point of view of the observer. (Figure 10) They will be seen to divide into four groups of three. The two middle groups, B and C, are *task-oriented;* that is, they comprise acts aimed at contributing to the solution of the task set to the group. The two outer groups, A and D, are oriented to the relief of *social emotional problems*. The starting point, for which empirical justification is claimed, is that every unit of verbal behavior is related either to task achievement or to the alleviation of strains induced in the group by the very process of task achievement.

It is difficult to justify this claim of the homogeneous character of individual acts. While it may be accepted that task achievement is likely to be intermittently interrupted by social and emotional strains, it does not follow from this that every contribution to the interaction process is fully identifiable as either instrumental or expressive. And yet what the observer is asked to do is to select the salient orientation of the act and to ignore or suppress the subsidiary orientation. This seems to conflict with the point made by Bales and already reported that "*every act* involves some characteristics which we can abstract and call cognitive (or symbolic), some characteristics we can abstract and call affective, and some we can abstract and call conative."[13] The theoretical justification is not made clear at this point; perhaps a better formulation would be that the action process, or series of acts, contains all three characteristics but that it is legitimate to classify each act as primarily concerned with either cognition, affect, or conation.

The next feature of these three categories, which is intellectually very satisfying, is their symmetry, so that, if a line is drawn between categories 6 and 7, each category has a mirror image; that is, 6 is symmetrical with 7, 5 with 8, 4 with 9, 3 with 10, 2 with 11, and 1 with 12. Categories 6 and 7 are concerned with communication, 5 and 8 with evaluation, 4 and 9 with control, 3 and 10 with decision, 2 and 11 with tension and tension reduction, 1 and 12 with solidarity and its opposite. Thus there is a fascinating Cartesian beauty about these categories.[14]

Mention must be made of the fact that there have been some minor revisions in the categories. For example, *jokes*, which appear in Category 1 in the version here reproduced, originally appeared in Category 2. There are, in fact, three categories in which jokes might be placed: a joke might be a verbal laugh (Category 2), as originally supposed; it might be a joke showing solidarity (Category 1); or it might be one of those sly jokes which are really designed to deflate another's status (Category 12).[15]

Clearly the observers must be rather skilled if they are to select the proper categories. The book in fact contains a most interesting description of the training and testing of observers, which makes it clear that the limitations of observation have had repercussions not only on the practical details of the experiments but also on their theoretical aspects. It was indeed because of the practical difficulty of training the observers to operate with a full set of categories that simplification to the finally adopted twelve categories took place. With this number observers were able to master not only the stenographic skills required but also the analytic assumptions underlying the classification system.

A routine was worked out for initiating trainees. The rationale of the program and its possible applications were first explained, and then the trainee was plunged into learning the extended definitions of which acts were to be placed in each category. These descriptions had clearly grown up from practical experience of acts observed in the course of experimental sessions and were spelled out in considerable detail. For example, Category 1, which in this chapter has been defined as "Shows solidarity, raises others' status, jokes, gives help, reward," has a full definition which occupies two pages, being split up into the following:

1. *Initial and responsive acts of active solidarity and affection,* such as hailing the other, waving, drawing near him in order to speak, and many other such acts.

2. *Initial and responsive status-raising acts,* such as saying "That's fine," "You've done a good job."

3. *Acts in response to Category 11,* such as giving support, reassurance, or comfort when there had been tension increase.

4. *Acts in response to the other negative reactions (Categories 10 and 12),* such as acts of pacification which might appear after a situation of difficulty or during a situation of estrangement.

By acquiring familiarity with this massive collection of special cases which had accumulated in the course of many years, the observer began to get the feel of the categories and learned to be sensitive not only to the isolated act but also to the act that had preceded it and the act that would follow it.

As a second step the trainees were set to practice on written protocols. This step gave them the opportunity to look up definitions and take their time generally, but it was found unwise to linger over this stage too long or else they became too much concerned with precise definitions and lost the art of operating at the fairly superficial level necessitated by the conditions of a *live* session.

The next stage made use of recordings of actual sessions; the trainees at first listened while the instructor would tap each time he recognized a unit. This is how it went: "Well [*tap*], Joe asked a question about what we were going to talk about in these sessions [*tap*]. In the first place I mentioned that these are emotional problems [*tap*], and each individual has a problem [*tap*]. Well, these problems are things we live through every day [*tap*], so we all know the subjects [*tap*]. It's a case of connecting it up right"—and so on. After a while the trainees would join in too and tap in time with the instructor. This was a rather gentle way of initiating them because, if one trainee tapped in the wrong place or failed to tap, he would not be too conspicuous. It was like learning to sing in a choir. Many detailed conventions had to be absorbed, such as that a laugh became a fresh unit each time the person had to draw an additional breath. When a certain proficiency was attained, the trainees moved on to classifying the interactions by categories.

Categories can be mastered by the use of recorded material, but the scoring of who-to-whom material can be done satisfactorily only with live subjects so that the trainees can watch the participants. For this live situation it was found best to start with a dramatized session acted out by two or three members of the training team and built up around certain chosen combinations of categories. The actors could talk slowly and make it quite explicit to whom they were speaking, while the trainees would sit around with their scoring pads and write: [(4) 1–2], [(3) 2–1], [(12) 3–0], [(6) 1–3], and so on.

After this trainees were ready for the real thing. But it had been found that in these last stages some resentment could arise among the trainees from remarks that exposed them to criticism of their judgment or common sense. As Bales points out, people may be more defensive about their powers of judgment than about their educational attainments or intelligence. They may not mind being thought relatively unintelligent so much as being thought lacking in common sense. It was therefore important to explain that the criteria for correctness were impersonal and that their own common-sense judgment was not at stake.

Besides gaining practical experience the trainees were taught two priority rules to be applied when any difficulty arose. The first rule was that each act should be viewed as a response to the last act of the "last other" (that is, the initiator of the previous act) or as an anticipation of the next act of the "next other" (that is, the initiator of the following act). This implies that the immediate social act takes precedence over the more general social context, that reactive or anticipatory characteristics take precedence over permanent personality traits, and that the emphasis is on immediate rather than on depth meanings. This rule has obvious practical advantages. The fact that a man has a stammer or is deeply disturbed before the interaction begins is not so relevant as the way in which, for example, his tension is increased or released by the interaction process itself; somebody who had come, say, to ask for financial assistance would be anxious, but what is important in this context is how his anxiety—not to mention his financial problem—is resolved by the session. It is the changes in the situation brought about by the interaction, not the permanent features of the situation, which are the focus of interest.

The second general rule taught to the trainees is that, if there is any doubt, they should always favor a category more distant from the middle. Thus, if one person says, "It's hot today" and the other smiles and replies, "Over ninety," this reply is interpreted as showing solidarity (category 1) rather than as giving information (category 6). It will be appreciated that this implies a preference for the affective tone of acts rather than for their cognitive content and explains how in practice the expressive-instrumental dilemma already discussed is always resolved in favor of the expressive categories.

It is clear that the training of observers was taken very seriously and was well worked out. At the same time it was recognized that scoring remained partly an intuitive procedure. While decisions were carefully regulated, too much cerebration was discouraged.

This naturally raises questions of reliability and repeatability of observations. There are three ways in which scoring might go wrong:

1. In "unitizing" (horrible word!), that is, distinguishing separate acts.

2. In "categorizing," the assignment of acts to interaction categories.

3. In "attributing," designating the originator and target for an act.

Bales points out that a simultaneous test for all three would require the enormous matrix of $(n + 2)(n + 2)(12k)$, where n is the number of persons in the group and k is the number of time intervals (say, the number of ten-minute periods) in the record. This would become quite unmanageable for analysis, and two partial tests are substituted: they test first the reliability of 1 and 2 and then of 1 and 3. In any tabulation of a session there is obviously no "objective" result with which the scores of an observer can be compared. The method is therefore to determine the correspondence between scores of two different observers. If these agree closely as to the number of units placed in each of the twelve categories in each of a succession of ten-minute periods, it is concluded that they have both performed reliably on "unitizing" and "categorizing."

The next question is how accurately the observers are able to repeat their scoring of the same session. For this purpose A and B listen to the recording and rescore it. Under the stimulus of the recording most observers can vividly recall the image of an interaction they have previously observed; observers, having "been there before," frequently score more acts the second time.

The next test (Phase 3) consists of a written description by observers A and B of what occurred in a selected period. At this stage an "anecdotal observer," C, is brought in to contribute notes on the content and tenor of the session. These three prepare a joint version of what took place. In Phase 4 the written protocol is submitted to three experienced judges, who compare and reconcile it with the recording; the judges may listen to the recording as many times as they choose. Phases 5 and 6 are concerned with reconciling and pooling the differences in the scores of individual observers.

This outline gives some indication of the elaborate steps taken to achieve reliability within the framework of what the investigators are aiming to do.

PRACTICAL APPLICATIONS

At this point we shall turn to some early examples of how this elaborate procedure was applied to actual problems. One case cited was taken from the field of counseling. William Perry, of the Harvard Bureau of Study Counsel, wished to develop an instrument that would check his performance as a counselor. His aim was to establish with his student counselees a relationship of such a nature that after an initial period the student would gain sufficient confidence to solve his own problems, while the counselor's role shifted from that of instruction to that of questioning and evaluating the student's problem. It is clear that the success of this aim could be readily tested by interaction process analysis. As Figure 11 shows, the test confirmed that this shift of emphasis did in fact take place. In the early sessions 75 per cent of the acts of the counselor fitted into Category 6 (gives orientation, information, repeats, clarifies, con-

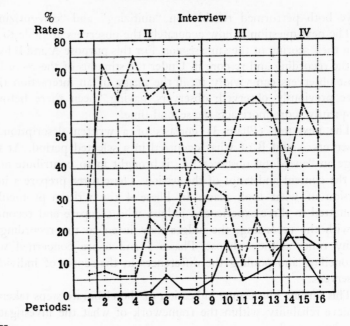

Key:

---------- Category 6 (gives orientation, etc.)
—·—·—·—·— Category 5 (gives opinion, etc.)
——————— Category 8 (asks for opinion, etc.)

FIGURE 11. Counselors' rates of activity in categories 6, 5, and 8, by ten-minute periods through four interviews.

firms), whereas in the later sessions, after about two hours, the share of this category dropped to between 10 and 20 per cent. Again, whereas at the beginning the counselor offered few evaluations or opinions, toward the end the share of this category had built up to 60 per cent. This particular counselor seems to have had to ask very few questions; for the first two sessions the share of Category 8 (Asks for opinion, evaluation, analysis, expression of feeling) was down well below 5 per cent, and it was only in the later stages that it went up to 15 per cent.

The acts initiated by the student counselee were also being observed and recorded; his record (Figure 12) shows that at the very beginning he displayed considerable tension. After this had declined, he seemed on the whole to be fairly passive, except for one period

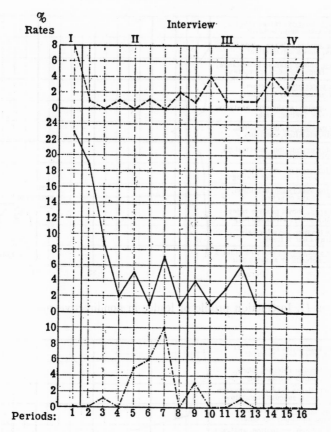

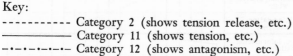

Key:

---------- Category 2 (shows tension release, etc.)
——————— Category 11 (shows tension, etc.)
—·—·—·—·— Category 12 (shows antagonism, etc.)

FIGURE 12. Students' rates of activity in categories 2, 11, and 12, by ten-minute periods through four interviews.

when he showed antagonism. This behavior (Category 12) was, however, directed not at the counselor but at his father, who had involved him in a difficulty. His father was, of course, not present and was thus part of his outer environment rather than of the interaction situation, and if it had not been for the overriding precedence given to expressive acts, these units might perhaps have been classi-

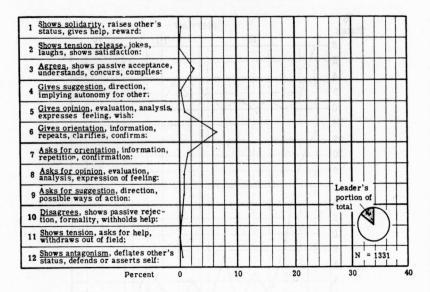

FIGURE 13. Interaction profile of leader in nondirective role.

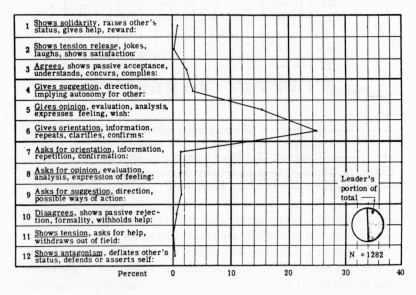

FIGURE 14. Interaction profile of leader in democratic-directive role.

fied in Category 6 (gives information . . .) rather than in Category 12, in which they were actually placed. Be that as it may, this analysis of counseling provides a good illustration of the use of interaction process analysis in systematizing information about a dyadic relationship.

A second example of the use of this method is concerned with the attempt to set up characteristic profiles of certain types of individual. In this case a comparison was made between different types of leader in a specially constituted group, so as to trace the contrast between what happened with a nondirective leader and what happened with a democratic-directive leader (Figures 13 and 14). For experimental purposes the same man assumed first one of these roles and then the other. The most important feature is that when he was being a nondirective leader, he said very little, his contribution constituting only 14 per cent of all the acts, whereas when he was being a democratic-directive leader, he contributed 52 per cent of all the acts. But apart from this striking contrast, obviously there are considerable differences according to the role being played. This is shown by comparing the frequencies with which the leader's acts fell into the twelve categories. For convenience these are drawn as frequency profiles, and it can be seen at a glance how different the two profiles are, even with the same leader playing the two roles. When being democratic-directive the leader was engaged mainly in "giving orientation, information, repetition, confirmation," but he also frequently "gave opinion, evaluation, analysis, expressed feeling or wish." By comparison, in the nondirective role he gave very few opinions or personal expressions; most of his interventions were to provide information, with a secondary peak of acts signifying agreement or acceptance.

There were also interesting differences between the profiles for the groups (Figures 15 and 16). In the "nondirective" group, since the leader spoke less, the other members spoke more. It was also found that although agreement was shown more frequently in this group, there was also a greater incidence of tension symptoms. In the "democratic-directive" group there was less display of tension but a higher frequency of tension release. Although a tentative explanation of these differences is offered, it is also emphasized that since only one meeting of each of only two groups was held, the

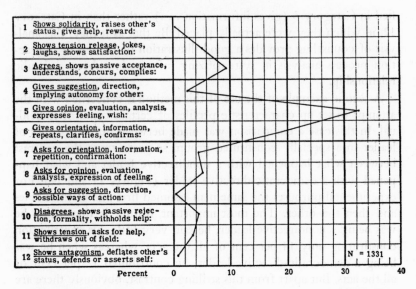

FIGURE 15. Interaction profile of members in group with nondirective leader.

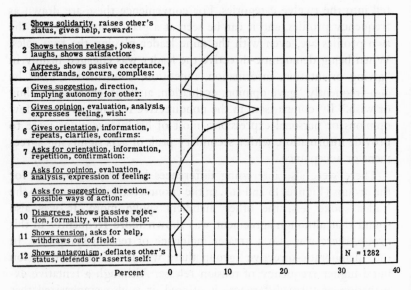

FIGURE 16. Interaction profile of members in group with democratic-directive leader.

results might be accounted for in terms of personality differences between members of the two experimental groups.

Other examples given are taken from material collected by Dorothy Swain Thomas at Teachers College as well as from other sources. Certain conclusions are drawn from the interaction profiles of the different groups examined. A preschool gang is high in the social-emotional categories, while in the task area most decisions are forced by direct suggestion rather than by subtler forms of influence. A group of ninth-grade boys shows more control over emotional expression, but tension release is exceptionally high, while cognitive agreement is relatively low.

A study of marital discussions has already been reported. This material was also used to construct interaction profiles. The results obtained from five separate couples were pooled for this purpose. Perhaps the most interesting result is that the rate of antagonism displayed was exceptionally high. Three possible explanations are suggested. The first is that this was one of the few instances in which the subjects were not aware that they were being observed; the second is that the marital relationship may by its very constancy engender more antagonism—and, indeed, emotional response of all kinds—than the transient relationships most commonly observed; the third is that the marital relationship implies sufficient basic solidarity to weather the free display of antagonism that might imperil the more fragile relationships of a casual group.

A fourth profile presented is derived from an academic discussion group of six persons, all either staff members or graduate students. As might be anticipated, this profile shows a striking concentration on information and analysis and a corresponding paucity of either positive or negative expressive behavior. The profile is thus at the other extreme from that of the preschool gang, and because of its qualities the discussion group was named the "Group Mind."

These cases virtually exhaust the empirical material available for inclusion in *Interaction Process Analysis*. In terms of results the achievement to that date was not particularly impressive. On the other hand, there was a well-devised technique and an exceptionally sophisticated and often exciting approach to both methodology and theory. Before leaving the book we shall follow Bales' statement on his position on these two issues at that date.

METHODOLOGY

It is natural that on the question of methodology Bales was deeply concerned about the problem of proof. He introduces this subject at the beginning of his thoughtful final chapter. As a theoretician who has embraced the empirical world in search of reinforcements and fresh insights for his theories he has been directly confronted with the need to reconcile concrete observations with general theoretical notions. As he sees it, there can be no single link between observations and theory, but rather a series of bridges, or what J. S. Mill called *axiomata media*, the middle principles of science, "which tell us, on the one hand, how to give operational content to the referents of our theoretical variables and, on the other, how to give theoretical meaning to the empirical uniformities in our data."[16]

Methodologically, Bales was both fascinated and troubled by what he calls the "flip-flop" problem. This is the familiar difficulty that arises when a hypothesis is not only nullified but is apparently reversed by empirical results. One is reminded of the classic example quoted by Merton in which two entirely different theories are produced, first to account for the apparent fact that the unemployed read less than average and secondly to account for the corrected fact that they actually read more than average.[17]

Merton was, however, pointing out the fallacy of the ex post facto explanation, whereas Bales is aiming at a rather different target. In his example he considers the logical steps involved in testing the extent to which an unspecified Factor A varies with solidarity. As acts in Category 1 are supposed to "show solidarity . . ." it would seem at first sight reasonable to assume that a group with a high rate in this category is more solidary than a group with a lower rate. The difficulty arises when it is seen that groups that could be presumed to possess high solidarity, such as married couples, actually have a lower rate on Category 1 than preschool children, who would be assumed to have achieved less solidarity.

The question is how to account for such an unexpected finding. According to Bales, "the almost irresistible tendency is to do a 'flip-flop' of the original criterion. We maintain our idea that the married couples are more solidary than the children's play groups—in fact we now believe they are so solidary that they do not need to show it in interaction!"[18] A very similar re-explanation actually put forward by Bales was innocently introduced earlier in this chapter.

Often, as Bales points out, the original confusion arises through equating the behavior in the immediate situation with all the more persistent structural influences on the group—the outer situation and the culture common to all members of the group, and certain pre-existing relationships and motivations. In this way, to imagine that a great display of solidary actions in the ingroup connotes structural solidarity in the group is to be confused over the meaning of the word "solidarity." It could genuinely occur that an underlying lack of structural solidarity would lead an individual into a stream of behavioral acts all of which could be interpreted as showing solidarity to other members of the group.

Clearly, however, the difficulty goes deeper than this. The truth is that without a mature theory of the function and meaning of group solidarity it is impossible to interpret or predict the sequence of events in an interacting group. Once a theory exists, every new accession of empirical data can be used to make the theory more nearly complete and hence to refine its predictive capacity. Within the bounds of the theory an apparent flip-flop may have to be accommodated. One example of this is the reaction-formation concept in psychoanalytic theory, which so infuriates critics, who feel that the theory should be able to predict *how* the individual will respond to a situation and not merely *that* he will respond.

It must also be noted that sometimes the confounding of an a priori prediction can be extremely valuable because it leads to a conceptually more sophisticated formulation of apparently self-evident popular sociological generalizations. In general, in the social sciences it is through the gradual and successive testing of a theory at all points rather than by a crucial experiment that we are likely to achieve predictive understanding of social events. Successful tests constitute the bridges by which hypotheses are established, modified, or rejected.

Bales lists ten questions that in his opinion should be asked about such hypotheses before they are adopted for testing.

1. Are the terms empirically specific, so that the concepts or variables can be distinguished in concrete situations?
2. Is the posited relationship between the variables one that could be verified or nullified by means of empirical operations?

3. Is there any prior evidence as to the truth or falseness of the posited relationship?

4. Can an appropriate study design be devised?

5. Are the variables "context-bound" (e.g., restricted to play group or gang), or could they be equally well applied to other interaction situations (e.g., work group or family)?

6, 7. Are the generalizations "culture-bound" (e.g., valid only in the United States or Western Europe), or can they also be applied realistically to other cultures?

8. If other relevant factors are subject to change in the course of the observations, are they adequately specified and enumerated so that the observers can ascertain whether they have changed during the period of observation?

9. Is the generalization part of a theoretical system from which it could be deduced as well as being verified by the proposed empirical induction?

10. Is the empirical system that is constructed sufficiently precise and articulated to permit predictions in concrete situations?[19]

Bales next turns again to what has been found to be a major stumbling block in the attempt to conceptualize the problem-solving sequence, the fact that two distinct but not entirely independent dichotomies, subject-object and past-future, must be incorporated. The idea of the functional sequence is found helpful here because it emphasizes that some kind of dynamic equilibrium is involved. The group proceeds to the solution of problems because its individual members are motivated by the need for a reduction of tensions. Tensions can be aroused in the individual either by the need for adaptation to the outer dimension—which in the case of problem solving involves the intellectual instrumental activity of finding an answer to a set question—or by the need for integration with the inner dimension under the new conditions created by the foregoing instrumental changes. At the end of one such cycle a problem-solving group is motivated to enter into another such cycle which will involve further processes within the group and further adaptations to the outer situation. Thus it seems to Bales that no reduction is possible in the number of the four basic concepts: *instrumental* and *expressive* are needed to describe the extension of the interaction system in time, and *adaptive* and *integrative* are needed to describe the extension of the interaction system in a structurally differentiated outer and inner dimension.

Perhaps the crucial feature of this formulation is that it leads to, or possibly arises out of, the novel form of classification of the interaction process in terms of a sequence of acts rather than in terms of the participating individuals. It is this fact that categorically divorces it from any form of psychological analysis. Furthermore, the innovation is shown to be empirically justified by the fact that certain regularities in interaction are found to occur. Thus an act in certain categories (e.g., Category 5—Gives opinion . . .) tends to evoke a second act in the same category, whereas an act in any other category tends to evoke a reversion to either Category 5 or Category 6 (Gives orientation, information . . .). Again, the tendency for symmetry already noted is shown to be a general one; for example, Category 7 often leads to Category 6, while Category 8 leads to Category 5.

Some of these results are perhaps less impressive than at first appears. The panoply of interaction process analysis is not needed to show that questions tend to provoke attempted answers. It is, however, interesting to have empirical confirmation of the fact that there tends to be an alternation of instrumental-adaptive and integrative-expressive functions. Analysis by subperiods of groups meeting under laboratory conditions is also revealing, showing that Categories 6 and 7, concerned with "Problems of Communication," are concentrated in the early stages of the meeting, whereas the incidence, for example, of Categories 4 and 9, concerned with "Problems of Control," and of Categories 2 and 11, concerned with "Problems of Tension Reduction," increases as the meeting proceeds.

The above results were obtained in the thesis discussion group of academically inclined individuals, the so-called "Group Mind," to which reference has already been made. As Bales admits, the fact that the results of this meeting so beautifully agree with the empirical predictions depends partly on the prior fact "that the order of events discovered in this group was a 'lucky find' under optimum conditions of some kind."[20] Whether this shows that the hypothesis is "context bound" or "culture bound" (for example, restricted to academic discussion groups) or whether the results were due to pure chance could obviously not be established from the analysis of one meeting. The result does seem to Bales at least to justify the setting-up of four hypotheses concerned respectively with communication, evaluation, control over the outer situation, and control of activity within the system. These can be briefly paraphrased as follows:

1. Without adequate perception of the situation and communication with one another, members of a group are unable to co-operate and will react to remove the consequent insecurity by adaptive-instrumental activity. Any residual insecurity will result in expressive-malintegrative behavior (for example, magic, rumor, obsessions, aggressions, described as "malintegrative" because, although they may reduce tensions in the short run, they solve nothing in the longer run and in fact set up circular developments).

Operationally, "Difficulty of Communication" is measured by a high rate of Category 7 acts compared with Category 6 (actually $7/(7 + 6)$ while "Expressive-Malintegrative Behavior" is measured in terms of a high rate of negative expressive acts (actually

$$\frac{(10 + 11 + 12)}{(10 + 11 + 12) + (1 + 2 + 3)}$$

and the relationship between the two can be expressed as

$$\frac{7}{7 + 6} = f \left[\frac{(10 + 11 + 12)}{(10 + 11 + 12) + (1 + 2 + 3)} \right]$$

where each number symbolizes the number of acts recorded in that category.

2. Without adequate agreement as to values, members of a group are unable to co-operate and will again react to remove the consequent insecurity by adaptive-instrumental activity. Any residual insecurity will again result in expressive-malintegrative behavior.

Operationally, the relationship between "Difficulty of Evaluation" and "Expressive-Malintegrative Behavior" can be expressed as

$$\frac{8}{8 + 5} = f \left[\frac{(10 + 11 + 12)}{(10 + 11 + 12) + (1 + 2 + 3)} \right]$$

3. Without effective achievement in controlling the situation, members of a group will react to remove the consequent frustration or deprivation by adaptive-instrumental activity. Any residual insecurity will again result in expressive-malintegrative behavior.

Operationally, the relationship between "Difficulty of Control over Situation" and "Expressive-Malintegrative Behavior" can be expressed as

$$\frac{9}{9+4} = f \left[\frac{(10 + 11 + 12)}{(10 + 11 + 12) + (1 + 2 + 3)} \right]$$

The next hypothesis is linked with this one in an interesting way. It seems inevitable that control over the situation also requires control over the action processes directed toward the situation and hence control by certain members of the group over other members. The process of deciding on action, before the action is actually rewarded, thus implies constraint over action and is felt as an increase in tension. Thus, as the point of decision approaches, tension tends to increase and malintegrative social behavior is more likely to occur.

This effect was noted in the analysis of the "Group Mind" in which a rise in the rate of Categories 9 + 4 acts (asking for and giving suggestions) coincided with a rise in the rate of Categories 1 + 12 acts (showing solidarity and antagonism). It also fits in with certain other classical psychological studies showing that authoritarian control generates tensions. This effect is stated as Hypothesis 4, paraphrased as follows:

4. Without integrated control over collective decisions of the group and without limitation of the authority of individual members of the group, the group will again react to remove the consequent insecurity by adaptive-instrumental activity. Any residual insecurity will again result in expressive-malintegrative behavior.

Operationally, the relationship between "Directiveness of Control" and "Expressive-Malintegrative Behavior" can be expressed as

$$\frac{4}{4+6} + \frac{5}{5+6} = f \left[\frac{(10 + 11 + 12)}{(10 + 11 + 12) + (1 + 2 + 3)} \right]$$

It will be noted that the four functions on the left of this series of equations take account of all the categories in the central portion, 4–9 inclusive, the so-called task area.

The foregoing analysis is concerned with the interacting group. It can just as fruitfully be applied to the study of the roles of individuals in the group.

The starting point is the plausible supposition that it makes a difference to the social status of an individual in the group whether he

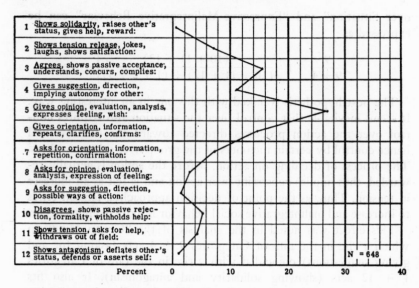

FIGURE *17*. Interaction profile of a five-person group.

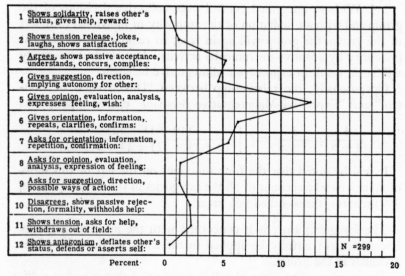

FIGURE *18*. Interaction profile of an active member (Member 1) of a five-person group.

is, for example, one who repeatedly asks questions or whether he is one who is frequently asked questions by others. It makes a difference whether his replies evoke positive or negative reactions and whether his own reactions to the acts of other members are typically positive or negative.

The data relating to a particular session are illustrated in the normal form of interaction profiles (Figures 17 to 20). These show that the individual profile of one particular member of the group (Member 1) are broadly similar to the composite profile for the group as a whole, whereas the profiles of other group members are quite different (Figures 19 and 20). This is due partly to the fact that the individual in question was the most active member of the group, so that his gross activity made up nearly half of the total. The observers were in agreement that he was the "leader" of the group, even though another member (Member 3) at the start of the meeting strode in confidently and sat down solidly in the middle chair. Once the session began, however, Member 3 was held in check by Member 1; whenever Member 3 made a suggestion as to how the group should proceed, Member 1 effectively drowned it in a flood of talk. The position of leadership thus achieved by Mem-

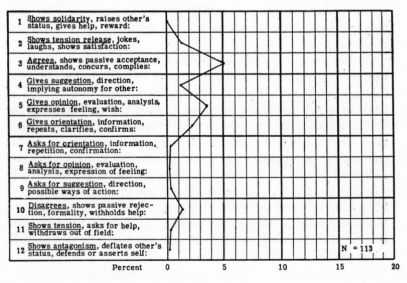

FIGURE *19*. Interaction profile of Member 2.

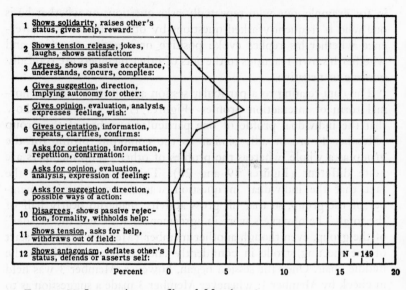

FIGURE 20. Interaction profile of Member 3.

ber 1 was greatly strengthened by Member 2, who was noticeably attentive and confirmatory to Member 1's suggestions. The other two members of the group contributed relatively little to the discussion.

On the strength of this analysis an attempt is made to present a general formulation applicable to all sorts of small groups. In brief, this suggests that the need to solve problems leads to a division of labor in which particular persons are given the responsibility for finding solutions, and thereby achieve enhanced social status, while those allotted less valued roles suffer a decline in social status. In due course those performing superior roles receive superior rewards and additional powers of direction, and these privileges are reflected in a further increase in social status. Meanwhile the gap between those of high social status and those of low social status is enlarged as the functional roles performed by persons in a group become more specific, differentiated, and formal, and this widening gap leads to a less solid relation between them.

Thus a sequence of changes in social relationship which is sparked by the group's need to solve problems leads to institutionalized differentiation in social status, in property owning, in authority, and in solidarity. The repercussions of this inevitable process can be very great. It may force individuals to compulsive competition for status; it may lead to compulsive rejection of approved status channels and the substitution of isolationism, schisms, sorcery, and other socially unacceptable solutions), or to compulsive rebelliousness, or to ritual and symbolic attempts to increase the solidarity of the whole group.[21]

Bales appears to advance the hypothesis at this stage that solidarity in the group between persons of different social status is incompatible with the efficiency achieved by division of labor, by the differentiation of rewards (in terms of status and property) and by the grading of authority. As he sees it, there is a constant dilemma between the "optimum adaptation to the outer situation at the cost of internal malintegration, or optimum internal integration at the cost of maladaptation to the outer situation."[22] This will be reflected by an unstable balance toward the crucial issues of functional diffuseness or functional specificity (division of labor), of communal or individualistic distribution of property rights, of informal or formal exercise of authority, of integration or efficiency, of subgroup association or over-all group solidarity.

THE AUTHOR

So much for *Interaction Process Analysis*. Perhaps this is the place to insert a word or two about Professor Bales. His first professional interest was in alcoholism. He has been described as "a kind of scientific patron" for Alcoholics Anonymous, which was founded in 1937, when he was a very young man. In the 1940's, while at the Yale School of Alcoholic Studies, he helped to establish at Hartford the first Yale Plan Clinic for Alcoholics. Emotionally, this human experience was clearly of the greatest importance to him. Intellectually, at least to the outsider, the connection of alcoholism with small groups appears tenuous. It may be that Bales' delight in interaction process analysis stems largely from the Cartesian simplicity and perfection of the resulting pattern, to which reference has already been made.

There is, however, an objective as well as a subjective element in fortune, and it is at least historically relevant that the earliest systematization of the method arose in 1946 from a program of study of subjects at the Harvard Psychological Clinic, into which Bales was drawn soon after his arrival at the Harvard Department of Social Relations. On the basis of this and other experiences Bales revised his categories, explicitly for use in observing therapeutic groups of patients in hospitals and clinics. It was only in the next academic year, 1947–48, that the method was applied in a fully generalized and theoretical context.

While Bales was working through the reconciliation of his interest in the pressing social problem of alcoholism with his strong theoretical inclinations, he was also exposed to the powerful influence of Professor Talcott Parsons, who, in collaboration with Professor Shils and others, was nearing the completion of his two books *Toward a General Theory of Action* and *The Social System*, both of which were first published in 1951. In his preface to *Interaction Process Analysis* Bales acknowledges the influence of "Professor Talcott Parsons, who, probably more than any other single person, has influenced my thinking in the analysis of social action and social systems."[23] There is, however, no direct reference to Parsons' *The Structure of Social Action*, which had been published in 1937, or to other published writings by Parsons. This is at first surprising in view of the central position taken in both theoretical presentations of the concepts of instrumental and expressive orientations (even though more symmetry is perceived by Bales than by Parsons), but it may be partly a reflection of the fact that between 1937 and 1951 Parsons had produced no major exposition of his theory.

Similarly, although there are passing references to, for example, "the small-group meetings which Bales and others have been observing so systematically,"[24] and although Bales' name is mentioned in conjunction with other names as having contributed fruitfully "in the more centrally sociological field,"[25] there was very little indication at this stage that a significant convergence was taking place. It was only in 1953, when Parsons, Bales, and Shils collaborated in producing *Working Papers in the Theory of Action*, that Bales' previous contribution was more fully acknowledged. "Though not formally a collaborator in the volume *Toward a General Theory of Action*, Bales participated actively in many of the discussions on which that publication was based and contributed much to them."[26]

SUBSEQUENT STUDIES

Working Papers in the Theory of Action is significant in the present context not only because it signalizes the arrival of Bales to full collaboration with the man who had most influenced his thinking but also because it provided the occasion for a report of the very considerable achievements of the observation project during the three years since the publication of *Interaction Process Analysis.*

The program described had consisted of the observation of a series of experimental discussion groups, each group meeting on four occasions to discuss and find solutions to four separate imaginary human-relations problems. The subjects, generally three to six in number, were obtained through the Harvard Employment Service and typically were previously unknown to one another. Each meeting lasted forty minutes, at the end of which the group was supposed to have decided (1) why the persons in the imaginary case were behaving as they did, and (2) what should be done about it. No leader was appointed.

The observations were made as previously described and were analyzed in the twelve categories. In addition, at the end of each meeting the members were asked to fill out a questionnaire stating their reactions, their satisfaction, their relations to one another, and their opinions about their discussion group.

The program was deliberately arranged so that the first meeting of each group began with the minimum of imposed structure. Thus, by the procedure adopted for giving them the facts of the case they were to discuss, the members were left uncertain as to whether they had all been given the same facts. The first task they were expected to solve in the course of the meeting was the *cognitive* one of arriving at a common definition of the situation.

Again, they started with somewhat different value systems, and the second task for the group was the *evaluative* one of arriving at the common value judgments needed for a joint decision. Thirdly, with no appointed leader but under pressure to arrive at a solution by joint decision, they were faced with problems of *control* within the group.

The question at issue was whether the different groups assembled for this series of experiments had significantly different interaction profiles and whether there were features in these profiles which correlated with the groups' feeling (as expressed in the questionnaires completed after the meetings) that their discussions had been satisfactory or unsatisfactory. To test this the profile of the "most satisfied" of the sixteen groups observed was compared with that of the "least satisfied." It will be appreciated that the sampling for this test, being based on only one case at each end of the satisfaction spectrum, is not adequate for reliable conclusions.

With this proviso it was found that between the two profiles there were broad similarities but also interesting differences. Both profiles followed the normal rule that attempted answers are more numerous than questions, and positive reactions more numerous than negative reactions. Without this constructive bias it may be presumed that group interaction would break down. It was noticeable, however, that with the "satisfied" group there was a much higher proportion of acts in Category 3 (Agrees . . .) and a much lower proportion of acts in Category 10 (Disagrees . . .). There was also less display of tension and antagonism.

The analysis next turned to an attempt to discover a typical sequence of events in the group interaction. This appeared to consist of a repetitive sequence of cycles consisting of an initial idea or suggestion followed by a "dwindling series of feedbacks" while the fresh idea was being assimilated or rejected by the group. This sequence was suggested by the psychologist Henry A. Murray, whose influence has been discussed in the chapter on *The Authoritarian Personality*.

Murray had suggested[27] that a distinction be made between *proaction*, in which the same person contributes the next act, and *reaction*, which follows an act contributed by some other member of the group. At least, the minute dissection used in interaction process analysis gives a reasonable chance that the same person will continue to hold the floor for several acts; in other words, proactive acts are frequent.

The detailed analysis shows, moreover, that even if an individual's first contribution is a reaction (positive or negative) to the act of another, which he interjects when the contributions of the previous participant have built up sufficient tensions within him, he is quite likely to follow up his first intervention with a "serial program" of proaction in which the same type of activity, namely, attempted answers, continues for some time, until other members feel that he is becoming too "directive" or "constrictive." If, however, his reaction is strongly affective, he is likely to continue in the same vein; it is only after tension release occurs, probably for several acts, that a return to the task area is possible. "The dilemma of all action systems is that no one disturbance can be reduced without creating another."[28]

It becomes much clearer at this stage that the group's sense of satisfaction with the outcome of a meeting is dependent far more on the preponderance of positive reactions over negative reactions in the affective area than on the preponderance of problem-solving successes in the task area. In terms of satisfaction the successful solving of the problems set is important primarily because it increases the proportion of positive affective reactions.

Another hypothesis is that the satisfaction felt by an individual member depends on the preponderance of positive reactions that he receives from other members of the group. It appeared that higher-status members did receive a disproportionate share of positive reactions and did in general have higher satisfaction ratings.

Perhaps the most productive fresh contribution arises out of a closer examination of the way in which participation tends to be distributed among members. It was found that groups with no designated leader tend to have more equal participation than groups with a designated leader. Either the designation of a leader or the working-out by the group of a system of control does, however, lead to regularities in the pattern of participation. It was found, for example, that each man received from other members a response roughly proportionate to his own contribution. Those ranking high in participation also tend to be more proactive, contributing more attempted answers, and also tend to address more of their contributions to the group as a whole rather than to individuals. Conversely, low-ranking members give out more agreement, disagreement, and requests for information than they receive.

It will be remembered that in Strodtbeck's experiments on marital discussions the spouse who contributed most to the discussion was the most likely to prevail in argument. In the present series a similar finding is reported, in that the members who participated most in the discussion were generally judged in the questionnaire results to have had the best ideas. There are exceptions, of course, as when a member who is "odd man out" in a group tends to attract or receive a disproportionate amount of attention.[29]

Size of group has an important influence on the distribution of activities. In large groups the "top man" is more likely to address the group as a whole, and remarks from other members are more likely to be addressed to him. By the process known in psychology as "reinforcement" he will tend to build up his contribution in a "generalized" way, so that his successful performance wins him an ascribed position in the group. This position will be stable provided he does not surrender it by failing to live up to the expectations of the group or by changing his behavior. The psychological mechanism involved was tested by setting up a working model with rules corresponding more or less to the behavior observed in real groups, and this test confirmed that equilibrium conditions may well incorporate the singling-out of a "top man."

It seems, however, that some initial stimulus is needed if the top man is to get far enough ahead to be ascribed the position of leadership by the group. He must gain the opportunity to go ahead by receiving agreement, possibly because he is more sure of himself and his normative judgments, in which case his judgment does not depend initially on rewards from other members of the group but will be reinforced by the group's expectation that whatever he says is likely to be right. His positive and negative reactions to the contributions of others will thus be seen as rewards and punishments, whereas he will be relatively invulnerable to their reactions.

How he receives the initial advantage is not always clear. He may be personally the target of positive affect—a "sociometric star." He may be the member most closely identified with the prevailing symbol system. Possibly, like the psychotherapist, he may be immunized against negative reactions by his superior knowledge which can "explain" hostile reactions in terms of the situation.

The questionnaires asked members of the group to name not only the member who in their opinion had succeeded best in the task area ("Best Ideas," "Guidance") but also to the members they liked most and disliked most. In twelve assorted meetings of five-man groups the five members were next placed in order of the contribution made to the meetings ("basic initiating rank"), and for each rank position the "number of votes received" in respect of "Guid-

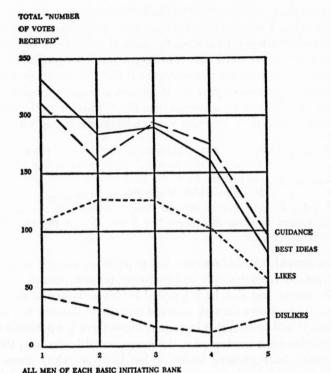

TOTAL "NUMBER
OF VOTES
RECEIVED"

GUIDANCE

BEST IDEAS

LIKES

DISLIKES

ALL MEN OF EACH BASIC INITIATING RANK

FIGURE 21. "Total Number of Votes Received" on each of four roles, pooled for men of each basic initiating rank as of each meeting. (Data from twelve assorted meetings of four five-man groups.) (From Talcott Parsons, Robert F. Bales, and Edward A. Shils, *Working Papers in the Theory of Action,* published by The Free Press of Glencoe in 1953.)

ance," "Best Ideas," "Likes and Dislikes" was plotted. The results of this analysis are shown in Figure 21.

This chart has a number of interesting features. The first point is that, as was anticipated, the number of votes received for providing "Guidance" and "Best Ideas" for the group varies with the number of contributions made. In other words, those talking most are felt by the group to have been the most helpful. However, the curve is not continuous, since on both these counts the "second man" receives fewer votes than would be expected.

A more serious departure from the prediction is found in the curve on likes. The top man is liked less than might have been expected, while the second man is liked more than anyone else. At the other end, the top man is actually disliked more than anyone else, the second most-disliked person being the smallest contributor.

How are these results to be accounted for? The belief is strengthened that the person most active in the task area often treads on some toes, so that he is more respected than liked. This leaves the need for someone whose main function is to maintain the group integration.

Such a man can be warm, receptive, responsive, and rewarding, can "conciliate" and "bind up the wounds," without diverting the movement of the system too far from the kind of movement in the instrumental-adaptive direction which is also felt to be necessary. He can do this because he does not assume the "responsibility" for the movement of the system in these directions, but leaves this to the technical or executive specialist.[30]

The second man is, however, less popular on average than might be expected from his role in promoting tension release; this may be due to the fact that he is tempted by his eminence in the group to try to break into the task area and contribute directly to problem solving. It will be seen that in various forms there is a potential status struggle between the top man, the instrumental leader, and the second man, the expressive leader, unless both are clear about their leadership roles in the group, so that the former is reconciled to a sacrifice of popularity and the latter to a sacrifice of respect.

It will also be noted that in this series there is one man cast for the unpopular role of scapegoat, receiving pathetically few votes for providing Guidance and Ideas, with few friendly votes and many hostile ones. There is some evidence that the presence in the group of such a scapegoat has the effect of diverting from the top man the hostility generated in the process of problem solving.

This distinction between instrumental and expressive leadership roles must be judged a most important result, with profound practical and theoretical implications. One immediate consequence is that we are forced to recognize that the question of who is the leader of a group is conceptually inadequate, as two quite distinct leadership roles have been demonstrated. We can, for example, cast our minds back to *Street Corner Society*, with the contrasting characters of Doc, the ideal expressive leader, and Chick Morelli, a typical instrumental leader. Doc was highly popular with his gang, but he did not lead them to any significant activity, whereas Chick was always bursting with ideas and always treading on toes in the process.

In the theoretical field the next important step was a paper contributed by Philip E. Slater, a colleague of Bales at the Laboratory of Social Relations at Harvard. This appeared in two slightly different versions. One version, *Role Differentiation in Small Groups*, appeared in the *American Sociological Review* in 1955 and was simultaneously printed in *Small Groups*. A second and apparently earlier version was printed in *Family Socialization and Interaction Process* by Bales and Slater, also published in 1955.[31]

The fresh empirical evidence in both papers was based on a series of studies generically similar to those already described. The sample size was in this instance systematically varied so that there were four groups of each size from a three-person group to a seven-person group, making twenty groups in all. As each group met four times, the observations covered a maximum of eighty meetings. The procedure was as before. The men were ranked according to who talked the most ("Talking") and who received the most interaction ("Receiving"). The questionnaires allowed the investigators to rank the men on the perceived quality of their ideas ("Best Ideas"), their perceived ability to guide the discussion ("Guidance"), and their personal popularity ("Liked").

As interest was focused on role differentiation, a measure of specialization was needed. This was set up by declaring a man a "specialist" if he held top rank in only one of the five measures mentioned above.

It was found that the commonest form of specialization was to be the Best-liked individual. In thirty of the eighty meetings the best-liked man held top rank only in that characteristic. Statistically this result was highly significant, indicating that "popularity is apparently a relatively specialized achievement."[32]

Closer analysis took into account the differences between those groups which had a high level of internal agreement on the choice of the instrumental leader (high status–consensus) and those which had a low level of internal agreement on this choice (low status–consensus). It was found that when consensus was high, role differentiation was bipartite along the lines already discussed. When, however, there was low status–consensus within the group, there seemed to be a tripartite role differentiation, with an active participator who was neither well liked nor highly rated on task ability, a more passive task specialist who was also not well liked, and a popular individual who was neither active nor highly rated on task ability.

It was found that role differentiation increased with time, being much more highly developed in the last of the four meetings than in the first. At the end of the fourth meeting the participants were asked to rank their fellow members on the criterion of leadership. The purpose of this was to discover which of the former measures fitted most closely to the measure of leadership. It was found that "Guidance" was the characteristic most closely associated with leadership, whereas "Liking" was least closely associated with leadership. This agrees with the other demonstrable fact that the "Idea man" (that is, the instrumental leader) is more likely than the Best-liked man (that is, the expressive leader) to initiate interaction in the task area (Categories 4, 5, and 6), while his affective reactions are more likely to be negative. Conversely, the Best-liked man is more likely to make his contribution in the task area by asking questions. This complementarity of the roles of the two leaders makes it not only possible but also fruitful for them to coexist, and to increase the group's interaction, without mutual antagonism.

An echo of *The Authoritarian Personality* is provided by the attempt to use the F scale to probe into the personality of the participants occupying the different leadership roles. The results were quite promising, but they were not followed up very vigorously. It was, however, shown that the mean F-scale scores for the top men tended to be higher in the low-consensus groups. It also appeared, perhaps surprisingly, that in the case of high-consensus groups the Idea men had significantly lower scores (that is, less authoritarianism) than the Best-liked men. These results suggest to Slater that there is a connection between personal rigidity and any kind of specialization, as specialization is supposedly a feature common to low-consensus groups and to the role of Best-liked man. It is therefore concluded that "the sharper the role differentiation in the group, or the more specialized the role played by the individual, the greater the rigidity in the personality or personalities involved."[33]

It is hypothesized elsewhere that "attribution of Leadership will tend to be associated with prominent performance of highly generalized rather than with highly specialized functions,"[34] and if this belief could be confirmed, it might lead to the conclusion that leaders are somewhat unlikely to have rigid and absolutist personalities. This clearly is not necessarily true, and the discrepancy suggests a certain limitation in the data, perhaps related to the highly atypical groups studied up to this point.

Slater's paper then proceeds to a highly illuminating discussion on the relation between these experimental results and certain other empirical findings. Slater starts with a telling reference to Chester I. Barnard's statement that the survival of any organization depends upon its ability to solve two problems: the achievement of the purposes for which the organization was formed and the satisfaction of the more immediate needs of the members of the organization.[35] In large organizations the latter function is left mainly to the leaders of informal groups. (Cf. Chapter 6 of this book.)

The question arises, Why should it be so rare for a single individual to fill the roles of both instrumental leader and expressive leader? This fact is accounted for at two levels. At the sociological level, the difficulty is seen as being related to the disturbances created in idea and value systems by the need to adapt to external change. It is difficult to achieve technological advance without disturbing social-emotional equilibrium, and some sacrifice of popularity is an almost automatic consequence of the assumption of the role of innovation.

At the psychological level, the choice of role may be determined by personality traits. One man may value popularity very highly and may do anything to avoid controversy and conflict, even seeking the conventional safety of the "average Joe." Another man may suffer a compulsive drive to achieve success in more or less abstract problem solving as a channel for his aggression or to compensate for his inability to respond to the needs of others. The presence in a group of such a person, with his inherent rigidity, may not only inhibit satisfactory problem solving by the group but may also *create* low status-consensus, thus effectively smothering any satisfactory structuring of the group.

Thus there are three characteristic patterns. The first, infrequently found, occurs when one participant is able to fulfill both the instrumental and the expressive requirements of the group. The second is the well-structured group in which, in the absence of an exceptionally talented leader, a satisfactory role differentiation occurs. The third is the low status-consensus group in which sharp and disruptive specialization is precipitated in response not so much to the needs of the group as to the inner personality needs of one or more members. Specialists perform in a particular role because they "have to" rather than because it is useful or desirable. In this third type of group there ceases to be any automatic relation between an individual's amount of participation and his rating on task ability by other members of the group.

He apparently does not adjust his amount of participation to the approval and acceptance he receives, but persists in interacting despite their absence. His participation time is determined by his own aggressiveness, by insensitivity rather than responsiveness to feedback from others.[36]

One of the most fascinating applications of this work and theory is to the case of the nuclear family. As a social system the nuclear family differs from the ephemeral groups thus far discussed in that it is essentially a continuous group, outliving even its participants. But the similarities overshadow the differences. Like any other "problem-oriented group," the family has the task of effecting change in the external environment while maintaining the integration of the group. It therefore needs both instrumental and expressive leadership. As the primary source of gratification to the nursing children the mother is "the more likely expressive focus of the system as a whole,"[37] while the father, as the breadwinner, is expected to manipulate the external environment[38] in the interests of the group. The socialization of the child is brought about by the sometimes threatening pressures of the father reinforced by the expressive role of the mother, whose love is made conditional on the child's acceptance of the joint parental authority. At some stage, however, the maturing child will assume an external as well as an internal role, thus challenging the instrumental leadership to the point at which fission takes place. Conversely, the aging father will gradually relinquish his instrumental roles and sink back into a sometimes plaintive support of things as they are.

The foregoing description is applicable most immediately to the "traditional" nuclear family of the Western world, and it is easy to see why such a family is particularly vulnerable if there is a "weak, ineffectual" father or a "cold, unyielding" mother.[39] It is obviously important, however, to discover how far the generalization stretches, whether it will cover the more extended families encountered in folk societies. In *Family, Socialization and Interaction Process* Morris Zelditch, Jr., analyzes a mass of anthropological data, including the material used by Margaret Mead in *Sex and Tempera-*

ment to examine very nearly the same question. He finds, not surprisingly, that the nuclear family, which in any case exists to some extent in almost all societies, provides the clearest exemplification of the instrumental-expressive dichotomy. He also finds that the line of descent is not crucial, the instrumental leadership being vested in a male even in a matrilineal society; the main difference is that when the nuclear family is well defined, the instrumental leader is the father, whereas when the nuclear family is weakly defined, the instrumental leader may be the mother's brother. Zelditch is not completely convinced by Mead's suggestion that in some societies, such as the Tchambuli, male and female roles are reversed.

Zelditch also asks whether the division of leadership obtains in the more egalitarian modern Western society. He concludes that it does. While father helps mother with the dishes, and mother can supplement income by working outside,

the American male, by definition, *must* "provide" for his family. He is *responsible* for the support of his wife and children. . . . There is simply something wrong with the American adult male who doesn't have a "job." American women, on the other hand, tend to hold jobs *before* they are married and to quit when "the day" comes; or to continue in jobs of a lower status than their husbands.[40]

In spite of democratization all the evidence is that executive decisions are referred to the father, even though this is explained in terms of his "good judgment" rather than of his position of authority. The "henpecked" husband is marked down simply because his executive primacy is not recognized in the home.

Side by side with this extension of the theoretical frontiers, interaction process analysis has yielded dividends in practical fields. As early as March, 1954, Bales contributed to the *Harvard Business Review* an article[41] abounding in practical suggestions for the conduct of a committee meeting. He explains that there will be an optimum balance between positive and negative reactions; he explains the three stages—information pooling, evaluation, suggestion —through which successful problem-solving groups pass. He calls attention to the probable emergence of a social leader as well as a task leader. He concludes with ten "rules of thumb" for success in committee work, which may be summarized as follows:

1. If possible, restrict committees to seven members, so placed that each member can readily communicate directly with every other member.

2. Avoid committees as small as two or three if the power problem between members is likely to be critical.

3. Choose members likely to participate in varying amounts. A group of all high participators will tend to clash, one of all low participators may find themselves short on ideas.

4. Try to include both a task leader and a social leader. If the social leader does not have a light touch, consider including a "humorist." "Difficult" members can be neutralized by creating an otherwise balanced group.

5. Proceed from facts to evaluation and thence to decisions. It is noted that this order is the exact opposite of normal parliamentary procedure.

6. Try to draw out from members a full description of the experiences on which their opinions are based. This helps to reduce disagreements due to verbal differences.

7. When listening, keep indicating your reactions actively. Most people are not much good at reading your mind.

8. Keep your eyes on the group, and not just on one or two special cronies or opponents. Search constantly for reactions to what you are saying. "Nothing tones up the general harmony of a group like a good strong undercurrent of direct eye contact."

9. If disagreement crops up, backtrack to further work on the facts and direct experience.

10. Keep your ear to the ground. Do not become so engrossed in getting the job done that you lose track of good relations between the committee members.

There is no doubt whatsoever that the work started by Bales and his colleagues has had great repercussions in the field of the sociology and psychology of small groups. Not only has the technical apparatus proliferated, but also the ideas have extended in scope and in their applications to real-world situations. Even by 1955, when *Small Groups* was published, it was possible to assemble an impressive first batch of material deriving from the pioneer work and applied to problems ranging from those of psychotherapy groups (whose sessions, not being task-oriented, failed to show the characteristic developmental phasing) to those of bomber crews (which start with a highly structured leadership pattern). Since then the work has expanded in many directions, which have tended to show the great variety of types of group that may be encountered in real life, and have worked toward typologies in terms of groups and individuals. Today any issue of *Sociological Abstracts* is likely to record a number of small group inquiries that owe their provenance to *Interaction Process Analysis*.

Bales, since 1960 director of the Laboratory of Human Relations at Harvard, has declared himself, in *Sociology Today*, reassured by the remarkable accumulation of knowledge in this area. Unlike workers in other fields that are still characterized by an untidy patternless maze of lonely furrows, "the researcher in small groups today can begin his study immeasurably further along than his colleagues of even five years ago. It may turn out that the distinguishing mark of the last five years of development in this field is the degree of accumulation and consolidation that the literature has undergone."[42]

And yet Bales is very conscious that the epitome of science, the capacity to predict and ultimately to control, still eludes the small-group man. Predictions are possible in psephology, for example, largely because the theory involved is simple, avoiding the need to specify the products of numerous and complicated interactions. In the smallest of groups the difficulties of prediction are far greater.

In such situations, what the therapist, leader, or any other interested participant wants to be able to do is to read the signs that appear in the behavior (his own as well as others)—to diagnose accurately what is going on, predict where it is going, and how it will change if he takes a given action—all of this soon enough for him to intervene and try to change the course of events if he deems it desirable.[43]

The drive to achieve this kind of success is still gathering force. Success depends first on learning how to approach and to measure the individual and group characteristics, to match task abilities with task requirements, to gauge the reconciliation of "social reality" with "physical reality." (See Chapter 13.) But even when this immensely difficult objective is in sight, it remains necessary to devise a technique for bringing all these variables simultaneously into the picture. On this point Bales is an optimist, believing that the rapid development of computer simulation methods will at least keep pace with the gathering of data worthy to be fed into the machines. Be that as it may, it cannot be doubted that interaction process analysis provides an exciting means of entry into the territory of social manipulation, and that even partial successes in prediction and control could have untold consequences.

13

THE GROUP DYNAMICS OF A NEW COMMUNITY

It is appropriate to introduce this chapter by a reference to Kurt Lewin, former professor of philosophy and psychology at the University of Berlin and one of the most influential social psychologists of the past twenty years. Like so many other eminent social scientists, Lewin was driven out of Germany by the Nazis and found refuge in the United States. After periods at Cornell University and at the University of Iowa, he was able in 1945 to set up the Research Center for Group Dynamics at Massachusetts Institute of Technology. Shortly afterward he died, and the Research Center moved to the University of Michigan, where it has been ever since. Dorwin Cartwright succeeded Lewin as director and was assisted by three program directors: Ronald Lippitt, a long-standing associate of Lewin; John French; and Leon Festinger, who with H. H. Kelley was the author of the book discussed in this chapter, *Changing Attitudes through Social Contact*.[1]

Lewin died in February, 1947. He was only fifty-seven years old, but it will be generally conceded that in spite of certain difficulties attached to his line of approach he had an abiding influence on the social sciences. Perhaps more than anyone else he had bridged the gap between social psychology and sociology. More than most other social psychologists he held out a hand to sociology.

One reason why his influence is likely to endure, and even to increase, is that he emphasized the need for experimentation. This emphasis was central in his thinking. In one of his papers he wrote:

I am persuaded that it is possible to undertake experiments in sociology which have as much right to be called scientific experiments as those in physics and chemistry. I am persuaded that there exists a social space which has all the essential properties of a real empirical space and deserves as much attention by students of geometry and mathematics as the physical space, although it is not a physical one. The perception of social space and the experimental and conceptual investigation of the dynamics and laws of the processes in social space are of fundamental theoretical and practical importance.[2]

And it was with this idea of the development of social space that Lewin worked out his celebrated conceptual scheme known as "field theory." This theory conceptualizes the impact of the environment on the individual by describing the decisions made by an individual in terms of his "locomotion" under social and psychological pressures acting in an environment described as "social space."

For this formulation, Lewin drew on the analogy of topology—the type of geometry that concerns itself with relationships between objects without paying much attention to measurements of the distances between them. This topological analogy accounts for the scribbles, strange at first sight, that serve as illustrations to Lewin's writings—freehand diagrams consisting of odd shapes that seem to have no significant details. It is perhaps in this spirit that they should be approached; they should be regarded as offering a visual device by which the reader can understand more clearly the ideas the author is aiming to convey.

Certainly in the simpler examples it is not difficult to grasp what is intended. For example, in one of his early classic papers, reproduced in *Resolving Social Conflicts*, Lewin describes differences in the social behavior of Americans and Germans. He illustrates his point with two diagrams, one representing the American, the other the German. Each diagram consists of a series of concentric circles; in each case one circle is thicker than the others. In the case of the German, the thick circle is not far from the periphery; in the case of the American, the thick circle is very near the center. These diagrams are intended to show a distinction between the typical American, who at first appears to be decidedly responsive and outgoing but retains at the core of his personality an impenetrable and private ego, and the typical German, who on first acquaintance presents a hard barrier but fundamentally has a greater capacity for true friendship. Lewin's formulation is interesting not only as a reminder of the European's bewilderment at the apparent contradictions in American behavior but also as a revelation of Lewin's German self-image.

Conceptually, perhaps the most important contribution of field theory is that it emphasizes that pressures are both external (sociological) and internal (psychological), and that the field which determines how the individual will actually behave responds to both these pressures. One of the principles that Lewin shares with the Gestalt psychologists is to refrain from trying to analyze situations in too much detail; it is better to grasp them as wholes.

The other merit of Lewin's diagrammatic approach is its suitability for showing change. Oddly enough, the diagram in Figure 8 in Chapter 12, showing the actor's range of external task achievement within the total situation of a small problem-solving group,

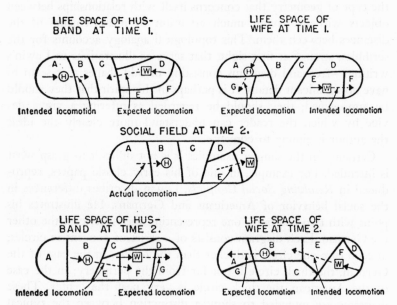

FIGURE 22. The life spaces of a husband and a wife and the social field containing them both. (Reprinted from Kurt Lewin, *Field Theory in Social Science*, edited by Dorwin Cartwright, by permission of Harper & Brothers, Publishers, New York. Copyright 1951 by Harper & Brothers.)

is a good example of the pictorial portrayal of a dynamic situation. It is almost Lewinian, but it is simpler and more axial than most of Lewin's diagrams. Lewin's own illustrations, such as those used to predict the course of a marriage, can become very complicated (see Figure 22). Unless one is constantly engaged in this form of representation, there comes a point when its helpfulness is exhausted. One must be a devotee, it seems, to derive from it everything that Lewin put into it.

But, apart from his field theory, the Lewin's other main preoccupation was his absorbing interest in experimentation, which has already been mentioned. Experiments appealed to him not only theoretically but also in practice. He was fertile in devising experimental designs for testing his ideas. Some of the experiments in which he participated, such as that concerned with the effectiveness of group decisions on the changing of food habits,[3] have become classics.

Although Festinger was closely associated with Lewin at Massachusetts Institute of Technology, where the study described in this chapter was undertaken, the report says very little about Lewin. The only reference is to one of Lewin's best-known studies, "Self-Hatred among Jews."[4]

Although Lewin's influence is discernible,* the ancestry is overtly attributed to others. In this instance the first reference is to a hypothesis of T. M. Newcomb that first appeared in *Human Relations* in 1947:

Members of one group who develop hostility towards members of some other group may be expected to cut off communication with that group. If the group against which the hostility is directed perceives it, they will probably not initiate contacts with the hostile group. Once possibilities for communication between them are removed, the hostile perceptions will be insulated against change.[6]

* More recently, H. H. Kelley, the junior author, has generously expressed his debt to Lewin.

"Acknowledgment should certainly be made of the various persons who have contributed to our intellectual orientation to group psychology. Although their specific concepts do not figure prominently in our present [1959] approach to this field, the attitudes toward research and theory expressed by Kurt Lewin and others of the original Research Center for Group Dynamics at the Massachusetts Institute of Technology form a central and enduring part of our outlook."[5]

Thus the initial hostility on the part of the first group removes any incentive to break down that hostility, so that a permanent insulation of the two groups is likely to ensue. The corollary of Newcomb's hypothesis is that in order to reduce hostility between two such groups one must take the initiative in reopening contacts between them. If this is true, it becomes a matter of considerable practical importance to discover how to renew contacts between groups that have cut themselves off from each other; the groups in question will not necessarily be actively hostile to each other, but they will be on neutral or distant terms or will try to ignore each other's existence.

Before examining the practical details of this study, we should look at the theoretical orientation, which on this occasion actually did precede the rather slight, simple, and straightforward empirical experiment needed to test the theory. The starting point was an elaboration of the Newcomb hypothesis. The initial issue concerned "the psychological situation of the low-status group member" and was covered by three related hypotheses.

The first hypothesis was: "Through contacts with the high-status group, the low-status person becomes aware of the limitations involved in his present group membership." The point to be noted about this statement is that, if the contacts do not exist, the low-status person is not aware of what he is missing. The privileges attached to a higher status will be observable to him only if he is to some extent exposed to members of the higher-status group, and it is under these conditions that he will tend to feel underprivileged and deprived. There was already much literature on this point. For example, Allison Davis had shown that as long as there is full segregation of children, as has been true in the Southern states, the low-status person—in that case the Southern Negro child—will be protected from the sense of deprivation. Of course, this protection acts only as a postponement; later in life, when the low-status person goes out to work in a subordinate position, he may suffer an even greater shock when he realizes how inescapably low in status he is.

The second hypothesis is: "Members of the low-status group desire to attain membership in the high-status group." This was expected to apply as a general rule, as there is a strong impulse to seek the privileges associated with high status, but other possible reactions caused by loyalty to a low-status in-group, or by apathy or despair, are recognized.

The third hypothesis points to the existence of a limiting factor: "There are restraints upon the member of the low-status group against leaving his group and entering the dominant group." Two restraining influences are here postulated. The first is the restraint from within—in the form of group loyalties that undoubtedly exist to some extent in all low-status groups. It seems likely, however, that these loyalties are normally very much overshadowed by the external restraints imposed by the dominant group in order to restrict their membership. The authors add:

There is little doubt that blunt rejections are early experiences in the lives of members of low-status groups and that they soon learn to anticipate rejection with the result that they give up any and all attempts to change their social position.[7]

In other words, they may give up trying to break into a high-status group and will rationalize their withdrawal from this struggle, by claiming, for example, their belief in the importance of class solidarity in order to avoid the pain that, as they had previously learned, followed attempts to join the dominant group. While it is true that the internal restraint may lead to a personal dilemma between the desire to rise and the sense of loyalty to the group, it may be expected that external restraints on advancement are even more powerful sources of personal maladjustment.

Following these first three points, which are concerned with the psychological situation of the low-status group member, the authors turn to a second set of five points concerned with the consequences of the low-status person's situation. These points describe either the solutions that he will find or the almost inevitable results of his situation.

Thus, his first tendency will be to take over many of the values of the high-status group. This hypothesis is supported by a number of investigations showing, for example, that within a Negro community the color preferences of whites have been taken over by Negroes and form part of their own evaluation of social status, the paler Negroes being generally regarded as of higher status.

A second consequence is that the low-status person is liable to become hostile toward his group. This was illustrated in Kenneth and Mamie Clark's famous experiment[8] in which three- to seven-year-old Negro children typically preferred white dolls, describing the brown doll as ugly or bad-looking. It is also noticeable that, possibly for the same reason, in Harlem and other similar neighborhoods, the wax models in the beauty salons and the clothing stores are all white.

Another example quoted is of an experiment by Radke,[9] who found that as they grew older, Jewish children tended increasingly to associate negative qualities with Jews.

Although some of these experiments have been criticized in respect of the methods used, the cumulative evidence is overwhelmingly in support of the belief that minority groups do try to take over the values of dominant groups. In psychoanalytic terms this behavior would be explained as an example of the introjection of aggressive feelings. It is a very plausible idea; one must blame someone for one's frustration, and if one cannot hate the external enemy, there may be a transformation into hate of one's own group.

Various examples of this effect have been given in previous chapters. In both *The Polish Peasant* (Chapter 3) and *The Gold Coast and the Slum* (Chapter 4), for example, attention was called to the rejection of parents by second-generation immigrants.

A third possible consequence of a subordinate situation is that the low-status person will move into the more privileged group if he is able to do so. In so doing he typically tries to avoid being identified with the low group and reduces further contact with them. This effect is easily recognized. An upwardly mobile person must not only acquire certain characteristics and habits that are the symbols of the dominant high-status group, such as money and education and fancy clothes, but must also reject certain characteristics and habits from his past, such as speech or behavior habits that betray his low-status origin. It is a reasonable hypothesis that he will cut down contacts with the low-status group because they might suggest to his new group that he was not completely emancipated from his origins.

In *Street Corner Society* (Chapter 7) the story of Chick Morelli and his College Boys provides a classic example of a group trying to break away from their origins, and in the process selecting higher-status associates from among non-Italians in preference to the male companions, girl friends, and work associates that they might have drawn upon from their own circle. Such people will avoid bringing their higher-status friends to their parental home. In extreme cases they will themselves leave home, not primarily because of conflicts and arguments but as a deliberate policy of rejection.

The next possible consequence of low status is perhaps equally important, but it embodies what might be described as a working-class form of social mobility as opposed to the previous course of action, which might be said to represent a middle-class viewpoint. In this case the low-status person may embark upon a program of improving his group in order to make his situation and that of his peers more tolerable. Such a man is trying, not to escape from his group, but to raise his whole group to a higher status. In a sense this is what Doc, of *Street Corner Society*, was doing, though not very vigorously. The last thing that Doc would contemplate was to desert his group, but, to the extent that he had a conscious purpose, it was perhaps to make life better for his companions.

It is suggested by Festinger and Kelley that people who adopt the policy of trying to improve their group are found more frequently among low-status people who have little possibility of what the authors call "locomotion" (Lewin's term) into the dominant group. It may be supposed that members of "visible" minorities, such as Negroes, who cannot move undetectedly into a higher-status group, might be more likely to adopt this policy of attempting to raise the status of their whole group.

Two slightly different goals seem to be involved. One goal is the self-improvement of the low-status group so that the dominant group will drop its negative evaluation of the low-status group. This is perhaps an unrealistic goal in that it is based on the assumption that the dominant group's rejection operates on a rational plane. The second goal is therefore probably more realizable; this is the mobilization of the subgroup into a position to win privileges and greater equality of treatment from the dominant group. For instance, a labor-union organizer does this when he mobilizes his workmen, not to secure general upward mobility into a dominant group, but by means of mass action to wrest certain concessions from the dominant group. Such concessions are seldom made freely by the dominant group because thereby they would lose to some extent privileges (relative advantages) they presently enjoy. This is therefore a classical situation that leads to some kind of struggle. Tempers will be frayed, whereas in individual upward mobility all is politeness and civility.

Failure for the lower group in these circumstances is quite common, and as a result the group that has not succeeded in raising itself may suffer from a sense of failure, so that morale may drop even lower than before. Furthermore, the frictions between the dominant group and the lower group will have been accentuated by the attempt at a mass rise, and the dominant group will be confirmed in the belief that the lower group are unco-operative. The concept of the "good," submissive Negro was discussed in *An American Dilemma*, and the authors here adduce further experimental evidence from an intensive study of middle-class Negro girls in which Brenman[10] found a high degree of intra-group hostility resulting from abortive attempts at self-improvement.

The final consequence of the situation in which the low-status person finds himself is that the frustration and conflict resulting from the failure to rise can bring about serious personality disturbances. This effect is supported by some quantitative studies which have shown that certain types of mental and emotional disturbance are more common in low-status groups.

It will thus be seen that hostility and conflict are very possible consequences of the uncertainty created by status interactions. One very awkward fact is that the hostile attitudes generated in inter-group relations tend to be highly stable and resistant to change, since they are strongly supported by the general situation. Following Krech and Crutchfield, the authors suggest several sources of stability in antagonistic social attitudes. The first are what they call the "internal motivational supports, which consist of repressed, frustrated and socially unacceptable need structures."[11] The second and third are the supports in the external world, consisting of "observable objects, events and relationships" and "the beliefs and attitudes of other people." All these will have a certain persistence that will consequently help to stabilize unfavorable social attitudes.

Given this inconvenient stability, it must be considered how such hostile attitudes can be broken down. In relation to personality, we have only to refer to the lessons of *The Authoritarian Personality* (Chapter 11) to remember how deep-rooted certain characteristics can be. It will, moreover, be recalled that the authors of *The Authoritarian Personality* were a little uncertain as to how to divert prejudiced personalities from antisocial channels. They suggested that if authoritarian personalities could be individually psycho-analyzed, it might be possible to dispose of their undesirable charac-teristics, but they recognized that this was not a practical procedure —if only because it would be very expensive in analysts' time—and they fell back on certain less convincing methods of breaking down the incidence of such prejudice in society as a whole.

If the method of *motivational control* seems unpromising, the same must be said of what can be called the method of *perceptual control*. The policy behind this method is based on the idea that hostile attitudes are the consequence of faulty or incomplete cog-nition and that therefore all that is needed to correct hostile attitudes is to confront the people in question with new sources of infor-mation. This idea is strongly held in some quarters, but Festinger and Kelley convincingly explain why it is very doubtful that this type of intervention will be effective. Their argument is the straight-forward one that a person's perceptions are as much regulated by his attitudes as his attitudes are by his perceptions. Whether the attitudes or the facts come first, there is abundant evidence that people tend to expose themselves to experiences that will support their attitudes and to retreat from experiences that will call their attitudes in question. This has been demonstrated in various studies concerned with such different issues as response to propaganda, first impressions of new social contacts, and the learning and forgetting of controversial material. Even though the intention and meaning of some particular act may seem to be perfectly obvious to the detached observer, if this is not in conformity with the preconcep-tions of the participant, the message may be entirely missed or garbled.

So the problem of changing attitudes by perceptual control is how to bypass the individual's selective perceptions, "to force the person to experience facts contrary to his attitudes, to push him into situations he would normally avoid, and to assure the presentation of experiences of such structural coherence and figural properties that they will resist distortion."[12] But, of course, as the authors point out, this is extremely difficult to achieve. Even if you do confront a person with factual information and experiences that should "logi-cally" change his attitudes, he will still retain his capacity to inter-pret the information and evaluate the experiences in the manner he wishes; and for this reason the effort does not have the intended result. In fact, Festinger and Kelley go so far as to say that "it seems doubtful theoretically whether information (as it is mediated) or knowledge (after it is internalized) ever has any *necessary* implications for a person's attitudes."[13] And this is the abiding limitation of perceptual control; if one tries to change attitudes by instilling facts, one will always come up at some point against the barrier of perceptual resistance. As was shown, for example, in *The Authoritarian Personality*, every experience can be twisted somehow to be a further confirmation of the rightness of the person's prejudices. Prejudice is a state of mind that cannot be penetrated by rational argument.

Having thus eliminated the methods of motivational control and perceptual control, the authors reach the conclusion that the only method left is to bring the person into social contact with people whose evaluations or attitudes differ from his own. This is called the method of *social control*, which lays stress not on information itself but on what other people think about it—how they *evaluate* it, interpret it, what attitudes they hold about it. The authors point out that to be most effective social control entails two processes, one designed to expose the person to the requisite fresh attitudes, and the other to cut him off in some way from the old attitudes. It is clearly not easy to achieve these two aims simultaneously. It is necessary first somehow to curtail the individual's existing social contacts with the persons and groups that were reinforcing his present attitudes; then, when his need for social supports drives him to make fresh social contacts, it must be arranged that his new circle of contacts is such as can be relied upon to express the requisite attitudes.*

One obvious difficulty is that the person's perceptions about other people's attitudes could be as distorted as his perceptions of other events and facts. This is a very interesting possibility, but the authors believe that it will rarely be found because the essence of social life is conformity with the social norms of one's particular

---

* C.f. Lewin's suggestion[14] "The effectiveness of camps or workshops in changing ideology or conduct depends in part on the possibility of creating . . . "cultural islands" during change. The stronger the accepted subculture of the workshop and the more isolated it is the more will it minimize that type of resistance to change which is based on the relation between the individual and the standards of the larger group."

circle. Failure to share norms with others entails cutting oneself off from people, which is psychologically a much more serious step than distorting or misusing information. The individual needs to conform to group standards to give him an anchorage for his own attitudes, and he cannot afford to be unrealistic about the social values of his chosen social group. Otherwise he exposes himself to the danger that they will reject him and that he will have no group affiliation left.

Indeed, it would seem that the most powerful determinants of attitudes are the standards and norms of groups in which people have membership. These "reference" groups help determine the formation of attitudes and, once formed, provide an anchorage for them.[15]

This underlines the importance of discovering what persons or groups will be the "reference group" for a given individual.

It should be noted in passing that the phrase "reference group" is here used by the authors in a rather narrow sense. They are here referring to what is normally called a "membership group," which is a special type of reference group to which the individual in question actually belongs. The whole range of possible reference groups, as will be discussed later, includes groups of which the individual is not a member and even groups about which he has little accurate information.

METHOD OF PROCEEDING

We may now turn to the practical details of the study. The authors set out to make a direct and experimental intervention in the life of a selected community to ascertain whether the attitudes of its members could be modified toward a better perception of their own status so that they might interact more comfortably with the town in which the community was located. Thus for the first time in the present book the design of the inquiry is deliberately experimental.

The study was located in "Baytown," an old New England town of some 30,000 inhabitants. It was a rather dispersed, economically stagnant town which suddenly regained much of its earlier importance during World War II because of the presence of a large

Naval installation. It was estimated that at some time or other during the war 60 per cent of the wage earners in Baytown had worked in the shipyards. Ecologically it does not appear to have been a very well-organized place; it seems to have had no one center but to have been divided into five separate neighborhoods. It was a town of few extremes, with neither great wealth nor poverty—rather above-average middle-class, with most people living in their own single-family houses. Predominantly Republican, the town was resentful of Federal interference, a fact that has a bearing on the present study.

The study was concentrated in a quite small project, here called "Regent Hill," consisting of only a hundred dwellings—seventy-two semidetached and twenty-eight single-family—which had been built in 1942 under the auspices of the Federal Housing Administration. The survey began in January, 1947, and the book was published in 1951.

This little housing project of Regent Hill occupies four square blocks in the center of the most northerly of the five neighborhoods in Baytown. It is in no way physically separated from the rest of the neighborhood, being bounded by ordinary streets. It was built very rapidly, being started a few months after Pearl Harbor to provide urgently needed housing for the shipyard workers. At the end of the war, work in the shipyard declined sharply, and by the date of the study, 1947, only 12 per cent of the Regent Hill residents were still working in the shipyard. Furthermore, only 40 per cent of the families then on the project were survivors from the original residents.

The report includes a brief history of the slightly checkered early days of this housing project. The Government first approached the Baytown Board of Selectmen in April, 1941, but the opposition to the project was so bitter that the plan was apparently shelved. After Pearl Harbor, however, it was put through as a crash program, and with the United States then at war nobody was inclined to continue opposition to the project. During 1942 the original plan for 50 dwellings was expanded to 100 dwellings.

These historical facts were pieced together from the newspapers of 1941 and 1942 and from an informal interview given in 1947 by the man who had been chairman of the Board of Selectmen in 1941–42. The current "official" attitudes toward the project in 1947 were obtained by interviewing twenty-eight community leaders. Extracts from four of these interviews included in the report suggest that although by 1947 the general tone was neutral, there was still a slight feeling among the community leaders that the project families were interlopers.

The investigators also undertook an initial sample interview survey of 200 residents of streets in the neighborhood of the project. In contrast with the residual feeling of the community leaders that the scheme had been rather imposed upon them, it was found that the other families in the neighborhood were to a remarkable extent indifferent to the whole scheme. Only about one-half of those living in the immediate vicinity were sufficiently aware of the project to recall its existence. Only 20 per cent of the total sample had any views on the project, and although two-thirds of these were against it, they expressed no great interest in the project as a whole, either for or against. When asked about the individual persons living on the project, 43 per cent had nothing to say, but the majority of those that expressed themselves were tolerant toward them, checking either "They are ordinary people" or even "They are wonderful people." It is therefore reasonable to point to a slight contrast between the community leaders, who were faintly hostile, and the ordinary townspeople, who were apathetic and neutral.

We turn next to the population of the project itself. Sociologically the population was rather typical of the town as a whole. If anything, their demographic characteristics were slightly superior to those of the town—the project had slightly more than its share of supervisory and clerical workers and slightly fewer unemployed. Definitely more respondents had had a high-school education or better than in the rest of the town, possibly because, as in many housing projects of this kind, the population was younger than in most communities. Also typically, the families were larger than average.

The book gives no general information on ethnic origin. This is rather surprising in view of the importance of ethnic origin in fomenting hostilities and in determining status.*

We now come to the reason for the choice of Regent Hill as the site for this study. Although they were tolerated and ignored by

* It will be noted later that Mrs. C., the active resident who was accused of being a Communist, was Jewish.

their neighbors, and although their occupational and educational status was at least as high as that of their neighbors, the residents of Regent Hill had come to believe that they were members of a low-status group, and that people outside the project regarded them as such and would repel any advances. When asked in the initial interview, "How do you get on with the townspeople?," a considerable minority of the project residents replied that the townspeople disliked the project and its residents, feeling that they were "low class." At one point or another in the interview 45 per cent of the project residents said that they were disliked or looked down upon by the townspeople.

At the other end of the scale, only 24 per cent of the project residents gave evidence of possessing specific friends in the town, while 24 per cent indicated that they were entirely without friends or acquaintances off the project. In the absence of comparative figures it is difficult to judge whether this is an unusually low friendship rate. Many community studies undertaken in England in recent years have suggested that the idea of "having friends" is not nearly so widespread as is sometimes supposed. On British housing projects the residents have neighbors, who live literally next door or near by, and relatives, who also may have lived very close before the residents at the new housing project moved there and who still are seen quite regularly. Both of these are functionally useful—the neighbor to borrow a loaf of bread from and the relative for more intimate forms of assistance. Friendships in the middle-class, shared-interest sense are much less common. If, as seems likely, the general pattern is the same in Baytown as in British housing estates, the absence of friends off the project is not so surprising.

It is more impressive to discover that 40 per cent of the residents belonged neither to clubs nor to churches, for this shows a considerable degree of social isolation. The comparable figure for the townspeople was only 11 per cent, so the project residents are very significantly more isolated in this respect. This fact and their verbalized belief that outsiders looked down on them make it appear that they were indeed a low-status group.

So the next consideration is whether this perception of low status was reflected in the internal social life of the project. The first question was included to determine how project residents felt toward one another. This evoked the rather serious result that 62 per cent of the informants on the project thought their neighbors were low class and undesirable. This is an example of self-hatred in a low-status group. The hostility extended to attitudes about children in the project—there must have been rather a spate of children—33 per cent said that there were too many children or that the children were bad, 23 per cent said that their children acquired bad habits from others, and a further 23 per cent said that their neighbors' children were low-class. These responses may overlap to some extent, but obviously many residents had some rude comments to make about neighboring families, an attitude that does not point to very good internal morale.

The second indication of poor community spirit is that not many had active social contacts even on the project. Only 35 per cent said they had friends on the project, and 20 per cent said they did not even have acquaintances on the project. As many as 37 per cent never invited friends to their homes. Here again, in the absence of comparable figures, it may be that formal invitations were not so common as the habit of dropping in, but even so the percentage appears rather high. And another indicator—60 per cent had met nobody new in the project during the previous two to three months; that suggests some stagnation in their already weak acquaintanceship pattern.

As the result of this review the authors felt justified in concluding that the low-status syndrome that they had suspected was indeed present in Regent Hill. Their next step was to attempt what they call a psychological analysis of the syndrome in the effort to explain how the hostility, isolation, and perceptions of rejection developed.

The first question was how the residents were selected and what expectations they had of their future neighbors. It was found that these people characteristically regarded themselves as having been forced into living on the project because of unusual circumstances. They thought that the circumstances which had brought their neighbors to the project were normal, but that the circumstances which had brought them there were unusual; for example, they had to work in the district and were therefore merely slumming it until they could get out. In respect of their neighbors, they arrived with the anticipation that the project would be tenanted by undesirable or low-class people, and this led them not to experiment with making contacts with them.

The next question was whether this lack of contact contributed to the persistence of their hostile attitudes. It was found that they moved into the project expecting to be hostile to their neighbors, and they did not put themselves in a position to change their views concerning their neighbors because they were so highly cautious as to the people they met on the project. They had no warm feelings toward people merely because they were fellow members of the project.

The third finding was that the hostile attitudes, once generated, persisted because there was no natural means of breaking them down. Residents took it for granted as a matter of habit that the people they saw on the project were low-class and undesirable, and so they kept away from them.

The fourth issue is concerned with what the authors call the relation of the residents' own attitudes with their perceptions of the attitudes of outsiders. Having decided in their own minds that the project consisted of low-class people, residents might be expected to believe that the people in the town as a whole thought the same. Unfortunately the first interview had no specific questions on this point, but it is of some interest that six people volunteered the opinion that outsiders were prejudiced against the project, and all of them also expressed the feeling that their neighbors were low-class, whereas nobody that did not mention low-class neighbors thought that the town as a whole was prejudiced against the project.

It may be mentioned in passing that the samples were very small, and some of the results quoted are not statistically significant. This last result is significant only at the 6 per cent level, which would be criticized as inadequate by most advocates of significance testing. In that particular case the authors repeated this point in a later survey, and the further data brought the significance down to the 3 per cent level. Even that is not entirely respectable, but the uncertainty is inevitable with such small samples.

The fifth finding is concerned with the relation between the residents' perception of town attitudes and the extent of their contacts with townspeople. Because the residents believed that they were likely to be rejected by the townspeople, they kept away from them and therefore had no opportunity to vary their perception of the townspeople's attitudes. If they had met the town, the residents would have discovered that the townspeople were in fact not so hostile as they feared. Contacts were further curtailed by the fact that residents avoided the normal mechanism for meeting new acquaintances through their own neighbors; in order to avoid being identified with the project, people would try to make contacts in the town in a more circuitous way.

THE ACTIVITY PROGRAM

These sets of facts lead naturally to a general conclusion that the "hostile-isolation" syndrome is fostered because of the residents' a priori unfavorable expectations concerning their neighbors. And so the authors set out to devise an experimental activity program specially aimed at breaking down these expectations. Although the ultimate objective was to improve contacts between the project and the town, Festinger and Kelley proposed to bring this about by improving the internal contacts on the project itself. Theoretical analysis had led the authors to believe that this would raise the morale of residents by their improved perception of their own status and of the townspeople's attitudes toward them. It was hoped that this would lead in turn to their becoming better integrated with the town. It is interesting to speculate that if the authors had been concerned solely to achieve community integration, they might have been better advised to concentrate on knitting the project residents into the life of the town, which should not have been very difficult in so small a place.

We now turn to the details of the activity program. Skilled community workers were hired and were given the task of working out, in conjunction with the project residents, an activity program designed to increase contacts among the project residents themselves. The community workers naturally wanted to bring the residents into town activities, but it was explained to them that the program mapped out for them was part of the experimental design and that they must work within that design. The community workers also acted as data collectors, keeping detailed descriptions of the day-to-day developments of the activity program and gathering information on the contacts, friendships, and attitudes among the project residents as revealed in their behavior and conversations.

At the same time the first two sets of interviews were undertaken. One set was administered to a random sample of 60 project residents, the other to 200 townspeople in the adjacent areas.

In the course of the complete activity program four sets of each of these interviews were undertaken; on each occasion a fresh sample was drawn. Overlapping could be avoided as far as the town sample was concerned, but it was not fully possible in the case of the project sample because there were only 100 families there. Oddly enough, by this design the investigators sacrificed what could have been a valuable feature of this material. If they had adopted what Lazarsfeld has named the "panel technique," returning to the same sample on each successive occasion, they could have watched the direct development of these chosen families, who at the same time would have provided a representative sample of the population as a whole.

The activities devised by the community workers comprised almost the first program of the kind to be developed on the housing project, although the project had been on the site more than four years. There had been a tenants' committee in existence that made a few desultory attempts to get activities under way—children's parties on special holidays and occasional dances—but there had been complaints that it was "always the same people who ran things," and the program had not been particularly successful. Thus the action program started in a general climate of pessimism on the part of the project residents, who could not believe that anything could be successfully started.

The activity program was divided into three periods. The first period ran for eleven weeks, from January 29 till April 15, 1947. The program was launched with a community-wide meeting. Although this meeting had been extensively advertised and carefully planned, only thirty-five of about two hundred adults on the project showed up. A representative from the Federal Public Housing Authority introduced the community worker, who began by suggesting certain projects in which these people might be interested, including a nursery school, a recreation program for school-age children, and various adult educational and recreational activities. The meeting set up three action committees, one to make plans for each of these proposed activities. A considerable number of women were drawn in, but at this stage only two men were persuaded to help.

Unfortunately resistances toward the activity program began to grow during the period of preliminary work. The pessimistic attitude proved very difficult to dispel, and the residents could not believe that anything could really get started in a project like this. There was some criticism about the conduct of the large meeting, focused on the silence of the experts and on the irrelevance of a movie that had been shown as a lure. There were also complaints about the proposals the action committees were working out. The earlier tenants' committee still existed, but it was more or less moribund. Its chairman was very dubious about the new development and succeeded in conveying his feelings to the other key people of the old leadership. Other people began to voice suspicions about the motives of the experts who were taking such an interest in the project, and they found it strange that the experts all came from the same educational institution. And then the secretary of the tenants' committee began to be openly obstructive; on two occasions she called off scheduled committee meetings.

In spite of these disruptive effects the first three action committees were becoming enthusiastic and were working out ambitiously constructive schemes. But tensions were obviously building up between the far-reaching aims of these new planning committees and the resistances to change that were increasingly showing themselves. One understandable reason was that the status of the old and rather inactive leaders was under threat from the new setup, which had been superimposed without much consultation with the established leadership.

Then suddenly the blow fell. The old leaders counterattacked and stopped all activities; they still controlled the community hall in which the new activities took place, and they exercised their legal power to stop these activities. Their grounds for doing so were that Mrs. C., who had become very active on the nursery-school program, was an "avowed Communist." On the strength of these "proven facts" the old leaders succeeded in persuading the local committee to drop the activities.

One of the key people in this crisis was the project manager. He had been put in charge of the project by the Federal Public Housing Authority, but he had been deliberately kept in the dark about the circumstances of the activity program, and could therefore not reassure these people or allay their genuine suspicion that this was some kind of Communist plot. The community worker had not informed him because of his initial hostility toward community activities, but events showed that it would have been wiser to explain the situation to him at the start.

The secretary of the tenants' committee, who had denounced Mrs. C. as a Communist, was able to produce sinister evidence, partly because she happened to live next door to Mrs. C. and had kept her under observation. Other neighbors seem to have interpreted past acts, which they had not fully understood at the time, as further evidence of a Communist plot. For example, Mrs. C. had become very friendly with the community worker. The true reason for this friendship was that they were both very enthusiastic about developing the nursery-school activities, but the accepted explanation was that Mrs. C. and the community worker were in collusion and that Mrs. C. had succeeded in introducing this particular community worker into the project for her own nefarious ends.

Also, the community worker had offered to provide temporarily the funds for a nursery-school teacher, which of course were thought to be Moscow gold. The fact that the money would be coming from the research funds had for obvious reasons not been disclosed.

Others recalled the movie that had been shown at the first general meeting, and on reflection it seemed to them that many of the incidents had been Red propaganda. The music (actually by Aaron Copland) now seemed to have "sounded Russian." Even the fact that the movie was shown at the end rather than at the beginning of the community meeting was thought to have been a Communist maneuver to prevent discussion. Actually the projector had broken down at the beginning of the meeting.

In their report the authors ask themselves three questions about the reasons for the inception and growth of the rumor. First, what functions did the rumor serve? Second, what roles did people play in its origin and spread? Third, what determined the nature of its content?

Functionally, to answer the first question, this rumor was thought somehow to have filled the gap created by the fact that the experimenters had quite unnecessarily kept people in ignorance of their intervention, with the result that everyone was seeking some explanation of the fresh external interest in the community affairs. This was coupled with the threat to the old leadership, which was undeniably real, and then in some way this threat had been identified with the then widely held belief in a Red menace. This had the usual effect: anyone who expressed doubt that there was a Red plot would in turn be accused of being a Red. Furthermore, the resistances to the rumor and to the consequent stopping of the activities were somehow undermined by the prevailing climate of pessimism, which even the extremely active program had not yet dispersed. People who thought that their neighbors were of a "low type" could not believe that anything could be started on the project, and the stopping of the activities thus in a sense confirmed their beliefs.

On the second question, role playing, it is evident that there had to be a scapegoat, and Mrs. C. seems to have fitted quite well into that role. She had previously been rather aloof and inactive on the project, and she suddenly burst forth when the new activities started; furthermore, the circumstance that she was Jewish increased her suitability as a scapegoat. Just as there was one main scapegoat, so there was one active instigator, her next-door neighbor, the secretary of the tenants' committee; and it is striking how well this woman was able to develop and propagate the rumor. Then, too, there were her passive supporters, who did not want to oppose the rumor lest they themselves be labeled Reds. Probably, too, they rather enjoyed the excitement of helping unearth a Red plot. But it should be noted that there was no concerted hostile action: deplorably the majority of the residents on the project never questioned the flimsy evidence on which the rumor was based.

The authors do not fully consider the third question, what determined the nature of the content of this rumor and how it became linked with the issue of Communism. Perhaps they thought it self-evident that Communism would be the natural tag at that date.

The experimenters did take fairly prompt action to combat the rumor. First, as they should probably have done at the beginning, they gave the residents detailed information about the experiment and its sponsorship. The principles of action research suggest that they would have lost nothing if they had done this at the start.

Second, they took another step which they might very well have taken at an earlier stage: they brought the old-established leaders into the picture as much as possible. It had been an obvious tactical error merely to ignore the chairman and the other officials of the tenants' committee; when these were brought in they became stanch supporters of the new program.

Third, by working both through regional management and directly with the local project manager the experimenters won the latter's support for the new program.

We can only conclude at this point that the experimenters learned by trial and error certain elementary practical details about conducting field studies which they should have known before they started. It is probably always necessary in such circumstances in some way to mollify all the active participants in the situation at all levels—the administrative and executive level, the local informal leadership level, and the level of the people whose actions one is directly going to affect.

The fourth step the experimenters took was to isolate the one irreconcilable opponent, the secretary of the tenants' committee, who was still intent on opposition.

Although these measures were effective, it had to be admitted that a very serious setback had occurred, and that the *status quo* could not easily be restored. The pessimism of the tenants as to the possibilities of community action was further confirmed, and any restarting of the activities had to be done in a very cautious and time-consuming way. Instead of the projected program the community worker concentrated on holding demonstration programs showing what could be done if nursery schools and school-age recreation facilities were to be provided.

The community worker also started a teen-age program which provided all the usual youth activities, run largely by the young people themselves. Attempts to resume adult activities were unsuccessful during this period, but an advisory committee of tenants and research workers was set up to obviate further difficulties and also to afford the local body a general overview of the welfare of the project.

The first period of the activity program thus ended in a situation slightly better than had obtained at the height of the rumor. During the second period, the 10½ weeks from April 16 to June 29, the situation improved. The nursery school was put on a regular basis with ten sessions a week, and four planning sessions were held to prepare a permanent setup for the school-age program. There were attempts at fund raising, but the prevailing response was pessimistic. A dance was adjudged successful, but only twenty-five people turned out, so that it could not have raised much money. The teenage program just survived but was not very active. The men began to show some interest. A softball team began hopefully but did not develop very vigorously.

The third period of the activity program, lasting the 11½ weeks from June 30 through September 21, was devoted to preparations for handing over the leadership and initiative from the experimenters and the community worker to the project people themselves. Steps were taken to explain to the residents that the research was about to end, and the attempt was made to develop in them a realistic appreciation of the effort they would have to put forth when the experimenters were withdrawn, and specifically to transfer responsibility to the project people and to train them in the skills they lacked.

The nursery school seemed to be settling down, and it was obviously filling a functional need. The school-age program was not properly emancipated from the community worker, and its future remained doubtful. The teen-agers were able to look after themselves, and their program was very well sustained. Leadership-training courses, with role-playing demonstrations of good and poor techniques, seemed to have been of value. As scheduled, the community workers withdrew on September 21.

So much for the activity program. In order to ascertain what it had achieved the investigators first made an analysis of the actual attendance records. This showed that as between Period I and Period III of the activity program there had been a modest increase (from 39 per cent to 50 per cent of all the women in the project) in the attendance of women and a striking increase (from 2 per cent to 43 per cent of all the men in the project) in the attendance of men. The main increase occurred between Period I and Period II. Taking the whole period, the activities attracted about one-half of all the project people, there being a somewhat higher proportion of men than of women. Most meetings were small, four-fifths of them attracting ten or fewer people and a very low proportion attracting more than twenty people, but analysis showed that the opportunities for interpersonal contacts steadily increased during the activity program.

As has already been mentioned, sample interview surveys were conducted on four occasions, before, during, and at the end of the activity program. The results of these surveys make it possible to determine the extent to which the program contributed to inter-action among the project people. Analysis shows that for those who directly participated the activity program was a salient feature in the residents' social lives and an important means of fostering new friendships.

The people were also questioned about the success of the activi-ties generally, and at the end of the activity program, of the partici-pation groups (that is, the half that had been participating) 95 per cent thought that this activity program had been a success; and 75 per cent of the people who had had nothing to do with the program also thought that it had been a success. Thus, the bitterness which had been rampant at the end of Period I was quite well forgotten by the end of Period III. Several people volunteered the opinion that the success was in the social content of the activities rather than in their more functional content. They stressed the social value of bringing people together and helping them to make friends.

However, although the majority felt that the program had been a success, there was a substantial minority who had participated but had reacted unfavorably to the experience, and a third group who had avoided any participation. The next stage of the analysis was to compare the attitudes of these three groups, which are described in brief as "favorable contact," "unfavorable contact," and "no con-tact," respectively.

One of the facts that emerge quite clearly from this second anal-ysis is that those who were favorable had for the most part joined the program rather early, whereas those who had joined in the later periods had probably been urged by the community worker to participate, with the result that they tended to be reluctant, "un-favorable contacts." Although the latter participated in the activities, they did not enjoy them, and their participation may even have done more harm than good.

It will be remembered that in the initial interview survey, most of those questioned felt that their neighbors were of low status. The subsequent surveys showed that these feelings were not systemati-cally changed as a result of the activity program. Furthermore, the feeling that others in the project were "not co-operative" was in

fact increased. This was particularly noticeable among the participants, who presumably felt that co-operation was very important.
They became very much annoyed with neighbors who refused to
attend the meetings they had been trying to arrange. At this point
there is a marked divergence between the "favorable contacts,"
whose complaints of nonco-operation tended to diminish as the program continued, and the "unfavorable contacts," whose complaints
reached the staggering figure of 82 per cent.

The third finding was that the percentage describing their project
neighbors as "nice neighbors" increased with the "favorable contact"
group and decreased steadily with the "unfavorable contact" group,
who became more and more hostile to neighbors. This is what one
might expect if the judgments were based on experiences gained
in the course of the activity program.

It thus becomes apparent that a real divergence in experiences
and attitudes had been taking place. On the other hand, the views of
the "no contact" people had hardly changed throughout the survey.
Those that had initially had hostile attitudes retained their hostile
attitudes; those that had initially had reasonably favorable attitudes
retained their favorable attitudes. In spite of this they were quite
detached from participation in the activities; they merely said, "I
think the program is very good, but I am not going to have anything to do with it." The "favorable contact" group, who had had
satisfactory experiences in the activity program, however, became
markedly less hostile to the project as a whole. They tended to revise
their views as to the status of the project families and consequently
began to have more confidence in themselves as members of a good
neighborhood. On the other hand, the "unfavorable contact" group
became more hostile, because of their unsatisfactory experiences, and
tended to feel more positive that the people around them were of
low status. Furthermore, satisfaction with their home increased for
the "favorable contact" group and declined very slightly for the other
two groups. This decline was not very marked, and for some reason
the general effect of the activity program was that people on average became somewhat better satisfied with their homes.

Those who had had some contact with the activity program,
whether their experience had been favorable or unfavorable, were
not found to have modified their usual reluctance to invite people
into their homes in spite of participating in the activities. All "con-

tacts" had about the same number of visitors as before, but the "favorable contacts" drew their visitors from a larger number of neighbors, so that the program had the effect of giving them a wider circle of acquaintances on the project.

The next major question was whether there had been any substantial change in relations between the project people and the townspeople. In the case of the "favorable contacts" the results fit nicely into the expectation that greater contacts with other project people would reduce their belief that the townspeople despised them. They showed an increased interest in activities off the project; furthermore, they thought that people on the project both *should* and *did* take some part in town activities. The former belief was symptomatic of their greater sense of belonging to the town, and the second clearly reflected the same sentiment, although the actual increase in contact was less impressive than the "favorable contacts" thought.

In contrast, the "unfavorable contacts" were not very much affected in their attitudes toward the townspeople by the activity program, except that they recognized that their group were taking a decreasing part in town activities.

Taking the project as a whole, contacts with the town seem to have increased fairly satisfactorily, particularly when account is taken of the fact that many residents with young children had little free time. It was also confirmed that the project people who were least in touch with their neighbors had the most difficulty in obtaining introductions to townspeople. In order to enter into town activities, often it is not enough simply to be present; in all except church activities it is necessary to be introduced by somebody.

The indirect impact of the project activities on townspeople does not seem to have been very considerable. Naturally the families living next to the project had more contacts with the project residents than did those living farther away. But the increases in contact due to the activity program were not striking.

As might be expected, the townspeople who had unfavorable opinions of the project had less and less to do with the project people. It did not follow, however, that contact with the project people automatically increased the townspeople's liking for the project; in fact, if their acquaintanceship was with "unfavorable contacts," the latter's unfavorable attitudes would be to some extent communicated to them. This was quite likely to occur because "unfavorable contacts" would prefer to make friends with townspeople rather than with the other project people whom they disliked. Conversely, the project people that became more favorable to the project would be alienated from their old friends in the town who remained unfavorable to the project, with the result that their contacts with the townspeople would tend to decline. One should perhaps here interpose a word of warning that these last explanations of the results have the weaknesses of all ex post facto arguments. If the results had been different, it is probable that some equally accommodating "explanation" could have been found.

IMPLICATIONS

The authors next consider the implications of the findings reported. As has been stated, the objectives of the study were both practical and theoretical. The practical aim was to lessen hostility within the project and also between project and town, and the theoretical aim was to find out what factors determine whether or not social contacts are effective in producing a desired attitude change.

The practical effects can be restated in the following sentences. Initially the project residents thought themselves to be of low status, and they had minimal contacts both inside and outside the project. They also had feelings of hostility toward neighbors because they considered them to be of low status. This evaluation was not particularly realistic; objectively the project people were not of lower status than the townspeople, nor were they perceived as of low status by the townspeople, who were generally neutral toward them. On the other hand, the residents entered the project with a negative stereotype of government projects and of the people that live in them. Their attempts at making contact with the town were restricted by these facts. They tried to dissociate themselves from the project; if they made a contact with somebody outside, they would keep the new contact to themselves and would not try to introduce their project neighbors, as that would emphasize their own association with the project. Furthermore, they would seek out

ople who would share their hostile attitudes to the project.
ctivity program was designed to counter these tendencies,
results were by no means all one way. The favorable-
contact people tended to become more favorable; the unfavorable-
contact people tended to become more hostile; and the indifferent
no-contact people remained unchanged in their attitudes.

Looking at the total project population in order to evaluate the overall
practical accomplishments of the program, it would appear that in many
instances matters became worse rather than better. For about half of
the project population matters had a tendency to become better, while
for the other half they remained unchanged or became considerably
worse.[16]

Thus, on balance, from a practical point of view the program had
not justified the cost.

On the theoretical side the results were much more productive.
In the first instance, Newcomb's thesis, quoted at the beginning of
this chapter, was supported by the results. It was corroborated in
this case that groups that imagine themselves to be the object of
hostility will tend to isolate themselves and withdraw. But the
authors also put forward the corollary, which is an elaboration of
Newcomb's formulation, that persons with hostile (or favorable)
attitudes toward a particular group will tend to establish and maintain contact with those who share their attitudes. This explains, for
example, the tendency to withdraw from contact with townspeople who were unfavorable to the project, a tendency that accompanied the lessening of hostility within the group.

This is a special case of the phenomenon, observed in innumerable
studies, that people belonging to the same group develop common
attitudes; and, conversely, people tend to move into groups that
share their attitudes and out of groups that do not share their attitudes. Such moves are partly voluntary and partly under pressure
—members of groups are likely to be rejected by fellow members
if they fail to share the prevailing attitudes. Group membership and
social contacts therefore tend to be chosen to reinforce existing attitudes.

Thus the no-contact group, who were distinguished by their refusal to enter into the activity program, would tend to seek out
and to maintain freindships with other no-contact people, which

would reinforce their bias against participation in activities. They were not unaware of what was going on—this must always be made clear—and they were not even unfavorable toward the activities (75 per cent of them were in favor of the existence of the activities), but this benevolent neutrality was dependent on their not having to do anything about it.

This, then, disposes of the no-contact people. They constitute a very interesting group, and they are always liable to be viewed with distaste by social workers who are dismayed by their failure to co-operate.

In the case of the contact people, whether their experiences had been favorable or unfavorable, the experiment provided a partial opportunity to test the hypothesis, already discussed, that the best way to change attitudes is to provide a program that not only exposes people to groups possessing the "suitable" new attitudes but also keeps them away from groups possessing the "unsuitable" old attitudes. By the nature of the experimental program adopted it was possible to arrange exposure to new attitudes but not to prevent exposure to old attitudes. On the other hand, the operation of the machinery already described makes it likely that those favorably disposed toward a change in attitude will gravitate toward like-minded people to the exclusion of those unwilling to make a shift in attitude. Thus the effect of the activity program was to bring together those that had favorable attitudes toward the program, giving them the opportunity to develop common attitudes on other matters. This illustrates the fact that attitudes are not unidimensional. If one can bring together people who share a favorable attitude toward participation, one exposes them to the possibility of agreeing on other points.

Thus the affiliations of every individual would tend to confirm his original stance. The initially favorable person would extend his positive attitude beyond the project to the town as a whole and would expect this positive attitude to be reciprocated by the town. Conversely, the initially unfavorable would undergo an equal and opposite confirmation of his position. By associating with other unfavorable individuals his hostile attitude would extend beyond the project to the town as a whole, and he would anticipate and avoid rejection by the townspeople by withdrawing from all contacts with them.

APPRAISAL

The experimental program, although relatively slight in comparison with some of the other studies described in this book, contains many interesting points. It shows something of the mechanism by which, in an adaptive society, both group upward mobility (by assimilation of the low-status group into the high-status group) and individual upward mobility (by rejection of the low-status group) can be achieved. Its results reinforce the lessons of previous works, for example, *Street Corner Society*, in stressing the crucial role of social action in facilitating upward mobility. Furthermore, it shows that it is possible in an experiment to achieve social control of the situation in such a way as to implement the upward mobility of members of a low-status group.

Nevertheless, the experiment was disappointingly unsuccessful in a number of respects. To some extent the mistakes were avoidable; it was both ethically unjustifiable and pragmatically inefficient to attempt to bring about changes without enlisting the understanding and support of the subjects. Moreover, from a practical point of view, greater integration between the project and the town might have resulted if the effort had been concentrated on more direct measures to bring this about.

Similarly, the theoretical explanation of what took place leaves something to be desired. Apart from the reliance on ex post facto explanations at certain points, there is perhaps too little consideration of the peculiarities of what did take place. One example will be given. Allowing for the vagaries of the sample which, it will be remembered, was drawn independently for each interview survey, it is a remarkable fact that the unfavorable-contact group appear to have continued to participate in the activity program more faithfully than the favorable-contact group. The explanation given is that the community workers applied particularly great pressure on the unfavorable-contact group, and this explanation is certainly supported in successive surveys by a fantastic increase in the proportion of unfavorable-contact people who replied that they had heard of the activities "from the community worker who contacted me" (7 per cent in Survey 1, 45 per cent in Survey 3), while the favorable-contact people were hearing less and less of the activities from this source. But what was there about the unfavorable-contacts that encouraged the community workers to continue pressure on them while they left the "no contacts" alone? (Only 6 per cent of "no contacts" in Survey 3 heard of activities through the community worker, although they were in no way isolated on the project.)[17]

Social workers usually believe that they should by one means or another draw in, by reformation if necessary, the entire population in their territory. The evidence of this part of the study is highly provocative. Not only does it highlight the no-contact people who have learned to evade the pressures of the community workers, or who have been rejected by them as hopeless,* but it also suggests that the community workers were expending a disproportionate effort on the unfavorable-contact people, whose only lasting response to the external pressures was hostility toward the activity program.

There is a practical indication here that any particular set of activities provided, and possibly all organized activities, will find favor with only a moderate proportion of a population. It may well be more beneficial to concentrate on providing the facilities that the volunteer participants need than to expend effort on attracting other people who though apparently suitable will participate only reluctantly and with veiled hostility.

This report by Festinger and Kelley is only a monograph with circumscribed aims, but it opens the door to an important area of modern sociological theory, to which Festinger and his colleagues have made a valuable contribution. At one level it enlarges the relevance of the small-group laboratory experiments described in Chapter 12. The studies on the Westgate project[18] showed the paramount importance of group standards (unanimity of attitude) in maintaining the cohesiveness of the group and in its internal power (the magnitude of the change which it can induce on its members). To the extent that shared attitudes are perceived by the group as necessary for goal achievement there will be pressures toward uniformity. In the many situations in which physical reality is not ascertainable a provisional truth is substituted by convergence with the opinions of other members of the group. This Festinger and his colleagues call "social reality," following Lewin's

---

* Recall the "roughnecks" who were thrown out of the Settlement House in *Street Corner Society* (Chapter 7) because they failed to conform to its middle-class norms.

comment that "experiments dealing with memory and group pressure on the individual show that what exists as 'reality' for the individual is, to a high degree, determined by what is socially accepted as reality."[19]

In the present context the most important evaluation required of the project people was that of their status in town and of their acceptance or rejection by the townspeople. Initially they were disoriented because they lacked group cohesion, which would have enabled them to arrive at a "socially realistic" evaluation of their own status, and also, it was said, interaction situations with the townspeople, which would have enabled them both to assess the status of the townspeople and to experience the "physical reality" of the townspeople's behavior toward them.

The preceding statement suggests a surprising degree of isolation. Yet the project residents seem to have had jobs in the town in the normal way and would thus have had ample opportunities to make friends at work or, at worst, to discover that their friendship was not sought by townspeople. It is true that they were all newcomers to the town, and it is possible (though this is speculation) that they belonged to ethnic minorities and therefore expected rebuffs. Or was it that residents of a Federal public housing project would automatically regard themselves as exposed to public hostility because they are being housed partly at the taxpayer's expense?

There are various possible consequences if an individual perceives himself, or if a group perceives itself, as of low status. A possible outcome is to suffer one of the many forms of disorientation caused by a gap between aspiration level and achievement level. Examples of such disorientation have accumulated throughout this book, from the anomic suicides of Durkheim and the disorganized youth delineated by Thomas and Znaniecki to the situation discussed in the present chapter.

Recently a formal model has been proposed by Thibaut and Kelley, who make use of the concepts of *comparison level* (CL), described as "the standard against which the member evaluates the 'attractiveness' of the relationship or how satisfactory it is," and the *comparison level for alternatives* (CLalt), described as "the standard the member uses in deciding whether to remain in or leave the relationship." The need for two levels is explained by the fact that "circumstances may require a person to remain in a relationship that he regards as unsatisfactory."[20] If he is thus frustrated, he may adapt either by lowering his CL or by finding means of "achieving the unattained outcomes."[21] The latter calls into operation the familiar frustration-aggression mechanism,[22] which, when it consists of hostility by a group against the external cause of frustration, may even provide additional rewards in the form of enhanced group solidarity.

If, however, the attempt to attain the CL fails, there may be a serious outbreak of discontent. The frustration will have been made more obvious, and the failure of the advancement program will accentuate the lack of achievement and the disillusionment with the power the group is able to mobilize. When success is perceived as virtually unattainable, the aggression can turn only inward.* On the other hand, successful attainments may increase the energy of outward aggression. Thibaut and Kelley report an experimental study by the former in which the experimenter arbitrarily varied the amount of concession to an *ad hoc* underprivileged group. They conclude:

When a group was successful in "influencing" the experimenter to grant better outcomes, there was a marked increase in the expression of aggression towards the previously favored persons. This suggests that successful action causes a general expansion in the perceived area of own control (and friendly power), with a consequent release of hostility that had previously been inhibited.[24]

This accords with the common observation that revolutionary movements are stimulated rather than appeased by concessions.

This part of the theory seems quite adequate, but very little is said about the criteria by which individuals, either singly or together, choose the group with which the comparison is made. As has been noted, the term "reference group" is used only once in *Changing Attitudes through Social Contact*, and then in an unusually narrow sense. Thibaut and Kelley make no use of the reference-group concept, their only relevant statement being to point out that outcomes have to be known to the person "either by direct experience or symbolically," and that the "salience" of each possible outcome will depend, for example, upon the recency of experiencing the outcome and the occurrence of stimuli which serve as reminders of the outcome.

* As described by Lewin[23] and also as exemplified by the intropunitive aggression of the authoritarian personality (Chapter 11).

Because these factors are likely to be absent or weak in the case of relationships and interactions that are unattainable, the latter will ordinarily have little weight in determining the location of CL.[25]

Although Festinger and Kelley have presented with great clarity the mechanism of upward social mobility and the restraints against it, there is thus one level of conceptualization in which their treatment disappoints. The situation in Baytown could not realistically be formalized into a straight dyadic relationship between the project people, self-evaluated as of low status, and the rest of the town perceived as of high status, yet this is the form required by the authors' own theoretical presentation. By this approach an accessible level of conceptualization has been sacrificed.

The critic is often tempted to complain that authors have not brought in a line of approach that he favors. In this case at least the omission is not due to ignorance, as is evidenced by Kelley's contribution to the 1952 edition of *Readings in Social Psychology*.[26] As a bridge between psychology and sociology, between individual motivations and group interactions, reference-group theory is, as has been shown in earlier chapters, an invaluable contribution. In fact, it seems very likely that the events described in this chapter might be explained rather differently if reference-group concepts were used. Festinger and Kelley, having once demonstrated that the occupational and educational levels of the project people were at least as high as those in the town as a whole, provide very little further information about the differences in behavior and attitude displayed by different sections of the project group. The results themselves show that the project people did not achieve the cohesiveness required of a group according to the theories of group dynamics. They had arrived at not one social reality but at two or three, and the group locomotion varied according to whether they were "favorable contacts," "unfavorable contacts," or "no contacts." It would have been worth while to devote some attention to the question why the marked divergences in behavior and attitude were consolidated, and one readily testable hypothesis would have been that the acts and thoughts of each section were regulated by identification with a different reference group.

Quite frequently individuals join in selected social activities in order to hoist themselves into the desired reference groups. The price they pay is submission to the social control of the group being penetrated. The program described in this chapter demonstrates once more that the activities traditionally devised by community workers and the work of the activity program have no appeal as a reference point to a considerable section of the public. But it also leaves the behavior and attitudes of the "no contacts" without adequate explanation. Do the "no contacts" want social activities but not the ones offered, or are they not motivated at all toward social interaction? If the explanation is the second one, does it matter that a community contains some voluntary isolates?

This relative indifference to the main-stream preoccupations of sociology is disturbing; one is left with the feeling that group dynamics has a most exciting contribution to make to the analysis and control of society, but that this contribution could be made still greater by a fuller awareness of sociological dimensions. In the words of Morton Deutsch:

These concepts have been largely developed in isolation from the body of sociological literature which deals with related topics. Nevertheless, the sociologically oriented reader will be able to detect many parallels between the concepts of group dynamics and of sociology. Whether or not the isolation from prior sociological theorizing has been sensible is hard to judge. The group dynamicist might argue that the isolation has produced concepts which have stimulated experimental research studies—studies which did not flow from the more general sociological conceptions. The sociologist might argue that the studies of group dynamicists might have been more sophisticated if they had been acquainted with the prior, relevant writings of sociologists.[27]

Whether or not group dynamicists would have benefited by more knowledge of sociology, it is certain that they have made an inestimable and enduring contribution to the science of sociology.

14

THE LESSONS In his paper on *Science and Economy of Seventeenth Century England*, first published in 1939, Merton addressed himself to the perennial question of how far social need precipitates inventions and canalizes scientific interests. He pointed out that a society, or at least its pioneering members, must first have perceived the need:

It is only when the goal is actually part and parcel of the culture in question, only when it is actually experienced as such by some members of the society, that one may properly speak of a need directing scientific and technological interest in certain channels.[1]

He declared the seventeenth century in England to have been one such period, finding it "indubitable . . . in the light of what the scientists themselves had to say about the practical implications of their work, that practical problems exercised an appreciable directive influence."[2] By an analysis of Royal Society meetings in four years between 1661 and 1687 he found that less than half of the investigations reported were classifiable as "pure science" and that more than a quarter were directly related to practical needs.

This was an age of scientific giants, like Newton, Halley, Wren, and Boyle. These men have not been accused of demeaning themselves because they devoted their efforts to the prosecution of both theory and practice.

Recently Merton has returned to a more contemplative examination of the relation between "idle curiosity" and "practical curiosity." Idle curiosity, the disinterested wish to know, is seen as a transitory phase.

The scientist may regard his deep interest in a question as reason enough for pursuing it. But sooner or later, if the question and its answers are to become part of the science rather than remaining a personal hobby, they must be shown to be relevant to other ideas and facts in the discipline.[3]

Whereas idle curiosity "ignores, rather than denies, the possibility that a new bit of knowledge will contribute to power, comfort, or pecuniary gain, to health, or repute, or anything other than knowledge,"[4] there is a supplementary, or alternative, rationale of practical curiosity.

Here the case is made for a question by indicating that its answers will help men achieve values other than knowledge itself: values of health, comfort, safety, efficiency, and the like. But the intent of a question need not, of course, coincide with the consequences of answering it. In sociology as in other disciplines, a question raised only because its answer promises to extend knowledge may nevertheless have practical consequences. . . . Conversely, a sociological question may be raised with an eye to the social value of finding an answer to it and still have important consequences for a set of sociological ideas, considered apart from practical implications.[5]

Clearly, everyone will be pleased if it is possible simultaneously to satisfy the appetite for pure knowledge and the thirst for instrumental knowledge. But clearly also there will be one primary purpose and one by-product. The individual scientist must make the choice, and it is difficult to avoid the conclusion that instrumental knowledge aimed at a purpose in which the scientist believes is more compatible with moral commitment to society than the intellectually fascinating pursuit of pure knowledge.

To nobody is this decision more urgent than to the human scientist. Rensis Likert, of whom we have heard at various points in this book, has recently written:

The important problems of our times concern human behavior. The problems of individuals, organizations and whole societies or nations are the result, to a great extent, of the way people behave in relation to each other. Achievement of the full measure of spiritual richness, personal satisfaction and material well-being which the people of every nation seek depends upon their ability to create effective personal relations.

Most people obtain their principal satisfactions and motivations from association with others. Conflict with others usually results in personal distress. However, we are only beginning to understand the complex attitudes and motivations that underlie social behavior.

As the complexity of societies and nations increases, the need for progress in our understanding of human behavior becomes even greater. The serious problems of how best to control the great resources made available by the physical and biological sciences depend primarily upon improving human co-operation and establishing new and appropriate social organizations. Whether nuclear energy serves or destroys man will depend upon the capacity of human beings to co-operate effectively with each other in developing social machinery for the control and use of nuclear energy and the other great contributions of physics and biology.[6]

It is so plain that mankind is confronted with a crisis in social relations that it seems almost incredible that we should be frittering away our opportunities for dealing with real problems. It is no longer just a matter of making the most of our resources, by a gradual process of perfection. Now the products of physical and biological science are valued for their capacity to destroy and kill, and there are those who would like to bend the social sciences to the same purpose.

In this situation we seem determined on self-destruction, or else we become obsessed with trivialities. It is not only, in the words of C. Wright Mills, that we "abdicate the intellectual and the political tasks of social analysis."[7] There is much scope for political analysis, but the sociologist is not exceptionally well equipped for this task and might contribute more by enlarging the vocabulary and the precision of our understanding of political action. On the other hand, there are forms of social understanding, and even of social action, at which, as this book has aimed to show, we have achieved the first levels of proficiency. Why, then, do we not contribute our skills more effectively?

This failure has, of course, been exhaustively ventilated and explained. There is Merton's "self-fulfilling prophecy," which promotes the very evils against which it is directed, saturating society with the ideas of family breakdown, delinquency, thought control, so that when these disasters occur they are treated as familiars and allowed hypnotically to engulf us; there is his counterpart, the "self-destroying belief," through which, "confident that they will win a game or a war or a cherished prize, groups become complacent, their complacency leads to lethargy, and lethargy to eventual defeat."[8]

But one can also point to a form of servility, presumably induced by the uncertainties of modern competitive existence. So many individuals are dependent on the benediction of their peers and bosses, so much hangs on a clean copybook, so often the future is pre-empted, that indiscretions of thought or action cannot be afforded. An executive is generally less vulnerable than a policy maker, for at least it can be said that he has done his best. Identically, an operator of research techniques is never so suspect as his colleague whose questions may undermine cherished prevailing assumptions. While the deviant is easily isolated and turned into a clown, the majority, being dutiful sociologists, busy themselves with academic niceties or with the less searching questions raised in the smooth application of social control.

SOCIAL PROBLEMS

At one time it seemed the province of the social worker to tidy up the problems attributed to social progress, while the sociologist worried about the social evils themselves and their prevention or cure. Today there has been a fuller integration of sociology with social action, which may or may not be desirable. If sociology is the docile handmaiden of administration, unable to question the assumptions of administrative decision, the current trend leads only to the bureaucratization of the science. On the other hand, sociology can itself become an autonomous form of social action; at this moment of challenge the questions and assumptions of sociology are tested by purposive action as by no other means.

Some of the social problems encountered in these pages are world-wide in their incidence. As Durkheim discovered, some citizens of every country die by their own hand. It is still significant, however, that Durkheim's attention was attracted to suicide by the fact that contemporary social conditions in France were increasing the incidence of suicide. Many of the other social problems attacked are characteristic of all modern adaptive societies. The United States has been exceptionally subject to the hazards of unplanned adaptation; and in accepting the premise that the home of empirically based sociology is in the United States, we also accept the corollary that the problems as well as the methods will be those most forcibly experienced and most clearly perceived in the United States. Later in this chapter we shall consider the theoretical implications of social disorganization. This is a phenomenon associated with social change, and America's own vivid history of change contains its share of practical problems associated with change.

Again, for decades the United States was the refuge of immigrants from all over the world. Practical problems of assimilating these newcomers were superimposed on the ancient and still open issue of how fully to accept the emancipated Negroes. Meanwhile the practical considerations that precipitated the research into authoritarianism were first most cogent in Nazi Germany and were only later experienced in the United States. Since then the universal rise in national consciousness and the massive population movements imposed by war and conquest and made possible by modern transportation have increased the prominence of ethnic prejudice. While traditional forms of class hatred have been muted by the rather general adoption of middle-class norms of attitude and behavior, there is little evidence that social prejudice has been laid to rest.

Perhaps the most immediately attractive contribution that sociologists can make is in the ratification of industrial morale and the stimulation of productivity. One of the prices paid for the establishment of a modern industrial society is the sacrifice of the old moral incentive to honest toil as a natural recompense for family and social solidarity. Men must still earn in order to maintain their families, but labor is now a calculated and negotiated commodity. Pride in work and determination to give value for money can no longer be automatically relied upon. Furthermore, the vagaries of consumption and production demand rapid and almost continuous adaptation both on the part of the industrial concern as a social institution and on the part of the individual worker. It is an objective fact that employees suffer unemployment, are forced to discard unwanted technical skills, are torn out of their social surroundings because of the basic need for a mobile labor force. By various devices—some spontaneous and largely unconscious, some quite strategically planned—the interests of labor are ranged against the powerful array of industrial management. Today society would no longer tolerate the power tactics once used by the industrial barons, and it is a most convenient parallel outcome for modern management that suitable social skills have been developed to accept, and to divert into mutually acceptable channels, the informal structure of worker resistance. Of course, like the military search for the ultimate weapon, the development of social skills is pursued in such a blaze of light that much of their objective effectiveness can be countered by greater sophistication in the opposing forces.

The United States also provides an important laboratory for the practical study of moral change. In recent years the revival of active religious affiliation has led to increased investigation of religious institutions. It is a curiously irrelevant fact that Robert Lynd initially set himself the task of studying the religious provision and practice in the town of his choice. Much more central to the theme of moral change are Kinsey's works on sexual behavior. The ingrained puritanism of the American culture appears to have constructed an exceptional chasm between the formal standards of morality and the pattern of sexual behavior as it was actually lived. This chasm must have generated an inordinate amount of guilt in individuals faced with this moral conflict, but even more it constituted a barrier between the generations. In 1925 Judge Lindsey, of the Juvenile and Family Court of Denver, opened the eyes of American parents to a whole new informal code evolved by their emancipated children and innocently imparted to him by the young people who came into his court. One girl of fifteen told him some of the rules:

I learned that one could go automobile riding at fifteen; that one could drink freely when one was eighteen; that love-making could begin at any time. Kissing, petting, and other tentative excursions into sex experience, provided they were not too pronounced, were taken for granted by this sweet-faced girl as part of what she might properly look forward to long before she should be eighteen—if she could manage not to get found out. Such was her code, and such was the code of her friends and intimates.[9]

Judge Lindsey's revelations breached the wall of silence. Parents and teachers were shocked but managed to preserve their belief that the Judge was a publicity-minded amoralist. In point of fact he was an entirely well-meaning, if somewhat muddled, man who wished to demonstrate his faith and trust in the youth of his country. He saw not merely the normal recurrence of youthful rebellion, like the "new woman" in the mid-Victorian period. This time he foresaw the growing effect of economic independence, the automobile, the telephone, the elimination of drudgery, the new mass media. All these influences led to the most fundamental development of all, the fact that new generations no longer had faith in the traditional code transmitted by their parents, but had the confidence to derive and to transmit their norms of behavior through the culture of their own generation of peers. The moral changes indicated by Lindsey's informal methods were confirmed by Kinsey's careful studies, but even more important than the facts of change was a growing awareness of the machinery of moral change. The implications of this knowledge are not yet understood or applied.

If we are concerned with social problems, we should expect to find a variety of social-welfare agencies operating in the area. The proliferation of such agencies is itself a recognition that individuals and families in an industrial society are not capable themselves of solving all their personal living problems, nor are they able to rely on the neighborly assistance of their community as they once would have done. In many instances the difficulty can be relieved by financial help. It seems, however, that social workers are at present treading an uneasy no-man's land between the simple duties of relieving distress and the much more demanding task of understanding and treating the many forms of social and psychological maladjustment to which men and women are prone.

Barbara Wootton has been spearheading an attack on the pretensions of the "godlike" social workers who after one interview with a new client can pronounce on

. . . such qualities as the degree of "zest for living" or of optimism manifested by the client, the extent of his energy, of his liking for people and of his sense of humor, his ability to verbalize his feelings, his articulateness and his capacity to take responsibility as well as the degree to which he was "motivated to change" or tended to disguise hostility or manifested paranoid tendencies or was "poorly organized" or wrapped up in himself or candid about his faults or mild-mannered or a social isolate.[10]

This actual example effectively parodies the self-assurance of certain types of social worker who are determined to display their professional grasp of the social and psychological sciences. In practice, social workers undoubtedly spend much of their efforts on giving practical help, but they do not stress this because,

. . . in the current ideology they are, unhappily, encouraged to despise it; it would be much better if they talked about it more. For the social worker whose practical assistance to a client in distress is prompt, efficient, and courteous has everything to be proud of. It may seem a small thing to arrange that someone's surgical boot should be ready at the time specified without his having to make several fruitless calls; but there are many who value such a service much above any "therapeutic relationship" with a caseworker.[11]

In the studies discussed in this book the main adverse lesson is that the social workers show too little awareness of the many possible forms of social organization and their related ideologies. By promoting one-way social adjustment to an approved middle-class image of a somewhat specialized kind, the social workers are not only destroying some of the richness of social life but are also partially failing to do their job, for by their attitude they are rebuffing a substantial section of the population. This is also a social problem of social workers. Caught in the transition from vocational to professional status, they are the victims of their own social insecurity; sometimes, as with Youth Board personnel, the requisite partial identification with deviant groups may win them social isolation and even punishment. In a world which reserves its main rewards for a quite different range of activities, it will always be difficult to recruit suitable men and women for what will remain, if they are to do their job properly, an outwardly unrewarding and unsuccessful life.

The question of the role and function of leadership is partly a theoretical one. The provision of leadership is, however, a matter of great practical importance. Among sociologists who have contributed to the consideration of this question is Homans, who has attempted to set down the mutual dependence, both within the group and in its external relations, of interaction, sentiment, and activity, by presenting a series of propositions, such as that *the more frequently persons interact with one another, the stronger their sentiments of friendship for one another are apt to be.*"[12] Although this is couched in theoretical terms, it will be noted that it can with the greatest of ease be transformed into a practical guide to action. It suggests that if you want to make friends with somebody, you should see as much of him as you can arrange. The results of the Festinger and Kelley study show, however, that these guides do not take all the necessary considerations into account, and that under some circumstances improved contacts may increase rather than decrease hostility to groups, if not to individuals. There seems to be an underlying American belief, which finds its way into much sociological research, that interaction is automatically a good thing, both reflecting and promoting social integration. This belief is not shared by all Europeans, some of whom see close contact sometimes as a desirable feature of social life and sometimes as a threat.[13]

This raises another important and unresolved issue. Because of differences in social and political institutions it is to be expected that social problems will vary substantially from place to place, and in terms of the sociology of knowledge it is extremely likely that even similar situations will be perceived differently in different places. Like various other well-known twentieth-century products that were either invented or first massively exploited in the United States, the sociology with which this book is concerned bears the American stamp. This is true even though similar ideas are adopted, and even improved upon, in other countries throughout the world. There has until recently been one major exception. The Soviet Union, which has not been too proud to borrow from Western technology while, for example, it was building up its automobile, aircraft, and electronic industries, has until the last few years held aloof from the Western brand of social sciences. For four decades the social principles of Marxist-Leninism were supposed to be able to supply all the necessary answers to social problems.

It is said that the jolt came in Amsterdam in 1956 at the Third World Congress of Sociology, where a potential ideological breach revealed itself between the Soviet delegates—meeting their Western colleagues for the first time—and the delegates from the other Eastern European members of the Soviet bloc who had had twenty-five years' exposure to Western sociology. Whatever the precipitating cause, it is now a well-known fact that a fundamental reversal of Soviet policy toward the social sciences is now in progress. The rather rigid Pavlovian determinism favored during the Stalin era is being replaced by a more dynamic and more complex model.

Administratively this has led to the reinstatement of the Academy of Social Sciences on an equal footing with the Academy of Sciences and the other leading scientific institutions. Parallel with this development there is emerging the concept of a "New Soviet Man" who will voluntarily and without coercion embrace the constructive principles of social science applied to social change. The Soviet authorities appear to believe that the apparatus of social control is sufficiently well developed for this program to be carried out, and they also appear understandably to believe that there is no satisfactory military or other countermeasure to this "threat," which has a potential spread throughout the world. No similarly ambitious program for the social sciences is yet entertained elsewhere. It has, of course, yet to be seen whether the Soviet premises are correct, and whether their intention will be sustained.

TECHNIQUES AND METHODOLOGY

We can now turn to the lessons in techniques and methodology that can be derived from an examination of the studies reported in this book.

The first question to be settled is whether there is a distinctive method of investigating group behavior and group attitudes and values. The answer would appear to be that there is no raw material relating to the group as a whole which would not have been more informative if it had been available in relation to the individuals in the group. It is useful to know that 8.5 per 100,000 inhabitants of a particular area committed suicide, or that 46 per cent of those eligible voted in Middletown in the presidential election of 1920. It would be even more valuable also to know more about the contrasting characteristics of the suicides and nonsuicides or of the voters and nonvoters. Even Durkheim, who reacted so forcibly against his contemporaries and their vulgar psychologism, was glad at one point in his analysis to desert the mass data and conduct a breakdown of particular cases so that the suicidal characteristics of individuals or classes of individuals could be compared.

The moral is that the point at which the data are tapped has, or should have, little relevance to the manner in which they are finally used. A "social fact" can be derived from the observed behavior of individuals, and individual attitudes and motivations can be inferred from analysis of mass data.

We must next be clear about the methodological relation between descriptive and explanatory surveys. Counts and descriptions are required for various administrative purposes: it is obviously necessary to enumerate and also to predict the number of children of school age if the task is to supply the requisite number of school places. But although census results often provide surprises and official forecasts are difficult to make accurately without them, they do not by themselves often satisfy scientific curiosity or add much to our understanding of the world. For this reason it is to be expected that the majority of the seminal books here discussed are concerned with explanations rather than enumerations.

This distinction is made so starkly by some scholars that the word "sociography" is used to describe studies which are primarily concerned with establishing facts and frequencies of occurrence, thereby preserving the purity of the higher-status cerebral activity known as sociology. The strict application of this rule might lead to the exclusion of several of the books here discussed. Much of the early Chicago work is perhaps primarily descriptive; it is otherwise difficult to justify Thrasher's laborious location of 1,313 gangs in the city, to take one example. Certainly Lynd as a young man was aiming to present a three-dimensional picture of a typical small town. In the first instance Stouffer and his colleagues were engaged in providing administrative data for the U.S. Army authorities.

Perhaps the most overtly deliberate determination to conduct a census was shown by Kinsey, and his most likely purpose in undertaking the task suggests what lay behind each of these essays in description. In all the cases cited one suspects that the descriptions and enumerations presented have an ulterior but not altogether declared purpose. There is more than a hint that in each case certain previously held notions of normality were being challenged. Thrasher wished to demonstrate that Chicago was riddled with gang formations, many of them delinquent, because this would help him to stir the public conscience to deal with the gangs and the environment that produced them. In the end, if not earlier, Lynd was concerned not only to portray but also to change life in a small American town.

It was consistent with Kinsey's attitude that he expressed a doubt whether the terms "normal" and "abnormal" belong in a scientific laboratory,[14] but it was undeniably a support to his generally permissive approach that he was able to declare that many items labeled "abnormal" or "perversions" in textbooks occur in as many as 75 per cent of certain populations, and that many of the socially and intellectually most significant persons in our histories have socially taboo items in their sexual histories.[15] Whether or not the use of the word "normal" is legitimate, it is apparent that data on incidence of forms of sexual behavior are felt by Kinsey to be relevant to normative judgments as to their general acceptability.

Another question related to the difference between description and exploration is the extent to which the investigator is aiming to achieve a proof (or a nullification) of his theories. If the investigation is designed to provide descriptive material, the main need is for validation to ensure that the data are accurate; any deeper question of proof or disproof does not arise. If, however, the purpose is to assist in theory building or at least to test general hypotheses, the contribution may lie at many points of the journey between exploration and proof. Provided his idea is formulated in such a way as to be, even remotely, susceptible of empirical testing, one of the most practical contributions that a sociologist can make is to point the way to some hitherto unsuspected relationship.

In this context Max Weber's classic suggestion that the Calvinist ethic favored the emergence of capitalism has had immense influence on subsequent thinking, yet it required no rigorous and systematic research and survives for us as a fragment of thought, much refined and elaborated by the great intellectual battle with historical materialism that it provoked.[16] In spite of its repute and broad acceptance, and in spite of its topicality in an era in which the "spirit of capitalism" is giving way, in England at least, before its arch enemy "traditionalism,"* no one, it appears, has sought to reappraise Weber's work in contemporary society.[18]

Similarly, Freud's many insights have been greedily absorbed into

---

* "Traditionalism is present when workers prefer less work to more pay, when during working hours they seek a maximum of comfort and a minimum of exertion, when they are unable or unwilling to adapt themselves to new methods of work. It is present also when entrepreneurs deal in goods of varied rather than standardized quality, when they work moderate hours and at a leisurely pace except for rush periods, when they are satisfied with earnings that permit a comfortable living, and when their relations with workers, customers and competitors are direct and highly personal."[17]

contemporary thought, but still there is a plaintive or sometimes exasperated outburst that his many interlinked hypotheses have never been put to adequate empirical test.

At the other end of the spectrum it is still an open question how far we can hope to achieve proofs of sociological hypotheses. In this respect one can perhaps detect a certain change of perspective among sociological methodologists. Logically there is still no substitute for the *experimentum crucis*, and indeed there cannot be. Carefully conceived experiment remains the aim, and such experiments have taken place on a number of occasions. But the practical possibilities of experimentation appear to remain pathetically few, a fact which perhaps reflects the low status of the sociologist in the power hierarchy, though it is also obviously connected with the nature of the subject matter.

In view of the many setbacks to the achievement of the experimental ideal, eyes have turned to the more propitious development of "theories of the middle range" and of models that rough out in coarse detail the main dimensions of small-scale social relations. Just as it is today realized that statistical significance, as tested by standard methods, may be less impressive than consistency of results over a replicated series of studies, so also there is more confidence in a theory that is consistently and repeatedly confirmed at a number of points in its structure. We may turn to an example already cited in this book; the reference group concept had been ventilated for many years when Merton and Kitt resolved to apply it to a secondary analysis of the *American Soldier* material. A passing application to one survey result would have been quite unimpressive, but it requires extreme skepticism to reject the applicability of the concept of relative deprivation after it has been successfully applied to a sequence of nine instances of results that might otherwise have appeared surprising and anomalous.

It must be recognized that although this is logically a much more powerful instrument than the solitary demonstration of a relationship, there remains a practical danger that the analyst will descend to ex post facto explanations, if necessary adopting the flip-flop technique pointed out by Bales. Moreover, it still seems true unfortunately that very few satisfactory predictive instruments have been based on such middle-range theories as that of the reference group. While it is possible to account for behavior or attitudes in terms of identifiable reference groups, it is not possible to predict with any regularity which particular group will be chosen for purposes of reference.

This is an inevitable consequence of the presence of a complex system of uncontrolled variables. There is, in fact, no substitute for experiment, in which the complex of variables is manipulated by control of certain key elements in the system. The precise form that such activity shall take will naturally vary, but for various reasons there appears to be a convergence on a particular pattern, which, according to the viewpoint, may be described either as "action research" or as "programmatic theory." This pattern is characterized by some identification of aims between the social scientist and the subjects involved.

The reason for this necessity is quite clear. It would naturally be repugnant to the social scientist to set in motion a process that he expected to be harmful to his subjects. Furthermore, he cannot knowingly encourage a group of people to continue in a situation that is harmful to them. On the other hand, if they are led blindly into a situation that is not explained to them, as happened in the study made by Festinger and Kelley, it is quite likely that they will rise in wrath and vitiate the experiment. Therefore, on both ethical and practical grounds, circumstances favor the combination of a morally committed social scientist with a consciously co-operating group. It will, of course, be appreciated that the investigator must be entirely clear as to his own relationship with the program. It will be remembered, for instance, that the test-room observer at the Hawthorne works was confronted with certain loyalty conflicts in relation to the girls under his surveillance, and other examples that have been cited will occur to the reader.

We turn now to a rapid review of the field techniques that have been described in successive chapters of this book. It is convenient to consider these separately under the three headings of documents, observation, and interview.

Documents

The documents used have varied widely. Some have been unsponsored raw personal documents, such as the sets of *Polish Peasant* letters. Some have been sponsored raw material, and have varied enormously in character, from the life-history supplied by Wladek and by the Jack-Roller to the elaborate test schedules devised for studying the authoritarian personality. Some have been records, official or otherwise; expert appraisals; newspaper reports; administrative forms; statistics.

If the researches described in the present book are at all characteristic of general trends in sociological research, it appears that the relative importance of documentary sources has greatly diminished. This impression is accentuated by the fact that the elimination of the documentary sources is particularly American. Of the twelve studies described in Chapters 2 through 13 of this book, six studies make substantial use of spontaneous documents of various kinds, and four of these include at least one European investigator (that is, Durkheim, Znaniecki, Myrdal, Adorno). The other two studies were made by the Chicago group and by Robert Lynd, both noted for their policy of tapping all available sources. Thus, while it is probably true that reliance on documents is declining, the apparent decline is exaggerated by the concomitant increase in the proportion of native-born Americans occupying leading positions in American sociological research.

To the extent that documents are currently used they tend to be standardized statements prepared under controlled conditions, so that they do not differ essentially from interview test material. The main *American Soldier* procedure is an example. Even with free response and projective questions, such as were used for the *Authoritarian Personality*, there is a rather serious loss of spontaneity, and in the case of many test and questionnaire data rigid precoding removes any possible richness. Apart from the obviously greater dangers of falsification, another unavoidable consequence of solicited documents is that the sense of history is likely to be sacrificed. If all the available raw material is contemporary, there is no opportunity to discern changes in attitudes, behavior, or relationships.

Some social scientists, and not only Americans, reject the merits of historical perspective. Kurt Lewin, for example, while naturally recognizing that the past indirectly affects behavior, believed that "behavior depends neither on the past nor on the future but on the present field,"[19] and there is awareness of time rather than emphasis on history in the work of Bales (Chapter 12) and of Festinger and Kelley (Chapter 13).

It is also common knowledge that the more "American" developments of psychoanalysis have been concerned to concentrate analytic attention on immediate precipitating causes rather than on the events of early childhood, and correspondingly to explore therapeutic methods that are more economical in time and effort than the procedures evolved by Freud. In this respect the psycho-analytic theory adopted in the *Authoritarian Personality* is "European" rather than "American," and explanations of authoritarianism and methods of combating this disorder are sought largely in terms of early family experience. It is significant that the facts of childhood were sought in the clinical interviews rather than in the written schedules.

Of the researches discussed in this book, none is more suffused with the idea of social change than the *Polish Peasant* studies. The essence of this study is the portrayal of the disorganization of life in rural Poland and among recent immigrants to the United States and the subsequent reorganization as the former peasant comes to terms with life in an industrial society. There is surely a connection between this historical preoccupation and the fact that the authors made extensive use of life histories and family correspondence. Apart from the panel method of interviewing which provides some follow-through in time, it is clear that the document in some form—objective, as Durkheim preferred, or subjective, "personal," as favored by Thomas and Znaniecki—provides the main hope of investigating the unfolding of social institutions, attitudes, and behavior under conditions of change. By their nature, observation and interviewing are instantaneous procedures, and it is a disproportionately difficult task to organize any substantial continuity in time while using either of these methods of investigation, so that a study which concerns itself with change over a long period of time necessarily involves some use of documents.

Observation

Observational techniques include not only much informal observation but also the specialized types that have developed in radically different directions. It will be recalled (Chapter 4) that Eduard

Lindeman was the first to offer systematic guidance in the use of observation for social discovery, and that he recommended the use not only of *participant observation,* with which his name is usually linked, but also of *objective observation.* In this way observation from the inside could be complemented by observation from the outside, a procedure which obviously required at least two investigators.

It is perhaps surprising that of the twelve descriptive studies discussed in this book only five contain references to extensive use of observation as a primary technique of investigation. Strangely, four of these five, including all those that make use of participant observation, were close together in time, being completed during the 1930's.

The pioneer participant observer was Nels Anderson, collaborator and fellow countryman of Eduard Lindeman, who lived the life of a hobo to obtain material for his book. His is perhaps the most dedicated example, but William Whyte also sank his cultural personality in the slum district of Cornerville. The other instances of participation were more informal and intermittent. The Lynds placed participation in the local life at the head of their list of research methods, and they found this an important access to otherwise remote information, even though "this constant interplay of spontaneous participation and detached observation presented difficulties which have not at all points been successfully overcome."[20]

The dilemma of the test-room observer at the Hawthorne Works has already been stressed, and it is revealing that in the bank-wiring observations special precautions were taken to withdraw the observer from participation in the social grouping. In this case he was allotted a role which, though geographically inside the observation room, was socially outside. He was able to record the workers' verbal and overt behavior, and in this case the elucidation of the more intimate attitudes, thoughts, and feelings was entrusted to an interviewer who in a fashion substituted for participant observation.

The extremes of outside observation are reached in the studies of interaction process analysis. Here the observers are withdrawn, shielded by their one-way mirrors, and the recording system is designed to be as objective and depersonalized as can be achieved. It is true that the observers are trained to empathize with the actors in the groups, but only in a fashion drained of content, evaluation, and commitment.

There is also the difficulty noted by Durkheim that often outside observers may be mistaken in interpreting the state of mind of others, attributing misery to people on the ground that their conditions of life would be intolerable to themselves. Such misinterpretations are regrettably common.

It is clear that it is not yet possible to obtain a record which is, on the one hand, insightful and complete and, on the other hand, rigorous and quantifiable. The pressures toward measurement must be respected, and the task is not complete until this degree of precision has been attained. But the pressures toward quantification are not purely technical. There are various attractions attached to this type of research, and certain deterrents against participant research, that have little or nothing to do with their relative scientific merits.

Participant research requires a high level of skill and cannot easily be delegated to assistants. It requires a quality of personal and vocational dedication that is not always in keeping with the individual's best career interests or with his desire to lead a reasonably normal life. One suspects, for example, that Whyte's researches in Cornerville were never quite the same after he went back with his bride.

In spite of these handicaps the exploratory value of participant observation is so great that it seems likely to survive and even possibly to increase. There are always individuals who are not ambitious for a career, unwilling perhaps to commit themselves to their native culture, or impelled by an absorbing interest in other manifestations of social life. Several such individuals are operating today in various countries, and some of the results of their work will become known and will throw fresh light on the inner operation of such traditional institutions as the neighborhood, the penitentiary, the hospital. There is also the likelihood that the growing dissemination of sociological concepts and techniques will encourage some of those whose primary participation in these institutions is action-oriented to give us the benefit of their unrivaled identification with their institution, which they could do by providing sociologically sophisticated participant records of their experiences and observations.

Interviewing

We turn next to interviewing, the primary method of the social sciences. Some interviewing was undertaken as part of almost all the investigations here described. The exceptions are *Suicide* and *An American Dilemma*, and in each case there is a ready explanation. Even today the use of interviews to study suicide has obvious difficulties, and in any case one would expect Durkheim to be opposed to this source of information on individuals. *An American Dilemma* was a compilation rather than a report of fresh field studies, so that none of the primary methods of data collection were featured.

As with the other methods discussed, the main development has been the increasing systematization of the interview techniques. The authors of *The Polish Peasant* were dealing with live material, but their contacts with individuals were not regulated by research considerations. The verbal sources included the experiences of Znaniecki while director of the Emigrants Protective Society in Warsaw and "private conversation" with a Polish-American priest in Boston and with court and social-welfare officials. The contribution of verbal contacts was obviously small compared with the massive use of documents. Taking the Chicago School as a whole, the balance had shifted somewhat toward face-to-face contacts, but no systematic interviewing was reported. In this respect the technique used in *Street Corner Society* was similarly informal.

The *Middletown* interviews, on the other hand, were clearly more deliberately engineered. While some were casual conversations, others were carefully planned. Apart from detailed questioning of religious leaders in the city, an inquiry was undertaken to obtain data from a group of working-class families and a group of business-class families, in which elaborate interviews were conducted. The description given in *Middletown* makes it clear that the interviewers had considerable discretionary powers.

In contrast with these relatively informal methods the techniques used in *Management and the Worker*, it will be seen, were amazingly advanced for their time. Even the initial interviews, with their rational approach to complaints, were deemed worthy of elaborate statistical analysis, while the counseling program was highly sophisticated. It is true that the clinical interviews used for elaborating the meaning of the more quantitative scale material in *The Authoritarian Personality* were conducted by highly trained psychologists, but the specific instructions given to the interviewers do not appear to have advanced greatly in the years since the counseling program described in *Management and the Worker*.

One recurring difficulty with the nondirective interview is that often the interviewer is uncertain how actively he should direct the course of the discussion. This hazard is reduced by the use of the *focused interview*, to which passing reference has been made (Chapters 6 and 9). This type of interview was designed to occupy an intermediate position between the test battery of fixed questions and the full clinical interview. The whole situation is carefully structured, with a standardized stimulus (for example, a film program) and with prepared hypotheses regarding probable responses to it. The major areas of inquiry and the criteria of relevance for interview data are mapped out, and the interview is conducted in such a way as to ascertain the informants' definition of a situation that has been concocted for the occasion. It is clear that, without accepting the artificialities introduced by the use of an entirely prestructured interview, the focused interview greatly decreases the amount of time spent on each interview and the length of the consequent record.

As a matter of fact the focused interview has been used less widely than might have been hoped, perhaps because it calls for exceedingly careful preparation and exceptionally sophisticated handling by the interviewers. In recent decades the available survey personnel, it seems, have not been prepared to make this effort. In its place there has grown up a highly standardized technique suitable for administrative and market research of all kinds. This routine application of the survey method has led to a very efficient procedure for handling the problems of sampling, question construction, interviewing, and the analysis of the results.

Unfortunately, although the procedures on these points have been reduced to an easily understood set of rules which eliminate the worst errors of handling, they have not led to the development of a method capable of handling any but the most simple and superficial of concepts. While it is understandably valuable to an automobile corporation to be able to gauge the reaction to a new product, if this can be done, the expenditure of vast sums on market research has

contributed incredibly little to our knowledge of attitudes, preferences, or behavior. Even the far more subtle and devious motivation
research has proved an exceedingly hit-and-miss affair.

In these circumstances it is not surprising that the scientific forerunners discussed in this book include no market or motivational
researchers. On the other hand, any increase in the number of
investigations covered would almost certainly include work in a
somewhat related field, namely, voting studies, in which Lazarsfeld
and various colleagues have pioneered a rigorous extension of mass-
interview methods, coupled with the panel method of repeated
interviews, to gain a much better understanding of the determinants
of voting behavior.*

The forms of interviewing mentioned thus far do not, however,
exhaust the full range. The report by Festinger and Kelley (Chapter
13) describes the use of a very simple form of interviewing in which
there is a remarkable contrast between the innocence of the questions
and the maturity of conceptualization on which the study is based.
This unusual relationship between methods and concepts appears to
be a recurrent and somewhat misleading feature of the group-
dynamics school.

This leaves the unique type of interview pioneered and developed
by Kinsey against the opposition of the majority of social scientists.
As the techniques of questioning were refined it came to be taken
almost for granted that some form of psychoanalytic penetration
into the near-unconscious was the proper method for handling
difficult affect-laden topics. Among such topics it would be assumed
that those dealing with sexual behavior would rank high, and that
exceptional psychological tact would be needed to obtain correct
answers on such questions. Then Kinsey came along, using as his
model the prosecuting lawyer rather than the psychoanalyst with
his couch-side manner, and by all accounts his strict and direct,
aggressive technique appeared to work. Kinsey found the efficacy of
a straight look between the eyes, and quite independently Bales
advocates the use of the eyes to hold a group together. "Nothing
tones up the general harmony of a group like a good strong undercurrent of direct eye contact." (See Chapter 12).

The differences between the questioning methods of psychoanalysts and those of attorneys are so great, not only in their

* Developments up to 1954 are well summarized by Lipset, et al.[21]

practical features but also in their implications, as to appear unbridgeable. To the extent that both methods have been used to elicit the same kinds of facts, it would seem prudent to conduct an experimental investigation to determine how the results obtained by both methods compare in their qualities.

METHODS OF ANALYSIS

Up to the end of the nineteenth century a variety of nominally inductive methods had been in use, leading to generalizations of various kinds, some precise and "scientific," some grandiose and speculative. There were, for example, the generalizations that postulated certain trends or cyclical processes in society as a whole. One such generalization was the belief of Marx and Engels that civilization was passing from a primitive state of classless society to an advanced state of classless society through a series of episodes dominated first by one class and then by another. Another generalization was Spencer's use of the analogy of biological evolution to explain the emergence of industrial types of society. During this period there was an imperfect distinction between social evolution and economic development, but the assumptions about economic behavior and motivation were being built up to the point where a whole theoretical system of economics could be constructed with only sporadic reference to how people actually behave.

Quite separate from this line of generalization, the science of statistics was growing up, specifically aimed at learning more about society and its variations. The impressive number of statistical societies founded in the early decades of the nineteenth century were interested not so much in the skilled manipulation of symbols as in the acquisition of basic data relating to social phenomena, particularly to those that posed problems of social control and amelioration. Even before the first Census Reports were published, *House of Commons Papers* began to contain social statistics, and it was not long before enough material was accumulating to enable statistical tests of the connections between different observable data.

In the case of "moral statistics" France was the pioneer. As early as 1833 A. M. Guerry, the criminal statistician for the City of Paris, was able to publish his *Essai sur la statistique morale de la France*,[22] which dealt with the connection between crime and other known facts such as levels of education, sex, age, and area of origin. This work was taken up in France by Quételet, and it quite logically led into the inquiries of Durkheim and his immediate predecessors, as described in Chapter 2.

This was by no means an isolated example. In England in 1840 the Statistical Society set up a Committee on Hospital Statistics. One of the leading members was Dr. William Farr, who had already declared his faith in medical statistics:

Science has nothing to offer more inviting in speculation than the laws of vitality, the variations of these laws in the two sexes at different ages, and the influence of civilization, occupation, locality, seasons and other physical agencies either in generating diseases and inducing death or in improving the public health.[23]

The proposals of the Statistical Society were not fully taken up, but the standardization of data was brought nearer to reality by the joint action of Farr and Florence Nightingale, who forcibly raised the question at an International Statistical Congress in 1860. The next year the metropolitan hospitals began the long process of convergence toward uniform hospital statistics; it was then recommended that a register kept at every hospital should comprise the following particulars relating to each patient: age, sex, social relation (married, single, widow), occupation, name of disease or injury, date of admission and discharge, result, and days in hospital.[24]

The point to be noted about both the above examples is that the pioneers were concerned to collect data that would not only count and describe but would also assist in explaining the incidence of crime, illness, or whatever phenomenon had their attention. This is in contrast with the social survey movement, which was generally concerned with the type of sociography needed to establish the incidence of social evils, primarily of poverty, with the purpose of arousing public opinion into taking practical measures to deal with such evils. One cannot disagree with the verdict of A. F. Wells that the social survey is not concerned with evolving any comprehensive sociological theory.[25]

This negative feature of the social survey has been highlighted in the Simeys' recent study of Charles Booth.[26] Booth was concerned with establishing the incidence of poverty, and his vivid presentation

of the concomitants of poverty—overcrowding, disrepair, lack of
sanitation, ill-lit, ill-paved, and dirty streets, squalor, noise, and
disorderly conduct—is a portrayal of certain total ways of life and
leads to the establishment of various immediate causes—casual occupations and irregular hours of work, lack of public responsibility
for living conditions—and to the rejection of various other popular
explanations, such as the influx of immigrants.[27] What is missing is
any grand theory of poverty and social submersion to set against
the theories, for example, of Marx and Engels.

When our chronicle begins, therefore, we find two traditions.
On the one hand, there are the descriptive and sociographic studies
that confine themselves mainly to the facts relating to definite
aspects of social life and to certain fairly simple and immediate
empirical correlations between these facts. On the other hand, we
have the grand theories that by their nature and by the manner in
which they are formulated do not lend themselves to empirical
verification.

Against this background the characteristic novelty of the works
introduced in this book becomes apparent. Each item of research is
unremittingly empirical, and, like the products of the social-survey
movement, almost all the studies are immediately concerned with
the alleviation of current social problems. At the same time, almost
without exception, each study makes a concurrent contribution to
verifiable knowledge. When viewed in this light the methods of
analysis are assigned a fresh role.

The grand theorists adopted the loose procedure that has been
given the generic title *comparative method:*

In essentials this method is an application of a general rule of inductive
logic: to vary the circumstances of a phenomenon with the object of
eliminating variables and inessential factors and so arriving at what is
essential and constant. What is peculiar to the method is the use of data
derived from different regions or different times.[28]

The feasibility of applying normal inductive methods to data scattered in space and time naturally varies with the scope desired by the
author and the availability of reliable data. Durkheim was able to
compare differences and trends in suicide rates because suicide is
properly recorded. At the other extreme, one could have foreseen
the lack of realism in Herbert Spencer's project for "making tabu-

lated arrangements of historical data, showing the co-existence and succession of social phenomena of all orders,"[29] which was to culminate in his proposed but never achieved *Descriptive Sociology*.

One of the pitfalls awaiting the user of the comparative method is the impossibility of defining some of the grandiose concepts that will be presented for manipulation. Definition and classification are essential preliminaries to analysis. Because of the inadequacies of definition, many important theories—and some trivial ones—remain in the purgatory between validation and rejection. The value of such theories is diminished but not obliterated. Durkheim's satisfactory definition of suicide may be contrasted with his almost casual introduction of the concept of anomie.[30] Merton's classic essay on *Social Structure and Anomie*, first published in 1938, showed that the twin ideas of anomie and deviant behavior were by then in widespread use among sociologists, but it was only when Merton returned to the subject in 1956 that he felt constrained to examine closely the anomie concept and the different ways in which it was then being used by scholars. At the latter date he was concerned to rescue the specifically sociological, as opposed to socio-psychological, references of the word as it had been adopted by Durkheim. By that time he could point not only to Srole's scaled five-item psychological test of *anomie* as perceived by an individual but also to Lander's identification of "an anomic factor" arrived at by the factor analysis of eight properties of certain census tracts in the city of Baltimore.

Although Merton found both the psychological and the sociological exercise only partially successful, this does not detract from the fact that an important step was being attempted in giving precision to what had started as a vague, if readily recognizable, concept. Merton drew from these attempts the further lesson that the looseness of fit of the empirical data to the concept of *anomie* was exaggerated by the fact that the investigators were restricted to the array of social data which *happened* to have been collected for administrative purposes.[31] This is a common experience among investigators who operate in the real world.

For example, Mannheim and Wilkins,[32] in setting out to predict the likelihood of recidivism by Borstal inmates, were limited in their statistical analyses mainly to the records normally kept in the Borstal files. On this basis their predictions, as compared with random predictions, were three times as valid as reports by prison governors or housemasters, who are expected to know the boys under their charge. This difference shows that a systematic approach can be better than the normal subjective judgment. On the other hand, the dependence on a fairly arbitrary collection of data is likely to neglect the guidance that can be given by an informed conceptual approach. One would expect that the indices constructed from data collected for the purpose will always be better than indices based on information chosen for its availability.

The next point to note is that even a relatively simple operational concept such as suicide needs very careful clarification with reference to particular instances. More complicated, higher-level abstractions, such as anomie, morale, leadership, authoritarianism, cannot by their nature be pinned down by a single empirical observation. The process of compounding is implicit in the use of such concepts. For this reason there has been serious concentration in recent decades on the search for an individual index that will "stand for" the concept. We have Thurstone's factor analysis, the Likert scale and item analysis, Guttman's scalogram analysis, Lazarsfeld's latent-structure analysis, together with a host of more informal scales in which the items are compounded in a more or less arbitrary manner.

Any empirical sociologist will have encountered the need to construct such a scale, knowing that he is forced to take decisions on weighting and other steps in the procedure that could not be justified by strict logic. He will probably console himself with the thought that the differences that the index is designed to detect are either so gross as to survive distortions caused by incorrect weighting or so fine that they could easily in any case be obscured by sampling errors or by some other deficiency in the empirical material. There is, in any case, a sense of safety in numbers which gives the investigator confidence in his material if the results of different parts tend in the same direction.

This is not the place to speculate on which of the formal scaling systems are to be preferred. This book has given examples of the use of the more important types together with various assertions as to the superiority of one over another. It may be noted that an investigator is in a strong position if he is able to justify the claim that a rival method constitutes a special case of his own. While the choice is presumably to be determined to a large extent by particular circumstances, such as the form of the problem and the extent of the data, there are undoubtedly many areas in which there is a choice between alternative methods. The insularity of the practitioners of the social sciences is illustrated by the fact that very few experiments have been conducted with the aim of comparing the suitability of one method with that of another.

The other questions related to analysis are not peculiar to the social sciences. One is the question of statistical sampling, which has progressed enormously in the decades since Durkheim. Many advances in technique have been brought about in studies in the field of the social sciences, but the works described in this book have contributed surprisingly little to the science of sampling. Some elementary sampling was involved in *Middletown* and in *Changing Attitudes through Social Contact*. One has a feeling of confidence in the sampling skills of Stouffer and his colleagues for *The American Soldier*, but the authors specifically state that their work led to no new contributions to sampling theory, no new mathematical constructs, and to little that would prove especially instructive for future civilian research, and they therefore kept very brief their descriptions of sampling methods.[33]

In most other cases, deficiencies rather than achievements in sampling procedures called for comment. The authors of *The Authoritarian Personality* and of the *Sexual Behavior* volumes were criticized because they attempted generalizations about the population as a whole although their sampling methods favored overweighting with students. There also appeared to be disappointingly little use made of longitudinal sampling methods; this weakness was pointed out in the chapter on *Changing Attitudes*, the design of which called for a panel sampling procedure.

Apart from inferences falsified by inadequate sampling, there are many other ways in which generalizations can be wrongly arrived at through a misuse of statistics. Taking the period under review as a whole, we note an undoubted increase in sophistication in the handling of statistical inference. To give one important example, the examination of the problems of the intervening variable has been helpful in protecting future generations from the pitfalls of spurious inference. As Kendall and Lazarsfeld point out, the two main difficulties in interpreting survey material are the danger that spurious factors are present and the difficulty of establishing clearly the time sequence of the variables involved. These difficulties do not arise in experimental studies because the investigator is able to eliminate irrelevant variables and can also control the time sequence. Survey material is never equivalent to experimental material because, however carefully the known spurious factors are filtered out, there is always doubt whether there are undetected spurious factors that have not been dealt with. Correct sequences in time can generally be determined, for example by longitudinal studies, but only if the investigator is alert enough to doubt the apparent meaning of associated events. Theories are not always so easy to puncture as the hypothesis that fire engines cause fires, based on the fact that the more appliances are present the larger the blaze is likely to be.

It must be remembered, however, that Durkheim fully understood the intervening variable. In the chapter on *Suicide* examples are given of how carefully he probed in order to determine whether the apparent influence of a given variable on suicide rates could be explained by a concomitant variation in the sample. What has been lacking in Durkheim, and in many of his successors described in this book, is a recognition of multiple causation. Durkheim, in his *Rules of Sociological Method*, explicitly adopts J. S. Mills' method of *concomitant variations* as the only available means of demonstrating causal connections.[34] From that point, however, he differs from Mills' acceptance of the *plurality of causes*, stating it to be axiomatic that *a given effect has always a single corresponding cause*.[35] He is therefore logically bound to declare that "if suicide depends on more than one cause, it is because, in reality, there are several kinds of suicides,"[36] just as there are several kinds of fever, all of which produce superficially similar symptoms.

In this respect Durkheim was handicapped by the relative immaturity of statistical analysis available in his epoch. Although his analysis of effects was based on differing rates, his analysis of causes was still based on the principle of all or nothing. He represented in this respect an intermediate stage between the traditional qualitative forms of comparison and the emergent quantitative forms. What we recognize today is that many effects result from a complex of causes; as each additional variable is woven into the fabric of explanation, understanding is enlarged. But to make this kind of manipulation practicable, a whole new set of mathematical procedures had to be brought into play. Lazarsfeld and Rosenberg use the generic name *multivariate analysis* to describe these procedures, though they also admit the derogatory phrase *IBM language*.[37]

It is perhaps a reflection on the choice of works included in this book that the use of multivariate analysis is rarely encountered.

A HERITAGE OF CONCEPTS

This book does not aim to be a treatise on sociological theory. It has been made clear, however, that many of the works discussed owe their importance less to their contribution to the techniques of fact finding and analysis than to their formulation and initial testing of significant empirical theories.

Just as we have seen in respect of other parts of the process of sociological research, there is a larger factor of inheritance in the growth of such theories than would at first appear. The amazing feature is that although closely similar concepts are put forward and used by different authors, there is typically very incomplete acknowledgment of the fact.

Without attempting a complete inventory of the theoretical contributions of the works cited and of their relation to the general corpus of sociological theory, we may profitably examine some of the principal threads that run through the half-century's development recorded in this book.

The Dynamics of Social Action

In one form or another the idea of change and of current action is implicit in all the works discussed. The sociological aim is directed not at inanimate objects, like the specimens of a geologist, nor even at objects in dynamic equilibrium, like the universe of the astronomer. The changes observed by the empirical sociologist, furthermore, are irreversible and to some extent internally generated. This feature is characteristic of organic systems, though it can be simulated by man-made servomechanisms.

It is a central feature of the reports discussed that they are all concerned with modern industrial society. As will be discussed later, many sociologists have been preoccupied with the nature of the dissolution which occurs when a folk society is supplanted by an industrial society and with the differences between the two social conditions. The present point is somewhat different. It was expressed most explicitly by Thomas and Znaniecki. Because "civilized society" is marked primarily by change, an appropriate social theory must make a central feature the idea of change. For this reason, as has been noted, sociological laws must be phrased in terms not of "stereotyped activity" but of "social becoming." Furthermore, Thomas and Znaniecki were very conscious of the time element in causal relationships:

> Social becoming, like natural becoming, must be analyzed into a plurality of facts, each of which represents a succession of cause and effect. The idea of social theory is the analysis of the totality of social becoming into such causal processes and a systematization permitting us to understand the connections between these processes.[38]

At the other end of the series, it will be remembered that Bales called attention to the central importance of the time factor in all problem solving and suggested an essentially dynamic process of tension increase and tension reduction to explain why individuals go through the interaction process.[39] This is a special application of the *action frame of reference*, which itself presupposes change through time.

The Question of Values

In various forms the question of values has arisen constantly throughout preceding chapters. Durkheim was somewhat shy of the evaluative processes of individuals. As Parsons comments, he "showed both that society was a moral phenomenon and that morality was a social phenomenon."[40] At the same time he was much concerned with the question of normality. This entered into his analysis in two ways. He recognized the strength of the control exercised by society which fixes limits on the appetites of its members, setting up certain normative standards and enforcing them by moral pressures:

> A regulative force must play the same role for moral needs which the organism plays for physical needs. This means that the force can only be moral. . . . Physical restraint would be ineffective; hearts cannot be touched by physio-chemical forces. So far as the appetites are not automatically restrained by physiological mechanisms, they can be halted

only by a limit that they recognize as just. Men would never consent to restrict their desires if they felt justified in passing the assigned limit. But, for reasons given above, they cannot assign themselves this law of justice. So they must receive it from an authority which they respect, to which they yield spontaneously. Either directly and as a whole, or through the agency of one of its organs, society alone can play this moderating role; for it is the only moral power superior to the individual, the authority of which he accepts. It alone has the power necessary to stipulate law and to set the point beyond which the passions must not go. Finally, it alone can estimate the reward to be prospectively offered to every class of human functionary, in the name of the common interest.[41]

While stating that social standards are generally stable, being imposed without the need for violence, Durkheim recognizes that they are constantly changing in response to economic fluctuations and the changes occurring in the moral ideas of society. He is also anxious, however, to set up a more constant and a more detached standard of normality which can be applied from outside in judgment upon social behavior. This question is argued at length in *Rules of Sociological Method.*

Durkheim starts with the analogy of health, discussing and rejecting the various criteria for health that had been proposed—absence of pain, adaptation to environment, maximum probability of survival. He concludes that, in both a biological and a sociological context, the best criterion of normality is frequency of occurrence. "We shall call 'normal' these social conditions that are the most generally distributed, and the others 'morbid' or 'pathological.' "[42] This is not a naïve starting point, and he concedes that what is normal relates only to a given society in a given phase of development. He also concedes that all that he has done is to give a definition of terms by grouping phenomena according to their characteristics and labeling the groups thus formed. It is clear, however, that his definition of normality retains an ethical judgment. "It would be incomprehensible if the most widespread forms of organization would not at the same time be, *at least in their aggregate,* the most advantageous."[43] It can generally be demonstrated, he writes, that the normal trait is either useful or it is an unavoidable consequence of a useful trait.

Durkheim's theories represent an impressive attempt to build an empirical concept of normality without introducing the psychological questions of motivation and meaning. It is on this point that the contrast with the approach of Thomas and Znaniecki is most marked. The latters' introduction of the question of meaning, of the "definition of the situation," had a decisive effect on subsequent sociological thought.

It is useful to distinguish the two adjustments to the concept of normality that are necessitated by the admission of this kind of relationism. The first is the psychological corollary of the sociology of knowledge. The recognition that moral judgments are subject to change with changes in the social climate is easily grasped, and it is instructive to observe that Kinsey, the zoologist, was much more sophisticated on this subject than Durkheim had been. This explains why habits are found to vary from culture to culture. There remains, however, the need to transcend the behaviorist reliance on overt manifestations. Thomas had stressed this in his comment, already quoted, that "if men define situations as real, they are real in their consequences." It is not simply that actions occur; they also possess meanings. These are the grounds for perhaps the most telling criticism of Kinsey, namely, that of Kubie, the psychoanalyst, that the same act can have different meanings according to the purposes it serves; at least as far as one individual is concerned a high frequency of occurrence of one form of behavior may connote obsessive tendencies, whether it is a form of sexual activity or any rational act such as hand washing (Chapter 10).

Just as an act may remain unjustified however frequently it occurs, so, we have also been reminded, certain characters or act syndromes may be regarded as neurotic or normal according to the prevailing ethos of the particular culture. Fromm found sado-masochism to be endemic in great parts of the lower middle class in Germany and elsewhere (Chapter 11). There is also a highly important vein of thought which shows the vital role of innovation that in the first instance entails deviant, abnormal behavior.

Actually, the role of the individual with respect to society is a double one. Under ordinary circumstances, the more perfect his conditioning and consequent integration into the social structure, the more effective his contribution to the smooth functioning of the whole and the surer his rewards. However, societies have to exist and function in an ever changing world. The unparalleled ability of our species to adjust to changing conditions and to develop ever more effective responses to familiar ones rests upon the residue of individuality which survives in every one of us after society and culture have done their utmost. As a simple unit in the social organism, the individual perpetuates the status quo. As an individual he helps to change the status quo when the need arises.[44]

By definition, however, the deviant character is in a minority, and the typical experience is socialization, which entails the acquisition not only of appropriate knowledge but also of appropriate values and attitudes. We saw first the heroic but unsuccessful attempt of Thomas and Znaniecki to distinguish values from attitudes, but this was not an important failure. What has survived is the recognition that social experiences, like all other experiences, must be interpreted by individuals who have to contribute their "definition of the situation." This idea is implied in almost all the works subsequently described.

The next fully explicit discussion is that of Myrdal, who constantly returns to the question of subjective interpretation. Three examples are his theoretical distinction between general and specific valuations, which allow the person to reconcile individual prejudices with a general attitude of tolerance; the story of the sculpture of a Negro lynching; and the extraordinary examples of rationalizations that prejudiced groups allow themselves in order to justify the maintenance of the myth of Negro inferiority (Chapter 8).

In later works there begins to emerge an indication of certain ways in which the definition of the situation is likely to operate. There is the interesting case of the students in Washington whose views on the "Jewish problem" were polarized by their living in a society with a high proportion of Jews—the prejudiced becoming more prejudiced and the unprejudiced even less anti-Semitic (Chapter 11). A similar polarization was found to occur in the housing project at Baytown, so that those who were already interacting freely were further encouraged by the activity program, whereas others were merely confirmed in their self-hatred and isolation (Chapter 13). Both examples run counter to the belief that exposure to a situation improves the individual's perception of it.

A somewhat different point was raised by Bales, whose study of small-group interaction (Chapter 12) led him to suggest the importance of adequate collective perception of the situation, which permits the intercommunication needed for instrumental problem solving. According to this line of thought two conditions appear to be necessary. A definition of the situation which does not reflect reality, even if collectively held, is likely to be disappointing because the attempted problem solving will not work. In the shorter run, the failure of any joint perception of the situation is even more devastating in its effects, leading to destructive forms of expressive behavior.

According to Bales, successful problem solving requires that a group reach both cognitive and evaluative agreement. There is, however, the interesting situation in which cognitive agreement is arrived at incorrectly, in the sense that it can be falsified by further information. One is tempted to assert that what appears to be objective truth is nothing more than the product of intersubjective agreement. But further verification or falsification is always possible, at least in theory. It is therefore more accurate to describe the product of intersubjective cognitive agreement as provisional truth, it being understood that further experience will provide such closer approximations to an instrumental truth as are required. It is clearly necessary that a group possess sufficient cognitive flexibility, or here again the shock of subsequent falsification may throw it back into some form of expressive-malintegrative behavior.

Two other important issues involving a definition of the situation deserve to be recalled. The first is the theory derived by Roethlisberger and Dickson from their studies in the Bank Wiring Observation Room. It will be remembered that the investigators came to recognize the importance of all environmental features as carriers of social value with socially determined meanings (Chapter 6). Furthermore, the behavior of individuals was also seen to be motivated by logically irrelevant considerations. In the case of executives and those in authority this motivation resulted in a formal organization that did not fit the real pattern of human interaction and that consequently led to the emergence of an informal organization which applied meanings and rules of conduct that were understandable to the workers in the work context. Provided the informal and the formal organizations possess aims that are compatible, the achievement of these aims will be facilitated by the coexistence of the two organizations, in that the positive sentiments generated by the informal organization will spill over onto the formal organization.

The other issue is the related one of the reference group, which, as has been indicated, received such a boost from the re-examination by Merton and Kitt of the *American Soldier* material. Here, as with the informal organization, the decisive effect is the identification of the individual with a particular group, but there the similarity ends. In the sense of relative deprivation the novel feature is not that the individual feels underprivileged but that the group with which he compares his lot is a group other than his own. It will be remembered that Merton and Kitt attempted, with some success, to explain the detailed thought processes by which individuals in one group select another external group with which to compare themselves. In the examination of the combat veterans, replacements, and green troops they showed that the differences in response could be explained not solely by differences in the desire to identify with the higher-prestige group but also by differences in the extent of their knowledge of the value system of the higher-prestige group (Chapter 10). Here again one can detect the fascinating interplay of cognitive and affective elements.

Social Mobility

The question of the reference group and of identification with a higher-status group leads naturally to a discussion of a topic that is constantly arising in the present series, namely, the process of upward social mobility. In most cases upward social mobility is treated as one of the self-evident background features of an adaptive society. In three chapters, however, the problems of mobility become explicit and constitute one of the major themes.

In *Street Corner Society* much attention is paid to the differences between Doc and Chick as characters and to how these differences were reflected in their careers. The distinctions are so clear and so compatible with theory that one might, unfairly, suspect that the evidence was doctored. The saving clause is that the theory itself has become much more explicit since, and partly owing to, the publication of *Street Corner Society*. As leaders both Doc and Chick would have been conspicuous in Cornerville, and they would also predictably have incorporated in their ideal form the traits looked for in the two types of group. If Doc had been able to save money for a more or less remote contingency, he would not have remained leader of a feckless street-corner gang, and if Chick had been a free spender, he would have attracted a different circle of friends (Chapter 7). The detailed character syndrome of Chick falls beautifully into place beside Max Weber's hypothesis of the connection between the ethos of personal thrift and the ethos of capitalistic enterprise.

Mention has already been made of the similar behavior observed in *The American Soldier* among enlisted men heading for promotion. Here, as in other examples cited, a combination of cognitive skill and readiness to tranfer allegiance was called for. Of these two capacities, the latter, it seems, was probably the more important. At least it appears that at that time promotion decisions were not based on objective tests of capacity or performance, and the commanding officer's choice of candidates suitable for promotion could hardly have failed to take account of the man's conformity with officially approved military mores.[45] In this context conformity represents the opposite of normal social conformity; in order to conform, the man must reject the mores and normal behavior of his group of origin and feel his way into the mores of the group to which he aspires. Merton and Kitt label this process *anticipatory socialization*. They point out that certain conditions must be fulfilled before such behavior will be observed. The most important condition is that there must be a relatively open social structure; otherwise the individual will not be acceptable to the group to which he aspires, and he will become a marginal man poised on the edge of two or more groups but fully accepted by none.[46]

It is worth remembering that in the adaptive society upward social mobility is not merely permitted, it is actively encouraged. Chick was helped to work his way through college, and after he left college he was able to take advantage of various institutional facilities to promote his rise. The role of the settlement house has been stressed, and it has been made clear that it was regarded by its sponsors as an instrument of anticipatory socialization.

Another point to be noted is that the upward mobility of an individual almost always produces some painful consequences. For the individual a certain amount of initial alienation from his original group would appear to be a precondition of a desire to change his membership group. The enlisted men who openly aspired to become officers had to bear the enhanced disapproval of the enlisted men whom they were intending to quit, and the process of assimilation by a new group will seldom be completed without rebuffs. It will be remembered that Festinger and Kelley incorporated this effect into their series of hypotheses on the conditions of social mobility (Chapter 13). Perhaps the most important point is the indication that if the rebuffs are severe, as will occur with a relatively closed social structure, the individual may give up the struggle and fall back on such alternative outlets as the promotion of the solidarity of his original groups. The implication here seems to be that solidarity is propagated by relative closure of the social structure and hindered by the development of an open society. If this argument is accepted—and it does not conflict with the observable support for competitiveness in an adaptive society—it means that we may have to choose between the solidarity value and the open-social-structure value.

Disorganization and the Secular Society

One of the most regularly recurrent theories in the earlier chapters of this book is that of disorganization and consequent reorganization. The idea of decay and replacement is implicit in any dynamic view of society, but in several of the works described it is a dominant theme. Durkheim's concept of anomie was the first to be encountered. His observation that suicides increase during times of disturbance of the collective order is accounted for in terms of an upset of the established relationship between aspiration and achievement, an explanation that was later so fruitfully elaborated and systematized by Merton.

Next came Thomas and Znaniecki, who observed the calamitous effect on morals and family solidarity produced by social disorganization when previously accepted social rules are discarded in favor of new attitudes provoked by foreign contacts or changed economic conditions (Chapter 3). What critically distinguishes these authors from Durkheim is that they recognize more clearly that a transition, however painful, is necessary in order to achieve a more appropriate new system of social values.

In terms of space rather than time, the Chicago ecologists explicitly borrow the idea of disorganization in the elaboration of their principle of succession (Chapter 4), explaining why a zone of transition around the central area and any other subsidiary nuclei tends to contain the most disorganized sections of the community. The reader will also recall, in the discussion of *The Gold Coast and the Slum*, the somewhat unsatisfactory attempt to explain the co-existence in a slum area of essentially alienated hoboes and the strict subculture of Sicilian families.

It is partly a matter of chance that the theme of disorganization-reorganization is not explicit in the works included in this book that were first published after 1930. It would have been possible to select works dealing with the disorganization caused by the great depression and World War II or with the rapid reshaping of society that has been occurring in country after country throughout the world. Since the countries of Western Europe and the United States were among the first to experience this change, and were the first to apply the methods of sociology to the study of its problems, the concentration on this theme in the early chapters may be regarded as a reflection of that fact.

Types of Society

Sociologists have, of course, been deeply preoccupied not only with the transient problems encountered during the period of reshaping but also with the essential differences in the societies before and after the decisive changes. Almost every major sociological theorist has expressed his thoughts on this subject.

Traditionally the distinction has been made in terms of a dichotomy which separates the relatively simple and static social structure of primitive societies from the relatively complex and dynamic social structure of civilized societies. There are, of course, great variations in detail between the ideal types postulated by different sociologists, but substantial convergence in their ideas will be noted.

One of the first statements of modern times was made in 1861 by the English historian Henry S. Maine, who traces the gradual dissolution of family dependency and the substitution of individual obligation. He describes this transformation as a movement "from status to contract."[47] Another early contributor was the German psychologist Wilhelm Wundt, whose *Völkerpsychologie* had a profound influence on the early stages of development of sociological thought. His immense scholarship enabled him to document the typically nineteenth-century belief (derived from Rousseau and subscribed to in one form or another by Marx and Comte among thinkers) that society was passing through innumerable travails from a state of primitive grace to a state of humanity and true brotherhood. This development was characterized by increasing social complexity, so that what was originally largely a matter of individual psychology would become more and more dependent upon social control.

The influence of Wundt's thinking on Durkheim's theories of social evolution appears plain. The *mechanical* solidarity reflects the natural order of a static society whose legal and other social institutions are designed to maintain the collective sentiments of the group. To Durkheim, following Comte, the division of labor necessitates a new moral system and a new *organic* form of social solidarity. Whereas legal sanctions in the mechanical stage of society are designed to serve the collective need for conformity, in the organic stage they are designed to safeguard individual right and the sanctity of the contract.[48]

Perhaps the most famous of all such dichotomies is that of Tönnies, who had also come under the influence of Wundt and whose formulation of the differences between *Gemeinschaft*, or community, on the one hand, and *Gesellschaft*, or society, on the other hand, has pervaded all subsequent sociological thought. Tönnies showed very clearly that although history appears to favor the extension of *Gesellschaft* at the expense of *Gemeinschaft*, the two can coexist, one in the city and the other in the countryside. He contrasted *Gemeinschaft*, the lasting and genuine form of living together still surviving in rural areas, with the transitory and superficial character of *Gesellschaft*. "Accordingly, *Gemeinschaft* should be understood as a living organism, *Gesellschaft* as a mechanical aggregate and artifact."[49] Rather confusingly, the connotations of mechanical and organic social structure are reversed from those adopted by Durkheim.

One may thus contrast the personal commitment of Durkheim, who accepted the division of labor as a necessary means for men's conquest over nature, with that of Tönnies, whose view of the world was nostalgic. It is interesting that his fellow countryman Max Weber appears also to have been motivated by nostalgic sentiments in undertaking his great work on *The Protestant Ethic and the Spirit of Capitalism*. Bendix has discerningly written of Max Weber:

His disenchantment with the world in which he lived led him to a search of the past for the origin of the values he prized. As an individualist Weber sought to uncover the historical sources of the individualism that prompted the farm workers to prefer the uncertainty of seasonal labor to the security of personal subservience. As a member of the middle class he inquired into the sources of the collectivism and rationality that prompted English and Hanseatic stockbrokers to impose an ethic of trade upon themselves—a practice that stood in marked contrast to the aping of aristocratic ways among his compatriots.[50]

Naturally it is easier to discover examples of a pure folk society in areas remote from industrial civilization. The social anthropologist Robert Redfield has made a significant contribution to the subject, primarily by setting up the characteristics of an ideal-type folk society and by demonstrating that the divergence from this pure form varies with the degree of contact with industrial civilization. He thus introduces the idea not of a clear-cut dichotomy but of a spectrum of circumstances which shade into one another by differences that are sometimes almost imperceptible. Initially, by studying four communities in Yucatan—city, town, peasant village, and tribal village— he showed that there was a regular gradation, so that the four communities are listed in the order in which they possess a syndrome of characteristics: heterogeneity, developed division of labor and money economy, secular rather than sacred professional specialists, relatively ineffective kinship ties and relative dependence on impersonal social control, less religion, more individuation.[51]

Redfield's study has been criticized on a variety of grounds.[52] It is possible that he aimed at greater generality than his data justified, but the main contention that greater differentiation and a looser type of solidarity are to be found at the urban end of the continuum was justified by his findings and is consistent with the mass of evidence from other—admittedly Western—sources.

The phrase *plural society* has been used to describe the typical urban community, to emphasize the fact that the city can accommodate a large number of subcultures, so that the individual has a corresponding freedom of choice. It will be remembered that Zorbaugh, in *The Gold Coast and the Slum*, made use of the teaching of W. I. Thomas to explain the difficulty of achieving community action in such a society because the requisite unanimity of opinion is impossible to achieve, so that decisions can represent only majority opinions (Chapter 4).

There is also no single prevailing culture in an urban community. The implications of this were pointed out by Linton:

> Folk cultures are borne by small, closely-integrated social units or by aggregates of such units which have already worked out satisfactory mutual adjustments. In such cultures, new items are not appearing with any great frequency and the society has plenty of time to test them and to assimilate them to its pre-existing pattern. In such cultures the core constitutes almost the whole.
>
> In modern civilization on the other hand, the small, closely integrated social units are being broken down, giving place to masses of individuals who are much more loosely interrelated than the members of the former local groups and classes. . . . In modern civilizations, therefore, the core of culture is being progressively reduced. Our own civilization, as it presents itself to the individual, is mainly an assortment of Alternatives between which he may or frequently must choose. We are rapidly approaching the point where there will no longer be enough items on which all members of the society agree to provide the culture with form and pattern.[53]

A fascinating feature of urban society is that to some extent the subcultures coexist and to some extent they isolate themselves geographically from one another. Zorbaugh reports that while the types of behavior that were most typical of the city were found largely within the central areas, the city had wrought less fundamental changes in the outlying areas, which retained a traditionally rural culture. Even the reformers, often highly civilized cosmopolites, lived in a settlement outside the city from which they attempted to impose on all Chicago the standards and ideals of their essentially rural culture.[54]

Examples have also accumulated of closely knit family cultures surviving relatively unaffected in the middle of raging disorganization. Little Sicily was one instance, and the works by Young and Willmott in Bethnal Green, London, and by Gans in Boston, provide modern cases of the same effect. In view of the demonstrated difficulty in communicating moral change (Chapter 13), this result is not altogether surprising. It is, however, significant that contemporary inquiries have tended to stress the integrative function of an established urban neighborhood in the face of the newer and increasingly depersonalized forms of suburban development.

Other recent research tends to show that under modern conditions there are interesting connections between how a married couple organize their conjugal-role relationship and how they organize their network of social relationships. There appears to be a spectrum ranging from one extreme in which both husband and wife come into marriage with a well-developed network of external social relationships so that they rely less on each other for mutual help and support, while at the other extreme there are relatively isolated families which are very dependent on each other. According to Bott, the type of family organization is not directly related to social class, except that the traditional areas with close-knit social networks tend to be working-class communities.[55]

Whichever type of social network is salient, one rather universal development has been noted. For various reasons the parental authority is seen to decline wherever a secular society is well established; with rapid growth in knowledge the function of educating children is very largely handed over by parents to the schools. At this stage the teacher acts *in loco parentis* and not only is the source of the child's knowledge but also originates many of his evaluations of the world. As a further development, which is becoming increasingly common in some cultures, the child ceases to absorb the norms of parent or parent-surrogate and instead derives his view of the world from his contemporaries. This habit of taste exchange is then frequently carried through to adult life. In the last decade or two, whole communities, for example, the Park Forest development described by William H. Whyte, Jr.,[56] have adopted this busy, depersonalized interactive way of life, and we must recognize today not only the classical dichotomy, now labeled by Riesman "tradition-direction" and "inner-direction," but also the new, previously unrecognized category of "other-direction." Nobody can as yet clearly see whether this third type is a stable social form or whether it is a symptom of transient malaise, but if it does establish itself, we may be sure that social life will evolve some surprising and distinctive features.

Functions and Characteristics of the Group

The scientific ideal is approached when the scientist is able to control and manipulate his material. This not only endears him to those in power, who can thereby make direct use of his knowledge, but also—in one sense more importantly—demonstrates to him that his theories and his techniques have consummated their union.

All this is true of the social scientist. The stakes are, in fact, exceptionally high not only because of the difficulties attached to social control but also because of the immense prizes that await the individual or group that succeeds in manipulating human social behavior and attitudes.

With a little exaggeration one might assert that almost every important figure in sociology has produced a formula for social control. We may start with the celebrated example of August Comte, the founder of sociology, whose scrupulous faith in a positive science became submerged in the grandiose vision of a new religion of humanity.

As has been noted, Durkheim was determined to pursue the practical consequences of the social problems that he studied; in the case of *Suicide* he inevitably considered the possible practical measures that could be taken to reduce suicide. At this stage in his book one is disappointed by his forecasts of what may be the effects of the measures that he considers—legislation, industrial corporations, increased restrictions on divorce, and so on. It is clear that, however incisive his analysis of the causes of suicide, he is groping in the dark in his search for cures.

Thomas and Znaniecki in *The Polish Peasant* were considerably more sophisticated on the subject of social control. The only disadvantage is that their contribution was mainly critical and negative. Recognizing the importance of social control in an era of rapid change, they mocked at the crude techniques actually applied by society—the exercise of power by the use of forcible legislation or the amateur methods of "practical" sociology, which neglected even the small knowledge of psychological motivation that had been gained by that date. As they saw it, any smooth change required attention both to the social environment itself and to the prevailing social attitudes; if a choice had to be made, they favored a concentration on attitudes. Furthermore, they commented with extraordinary foresight on the need to enlist the active and understanding co-operation of the individual on whom they desired to exercise social control (Chapter 3).

In contrast with their critique of the uncertain methods of social control normally adopted by legislators and others, Thomas and Znaniecki presented an imaginative analysis of the traditional forms of social control exercised in those Polish circles that had not yet been infected with the disorganizing pressures of industrial society. It is particularly interesting to compare this with the high degree of social cohesion retained by the ex-peasant families living in Little Sicily, as described by Zorbaugh in *The Gold Coast and the Slum*. The disorganizing conditions that had attracted the riffraff of Chicago had not tainted their neighbors, the Sicilians, presumably because the social attitudes of the Sicilians remained strong and constant enough to resist (Chapter 4).

The next relevant study shows clearly the important role that social control can play in resisting change. This is the phase in *Management and the Worker* during which Roethlisberger and Dickson were concerned with the Bank Wiring Observation Room. Under these conditions, in which the participants were expected merely to be themselves, a great variety of apparently pointless types of interaction took place (Chapter 6). Similarly, the activities of the young men of Cornerville in *Street Corner Society* were in many cases supposedly aimless—so much so that Whyte was rather ashamed at spending his time on them. It is only when their behavior is looked at in terms of its function of social control that the apparently trivial events begin to make sense. Nearly all the activities of the Observation Room were seen as methods of social control to protect the work group from internal indiscretions and from outside interference (Chapter 6). Similarly, the activities of the street-corner boys were designed to determine and reinforce the group structure and to assert the position of the group in relation to outside groups. An illuminating example of social control in action was the behavior of the group in disciplining Alec, one of its members, who boasted of skill at bowling that would have exceeded that expected of one of his stature in the group (Chapter 7).

One may indeed assert that a collection of individuals in regular contact can hardly fail to develop a social function of one kind or another. Any such group very consistently also evolves some kind of hierarchical structure. The group develops both function and form because it cannot survive without these features. This is true in terms both of the satisfaction to participating individuals and of the achievements of the group. It has already been shown (see Chapter 12) that the external achievements of the group presuppose an essentially correct cognitive appreciation of the situation, and the realization that the group view of the world is false is likely to have a devastating effect on group cohesion.

The works examined also show that knowledge of the world is not enough, and that the group must evolve a stable structure. This specification is again helped by the fact that the individuals look to the group as such for certain satisfactions. Outstanding among these, as Shils reminded us (see Chapter 9), is the human desire for a "protective personal relationship" which is evidenced in army units; if one member of the group is able to supply this need, the other members are quite likely to accept his commands, even if these lead them to certain deprivations. It is a corollary of this that the conditions for the rapid growth of solidarity within the primary group are accentuated by the existence of an immediate external task such as combat provides for military units, particularly when, as in this instance, the normal disparity of privileges between the leader and the led is blurred by combat conditions.

Shils, with Talcott Parsons, was influential in introducing the work of Max Weber to American sociologists. With Talcott Parsons he played a leading part in the later systematization of the theory of action, and it is clear that their collaboration strongly influenced Bales while he was working on *Interaction Process Analysis*. Bales incorporated both Weber's emphasis on leadership as legitimized authority—the instrumental function needed for the enforcement of orders—and Weber's famous category of charismatic leadership—which stresses its expressive function. The special contribution of Bales and his colleagues was that they gave precision to these ideas and to the relationship between them by the use of controlled laboratory experimentation. This is a rather exceptional example of the way in which empirical work, by making use of some theoretically sophisticated but otherwise somewhat unapproachable ideas, not only confirms earlier theory but gives a previously unattained specificity to them. It is found not merely, as Weber suggested, that the word leadership subsumes distinct func-

tions but, furthermore, that there is a relationship between these instrumental and expressive functions, so that in various circumstances the solidarity of the group will be sustained only if both
functions are provided for.

SOCIOLOGY AND OTHER CONTEMPORARY THEORIES

It would, of course, be absurd to suggest that the development of
sociological theory hinted at in previous sections has proceeded
without cross infection with other germinal theories that have swept
Western thought over the same period. Without attempting a profound analysis of the interrelationship between the thought inside
and outside the sociological camp, it may still be profitable to pick
up some of the most obvious communications that have penetrated
the stockades.

We need not linger over the seminal influence of the Enlightenment. We may also skim over the analogies aroused by the impact of
Darwin's theories and of the peculiar fascination that the idea of the
"survival of the fittest" seems to have had for late-nineteenth-
century thinkers. Such analogies have their uses provided the thinker
does not allow himself to be hypnotized by them. Evolution, organism, mechanism, the principle of uncertainty—all such borrowings
have a place in the development of sociological thought.

There are, however, two sets of ideas, poised in each case between science and philosophy, that have potentially an altogether
more basic influence. The first of these sets of ideas is associated
with the name of Karl Marx and the second with that of Sigmund
Freud.

The wave of social uncertainty in the 1840's that led Comte, dis-
ciple of the socialist Saint-Simon, toward the positive philosophy of
sociology also gave a powerful impetus to socialism, particularly in
its more active and revolutionary political forms. Karl Marx with
Friedrich Engels participated in the 1848 uprising, preparing the
celebrated *Communist Manifesto*. Later Marx, with the help of
Engels, devoted himself to a radical reformulation of the social
sciences. His influence on sociology has been indirect but is believed
by some to have been profound. European scholars in the last
century have been exposed to a continuous debate with Marxism,

and even when the antagonist has not been specified, one can detect fragments of dialogue aimed toward Marxism.[57]

In the United States for some decades there has been almost a deliberate silence as to the intellectual content of Marxism. It might be thought that for some reason American non-Marxist sociologists had never coolly examined these doctrines, and it comes as some surprise to learn that Albion Small, founder of the department of sociology at the University of Chicago, regarded Marx as a key figure, if a misguided one. Since he spent a couple of years as a young man in the Universities of Leipzig and Berlin, Small had continued to keep abreast of German sociological thinking, and it may have been this fact that made him declare himself some thirty years later in such categorical terms:

> Marx was one of the few really great thinkers in the history of social science. . . . Up to the present time the appellate court of the world's sober second thought has not given him as fair a hearing as it has granted to Judas Iscariot. . . . I do not think that Marx added to social science a single formula which will be final in the terms in which he expressed it. In spite of that, I confidently predict that in the ultimate judgment of history Marx will have a place in social science analogous with that of Galileo in physical science.[58]

Of the works described in this book, the earlier ones give the impression of taking Marx in their stride. In *Division of Labor* Durkheim quotes in passing a phrase of Marx that he found appropriate and colorful, but there is no evidence of any direct influence even though some points of similarity can be discerned.[59] Thomas and Znaniecki, writing at about the time of the Russian revolution, bracket Marx with Charles the Great, Napoleon, and Bismarck as a transformer of the social world, but do not appear to have taken particular account of him as a thinker.

Ten years later the contribution of Marx appeared to be asserting itself. As has been pointed out, Lynd—probably unconsciously— followed the Marxist dichotomy between proletarians and bourgeoisie, and by *Middletown in Transition* he had clearly gained much from his knowledge of Marxist writings. By the time that he was preparing *Knowledge for What?** Lynd, though still critical of the

* In this book Lynd also refers to the "relatively short shrift which Karl Marx receives from the social scientists in our universities."

"too-externalized drama of Marxism," called for a more forthright approach by social scientists to problems explicitly concerned with fundamental change, specifying Marx's economic determinism as one problem demanding study.[60]

In the case of *Management and the Worker* we might expect a recognition of the factory milieu as the natural focus for the class struggle in action. Instead we find an almost contemptuous neglect of any element of conflict in the industrial situation. That this is not a chance omission on the part of the authors is suggested by Mayo's assertion elsewhere that "Socialism, Communism, Marxism would seem to be irrelevant to the industrial events of the twentieth century."[61] Myrdal commented: "Modern social engineering has actually had practically no inspiration from Marx's 'scientific' socialism."[62]

Similarly, we are bound to conclude that the writings of Marx have had a remarkably small influence on the other empirical studies described in this book. It is true that we could have tuned in to that dialogue if we had examined Weber or Mannheim or, for example, C. Wright Mills, whose study of *The Power Elite* borrows from Marx as from many other thinkers. As a thought system, however, the light of Marxism in the United States shone for a while in the depression and then went out; the chasm that opened in the 1840's between sociology and socialism has remained unbridged.

In the case of psychoanalysis the course has been somewhat different. With his interest in the "four wishes" it is natural that W. I. Thomas should have followed up any available method of studying the personality. At least by 1923, in *The Unadjusted Girl*, he recognized the merits of the psychoanalytic school for this purpose, to be weighed against what he regarded as a lack of objectivity which overemphasized sex as the basis of life organization. He concluded that psychoanalytic records as case material were increasingly important for the study of behavior.[63] At the 1938 conference Thomas made it clear that his "four wishes" formulation had developed quite independently of psychoanalysis. Asked whether he thought that the current concern of psychoanalysts with anxieties was related to his *wish for security*, he replied:

I don't think there was an appreciable influence in that direction. And there was none in the other direction either. Some sociologists have assumed that I derived the idea of the wish from Freud, but, in fact, I was using the term in about the year 1905, and before I had heard of Freud.[64]

Similarly, one can turn the pages of the other works of the Chicago School without finding any reference to Freud or psychoanalytic theory. In this context it is interesting to recall that Dollard, in his *Criteria for the Life History*, subjected to analysis both Wladek's life history in *The Polish Peasant* and *The Jack-Roller*, one of Clifford Shaw's contributions to the Chicago series. As a psychoanalyst Dollard paid particular attention to the examination of materials in these life histories that had a bearing on psychoanalytic theory. *The Jack-Roller* makes a very bad showing in this respect; Dollard found a lack of specification of what had turned the principal character into a delinquent or of what motivated him in his career of jack-rolling. The same lack of concern with individual personality formation and motivation appears to characterize other works of the Chicago School.

The case of the Lynds is also an instructive one. Not surprisingly, the minimum of speculation on individual personalities is found in *Middletown*. In the sequel, *Middletown in Transition*, interest in this approach is beginning to show itself in a tentative fashion; the section on "Training the Young," for example, has nothing to say on the psychological basis of character, but there is a passing reference in "Spending Leisure" to the masochistic tendencies in our culture which make acquisition more important than living.[65] This is Weber's old point, but significantly it is here attributed to Horney and Fromm. *Knowledge for What?*, on the other hand, contains various comments on psychoanalysis, reflecting both Freud and Horney. It seems that psychoanalytic theory reached the Lynds substantially through the "American" writers on the subject. Today Helen Lynd has moved far into the realm of psychoanalysis, as her recent book, *On Shame and the Search for Identity*, reveals.

The position of Mayo and his Harvard colleagues appears to have been a little ambivalent. In 1933 Mayo is critical of "the doctrines of psychoanalysis with respect to the development of the childish mentality" and adds that "the concealed assumption of the doctrine of original sin invalidates the psychoanalytic findings."[66] In 1939 Roethlisberger and Dickson include Freud in a list of theoretical sources that range from Pierre Janet and Piaget to Pareto and Pitt-Rivers.[67] Later Mayo, in his notes on Pierre Janet, appears to go out of his way to show the close resemblances between Janet's studies of obsession and Freud's work on psychoneurosis. The time sequence suggests a growing interest in psychoanalysis, and at the very least Mayo demonstrated his familiarity with its psychoneurosis aspects.

As the practice of psychiatry has developed, the technical meaning of psychoneurosis has become somewhat simplified, and the term is now used to cover those suffering from virtually all mental disorders provided they are not actually psychotic.* In this sense the *American Soldier* team were much concerned with the recognition of psychoneurosis and the prediction of the outcome. John Dollard, serving in the Research Branch, prepared a memorandum on the conditions under which such predictions might be successful, but, although psychoanalytically oriented, he apparently did not use this occasion as an opportunity for psychoanalytic treatment. Likewise, his colleagues who prepared a variety of test batteries did so with only the faintest side glance at psychoanalysis; most of the questions asked seem to have been of the common-sense subtheoretical type, for example, "Do you often have trouble in getting to sleep or staying asleep?" and "Do your hands ever tremble enough to bother you?"[68]

In the case of the Kinsey reports the comment has already been made in this chapter that the orientation was consistently behaviorist. In spite of this the Kinsey team show themselves remarkably well read in Freud's writings and remarkably appreciative of his findings. It is stated, for example, that Freud's view of infant sexuality is confirmed by the interview material.[69] The authors also approve of Freud's interpretation of sex as a normal biologic function, adding that Freud has contributed more than biologists toward an adoption of this biologic viewpoint.[70] The *Human Female*, which is exceptionally well documented, is even more attentive to Freud and to psychoanalytic theory, differing mainly in orthodox post-Freudian respects; for instance, the paramount importance of early childhood experience is questioned.[71] The two Kinsey volumes are more sophisticated about psychoanalysis than any of the foregoing works discussed in this book; unfortunately they restricted themselves to

* Some authorities distinguish a third class of so-called "psychopathic" individuals.

describing sexual *activities* and left to others the consideration of the *meaning* of sexual behavior.

Naturally the outstanding example of applied psychoanalytic theory among the works discussed in this book is found in *The Authoritarian Personality*. In this case the ideas of Freud are all-pervasive —in the search for sentiments whose latent meanings point to authoritarianism, in the use of psychoanalytic clinical interviews, in the explanation of authoritarian personality in terms of early childhood experience (Chapter 11). It has been demonstrated how valuable it can be to a team of investigators to set out with a developed theory. In the present instance the only difficulty is that psychoanalytic concepts still arouse such powerful antipathies. Mention has been made of Hyman and Sheatsley's unnecessarily vigorous attack on the authors' use of psychodynamic explanations, and one cannot help feeling that at least on some occasions it is not the admittedly speculative form of psychological theory so much as its disturbing implications that lead to such fervent antagonism.

While the last two works studied in this book are not explicitly concerned with psychoanalysis, it is evident that in both cases the authors are very conscious of the challenge of psychoanalytic concepts. As a refugee from Europe, Kurt Lewin was well aware of the seductive power of psychoanalytic thought; but he and his colleagues rejected psychoanalysis both theoretically—for example, because Freud was concerned with the effects of early experiences, while Lewin was interested only in the contemporaneous field—and methodologically—because of Lewin's insistence on visible behavior.* At the same time Lewin borrowed certain psychoanalytic concepts, including *displacement* and *conflict*. Furthermore, the Research Center for Group Dynamics has always been open to psychoanalytic contacts, as is evidenced by the fact that since 1947 they have been cosponsors of the journal *Human Relations* jointly with the psychoanalytically oriented Tavistock Institute of Human Relations.

The influence on Bales was, as we have seen, rather more direct. It is made clear that he made use of the psychoanalytic concepts of ego, id, and ego ideal, but in an indirect way in keeping with his

---

* "Field theory, as any scientific approach to psychology, is 'behavioristic,' if this means the tendency to provide 'operational definitions' (testable symptoms) for the concepts used."[72]

decision to concentrate on the form of interaction to the exclusion of subject matter or of values and attitudes.

These examples suggest that an awareness of psychoanalysis has tended to become a normal quality in an American social scientist. In contrast with Marxism, the overt influence of which has declined, Freudianism has increased its indirect hold. Yet the direct effect of psychoanalysis on the social sciences is remarkably slight. The situation is still much as Hall and Lindzey described it in 1954. Their general comment refers to Freudian thought as one of the main currents of the intellectual stream of modern life. But when they turn to the self-conscious attempts to apply Freudian theory in the social sciences the picture is very different. It is only in anthropology that the record is at all impressive; even here there is anything but a blind acceptance of the general merit of psychoanalysis as a tool for the ethnologist. In social psychology there is a similar semicritical preoccupation with psychoanalysis. Newcomb is perhaps the most prominent among social psychologists who have explicitly used a psychoanalytic approach, and even he felt the need to translate Freud's concepts into the language of a later day.

The position is similar in the field of sociology. Sociologists have toyed with psychoanalysis, but few have attempted a thorough assimilation. The normal excuse has been that psychoanalysis has overconcentrated on instinctlike motivations, while sociology is more concerned with cultural developments, but it is again noticeable that Parsons and his collaborators draw heavily upon psychoanalytic sources in their attempt at the interdisciplinary theory of behavior presented in *Toward a General Theory of Action*. Riesman is another sociologist who has used psychoanalytic theory, in his case to account for the mechanism of inner direction, which relates so closely to Freud's concept of the superego.[73]

Ultimately, of course, the fact that sociology and the other social sciences have tried to plow their own furrows is not surprising. The social sciences have been eclectic enough, borrowing freely, though selectively, from the sciences, the arts, and the world of affairs. If any existing branch had been outstandingly suitable for handling the intellectual and practical problems with which the social sciences are concerned, the presumption is that it would have been used for this purpose. The future lies in more ready absorption of all and

every assimilable line of thought and not in the attempt to force
the matter of the social sciences into any predetermined mold.

THE PRESENT AND THE FUTURE OF SOCIOLOGY

Sociology today is a quite respectable occupation in most countries, and in the United States it is a thriving industry. Nearly fifteen
years ago Edward Shils could write:

> In this half century, as our universities exfoliated and lost whatever
> humanistic center of gravity they might once have had, sociology also
> developed in the same amorphous way. It has produced during this
> period a huge literature and has entered into the life of the nation in a
> great variety of ways. Sociologists are now employed in government
> departments and in numerous private bodies. They are firmly established
> in the system of higher education and they exercise some influence over
> the educational system on its lower and intermediate levels; vast sums
> of money are spent annually on sociological researches.[74]

What Shils wrote is even truer today. In terms of scale, an impressive effort is going into sociology in the form of teaching, research, and application. Furthermore, sociologists have lost some of
the self-consciousness that Shils detected. While the discipline of
sociology still receives its share of hostility from other academics,
sociologists are no longer so defenseless. To an increasing extent
they feel that they are needed.

The growing institutionalization of the professional practice is
one of the historical trends that emerge from this book. In their
early days sociologists were to be found in the thick of contemporary problems, often taking an independent line that brought them
into conflict with authority. In this same period, as we have seen,
methods were rough-and-ready, being aimed not at some paradigm
of science but at the level of problem solving that would be adequate to influence informed lay opinion. In social engineering, as in
other purposive activities, the tools must be good enough to do the
job, but to be too good is only wasteful.*

But, as so frequently happens, what started as a form of social
amelioration grew in maturity into an academic discipline and a

---

* This evaluation, it will be remembered, is the mark of a secular society.

status-conferring profession. With this came a greater perspective and increased concern with empirical theory. The human miseries that had previously appeared to be in need of local remedies began to be seen in a wider context, in terms both of theory and of functional interdependence. Specifically sociological concepts—such as *norms*, *values*, or *interaction*—began to be used confidently in empirical research. Specifically sociological methods of quantitative and qualitative analysis of field material were increasingly devised.

We must be very circumspect in criticizing such developments. Without the advances in systematic inquiry described in this book we should still be operating at the level of vague generality. Without the emergence of a specifically sociological frame of reference we should be unable to discipline the data that modern techniques enable us to collect. And yet these advances, indispensable as they may be, are only the means to an end for those who believe that the value of knowledge is control over nature, and that the world still has an overwhelming need for the large instrumental truths of sociology.

NOTES

CHAPTER 1

1. Robert E. Park and Ernest W. Burgess, *The City* (Chicago: University of Chicago Press, 1925), p. 14.

CHAPTER 2

1. Émile Durkheim, *Le Suicide: Étude de sociologie* (Paris: Alcan, 1897). Translated by John A. Spaulding and George Simpson, edited by George Simpson, and published as *Suicide* (New York: The Free Press of Glencoe, 1951).

2. The main source of this brief biography is Harry Alpert, *Émile Durkheim and His Sociology* (New York: Columbia University Press, 1939).

3. Émile Durkheim, *De la division du travail social: Étude sur l'organisation des sociétés supérieures* (Paris: Alcan, 1893). Translated by George Simpson as *The Division of Labor in Society* (New York: The Free Press of Glencoe, 1947).

4. Émile Durkheim, *Les règles de la méthode sociologique* (Paris: Alcan, 1895). Translated by Sarah A. Solvay and John H. Mueller and edited by George E. G. Catlin as *The Rules of Sociological Method* (New York: The Free Press of Glencoe, 1938).

5. Émile Durkheim, *Les formes élémentaires de la vie réligieuse: Le système totémique en Australie* (Paris: Alcan, 1912). Translated by Joseph Ward Swain as *Elementary Forms of the Religious Life* (New York: The Free Press of Glencoe, 1954).

6. The question is first discussed in *Division of Labor*, p. 246.

7. *Loc. cit.*

8. *Suicide*, p. 49.

9. *Ibid.*, p. 51.

10. *Division of Labor*, p. 33.

11. *Suicide*, p. 75.

12. Peter Sainsbury, *Suicide in London: An Ecological Study* (London: Institute of Psychiatry, 1955), pp. 60–61.

13. *Suicide*, p. 88.

14. *Ibid.*, p. 89.

15. *Ibid.*, p. 110.

16. Paul F. Lazarsfeld and Morris Rosenberg, eds., *The Language of Social Research* (New York: The Free Press of Glencoe, 1955), pp. 119 *et seq.*

17. *Suicide*, pp. 148–149.

18. *Ibid.,* p. 168.

19. *Ibid.,* p. 209.

20. *Ibid.,* p. 222.

21. *Ibid.,* p. 254.

22. *Division of Labor,* pp. 244–245.

23. *Suicide,* p. 256.

24. David Riesman, *The Lonely Crowd* (New Haven: Yale University Press, 1950), p. 129.

25. *Suicide,* p. 269.

26. *Ibid.,* p. 274.

27. Robert K. Merton, *Social Theory and Social Structure,* (revised edition, New York: The Free Press of Glencoe, 1957), p. 132.

28. *Rules of Sociological Method,* p. 6.

29. *Ibid.,* p. 8.

30. *Suicide,* p. 299.

31. *Rules of Sociological Method,* pp. 54–55.

32. *Ibid.,* p. 55.

33. *Ibid.,* p. 60.

34. *Ibid.,* pp. 56, 60.

35. *Suicide,* p. 309.

36. *Ibid.,* p. 311.

37. Alpert, *op. cit.,* p. 136.

38. Maurice Halbwachs, *Les causes du suicide* (Paris: Alcan, 1930).

39. *Suicide,* p. 370.

40. *Ibid.,* p. 378.

41. *Ibid.,* p. 382.

42. *Ibid.,* p. 384.

43. For example, Erich Fromm, particularly in his *Escape from Freedom* (New York: Rinehart, 1941), and Percival and Paul Goodman, whose *Communitas* (reissued, 1960, New York: Vintage Books) has had a lasting influence.

44. Alpert, *op. cit.,* p. 98.

45. This point was explored by R. E. L. Faris and H. W. Dunham in their classic study *Mental Disorders in Urban Areas* (Chicago: University of Chicago Press, 1939) and has since been taken up by Peter Sainsbury, *op. cit.,* and others.

46. Cf. Alpert, *op. cit.,* p. 120, and Merton, *op. cit.,* p. 92.

CHAPTER 3

1. William I. Thomas and Florian Znaniecki, *The Polish Peasant in Europe and America* (1st ed., Boston: Gorham Press, 1918–20, used for reference; 2nd ed., New York: Knopf, 1927).

2. Harry Elmer Barnes, *An Introduction to the History of Sociology* (Chicago: University of Chicago Press, 1948), p. 797.

3. See Herbert Blumer, *An Appraisal of Thomas and Znaniecki's "The Polish Peasant in Europe and America"* (New York: Social Science Research Council, Bulletin 44, 1939), p. 103.

4. *The Polish Peasant,* vol. 1, p. 400.

5. *Ibid.,* vol. 1, p. 316.

6. Blumer, *op. cit.,* p. 104.

7. *Ibid.,* p. 105.

8. *The Polish Peasant,* vol. 5, p. 62. This quotation is footnoted: "Most of the materials published at the end of this chapter come from such albums, particularly from those of the parishes of St. Stanislaus and of the Holy Trinity in Chicago."

9. See also *ibid.,* p. 26.

10. *Ibid.,* vol. 3, p. 1.

11. Blumer, *op. cit.,* p. 83.

12. *The Polish Peasant,* vol. 1, p. 24.

13. *Ibid.,* vol. 1, p. 22.

14. Robert E. Park, *Society* (New York: The Free Press of Glencoe, 1955), especially pp. 252–266. See also *The Polish Peasant,* vol. 1, pp. 30–32.

15. *The Rules of Sociological Method,* p. 110.

16. *The Polish Peasant,* vol. 1, p. 55.

17. *Ibid.,* vol. 1, pp. 64–65.

18. *Ibid.*, vol. 1, p. 65.

19. *Ibid.*, vol. 1, p. 66.

20. *Ibid.*, vol. 1, p. 68.

21. *Ibid.*, vol. 1, p. 72.

22. William I. Thomas, *The Unadjusted Girl* (Boston: Little, Brown, 1923), p. 4.

23. Barnes, *op. cit.*, p. 801.

24. C. M. Child, *et al.*, *The Unconscious, a Symposium* (New York: Knopf, 1927), pp. 145–146.

25. *The Polish Peasant*, vol. 1, pp. 76–78.

26. *Ibid.*, vol. 1, p. 76.

27. *Ibid.*, vol. 1, p. 76.

28. *Ibid.*, vol. 1, pp. 77–78.

29. John Dollard, *Criteria for the Life History* (New York: Peter Smith, 1949), pp. 155–171.

30. Blumer, *op. cit.*, p. 85.

31. *The Polish Peasant*, vol. 1, p. 73.

32. Blumer, *op. cit.*, p. 61.

33. *The Polish Peasant*, vol. 5, pp. 165–166.

34. Robert S. Lynd and Helen M. Lynd, *Middletown: A Study in Contemporary American Culture* (New York: Harcourt, Brace, 1929), p. 21.

35. *The Polish Peasant*, vol. 1, p. 137.

36. Blumer, *op. cit.*, pp. 69 *et. seq.*

37. *Ibid.*, p. 75.

38. *Ibid.*, pp. 75–77.

39. *Ibid.*, p. 76.

40. *Ibid.*, p. 77.

41. *Ibid.*, p. 81.

42. *Ibid.*, p. 116.

43. Gordon W. Allport, *The Use of Personal Documents in Psychological Science* (New York: Social Science Research Council, Bulletin 49, 1942), p. 148.

44. Louis Gottschalk, Clyde Kluckhohn, and Robert C. Angell, *The Use of Personal Documents in History, Anthropology, and Sociology* (New York: Social Science Research Council, Bulletin 53, 1945).

45. *Ibid.*, p. 183.

CHAPTER 4

1. Robert E. Park, *Human Communities* (New York: The Free Press of Glencoe, 1952), p. 5.

2. *Ibid.*, pp. 13–51.

3. In Robert E. Park and Ernest W. Burgess, *The City* (Chicago: University of Chicago Press, 1925).

4. Nels Anderson, *The Hobo: The Sociology of the Homeless Man* (Chicago: University of Chicago Press, 1923).

5. Frederic M. Thrasher, *The Gang* (Chicago: University of Chicago Press, 1927).

6. Louis Wirth, *The Ghetto* (Chicago: University of Chicago Press, 1928).

7. Calvin F. Schmid, "A Generalization Concerning the Ecology of the American City," *American Sociological Review*, vol. 15 (1960), pp. 264–281, and many later papers in the *American Sociological Review* and elsewhere.

8. Two notable recent examples are John Mogey, *Family and Neighbourhood* (New York: Oxford University Press, 1956); and Michael Young and Peter Wilmott, *Family and Kinship in East London* (London: Routledge, 1957).

9. Roderick McKenzie, *The Metropolitan Community* (New York: McGraw-Hill, 1933).

10. Harvey W. Zorbaugh, *The Gold Coast and the Slum* (Chicago: University of Chicago Press, 1929).

11. *Ibid.*, p. 3.

12. *Ibid.*, p. 5.

13. *Ibid.*, p. 6.

14. *Ibid.*, pp. 5–6.

15. Norman S. Hayner, "Hotel Life and Personality," in Ernest W. Burgess, ed., *Personality and the Social Group* (Chicago: University of Chicago Press, 1929) pp. 108–120.

16. Zorbaugh, *op. cit.*, p. 74.

17. *Ibid.*, p. 82.

18. *Loc. cit.*

19. Ruth S. Cavan, *Suicide* (Chicago: University of Chicago Press, 1928).

20. Robert K. Merton, *Social Theory and Social Structure* (revised edition, New York: The Free Press of Glencoe, 1957), pp. 155 *et seq.*

21. Zorbaugh, *op. cit.*, p. 92.

22. Henry Mayhew, *London Labour and the London Poor* (London: Griffin, 1851).

23. Zorbaugh, *op. cit.*, p. 141.

24. *Ibid.*, p. 154.

25. Wirth, *op. cit.*, p. 290.

26. As in Thrasher's Map of Chicago's Gangland, 1923–26, *op. cit.*, p. 24.

27. Zorbaugh, *op. cit.*, p. 182

28. *Ibid.*, p. 196.

29. *Ibid.*, p. 205.

30. *Ibid.*, Document 71, p. 214.

31. *Ibid.*, p. 235, fn.

32. *Ibid.*, p. 251.

33. Paul G. Cressey, *The Taxi Dance Hall* (Chicago: University of Chicago Press, 1932), p. xviii.

34. Eduard C. Lindeman, *Social Discovery* (New York: Republic, 1924), pp. 178–179.

35. *Ibid.*, pp. 181–182.

36. *Ibid.*, pp. 182–183.

37. *Ibid.*, p. 183.

38. Nels Anderson and Eduard C. Lindeman, *Urban Sociology* (New York: Knopf, 1930).

39. Anderson, *op. cit.*

40. Clifford H. Shaw, *The Jack-Roller: A Delinquent Boy's Own Story* (Chicago: University of Chicago Press, 1930).

41. *Ibid.*, p. 1.

42. *Ibid.*, p. 23.

43. *Ibid.*, p. 2.

44. *Ibid.*, pp. 3–4.

45. Clifford H. Shaw, *The Natural History of a Delinquent Career* (Chicago: University of Chicago Press, 1931); *Brothers in Crime* (Chicago: University of Chicago Press, 1938).

46. Walter C. Reckless, *Six Boys in Trouble* (Ann Arbor: Michigan University Press, 1929).

47. Shaw, *The Jack-Roller*, p. 296.

48. The main work was Clifford H. Shaw and Henry D. McKay, *Delinquency Areas* (Chicago: University of Chicago Press, 1929), followed by *Juvenile Delinquency and Urban Areas* (Chicago: University of Chicago Press, 1942). See also "Correlation of Rate of Juvenile Delinquency with Certain Indices of Community Organization and Disorganization," *Publications of the American Sociological Society*, vol. 22 (1928), p. 175; and "Social Factors in Juvenile Delinquency," National Commission on Law Observance and Enforcement (Washington, 1931).

49. The Bureau of the Census of the United States Department of Commerce has published a useful *Census Tract Manual* that outlines the history of the growth of census tract analysis in the United States and an *Annotated Bibliography of Census Tract Publications*.

50. Walter C. Reckless, *Vice in Chicago* (Chicago: University of Chicago Press, 1933).

51. *Ibid.*, p. 13.

52. *Ibid.*, p. 183.
53. *Ibid.*, p. 188.
54. *Ibid.*, p. 232.
55. Cavan, *op. cit.*

56. Robert E. Faris and H. W. Dunham, *Mental Disorders in Urban Areas* (Chicago: University of Chicago Press, 1939).

CHAPTER 5

1. Robert S. Lynd and Helen M. Lynd, *Middletown: A Study in Contemporary American Culture* (New York: Harcourt, Brace, 1929); *Middletown in Transition: A Study in Cultural Conflicts* (New York: Harcourt, Brace, 1937).

2. Clark Wissler, *Man and Culture* (New York: Crowell, 1923).

3. W. H. R. Rivers, *Social Organization* (New York: Knopf, 1924).

4. *Middletown*, p. vi.

5. *Ibid.*, p. xi.

6. *Middletown in Transition*, p. ix.

7. Harry Elmer Barnes, *An Introduction to the History of Sociology* (Chicago: University of Chicago Press, 1948), p. 764.

8. Quoted from a review by Hans L. Zetterberg in the *American Sociological Review*, vol. 22 (1937), p. 768.

9. Robert S. Lynd, *Knowledge for What?* (Princeton, N.J.: Princeton University Press, 1948).

10. *Ibid.*, p. 1.

11. *Ibid.*, p. 241.

12. A frank discussion of serendipity in survey design has been contributed by Edward Shils, "Primordial, Personal, Sacred and Civil Ties," *British Journal of Sociology*, vol. 8 (1957), pp. 130–145.

13. Elihu Katz and Paul F. Lazarsfeld, *Personal Influence* (New York: The Free Press of Glencoe, 1955), p. 339.

14. George Lundberg, *Social Research* (New York: Longmans, 1929).

15. *Middletown*, p. 507.

16. *Ibid.*, p. 277.

17. *Ibid.*, p. 509.

18. *Ibid.*, p. 200.

19. *Ibid.*, p. 95, fn.5.

20. *Ibid.*, p. 94.

21. *Ibid.*, p. 95–96, fn.7.

22. *Ibid.*, p. 99, fn.13.

23. *Ibid.*, p. 99, fn.14.

24. *Ibid.*, pp. 99–100.

25. *Ibid.*, p. 102.

26. See the discussion in John Madge, *The Tools of Social Science* (London: Longmans, 1953), p. 140.

27. *Middletown*, p. 103.

28. Arthur J. Vidich and Joseph Bensman, *Small Town in Mass Society* (Princeton, N.J.: Princeton University Press, 1958).

29. *Middletown in Transition*, p. 4.

30. *Ibid.*, pp. 74–75.

31. *Ibid.*, p. 75.

32. *Ibid.*, p. 77.

33. *Ibid.*, p. 79.

34. *Middletown*, pp. 58–59.

35. *Middletown in Transition*, p. 82.

36. *Ibid.*, p. 83.

37. *Ibid.*, pp. 85–86.

38. *Ibid.*, p. 422.

39. *Ibid.*, p. 423.

40. *Ibid.*, p. 426.

41. *Ibid.*, p. 426.

42. *Ibid.*, p. 427.

43. *Ibid.*, p. 439.

44. *Ibid.*, p. 446.

45. *Ibid.*, p. 447.

46. *Ibid.*, p. 450.

47. *Ibid.*, p. 451.

48. Reinhard Bendix and Seymour Martin Lipset, eds., *Class, Status and*

Power (New York: The Free Press of Glencoe, 1953), pp. 172–173.

49. *Middletown in Transition*, p. 463.

50. *Ibid.*, p. 469.
51. *Ibid.*, p. 489.
52. *Ibid.*, p. 510.

CHAPTER 6

1. F. J. Roethlisberger and William J. Dickson, *Management and the Worker* (Cambridge, Mass.: Harvard University Press, 1939).

2. This description of the antecedents to the Hawthorne Experiment is based primarily on Elton Mayo, *The Human Problems of an Industrial Civilization* (New York: Macmillan, 1933; 2nd ed., Boston: Graduate School of Business Administration, Harvard University, 1946); on George C. Homans, *Fatigue of Workers* (New York: Reinhold, for the National Research Council, 1941); and on a personal communication from P. Sargant Florence.

3. Josephine Goldmark and Mary D. Hopkins, *Comparison of an Eight-Hour Plant and a Ten-Hour Plant*, Public Health Bulletin No. 106 (Washington: U.S. Public Health Service, 1920).

4. *Ibid.*, p. 91.

5. Mayo, *op. cit.*

6. T. North Whitehead, *The Industrial Worker* (Cambridge: Harvard University Press, 2 vols., 1938).

7. *Management and the Worker*, p. 54.

8. S. Wyatt, J. A. Fraser, and F. G. L. Stock, *The Effects of Monotony in Work* (London: Industrial Fatigue Research Board, 1929), p. 42.

9. *Management and the Worker*, pp. 159–160.

10. *Ibid.*, p. 153.

11. Cf. Chapter 3, pp. 68 and 79.

12. John Madge, *The Tools of So-cial Science* (London: Longmans, 1953), pp. 286 *et seq.*

13. *Management and the Worker*, pp. 183–184.

14. *Ibid.*, p. 194.

15. *Ibid.*, p. 240.

16. Sigmund Freud, *Introductory Lectures in Psychoanalysis*, translated by Joan Riviere (London: Allen & Unwin, 1922), p. 100.

17. Madge, *op. cit.*, pp. 161 *et seq.*

18. Elton Mayo, *The Social Problems of an Industrial Civilization* (Boston: Graduate School of Business Administration, Harvard University, 1946), p. 65 (English ed., 1949).

19. Robert K. Merton, Marjorie Fiske, and Patricia M. Kendall, *The Focused Interview* (New York: The Free Press of Glencoe, 1956).

20. *Ibid.*, pp. 103–104.

21. Mayo, *Human Problems, op. cit.*, p. 94.

22. Mayo, *Social Problems, op. cit.*, p. 70.

23. *Management and the Worker*, p. 522.

24. *Ibid.*, p. 519.

25. The theoretical antecedents of the Mayo school of "Industrial Sociology" are discussed by Conrad Arensberg, "Behavior and Organization," in John H. Rohrer and Muzafer Sherif, eds., *Social Psychology at the Cross Roads* (New York: Harper, 1951), pp. 326 *et seq.*

26. This point was made by T. T.

Paterson in a BBC broadcast, reprinted in *The Listener* (London: December 6, 1956).

27. *Management and the Worker*, p. 552.

28. *Ibid.*, p. 557.

29. *Loc. cit.*

30. In the twenty years since the publication of *Management and the Worker* there has grown up a massive array of criticisms of the Mayo school. The following are of particular interest: Herbert Blumer, "Sociological Theory in Industrial Relations," *American Sociological Review*, vol. 12 (1947), pp. 271–278; Wilbert E. Moore, "Industrial Sociology: Status and Prospects," *American Sociological Review*, vol. 13 (1948), pp. 282–291; Delbert C. Miller and William H. Form, *In-dustrial Sociology* (New York: Harper, 1951); Harold L. Sheppard, "Approaches to Conflict in American Industrial Sociology," *British Journal of Sociology*, vol. 5 (1952), pp. 324–341.

31. Jeanne L. Wilensky and Harold L. Wilensky, "Personal Counseling: The Hawthorne Case," *American Journal of Sociology*, vol. 57 (1951), pp. 265–280.

32. *Ibid.*, p. 280.

33. Arensberg, *op. cit.*, pp. 336 *et seq.*

34. *Ibid.*, p. 337.

35. Henry A. Landsberger, *Hawthorne Revisited* (Ithaca: Cornell University Press, 1958).

36. George C. Homans, *The Human Group* (New York: Harcourt, Brace, 1950).

CHAPTER 7

1. William Foote Whyte, *Street Corner Society* (Chicago: University of Chicago Press, 1943; 2nd ed., 1955).

2. The first of these was W. Lloyd Warner and Paul S. Lunt, *The Social Life of a Modern Community* (New Haven: Yale University Press, 1941).

3. Caroline M. Ware, *Greenwich Village, 1920–1930* (Boston: Houghton Mifflin, 1935).

4. See Chapter 5 of this book.

5. Conrad M. Arensberg and Solon Kimball, *Family and Community in Ireland.*

6. *Street Corner Society*, p. 291.

7. See Chapter 4, pp. 118–119.

8. Elihu Katz and Paul F. Lazarsfeld, *Personal Influence* (New York: The Free Press of Glencoe, 1955), p. 48.

9. Kurt Lewin, "Group Decision and Social Change," in Maccoby, Newcomb, and Hartley, eds., *Readings in Social Psychology* (New York: Holt, 1958), pp. 197–211. Discussed in Katz and Lazarsfeld, *op. cit.*, p. 119.

10. *Street Corner Society*, p. 301.

11. *Ibid.*, p. 301.

12. *Ibid.*, p. 303.

13. *Ibid.*, p. 306.

14. *Ibid.*, p. 304.

15. *Ibid.*, p. 313.

16. The example is taken from Harold D. Lasswell, *The Analysis of Political Behavior* (London: Kegan Paul, 1948), pp. 101–102.

17. *Ibid.*, p. 321.

18. *Ibid.*, p. 335.

19. *Ibid.*, p. 358.

20. *Ibid.*, p. xx.

21. *Ibid.*, p. 12.

22. *Ibid.*, p. 14.

23. *Ibid.*, p. 17.

24. *Ibid.*, p. 20.

25. *Ibid.*, p. 21.
26. *Ibid.*, p. 259.
27. *Ibid.*, pp. 25–26.
28. *Ibid.*, p. 32.
29. *Ibid.*, p. 33.
30. *Ibid.*, p. 39.
31. *Ibid.*, p. 343.
32. *Ibid.*, p. 54.
33. *Ibid.*, p. 56.
34. *Ibid.*, pp. 57–58.
35. *Ibid.*, p. 71.
36. *Ibid.*, p. 72.
37. *Ibid.*, p. 96.
38. *Ibid.*, p. 97.
39. *Ibid.*, pp. 259–260.
40. *Ibid.*, p. 258.
41. *Ibid.*, pp. 73–78.
42. *Ibid.*, p. 70.
43. *Ibid.*, p. 53.
44. *Ibid.*, pp. 67–70.
45. George C. Homans, *The Human Group* (New York: Harcourt, Brace, 1950), p. 269.
46. Talcott Parsons, "A Revised Analytical Approach to the Theory of Social Stratification," in Reinhard Bendix and Seymour M. Lipset, *Class, Status and Power* (New York: The Free Press of Glencoe, 1953), pp. 92–128.
47. *Ibid.*, p. 93.
48. *Ibid.*, p. 100.
49. *Ibid.*, p. 108.
50. *Ibid.*, p. 115.
51. *Street Corner Society*, p. 12.
52. *Ibid.*, p. 255.

53. *Ibid.*, p. 255.
54. *Ibid.*, p. 58.
55. *Ibid.*, p. 257.
56. *Ibid.*, p. 55.
57. *Ibid.*, pp. 60–61.
58. *Ibid.*, p. 62.
59. *Ibid.*, p. 71.
60. *Ibid.*, p. 73.
61. *Ibid.*, p. 85.
62. *Ibid.*, p. 108.
63. Cf. p. 226.
64. Helen Hall Jennings, "Leadership and Sociometric Choice," in Maccoby, Newcomb, and Hartley, *op. cit.*, p. 486.
65. *Ibid.*, pp. 488–489.
66. Homans, *op cit.*, pp. 188–189.
67. *Street Corner Society*, p. 257.
68. Homans, *op. cit.*, pp. 246–247.
69. *Street Corner Society*, p. xx.
70. *Ibid.*, p. 258.
71. *Ibid.*, p. 106.
72. Samuel A. Stouffer, *et al.*, *The American Soldier:* vol. 1, *Adjustment during Army Life* (Princeton, N.J.: Princeton University Press, 1949), pp. 259–263.
73. *Street Corner Society*, p. 54.
74. *Ibid.*, p. 54.
75. *Ibid.*, p. 55.
76. *Ibid.*, p. 93.
77. *Ibid.*, p. 347.
78. *Ibid.*, p. 107.
79. *Ibid.*, pp. 99–100.
80. *Ibid.*, p. 276.

CHAPTER 8

1. Gunnar Myrdal, *An American Dilemma* (New York: Harper, 1944).
2. *Ibid.*, pp. x–xi.
3. *Ibid.*, p. v.
4. *Ibid.*, p. xiv.
5. *Ibid.*, p. xlvii.

6. *Ibid.*, p. 4.
7. *Ibid.*, p. 4.
8. *Ibid.*, p. 8.
9. *Ibid.*, p. 21.
10. *Ibid.*, p. 21.
11. The parallel between the status

of Negroes and the status of women is discussed in Appendix 5 of *An American Dilemma*, pp. 1073–1078.

12. *Ibid.*, p. 34.

13. *Ibid.*, p. 36.

14. *Ibid.*, p. 41.

15. John Dollard, *Caste and Class in a Southern Town* (New York: Harper, 1937); Allison Davis, Burleigh B. Gardner, and Mary R. Gardner, *Deep South* (Chicago: University of Chicago Press, 1941).

16. *An American Dilemma*, p. 60.

17. *Ibid.*, Appendix 3, "A Methodological Note on the Principle of Cumulation," pp. 1065–1070.

18. Anthony Richmond, *Colour Prejudice in Britain* (London: Routledge, 1954), pp. 6–7.

19. George C. Homans, *The Human Group* (New York: Harcourt, Brace, 1950), pp. 134–136.

20. *An American Dilemma*, pp. 28–29.

21. *Ibid.*, Appendix 1, pp. 1027–1034.

22. *Ibid.*, p. 1028.

23. *Ibid.*, p. 1032.

24. *Ibid.*, p. 1034.

25. *Ibid.*, Appendix 2, "Facts and Valuations in Social Science," pp. 1035–1064.

26. *Ibid.*, p. 1035.

27. *Ibid.*, p. 1041.

28. *Ibid.*, pp. 1060–1061.

29. H. H. Gerth and C. Wright Mills, *From Max Weber* (London: Kegan Paul, 1948), p. 25.

30. *Ibid.*, pp. 145–146.

31. *An American Dilemma*, p. 1061.

32. *Ibid.*, pp. 1062–1063.

33. *Ibid.*, pp. 1063–1064.

34. Arnold M. Rose, *Theory and Method in the Social Sciences* (Minneapolis: University of Minnesota Press), pp. 126–127.

35. Gunnar Myrdal, "Social Theory and Social Policy," *British Journal of Sociology*, vol. 4 (1953), p. 215.

36. *Ibid.*, p. 216.

37. *Loc. cit.*

CHAPTER 9

1. "Studies in Social Psychology in World War II" (Princeton, N.J.: Princeton University Press). Vol. 1: S. A. Stouffer, E. A. Suchman, L. C. De Vinney, S. A. Star, and R. M. Williams, Jr., *The American Soldier: Adjustment during Army Life* (1949). Vol. 2: S. A. Stouffer, A. A. Lumsdaine, M. H. Lumsdaine, R. M. Williams, Jr., M. B. Smith, I. L. Janis, S. A. Star, and L. S. Cottrell, Jr., *The American Soldier: Combat and Its Aftermath* (1949). Vol. 3: C. I. Hovland, A. A. Lumsdaine, and F. D. Sheffield, *Experiments in Mass Communication* (1949). Vol. 4: S. A. Stouffer, L. Guttman, E. A. Suchman, P. F. Lazarsfeld, S. A. Star, and J. A. Clausen, *Measurement and Prediction* (1950). Robert K. Merton and Paul L. Lazarsfeld, eds., *Continuities in Social Research: Studies in the Scope and Method of "The American Soldier"* (New York: The Free Press of Glencoe, 1950).

2. *Ibid.*, vol. 1, p. 12.

3. *Ibid.*, p. 15.

4. *Ibid.*, p. 18.

5. Robert K. Merton, Marjorie Fiske, and Patricia L. Kendall, *The Focused Interview* (New York: The Free Press of Glencoe, 1956).

6. Stanley L. Payne, *The Art of Asking Questions* (Princeton, N.J.:

Princeton University Press, 1951). The effect of the interviewer on informants' responses is discussed in Herbert Hyman, *Interviewing in Social Research* (Chicago: University of Chicago Press, 1954).

7. Merton and Lazarsfeld, eds., *Continuities*, p. 138. This case is based on material appearing in *The American Soldier*, vol. 1, p. 157.

8. *The American Soldier*, vol. 1, p. 51.

9. Herbert Hyman, *Survey Design and Analysis: Principles, Cases and Procedures* (New York: The Free Press of Glencoe, 1955), pp. 66 et seq.

10. Quoted in Merton and Lazarsfeld, *op. cit.*, p. 220.

11. Hyman, *Survey Design and Analysis, op. cit.*, p. 81.

12. Anthony H. Richmond, *Colour Prejudice in Britain* (London: Routledge, 1954), p. 78.

13. *Measurement and Prediction*, pp. 60–90.

14. *Ibid.*, p. 10.

15. *Ibid.*, pp. 80–81.

16. *Ibid.*, p. 71.

17. *Ibid.*, p. 159.

18. *Ibid.*, p. 163.

19. *Ibid.*, p. 192.

20. H. Menzel, "A New Coefficient for Scalogram Analysis," *Public Opinion Quarterly*, vol. 17 (1953), pp. 268–280. See also the developments discussed by Leo Srole, "Social Integration and Certain Corollaries," *American Sociological Review*, vol. 21 (1956), pp. 709–716 and by Dorothy L. Meier and Wendell Bell, "Anomia and Differential Access to the Achievement of Life Goals," *American Sociological Review*, vol. 24 (1959), pp. 189–202.

21. *Measurement and Prediction*, p. 19.

22. *Ibid.*, pp. 417 et seq.

23. *Ibid.*, pp. 21 et seq.

24. Max Lerner, *America as a Civilization* (New York: Simon and Schuster, 1957), p. 913.

25. Merton and Lazarsfeld, *op. cit.*, p. 221.

26. *Ibid.*, pp. 221–222.

27. *Ibid.*, pp. 200–201.

28. *Ibid.*, p. 115.

29. *Ibid.*, p. 22.

30. *Ibid.*, p. 30.

31. *Ibid.*, p. 28.

32. *Ibid.*, p. 32.

33. *Ibid.*, p. 32.

34. *Ibid.*, p. 37.

35. Paul Hare, Edgar F. Borgatta, and Robert F. Bales, eds., *Small Groups* (New York: Knopf, 1955).

36. *Ibid.*, p. 236.

37. Merton and Lazarsfeld, *op. cit.*, p. 45, quoting *The American Soldier*, vol. 1, p. 563.

38. *Ibid.*, p. 46.

39. *Ibid.*, p. 50.

40. *Ibid.*, p. 53, quoting *The American Soldier*, vol. 1, p. 256.

41. *Ibid.*, p. 54, quoting *The American Soldier*, vol. 1, p. 251.

42. Quoted in Merton and Lazarsfeld, *op. cit.*, pp. 73–74.

CHAPTER 10

1. Alfred C. Kinsey, Wardell B. Pomeroy, and Clyde E. Martin, *Sexual Behavior in the Human Male* (Philadelphia: Saunders, 1948). Alfred C. Kinsey, Wardell B. Pomeroy, Clyde E. Martin and Paul H. Bebhard, *Sexual Behavior in the Human Female* (Philadelphia: Saunders, 1953).

2. *Human Female,* p. 433.

3. *Human Male,* p. 13.

4. *Ibid.,* p. 17.

5. *Ibid.,* p. 19.

6. Ernest W. Burgess and Leonard S. Cottrell, *Predicting Success or Failure in Marriage* (New York: Prentice-Hall, 1939).

7. *Human Male,* p. 19.

8. *Loc. cit.*

9. G. W. Hamilton, *A Research in Marriage* (New York: Boni, 1929).

10. *Human Male,* p. 33.

11. *Human Female,* p. 4.

12. *Human Male,* p. 18.

13. *Ibid.,* p. 34.

14. *Ibid.,* p. 82.

15. *Ibid.,* p. 218.

16. Herbert H. Hyman, *Survey Design and Analysis: Principles, Cases, and Procedures* (New York: The Free Press of Glencoe, 1955), p. 81.

18. *Ibid.,* p. 35.

19. *Ibid.,* p. 43.

20. *Ibid.,* p. 43.

21. *Ibid.,* p. 44.

22. *Ibid.,* pp. 63–70.

23. *Ibid.,* p. 57.

24. *Ibid.,* pp. 57–58.

25. *Ibid.,* pp. 202–203.

26. *Ibid.,* p. 385.

27. *Ibid.,* p. 59.

28. *Human Female,* pp. 450–451.

29. *Human Male,* p. 81.

30. B. Seebohm Rowntree, *Poverty: A Study of Town Life* (London: Macmillan, 1901), p. 26.

31. B. Seebohm Rowntree, *Poverty and Progress* (London: Longmans, 1941), p. 479.

32. *Human Male,* p. 93.

33. *Ibid.,* p. 93.

34. *Loc. cit.*

35. William G. Cochran, Frederick Mosteller, and John W. Tukey, "Statistical Problems of the Kinsey Report," *Journal of the American Statistical Association,* vol. 48 (1953), pp. 673–716. Reprinted in Jerome Himelhoch and Sylvia Fleis Fava, eds., *Sexual Behavior in American Society* (New York: Norton, 1955), pp. 68–167.

36. *Human Male,* p. 103.

37. This device is described in John Madge, *The Tools of Social Science* (London: Longmans, 1953), p. 251.

38. *Human Male,* pp. 104–105.

39. *Ibid.,* p. 109.

40. *Ibid.,* pp. 122–123.

41. *Ibid.,* p. 123.

42. Cochran, *et al., op. cit.*

43. *Ibid.,* pp. 86–87.

44. Harvey J. Locke, "Are Volunteer Interviewees Representative?," *Social Problems,* vol. 1 (1954), pp. 143–146. Reprinted in Himelhoch and Fava, *op. cit.,* pp. 113–118.

45. Abraham H. Maslow and James M. Sakoda, "Volunteer-Error in the Kinsey Study," *Journal of Abnormal and Social Psychology,* vol. 47 (1952), pp. 259–262. Reprinted in Himelhoch and Fava, *op. cit.,* pp. 119–125.

46. Judson T. Landis, "The Women Kinsey Studied," *Social Problems,* vol. 1 (1954), pp. 139–142. Reprinted in Himelhoch and Fava, *op. cit.,* pp. 108–112.

47. John A. Clausen, "Biological Bias and Methodological Limitations in the Kinsey Studies," *Social Problems,* vol. 1 (1954), pp. 126–133. Reprinted in Himelhoch and Fava, *op. cit.,* pp. 39–49.

48. Manford H. Kuhn, "Kinsey's View of Human Behavior," *Social Problems,* vol. 1 (1954), pp. 119–125. Reprinted in Himelhoch and Fava, *op. cit.,* pp. 29–38.

49. Geoffrey Gorer, "Nature, Science and Dr. Kinsey," *Encounter,*

vol. 2 (1954), pp. 69–76. Reprinted in Himelhoch and Fava, *op. cit.*, pp. 50–58.

50. Jule Eisenbud, *Problems of Sexual Behavior* (New York: American Social Hygiene Association, 1948). Extracts included in Himelhoch and Fava, *op. cit.*, pp. 294–300. Quotation from p. 296.

51. Lawrence S. Kubie, "Psychiatric Implications of the Kinsey Report," *Psychosomatic Medicine*, vol. 10 (1948), pp. 95–106. Reprinted in Himelhoch and Fava, *op. cit.*, pp. 270–293.

52. *Loc. cit.*

53. Gorer, *op. cit.*, p. 57.

CHAPTER 11

1. T. W. Adorno, Else Frenkel-Brunswick, Daniel J. Levinson, and R. Nevitt Sanford, *The Authoritarian Personality* (New York: Harper, 1950).

2. *Ibid.*, p. 1.

3. *Ibid.*, p. 971, fn.

4. M. B. Smith, "Review of *The Authoritarian Personality*," *Journal of Abnormal and Social Psychology*, vol. 45 (1950), pp. 775–779. Quoted in Richard Christie and Marie Jahoda, eds., *Continuities in Social Research: Studies in the Scope and Method of "The Authoritarian Personality"* (New York: The Free Press of Glencoe, 1954), p. 123.

5. Christie and Jahoda, *op. cit.*, p. 126, also footnote.

6. Erich Fromm, *The Fear of Freedom* (London: Routledge, 1942), pp. 140–141. [American edition titled *Escape from Freedom* (New York: Farrar and Rinehart, 1941).]

7. *Authoritarian Personality*, p. 224.

8. Max Horkheimer, *Autorität und Familie* (Paris: Alcan, 1936).

9. *Authoritarian Personality*, pp. 11–12.

10. See, for example, *ibid.*, p. 225.

11. *Ibid.*, p. 13.

12. Herbert H. Hyman and Paul B. Sheatsley, "The Authoritarian Personality—a Methodological Critique," in Christie and Jahoda, *op. cit.*, p. 120.

13. *Authoritarian Personality*, p. 13.

14. *Ibid.*, pp. 225 *et seq.*

15. See Chapter 9.

16. See *The Authoritarian Personality*, p. 77.

17. *Ibid.*, p. 80.

18. *Ibid.*, p. 89.

19. *Ibid.*, p. 150.

20. *Ibid.*, p. 207.

21. *Ibid.*, pp. 201–262.

22. R. Likert, "A Technique for the Measurement of Attitudes," *Archives of Psychology*, No. 140, 1932.

23. Theodore M. Newcomb, *Social Psychology* (London: Tavistock, 1952), p. 162.

24. *Authoritarian Personality*, p. 14.

25. Christie and Jahoda, *op. cit.*, p. 15.

26. *Authoritarian Personality*, p. 19.

27. Christie and Jahoda, *op. cit.*, pp. 61 *et seq.*

28. *Ibid.*, p. 56.

29. *Ibid.*, p. 67.

30. *Authoritarian Personality*, p. 24.

31. Compare Myrdal's *An American Dilemma*, discussed in Chapter 8.

32. *Authoritarian Personality*, p. 279.

33. *Ibid.*, p. 291.

34. *Ibid.*, p. 314.

35. *Ibid.*, p. 373.

36. *Ibid.*, p. 375.

37. Christie and Jahoda, *op. cit.*, p. 122.

38. *Authoritarian Personality*, pp. 22–23.

39. *Ibid.*, p. 97.

40. *Ibid.*, p. 836.

41. Christie and Jahoda, *op. cit.*, pp. 93–95.

42. *Authoritarian Personality*, p. 94.

43. Christie and Jahoda, *op. cit.*, p. 72.

44. *Ibid.*, p. 73.

45. For example, *Authoritarian Personality*, pp. 302, 304.

46. *Ibid.*, p. 189.

47. Paul F. Lazarsfeld, Bernard Berelson, and Hazel Gaudet, *The People's Choice* (New York: Columbia University Press, 1944), pp. 21 *et seq.* and 148–149.

48. Christie and Jahoda, *op. cit.*, p. 120.

49. *Authoritarian Personality*, p. 744.

50. *Ibid.*, p. 747.

51. *Ibid.*, p. 758.

52. *Ibid.*, p. 759.

53. *Ibid.*, p. 760.

54. Robert M. Lindner, *Rebel Without a Cause* (New York: Grune and Stratton, 1944). Reprinted in a paper-back edition with the subtitle, *Hypnoanalysis of a Criminal Psychopath* (New York: Grove, 1956).

55. *Ibid.*, p. 757.

56. *Ibid.*, p. 771.

57. *Ibid.*, p. 781.

58. *Ibid.*, p. 973.

59. *Ibid.*, p. 224.

60. Christie and Jahoda, *op. cit.*, p. 129.

61. *Ibid.*, p. 132.

62. *Ibid.*, p. 166.

63. Harold Webster, Nevitt Sanford, and Marvin Freedman, "A New Instrument for Studying Authoritarianism in Personality," *Journal of Psychology*, vol. 40 (1955), pp. 73–84.

64. Marvin Freedman, Harold Webster, and Nevitt Sanford, "A Study of Authoritarianism and Psychopathology," *Journal of Psychology*, vol. 41 (1956), pp. 315–322.

65. R. Christie and J. Garcia, "Subcultural Variation in Authoritarian Personality," *Journal of Abnormal and Social Psychology*, vol. 46 (1951), pp. 457–469.

66. W. M. O'Neil and D. J. Levinson, "A Factorial Exploration of Authoritarianism and Some of Its Ideological Concomitants," *Journal of Personality*, vol. 22 (1954), pp. 449–463.

67. Santo F. Camilleri, "A Factor Analysis of the F-Scale," *Social Forces*, vol. 37 (1959), pp. 316–323, failed to verify the theoretical structure of the F-Scale.

68. Seymour M. Lipset, *Political Man* (London: Heinemann, 1960), pp. 104 *et seq.*

69. Samuel A. Stouffer, *Communism, Conformity and Civil Liberties* (New York: Doubleday, 1955).

CHAPTER 12

1. Robert Freed Bales, *Interaction Process Analysis* (Reading, Mass.: Addison-Wesley, 1951).

2. *Ibid.*, p. 33.

3. *Ibid.*, p. 34.

4. *Ibid.*, p. 35.

5. *Ibid.*, p. 41.

6. *Ibid.*, p. 43.

7. *Ibid.*, p. 65.

8. *Ibid.*, p. 82.

9. Robert F. Bales and Ned A. Flanders, "Planning an Observation

Room and Group Laboratory," *American Sociological Review*, vol. 19 (1954), pp. 771–781.

10. *Interaction Process Analysis*, p. 1.

11. Fred L. Strodtbeck, "Husband-Wife Interaction over Revealed Differences," *American Sociological Review*, vol. 16 (1951), pp. 468–473. Reprinted in Hare, Borgatta, and Bales, eds., *Small Groups* (New York: Knopf, 1955), pp. 464–472.

12. Bales and Flanders, *op. cit.*, p. 775.

13. *Interaction Process Analysis*, p. 52.

14. See also *ibid.*, pp. 128 *et seq.*

15. See also the discussion in Talcott Parsons, Robert F. Bales, and Edward A. Shils, *Working Papers in the Theory of Action* (New York: The Free Press of Glencoe, 1953), p. 123.

16. *Interaction Process Analysis*, p. 116.

17. Robert K. Merton, *Social Theory and Social Structure* (revised edition, New York: The Free Press of Glencoe, 1957), p. 94.

18. *Interaction Process Analysis*, p. 117.

19. *Ibid.*, pp. 124–126.

20. *Ibid.*, p. 137.

21. These repercussions may be compared with the types of individual adaptation described in Merton, *op. cit.*, pp. 139, *et seq.*

22. *Interaction Process Analysis*, p. 157.

23. *Ibid.*, p. xi.

24. Talcott Parsons and Edward A. Shils, eds., *Toward a General Theory of Action* (Cambridge, Mass.: Harvard University Press, 1952), p. 437.

25. Talcott Parsons, *The Social System* (New York: The Free Press of Glencoe, 1951), p. xi.

26. Parsons, Bales, and Shils, *op. cit.*, p. 9.

27. Parsons and Shils, *op. cit.*, pp. 439–440.

28. Parsons, Bales, and Shils, *op. cit.*, p. 123.

29. *Ibid.*, p. 131, contains a reference to an experiment by Festinger and Thibault which reflected this "odd man out" situation.

30. *Ibid.*, p. 148.

31. Philip E. Slater, "Role Differentiation in Small Groups," in Hare, Borgatta, and Bales, *op. cit.*, pp. 498–515. Robert F. Bales and Philip E. Slater, "Role Differentiation in Small Decision Making Groups," in Talcott Parsons and Robert F. Bales, *Family, Socialization and Interaction Process* (New York: The Free Press of Glencoe, 1955).

32. Hare, Borgatta, and Bales, *op. cit.*, p. 501.

33. *Ibid.*, p. 511.

34. Bales and Slater, *op. cit.*, p. 292.

35. Hare, Borgatta, and Bales, *op. cit.*, p. 511.

36. *Ibid.*, p. 514.

37. Morris, Zelditch, Jr., "Role Differentiation in the Nuclear Family: A Comparative Study," in Parsons and Bales, *op. cit.*, p. 314.

38. *Loc. cit.*

39. *Loc. cit.*

40. *Ibid.*, p. 339.

41. Robert F. Bales, "In Conference," *Harvard Business Review*, vol. 32 (1954), pp. 44–50.

42. Robert F. Bales, "Small Group Theory and Research," in Robert K. Merton, Leonard Broom, and Leonard S. Cottrell, Jr., eds., *Sociology Today* (New York: Basic Books, 1959), p. 294.

43. *Ibid.*, p. 296.

CHAPTER 13

1. Leon Festinger and Harold H. Kelley, *Changing Attitudes through Social Contact* (Ann Arbor: University of Michigan Press, 1951).

2. Kurt Lewin, "Experiments in Social Space," *Harvard Educational Review* (1939), vol. 9, p. 21. Reprinted in Kurt Lewin, *Resolving Social Conflicts* (New York: Harper, 1948), p. 71.

3. Kurt Lewin, "Group Decision and Social Change" in Maccoby, Newcomb, and Hartley, eds., *Readings in Social Psychology* (New York: Holt, 1958), pp. 197–211.

4. Chapter 12 of *Resolving Social Conflicts*.

5. Thibaut and Kelley, *The Social Psychology of Groups* (New York: Wiley, 1959), p. x.

6. Festinger and Kelley, *op. cit.*, p. 1.

7. *Ibid.*, p. 3.

8. K. B. Clark and M. P. Clark, "Racial Identification and Preference in Negro Children," in Maccoby, *et al.*, *op. cit.*, pp. 602–611.

9. M. Radke, unpublished study reported in *Christian Science Monitor*, July 17, 1946, p. 4.

10. M. Brenman, "The Relationship between Group Membership and Group Identification in a Group of Urban Middle Class Negro Girls," *Journal of Social Psychology*, vol. 11 (1940), pp. 171–197.

11. Festinger and Kelley, *op. cit.*, p. 8.

12. *Ibid.*, p. 9.

13. *Ibid.*, p. 9.

14. Kurt Lewin, *Field Theory in Social Science* (New York: Harper, 1951), p. 232–233.

15. Festinger and Kelley, *op. cit.*, p. 10.

16. *Ibid.*, p. 70.

17. *Ibid.*, Table 14, p. 53.

18. L. Festinger, S. Schachter, and K. Back, *Social Pressures in Informal Groups* (New York: Harper, 1950).

19. *Resolving Social Conflicts*, p. 57. Compare also the dictum of W. I. Thomas that "if men define situations as real, they are real in their consequences." (See p. 76.)

20. Thibaut and Kelley, *op. cit.*, p. 21.

21. *Ibid.*, p. 181.

22. John Dollard, *et al.*, *Frustration and Aggression* (New Haven: Yale University Press, 1939).

23. Lewin, "Self-Hatred among Jews," Chapter 12 of *Resolving Social Conflicts*.

24. Thibaut and Kelley, *op. cit.*, p. 183.

25. *Ibid.*, p. 21.

26. H. H. Kelley, "Two Functions of Reference Groups," in Swanson, Newcomb, and Hartley, *Readings in Social Psychology* (New York: Holt, 1952), pp. 410–414.

27. Morton Deutsch, "Field Theory in Social Psychology," in Gardner Lindzey, ed., *Handbook of Social Psychology* (Reading, Mass.: Addison-Wesley, 1954), p. 214.

CHAPTER 14

1. Robert K. Merton, *Social Theory and Social Structure* (revised edition, New York: The Free Press of Glencoe, 1957), p. 610.

2. *Ibid.*, p. 624

3. Robert K. Merton, "Introduction" to Merton, Broom, and Cottrell, eds., *Sociology Today* (New York: Basic Books, 1959), p. xx.

4. *Loc. cit.*

5. *Ibid.*, pp. xx–xxi.

6. Rensis Likert, *Behavioral Research* (UNESCO, 1957).

7. C. Wright Mills, *The Sociological Imagination* (New York: Oxford University Press, 1959; reprinted, New York: Evergreen, 1961), p. 21.

8. Merton, *op. cit.*, p. 128.

9. Ben B. Lindsey and Wainwright Evans, *The Revolt of Modern Youth* (London: Brentano, 1928), pp. 25–26.

10. Barbara Wootton, "The Image of the Social Worker," *British Journal of Sociology*, vol. 11 (1960), pp. 373–385.

11. *Ibid.*, pp. 382–383.

12. George C. Homans, *The Human Group* (New York: Harcourt, Brace, 1950), p. 133 (English edition).

13. This point has been made several times, e.g., in Leo Kuper, ed., *Living in Towns* (London: Cresset, 1953), pp. 42 *et seq.*

14. Kinsey, Pomeroy, and Martin, *Sexual Behavior in the Human Male* (Philadelphia: Saunders, 1948), p. 199.

15. *Ibid.*, p. 201.

16. See Reinhard Bendix, *Max Weber: An Intellectual Portrait* (New York: Doubleday, 1960), p. 72.

17. *Ibid.*, p. 73, where Bendix paraphrases a passage from Weber's *Protestant Ethic and the Spirit of Capitalism.*

18. See Merton, Broom, and Cottrell, *op. cit.*, p. 174.

19. Kurt Lewin, *Field Theory in Social Science* (New York: Harper, 1951).

20. Robert S. Lynd and Helen M. Lynd, *Middletown: A Study in Contemporary American Culture* (New York: Harcourt, Brace, 1929).

21. Seymour M. Lipset, Paul F. Lazarsfeld, Allen H. Barton, and Juan Linz, "The Psychology of Voting: An Analysis of Political Behavior," in Gardner Lindzey, ed., *Handbook of Social Psychology* (Reading, Mass.: Addison-Wesley, 1954), pp. 1124–1175.

22. See Terence Morris, *The Criminal Area* (London: Routledge, 1957), p. 44.

23. Quoted in the General Register Office, *Hospital Morbidity Statistics* (London: H.M. Stationery Office, 1951), p. 8.

24. *Ibid.*, p. 9.

25. A. F. Wells, *The Local Social Survey in Great Britain* (London: Allen and Unwin, 1935), p. 18.

26. T. S. Simey and M. B. Simey, *Charles Booth: Social Scientist* (New York: Oxford University Press, 1960).

27. Beatrice Webb, *My Apprenticeship* (Second ed., London: Longmans, N. D.), pp. 213–214.

28. Morris Ginsberg, "The Problems and Methods of Sociology," in F. C. Bartlett, *et al.*, eds., *The Study of Society* (London: Kegan Paul, 1939), p. 476.

29. David Duncan, *Life and Letters of Herbert Spencer* (London: Methuen, 1908), p. 141.

30. Émile Durkheim, *Suicide* (New York: The Free Press of Glencoe, 1951), p. 253.

31. Merton, *op. cit.*, pp. 164–165.

32. Hermann Mannheim and Leslie T. Wilkins, *Prediction Methods in Relation to Borstal Training* (London: H.M. Stationery Office, 1955).

33. Stouffer, *et al.*, *Measurement and*

Prediction (Princeton, N.J.: Princeton University Press, 1950), p. 709.

34. Émile Durkheim, *The Rules of Sociological Method* (New York: The Free Press of Glencoe, 1938), p. 125.

35. *Ibid.,* p. 128.

36. *Ibid.,* p. 129.

37. Paul F. Lazarsfeld and Morris Rosenberg, eds., *The Language of Social Research* (New York: The Free Press of Glencoe, 1955), p. 111.

38. William I. Thomas and Florian Znaniecki, *The Polish Peasant,* vol. 1, p. 36.

39. Robert F. Bales, *Interaction Process Analysis* (Reading, Mass.: Addison-Wesley, 1951), p. 49.

40. Talcott Parsons and Edward A. Shils, *Toward a General Theory of Action* (Cambridge, Mass.: Harvard University Press, 1952), p. 423.

41. Durkheim, *Suicide,* pp. 248–249.

42. Durkheim, *Rules of Sociological Method,* p. 55.

43. *Ibid.,* p. 58.

44. Ralph Linton, *The Cultural Bcakground of Personality* (New York: Appleton-Century, 1945), pp. 22–23.

45. Robert K. Merton and Paul F. Lazarsfeld, *Continuities in Social Research: Studies in the Scope and Method of "The American Soldier,"* (New York: The Free Press of Glencoe, 1955), p. 85.

46. *Ibid.,* p. 88.

47. Henry S. Maine, "From Status to Contract," in Edgar F. Borgatta and Henry J. Meyer, eds., *Sociological Theory* (New York: Knopf, 1956), pp. 164–167.

48. Émile Durkheim, *The Division of Labor in Society* (New York: The Free Press of Glencoe, 1947), p. 62.

49. Ferdinand Tönnies, *Gemeinschaft und Gesellschaft.* Translated and edited by Charles P. Loomis, *Community and Society* (East Lansing: Michigan State University Press, 1957), p. 35.

50. Bendix, *op. cit.,* p. 70. See also Talcott Parsons.

51. Robert Redfield, *The Folk Culture of Yucatan* (Chicago: University of Chicago Press, 1941), pp. 338–339.

52. See, for example, Horace Miner, "The Folk-Urban Continuum," in Lazarsfeld and Rosenberg, *op. cit.,* pp. 334–344.

53. Ralph Linton, *The Study of Man* (New York: Appleton-Century, 1936), pp. 283–284. Quoted in Redfield, *op. cit.,* p. 349.

54. Harvey W. Zorbaugh, *The Gold Coast and the Slum* (Chicago: University of Chicago Press, 1929), p. 269.

55. Elizabeth Bott, *Family and Social Network* (London: Tavistock, 1957), pp. 103 *et seq.*

56. William H. Whyte, Jr., *The Organization Man* (New York: Simon and Schuster, 1956; reprinted, New York: Doubleday Anchor, 1956), pp. 295 *et seq.*

57. This point is made by Mills, *op. cit.,* pp. 48, 82.

58. Albion W. Small, "Socialism in the Light of Social Science," *American Journal of Sociology,* vol. 17 (1912), pp. 809–810. Quoted by Howard Becker and Harry E. Barnes, *Social Thought from Lore to Science* (Washington: Harren, 1952), p. 637.

59. Cf. Merton, *op. cit.,* pp. 489 *et seq.*

60. Robert S. Lynd, *Knowledge for What?* (Princeton, N.J.: Princeton University Press, 1948), p. 41.

61. Elton Mayo, *The Human Problems of an Industrial Civilization* (New

York: Macmillan, 1933), pp. 174–175.

62. Gunnar Myrdal, *An American Dilemma* (New York: Harper, 1944), p. 1051.

63. William I. Thomas, *The Unadjusted Girl* (Boston: Little, Brown, 1923), p. 253.

64. Quoted in Herbert Blumer, *An Appraisal of Thomas and Znaniecki's "The Polish Peasant in America"* (New York: Social Science Research Council, Bulletin 44, 1939), pp. 131–132.

65. Robert S. Lynd and Helen M. Lynd, *Middletown in Transition: A Study in Cultural Conflicts* (New York: Harcourt, Brace, 1937), p. 244.

66. Mayo, *op. cit.*, p. 152.

67. F. J. Roethlisberger and William J. Dickson, *Management and the Worker* (Cambridge, Mass.: Harvard University Press, 1939), p. 272.

68. Stouffer, *et al.*, *op. cit.*, p. 535.

69. Kinsey, Pomeroy, and Martin, *op. cit.*, p. 180.

70. *Ibid.*, p. 263.

71. Kinsey, *et al.*, *Sexual Behavior in the Human Female* (Philadelphia: Saunders, 1953), p. 643.

72. Lewin, *Field Theory in Social Science*, *op. cit.*, p. 61.

73. Compare the discussion in Gardner Lindzey, ed., *Handbook of Social Psychology* (Reading, Mass.: Addison-Wesley, 1954), pp. 174–175.

74. Edward A. Shils, *The Present State of American Sociology* (New York: The Free Press of Glencoe, 1948), p. 3.

NAME INDEX

SUBJECT INDEX